User's Guide

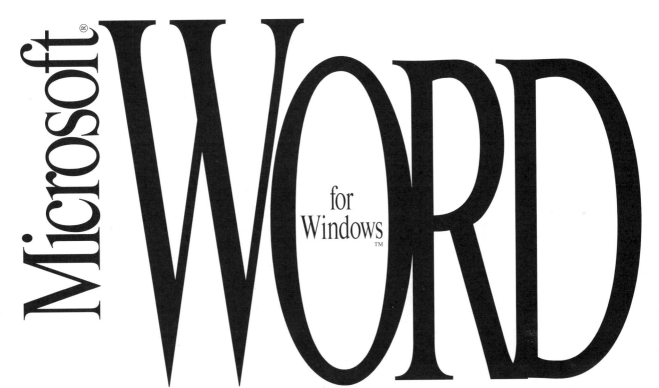

Microsoft® WORD for Windows™

Word Processing Program Version 2.0

Document Number WB37584-1092

Contents

Part 3   Formatting a Document

Part 4   Editing and Proofing Tools

Part 5   Arranging Text and Graphics on the Page

Part 7   Special Features for Documents

Part 8   Merging Documents

Part 9 Using Word with Other Applications

Part 10 Customizing Word

About This Manual

The *Microsoft Word User's Guide* is a comprehensive guide that contains all of the procedures you need to work with Microsoft® Word. To help you learn and use Word efficiently, this manual is organized by tasks, beginning with the most common word-processing tasks (parts one through three), and moving on to more advanced Word features (parts four through eleven).

Many of the skills described in this manual are also covered in the online tutorial, Learning Word. If you'd like to get hands-on experience right away, install and start Word as described in *Microsoft Word Getting Started*. Then choose the Getting Started command from the Help menu and follow the directions on your screen.

Before You Begin

Before you can use Word, you must install Microsoft Windows™ on your computer and then install Word. For information on installing Windows, see your Windows documentation.

To install Word, you must use the Setup program. Word files are compressed; you use the Setup program to decompress and install the Word files. For information on setting up Word on an individual computer, see *Microsoft Word Getting Started*. For information on setting up Word on a network, see Appendix A, "Setting Up and Using Word on a Network."

Symbols and Conventions

The Word documentation uses a few special symbols and conventions.

The Keyboard

- The keys on your keyboard may not be labeled exactly as they are in this manual. All key names are shown using small capital letters. For example, the Control key is shown as CTRL; the Escape key is shown as ESC.

- Keys are frequently used in combinations or sequences. For example, SHIFT+F1 means to hold down the SHIFT key while pressing F1, and ALT, F, A means to press and release each of these keys in order: first ALT, then F, and then A.

- *Arrow keys* is the collective name for the UP ARROW, DOWN ARROW, LEFT ARROW, and RIGHT ARROW keys.

- To choose a command from a menu, you can use the mouse or press a key combination. In procedures, key sequences follow the menu and command names. For example: From the File menu, choose Open (ALT, F, O).

Text

- Specific text you are to type is shown in bold. For example, if the manual says to type **cd word** you type the lowercase letters "cd" followed by a space and the lowercase word "word." What you type is always shown in lowercase letters, unless it must be typed in uppercase letters to work properly.

- Placeholders for items such as filenames that you must supply yourself are shown in italic. For example, when the manual says to type **cd** *directory_name* you type the letters "cd" followed by a space and the name of a directory. For a directory called BUDGET, you would type **cd budget**

- Examples of field syntax and macro listings are displayed in monospace font—for example, `Sub MAIN`.

Procedures

You can use the mouse or the keyboard for most actions in Word. Whenever possible, procedures apply to both the mouse and the keyboard.

 The mouse symbol in the margin directs you to the procedures for accomplishing a task with the mouse.

 The keyboard symbol in the margin directs you to the procedures for accomplishing a task with the keyboard.

Microsoft Support Services

Microsoft offers a variety of support options to help you get the most from your Microsoft® product. This section summarizes these options.

If you have a question about your Microsoft product, first look in the printed product documentation or consult Help. If you cannot find the answer, contact Microsoft Product Support.

Outside the United States, contact Microsoft Product Support at the Microsoft subsidiary office that serves your area. For information about Microsoft subsidiary offices, see the following section, "Microsoft Product Support Services Worldwide." If you purchased this package in a country other than the United States, you can also refer to an enclosed card that lists all the subsidiaries and how to reach them.

Product Support Within the United States

You can obtain product support in several ways, and locate additional training and consultation services in your area.

You have the following means of obtaining product support:

Use Microsoft® FastTips Automated Telephone Support and Fax Services If you have a touch-tone telephone, you can use Microsoft FastTips to hear recorded responses in English to common questions about Microsoft® Word for Windows™. Microsoft FastTips is available 24 hours a day, seven days a week. You can also order application notes that will be sent to your fax machine.

Call the Interactive Voice Support Service You can hear recorded responses to common questions about Microsoft Word. You can also order application notes that will be sent to your fax machine. This automated service is always available, and requires a touch-tone telephone.

- For assistance with Microsoft Word for Windows, dial (206) 635-7231.

After you reach the Interactive Voice Support Service:

- To advance to the next message, press *.
- To repeat the current message, press 7.
- To return to the beginning of the Interactive Voice Support Service, press #.

Use the Microsoft Forums on CompuServe Microsoft Product Support staff is available on several CompuServe forums. For an introductory CompuServe membership kit specifically for Microsoft users, dial (800) 848-8199 and ask for operator 230. If you are already a CompuServe member, type **GO MICROSOFT** at any ! prompt.

Call Microsoft Product Support Staff   You can reach Microsoft Product Support staff between 6:00 A.M. and 6:00 P.M. Pacific time, Monday through Friday.

■   For assistance with Microsoft Word for Windows, dial (206) 462-9673 or (206) 462-WORD.

When you call, you should be at your computer and have the appropriate product documentation at hand. Be prepared to give the following information:

■   The version number of the Microsoft product you are using

■   The type of hardware you are using

■   The exact wording of any messages that appeared on your screen

■   What happened and what you were doing when the problem occurred

■   How you tried to solve the problem

Getting Product Support with a Text Telephone (TDD/TT) for the Deaf and Hard of Hearing You can contact Microsoft Product Support staff with a Telecommunications Device for the Deaf/Text Telephone (TDD/TT) by dialing (206) 635-4948. Call between 6:00 A.M. and 6:00 P.M. Pacific time, Monday through Friday.

Microsoft's support services are subject to Microsoft prices, terms, and conditions at the time the service is used.

Getting Product Training and Consultation Services

Within the United States, Microsoft offers the following services for training and consultation:

Authorized Training Centers   Microsoft Authorized Training Centers offer several services for Microsoft product users. These include:

■   Customized training for end users and trainers

■   Training material development

■   Consulting services

For information about the training center nearest you, call Microsoft Sales and Service at (800) 426-9400.

Consultant Referral Service   Microsoft's Consultant Relations Program can refer you to an independent consultant in your area. These consultants are skilled in:

■   Macro development and translation

■   Database development

■   Custom interface design

For information about the consultants in your area, call the Microsoft Consultant Relations Program at (800) 227-4679, extension 56042.

Microsoft Product Support Services Worldwide

If you are outside the United States and have a question about Microsoft Word, Microsoft offers a variety of no charge and fee-based support options. To solve your problem you could:

1 Consult the manual's index and other printed product documentation.

2 Check context sensitive online Help from the menu.

3 Check the README files that come with your product disks.

4 Consult electronic options such as CompuServe forums or Bulletin Boards if available in your country.

If you cannot find the solution, you can receive information on how to receive product support by contacting the Microsoft subsidiary office that serves your country.

Microsoft's support services are subject to Microsoft's prices, terms, and conditions in place in each country at the time the service is used.

Telephoning Microsoft Product Support Services

When you call, you should be at your computer with Microsoft Word running and the product documentation at hand. Have your file open and be prepared to give the following information:

- The version of Microsoft Word that you are using.

- The type of hardware you are using, including network hardware, if applicable.

- The operating environment that you are using.

- The exact wording of any messages that appeared on your screen.

- A description of what happened and what you were doing when the problem occurred.

- How you tried to solve the problem.

Microsoft subsidiary offices and the countries they serve are listed below.

Countries	Telephone Numbers
Argentina	Microsoft de Argentina S.A. Phone: (54) (1) 814-0356 Fax: (54) (1) 814-0372

Australia	Microsoft Pty. Ltd.
	Phone: (61) (02) 870-2200
	Telex: MSOFT AA 75253
	Fax: (61) (02) 805-1108
	BBS: (612) 870-2348
	Technical support: (61) (02) 870-2131
Austria	Microsoft Ges.m.b.H.
	Phone: 0222-68 76 07
	Fax: 0222-68162710
Baltic states	See Germany
Belgium	Microsoft NV
	Phone: 02-7322590
	Fax: 02-7351609
	Technical Support Bulletin Board Service: 02-7350045
	(1200/2400/9600 baud, 8 bits, no parity, 1 stop bit, ANSI terminal emulation)
	Technical Support Phone Service:
	(Dutch) 02-5133274
	(English) 02-5023432
	(French) 02-5132268
	Technical Support Fax: (31) 2503-24304
Bermuda	See Venezuela
Bolivia	See Argentina
Brazil	Microsoft Informatica Ltda.
	Phone: (55) (11) 530-4455
	Fax: (55) (11) 240-2205
	Technical support: (55) (11) 533-2922
Canada	Microsoft Canada Inc.
	Phone: 1 (416) 568-0434
	Fax: 1 (416) 568-4689
	Technical support: 1 (416) 568-3503
Caribbean Countries	See Venezuela
Central America	See Venezuela
Chile	See Argentina
Colombia	See Venezuela

Denmark	Microsoft Danmark AS
	Phone: (45) (44) 89 01 00
	Fax: (45) (44) 68 55 10
Ecuador	See Venezuela
England	Microsoft Limited
	Phone: (44) (734) 270000
	Fax: (44) (734) 270002
	Upgrades: (44) (81) 893-8000
	Technical support:
	Main Line (All Products) (44) (734) 271000
	Bulletin Board Service (44) (734) 270065
	2400 Baud
	Fax Information Service (44) (734) 270080
Finland	Microsoft OY
	Phone: (358) (0) 525 501
	Fax: (358) (0) 522 955
France	Microsoft France
	Phone: (33) (1) 69-86-46-46
	Telex: MSPARIS 604322F
	Fax: (33) (1) 64-46-06-60
	Technical support: (33) (1) 69-86-10-20
French Polynesia	See France
Germany	Microsoft GmbH
	Phone: 089-3176-0
	Telex: (17) 89 83 28 MS GMBH D
	Fax: 089-3176-1000
	Technical support:
	089-3176-1131 Word for Windows
Hong Kong	Microsoft Hong Kong Limited
	Technical Support: (852) 804-4222
Ireland	See England
Israel	Microsoft Israel Ltd.
	Phone: 972-3-752-7915
	Fax: 972-3-752-7919

Italy	Microsoft SpA
	Phone: (39) (2) 269121
	Telex: 340321 I
	Fax: (39) (2) 21072020
	Technical support:
	(39) (2) 26901362 Word, PC Works
Japan	Microsoft Company Ltd.
	Phone: (81) (3) 3363-1200
	Fax: (81) (3) 3363-1281
	Technical support:
	(81) (3) 3363-5040 Windows Applications
	Fax: (81) (3) 3363-9901 All products
Korea	Microsoft CH
	Phone: (82) (2) 552-9505
	Fax: (82) (2) 555-1724
	Technical support: (82) (2) 563-9230
Liechtenstein	See Switzerland
Luxembourg	Microsoft NV
	Phone: (32) 2-7322590
	Fax: (32) 2-7351609
	Technical Support Bulletin Board Service: (31) 2503-34221
	(1200/2400/9600 baud, 8 bits, No parity, 1 stop bit, ANSI terminal emulation)
	Technical Support Phone Service:
	(Dutch) (31) 2503-7787
	(English) (31) 2503-77853
	(French) (32) 2-5132268
	Technical Support Fax: (31) 2503-24304
Mexico	Microsoft Mexico, S.A. de C.V.
	Phone: (52) (5) 325-0910
	Fax: (52) (5) 202-0399
	Technical support: (52) (5) 325-0912
	Sales: (52) (5) 325-0911

Netherlands	Netherlands
	Microsoft BV
	Phone: 02503-13181
	Fax: 02503-37761
	Technical Support Bulletin Board service: 02503-34221
	(1200/2400/9600 baud, 8 bits, No parity, 1 stop bit, ANSI terminal emulation)
	Technical Support Phone service:
	(Dutch) 02503-77877
	(English) 02503-77853
	Technical Support Fax: 02503-24304
New Zealand	Technology Link Centre
	Phone: (64) (9) 358-3724
	Fax: (64) (9) 358-3726
	For Applications Support, Call:
	(64) (9) 375-5575
Northern Ireland	See England
Norway	Microsoft Norway AS
	Phone: (47) (2) 95 06 65
	Fax: (47) (2) 95 06 64
	Technical support: (47) (2) 18 35 00
Papua New Guinea	See Australia
Paraguay	See Argentina
Peru	See Venezuela
Puerto Rico	See Venezuela
Portugal	MSFT, Lda.
	Phone: (351) 1 4412205
	Fax: (351) 1 4412101
Republic of China	Microsoft Taiwan Corp.
	Phone: (886) (2) 504-3122
	Fax: (886) (2) 504-3121
Republic of Ireland	See England
Scotland	See England

Spain	Microsoft Iberica SRL
	Phone: (34) (1) 804-0000
	Fax: (34) (1) 803-8310
	Technical support: (34) (1) 803-9960
Sweden	Microsoft AB
	Phone: (46) (8) 752 56 00
	Fax: (46) (8) 750 51 58
	Technical support:
	(Applications) (46) (8) 752 68 50
Switzerland	Microsoft AG
	Phone: (41) (1) 839 61 11
	Fax: (41) (1) 831 08 69
	Technical support:
	German
	01-342-40-87 Word for Windows
	French
	022-738-96-88 All Microsoft products
Uruguay	See Argentina
Venezuela	Phone: 0058.2.914739
	Fax: 0058.2.923835
Wales	See England

Your First Word Document

This chapter presents the basic skills and concepts that you need to start using Microsoft Word immediately. In this chapter, you'll learn how to:

- Start Word and display a document on your screen.
- Type and edit text.
- Create a new document and open an existing document.
- Save your work for future use.
- Make simple changes to your document's appearance, such as making text bold, centering a heading, and indenting a paragraph.
- Print a document.
- Close a document and quit Word.

Is This Chapter for You?

This chapter provides enough information to get you started using Word and to produce a simple document. The following paragraphs may help you to determine whether or not this chapter is appropriate for you.

If you haven't yet installed Word   You must run the Setup program to install Word. Then refer to this chapter for basics about using Word. For information on installing Word, see *Microsoft Word Getting Started*.

If you're new to the Windows operating environment   You should learn Windows fundamentals—using the mouse, working with windows, and opening and closing documents—before you begin your work with Word. However, if you are short of time or don't have a Windows manual available, this chapter briefly covers the techniques you'll need to start working with Word for Windows.

If you're new to word-processing   If you've always worked on a typewriter, you may not know where to begin or how to use a word processor. This chapter guides you through a typical work session—from starting a new document to printing the final version. It also points out some typing habits to avoid when working in Word.

If you're new to Word   If you are changing to Word from another word processor, you probably already know the tasks you want to accomplish, but you may not know how to accomplish them in Word. The techniques and features introduced in this chapter are those you'll use most often. If you don't find a specific term, it may have a different name in Word; refer to the index in this book for its equivalent.

If you want to use your computer to learn about Word   Start Word and choose the Getting Started command from the Help menu to use the online lessons. For information about starting Word and choosing commands from menus, see "Choosing

Commands" and "Starting Word," later in this chapter. If you need more information, see Chapter 5, "Using Help and Online Lessons."

Before You Begin Your Work with Word

Before you start work on your first document, make sure you have installed Windows, a printer driver for your printer, and the necessary fonts. For more information on installing printers and fonts, see your Windows documentation.

You can use the keyboard or the mouse to carry out any action in Word. If you are not familiar with using the mouse or keyboard, or with choosing commands in Windows, read the following information.

Using the Mouse

The mouse controls a pointer on the screen. You move the pointer by sliding the mouse over a flat surface in the direction you want the pointer to move. You don't press the mouse button when you move the mouse. If you run out of room to move the mouse, lift it and then put it down. The pointer doesn't move while the mouse is in the air.

The mouse has two buttons; you use the left button for most tasks in Word. Moving the mouse and pressing the mouse button are the only actions involved in the basic skills of *pointing, clicking,* and *dragging*.

Pointing   Moving the mouse to place the pointer over an item is called pointing.

Clicking   Pointing to an item on your screen and then quickly pressing and releasing the mouse button is called clicking. You select items on the screen and move around in a document by clicking. Double-clicking—pointing to an item and quickly pressing the mouse button twice—is a convenient shortcut for many of the tasks you'll do in Word.

Dragging   Holding down the mouse button as you move the pointer is called dragging. You can use this technique to select text in your documents.

Using the Keyboard

To provide keyboard information, the Word documentation uses some special conventions:

- The keys on your keyboard may not be labeled exactly as they appear in this manual. For example, the Control key is shown as CTRL, and the Escape key is shown as ESC.

- Keys are often used in combinations or sequences. For example, SHIFT+F1 means to hold down the SHIFT key while pressing the F1 key, and ALT, F, A means to press and release each of these keys in order: first ALT, then F, and then A.

- *Arrow keys* is the collective name for the UP ARROW, DOWN ARROW, LEFT ARROW, and RIGHT ARROW keys.

Choosing Commands

For more information about choosing commands and selecting options in dialog boxes, see Chapter 1, "The Word Workplace."

To choose a command from a menu, you can use the mouse or press a key combination. In Word documentation, key combinations are provided after the menu and command names. For example, if a procedure step states "From the File menu, choose Open (ALT, F, O)," use the mouse and/or keyboard as described in the following procedure.

To choose a command

1   Point to the File menu, and then click the left mouse button.

2   Point to the Open command, and then click the left mouse button.

1   Press the ALT key to activate the menu bar, and then press F to open the File menu.

2   Press O to choose the Open command.

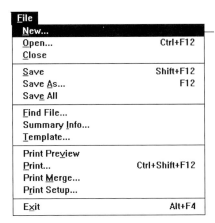

— When you open a menu, the first command is selected.

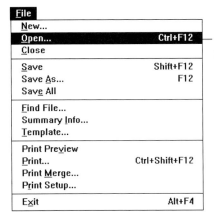

— Use the mouse or the keyboard to choose a command.

If you choose a command name that is not followed by three dots—an ellipsis—the command is carried out immediately. If the command name is followed by an ellipsis, like the Open command in the preceding illustration, Word displays a dialog box, in which you can select the options you want. Information on selecting options is included for each procedure in this chapter.

Starting Word

Word Setup automatically creates the Word for Windows 2.0 program group, the Word Setup icon, and the Word application icon. The Dialog Editor is a tool you can use to create dialog boxes for WordBasic macros.

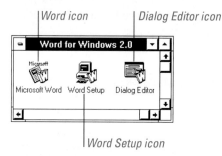

In Windows, the Word icon is displayed in the Word for Windows 2.0 group.

To start Word

You can start Word using either the mouse or the keyboard. If Windows is not already running, type **win** at the command prompt.

▶ Double-click the Microsoft Word icon.

–Or–

▶ Do one of the following:

■ If the Microsoft Word icon is selected, press ENTER.

■ If the Microsoft Word icon is not selected, use the arrow keys to select the Word icon, and then press ENTER.

■ If the Microsoft Word icon is not selected and the Word for Windows 2.0 group window is not active, press CTRL+TAB until the group is active. A group is active when the title bar and an icon in the group are highlighted. Then select the Microsoft Word icon and press ENTER.

Selecting a Printer

If you installed more than one printer when you set up Windows, the first time you start Word you'll need to make sure that the active printer is the one you want to use to print your Word documents. If you have one printer selected while you work in a document and then select a different printer to print it, some fonts, sizes, and other character formatting options may not be available when you print the document.

Once you select a printer, you won't need to do so again, unless you install a new printer or want to change to a different printer. For information about selecting a printer, see Chapter 4, "Printing a Document."

Beginning Work on a Document

When you start Word, you see the basic Word screen, or *workplace,* where a new, empty document is automatically opened for you.

A new document is preset to use standard 8.5-by-11-inch paper, with 1.25-inch left and right margins and 1-inch top and bottom margins. You can use these and other default settings until you want to change the document's appearance.

You can begin typing in the document, just as you would on a clean sheet of paper in a typewriter. You can also open an existing document.

The Word Screen

For more information about the screen, see Chapter 1, "The Word Workplace."

The following illustration shows some important parts of the Word screen, followed by a brief description of each part.

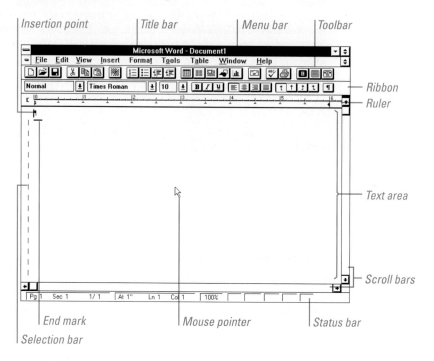

A new document window

Title bar   Displays "Microsoft Word" and the name of the active document.

Menu bar   Contains a list of menus. You open menus and then choose commands from them to instruct Word to perform actions.

Toolbar   With the mouse, provides instant access to frequently used Word commands.

Ribbon and ruler   Help you quickly change the appearance of text.

Text area   Displays text and graphics.

Insertion point   Shows where text will be inserted when you type.

Mouse pointer   Shows where the next action will occur if you click the mouse button. The mouse pointer is shaped like an I-beam when you point at text and an arrow when you point at selected text or the selection bar on the left side of the screen.

End mark   Shows the end of the document; the end mark moves as you type.

Scroll bars   Indicate your location in a document. With the mouse, display other pages by clicking the scroll bar or the scroll arrow, or by dragging the scroll box.

Status bar   Displays information about the active document or selected command.

Selection bar   An unmarked area along the left side of the window that helps you select text with the mouse. In the selection bar, the mouse pointer is an arrow.

Typing in a Document

Working in Word is easier than typing on a typewriter. Nothing is on paper until you print your document, so you can reword a phrase as many times as you like and correct errors as you go.

Before you begin typing, position the insertion point where you want to insert the text. If the document doesn't contain any text, the insertion point is already positioned for you.

To position the insertion point

▶   Click the mouse where you want to position the insertion point.

–Or–

1   Make sure that NUM LOCK is not on.

2   Press the arrow keys or the HOME, END, PAGE UP, and PAGE DOWN keys.

For more information on using keys to position the insertion point, see Chapter 3, "Typing and Revising a Document."

Tip   You can't position the insertion point past the end mark at the end of the document. If you want to create some blank space before typing, press the ENTER key.

To add text to a document

1   Position the insertion point where you want to insert new text.

2   Type the new text.

As you type, the insertion point advances to the right. Word automatically adjusts the text between the right and left margins, starting a new line where necessary. This is called *wordwrap*.

If the Show/Hide ¶ button is selected on the ribbon, or the All check box is selected in the View category in the Options dialog box (Tools menu), your document will look similar to the following illustration.

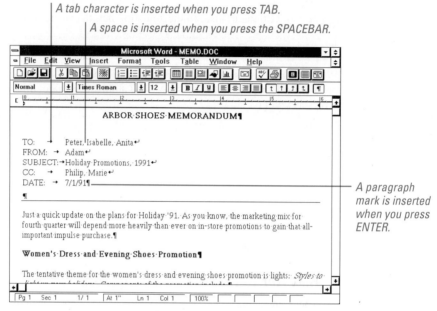

A document with paragraph marks and other nonprinting characters displayed

Note   If you press the INS key on the numeric keypad, the status bar at the bottom of the screen displays "OVR," for overtype mode. The next text you type replaces the text that follows the insertion point. If you press INS again, the text you type is inserted to the left of any existing text; the existing text moves to the right.

Displaying ¶ Marks and Other Nonprinting Characters

Paragraph marks play an important role in formatting your documents. You'll learn about formatting later.

A paragraph mark (¶) is inserted each time you press ENTER. Paragraph marks store information about the paragraph; if you delete a paragraph mark, the paragraph takes on the formatting of the next paragraph in your document.

Because paragraph marks are important, it is best to work with them displayed. Paragraph marks aren't printed, even when they are displayed on your screen. Word uses other nonprinting characters, such as spaces and tab characters, that you may also want to display.

To display ¶ marks and other nonprinting characters

▶ On the ribbon, click the Show/Hide ¶ button.

Word displays all paragraph marks, tabs, spaces, and other nonprinting characters on the screen.

1 From the Tools menu, choose Options (ALT, O, O).

In the Category box, View may already be selected.

2 If View isn't already selected in the Category box, press the UP ARROW or DOWN ARROW key until View is selected.

3 Under Nonprinting Characters, select the Paragraph Marks check box by pressing ALT+M.

4 To view other nonprinting characters, such as tab characters and spaces, hold down the ALT key and press the underlined letter for the appropriate option. For example, to display tab characters, select Tabs by pressing ALT+T.

5 Press ENTER.

Word displays paragraph marks and spaces on the screen. If there are optional hyphens, tab characters, or hidden text, they are also displayed.

How *Not* to Type in a Word Processor

Your computer keyboard may remind you of a typewriter, but using a word processor is different from working on a typewriter. If you're coming to Word from a typewriter, remember the following:

Do not press the ENTER key at the end of each line. Instead, press ENTER only to start a new paragraph. If you press ENTER at the end of each line, Word can't adjust the line breaks when you add or delete text. Take advantage of wordwrap; it is one of the many benefits of using a word processor.

Do not use the SPACEBAR to move the insertion point or to indent or align text. Instead, use the arrow keys or click the mouse to move the insertion point. Use tabs or paragraph formatting to indent or align text. Press the SPACEBAR only to insert a space between words. To your computer and Word, spaces are not just blanks on the page: They are characters just like the letter "a" or the 0's in 1,000,000. For more information about setting tabs and indenting or aligning text, see Chapter 7, "Paragraph Formatting."

Opening an Existing Document

Before you can work on an existing document, it must be open on the screen.

To open an existing document

1   From the File menu, choose Open (ALT, F, O).

Word displays the Open dialog box.

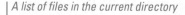
A list of files in the current directory

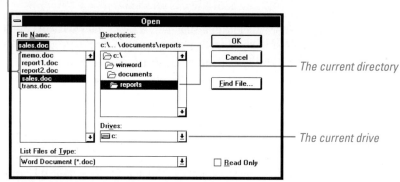

The current directory

The current drive

2   In the File Name box, double-click the name of the document you want to open.
    −or−
    In the File Name box, type the filename, or press the UP ARROW or DOWN ARROW key to select the filename. Press ENTER.

To list a document in the File Name box

If the document you want is not listed in the File Name box, select a new drive or directory in the Open dialog box. If the document you want is not a Word for Windows document, select a different type of file in the List Files Of Type box.

1   From the File menu, choose Open.

2   Do one of the following:

If the file is	To display its name in the File Name box
In a different subdirectory	Double-click the directory in the Directories box.
On a different drive	Click the arrow in the Drives box, and then click the drive letter.
Of a different file type	Click the arrow in the List Files Of Type box, and then click the type of file.

1 From the File menu, choose Open (ALT, F, O).

2 Press ALT+D to select from the Directories box, ALT+V to select from the Drives box, or ALT+T to select from the List Files Of Type box.

3 Press the UP ARROW or DOWN ARROW key until the directory, drive, or file type you want is selected.

4 Press ENTER.

Note If the directory that contains the file is not displayed in the Directories box, you may have to move higher in the directory hierarchy to find the file. For example, suppose you have two subdirectories under drive C. The contents of the first subdirectory are listed, and you want to list the contents of the second subdirectory. In the Directories box, you must first double-click the C:\ directory and then double-click the second subdirectory.

Quickly Locate a File

You can quickly locate a file using the Find File command on the File menu. With Find File, you can search for a file by its filename, file type, specific text in the file, and other information. You can also make sure you've located the file you want by viewing its contents without opening it. For more information about Find File, see Chapter 26, "Finding and Managing Files."

Creating a New Document

You can create new blank documents in Word.

To create a new document

1   From the File menu, choose New (ALT, F, N).

Word displays the New dialog box.

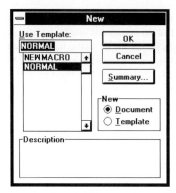

You can make changes in this dialog box, but for now, use the Word defaults, which are already selected for you.

2   Click the OK button, or press ENTER.

Word gives the new document a temporary name, such as Document1. You give the document a unique name when you save it.

Note   You can have as many as nine documents open in Word. You can switch between them as you work, and size and move them so you can see more than one at a time. For more information, see Chapter 1, "The Word Workplace."

Editing a Document

Selecting text is an important first step for much of the work you'll do with Word.

Editing, or revising, document text is easy with Word. You can delete, replace, or rearrange text in a document. To indicate which text you want to change, you must first select it. For example, to remove text from a document quickly, you first select the text and then choose a command or press a key to delete it.

Selected text is highlighted, that is, shown in white letters against a dark background or in dark letters against a colored background. How selected text appears depends on your computer settings.

> **Introduction¶**
>
> The Trey Research FilmWatch Division represents Trey's best opportunity to dominate market research for the film industry. This new Trey division will be one of the first research organizations devoted exclusively to quantitative research and analysis for motion picture producers. We see two main target markets: ¶

The selected, or highlighted, area in your document is called the selection.

To select text

1   Position the insertion point at the beginning of the text you want to work with.

2   Hold down the left mouse button and drag the pointer to the end of the text.

1   Position the insertion point at the beginning of the text you want to work with.

2   Hold down the SHIFT key and use the arrow keys to move the insertion point to where you want the selection to end.

To select specific amounts of text

When you're formatting text, the same general rule applies as for editing: You must first select the text you want to format. If you are using a mouse, you can always drag to select any amount of text. Here are some additional shortcuts you can use.

▶   Do one of the following:

To select	Do this
A word	Point to the word and double-click.
A paragraph	Double-click the selection bar.*
An entire document	Hold down CTRL and click the selection bar.*

*The selection bar is at the left edge of the text area; when the mouse pointer is in the selection bar, the pointer is shaped like an arrow.

1   Place the insertion point in the text you want to select.

2   Press F8.

The status bar displays "EXT," for extend mode.

3   To select a word, sentence, paragraph, section (if applicable), or entire document, press F8 repeatedly until the amount of text you want is selected.

To reverse a selection made with F8, press SHIFT+F8.

4   Press ESC to cancel extend mode.

For more information about selecting text, see Chapter 3, "Typing and Revising a Document."

To cancel a selection

If you select text and then decide not to change it, or if you select the wrong text, cancel the selection before you continue typing. If text is selected, the next text you type will replace it.

▶ Click anywhere in the document window.

–Or–

▶ Press any arrow key.

To delete characters

▶ Do one of the following:

To delete	Do this
A character to left of insertion point	Press BACKSPACE.
A character to right of insertion point	Press DEL.
Several characters	Select them, and then press DEL or BACKSPACE.

To type over text

1   Select the text you want to replace with new text.

2   Begin typing the new text.

As soon as you press a key, Word deletes the selected text and inserts the new text.

Tip   If you don't want Word to replace selections when you type, you can clear the Typing Replaces Selection check box in the General category in the Options dialog box (Tools menu). For more information, see Chapter 39, "Setting Preferences."

To move text

Moving text from one place to another in your document is sometimes called cutting and pasting. You move text using the Cut and Paste commands on the Edit menu. You can also copy text to another place in your document by using the Copy command, also on the Edit menu.

1   Select the text you want to move.

2   From the Edit menu, choose Cut (ALT, E, T).

Word removes the selected text from your document and stores it on the Clipboard, a temporary storage area. A copy of the text stays on the Clipboard until you next choose the Cut or Copy command.

3   Position the insertion point where you want to move the text.

4   From the Edit menu, choose Paste (ALT, E, P).

Word inserts the text from the Clipboard. You can choose Paste as many times as you want to insert the same text at other locations in your document.

To undo a command or editing action

You can often reverse your most recent action—typing, deleting text, or choosing most Word commands. If something happens that is confusing or is not what you intended, choose the Undo command as the next action.

▶   From the Edit menu, choose Undo (ALT, E, U).

Speeding Up Basic Tasks

If you have a mouse, you can use the buttons on the Toolbar to perform many basic tasks quickly, such as creating, opening, saving, and printing documents; cutting, copying, and pasting text; and undoing the most recent action. For example, you can quickly create a new document by clicking the New button.

Click to create a new document.

The Toolbar groups buttons by type of task. New is in the first group.

If you forget which button accomplishes a particular task, you can view a brief description in the status bar at the lower-left corner of the screen. Point at a button on the Toolbar and hold down the left mouse button. To avoid activating the button, continue to press the mouse button. Drag the mouse pointer away from the button on the Toolbar, and then release the mouse button. The Toolbar is described in more detail in Chapter 1, "The Word Workplace."

Saving Your Work

It's a good idea to save your document at least every 10 minutes.

When you're working in Word, you're actually working on a copy of your document temporarily stored in the computer's memory. To save your work for future use, you must give the document a name and store it on a disk—either a hard disk or a floppy disk. If a power failure or other problem interrupts your Word session, any work you haven't saved will be lost.

To save a document

1   From the File menu, choose Save (ALT, F, S).

If you're saving the document for the first time, Word displays the following dialog box.

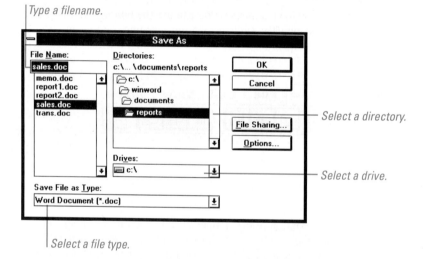

Type a filename.

Select a directory.

Select a drive.

Select a file type.

2   In the File Name box, type a name (maximum of eight characters without spaces).

Word saves the document in the current drive and directory and automatically adds a .DOC extension to the filename unless you specify another extension.

If you make a mistake, you can use the LEFT ARROW, RIGHT ARROW, or BACKSPACE key to correct it.

3   If you want to save the document in a different drive or directory, see "To save a document in another drive or directory," later in this section.

4   Click the OK button, or press ENTER.

Word displays the Summary Info dialog box, in which you can fill in information about your document. The information is optional, but it may make it easier for you to locate the document later. For now, just choose the OK button to close the dialog box and return to your document.

To save a document in another drive or directory

1 From the File menu, choose Save As (ALT, F, A).

2 In the File Name box, type the complete path and filename.

   For example, to save SALES.DOC in the REPORTS directory on drive A, type
   a:\reports\sales.doc
   –or–
   In the File Name box, type a filename, and then select a new drive or directory as
   follows:

If you want to save the document	Do this
In a different directory	Double-click the directory in the Directories box. –or– Press ALT+D to move to the Directories box, and then press the UP ARROW or DOWN ARROW key until the directory you want is selected.
On a different drive	Click the arrow in the Drives box, and then click the drive letter. –or– Press ALT+V to move to the Drives box, and then press the UP ARROW or DOWN ARROW key until the drive you want is selected.

3 If you want to save the document in a different file format, select the format you
   want in the List Files Of Type box.

4 Click the OK button, or press ENTER.

Have Word Save Your Work Automatically

It's easy to forget to save your documents regularly, especially if you aren't accustomed
to working on a computer. To have Word periodically save your work, you can use the
Options command on the Tools menu. Select the Save category, and then select the
Automatic Save check box. Word proposes to save your work every 10 minutes, but you
can type or select a different interval in the Minutes box. For more information about the
Save options, see Chapter 2, "Opening, Saving, and Deleting Documents."

Changing the Look of Text

You control the way your document looks through the formatting you apply. This section covers the simple formats you'll use most often, including ways to emphasize text, such as bold and italic formatting, and ways to arrange text on the page, such as centering and indenting paragraphs.

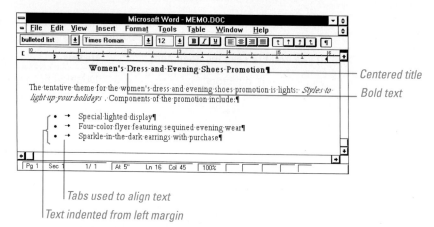

A document with simple formatting. The ruler and ribbon show paragraph and character formatting at the insertion point.

Formatting Commands Apply to Different Parts of the Document

Some formats, such as bold and underline, can be applied to any amount of text—to a single character or to the entire document. Formats of this type are called *character formats*. Other types of formatting—such as line spacing and indents—affect whole paragraphs of text. These formats are called *paragraph formats*. Still other formats affect a section of the document. For example, margin settings and the page number format can differ in each chapter or section. For more information about using formatting commands to control the appearance of your documents, see Part 3, "Formatting a Document."

To make text bold, italic, or underlined

Bold, italic, and underline are formats you can apply or remove quickly by clicking buttons on the ribbon or by using key combinations. You can apply more than one format to the selected text—for example, you can make text both bold and italic.

1   Select the text.

2   On the ribbon, click the buttons for the formats you want.

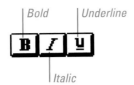

Bold   *Underline*

Italic

1   Select the text.

2   Press any of the following key combinations.

To apply this character format	Press
Bold	CTRL+B
Italic	CTRL+I
<u>Underline</u>	CTRL+U

You apply a format by selecting it and remove the format by selecting a different format.

If you prefer to make text bold, italic, or underlined as you type, you can select the format and then type the text.

To change the font and point size

A font is the design of characters; the point size is their height. The active font and size are shown in the Font and Points boxes on the ribbon.

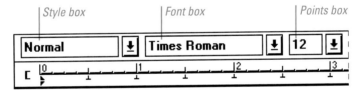

Style box   *Font box*   *Points box*

The Font and Points boxes are to the right of the Style box on the ribbon.

1   Select the text you want to change.

2   On the ribbon, click the arrow next to the Font or Points box, and then click the font or size you want in the box.

1   Select the text you want to change.

2   To select the Font box, press CTRL+F.
    –or–
    To select the Points box, press CTRL+P.

3   In the Font or Points box, type the font name or the point size, and then press ENTER.
    –or–
    Press the DOWN ARROW key to display the Font or Points box. Then use the DOWN ARROW or UP ARROW key to select a font name or point size and press ENTER.

Tip   All of your Word documents have a preset, or default, font and point size. If you frequently use a different font or point size, you can change the defaults. For more information, see Chapter 6, "Character Formatting."

Left margin

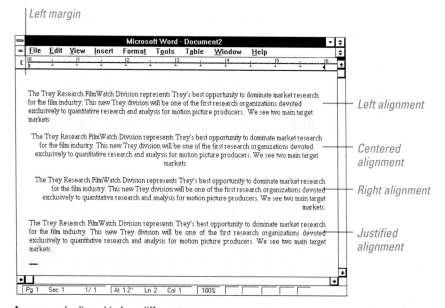

A paragraph aligned in four different ways.

To change a paragraph's alignment

You can align a paragraph in four different ways relative to the margins. Word is preset to align text flush with the left margin.

1   Select the paragraphs.

2   On the ribbon, click the button for the format you want.

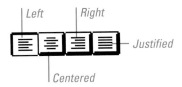

Alignment buttons

1   Select the paragraphs.

2   Press one of the following key combinations.

To align	Press
Left	CTRL+L
Center	CTRL+E
Right	CTRL+R
Justified	CTRL+J

You apply a format by selecting it and remove the format by selecting a different format.

If you prefer to align paragraphs as you type, you can select the format and then type the paragraphs.

Tip   You can change the spacing within a paragraph and the spacing between paragraphs. For example, you can have double-spacing between the lines in a paragraph and single-spacing between paragraphs. For more information, see Chapter 7, "Paragraph Formatting."

Setting Tab Stops

If you're using tabs to set up columns of text or numbers, consider using the Word table feature instead. See Chapter 17, "Tables."

Tab stops are preset every half inch. When you press the TAB key, the text following the insertion point lines up at the next tab position in the paragraph. You can set four different types of tab stops in Word.

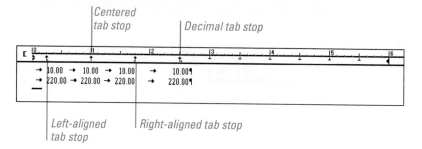

Document with four types of tab stops. Tab characters are displayed.

To set a tab stop

Before you use the following procedure to set tab stops, display tab characters in your document as explained under "To display ¶ marks and other nonprinting characters," earlier in this chapter.

1   Select the paragraphs for which you want to set the tab stop.

2   On the ribbon, click the button for the type of tab stop you want.

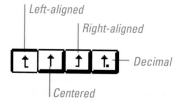

Tab stop buttons

3   In the lower half of the ruler, click where you want the tab stop.

4   To set other tab stops, repeat steps 2 and 3.

1   Select the paragraphs for which you want to set the tab stop.

2   To activate the ruler, press CTRL+SHIFT+F10.

3   To move the ruler cursor to where you want the tab stop, press the LEFT ARROW or RIGHT ARROW key.

4   Select an alignment for the tab stop.

For this tab stop	Press
Left-aligned	1
Centered	2
Right-aligned	3
Decimal	4

5   Press INS to set the tab stop.

6   To set other tab stops, repeat steps 3 through 5.

7   To return to the document, press ENTER.

Indenting Paragraphs

The text of a paragraph normally extends from the left margin to the right margin. You can quickly indent selected paragraphs from the left margin by clicking the Indent button on the Toolbar. Clicking the Indent button indents the paragraphs to next default tab stop. The default tab stops are set at 0.5-inch intervals.

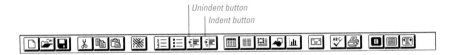

| Unindent button
| Indent button

If the Toolbar is not displayed, choose Toolbar from the View menu (ALT, V, T).

To indent a paragraph to the next default tab stop

With the selection or insertion point in the paragraph, click the Indent button on the Toolbar.

To move the paragraph back to the left, click the Unindent button on the Toobar.

Press CTRL+N.

To move a paragraph back to the left, press CTRL+M.

If you want to apply special left, right, hanging, or first-line indents, you can use the indent markers on the ruler.

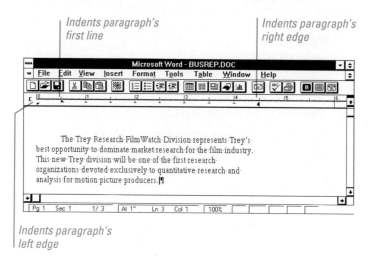

Indents paragraph's first line

Indents paragraph's right edge

Indents paragraph's left edge

For the most precise control over indentation, choose the Paragraph command from the Format menu (ALT, T, P) and change the settings under Indentation in the Paragraph dialog box.

For more information about setting indents, see "Indenting Paragraphs" in Chapter 7, "Paragraph Formatting."

About paragraphs and paragraph formatting

To Word, a paragraph is any amount of text or graphics followed by a paragraph mark (¶). A paragraph mark by itself on a blank line is also considered a paragraph.

The formatting you apply to the paragraph is "stored" in the paragraph mark that indicates the end of the paragraph. This is why if you delete a paragraph mark, the text of that paragraph takes on the formatting of the next paragraph in your document. If this is not what you want, choose Undo from the Edit menu as your next action.

Word considers the paragraph you're typing in—the paragraph containing the insertion point—to be selected, so any paragraph formatting commands you choose are applied to the current paragraph.

Once you format a paragraph, you can continue typing additional paragraphs in the same format. When you press ENTER, each new paragraph has the same format as the preceding paragraph until you change the format.

Previewing and Printing Your Document

For information on adjusting your document in print preview, see Chapter 24, "Viewing Documents."

In Word, you can view your document in a variety of ways to best suit the work you are doing. One view, print preview, allows you to see whole pages as they will look when printed. If you don't like the way your pages look, you can return to your document and make changes to your text and layout, or you can remain in this view and make changes to the overall layout of the document. When you're satisfied with how things look, you're ready to print.

To preview your document before you print

1   From the File menu, choose Print Preview (ALT, F, V).

Word displays the document in a reduced size so you can see the overall appearance of the pages.

Print the document.   *View two pages simultaneously.*

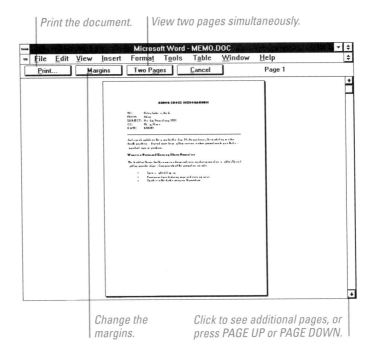

Change the margins.   *Click to see additional pages, or press PAGE UP or PAGE DOWN.*

2   To return to your document, choose the Cancel button or press ESC.
–or–
To print the document, choose the Print button or press P.

To print a document

1   From the File menu, choose Print (ALT, F, P).

Word displays the Print dialog box.

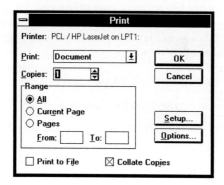

You can make changes in this dialog box, but for now, use the Word defaults, which are already selected for you.

2   Click the OK button, or press ENTER.

Word displays a message to tell you that your document is being printed. If you need to cancel printing in progress, choose the Cancel button or press ESC.

Closing a Document and Quitting Word

If you're ready to begin work on another document, you can close the active document's window and open another document, or if you're finished working, you can quit Word.

If a document has changes you haven't saved, Word asks if you want to save changes before closing the document or quitting Word. If you choose the Yes button, but haven't yet named the document, Word displays the Save As dialog box. For information on saving a document, see "Saving Your Work," earlier in this chapter.

To close a document

▶ Double-click the document Control-menu box in the upper-left corner of the document window.

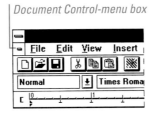

Document Control-menu box

The document Control menu box is to the left of the File menu.

–Or–

▶ From the File menu, choose Close (ALT, F, C).

To quit Word

▶ From the File menu, choose Exit (ALT, F, X).

Where to Go from Here

To get help with your word-processing tasks, press F1 at any time. Pressing F1 displays help on your task and the active dialog box, and any error messages on your screen. You can even get help on using Help. For more information, see Chapter 5, "Using Help and Online Lessons."

Word contains many useful features, such as outlining and tables, that can help you to work more accurately and productively. For more information on Word features, see the next chapter, "Putting Word to Work."

If you want more information on any of the topics covered in this chapter, refer to the table of contents or index.

Putting Word to Work

Microsoft Word is a powerful word-processing program with features that make it easy for you to create all kinds of documents. However, as with anything that's rich with possibilities, you sometimes can't immediately see all that's there. Whether you learn by experimentation, by reading, or from a friend or colleague, it takes time to explore the program's versatility. Sometimes, the first methods you learn become habits, even though there may be more efficient ways to accomplish your tasks.

This chapter provides a quick overview of some of the most important features in Word. You'll see examples of techniques you'll want to use right away, and others you'll file away to use later when you are more familiar with Word.

To demonstrate how you can use these features in your work, some of these techniques are illustrated as parts of several typical kinds of documents, including:

- A business letter and memo
- A business report
- A book or long document
- A brochure and newsletter

The examples illustrate how Word can work for you. You can use each basic feature as shown or modify it to fill a specific need. As you learn the features shown here, you can apply them to other types of documents. For example, you can insert a graphic into any kind of document using the same easy method you learn to insert a company logo into a business letter. For details about the features introduced in this chapter, see the chapter mentioned at the end of each feature.

Business Letters and Memos

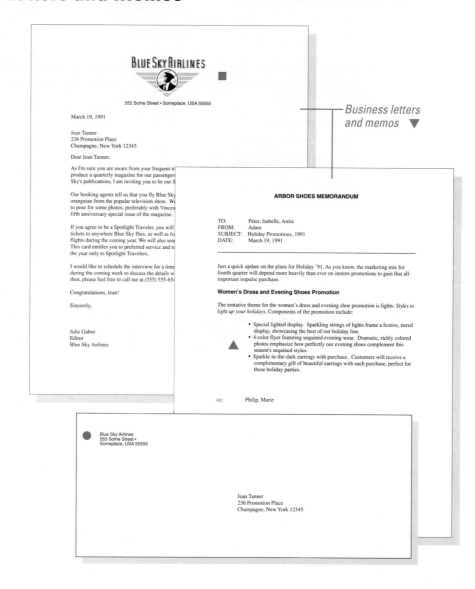

Business letters and memos ▼

▼ **Do you often create the same type of memo or letter?**

Create a template If you often create documents that are similar in layout and format, you can create a *template* that includes all the formatting you need. For example, you may have a standard business letter in which you only need to change the name and address and a phrase or two. By saving this letter as a template, you can use it repeatedly without changing the original letter. You create a new document based on the template, make the needed changes to the name and address, and print it for mailing.

See Chapter 37, "Document Templates."

■ **Do your letters often include the company logo and address?**

Store items you want to use again   You can use the *glossary* feature to store text and graphics so you can add them to any document. For example, when creating a new business letter, you can select a logo and address you saved in the glossary and insert them into the letter.

See Chapter 13, "Glossaries: Storing Items for Reuse."

▲ **Do you want an easy way to create bulleted lists?**

Let Word insert the bullets   It's often useful to break out key points and put a bullet in front of each item for emphasis. It can be tricky, though, to insert a bullet and get the second line of text to line up under the first. You can simplify this task with the Bullets And Numbering command. Just type the paragraphs, choose the command, select the bullet you want, and Word adds bullets to the list for you.

See Chapter 28, "Adding Bullets and Numbers."

● **Does that letter need an addressed envelope?**

Address it in Word   If you need to address an envelope, choose the Create Envelope command to copy the address from the letter, insert your return address, and position them correctly on your printed envelope. If you plan on using the letter again, you can attach the envelope to the letter so it is printed every time you use the letter.

See Chapter 4, "Printing a Document."

Do you want to personalize form letters?

Merge information from your client database   Many business letters contain standard text in which only the addresses vary. The print merge feature in Word combines information from a database with a form letter to print such letters automatically. However, the process of setting up the main document and data file can be confusing. To help, the Print Merge command uses dialog boxes and instructions to guide you through the entire process. For instant Help, press F1 at any time.

See Chapter 32, "Print Merge Basics," and Chapter 34, "Form Letters and Other Merged Documents."

Articles and Reports

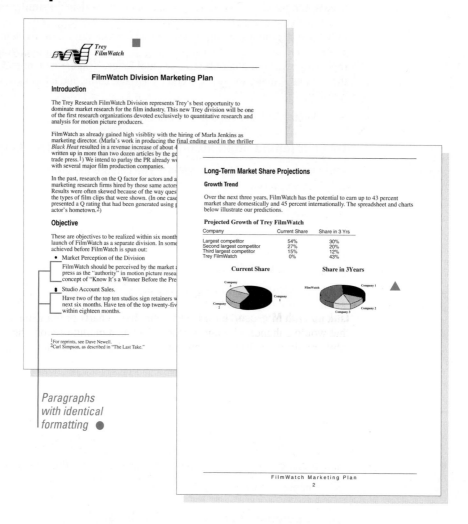

*Paragraphs
with identical
formatting* ●

- ### Do you want to apply the same formatting to many paragraphs?

  Save your formats in a style and apply them all at once   Paragraphs in a document often require the same look. The text in a report may require a certain font, tab settings, and justification. Applying this formatting to each paragraph can be tedious. You can save time by saving formatting as a *style*. Give the style a unique name, and then, using that name, apply the style any time you need that formatting.

  The Styles box on the ribbon

  See Chapter 8, "Formatting with Styles."

- ### Do you want to include pictures or graphics?

  Import a graphic   You can include pictures from most graphics applications by opening the picture in its application, copying it, and pasting it into Word. Once in Word, you can position the graphic, size it, crop it, and have text flow around it.

  See Chapter 20, "Importing Graphics."

- ### Do you need to show worksheets or charts in your documents?

  Link up with Microsoft Excel   You may have charts or worksheets in Microsoft Excel that would enhance a business report. You can include a worksheet or chart in Word while retaining its link to Microsoft Excel. When linked, the worksheet or chart appears in your Word document while remaining connected to the original information. If the worksheet or chart changes in Microsoft Excel, you can update the chart in Word with one keystroke.

  See Chapter 36, "Exchanging Information."

Do you prefer choosing commands with the mouse?

Click the Toolbar   Choosing commands you frequently use is easy with the Toolbar. The Toolbar, located just below the menu bar, displays a row of buttons for commands that you can choose without hunting through menus or trying to remember a key combination. In some cases, you can even avoid dialog boxes. For example, by choosing the Print button, you can immediately print one copy of the active document without displaying the Print dialog box. If the commands on the Toolbar are not those you use frequently, change them using the Options command on the Tools menu. And if you write your own macros, you can also assign them to a button on the Toolbar.

The Toolbar

See Chapter 1, "The Word Workplace."

Books and Manuals

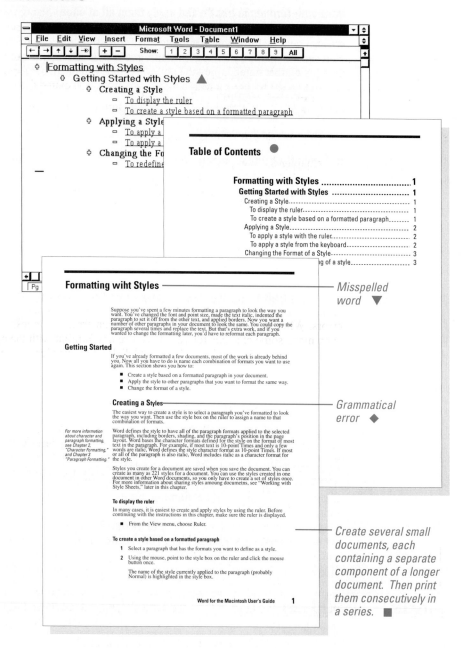

▲ **Do you often reorganize large sections of documents?**

Use outline view to simplify the task   It can be time-consuming and confusing to change the structure of a large, complex document by cutting and pasting chunks of text throughout the document. The structure of large documents can also be hard to visualize. Using outline view, you can choose to see only the document headings so you can concentrate on the structure of your document. To restructure the document, you only need to move a heading to move all its associated text to the new location.

See Chapter 27, "Outline View: Creating Outlines and Reorganizing Documents."

■ **Do you work with large documents?**

Connect smaller documents   Instead of trying to create an entire book in one document, it is often more efficient to create smaller documents and then print them in a series as one integrated document. When you work with smaller documents, more than one person at a time can work on the book or manual.

See Chapter 11, "Setting Up Long Documents."

◆ **Do you want to check the grammar in your document?**

Check your grammar with Word   While not a replacement for a skilled editor, the grammar checker in Word can help you polish your documents. The grammar checker reviews your document sentence by sentence and alerts you to possible grammatical errors. When the grammar checker identifies an error, it suggests a correction and can even make some changes for you. If you're not familiar with the applicable grammar rule, the Explain button in the Grammar dialog box provides more information.

See Chapter 14, "Proofing a Document."

▼ **Do you want to check for typos and misspelled words?**

Check the spelling in your document   Checking for spelling or typographical errors is an important part of polishing your work. The spelling feature in Word can review your document before you print it. You can add to the dictionary any special words or terms that you use often, including proper nouns, special terminology, and other words that Word might not recognize.

See Chapter 14, "Proofing a Document."

● **Do you want to add a table of contents?**

Compile tables of contents automatically   You don't have to take the time to type a table of contents for your book when Word can generate it for you, complete with page numbers. After marking the headings in your document, you can generate a table of contents that is inserted at the beginning of your document. If you make changes to the document, just choose the command again to update the table of contents.

See Chapter 29, "Indexes and Tables of Contents."

Brochures and Newsletters

● **Do you want text to flow around graphics?**

Use frames to position graphics   When you paste a graphic in Word, the graphic usually moves on the page to accommodate changes you make to the text. By placing the graphic inside a *frame,* Word anchors a graphic at a specific location on a page, so that changes made to the text flowing around it will not change the graphic's position. In page layout view, you can use the mouse to drag a framed graphic to a new location on the page. You can also place text inside a frame for the same effect.

See Chapter 21, "Positioning Text and Graphics on the Page."

▼ **Do you want a simple way to emphasize special text?**

Add a border or shading   When you need to make some text stand out, add a border or apply some shading. One paragraph may require a simple box border, while a table would stand out with 10-percent shading. Still another may use both a border and shading.

See Chapter 19, "Borders and Shading."

■ **Do you want to format side-by-side columns of text?**

Place them in columns or tables   Word provides two ways to place more than one column of text on a page: columns and tables. Text in newspaper-style columns flows from the bottom of one column to the top of the next. Tables provide more precise positioning across rows of columns. The method you use depends on the amount of control you need. For example, for a three-column brochure, newspaper-style columns work best; to show a comparison in a report, use tables.

See Chapter 17, "Tables," and Chapter 18, "Columns."

▲ **Do you want to add a graphic quickly?**

Draw without leaving Word   You may want to illustrate a point by adding a graphic. With the optional draw feature, you can create and insert graphics in your documents without leaving Word. One command displays a new window where you create the graphic. Close the special window when you're ready to insert the graphic into your document. If you need to work on the drawing again, just double-click the graphic and the drawing window opens again.

See Chapter 20, "Importing Graphics."

Do you need a closer look at your document?

Scale the view   If you've ever tried to type and edit in a small, hard-to-see font size, you know it can be hard on your eyes. By magnifying or zooming in on your view of a document with the zoom feature, you can magnify a document up to 200 percent of its size. You can also reduce your view, or zoom out, to 25 percent to eliminate horizontal scrolling as you type and edit. The zoom feature affects only the screen display and does not change the look or size of the printed document.

See Chapter 24, "Viewing Documents."

Chapter 1

The Word Workplace

Word is a great place to work. All you need to produce professional-looking letters, memos, reports, and other documents is either on the screen or at your fingertips. The Word menus list commands that automate many tasks, and the Toolbar, ribbon, and ruler put commonly used commands and options in easy reach. This chapter shows you around the Word workplace, describing the numerous features that will make your work more efficient and the results more polished and professional. If you need help with a particular task, online Help can give you step-by-step instructions.

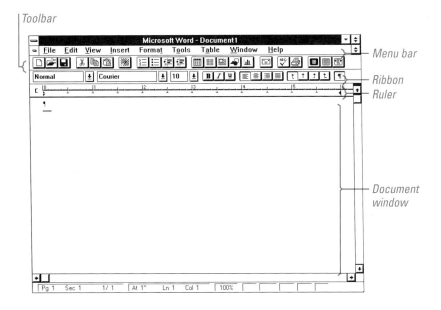

Note In Word, the mouse works as it does in most other applications. If you need to review how to point, click, and drag, see "Your First Word Document," in Part 1, and "Mouse Pointers and Techniques," later in this chapter.

Word Menus and Commands

Choosing a command tells Word what to do next—print a document, format text, and so on. Commands that carry out similar actions are grouped on a menu. For example, the File menu contains commands you use to open, print, and file away your documents. The menus are listed on the menu bar at the top of the Word window.

You can use the mouse or the keyboard to display the commands on each menu. To open the menus and browse through the commands, drag across the menu bar with the mouse, or press the ALT key, and then press the underlined letter in the name of the menu you want to open.

To use some commands, you must first select the text or part of your document you want the command to act on. These commands are unavailable and appear dimmed on a menu until a selection is made. For example, you can't choose the Cut command on the Edit menu until you select the item you want removed from your document.

Word carries out some commands right away. If more information is needed to complete a command, Word displays a dialog box. You select options in the dialog box to control how the command is carried out.

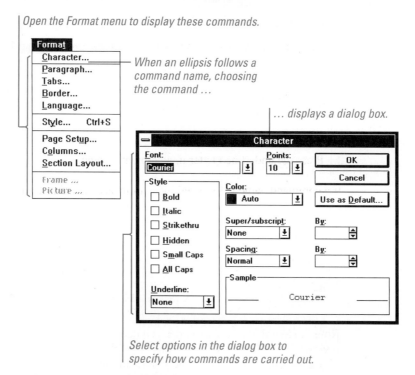

Open the Format menu to display these commands.

When an ellipsis follows a command name, choosing the command ...

... displays a dialog box.

Select options in the dialog box to specify how commands are carried out.

Choosing Commands

You can choose commands from the menus or press the shortcut key assigned to commonly used commands. A bullet or check mark next to a command name indicates the command is in effect at the moment. On the menus, the shortcut key is shown to the right of the command. Keys also are assigned to many Word commands not listed on the menus. These commands are described in later chapters.

Note   Certain commands and features are optional at the time you install Word. If, while working in Word, you choose a command or feature that has not been installed, a message tells you that Word cannot locate the command or feature. The following commands are optional when you install Word:

- Spelling, Hyphenation, Grammar, Thesaurus (Tools menu)
- Help Index, Getting Started, Learning Word (Help menu)
- Draw, Graph, Equation Editor (Object command, Insert menu)

For information about installation, see *Microsoft Word Getting Started.*

To choose a command from a menu

1   Point to a menu name and click the left mouse button.

For example, point to the File menu and click to display the File commands.

2   Point to a command name and click the left mouse button.

For example, point to the Save command and click to save the document.

1   Press the ALT key to activate the menu bar.

2   Press the underlined letter in a menu name.

3   Press the underlined letter in a command name.

If a command name is followed by an ellipsis (...), a dialog box appears so you can set the options you want.

Tip   You can easily change menus in Word, adding commands and options you use frequently and removing those you seldom use. You can also change the shortcut keys assigned to commands. For details, see Chapter 38, "Customizing Menus, the Keyboard, and the Toolbar."

To cancel a menu

You can close a menu without choosing a command.

▶   Click outside the menu.

–Or–

1   Press ESC to cancel the menu.

2   To return to your document, press ESC again.

Selecting Options in a Dialog Box

A dialog box is a special window containing options that you select to tell Word how to carry out a command. The dialog boxes displayed when you choose the Character command from the Format menu and the Save As command from the File menu illustrate some features common to dialog boxes.

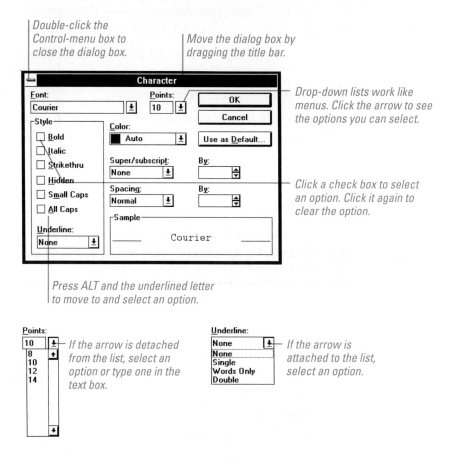

Double-click the Control-menu box to close the dialog box.

Move the dialog box by dragging the title bar.

Drop-down lists work like menus. Click the arrow to see the options you can select.

Click a check box to select an option. Click it again to clear the option.

Press ALT and the underlined letter to move to and select an option.

If the arrow is detached from the list, select an option or type one in the text box.

If the arrow is attached to the list, select an option.

Type information in text boxes.

Commands that appear dimmed are unavailable.

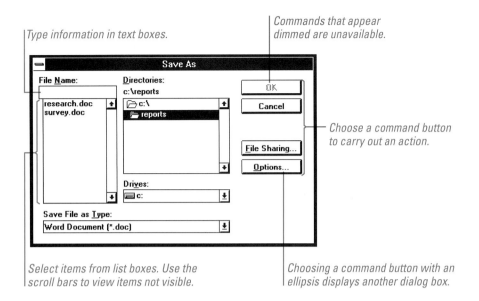

Choose a command button to carry out an action.

Select items from list boxes. Use the scroll bars to view items not visible.

Choosing a command button with an ellipsis displays another dialog box.

Typing Measurements in Text Boxes

For formatting options, you need only type or select a number to specify a measurement. Word supplies the unit of measure or uses the default that you choose from the General options in the Options dialog box (Tools menu). To specify a different unit of measure, type one of the following abbreviations after the number. You do not need to leave a space between the number and the measurement. For example, you could type either **3cm** or **3 cm** to indicate three centimeters.

To specify	Type	Conversion
Centimeters	**cm**	2.54 cm = 1 in.
Inches	**in** or **"**	1 in. = 72 pt = 6 pi
Lines	**li**	1 li = 1/6 in. = 12 pt
Picas	**pi**	1 pi = 12 pt = 1/6 in.
Points	**pt**	1 li = 1/6 in. = 12 pt

The OK, Cancel, and Close Command Buttons

The OK, Cancel, and Close command buttons appear in many dialog boxes. You choose one of these buttons when you finish setting options in a dialog box.

OK   Choosing the OK button closes the dialog box and completes the command using the selected options. For example, choosing the OK button in the Print dialog box starts printing the document. To choose the OK button, you can either click the button or press ENTER.

Cancel and Close   Choosing the Cancel button discards the options you have selected, closes the dialog box, and returns you to your document. When Word completes an action that cannot be canceled, the Cancel button changes to the Close button. The Close button closes the dialog box without reversing any completed changes. To choose the Cancel button, you can click the button or press ESC. To choose the Close button, you click the button or press ESC or ENTER. You can also use the Close command on the Control menu in the upper-left corner of the dialog box. For more information about the Control menu, see "Word Document Windows," later in this chapter.

Selecting Options Using Keys

Use the following shortcut keys to select and edit options in a dialog box.

To	Press
Move to the next text box, option, or command button	TAB
Move to the previous text box, option, or command button	SHIFT+TAB
Move directly to an option and select it	ALT+*underlined letter in the option name*
Display a drop-down list	ALT+*underlined letter in the option name*
Select an item on a list	UP ARROW or DOWN ARROW and then ALT+DOWN ARROW to close the list
Close a list without selecting an item	ALT+DOWN ARROW
Adjust a measurement up or down	UP ARROW or DOWN ARROW
Clear a selected option	ALT+*underlined letter in the option name*

Typing and Editing in Dialog Boxes

Some dialog boxes contain text boxes where you type information or a response, such as a filename or a word that you want to find in a document.

To replace text in a text box

1   Select the text you want to replace by pointing to the text box and dragging over the text.
    –or–
    Hold down the ALT key and press the underlined letter in the text box name.

2   Type your replacement text.

    Word replaces the selected text with the new text as soon as you start typing.

To edit text in a text box

1   Move the insertion point to the text box.

2   Edit and type text the same way as in a document window.

Undoing and Repeating Commands

As you work, it helps to keep in mind the Undo and Repeat commands on the Edit menu. Undo cancels the most recent command or action you completed. If you don't like the results of a command or accidentally delete some text, choose Undo as the next action. The fastest way to choose Undo is to click the Undo button on the Toolbar. Some actions, such as saving a document, can't be reversed. In this case, Undo changes to Can't Undo and appears dimmed on the menu, indicating it is unavailable.

The Repeat command repeats the last command or action you completed. It's often easier to choose Repeat than to choose the same command several times, particularly if the last command involved a complex formatting change you applied using the Character or Paragraph command. You can select other text and then choose Repeat to apply the same formatting in one step. Repeat also duplicates typing. Choose Repeat if you've typed a long paragraph and want to type the same text elsewhere in your document. The fastest way to choose Repeat is to press F4.

To undo a command or editing action

▶   On the Toolbar, click the Undo button.

–Or–

▶   From the Edit menu, choose Undo (ALT, E, U), or press the Undo key (CTRL+Z).

The Undo command changes to Undo Undo. After choosing Undo Undo, you can choose Undo again to reverse the same action.

To repeat a command or editing action

▶ From the Edit menu, choose Repeat (ALT, E, R), or press F4.

The name of the Repeat command changes to reflect the last action taken. For example, the command name might be Repeat Copy or Repeat Paste, depending on the last action. If a command cannot be repeated, Repeat changes to Can't Repeat and appears dimmed on the menu, indicating it is unavailable.

To cancel an action that is in progress

▶ Press ESC.

If the process does not stop, press ESC again.

Note   You cannot interrupt an operation if doing so might damage a file or an open document.

The Toolbar

If you use a mouse, the Toolbar gives you instant access to the most frequently used Word commands. By simply clicking a button, you can open a document, check your spelling, save a document, or print. You can also click a button to change the look of the document—to cut, copy, or paste text, to change the number of newspaper-style columns, or to insert a table. Clicking a button can turn selected paragraphs into a bulleted or numbered list.

Toolbar

To display or hide the Toolbar

▶ From the View menu, choose Toolbar (ALT, V, T).

The Default Toolbar

The following table describes the default buttons that appear on the Toolbar.

Click		To
	New	Open a new document based on current default settings.
	Open	Open an existing document or template. Word displays the Open dialog box, where you can locate and open the file you want.
	Save	Save the active document or template with its current name. If you have not named the document, Word displays the Save As dialog box for you to do so.
	Cut	Remove selected text and graphics from the document and store them on the Clipboard.
	Copy	Copy selected text and graphics and store them on the Clipboard.
	Paste	Insert the contents of the Clipboard at the insertion point or selection.
	Undo	Reverse the last action you took. (You cannot undo some commands.)
	Numbered List	Number selected paragraphs sequentially, inserting an arabic numeral (1, 2, 3) in front of each paragraph and aligning paragraph text one-quarter inch to the right of the numbers.
	Bulleted List	Place a bullet in front of each selected paragraph and align the paragraphs one-quarter inch to the right of the bullets.
	Unindent	Move selected paragraphs left, back to the previous default tab stop.
	Indent	Move selected paragraphs right, forward to the next default tab stop.
	Table	Insert a table. To select the number of rows and columns you want, drag over the sample table that is displayed. The sample expands as you drag.
	Text Columns	Format the current section of your document with one or multiple newspaper-style columns. To select the number of columns, drag over the sample columns that are displayed.

(continued)

Click		To
	Frame	Place a nonprinting "frame" around selected text, tables, or graphics, or insert an empty frame.
	Draw	Start the Microsoft Draw program.
	Graph	Start the Microsoft Graph program.
	Envelope	Create an envelope that will print along with the active document.
	Spelling	Check the spelling of the entire document, or if you've selected text, check the spelling of the selection. Displays the Spelling dialog box if a word is not found in the dictionary.
	Print	Print all pages of the active document.
	Zoom Whole Page	Display a document in page layout view, reduced to show an entire page on the screen. You can view the document just as it will print and adjust the layout.
	Zoom 100 Percent	Display the document at full size in normal view—the best view for most typing and editing. Multiple columns appear in their actual width but not side by side.
	Zoom Page Width	Display the full width of the page.

You can customize the Toolbar, adding commands or macros to it, or replacing the commands that appear on the Toolbar with commands of your own choosing. You can also create a customized Toolbar for each type of document that you regularly produce by saving the Toolbar with a template. For example, you could create a Toolbar that has the commands you use most often when working on the graphics and columns of a monthly newsletter, and save it with the newsletter's template. For more information about customizing the Toolbar, see Chapter 38, "Customizing Menus, the Keyboard, and the Toolbar."

The Ribbon and Ruler

The ribbon and ruler make formatting your document convenient and fast. To use them, you select the text you want to change and click a button or drag a marker. The settings on the ribbon and ruler indicate the format you applied to the selected paragraph or the paragraph containing the insertion point. When you move the insertion point to a paragraph with a different format, the settings on the ribbon and ruler change to show the formatting for that paragraph.

The Ribbon

You can use the ribbon to change the appearance of any selected text characters, changing the font or point size, or making a word bold or underlined, for example. You can also control paragraph alignment or customize tab settings.

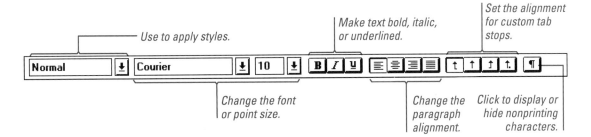

The Ruler

With the ruler, you can change the indents of paragraphs, adjust the margins, change the width of newspaper-style columns, or change the width of table columns.

On the left side of the ruler, click the Margin Scale symbol (**⌐**) to work with margins and multiple columns. Click the Indent Scale symbol (**↳**) to work with indents or to set tab stops. Click the Table Scale symbol (**T**) to adjust the width of table columns.

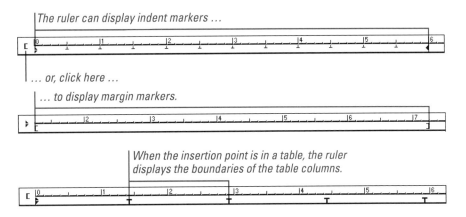

If your present work mainly involves typing and editing text, you can hide the ruler and ribbon to see more of your document in the window. The Ribbon and Ruler commands on the View menu display or hide the ribbon and ruler.

To display or hide the ribbon

▶   From the View menu, choose Ribbon (ALT, V, B).

To display or hide the ruler

▶   From the View menu, choose Ruler (ALT, V, R).

Note   A ruler is displayed in each document window that you open. However, there is only one ribbon and only one Toolbar at any time. You can use them in any window.

For more information about using the ribbon and ruler to format a document, see the following chapters.

For information about	See
Changing the typeface (font), point size, or characteristics such as bold and italic	Chapter 6, "Character Formatting"
Applying styles	Chapter 8, "Formatting with Styles"
Setting tab stops, aligning paragraphs, and setting indents	Chapter 7, "Paragraph Formatting"
Changing the width of newspaper-style columns	Chapter 18, "Columns"
Changing the column widths of tables	Chapter 17, "Tables"
Changing margins using the ruler	Chapter 9, "Margins, Paper Size, and Page Orientation"

Word Document Windows

Although document windows in Word are similar to those in other applications, some elements are unique to Word. The following section describes the main elements of Word windows and introduces terms used in this documentation. To learn more about windows, see your Windows documentation.

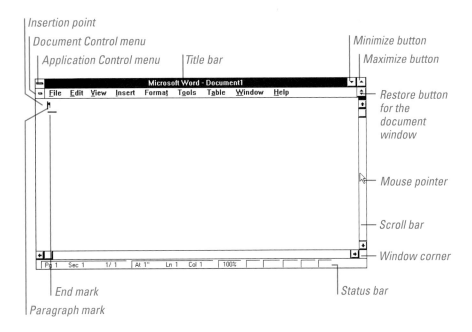

Title bar   Displays the name of the document. Until you save and name the document, the window is named DocumentX, where X denotes the number of the document. Documents are numbered sequentially each session.

Application Control menu   Displays a menu with commands for sizing and moving the Word window, switching to other applications, and closing Word.

Document Control menu   Displays a menu with commands for sizing, moving, splitting, and closing the document window, and for moving the insertion point between windows.

Maximize button for Word   Fills the screen with the Word window. When you click the Maximize button, it is replaced by the Restore button, which returns the window to its previous size.

Maximize button for a document window   Fills the Word application window with a document window. When you click the Maximize button, it is replaced by the Restore button, which returns the window to its previous size.

Restore button   Returns the window to its previous size. This button is displayed when you click the Maximize button.

Minimize button   Shrinks Word to an icon. The Minimize button performs the same function as the Minimize command on the Control menu.

Insertion point   This blinking vertical bar shows where the next character you type will be entered. Any item that you add to your document—a graphic pasted from the Clipboard, for example—is inserted at the insertion point.

Mouse pointer   The mouse pointer changes shape depending on where you point on the screen. To move the pointer, move the mouse across a flat surface. For a description of common pointer shapes, see "Mouse Pointers and Techniques," later in this chapter.

Paragraph mark   A new document window contains one empty paragraph, indicated by the ending paragraph mark. You can't delete this paragraph mark unless you add others. To see the mark, click the Show/Hide ¶ button on the ribbon, or from the Tools menu choose Options, select the View category, and then select Paragraph Marks.

End mark   Marks the end of the document. You can't type or move the insertion point past the end mark.

Window corner   Dragging a window corner changes the window size.

Scroll bars   Clicking in the vertical or horizontal scroll bar or dragging the box in the scroll bar brings other parts of the document into view. For information about scrolling, see Chapter 3, "Typing and Revising a Document."

Status bar   Displays the following information about the page that contains the insertion point: the page number, the section number, the total number of pages from the beginning of the document followed by the total number of pages in the whole document, the position of the insertion point measured from the top edge of the page, the line number, and the column number calculated by counting the number of characters between the insertion point and the left margin. The status bar also shows the level of magnification, as well as the status of several keys on your computer, such as CAPS LOCK and NUM LOCK, and various Word features, such as macro recording and revision marking.

Switching to a Different Document Window

With Word, you can have more than one document open at a time. You can open as many as nine, depending on how much memory is available on your computer. Each document that you open is displayed in a separate document window, which is listed on the Window menu.

The window you are currently working in—the window containing the insertion point or a selection of text—is called the active window, and the document you are working in is called the active document. Text that you type is entered in the active document, and most commands or actions you carry out affect only the active document. To work in a different document, you must make that document window active.

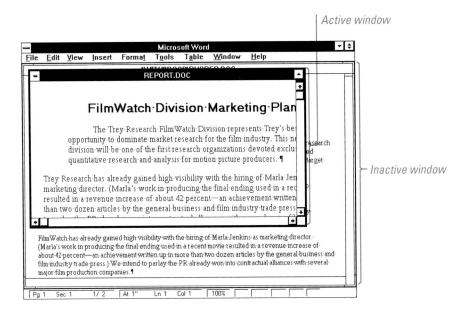

Active window

Inactive window

To make a document window active

▶ From the Window menu, choose the name of the document that you want to make active.

The order in which the documents are listed on the Window menu follows the order in which the documents were opened.

To make the next open window active

▶ If the window you want to work in is visible, click anywhere within its borders.

– Or –

▶ From the document Control menu, choose Next Window (ALT, HYPHEN, N), or press CTRL+F6 until the window you want is active.

To make the previous window active, press CTRL+SHIFT+F6.

Moving and Sizing Windows

You can size and move the Word application window or any open document window. If you're working with several open documents, you may want to view all open documents at once, or move windows out of your way or make them smaller so you can see a few of the documents at once. To avoid cluttering the screen, close any windows you no longer need.

To view all open documents

▶ From the Window menu, choose Arrange All (ALT, W, A).

Word arranges all open documents on the screen. To move from one to the next, press CTRL+F6, or click the window you want to work in.

To move a window or dialog box

You sometimes need to move a window to see another window behind it. You can't drag a window completely off the screen; at least some of the title bar must remain visible. Also, if the Word window is maximized, you cannot move it until you restore it. You can move a dialog box at any time.

▶ Point to the title bar of the window or dialog box and drag it to the new position.

–Or–

1 To move a document window, choose Move from the document Control menu (ALT, HYPHEN, M), or press CTRL+F7.
   –or–
   To move a dialog box, choose Move from the dialog box Control menu (ALT, SPACEBAR, M).

2 Press the arrow keys to position the outline of the window or dialog box.

   To return the window or box to its former location, press ESC.

3 When the window or dialog box is where you want it, press ENTER.

Tip   You can move and size the Help window and the document window so they appear side by side. This allows you to view Help as you work in your document.

To expand a document window to maximum size

You can enlarge any document window to fill the entire Word window. When you maximize a document window, other open document windows remain open, even though they are hidden.

▶ Click the Maximize button in the upper-right corner of the window you want to expand.

–Or–

▶ From the document Control menu, choose Maximize (ALT, HYPHEN, X), or press CTRL+F10.

To resize a document window

A window cannot be moved or sized if it is currently maximized.

1 If the window has been enlarged to its maximum size, click the Restore button.

2 Point to the border or corner of the window you want to size.

3 When the mouse pointer displays a two-headed arrow, drag the window border or corner until the window is the size you want it.

1 If you are sizing a document window that has been enlarged to its maximum size, choose Restore from the document Control menu (ALT, HYPHEN, R), or press CTRL+F5.

2 From the document Control menu, choose Size (ALT, HYPHEN, S), or press CTRL+F8.

The pointer displays a four-headed arrow.

3 Press an arrow key to indicate the border you want to move.

The pointer displays a two-headed arrow.

4 Use the appropriate arrow keys to move the border.

To return the window to its former size, press ESC.

5 When the window is the size you want, press ENTER.

To close a document window

▶ Double-click the document Control-menu box in the upper-left corner of the document window.

–Or–

▶ From the document Control menu, choose Close (ALT, HYPHEN, C), or press CTRL+F4.

Tip   You can exit Word by double-clicking the application Control-menu box. If you have any open documents that you have not saved, Word prompts you to save them.

Viewing a Document in Several Windows

Sometimes you need to see different parts of a document at the same time. Instead of scrolling back and forth, you can open additional windows for the document or split the document window horizontally into *panes*. You can scroll independently in each window or pane, making it easy to compare different parts of the document or to move and copy text over long distances. Changes that you make to the document in one window are reflected immediately in other windows.

For example, suppose that you're working in a large table and you want to keep the column headings in view as you enter information. To do this, you can split the window and display the column headings in the upper pane. If the table is very wide, you may want to keep the first column in view as you work with the columns on the far right. In this case, you can open a second window for the document and arrange the windows side by side.

To open another window for the active document

▶ From the Window menu, choose New Window (ALT, W, N).

The new window becomes the active window. A number identifying the window is added to the document name in the title bar and on the Window menu.

To split or unsplit a window

Before a window is split, the split box is at the top of the vertical scroll bar. After a window is split, the split box is located at the split position. When the mouse is pointing to the split box, Word displays a ⬍ .

▶ To split the window into two equal panes, point to the split box on the vertical scroll bar. When the mouse pointer changes shape, double-click.
  –or–
  Drag the split box to the position you want.

1 From the document Control menu, choose Split (ALT, HYPHEN, T).

  Word displays a split bar and the pointer changes to a two-headed arrow positioned over the split bar.

2 Press the UP ARROW or DOWN ARROW key to position the split bar.

3 Press ENTER to insert the split.

  To remove a split, repeat this procedure, using the arrow keys to move the split bar off the window, and then pressing ENTER.

To move between panes

▶ Click in the inactive pane, or press F6, to make it active.

Tip   To copy or move text between parts of a long document, split the window into two panes and display the text you want to move or copy in one pane and the destination in the other.

Splitting a window also allows you to show field codes in one pane and results of field codes in the other.

Changing Your View of a Document

When you use Word for the first time, documents are displayed in normal view, which is ideal for most of your daily work. Text formatting is shown—for example, line spacing, the font and point size, and italic—but the layout of the page is simplified. If you have multiple-column text, it is displayed in one continuous column, with page breaks represented by dotted lines.

With the Outline and Page Layout commands on the View menu, and the Print Preview command on the File menu, you can change your view of a document to focus on different aspects of your work.

- *Outline view* helps you examine the logical structure of your document. You can choose to display only headings, temporarily hiding the text beneath them. To reorganize your document, you can simply drag a heading to another place in the outline—all supporting subheadings and text automatically move with the heading. You also can raise or lower a heading's level of importance in the outline.

- *Page layout view* shows you how each page of your document will look when printed. You can edit and format the text and see the results on the screen. A similar command, Print Preview on the File menu, displays whole pages at a reduced size and allows you to adjust margins, page breaks, and other aspects of the page layout. However, text cannot be edited in print preview.

- *Print preview* shows a miniature version of your document exactly as it will print, reduced in size to display one or two pages on the screen. Although you can't edit text in this view, it provides a quick and convenient way to review the final page layout and adjust page breaks and margins.

You can change the display size of a document as you work on it, magnifying it for a closer look at text that is in a small font size and reducing it for an overview of an entire page. The magnification or reduction affects only the screen display; it does not change the look or size of the printed document. Using the Zoom command on the View menu, you can reduce or magnify the display size from 25 percent through 200 percent. If you are using a mouse, you can reduce the display size by clicking buttons on the Toolbar. Click the Zoom Whole Page button to view an entire page on the screen in page layout view. Or click the Zoom Page Width button to reduce the size of a wide document so the entire page width fits on the screen in page layout view. Clicking the Zoom 100 Percent button returns the document to 100 percent magnification in normal view.

For more information about working in the different document views or changing the display size, see Chapter 24, "Viewing Documents." For information about working in outline view, see Chapter 27, "Outline View: Creating Outlines and Reorganizing Documents."

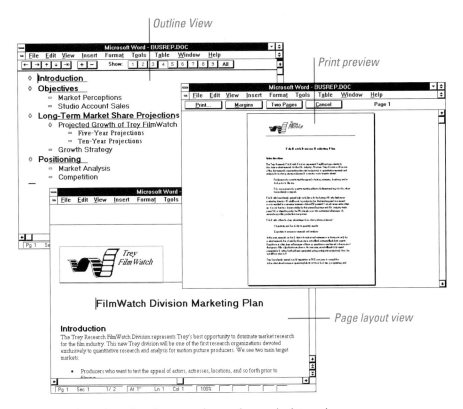

A document shown in outline view, page layout view, and print preview

You may find it helpful to see where you started a new paragraph or used tabs to align text, especially if you are new to Word. When you display nonprinting characters, spaces are represented by raised dots, paragraph marks (¶) show where you pressed ENTER, and tab marks (→) show where you pressed the TAB key. These characters are never printed, even when they're displayed in the document. You can choose to display or hide nonprinting characters at any time.

To display or hide nonprinting characters

▶ Click the Show/Hide ¶ button on the ribbon.

–Or–

1 From the Tools menu, choose Options (ALT, O, O).

2 Select the View category.

3 Under Nonprinting Characters, select the characters that you want to display.

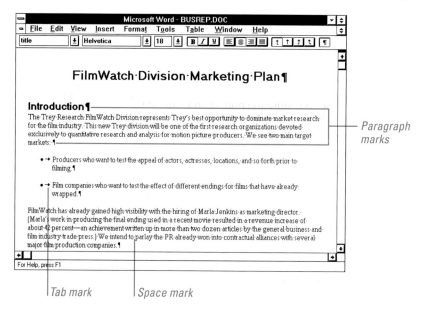

Normal view with nonprinting characters displayed

Some elements of your document aren't shown in normal view. To see these elements, you must choose a command from the View menu. For example, to see headers and footers (the text printed in the top and bottom margins of each page), you open the appropriate header or footer pane using the Header/Footer command on the View menu.

You can control other aspects of how documents are displayed by selecting options in the View category of the Options dialog box (Tools menu). For more information, see Chapter 39, "Setting Preferences."

Mouse Pointers and Techniques

The mouse works about the same in Word as it does in other applications, with a few variations. This section summarizes basic mouse shapes and techniques.

Pointer Shapes

When you point with the mouse to different parts of your screen, the pointer shape changes, allowing you to perform different tasks. Some commands also change the pointer shape.

If the pointer assumes a shape you don't want to use—for example, if you accidentally press the Help key (SHIFT+F1), changing the pointer to a bold question mark—press ESC to restore the pointer to its usual shape.

The following table lists the common pointer shapes.

Pointer shape	Significance
$\text{I}\quad\text{I}$	The pointer is in the text area. This is sometimes called the "I-beam" pointer. In italic text, this pointer slants to make positioning and selecting easier. You use this pointer to indicate where you want to begin typing.
+	This pointer appears in print preview when margins are displayed and the pointer is over an object you can drag, such as a margin or page break.
↖	The pointer is in the menus, inactive windows, scroll bars, ribbon, ruler, or Toolbar. You can choose a menu and command, click a button, or drag a tab stop marker. This is also the sizing arrow when you have a picture selected. You drag the sizing handles to scale or crop the picture.
↗	The pointer is in the selection bar or the style name bar along the window's left edge. You can select a line, paragraph, or the entire document. This pointer also appears in table selection bars.
⌛	Word is performing a task that will take a few seconds.

(continued)

Pointer shape	Significance
	The pointer appears after you press the Help key (SHIFT+F1). You can point to a command name or a region on the screen and click to view a Help topic about the item you clicked.
	This pointer appears when you choose the Split command on a Control menu or when the mouse pointer is on the split box in the vertical scroll bar.
	The pointer is on the style name area split line. Drag to change the width of the style name area, displaying more or less of each style name.
	The pointer is in a window border. You can change the size of a window vertically.
	You can change the size of a window horizontally.
	You can change the size of a window diagonally.
	This pointer appears after you choose the Move or Size command from the Control menu. You can move the window to a new position or drag a window border.
	This pointer appears in outline view, when positioned on a selection symbol. It indicates you can drag the heading. It also appears when positioned over a frame, indicating you can drag the frame to a new position.
	This pointer appears in outline view as you drag a heading left or right to a new level in the outline. It also appears when positioned over a frame handle, indicating you can size the frame by dragging the handle.
	This pointer appears in outline view as you drag a heading up or down to a new position. It also appears when positioned over a frame handle, indicating you can size the frame by dragging the handle.
	The pointer is over a column in a table. Click to select the column.
	A small, dotted box and dotted insertion point appear when you select text or a graphic and press a mouse button to drag the selection itself to a new location, where you "drop," or insert, it.

Basic Mouse Techniques

The following table provides a review of basic mouse techniques you'll need to know to work in Word. For more information and practice using these skills, see the documentation that came with your mouse.

To	Do this
Point	Position the mouse pointer on or next to something.
Click	Position the pointer and then quickly press and release the left mouse button.
Double-click	Position the pointer and then quickly press and release the left mouse button twice.
Drag	Position the pointer. Press and hold down the left mouse button as you move the mouse to the desired position. Then release the button.

Basic Mouse Techniques

Chapter 2

Opening, Saving, and Deleting Documents

Before you can work on a document, you must open it—that is, display it on your screen. You can type and edit text, change the appearance of the document, and print it. To preserve your work, you save the document. Saving a document stores it, in its current version, in a file on a disk. Saving your documents regularly is a very good idea—and if you've never used a word processor before, you should get into the habit from the start.

If you'd like a quick demonstration of these skills, choose the Getting Started command from the Help menu. Then choose Basic Skills from the Main menu and then Working With Documents from the Lesson menu. In addition to the demonstration, this lesson offers opportunities for hands-on practice without affecting the document you are working on. You can quit the lesson at any time by choosing the Controls button and then choosing the Exit button.

Opening a Document

When you start Word, a blank document temporarily named Document1 opens in a window on the screen. If you're ready to start a new document, you can simply start typing. At any time during a Word session, you can open a new document window from the File menu; see "To create a new document," later in this chapter.

To work on an existing document stored on a disk, you open the document using the Open button on the Toolbar or the Open command on the File menu. If you have worked on the document recently, you may be able to open it again by choosing its name from the File menu. Word lists the four documents you most recently opened at the bottom of the File menu. This is the fastest way to open a document and is especially handy when you work on a small group of documents over a period of time.

For instructions on using Find File, see Chapter 26, "Finding and Managing Files."

If you can't remember the name of a document or the directory where it's stored, you can search for it with the Find File command on the File menu. For example, you can locate documents having a certain sequence of letters in their filename, documents written by a particular person, or those containing a particular word or phrase. You can open more than one document at a time and move between document windows as you work.

Creating a New Document

You can begin a new document at any time while you're working in Word.

To create a new document

1 From the File menu, choose New (ALT, F, N).

To base your document on a template other than NORMAL.DOT, the default template, type or select the name of the appropriate template in the Use Template box.

2 Choose the OK button.

Word gives the new document a temporary name, such as Document1. You give the document a unique name when you save it.

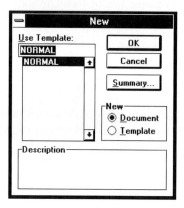

For more information on creating and using templates, see Chapter 37, "Document Templates."

New Document   Creates a new document.

New Template   Creates a new document template rather than a document.

Use Template   Lists available templates and lets you select a template for the type of document you want to create. All documents are based on a document template. New documents are automatically based on the default template, NORMAL.DOT, unless you choose a different template.

Summary   Opens the Summary Info dialog box. Summary information can help you locate documents by their title, subject, author, specific words contained in the document, and comments.

Tip   Starting from templates can save you the work of typing and formatting each new document from scratch. Templates contain the standard text and formatting that you routinely use for certain documents. They can also place some of the more powerful Word features at your fingertips. You can produce your own templates or use the ones that Word provides for memos, letters, and other common documents.

Opening an Existing Document in Word

You can quickly open any of the last four documents you worked on—their names appear at the bottom of the File menu. You can open any other document using the Open command on the File menu.

To open a recently closed document

1 Open the File menu (ALT, F).

2 Click the name of the document you want.
   –or–
   Type the underlined number that corresponds to the document you want to open.

Picking Up Where You Left Off

To continue working where you stopped in a previous session, press the Go Back key (SHIFT+F5) as soon as you open the document. Word returns the insertion point to its last position or to the last selection.

While you are working on a document, Word stores the three latest editing locations. Each press of the Go Back key moves the insertion point back one previous position. On the fourth press, the cycle starts again at the point where the Go Back key was first pressed.

To open an existing document

1 From the File menu, choose Open (ALT, F, O), or press CTRL+F12.

2 In the File Name box, type or select the name of the document you want to open.

   If you do not see the name of the file you want, select a new drive or directory, or select a different type of file from the List Files Of Type box.

3 Choose the OK button.

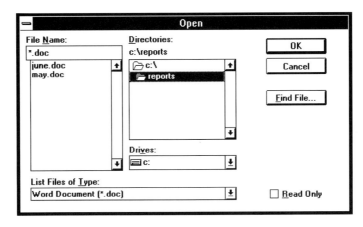

File Name   Lists files in the current directory and provides a box for you to type or select a filename.

List Files Of Type   Lists the file formats supported by Word. For more information on file formats, see Chapter 35, "Converting File Formats."

Directories   Lists the directories available on the current drive.

Drives   Lists the drives available on your system.

Find File   Searches the current path and then opens the Find File dialog box so you can search for the documents with the title, subject, author, keywords, or comments that you are interested in. For more information on finding files, see Chapter 26, "Finding and Managing Files."

Read Only   Prevents accidental changes to the document you are about to open. If you select this option, you can view the document, but if you make changes to it, you must save it with a different name. For more information, see "Protecting Documents from Changes," later in this chapter.

Tip   To see a list of all files in a drive or directory with a specific filename extension, in the File Name box, type an asterisk (*), a period (.), the filename extension, and then choose the OK button. For example, to see all the files with a .DOT filename extension in a directory, type ***.DOT** in the File Name box. To see all the files in a directory, type ***.*** in the File Name box.

To insert a second document into an open document

1   Position the insertion point at the place in your open document where you want the second document to begin.

2   From the Insert menu, choose File (ALT, I, L).

3   Under File Name, type or select the name of the document you want to insert.

If you don't see the name of the file you want, select a new drive or directory, or select a different type of file from the List Files Of Type box.

4   Choose the OK button.

Word inserts the complete document, beginning at the location where you placed the insertion point. If that location was before the end of your first document, the remaining portions of the first document now follow the end of the newly inserted file.

Opening Several Documents at Once

For more information
about document
windows, see
Chapter 1, "The
Word Workplace."

You can open as many as nine documents simultaneously, each in a separate document window. If you are beginning a Word session and plan to work on several documents, you can open them all at once.

To open several documents at once

1   From the File menu, choose Find File.

    Under File Name, look for the names of the documents you want to open. If any are not listed, choose the Search button and, under Location, specify the location of the files you want to open. Then choose the Start Search button.

    For more information about locating documents with the Find File command, see Chapter 26, "Finding and Managing Files."

2   Click the first file you want to open; then hold down CTRL while clicking each additional file you want to open.

    If you make a mistake, hold down CTRL and click any selected filename to remove the selection.

3   Choose the Open button.

1   From the File menu, choose Find File (ALT, F, F).

    Under File Name, look for the names of the documents you want to open. If any are not listed, choose the Search button and, under Location, specify the location of the files you want to open. Then choose the Start Search button.

    For more information about locating documents with the Find File command, see Chapter 26, "Finding and Managing Files."

2   If the filename that is highlighted is not one that you want to open, press the DOWN ARROW or UP ARROW key until you've highlighted a file you want. Then press SHIFT+F8 to select the filename.

3   Use the DOWN ARROW or UP ARROW key to place a dotted frame around the next filename you want to open. Then press the SPACEBAR to select the filename.

4   Repeat step 3 for each additional file you want to open.

    If you make a mistake, press the arrow key to move to the filename again and press the SPACEBAR to remove the selection.

5   Choose the Open button.

Tip   If the files you want to open are listed consecutively, you can select them more quickly with the mouse by clicking the first filename and, while holding down SHIFT, clicking the last filename in the sequence that you want to open. Word selects all files between the two points. With the keyboard, select the first filename and, while holding down SHIFT, press the DOWN ARROW key to select the subsequent filenames.

To switch to a different open document

No matter how many documents you have open, only one can be the active document at any given time. The active document contains the insertion point, and the editing and formatting actions you take affect only that document. To work with a different open document, you must first make it the active document.

▶ From the Window menu, choose the filename of the document you want to work in.

The document becomes the active document and is displayed on top of any other open documents.

Opening a Document with a Different File Format

For details about opening documents in file formats other than Word, see Chapter 35, "Converting File Formats."

You can open documents in Word that were created with different word-processing applications. Word converts the documents to Word format.

To open a document with a different file format

1   From the File menu, choose Open (ALT, F, O), or press CTRL+F12.

2   In the File Name box, type or select the name of the document you want to open.

    If you do not see the name of the file you want, select a new drive or directory, or select a different type of file from the List Files Of Type box.

3   Choose the OK button.

4   Choose the OK button to convert the file to Word format.

If you save this document later with the same name, you can choose between saving it in its original format and converting its format. See the following section, "Saving a Document."

Saving a Document

When you open a document, Word copies it from the disk and displays the copy in a document window. As you work, you're actually making changes to the copy of the document temporarily stored in the computer's memory. To keep your latest work safely on the disk, you should periodically save your document. You should also save backup copies of important documents. For information about backing up your work, see "Good Saving Habits," later in this chapter.

Saving Open Documents

A good rule of thumb is to save every 10 to 15 minutes, or after you've completed any work you wouldn't want to redo. If you save frequently, you won't lose much work in the event of a power failure or other problem. It's also a good habit to save a document before you print or make a major change to it.

It's easy to neglect saving your work as often as you should. You can have Word automatically save your documents on a regular basis. See "Controlling How Word Saves Documents," later in this chapter.

When you save a document, the document remains open on your screen so you can continue working. If you are finished with a document, close it to prevent cluttering your screen with unneeded document windows. When you quit Word, if any changes have not been saved, a message asks if you want to save the changes.

When you save a document for the first time, Word displays the Summary Info dialog box, shown in the following illustration. The information you type can help you recall important details about a document later. You can also use the summary information when searching for documents with the Find File command.

For details on summary information, see Chapter 26, "Finding and Managing Files."

You can add or update summary information at any time by choosing the Summary Info command from the File menu.

If you lose data because of a power failure or other problem while working on a document, you can often recover the file. For more information on retrieving lost information, see "Restoring Your Work," later in this chapter.

Saving Your Document in Other File Formats

You can save a Word document in many common file formats, making it easy to transfer documents to other word processors. For information about saving in other file formats, see Chapter 35, "Converting File Formats."

To save an existing document

▶ On the Toolbar, click the Save button.

–Or–

▶ From the File menu, choose Save (ALT, F, S), or press SHIFT+F12.

Tip   If you want to save changes to a read-only document, you can save the document with a new name. If you edit a read-only document and try to save it, Word displays the Save As dialog box, prompting you to save your changes with a new name.

To save a new, unnamed document

1   From the File menu, choose Save (ALT, F, S).

2   In the File Name box, type a name (maximum eight characters).

   Word saves the document in the current drive and directory and automatically adds a .DOC filename extension unless you specify another filename extension.

3   If you want to save the document to a different drive or directory, do one of the following:

   ■   Select a drive and a directory.

   ■   Type the complete path in the File Name box—for example, **a:\reports\sales**

4   Choose the OK button.

5   If Word displays the Summary Info dialog box, type any of the optional information you want to add, and then choose the OK button.

   If you choose the Cancel button instead of the OK button, Word saves the document but records no summary information. The next time you save this document, the Summary Info dialog box is again displayed.

Tip   By default, Word displays the summary information dialog box each time you save a new document or choose the Save As command. If you do not want this to happen automatically, choose the Options command from the Tools menu. In the Save category, clear the Prompt For Summary Info option.

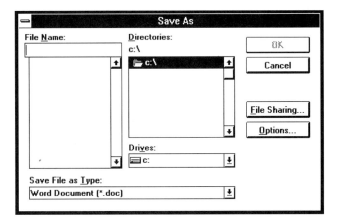

File Name   Provides a box for you to type a filename for a new file.

Directories   Lists the directories available on the current drive.

Drives   Lists the drives available on your system.

Save File As Type   Lists the file formats supported by Word. For more information on file formats, see Chapter 35, "Converting File Formats."

File Sharing   Contains the Lock File For Annotations check box and the Protection Password option. You can use these to protect the file from unintentional changes. For more information, see "Protecting Documents from Changes," later in this chapter.

Options   Opens the Options dialog box with the Save category selected. This category controls special options for saving. For more information on these features, see "Controlling How Word Saves Documents," later in this chapter.

To save all open documents

When you quit Word by choosing Exit from the File menu, Word closes all documents and verifies that you want to save changes. If, while you are working, you want to save all open documents, templates, dictionaries, and glossary files at once, use the following procedure.

▶   From the File menu, choose Save All (ALT, F, E).

If a document has changes you have not saved, Word asks if you want to save changes to the document. If you choose Yes but have not yet named the document, Word displays the Save As dialog box.

If you have changed glossary entries, macros, or the commands on your menus, Word asks if you want to save global glossary or command changes. Choose Yes to make these changes available to all documents. Choose No to lose the changes.

Saving Another Copy

When you choose the Save command, Word saves the active document under the name and location you last gave it. You can use the Save As command to create more than one version of a document and to save copies on another disk for safekeeping. You can save each version under a different name, or you can save them under the same name in different directories or on different disks.

Before saving a copy to another disk, you should first make sure to save the document on your hard disk.

To save a copy of the active document

1   From the File menu, choose Save As (ALT, F, A), or press F12.

Word displays the name of the active document in the File Name box.

2   If you want to save the document under another name, in the File Name box, type a new name for the document.

The document's old name remains attached to its last-saved version.

3   If you want to save the document to a different drive or directory, do one of the following:

■   Select a drive and a directory.

■   Type the complete path in the File Name box—for example, **a:\reports\sales**

4   Choose the OK button.

If you type a filename that already exists within the directory you've designated, Word displays a message asking whether you want to replace the existing file with the active document. Choose the Yes button to save the new document and replace the old one, or choose the No button and type a different filename. Choose the Cancel button to return to the document without saving it.

To save a copy of several documents at once

1   From the File menu, choose Find File (ALT, F, F).

Under File Name, look for the names of the documents you want to save. If any are not listed, choose the Search button and, under Location, specify the location of the files you want to save. Then choose the Start Search button.

For more information about locating documents with the Find File command, see Chapter 26, "Finding and Managing Files."

2   Click the first file you want to save; then hold down CTRL while clicking each additional file you want to save.

If you make a mistake, hold down CTRL and click any selected filename to remove the selection.

3   Choose the Copy button.

4   Type or select the directory in which you want the files saved.

If the directory you specify contains one or more files whose names match those you are now saving, Word prompts you to confirm that you want to replace the existing files with the new ones.

5   Choose the OK button.

1   From the File menu, choose Find File (ALT, F, F).

Under File Name, look for the names of the documents you want to save. If any are not listed, choose the Search button and, under Location, specify the location of the files you want to save. Then choose the Start Search button.

For more information about locating documents with the Find File command, see Chapter 26, "Finding and Managing Files."

2   If the filename that is highlighted is not one that you want to save, press the DOWN ARROW or UP ARROW key until you've highlighted a file you want. Then press SHIFT+F8 to select the filename.

3   Use the DOWN ARROW or UP ARROW key to place a dotted frame around the next filename you want to save. Then press the SPACEBAR to select the filename.

4   Repeat step 3 for each additional file you want to save.

If you make a mistake, press the arrow key to move to the filename again and press the SPACEBAR to remove the selection.

5   Choose the Copy button.

6   Type or select the directory in which you want the files saved.

If the directory you specify contains one or more files whose names match those you are now saving, Word prompts you to confirm that you want to replace the existing files with the new ones.

7   Choose the OK button.

Tip If the files you want to save are listed consecutively, you can select them more quickly with the mouse by clicking the first filename and, while holding down SHIFT, clicking the last filename in the sequence that you want to save. Word selects all files between the two points. With the keyboard, select the first filename and, while holding down SHIFT, press the DOWN ARROW key to select the subsequent filenames.

Saving to and from Different File Formats

For more information, see Chapter 35, "Converting File Formats."

If you have opened a document that was created with a different word-processing program and want to save it for future use in Word, you must change that document's file format. Conversely, you may need to save a Word document in a format other than the Normal Word format—for example, when it must be saved as a text-only file.

To save a document in Word that was created in a different format

1   From the File menu, choose Save (ALT, F, S).

    Word asks if you want to overwrite the original format of the file with Normal Word format.

2   Choose Yes.

3   Fill in the summary information you want to record, and choose the OK button.

To save a Word document with a different file format

1   From the File menu, choose Save As (ALT, F, A), or press F12.

2   In the File Name box, type a new name for the document.

3   In the Save File As Type box, select the file format.

4   Choose the OK button.

Tip Save a document in Normal Word format until you've finished working on it in Word. Wait to convert it to another format until you are ready to open it in another application.

Guidelines for Naming Documents

Word documents can have any acceptable DOS filename. This means that the filename can be from one to eight characters long, followed—optionally—by a period and a one-to-three-character filename extension. You can use any characters except spaces and the following characters: * ? , ; [ ] + = \ /: | < >. You cannot use a period except to separate the filename from the extension.

Do not use DOS command names for filenames.

Filename extensions are used to distinguish between the types of files. For example, document files generally have the extension .DOC, backup files have the extension .BAK, and document templates have the extension .DOT.

If you do not add a filename extension to document filenames, Word adds .DOC by default. If you want, you can add a different extension by typing a period and then the extension—for example, DOCUMENT.ABC. If you don't want an extension, type the filename and end it with a period.

Do not use the filename extension .RTF. Word uses this extension when converting Word files to RTF format.

Word assumes specific filename extensions. If you use other extensions for your files, type the extension every time you type the filename.

Word uses the following filename extensions.

Filename extension	Meaning
.DOC	Current version of a document
.DOT	Document template file
.BAK	Previous version of a document (a backup file)
.DIC	Dictionary file
.DLL	Dynamic-link library file
.DRV	Device driver file
.EXE	Program file
.FON	Font file
.INI	Initial settings file
.LEX	Data files for spelling checking, hyphenation, and thesaurus
.TIF	Default picture file (TIFF)
.TMP	Temporary file used by Word only during a Word session

Good Saving Habits

If you usually store your documents on your hard disk, you should also store copies of important documents on a floppy disk or file server. That way, if there is ever a problem with your computer, you'll have a safe copy of your work. If you store your documents only on floppy disks, you should store copies of the disks separately. For instructions on making duplicate copies of files, see the procedure "To save a copy of the active document," earlier in this chapter.

Selecting the Always Create Backup Copy check box in the Options dialog box (Tools menu) preserves the previously saved version of a file each time you save it. This is a good way to protect the document as you work, but it is not a good way to provide long-term safety for your files. The backup file, named *DOCUMENT NAME*.BAK, does not contain the most recent changes—it's always one version behind. In addition, because it is saved in the same disk and directory as the original, problems with the disk or directory can affect both the backup and the original.

Protecting Documents from Changes

Word provides several methods of preventing accidental changes to an important file:

- The Read Only option keeps you from accidentally making changes to a document that you open. If you choose the Read Only option when you open a document and then try to save changes, Word displays a message that the file is read-only, and then displays the Save As dialog box so you can save your changes under a different filename.

- A protection password prevents others from viewing or making changes to your document without the password. You can remove a password when you no longer need it.

For more information on annotations, see Chapter 31, "Footnotes, Annotations, and Revision Marks."

- The Lock For Annotations option permits others to add comments to a document that are similar to footnotes, but not to edit or format the document text. When a document is locked for annotations, only its author can make changes to text, and only the author can unlock the document.

Some operating systems and local area networks (LANs) also provide a means of protecting files. To find out if your system has this feature, see your operating system or network documentation.

To open a document as read-only

1   From the File menu, choose Open (ALT, F, O), or press CTRL+F12.

2   In the File Name box, type or select the name of the document.

3   Select the Read Only check box.

4   Choose the OK button.

To protect a document with a password

The password can be from 1 to 15 characters long, and it can include spaces, uppercase and lowercase letters, and any character on the keyboard. If you have several open documents, the insertion point must be in the document you want to protect with a password.

1   From the File menu, choose Save As (ALT, F, A), or press F12.

2   If you have not given the document a name, type a document name in the File Name box.

3   Choose the File Sharing button.

4   Type a password in the Protection Password box, and then choose the OK button.

5   Retype the password to verify it.

6   Choose the OK button.

7   To save the document, choose the OK button again.

8   If Word displays the Summary Information dialog box, type any of the optional information that you want to add, and then choose the OK button.

Word asks for the password each time the document is opened.

Important   If you forget a password, you cannot open the document or remove the password. It's a good idea to keep a list of your passwords and their corresponding document names in a safe place.

To change or delete a password

If you have several open documents, the insertion point must be in the document whose password you want to change or delete.

1   From the File menu, choose Save As (ALT, F, A), or press F12.

2   Choose the File Sharing button.

3   To change the password, type the new password.
    –or–
    To delete the password, press the DEL key.

4   Choose the OK button.

    If you changed the password, Word asks you to retype the new password.

5   To save the document with the change to the password, choose the OK button.

6   If Word displays the Summary Info dialog box, type any of the optional information that you want to add, and then choose the OK button.

To lock or unlock a document for annotations

Only the author can unlock a document that has been locked for annotations.

1 From the File menu, choose Save As (ALT, F, A), or press F12.

2 Choose the File Sharing button.

3 To lock the document, select the Lock File For Annotations check box.
  –or–
  To unlock the document, clear the Lock File For Annotations check box.

4 Choose the OK button.

5 To save the document, choose the OK button.

6 If Word displays the Summary Info dialog box, type any of the optional information that you want to add, and then choose the OK button.

Closing a Document and Quitting Word

When you finish working with a document, close the document to prevent cluttering your screen with unneeded document windows and to free memory.

To close a document

You can close a document without quitting Word. If a document has changes you haven't saved, Word asks if you want to save changes before closing. If you choose Yes, but haven't given the document a name, Word displays the Save As dialog box.

▶ Double-click the document Control-menu box in the upper-left corner of the document window.

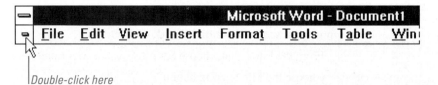

	Microsoft Word - Document1

File **Edit** **View** **Insert** **Format** **Tools** **Table** **Win**

Double-click here

This closes only the active window. If other windows are open for the same document, they will remain open.

▶ From the File menu, choose Close (ALT, F, C).

This closes the active window and any other windows that are open for the same document.

To quit Word

▶ From the File menu, choose Exit (ALT, F, X), or press ALT+F4.

If you've made changes to any open document since you last saved it, Word displays a message asking if you want to save the changes. Choose Yes to save the changes or No to discard them. Choose Cancel to continue working in Word without saving.

If you've made changes to the glossary, macros, or menu commands and have not saved them, Word displays a message asking if you want to save the changes. Choose Yes to save the changes or No to discard them.

Controlling How Word Saves Documents

When you save a document in Word, you can use any of the following special options:

- Automatic Save, which saves a document every 10 minutes or at an interval you set. This saves your changes regularly between the times that you choose the Save or Save As command.

- Allow Fast Saves, which saves documents quickly in Normal Word format.

- Always Create Backup Copy, which automatically creates a copy of your active document when you save.

- Prompt For Summary Info, which automatically displays the Summary Information dialog box when you save a document for the first time. Using summary information, you can search for a file based on its author, title, subject, keywords, or comments. For more information on using summary information, see Chapter 26, "Finding and Managing Files."

Tip   The procedures that follow describe how to set various save options using the Options command on the Tools menu. For convenience, you can display the same dialog box when you choose the Save As command and choose the Options button.

Saving Documents Automatically at Regular Intervals

If you have Automatic Save selected, Word saves your document for you at specific intervals. If there's a power outage or system failure, you can retrieve your work from the autosave backup files.

The first time Word performs an autosave backup, it saves the entire document. For subsequent backups, Word saves only those parts of the document that have changed since the last save. The first autosave may take a moment, but later backups are fast and hardly noticeable as you work. Automatic Save does not take the place of the Save or Save All commands. These commands completely save and update the versions of a document on disk each time you choose them.

Word creates autosave backup files only as necessary. Any time you choose the Save command, Word deletes the autosave backup file for the document you're saving.

Word creates the files again at the next autosave interval for documents active at that time. If you choose Save All or quit Word, Word deletes all of the autosave backup files.

In addition to performing backups at regular intervals, Word performs an autosave backup whenever the word "SAVE" appears in the status bar. This prevents you from accidentally losing work by your computer's running out of memory.

To save the current document automatically

1   From the Tools menu, choose Options (ALT, O, O).

2   Under Category, select Save.

3   Select the Automatic Save Every check box.

4   In the Minutes box, type or select how often (in minutes) you want Word to save your work. For example, to save every 15 minutes, type or select **15**

   You can choose a time interval from 1 to 120 minutes.

5   Choose the OK button.

As soon as you save a file using the Save, Save As, or Save All commands, the autosave backup files are deleted. In case of a power failure or other trouble with your computer, you can open an autosave backup file the next time you start Word. For more information, see "Restoring Your Work," later in this chapter.

Using the Allow Fast Saves Option

To save changes quickly as you work, you can use the Allow Fast Saves option. Fast saves are useful most of the time. You should use a normal save, however, to store more complete information about your document before you:

■   Begin a task that uses a lot of memory, such as searching for text or compiling an index.

■   Transfer the document text to another application.

■   Convert the document to a different file format.

To select or clear fast saves

1   From the Tools menu, choose Options (ALT, O, O).

2   Under Category, select Save.

3   To allow fast saves on all open documents, select the Allow Fast Saves check box.
   –or–
   To allow normal saves only on all open documents, clear the Allow Fast Saves check box.

4   Choose the OK button.

Saving: Fast vs. Normal

As you work on a document, Word records the editing and formatting changes you make. The first time a new document is saved, Word performs a normal (complete) save. When you save the document subsequently, Word by default performs a fast save—that is, it stores the list of changes on the disk with the file rather than taking the time (actually only a few seconds) to rearrange all the text in the file.

When the Allow Fast Saves option is cleared, Word performs a normal save, which consolidates all changes, clears the list of changes from memory, and reorders the text in the stored file.

Fast saves speed up saving but require more memory as you work and usually require more disk space for the saved documents.

Word occasionally performs a normal save to clear the edit list and free memory, even when fast saves are in effect. Word also performs a normal save when making a backup copy of a document.

Your documents are safely stored regardless of how they are saved. However, it's best to perform a normal save before you begin a task that uses a lot of memory, such as compiling an index, and before you transfer text from a Word document to another application.

If you select the Always Create Backup Copy check box in the Options dialog box (Tools menu), Word always performs a normal save on documents.

To make a backup copy when you save

You can choose to have Word create a backup copy of a document whenever you save the active document, beginning with the second time you save it. Word gives the backup copy a .BAK filename extension. Each new backup copy overwrites the previous backup for that document.

1   From the Tools menu, choose Options (ALT, O, O).

2   Under Category, select Save.

3   Under Save Options, select the Always Create Backup Copy check box.

4   Choose the OK button.

Deleting a Document

When you no longer need a document, you should delete it to make the disk space available for other documents. You can use the Find File command to delete documents that are no longer needed.

To delete one or more files

1 From the File menu, choose Find File (ALT, F, F).

   Under File Name, look for the names of the files you want to delete. If any are not listed, choose the Search button and, under Location, specify the location of the files you want to delete. Then choose the Start Search button.

   For more information about locating documents with the Find File command, see Chapter 26, "Finding and Managing Files."

2 Click the first file you want to delete; then hold down CTRL while clicking each additional file you want to delete.

   If you make a mistake, hold down CTRL and click any selected filename to remove the selection.

3 Choose the Delete button.

   Word asks if you want to delete the selected files.

4 Choose the Yes button.

5 To close the Find File dialog box, choose the Close button.

1 From the File menu, choose Find File (ALT, F, F).

   Under File Name, look for the names of the files you want to delete. If any are not listed, choose the Search button and, under Location, specify the location of the files you want to delete. Then choose the Start Search button.

   For more information about locating documents with the Find File command, see Chapter 26, "Finding and Managing Files."

2 If the filename that is highlighted is not one that you want to delete, press the DOWN ARROW or UP ARROW key until you've highlighted a file to delete. Then press SHIFT+F8 to select the filename.

3 Use the DOWN ARROW or UP ARROW key to place a dotted frame around the next filename you want to delete. Then press the SPACEBAR to select the filename.

4 Repeat step 3 for each additional filename you want to delete.

   If you make a mistake, press the arrow key to move to the filename again and press the SPACEBAR to remove the selection.

5 Choose the Delete button.

   Word asks if you want to delete the selected files.

6 Choose the Yes button.

7 To close the Find File dialog box, choose the Close button.

Tip If the files you want to delete are listed consecutively, you can select them more quickly with the mouse by clicking the first filename and, while holding down SHIFT, clicking the last filename in the sequence that you want to delete. Word selects all files between the two points. With the keyboard, select the first filename and, while holding down SHIFT, press the DOWN ARROW key to select the subsequent filenames.

Restoring Your Work

For more information, see Chapter 26, "Finding and Managing Files."

Word provides two options that can help you recover your work in the event of a power failure or other problem. You must select one or both of these options before the problem occurs for them to be of use.

If the Automatic Save option was selected when the problem occurred, all files that were open at the time of the problem are automatically displayed the next time you start Word. Word adds "(Recovered)" to the title of each window. If you were working with a document on a floppy disk when the problem occurred and you haven't made changes to your WIN.INI file, the backup files are stored in the Word program directory on your hard disk. The only work you may have lost will be the work you did following the last automatic save.

If the Automatic Save option was not selected when the problem occurred, and you cannot open the file you were working on, you may still have a backup version of the file. If the Always Create Backup Copy option was selected before the problem occurred, and you've saved the file more than once, you can open the backup file this option creates. If the document you were working with was on your hard disk, the backup version will be in the same directory; if you were working from a floppy disk, the backup version will be on the floppy disk. This file has the same name as your original file, with the filename extension .BAK. For example, if the file was named SALES.DOC, type **sales.bak** in the Open dialog box to open the backup version. This file contains the next-to-last version of your original file.

Chapter 3

Typing and Revising a Document

When you open a new document in Word, the insertion point is at the top of the window, ready for you to start typing. You'll find that using a word processor like Word is much easier than using a typewriter. Nothing's on paper until you print the document, so you can easily make corrections and move or copy items until you're satisfied with the results.

You make changes in a document by first *selecting* the text and graphics you want to revise and then choosing a command that tells Word how to change the selected copy. Selecting is how you mark the text you want to revise; it is the first step for much of the work you do in Word. You can select text a variety of ways using the mouse or the keyboard.

This chapter shows you how to type text, move around in the document, and select and edit text. Once you're familiar with the basic techniques covered here, make sure you investigate commands on the Edit and Tools menus. They can help automate many of the routine changes you make to documents.

Typing Text

Like most word processors, Word automatically "wraps" the lines of text to fit between the margins as you type, starting a new line when needed. If you add or delete text, change the margins, or change the format of the text, Word adjusts the line breaks for you. To allow Word to work effectively, keep the following points in mind when you're typing:

- Press ENTER only to start a new paragraph, not at the end of each line of text.

- Don't use spaces to align text.

   Instead, use a tab, an indent, a table, or one of the paragraph alignment options. In most cases, you'll get just the effect you want with a few keystrokes or with a few clicks of the mouse.

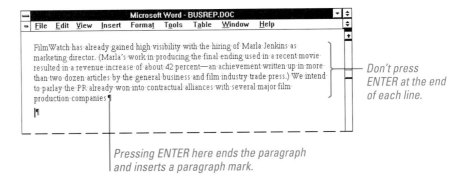

Don't press ENTER at the end of each line.

Pressing ENTER here ends the paragraph and inserts a paragraph mark.

For information about paragraph formatting techniques, see Chapter 7, "Paragraph Formatting."

The formatting commands in Word make spacing and aligning text fast, easy, and accurate. You don't have to guess how many spaces to insert, and text remains aligned even if you edit or reformat the text. The following illustration shows how tabs and paragraph alignment are used to position text in a custom letterhead.

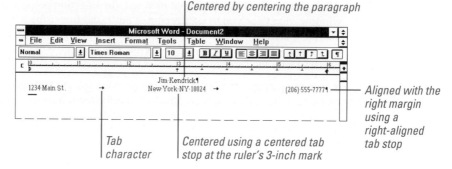

Centered by centering the paragraph

Aligned with the right margin using a right-aligned tab stop

Tab character

Centered using a centered tab stop at the ruler's 3-inch mark

To add to text you've already typed

1   Using the mouse, position the I-beam pointer where you want to begin typing, and then click.
    –or–
    Use the arrow keys to move the insertion point where you want to begin typing.

2   Type the new text.

Word adjusts the rest of the paragraph to accommodate the new text.

To type words in uppercase letters

▶ Press the CAPS LOCK key.

Word displays the letters "CAPS" in the status bar at the bottom of the window. To type lowercase letters, press the CAPS LOCK key again.

To start a new paragraph

▶ Press ENTER.

Word inserts a paragraph mark (¶) and moves the insertion point to the first line of the new paragraph.

To start a new line in the same paragraph

Use this technique to force a line break as you type a series of short lines, as in an address or list. You can then format all the lines as a single paragraph.

▶ Press SHIFT+ENTER.

If you have chosen to display paragraph marks, you'll see a newline character (↵) on the screen. Newline characters do not print.

Tip   Paragraph marks store the formatting instructions for the text that precedes them. It's a good idea to work with paragraph marks displayed. They do not print. To display paragraph marks and other nonprinting characters, such as space marks and tab characters, click the Show/Hide ¶ button on the right side of the ribbon. If you want Word to display only paragraph marks and newline characters, select the Paragraph Marks check box, an option in the View category of the Options dialog box (Tools menu).

To repeat text you just typed

Word stores in memory the last characters you typed until you perform an action other than moving the insertion point. You can repeat text you just typed, inserting it again anywhere in your document.

1   Position the insertion point where you want to repeat the text you just typed.

2   From the Edit menu, choose Repeat Typing (ALT, E, R), or press F4.

Tip   You probably will find yourself typing some text again and again—for example, your company's name, policy statements, names and addresses of clients and vendors, or people you correspond with regularly. If you store these items as glossary entries, you can insert them in other documents using only a few keystrokes. You also can store graphics as glossary entries. For more information, see Chapter 13, "Glossaries: Storing Items for Reuse."

To type over existing text

By default, Word inserts new characters you type by moving existing text to the right. You can change this so that new text replaces existing text, character by character. This is called overtype. Before using the following procedure, make sure the Use The INS Key For Paste check box is cleared in the General category of the Options dialog box (Tools menu).

1   Press the INS key.

The letters "OVR" appear in the status bar at the bottom of the window, indicating that the overtype mode is on.

2   Type the new text.

The new text you type replaces existing text.

To turn the overtype mode off, press INS again.

To type numbers using the numeric keypad

When typing numbers, you may prefer to use the numeric keypad, which is available on some keyboards. The keys and numbers on the keypad are arranged like those on a conventional adding machine. Normally, pressing keys on the keypad moves the insertion point. With NUM LOCK on, you can type numbers and math symbols using the keypad.

▶ Press the NUM LOCK key.

Word displays the letters "NUM" in the status bar at the bottom of the window. When you want to use the numeric keypad to move the insertion point, press NUM LOCK again.

Typing Special Characters

① ❷ ③ ❏ ◆ ⇨ ¢ fl Œ ì Æ § £ ¥ ¢ Ò   α β χ δ ε Φ Γ 📱 📠 ☆

In many fonts (typefaces), you can type characters that aren't displayed on the keyboard. For example, some fonts provide the Greek alphabet and many math symbols. Other fonts consist of graphic "clip art" characters, while others have bullets, numbers, and other graphics to enliven your document's design. Some fonts consist entirely of special characters. For information about inserting these special font characters in your document, see Chapter 6, "Character Formatting."

If you frequently create documents in languages other than English, you can change your keyboard driver to assign international characters to keys on your keyboard. For more information on changing keyboard drivers, see your Windows documentation.

Typing Hyphens and Nonbreaking Spaces

You can use special hyphens and nonbreaking spaces to control line breaks in a paragraph. When printed, these characters look like ordinary hyphens and spaces, but you can tell them apart when you view your document if you work with nonprinting characters displayed.

Normal hyphen   Use for words such as "great-grandson" that should always be hyphenated, regardless of where they fall in a line of text. If the hyphenated word falls at the end of a line, Word breaks the word at the normal hyphen.

For more information about hyphenating words, see Chapter 14, "Proofing a Document."

Optional hyphen   Use optional hyphens to indicate where Word should hyphenate a word that falls at the end of a line. If adding or deleting text moves the whole word back to the middle of the line or down to the next line, the optional hyphen disappears and does not print.

If you want all optional hyphens to be visible on the screen, including those that don't occur at line breaks, select the Optional Hyphens check box, an option in the View category of the Options dialog box (Tools menu). Word will still print only those optional hyphens that occur at line breaks.

Although you can insert optional hyphens as you type, you will find it more efficient to insert them using the Hyphenation command on the Tools menu. Use this command to insert optional hyphens after you complete final editing changes in the document.

Nonbreaking hyphen Use this hyphen when you don't want a hyphenated word divided at a line break. For example, you could use nonbreaking hyphens for hyphenated proper names such as Stratford-upon-Avon, or for minus signs used with negative numbers. Word moves the entire word to the next line instead of breaking it. Nonbreaking hyphens are always visible and are printed as ordinary hyphens.

Nonbreaking space A nonbreaking, or "hard," space keeps Word from breaking a line between two words. For example, you would not want a line break between the numeral and the unit of measure in a measurement such as 2 feet. Unlike spaces inserted with the SPACEBAR, nonbreaking spaces aren't expanded to fill out lines in justified text. Nonbreaking spaces are useful in math formulas or computer command syntax in which you don't want the spacing adjusted.

The following table lists the keys you type to insert these characters in your document. If you choose to display nonprinting characters, the hyphens are displayed as shown in parentheses.

To type	Press
Normal hyphen (-)	HYPHEN
Optional hyphen (¬)	CTRL+HYPHEN
Nonbreaking hyphen (—)	CTRL+SHIFT+HYPHEN
Nonbreaking space (◊)	CTRL+SHIFT+SPACEBAR

To display or hide nonprinting characters

You can have Word display or hide nonprinting characters such as paragraph marks, tab characters, space marks, and all optional hyphens in the document. Even when these characters are visible on the screen, they are not printed.

▶ On the ribbon, click the Show/Hide ¶ button.

– Or –

1 From the Tools menu, choose Options (ALT, O, O).

2 Under Category, select View.

3 Under Nonprinting Characters, select or clear the check boxes for the nonprinting characters you want to display or hide.

   To display or hide all nonprinting characters, select or clear the All check box.

4 Choose the OK button.

Tips for Making Attractive Documents

Here are some ideas for adding polish to your printed documents.

- After a period or colon, type one space instead of two. Using only one space is standard practice in the publishing industry.

- Don't type two hyphens in place of a dash character. Instead, insert an em dash— like the two dashes here—or insert an en dash, like the dash used in ranges of numbers such as 22–34. With NUM LOCK on, press ALT+0150 to insert an en dash and ALT+0151 to insert an em dash.

- Instead of inserting blank lines to add space between paragraphs, use the Paragraph command on the Format menu to add space before or after them. You can control the spacing more precisely, adding one-half of a line, one-third of a line, and so forth. If you define the spacing as a style, you can apply it to other paragraphs.

- Instead of typing three periods for an ellipsis, use the Symbol command on the Insert menu to insert an ellipsis as one character, so that the periods cannot be separated at a line break.

- Use italic, not underlining, for titles of books and other publications.

- Instead of using straight quotation marks (" or '), use the curled opening and closing quotation marks (' ' or " "). To insert them, make sure NUM LOCK is on, and then press ALT+0145 ('), ALT+0146 ('), ALT+0147 ("), or ALT+0148 (") on the numeric keypad.

- Depending on the printer you are using and the fonts installed in your system, you may be able to easily insert true publishing characters into your document by using the symbol command on the Insert menu. For more information, see Chapter 6, "Character Formatting."

- As already mentioned, use tabs, indents, tables, or paragraph alignment options to align text; don't use the SPACEBAR.

Setting Typing Preferences

In Word, there are several different ways text can be inserted and deleted as you type. Using the Options command on the Tools menu, you can specify how you want Word to insert and delete text.

To set the function of the INS key

The default function of the INS key is to switch in and out of overtype mode. You can change this default to have the INS key insert the contents of the Clipboard into a document instead. The Clipboard is a temporary storage area for text or graphics you have removed or copied from your document using the Cut or Copy command on the Edit menu. For more information about the Clipboard, see "Moving and Copying Text," later in this chapter.

1   From the Tools menu, choose Options (ALT, O, O).

2   Under Category, select General.

3 Under Settings, do one of the following:

- To use INS to paste items from the Clipboard into the document, select the Use The INS Key For Paste check box.

- To use INS to switch between overtype mode and regular typing mode, clear the Use The INS Key For Paste check box.

4 Choose the OK button.

To set the overtype mode as the default

By default, Word makes room for new characters you type by moving existing characters to the right. You can change the default to have Word replace existing text with new text, character by character. This is called overtype. For procedures for using overtype, see "To type over existing text," earlier in this chapter.

1 From the Tools menu, choose Options (ALT, O, O).

2 Under Category, select General.

3 To have Word automatically replace existing characters with new characters you type, select the Overtype Mode check box.

4 Choose the OK button.

To return to regular typing mode, in which Word inserts new text without replacing the old, clear the Overtype Mode check box.

To set the Typing Replaces Selection option

You can have Word replace a selection with new text you type or insert the new text at the end of the selection.

1 From the Tools menu, choose Options (ALT, O, O).

2 Under Category, select General.

3 Under Settings, do one of the following:

- To replace a selection with typing, select the Typing Replaces Selection check box.

- To preserve the selection when you type, clear the Typing Replaces Selection check box.

4 Choose the OK button.

Adding the Date or Time

You can always add the date or time to a document by typing it in; however, it's handier to use the Date And Time command on the Insert menu. With this command, you can add the date in any of a number of formats or add the time based on either a 12- or 24-hour clock. Unless you specify otherwise, Word updates the date or time to be current at the time of printing.

To add the date or time

1   Place the insertion point where you want to add the date or time.

2   From the Insert menu, choose Date And Time (ALT, I, T).

3   In the Available Formats box, select the date or time format you want.

4   Choose the OK button.

Word inserts the date or time as a field code, which it updates at printing. If you want, you can update as you work by positioning the insertion point in the date or time and pressing the Update Field key (F9). If you don't want the date or time to be updated at all, position the insertion point and press the Unlink Field key (CTRL+SHIFT+F9).

You cannot delete the date or time by backspacing over it; you have to select it as a whole, and then delete it. You can, however, position the insertion point in the date or time and backspace to edit the text.

The date or time is displayed in the format you selected—for example, December 12, 1991—unless you choose Field Codes from the View menu. Then the underlying field code—{TIME \@ "MMMM d, yyyy"} for this example—is displayed. For more information about fields, see Chapter 41, "Fields."

Moving the Insertion Point and Scrolling

When you type, text is inserted in your document at the insertion point, the blinking vertical bar. As you type or edit text, Word automatically scrolls through the document, displaying a different portion of it and keeping the insertion point or selection visible in the window.

To bring other parts of your document into view, use the scroll bars along the right side and bottom of the window. Scrolling moves your document in the document window in much the way film rolls past the lens of a movie camera.

Keep in mind that scrolling doesn't necessarily move the insertion point. After scrolling to another part of your document, point with the mouse and click to move the insertion point where you want to start work. If you are working on page 4, for example, and then scroll to page 7 and begin typing without clicking the page, Word automatically scrolls back to page 4 to display the new text at the insertion point.

Moving the Insertion Point

The simplest way to move the insertion point is to point and click with the mouse when the I-beam pointer is displayed. Just pointing with the mouse won't move the insertion point. If you prefer, you can move the insertion point using keys.

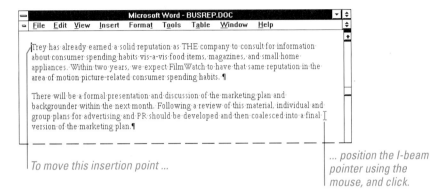

To move this insertion point ...

... position the I-beam pointer using the mouse, and click.

To move the insertion point using the mouse

▶ Point the I-beam pointer where you want to type, and then click.

The insertion point always stays within the text area. If you click in the right margin or after the final paragraph mark of your document, the insertion point moves to the closest text.

To return to a previous editing location

Word remembers the last three locations where you typed or edited text. The Go Back key combination returns the insertion point to each of the previous locations.

▶ Press SHIFT+F5 until you reach the location you want.

The insertion point moves to each of the three previous editing locations in turn and then returns to its original position.

Tip   When you save a document, Word stores the last location of the insertion point. When you next open the document, use the Go Back key (SHIFT+F5) to continue working where you left off.

To go to a specific page, bookmark, or other location

If you want to move quickly to a specific place in a document, such as a particular page or a bookmark, use the Go To command.

1   From the Edit menu, choose Go To (ALT, E, G), or press F5 twice.

2   In the Go To box, type one of the following instructions.

To go to	Type
Line	**l** (el) followed by a line number
Page	**p** for next page, or **p** followed by a page number, or the page number by itself; for example, to move to page 14 of the document, type **p14** or **14**
Section	**s** for the next section, or **s** followed by a section number
Bookmark	The bookmark name, or select it from the list
Footnote	**f** for next footnote, or **f** followed by a footnote number
Annotation	**a** for next annotation, or **a** followed by an annotation number
Specified distance through the document	A number followed by **%** (percent sign); for example, to move to the middle of your document, type **50%**
Specific location	A combination of instructions, in the order they appear in this table; for example, to go to section 2, page 5, line 4, type **s2p5l4**

3   Choose the OK button.

Tip   You can type any of the preceding instructions without displaying the Go To dialog box. Instead, press F5 to display the "Go To" prompt at the bottom of the Word window, type the instruction, and then press ENTER.

To move the insertion point using key shortcuts

▸ To move the insertion point quickly, press the following keys.

Make sure NUM LOCK is off before using the numeric keypad.

Pressing some keys has a different effect in page layout view and within a Word table. For details, see Chapter 24, "Viewing Documents" and Chapter 17, "Tables."

To move the insertion point	Press this key
Up one line	UP ARROW or 8 on keypad
If text is selected, the insertion point moves to the line above the beginning of the selection.	
Down one line	DOWN ARROW or 2 on keypad
If text is selected, the insertion point moves to the line below the beginning of the selection.	
One character to the left	LEFT ARROW or 4 on keypad
If text is selected, the insertion point moves back from the first character of the selection.	
One character to the right	RIGHT ARROW or 6 on keypad
If text is selected, the insertion point moves one character to the right of the last character of the selection.	
One word to the left	CTRL+LEFT ARROW
One word to the right	CTRL+RIGHT ARROW
Beginning of the line	HOME
End of the line	END
One paragraph up	CTRL+UP ARROW
One paragraph down	CTRL+DOWN ARROW
Down one window	PAGE DOWN
Up one window	PAGE UP
To the bottom of a window	CTRL+PAGE DOWN
To the top of a window	CTRL+PAGE UP
Beginning of the document	CTRL+HOME
End of the document	CTRL+END

Tip   In Word, outline view makes moving the insertion point through long documents easy because you can collapse your document to show only the headings. For more information, see Chapter 27, "Outline View: Creating Outlines and Reorganizing Documents."

Scrolling

To scroll quickly to another part of your document, you can use the vertical scroll bar along the right side of the document window. The position of the scroll box indicates your approximate location in the document. If you're working with a wide document or a narrow window, you can use the horizontal scroll bar at the bottom of the window to scroll horizontally.

When you stop scrolling, click in the text to position the insertion point. Word displays the current page number in the status bar at the bottom of the window.

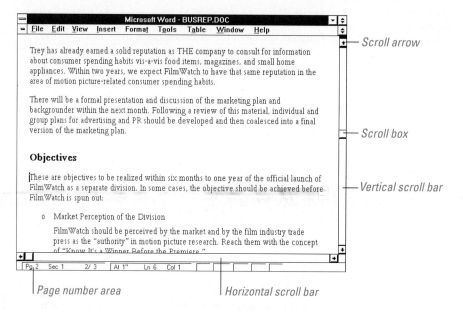

Scroll arrow

Scroll box

Vertical scroll bar

Page number area

Horizontal scroll bar

Note   If the scroll bars are not displayed, choose the Options command from the Tools menu. In the View category, select the Horizontal Scroll Bar and Vertical Scroll Bar check boxes.

To scroll using the mouse

▶ To scroll through the document, use the mouse to do any of the following:

To scroll	Do this
Up or down one line	Click the up or down scroll arrow on the vertical scroll bar.
Up or down one screen	Click the scroll bar above or below the scroll box.
A percentage of document length	Drag the scroll box up or down.
Left or right	Click the left or right scroll arrow on the horizontal scroll bar.
A percentage of document width	Click the scroll bar to the left or right of the scroll box on the horizontal scroll bar.
Into the left margin in normal view, past the 0 (zero) mark on the ruler	Hold down SHIFT and click the left scroll arrow.

To view this text ...

... hold down SHIFT and click here.

In page layout view, you can also use the Page Forward and Page Back buttons on the vertical scroll bar to move quickly through your document. For more information about working in page layout view, see Chapter 24, "Viewing Documents."

To scroll using the keyboard

▶ Use the following keys to scroll in normal view.

Make sure NUM LOCK is off before using the numeric keypad.

To scroll	Press
Up approximately one screen and also move the insertion point up	PAGE UP or 9 on keypad
Down approximately one screen and also move the insertion point down	PAGE DOWN or 3 on keypad

To scroll into the left margin

Word usually stops scrolling at the left margin. You sometimes may need to scroll farther, for example, to set a negative indent using the ruler.

▶ Hold down the SHIFT key and click the left scroll arrow on the horizontal scroll bar.

To return the document to its usual horizontal placement, click the right scroll arrow.

1   Press CTRL+SHIFT+F10.

A gray box called the ruler cursor appears on the left end of the ruler.

2   Hold down the SHIFT key and press the LEFT ARROW key.

The ruler cursor moves into the left margin.

To return the document to its usual horizontal placement, press the END key until the 0 (zero) point on the ruler is no longer visible, and then press the HOME key. To return the insertion point to the document text, press ESC.

Selecting Text

For information about selecting graphics for sizing and scaling, see Chapter 20, "Importing Graphics."

To identify the text and graphics in your document that you want the command you choose to act on, you select the area. This is an important first step for much of the work you do in Word. For example, to delete a sentence, you select it and then delete it. You can select text a variety of ways using the mouse or the keyboard.

One technique, dragging over text with the mouse, is a standard way of selecting text. Often, however, the editing and formatting changes you make involve whole words, sentences, lines, and paragraphs. In Word, you can quickly select the appropriate amount of text with a few keystrokes or clicks of the mouse. You will work more quickly if you learn several techniques and use the one best suited to a task.

The selected area in your document is called the *selection* and is highlighted on your screen. Text may remain highlighted after commands are completed. For example, if you select text and choose a formatting command, the text remains selected. You don't have to select the text again to apply additional formatting. When you finish working with the text, be sure to cancel the selection—just click where you want to begin typing, or press an arrow key.

To make selecting italic text easier, Word slants the insertion point when you position it in italic text.

Note   When applying paragraph formats or styles to text, you don't need to select all the text in the paragraph. The paragraph containing the insertion point or any part of a selection is considered selected.

To select any item or area of text

You can use this technique to select any item or any text in your document, including nonprinting characters such as paragraph marks and tab characters.

▶ Point to where you want the selection to begin, hold down the left mouse button, and drag the mouse pointer to where you want the selection to end.

–Or–

▶ Position the insertion point where you want the selection to begin. Hold down SHIFT as you use the arrow keys to move the insertion point to where you want the selection to end.

A character is selected if at least half of the character is within the selection.

Note   To display nonprinting characters and make it easier to select them, click the Show/Hide ¶ button on the ribbon. You can also use the Options command on the Tools menu to display nonprinting characters. Select the All check box in the View category of the Options dialog box.

To adjust a selection

If you initially selected too much or too little text, use one of the following methods to adjust the amount of text selected.

▶ Hold down SHIFT and click where you want the selection to end.

If you initially selected whole units of text, such as sentences or paragraphs, the selection expands or contracts by those units.

–Or–

▶ Hold down SHIFT while pressing any arrow key.

You can expand or contract the original selection using this method.

–Or–

▶ Press SHIFT+F8.

The selection is reduced first to a paragraph, then a sentence, then a word.

Tip   If you begin typing or accidentally press a key while text is selected in your document, Word may replace the selected items with the new text you type. Choose Undo from the Edit menu as the next action to restore the deleted text to your document.

To cancel a selection

Do one of the following to cancel a selection made by using the mouse or key combinations.

▶   Click anywhere in the text of the document window.

– Or –

▶   Press an arrow key.

If you pressed F8 to extend a selection, first press ESC to cancel extend mode, and then press an arrow key to cancel the selection.

To select whole units of text with the mouse

The *selection bar* is an unmarked area along the left side of the document window. In the selection bar, the pointer shape changes to a right-pointing arrow. You can then select a line, paragraph, or entire document with one or two mouse clicks. To select words and sentences, you click the text itself.

▶   Using the mouse, do one of the following:

To select	Do this
Word	Double-click in the word.
Sentence	Hold down CTRL and click anywhere in the sentence.
Line of text	With the pointer in the selection bar, point to the line and click. To select multiple lines, drag in the selection bar next to the lines.
Paragraph	With the pointer in the selection bar, point to the paragraph and double-click. To select multiple paragraphs, drag in the selection bar.
Document	Hold down CTRL and click anywhere in the selection bar.

If you want to select additional words, sentences, lines, or paragraphs after making an initial selection, hold down SHIFT and click anywhere in the unit of text you want included in the selection.

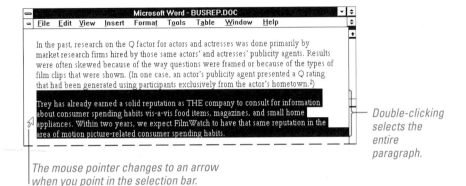

Double-clicking selects the entire paragraph.

The mouse pointer changes to an arrow when you point in the selection bar.

Note   When you select a document, the headers and footers aren't included. To select all of a header or footer, open the appropriate header or footer pane using the Header/Footer command on the View menu. Then use the Select All command on the Edit menu to select the contents of the header or footer pane.

To select a large area with the mouse

If you're selecting more than a few words or paragraphs, this technique is faster than dragging the pointer over text. You establish an anchor point and then indicate where you want the selection to end.

1 Click where you want the selection to begin.

2 Hold down SHIFT and click where you want the selection to end.

You may have to scroll to reach the end of the text you want to select.

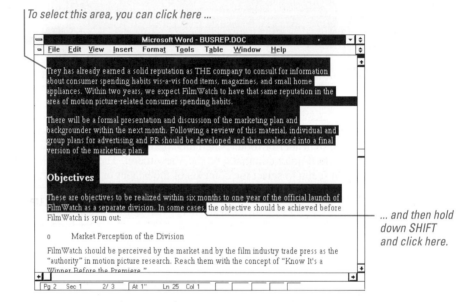

To select this area, you can click here ...

... and then hold down SHIFT and click here.

You can also position the insertion point where you want the selection to end, hold down SHIFT, and click where you want the selection to begin.

To select whole units of text with keys

You can select text by holding down the SHIFT key and pressing keys that move the insertion point. You can also use the Extend key (F8) to select text.

▶   Use any of the following key combinations to select text.

To select	Press
One character to the right	SHIFT+RIGHT ARROW
One character to the left	SHIFT+LEFT ARROW
To the end of a word	CTRL+SHIFT+RIGHT ARROW
To the start of a word	CTRL+SHIFT+LEFT ARROW
To the end of a line	SHIFT+END
To the start of a line	SHIFT+HOME
One line down	SHIFT+DOWN ARROW
One line up	SHIFT+UP ARROW
To the end of a paragraph	CTRL+SHIFT+DOWN ARROW
To the start of a paragraph	CTRL+SHIFT+UP ARROW
One screen down	SHIFT+PAGE DOWN
One screen up	SHIFT+PAGE UP
To the end of a document	CTRL+SHIFT+END
To the start of a document	CTRL+SHIFT+HOME
An entire document	CTRL+5 on keypad
An entire table	ALT+5 on keypad

To extend a selection using the Extend key (F8)

1   Place the insertion point in the text you want to select.

2   Press F8.

The letters "EXT" appear in the status bar.

3   To select a word, sentence, paragraph, section, or entire document, press F8 repeatedly until the amount of text you want is selected.
–or–
To extend the selection to a particular character, press the key for that character. You can press the key for an uppercase or lowercase letter or other character, including PERIOD, TAB, or ENTER.

Press ESC to cancel Extend mode.

Tip You can press F8 and then choose the Find or Go To commands on the Edit menu to extend the selection. Use the Find command to extend the selection to a specific piece of text; use Go To to extend the selection to a specific page, bookmark, footnote, or annotation.

To select a column of text

For information about selecting in a Word table, see Chapter 17, "Tables."

This technique most often is used to select columns of text or numbers set up using tabs. You use a different technique to select a column of cells in a Word table. To keep the proper alignment if you move or copy the column elsewhere, make sure you include the trailing tab mark in each line you select.

1   Point to one corner of the column of text you want to select.

2   Hold down the right mouse button and drag to the opposite corner.

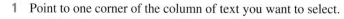
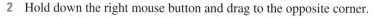

Point here, and then hold down the right mouse button ...

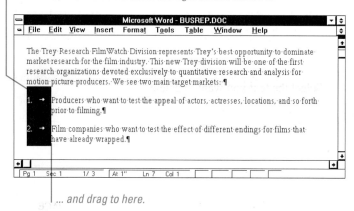

... and drag to here.

1   Position the insertion point at one corner of the column of text you want to select.

2   Press CTRL+SHIFT+F8.

The letters "COL" appear in the status bar at the bottom of the window.

3   Use the arrow keys to extend the selection to the opposite corner.

Press ESC to cancel the column selection mode.

Correcting and Deleting Text

To correct mistakes as you type, press BACKSPACE or DEL. The BACKSPACE key deletes the character preceding the insertion point. The DEL key deletes the character following the insertion point. To delete more than a few characters, it's faster to first select the text you want deleted and then press DEL or BACKSPACE. You can also select text and then type new text to replace the selection, similar to a "typeover" mode on some word processors.

If you think you might use the text somewhere else in your document, use the Cut command on the Edit menu to remove it. This stores the text on the Clipboard, and you can use the Paste command to insert it in another location. For more information about the Cut command, see "Moving and Copying Text," later in this chapter.

Note If two paragraphs are formatted with different styles, you cannot use the BACKSPACE key to delete the paragraph mark of the first paragraph. This feature prevents accidental loss of the formatting stored in the paragraph mark. Instead, select the paragraph mark and then press DEL. The combined paragraphs take the formatting of the second paragraph.

To delete selected text

1 Select the text you want to delete.

2 Press the DEL or BACKSPACE key.

To delete text using the keyboard

▶ Position the insertion point, and then press one of the following keys.

To delete	Press
Character before the insertion point	BACKSPACE
Character after the insertion point	DEL
Word before the insertion point	CTRL+BACKSPACE
Word after the insertion point	CTRL+DEL

To restore deleted text

▶ From the Edit menu, choose Undo (ALT, E, U).

You must choose Undo as the next action after deleting the text.

Tip You can also quickly restore deleted text by pressing the Undo key (CTRL+Z) or clicking the Undo button on the Toolbar before taking any other action.

To replace a selection with typing

1   Select the text you want to replace.

2   Type the replacement text.

Word replaces the highlighted selection with the first character of the replacement text.

Note   You can have new text you type be inserted after a selection, instead of replacing the selection. To do this, clear the Typing Replaces Selection check box, an option in the General category of the Options dialog box (Tools menu). For more information, see "Setting Typing Preferences," earlier in this chapter.

Moving and Copying Text

Moving text to another place in your document typically involves cutting and pasting using the Cut and Paste commands on the Edit menu or the Cut and Paste buttons on the Toolbar. To copy material, leaving the original text in place, you use the Copy and Paste commands or buttons in a similar way. Use the Cut, Copy, and Paste commands to move and copy text within the same document, to another open document, or from or to a document created in another application.

Text that you cut or copy is placed on the Clipboard, a temporary storage area. An item placed on the Clipboard remains there until you choose the Cut or Copy command again, when it is replaced with the new item. You can paste an item from the Clipboard into your document as many times as you like.

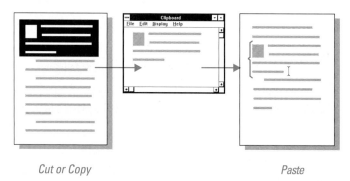

Cut or Copy   Paste

If you choose the Cut or Copy command and accidentally replace material on the Clipboard, choose Undo from the Edit menu as the next action. This reverses the Cut or Copy command and restores the previous material to the Clipboard.

Items generally remain on the Clipboard when you quit Word, allowing you to paste them into other applications. When you quit Word after copying or moving large amounts of text on the Clipboard, you may get a message asking if you want to save the Clipboard contents. Save the Clipboard if you plan to use its contents. If not, choose No to clear the Clipboard and make more memory available to your applications.

You may find it more convenient to move and copy text using the Move Text and Copy Text keys. These key combinations and the alternative mouse procedures provide a quick way to move a selection directly to its new location without using the Clipboard. You can also use the mouse to drag selected text or a graphic to a new location within a document.

Tip   If you're pasting material from another Word document or another application such as a Microsoft Excel worksheet, consider using the Paste Special command instead of Paste. The Paste Special command links the item pasted in your Word document with the original item in its source document or application. The item in the Word document is updated automatically when changes are made to the original. For information about various ways to use the Paste Special command, see Chapter 36, "Exchanging Information."

Moving and Copying Text Using the Clipboard

The following instructions tell how to move and copy text, but you use the same techniques to move and copy any item or character you can select in a Word document. These include graphics, special screen symbols, and items you insert from other applications. With few exceptions, you also use the Cut, Copy, and Paste commands in the same way to edit text within a cell of a Word table.

If you include paragraph marks in your selection when you copy or move text between documents, the formatting and styles applied to the paragraphs are also copied. If you copy more than 50 paragraphs in a document you have saved at least once, all styles in the document are copied along with the paragraphs.

To move or copy text

1   Select the text.

2   To move text, choose Cut from the Edit menu (ALT, E, T), press CTRL+X, or click the Cut button on the Toolbar.
    –or–
    To copy text, choose Copy from the Edit menu (ALT, E, C), press CTRL+C, or click the Copy button on the Toolbar.

    This places the text on the Clipboard.

3   Position the insertion point in a new location.

    If the new location is in another document, open the document, or choose the filename from the Window menu if it's already open.

4   From the Edit menu, choose Paste (ALT, E, P), press CTRL+V, or click the Paste button on the Toolbar.

You can adjust Word so that pressing the INS key inserts the contents of the Clipboard. For more information, see "Setting Typing Preferences," earlier in this chapter.

Tip If you need to move many pieces of text to the same place, using the Spike is faster than repeatedly using the Cut and Paste commands. The Spike is a special glossary entry that is similar to the Clipboard. Unlike using the Clipboard, which holds only one entry at a time, you can continue adding text and graphics to the Spike without replacing what's already there. For more information, see Chapter 13, "Glossaries: Storing Items for Reuse."

To see the contents of the Clipboard

The Clipboard is a temporary storage area for text or graphics that you are copying or moving from one location to another. The Clipboard is shared among applications.

1　From the Word Control-menu box, choose Run (ALT, SPACEBAR, U).

　　The Clipboard option is selected.

2　Choose the OK button.

To close the Clipboard

▶　From the Clipboard Control-menu box, choose Close (ALT+F4).

Tips for Moving and Copying Text

■　To return to text you just selected or edited in another part of your document, press the Go Back key (SHIFT+F5) to jump back to the text. Use the Go Back key to move around in the document quickly.

■　Instead of reorganizing long passages of text using the Cut and Paste commands, switch to outline view and collapse the text to show only the outline headings. Then drag the headings to reorder them. When you leave outline view, the headings and all their supporting subheadings and text are in their new order. For details, see Chapter 27, "Outline View: Creating Outlines and Reorganizing Documents."

To copy or move text between Word and another application

Because most applications use the Clipboard to transport text, graphics, and other data, you can copy and move text between different applications just as you do within a Word document.

1　Select the text you want to copy or move.

2　To copy text, choose Copy from the Edit menu (ALT, E, C), or press CTRL+C.
　　–or–
　　To move text, choose Cut from the Edit menu (ALT, E, T), or press CTRL+X.

　　This places the text on the Clipboard.

3 Switch to the other application by doing one of the following:

- If the other application is not yet open, start the other application.

- If the other application is already open, press CTRL+ESC and choose the application from the Task List dialog box.

  You can also press ALT+ESC until you switch to the application.

4 Position the insertion point where you want to insert the text.

5 From the Edit menu, choose Paste (ALT, E, P), or press CTRL+V.

Tip Instead of copying information between documents or applications, you can link a document to other applications. For example, you can link a table in a Word document to data in a Microsoft Excel worksheet. When the worksheet changes, the table in the Word document is updated automatically. For more information, see Chapter 36, "Exchanging Information."

Bypassing the Clipboard

When you move or copy text within a document, you often need to scroll back and forth between two locations—the old and the new. The Move Text and Copy Text keys can simplify this. You can position the insertion point in the new location for the text, and then scroll to select the text you want to move or copy. When you press ENTER, Word inserts the text at the location of the insertion point and scrolls to display it. You don't have to find your place in the document again.

Another advantage to using these keys is that they don't send text to the Clipboard, so they're useful when you need to preserve the material currently on the Clipboard. Use these keys when you are working within Word. You can't use them to move or copy text to other applications.

You can also use the mouse to move or copy text or to drag a selection to a new location.

To move or copy text using the mouse

If you are moving text to another Word document, make sure the new location is visible before you select the text to move.

1 Select the text.

2 To copy text, hold down the CTRL and SHIFT keys, point to where you want to insert the copied text, and click the right mouse button.
   –or–
   To move text, hold down the CTRL key, point to the new location, and click the right mouse button.

To move text by dragging it

Using the left mouse button, you can quickly drag a selection to a new location. Use this procedure to move selections short distances within a document.

1   Select the text or graphic.

2   Point to the selection.

The mouse pointer becomes an arrow.

3   Press the left mouse button to display a small, dotted box and a dotted insertion point. Drag the dotted insertion point to the new location, and then release the mouse button.

Word inserts the selection in the new location.

If you change your mind after moving the selection, click the Undo button on the Toolbar or choose Undo from the Edit menu as your next action. Word returns the selection to its original location.

Tip   You can choose not to have the left mouse button function as described in the preceding procedure. Display the Options dialog box by choosing Options from the Tools menu. Under Category, select General, and then clear the Drag-And-Drop Text Editing check box.

To move or copy text using keys

1   Position the insertion point where you want to insert the text.

2   To move text, press the Move Text key (F2).
–or–
To copy text, press the Copy Text key (SHIFT+F2).

The message "Move from where?" or "Copy from where?" is displayed in the lower-left corner of the status bar, at the bottom of the window.

3   Scroll to the material you want to move or copy, and then select it.

Word marks the text you select with a dotted underline.

4   Press ENTER.

Word inserts the selected text back at the insertion point, and scrolls to that location.

To cancel this procedure, press ESC anytime before you press ENTER.

Tip   The preceding keyboard procedure shows how to select the new location, and then select the text you want to move or copy. If you prefer, you can select the text you want to move or copy, press the Move Text or Copy Text key, position the insertion point where you want to place the text, and then press ENTER.

Printing a Document

Once you select a printer and the appropriate Print Setup options, printing is simple—just choose the Print command from the File menu. In this chapter, you will learn how to print all or part of a document and use options in the Print dialog box to control how Word prints your document. You will also learn how to print more than one file at a time and how to print envelopes.

The printer you use affects how Word displays and prints your document. Before formatting a document, check to make sure that you have selected the correct printer. For instructions on installing your printer and connecting it to your computer, see your Windows documentation and your printer manual. For troubleshooting information on printing problems, see PRINTERS.DOC, a file that came with your Word package.

Printing Documents

Before you print, it's a good idea to check your document using the Print Preview command on the File menu or the Page Layout command on the View menu. In print preview, you can see whole pages, one or two at a time, and adjust such things as page breaks and margins. In page layout view, you can make last-minute changes to the text and formatting.

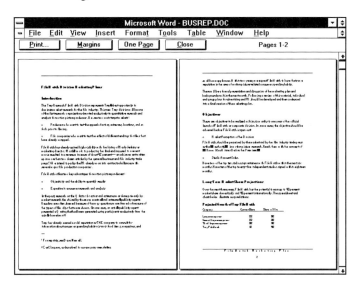

To print a document

It's a good idea to save your document before you print. That way, if a printer error or other problem occurs, you won't lose any of the work you've done since you last saved.

1   Display the document you want to print in the active window.

2   From the File menu, choose Print (ALT, F, P).

3   Select the options you want, and then choose the OK button.

See the rest of this chapter for information on different printing options.

To cancel printing

▶ Press ESC.

To print a range of pages

If you have edited a document recently, it's a good idea to repaginate and verify the starting and ending pages you want to print. Note that the page number in the status bar identifies the page that contains the insertion point.

1   With the document in the active window, choose Repaginate Now from the Tools menu (ALT, O, A).

    Word repaginates the document.

2   From the File menu, choose Print (ALT, F, P).

3   In the From box, under Range, type the beginning page number.

    To specify a page within a section, specify the page number first, then "s" for section and the section number. For example, type **6s1** to specify page 6 of section 1.

4   In the To box, under Range, type the ending page number.

5   Choose the OK button.

To print the current page or a selected part of a document

Use this procedure to print the current page or only a small area of your document—for example, the contents of the screen. Printing just a selected part of a document is particularly useful if you want to print a paragraph or table that spans a soft page break. That way, you don't have to print both pages.

1   With the document in the active window, position the insertion point within the page you want to print, or select the text or graphics you want to print.

2   From the File menu, choose Print (ALT, F, P).

3   Under Range, select the Current Page or Selection option button.

When you choose the Print command from the File menu, the Print dialog box displays the Selection option if you have selected some text or graphics in your document. If there is no selection in your document, the Print dialog box displays the Current Page option instead.

4   Choose the OK button.

To print more than one copy of a document

By default, Word prints every copy of a page before printing the next page. You can print collated copies by selecting the Collate Copies check box. Printing is considerably slower with this option selected since Word has to resend the entire document to the printer for each copy it prints.

1   From the File menu, choose Print (ALT, F, P).

2   In the Copies box, type or select the number of copies you want to print.

3   Select the Collate Copies check box if you want Word to print a complete copy of the document before printing the next copy.

4   Choose the OK button.

Some printers are unable to print uncollated copies. When this is the case with the active printer, the Collated Copies check box is selected and cannot be cleared.

To print to a file

You can save a printed version of a document in a file if you want to print it later or transfer it to another program.

1   From the File menu, choose Print (ALT, F, P).

2   Select the Print To File check box.

3   Choose the OK button.

4   Type a name for the file to which you want to print.

The name you type should be different from the original filename.

5   Choose the OK button.

Printing Related Document Information

It's often useful to print the different elements of a document or template—glossary entries, styles, key assignments, for example—that aren't part of the document text itself. You can print these different elements using the Print command.

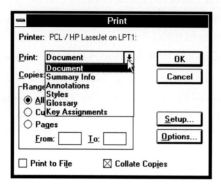

Word can print the annotations, styles, or summary information associated with the active document.

When you select Glossary or Key Assignments in the Print dialog box, Word prints the glossary entries or key assignments of the template attached to your document as well as those that are available globally. If the document has no template attached, Word prints the global glossary entries and key assignments only. If you're not sure whether a template is attached to your document, you can check by choosing the Template command on the File menu.

Annotations and summary information can be printed separately or with the document with which they're associated. To print them with their document, select the appropriate options in the Options dialog box. For more information on printing annotations and summary information with their document, see, "More Printing Options," later in this chapter.

To print related document information

1   From the File menu, choose Print (ALT, F, P).

2   In the Print box, select the option you want.

3   Choose the OK button.

More Printing Options

For additional printing options, you can choose the Options button in the Print dialog box. These options are also available when you choose the Options command from the Tools menu.

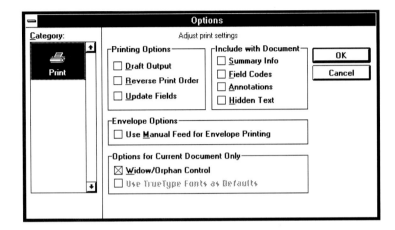

Once you set one of the print options in the Options dialog box, it remains in effect until you change it.

Draft Output   Prints the document using the printer's draft mode. The effect of draft mode varies according to the kind of printer you have, but most printers can print output more quickly in draft mode. Some printers do not print graphics in draft mode; others do not print character formatting, such as bold or italic.

Note   Some printers cannot print Adobe Type Manager fonts when you select the Draft Output option.

Reverse Print Order   Prints the pages from last to first. This option is useful for printers that stack the pages face up as they are ejected from the printer.

Update Fields   Directs Word to update all the fields in a document before printing. This option is useful for updating fields that are not updated by the regular printing process. For more information on fields, see Chapter 41, "Fields."

Summary Info   Prints the summary information on a separate page after the document is printed. If you are printing the document and include annotations, the summary information is printed after the annotations. Available only when you select Document in the Print box within the Print dialog box.

Field Codes   Prints the field codes instead of the field results in the document. Available only when you select Document, Annotations, or Glossary in the Print box.

Annotations   Prints the annotations on separate pages at the end of the document. When you select this option, Hidden Text is automatically selected because the annotation marks are formatted as hidden text. If you print only part of a document, say pages 10 through 20, Word prints annotations for only pages 10 through 20. Available only when you select Document in the Print box.

Hidden Text   Prints any text that has the hidden text character format, even if hidden text is not displayed in the document. Use this option to print notes to yourself that are formatted as hidden text.

Printer's Envelope Feeder Has Been Installed   Tells Word to use the printer's envelope feeder as the paper source for envelopes. Select this option if you have installed an envelope feeder on your printer. If your printer cannot support an envelope feeder, selecting this option has no effect; when the printer is ready to print the envelope, it prompts you to insert an envelope manually.

Widow/Orphan Control   Automatically checks to prevent widow and orphan lines. A widow is a single line at the top of a page; an orphan is a single line at the bottom of a page.

Printing Multiple Documents

Word provides two ways to print more than one document at a time:

- You can use the Find File command on the File menu to find, select, and print several documents. For more information about finding and selecting multiple documents, see Chapter 26, "Finding and Managing Files."

- You can create a master document, so that you can print several documents at once and also compile a table of contents and an index for all of the documents. For more information, see Chapter 11, "Setting Up Long Documents."

Creating and Printing Envelopes

You can use the Create Envelope command on the Tools menu to print an envelope immediately or to add an envelope address to your document. If you have already typed an address in your document, the Create Envelope command can find it and create the envelope address. Or you can type the address in the Create Envelope dialog box.

Word includes a return address on the envelope unless you choose to omit it. The first time you use the Create Envelope command, you may have to fill in the return address yourself, but on subsequent uses Word remembers the address and supplies it automatically. Word stores the return address in the User Info category of the Options dialog box (Tools menu).

If you use the Create Envelope command to add an envelope to your document, Word automatically positions the address and return address on the envelope and selects an appropriate printer paper source.

The Create Envelope command uses two standard styles to format the envelopes it creates: Envelope Address for the envelope address and Envelope Return for the return address. You can change the definitions of these styles if you want to change the formatting of the envelope addresses. For example, you could change the font used for the return address.

If your printer has an envelope feeder installed, select the Printer's Envelope Feeder Has Been Installed check box in the Print category of the Options dialog box (Tools menu). When you select this option, the Create Envelope command uses the envelope feeder to print envelopes.

To create an envelope

1   To create an address for the envelope, do one of the following:

Envelope button

If you	Do this
Have typed an address in your document	Select the address, and then choose Create Envelope from the Tools menu (ALT, O, E) or click the Envelope button on the Toolbar. Word displays the address in the Addressed To box.
	If you do not first select the address, Word looks for consecutive lines in your document that look like an address.
Have not already typed an address in your document	From the Tools menu, choose Create Envelope (ALT, O, E), or click the Envelope button on the Toolbar. In the Addressed To box, type the address.

2   If you do not want to print a return address on the envelope, select the Omit Return Address check box.

3   In the Envelope Size box, select the correct envelope size.

4   Choose the Print Envelope button to print the envelope immediately.
   –or–
   Choose the Add To Document button to add the envelope in a new section at the beginning of the document.

You can insert bookmarks in your document called EnvelopeAddress and EnvelopeReturn to mark an envelope address and return address. The Create Envelope command recognizes these bookmarks and inserts their text in its dialog box.

To print an envelope

You can print an envelope by itself or as part of a larger document.

▶ Do one of the following:

Envelope button

To print	Do this
An envelope by itself	From the Tools menu, choose Create Envelope (ALT, O, E), or click the Envelope button on the Toolbar. Type the envelope addresses, and then choose the Print Envelope button.
An envelope with the document to which it is attached	From the File menu, choose Print (ALT, F, P), and then choose the OK button.

Note When you've used the Create Envelope command to insert an envelope in a document, you can use the Print command to print the envelope only. Word inserts the envelope on a separate page, numbered page 0 (zero). In the Print dialog box, you can type **0** in the From box and **0** in the To box to print the envelope only.

Envelope Printing Tips

Although the Create Envelope command takes care of the formatting and positioning of envelope addresses and the sizing of envelopes, printers handle envelopes in many different ways. The following are some tips on how to get the best results from your printer.

Using a Laser Printer

Use a "straight-through" printing path if your printer provides one. A "straight-through" printing path is designed for envelopes or heavy paper that may smear or become jammed along the normal printing path.

If your laser printer does not have a special envelope feeder installed, it is probably set up to accept envelopes through "manual" feed. The printer may prompt you for an envelope or for letter-sized paper. If you are prompted for letter-sized paper, it is important to center the envelope in the paper feeder; otherwise the envelope addresses won't print in the correct position.

Using a Dot-matrix Printer

With many dot-matrix printers, printing an envelope requires removing tractor-fed paper and inserting an envelope. With these printers, it's easiest to print several envelopes at the same time. To align an envelope so that the address is positioned properly, align the left edge of the envelope with the zero mark on the printer's metal paper holder. If possible, align the top edge of the envelope with the top edge of the dot-matrix print head. On some printers, however, you may need to roll up the envelope a little further, so that the top edge fits beneath the metal paper holder.

The printer software for Microsoft Windows directs most dot-matrix printers to roll paper up 0.5 inch before printing. Normally, then, an envelope's return address is printed at least 0.5 inch from the top of the envelope. If you want the return address to be printed closer to the top of the envelope, you may be able to position the envelope below the top of the print head with which it should normally be aligned.

Because many printers cannot handle catalog-sized envelopes (12" x 9"), Word does not include that size in the Envelope Size list in the Create Envelope dialog box. You can use the Create Envelope command to print it, however, if your printer is large enough to accept an envelope of this size.

The Create Envelope Command and Printing Merged Documents

You can use the Create Envelope command to create envelopes for merged documents. For example, if you have a form letter that uses a series of merge fields to insert an address, you can use the Create Envelope command to add an envelope to the form letter so that for each form letter you print, a correctly addressed envelope is printed also. To add an envelope to a form letter, you select the address in the letter, choose the Create Envelope command, and then choose the Add To Document button. The address you select must consist of merge fields. For more information on printing merged documents, see Chapter 32, "Print Merge Basics."

Preparing to Print

Preparing to print has two aspects:

- Preparing the printer itself—plugging it in; adding paper, a ribbon, or a toner cartridge; and connecting it to your computer.

- Preparing your computer—telling it what kind of printer you use by installing the appropriate printer driver software and setting up the printer driver correctly for your printer.

For information about installing printer drivers, see your Windows documentation. In Word, you can change printers, if you use more than one, and you can select printer settings such as the paper source and orientation (portrait or landscape).

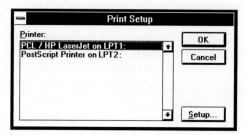

Note You should always select your printer before formatting your documents. The choice of fonts Word offers depends on the printer you have selected. If you have not selected a printer, or have selected the wrong one, you won't be able to format your document with the correct fonts for your printer.

Selecting a Printer

You can only select a printer in Word that you have installed on your system. For information on installing printer software, see your Windows documentation.

To select a printer

1 From the File menu, choose Print Setup (ALT, F, R).

2 In the Printer box, select the printer you want to use, and then choose the OK button.

    If you select a laser printer, you may also need to select a font cartridge.

Selecting Printer Setup Options

Because different printers have different printing capabilities, the dialog box that appears when you choose the Setup button in the Print Setup dialog box depends on the printer. Many laser printers, such as the Hewlett-Packard LaserJet, whose setup options are shown in the following illustration, can accept different font cartridges. If your printer uses a font cartridge, it is important to select it; otherwise you won't have access in Word to all of the fonts available on your printer.

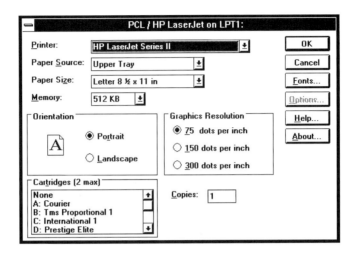

Most printers can accommodate different paper sizes, orientations, and paper sources. You can set the default paper size, orientation, and paper source for your documents in this dialog box. You can also use the Page Setup command on the Format menu to set the paper size, orientation, and paper source for individual documents and parts of documents. If there is a conflict between the settings in the Page Setup dialog box and those in the Print Setup dialog box, the settings in the Page Setup dialog box take precedence. For example, you can use the Page Setup command to specify landscape orientation for a particular document or as the default for all documents based on a template. In the Print Setup Options dialog box, the orientation setting can remain portrait, but it does not affect the orientation of documents or sections of documents that are formatted with landscape orientation using the Page Setup command on the Format menu.

To select printer setup options

1   From the File menu, choose Print Setup (ALT, F, R).

2   In the Printer box, select the printer you want to use, if more than one is available.

3   Choose the Setup button.

4   Select the appropriate options.

5   Choose the OK button.

Using Help and Online Lessons

To get help quickly as you work, just press the F1 key. When the Help window appears, you can display the procedure for a particular task, get a definition for a term you don't understand, or see information about any Word command. You can also get help whenever you see an error message or if you need more information about an option in a dialog box or part of the Word screen.

If you'd like to take a short time-out from your work to practice a skill or learn about a feature without making any changes to your document, you can use the online tutorial that comes with Word. Just choose the Getting Started command or the Learning Word command from the Help menu. All of the skills presented in these lessons are also listed in an index for quick reference.

The first part of this chapter describes how you can get help as you work. The second part of the chapter describes the online tutorial.

Getting Help as You Work

To get information quickly about a command or task, use online Help. You can display step-by-step instructions and then complete your tasks without having to turn away from the screen. With Help you can:

- Press F1 to display the Help Index for Word, to get help on a selected command, to find out more about the options in the current dialog box, or to see an explanation of an error message.

- Press SHIFT+F1 to get help on the next command you choose, a key combination, or a screen region such as the ruler.

- Search for topics associated with a word or phrase. For example, you can get a list of all topics associated with "saving documents."

- View step-by-step instructions in Help while you perform a task in Word.

- Add your own notes to a Help topic.

- Mark topics that you use frequently so you can quickly jump to them.

- Print a copy of a Help topic.

You can view Help side by side with a document so that both windows remain fully visible while you work. To display Help and your document at the same time, resize the windows so they don't overlap.

There may be other times when you want to resize the Help window. For example, you can expand the Help window to see all the information in a Help table. The next time you start Word and open Help, the Help window appears with the size and location it had when it was last open.

Using the Help Window

The Help window has buttons you can use to move around the Help system easily. If a particular feature is not available, the button associated with it is dimmed.

By choosing a button at the top of the Help window, you can display a list of Help topics, search for a list of topics that include a particular keyword, and move forward and backward through the Help topics you have used in the current Help session.

Some words in a Help window are marked with a dotted or solid underline and appear in color if you have a color video display.

Words marked with a solid underline are *jump terms* you can use to move around the Help system quickly. When you click a jump term, you immediately move to a Help topic associated with that word.

Clicking a word or phrase marked with a dotted underline displays a definition of that term.

You can get help about all of the Help system's features and practice using them within Help itself.

To get help about using the Help system

1   From the Help menu in Word, choose Help Index (ALT, H, I).

2   In the Help window, press F1, or choose Using Help from the Help menu (ALT, H, H).

3   From the list of Using Help Topics, choose the information you want to see.

Finding the Information You Want in Help

There are three ways to find the information you need:

- Use the Search feature in Help. For example, to find background information and procedures for saving a document, search the Help system for the phrase "saving documents." Word displays a list of topics and procedures related to saving. You can choose a topic and read its contents.

- Get context-sensitive Help as you work. For example, if you display the Save As dialog box and need help about its options, press F1. Word displays information about the options.

- Use the Help Index. You can go to the chapter listing in the Help Index and find the Opening, Saving, and Deleting "chapter" of procedures, and then select the procedure you need. Or you can look in the alphabetical listing of topics for an entry about saving documents.

The information in a Help topic may lead you to other related topics. You can always backtrack through the Help topics you have viewed in the order you viewed them. Note, however, that the record of topics you have viewed is erased each time you close the Help window.

To get help on a dialog box

▶ With the dialog box displayed on the screen, press F1.

Word displays information about the options in the dialog box.

To get help on a command

1 Press SHIFT+F1.

   The pointer changes to a question mark.

2 Choose the command from the menu.

1 Open the menu, and then press the arrow keys to select the command name.

2 Press F1.

Word displays information about the command.

Note You cannot press SHIFT+F1 to get Help on unavailable commands that appear dimmed. Instead, select the unavailable command by pressing ALT+the underlined letter on the menu, and then use the arrow keys to select the command. Press F1 to display information about the command. Or use the mouse to select the command name and then, while you hold down the left mouse button, press F1.

To get help on a key, key combination, or screen region

1 Press SHIFT+F1.

   The pointer changes to a question mark.

2 Press a key or key combination.
   –or–
   Click a screen region.

Word displays information about the item you chose.

To jump to a cross-reference

1 In a Help topic, point to a term or phrase with a solid underline.

   The pointer changes to a hand symbol.

2 Click the left mouse button.

1 Press TAB to select a term or phrase with a solid underline.

2 Press ENTER.

To display a definition

1 In a Help topic, point to a term or phrase with a dotted underline.

The pointer changes to a hand symbol.

2 Hold down the left mouse button until you have finished reading the definition.

1 Press TAB to select a term with a dotted underline.

2 Hold down ENTER until you have finished reading the definition.

To minimize Help

This procedure closes the Help window, but the Help icon remains on the desktop. When you press F1, Help reappears, showing the last topic you viewed.

▶ Click the Minimize button in the upper-right corner of the Help window.

–Or–

▶ From the Control menu, choose Minimize (ALT, SPACEBAR, N)

To close Help

▶ In the Help window, choose Exit from the File menu, or press ALT+F4.

The next time you choose Help, the Help window retains its size and location, even if you have quit Windows in the interim.

Marking the Topics You Frequently Use

Just as you can use bookmarks to mark specific references in a book, you can place bookmarks at Help topics you use frequently. Once you have placed a bookmark at a topic, you can display that topic quickly by choosing the bookmark from the Bookmark menu in Help.

To place a bookmark at a topic

1 Display the topic.

2 In the Help window, choose Define from the Bookmark menu (ALT, M, D).

3 To use the topic title as the bookmark name, choose the OK button.
–or–
To use a different name, type a name for the bookmark, and then choose the OK button.

The bookmark name now appears on the Bookmark menu in Help.

To go to a marked topic

1 In the Help window, open the Bookmark menu (ALT, M).

2 Choose the name of the bookmark you want to view.

   Underlined numbers precede the first nine bookmark names. You can press the corresponding number key to display the topic. If you have defined more than nine bookmark names, you can choose More from the Bookmark menu to see a list of all the bookmarks you have defined.

To remove a bookmark

1 In the Help window, choose Define from the Bookmark menu (ALT, M, D).

2 Select the bookmark you want to remove.

3 Choose the Delete button, and then choose the OK button.

Adding Your Own Notes to Topics

You can add your own comments, called *annotations*, to Help topics. Annotations can be up to 2000 characters long, using any characters on the keyboard. When you make an annotation, Help places a paper clip symbol to the left of the title of the topic to remind you that you have added text to that topic. Annotations are not printed if you print the topic.

To add text to a Help topic

1 Display the topic.

2 In the Help window, choose Annotate from the Edit menu (ALT, E, A).

3 Type the text you want to add.

   If you make a mistake, press BACKSPACE to erase any unwanted characters and then continue typing. Text wraps automatically as you type, but you can end a line before it wraps by pressing CTRL+ENTER.

4 When you have finished the annotation, choose the OK button.

To view an annotation

1 Display the topic that has the annotation.

2 Click the paper clip symbol.
   –or–
   Press TAB to highlight the paper clip symbol, and then press ENTER.

3 When you have finished reading the annotation, choose the Cancel button.

To remove an annotation

1   Display the topic that has the annotation you want to remove.

2   Click the paper clip symbol.
     –or–
     Press TAB to highlight the paper clip symbol, and then press ENTER.

3   Choose the Delete button.

If Help Is Not Installed

Installing Help is an option when you set up Word. If a message indicates that Help is not installed, you can install it using the following procedure.

To install Help

1   In the Program Manager, double-click the Word Setup icon.
     –or–
     Select the Word Setup icon, and then press ENTER.

2   In the Install To box, type the path to Word and choose the Continue button.

     Setup displays a message that it detects a version of Word in this directory.

3   Choose the Yes button to change the installation.

4   Choose the Custom Installation button.

     Make sure that you clear the check boxes for any options you don't want to add. Note the Available Space information toward the bottom of the dialog box. If you do not have enough room on your hard disk to install the Help files, exit Setup, move documents to other disks, and then return to step 1 of this procedure.

5   Select Help and any other options you want, and then choose the Setup button.

6   Insert the disk specified in the message and follow the instructions on the screen.

Word adds the Help files to the directory you specified. Or, if your computer does not have enough disk space to store the files, Word displays a message. If this occurs, choose the Cancel button to cancel Setup.

Learning About Word: Hands-On Practice

Word provides two sets of online lessons. The first set of lessons, Getting Started, presents the basic skills you need to produce documents in Word. It also offers a 5-minute overview of document production that includes strategies to speed your work. The second set of lessons, Learning Word, presents the most popular features in Word.

With the online lessons you can practice using features without affecting your real Word documents. To start the lessons, choose the name of the set of lessons you want to use from the Help menu.

Both sets of lessons provide a main menu from which you can choose the lesson you want to view. Once you choose a lesson, you have the choice of a short overview or a variety of short practices. You may want to go through the overview and then try the practices that are most suited to your work.

You move through the lessons at your own pace. You can back up to review a screen of information, or move forward one screen at a time. Some screens contain highlighted words with underlined letters. You can view definitions of these words by clicking the word with the mouse or pressing ALT+the underlined letter.

When you choose a practice, Word gives you a general description of the task and then demonstrates the steps needed to complete the task. You can try the task on your own, or if you need help remembering the steps, you can choose the Show Steps button to see the list of steps. If you make a mistake while practicing, Word gives you helpful reminders and a chance to try again.

If you'd like to practice a specific task, you can select a topic from the Index. This takes you to a sublist of tasks or directly to the appropriate practice.

You can exit the lessons and return to your work at any time by choosing the Controls button and then choosing the Exit button. When you exit the lesson, Word displays any open documents as they were when you began the lesson.

Choosing a Starting Point

If you are new to word-processing   Begin with Getting Started, the lessons that teach basic skills. Move on to Five Minutes to Productivity for a quick demonstration of how to produce your first Word document. To view the lessons, from the Help menu, choose the Getting Started command.

If you are familiar with word-processing, but new to Word   Begin with the Five Minutes to Productivity lesson for an overview of basic Word skills. To view this lesson, choose Getting Started from the Help menu, and then select the lesson. If, after viewing the lesson, you'd like more background information, choose another lesson in Getting Started. When you are comfortable with the basic skills, choose Learning Word from the Help menu for practice with some of the most useful features in Word.

If you've used Word before   The Learning Word lessons are a good starting point. They cover intermediate skills and new features. You can also check the index for particular skills you'd like to practice. To view the lessons or the index, choose Learning Word from the Help menu, and then select the lesson you want to view or choose the Index button.

Viewing a Lesson

Once you begin a lesson, you use the arrow buttons at the bottom of the screen to move forward and backward in the lesson. If you don't have a mouse, you use the LEFT ARROW and RIGHT ARROW keys on the keyboard. You use the Control button at the bottom of the screen to display other options. For example, you use the Control button to move to another lesson or to exit the lessons and return to your document.

To begin a lesson

1   From the Help menu, choose Getting Started (ALT, H, G) to learn basic skills.
    –or–
    For lessons on Word features, choose Learning Word (ALT, H, L).

    If you have made any changes to your documents, Word prompts you to save the changes.

2   Click a lesson button, or press ALT+the underlined letter of a lesson title.

    Word displays the names of the lessons. Note the buttons at the bottom of the screen; similar buttons appear throughout the lessons.

3   Do any of the following to move through a lesson:

To	Do this
Move to the next screen	Click the button with the right arrow on it or press the RIGHT ARROW key.
Move to the previous screen	Click the button with the left arrow on it, or press the LEFT ARROW key.
Return to the main menu	Choose the Controls button, and then choose the Main Menu button.
Return to the lesson menu	Choose the Controls button, and then choose the Lesson Menu button.
View instructions for using the lessons	Choose the Controls button, and then choose the Instructions button.
Exit a lesson	Choose the Controls button, and then choose the Exit button.

To go to a practice from the index

1   From the main menu or lesson menu, choose the Index button.
    –or–
    From within a lesson, choose the Controls button, and then choose the Index button.

2   Click the topic you want.
    –or–
    Press the arrow keys or the TAB key to select a topic, and then choose the Go To button.

Part 1: Getting Started

When you choose the Getting Started command from the Help menu, Word displays a menu of lesson titles. The following table lists the tasks taught in each of the lessons. All lessons except Five Minutes to Productivity include hands-on practices.

Lesson	Skills
The Word Screen	Choosing commands and working in dialog boxes Scrolling and splitting windows Using the ruler, ribbon, and Toolbar
Basic Skills	Working with Documents 　　Starting a document 　　Saving a document 　　Closing a document 　　Opening an existing document 　　Typing and deleting text 　　Moving the insertion point 　　Creating a new paragraph Basic Editing 　　Selecting text 　　Moving text 　　Finding and replacing text 　　Checking your spelling Basic Formatting 　Character Formatting 　　　Applying bold and underline formatting 　　　Changing the color of the text 　　　Changing the default character format Setting Margins and Tabs 　　Adjusting margins 　　Setting tab stops Paragraph Formatting 　　Changing line spacing 　　Adjusting paragraph indents 　　Changing paragraph alignment
Five Minutes to Productivity	A quick look at creating and printing a document

Part 2: Learning Word

These lessons present many of the most useful features in Word. The hands-on practices do not affect any of your documents.

Lesson	Skills

Formatting	Formatting Paragraphs
	    Creating hanging indents
	    Adding borders and shading
	
	Formatting Columns
	    Creating newspaper-style columns
	    Inserting vertical lines between columns
	    Varying the number of columns in a document
	
	Formatting Pages
	    Changing the page orientation
	    Adding headers and footers
	
	Creating Styles
	    Applying styles
	    Creating a new style
	    Basing a style on an existing style
	    Assigning a key combination to a style
	
	Modifying Styles
	    Modifying an existing style
	    Deleting a style
	    Specifying a "next style"

Editing	Replacing formatted text and styles Creating, saving, and using glossaries Working with footnotes Creating annotations Locking a document for annotations Working with revision marks
Proofing	Using the spelling checker Using the grammar checker Using the thesaurus
Tables, Frames, and Pictures	Creating and modifying tables Creating and modifying frames Working with pictures and objects
Organizing Documents	Creating, viewing, and modifying an outline Creating a table of contents Finding files
Viewing and Printing	Working in different views Printing all or part of a document Printing information about a document Printing more than one document Using print merge

If the Online Lessons Are Not Installed

When you install Word on your computer, you have the option of installing the online lessons. If the lessons are not installed, Word displays a message when you choose the Getting Started command or the Learning Word command from the Help menu. You can return to the Setup program for Word and install the lessons at any time.

To install the lessons

1   In the Program Manager, double-click the Word Setup icon.
    –or–
    Select the Word Setup icon, and then press ENTER.

2   In the Install To box, type the path to Word and choose the Continue button.

    Setup displays a message that it detects a version of Word in this directory.

3   Choose the Yes button to change the installation.

4   Choose the Custom Installation button.

    Make sure that you clear the check boxes for any options you don't want to add. Note the Available Space information toward the bottom of the dialog box. If you do not have enough room on your hard disk to install the lessons, exit Setup, move documents to other disks, and then return to step one of this procedure.

5   Select Online Lessons and any other options you want to install, and then choose the Setup button.

6   Insert the disk specified in the message and follow the instructions on the screen.

Word adds the online lessons to the directory you specified. Or, if your computer does not have enough disk space to store the lesson files, Word displays a message. If this occurs, choose the Cancel button to cancel Setup.

Chapter 6

Character Formatting

Characters are the letters, punctuation marks, numbers, and symbols—such as @, *, and &—that you type as text. Character formatting determines how characters appear on the screen and in print. With character formatting, you can:

- Change the font (type style) and point size (height) of characters.
- Make text bold or italic, or apply other formats such as strikethrough.
- Create superscript or subscript text.
- Adjust the spacing between characters to make them more readable or to create special effects.
- Add color to characters.
- "Hide" text so your document can include information such as notes or comments that you don't want to print.
- Change the case of characters—for example, from lowercase to uppercase.

Word provides several shortcuts for applying character formatting. You can repeat character formatting quickly using a key combination and copy the formatting of one character to other text.

In Word, you can also insert special characters such as mathematical symbols, bullets, and characters used in other languages (ü, é, and ç, for example) that may not be available on your keyboard.

Tip   You can use WordArt to rotate or flip text, to print the text in a half-circle, circle, or vertical line, or to get other special effects. To start WordArt, choose Object from the Insert menu; then select WordArt in the Object Type box, and choose the OK button. For instructions on using WordArt, see WordArt Help. To get Help in WordArt, press F1 or choose a command from the Help menu.

Methods for Formatting Characters

Word uses preset, or default, formats to determine the font, size, and other character formatting of the text you type. You can change the formatting by choosing new formats before you type, or by selecting text and applying the new formats after you type.

You can also change the defaults so that any text you type automatically has the new formatting. For more information, see "Changing the Default Formatting," later in this chapter.

You can use the ribbon, the Character command on the Format menu, or key combinations to apply character formatting. Each method has its advantages.

Method	Advantages
Ribbon	Offers the quickest way with the mouse to apply fonts, sizes, and commonly used formats.
Character command (Format menu)	Provides all character formatting options and previews formatting before you make final changes in your document. It is especially useful for changing several formats at one time.
Key combinations	Provide quick ways to format text while you keep your hands on the keyboard.

For more information on styles, see Chapter 8, "Formatting with Styles."

You can also apply character formatting as part of a paragraph style. For more information about using character formatting with styles, see "Character Formatting and Styles," later in this chapter.

Using the Ribbon

With the ribbon, you can quickly change the font or point size of text, or format the text as bold, italic, or underlined.

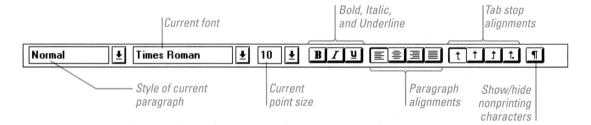

The ribbon shows the current font and point size for the selection. If there is no selection, it shows the font and size that will be applied to the next text you type. If a selection includes several fonts and sizes, the Font and Points boxes are empty.

Word displays a list of the fonts available on your printer when you click the arrow to the right of the Font box or press CTRL+F (for fonts) and then the DOWN ARROW or UP ARROW key. A printer symbol identifies each printer font. The Points box displays the sizes available for the selected font. Use the mouse to display the point size list, or press CTRL+P (for point sizes) and then the DOWN ARROW or UP ARROW key. To apply a format, you can select an option from either list. Or you can type the option in the box, and then press ENTER or click in the text area. The format is applied to all the characters in the selection or, if there is no selection, to the next text you type at the insertion point's current location.

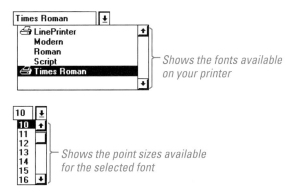

Font and Points lists

The ribbon also has buttons for applying bold, italic, and single underline formats. If one of these formats has been applied to the selected text, the button is selected. If a selection has mixed formatting, the related buttons are dimmed. For example, if one word in a selection is bold and another is italic, the Bold and Italic buttons are dimmed.

You apply a format by clicking the appropriate button, and you remove the format by clicking the button again. To apply a format as you type, position the insertion point where you want to start typing, and click the button on the ribbon. The format is applied to all text you type until you click the button again or reposition the insertion point. If you have selected text, the format is applied to all characters in the selection.

Note   From the ribbon, you can also choose a new style and paragraph alignment, and insert one of four types of tab stop. In addition, you can view or hide hidden text and other nonprinting characters. For information on paragraph alignment, tab stops, and nonprinting characters, see Chapter 7, "Paragraph Formatting." For information on styles, see Chapter 8, "Formatting with Styles." For information on hidden text, see "Using Hidden Text," later in this chapter.

When you start Word, the ribbon is displayed beneath the Toolbar. You can hide the ribbon to allow more room for document text, and then display the ribbon again when you want to work with it.

To display or hide the ribbon

▶ From the View menu, choose Ribbon (ALT, V, B).

Using the Character Command

The Character command on the Format menu displays the Character dialog box. This dialog box provides an alternative to the ribbon and includes formatting options that are not available on the ribbon. The Character dialog box is especially useful if you want to apply several character formats or if you want to preview proposed changes before you make them in your document.

You can display the dialog box by double-clicking in a space between any of the buttons on the ribbon or by choosing Character from the Format menu.

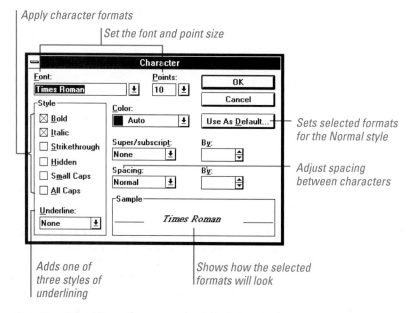

Character dialog box

The Character dialog box shows the formats for the current selection. If there is no selection, it shows the formats that will be applied to the next text you type. If a selection includes characters with different formats, check boxes are filled with gray, text boxes are blank, and list boxes have no item selected. When you apply a new format, the format is added to the existing formats for all characters in the selection.

The Sample box shows the effects of your formatting choices before you apply them. You can change the formatting selections in the dialog box until the sample shows the look you want. When you are satisfied with the formatting, choose the OK button.

Tip For quick access, you can add any of the character formatting options to a menu or to a Toolbar button, or you can assign a key combination to a formatting option. For information, see Chapter 38, "Customizing Menus, the Keyboard, and the Toolbar."

Using Key Combinations

Pressing a key combination is often the quickest way to apply formatting, especially a format such as small caps or hidden text. Key combinations are particularly useful for applying formats while you type, for repeating formatting, and for copying the formatting of one selection to another. For a list of character formats and the key combinations assigned to them, see "Applying and Removing Character Formats," later in this chapter. For information about repeating or copying formatting, see "Repeating and Copying Character Formats," also in this chapter.

Changing Fonts and Point Sizes

Fonts and point sizes establish the basic look of characters in your document. A font is a set of characters with a unique design. The following are some commonly used fonts.

Courier   Σψμβολ (Symbol)

Helvetica   Times Roman

LinePrinter

Each font comes in a range of sizes, measured in points. A point is a typographical measurement equal to 1/72 inch. In Word, you can specify any size from 4 points through 127 points, in 0.5-point increments.

Important Before you start work on a new document, make sure you have installed a printer driver for your printer and that you have selected the correct printer and setup options using the Print Setup command on the File menu. The printer fonts (those with a printer symbol) that you see and the point sizes that Word displays for them are for the selected printer. If a printer different from the one you will print on is selected when you format a document, some of the fonts, sizes, and other character formatting options may not be available when you print the document. For information on installing printers, see your Windows documentation.

To change the font or point size

If the ribbon is not displayed, choose Ribbon from the View menu (ALT, V, B).

1 Select the characters you want to format, or position the insertion point where you want to type characters in the new font or point size.

2 On the ribbon, select a font or size from the Font or Points box, or type the font name or point size in the box.

3 To return to the document, click in the text area.

1 Select the characters you want to format, or position the insertion point where you want to type characters in the new font or point size.

2 To select the Font box, press CTRL+F.
   –or–
   To select the Points box, press CTRL+P.

3 Type the font name or the point size.
   –or–
   Press the DOWN ARROW or UP ARROW key to display the list and to select an option.

4 To apply the change and return to the document, press ENTER.

You can also change the font and point size by choosing the Character command from the Format menu. In the Font or Points box, type or select a font or point size, and then choose the OK button.

Note If the ribbon is not displayed, pressing CTRL+F or CTRL+P displays a message in the status bar. Type a font name or point size and then press ENTER. You can also press CTRL+F or CTRL+P twice to display the Character dialog box.

To increase or decrease the point size quickly

1 Select the characters you want to format, or position the insertion point where you want to type characters in the new size.

2 To increase the point size to the next available size, press CTRL+F2.
   –or–
   To decrease the point size to the next available size, press CTRL+SHIFT+F2.

The available sizes depend on which printer you selected using the Print Setup command on the File menu. For example, if the printer supports point sizes 9, 10, and 12 and the current point size is 10, pressing CTRL+F2 increases the point size to 12; pressing CTRL+SHIFT+F2 decreases the point size to 9.

About Screen and Printer Fonts

There are two kinds of fonts: screen fonts, which display characters on the screen, and printer fonts, which you use to print your documents. In the Font box, a printer symbol identifies each printer font. You can also print the Modern, Roman, and Script fonts, which aren't printer fonts.

For information on installing screen and printer fonts, see your Windows documentation or printer documentation.

To be displayed on the screen, a font must be installed as a screen font on your computer. Microsoft Windows comes with basic screen fonts installed in several point sizes; you can purchase and install additional fonts and point sizes. To be printed, a font must be installed for the printer that you selected using the Print Setup command on the File menu.

You can use fonts that display on your screen but cannot be printed and fonts that can be printed but not displayed. If each screen font you use has a matching printer font, the screen display of the document will closely match the printed document. However, because of differences between display technology and printer technology, they may not match exactly.

To view a document as it will print, make sure that the Line Breaks And Fonts As Printed option is selected in the View category of the Options dialog box (Tools menu). To display screen fonts without regard to how they will print, clear this option.

Note You can also view the document as it will print by choosing Page Layout from the View menu. In page layout view, the Line Breaks And Fonts As Printed option is selected automatically.

The Font boxes on the ribbon and in the Character dialog box show the printer fonts that are available on the current printer. The Points boxes show the sizes available for the selected font.

If you want to choose a font that is not available on the current printer (but is available on another printer to which you have access), you can type the font name in the Font box. Word displays a screen font that matches the printer font as closely as possible. If you type a point size that isn't available for the current font, the closest available size is displayed. When you open the document on a computer that has the screen font and printer font you chose, Word displays and prints the font correctly.

The fonts in the Font box are printer fonts, and the fonts installed in your operating environment are screen fonts. If you select a font in your document that is not available on your printer or on the cartridge you selected in the Print Setup dialog box, the font name will be displayed in the Font box, but the font won't be available in the list.

Applying and Removing Character Formats

You can use character formats to emphasize text, mark editing changes, and create special effects in your documents. The following character formatting options are available in Word:

bold	sub Script	super Script
italic	ALL CAPS	SMALL CAPS
~~strikethrough~~	continuous underline	character s p a c i n g
hidden	word underline	Character Case
colors	double underline	

You apply a format by choosing it and remove the format by choosing it again. You can apply multiple character formats to the same text. For example, you can make a word both bold and italic.

Word provides 16 colors. Auto is the Window Text color you set in the Color dialog box in the Control Panel for Windows. You can choose character colors even if you don't have a color monitor. You won't see the colors on your screen, but you will be able to print in color if you have a plotter or color printer.

The All Caps and Small Caps options display lowercase characters as uppercase characters. If you apply All Caps formatting to numbers or to text that has been capitalized using the SHIFT or CAPS LOCK key, the characters do not change in appearance. The Small Caps option converts lowercase characters to uppercase characters in a smaller point size.

You use the same basic procedure to apply and remove all character formats, as explained in the following procedure. Superscript and subscript, spacing between characters, hidden text, and character case formatting are covered in more detail later in this chapter.

To apply or remove character formats

1 Select the characters you want to format, or position the insertion point where you want to type characters with new character formats.

2 From the Format menu, choose Character (ALT, T, C).

3 Select or clear options to specify the formats you want.

The Sample box shows the effects of the selected formats. You can make as many changes as you like.

4 Choose the OK button.

Shortcuts

Use this technique to quickly apply or remove bold, italic, or an underline.

1 Select the characters you want to format, or position the insertion point where you want to type characters with new character formats.

2 On the ribbon, click the Bold, Italic, and Underline buttons to add or remove formats.

1 Select the characters you want to format, or position the insertion point where you want to type characters with new character formats.

2 Press one or more of the following key combinations.

To apply	Press CTRL+
Bold	B
Italic	I
Underline	U
Word Underline	W
Double Underline	D
Small Caps	K
All Caps	A
Hidden Text	H

Note   To cancel any of the text formats, press CTRL+SPACEBAR to return the text to the
character formatting in the current style.

Making Characters Superscript or Subscript

All characters in a document are positioned in relation to the baseline of the text.
When you format characters as superscript or subscript, Word positions them either
above or below the baseline, as shown in the following illustration.

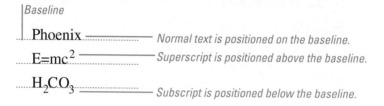

Baseline

Phoenix —————————— *Normal text is positioned on the baseline.*

$E=mc^2$ —————————— *Superscript is positioned above the baseline.*

H_2CO_3 —————————— *Subscript is positioned below the baseline.*

To make characters superscript or subscript

1   Select the characters you want to format, or position the insertion point where you
    want to type superscript or subscript characters.

2   From the Format menu, choose Character (ALT, T, C).

3   Select the appropriate Super/Subscript option.

4   If you want to change how far above or below the baseline Word positions the
    characters, type or select a number in the By box.

    You can specify a measurement to the half-point (a decimal fraction). You can type
    any number from 0 through 63.5 in 0.5-point increments.

5   To make the characters larger or smaller, select a different font size in the Points
    box.

6   Choose the OK button.

Shortcut

1   Select the characters you want to format, or position the insertion point where you
    want to type superscript or subscript characters.

2   For 3-point superscript, press CTRL+SHIFT+PLUS SIGN.
    –or–
    For 3-point subscript, press CTRL+EQUAL SIGN.

To remove superscript or subscript formatting, select the None option under
Super/Subscript in the Character dialog box or repeat the appropriate key combination.

Note If you want to enter a formula that includes a superscripted expression, and you don't want the underline to be superscripted, use the Equation Editor to create the formula. You can also use the Equation Editor for non-mathematical expressions that you want to underline. Or you can prevent the superscripting of an underline by converting the information to a table and applying a bottom border. For information about the Equation Editor, see the *Microsoft Equation Editor User's Guide*. For information about working with tables, see Chapter 17, "Tables," in this manual.

Changing the Space Between Characters

Word automatically establishes the spacing between characters. You can expand or condense the character spacing to make the text more readable or to create special effects such as dramatic spacing between the characters in a title. This process is known as kerning.

The ability to control character spacing is especially important when you work with large headings and when you use italic and bold-italic formatting.

When you use the Character command on the Format menu to kern text, Word expands the space between characters by 3 points or condenses the space by 1.75 points unless you specify a different measurement. The following illustration shows the effects of expanding and condensing text.

Conceptual Art————— *Chicago font, 12-point size*

Conceptual Art————— *Character spacing condensed by 1.5 points ...*

Conceptual Art—— *... and expanded by 3 points.*

To change the space between characters

1 Select the characters you want to format, or position the insertion point where you want to type characters with the new spacing.

2 From the Format menu, choose Character (ALT, T, C).

3 To increase the space between characters, choose Expanded under Spacing.
   −or−
   To decrease the space between characters, choose Condensed under Spacing.

4   To change the suggested spacing measurement, type or select a number in the By box.

You can specify a measurement to the quarter of a point. If you're expanding the space, type any number from 0 through 14 (type fractions as decimals). If you're condensing space, type any number from 0 through 1.75.

5   Choose the OK button.

To return to the default spacing, select the Normal option under Spacing in the Character dialog box.

Using Hidden Text

When you format text as hidden, you can choose whether or not to display or print the text. For example, you can use the hidden text format to type notes or comments to yourself. You can see the comments while you are working and later print the document without including the comments. Word also uses the hidden text format to hide the coding for table of contents entries, index entries, and annotations.

You display hidden text using the Hidden Text option in the View category of the Options dialog box (Tools menu). Hidden text also is displayed when All is selected. With either of these options selected, Word displays hidden text with a dotted underline in all your documents.

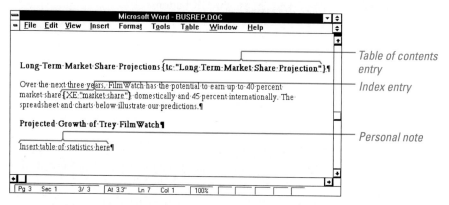

A document with hidden text displayed

If you want to print hidden text in a document, regardless of whether it is displayed on screen, select the Hidden Text option in the Print category of the Options dialog box (Tools menu). You also can select this option at printing after choosing the Options button from the Print dialog box (File menu). With this option selected, Word prints hidden text where it occurs in the document, without any special formatting.

When hidden text is displayed, it affects your document's line and page breaks in normal and page layout views regardless of whether you have selected the Hidden Text option for printing. When you select the Hidden Text option for printing, hidden text affects the line and page breaks in print preview and in the printed document regardless of whether you have hidden text displayed in normal and page layout views.

Tip Hidden text can affect the page numbering in a document, which can affect the accuracy of the page numbering in a table of contents and index. To ensure accurate page numbers, make sure that hidden text is not set to display or print.

If your page numbers still are not accurate, you may have page or section breaks formatted as hidden text. Use the Replace command on the Edit menu to find and clear hidden text formatting. For more information about the Replace command, see Chapter 12, "Finding and Replacing Text or Formatting."

To format hidden text

1   Select the characters you want to format as hidden text, or position the insertion point where you want to type hidden text.

2   Press CTRL+H.
    –or–
    From the Format menu, choose Character (ALT, T, C). Then select the Hidden check box, and choose the OK button.

Word displays hidden text with a dotted underline if either the Hidden Text option or the All option is selected in the View category of the Options dialog box (Tools menu). When All is selected, hidden text is displayed regardless of whether the Hidden Text option is selected.

To display or hide hidden text

1   From the Tools menu, choose Options (ALT, O, O).

2   Under Category, select View.

3   Under Nonprinting Characters, do one of the following:

- To display hidden text, make sure that either the Hidden Text or the All check box is selected.

- To hide hidden text, make sure that both the Hidden Text and the All check boxes are not selected.

4   Choose the OK button.

Selecting either the Hidden Text or the All option in the View category displays hidden text in all your documents until you clear the option.

To print the hidden text in a document

If Hidden Text is selected in the Printing category of the Options dialog box, the Hidden Text option in the Print dialog box will already be selected.

1 From the File menu, choose Print (ALT, F, P).

2 Choose the Options button.

3 Under Include With Document, select the Hidden Text check box.

4 Choose the OK button.

To view hidden text as it will print

1 From the Tools menu, choose Options (ALT, O, O).

2 Under Category, select Printing.

3 Under Include With Document, select the Hidden Text option.

4 Choose the OK button.

When you print your document, the hidden text will be printed. Accurate line and page breaks will be displayed in print preview.

Note Hidden text affects the cells in tables differently from normal paragraphs. When you hide hidden text during printing, the hidden text in a table does not print, but the cell that contains the text still occupies space in the printed document. To remove the space, convert the table to text or temporarily remove the cells from your table. For information about working with tables, see Chapter 17, "Tables."

Viewing and Printing Hidden Text

If the Hidden Text option or the All option is selected in the View category of the Options dialog box (Tools menu) and the Hidden Text option is cleared in the Print category (or vice versa), you may see different page breaks in print preview than you see in page view.

This is because the View category options affect only the display of text on the screen. Any time you can edit text—in normal view or in page layout view—what you see depends on the state of the View options.

The Hidden Text option in the Print category affects how your text will print and what you see in a print preview.

To view hidden text in print preview, choose Options from the Tools menu. Select the Print category, and choose the Hidden Text option. Then display your document as it will print by choosing the Print Preview command from the File menu.

Changing the Case of Characters

You use the Change Case key (SHIFT+F3) to change the case of characters. For example, you can change all selected characters from lowercase to uppercase or capitalize the first letter of each word in an uppercase selection. When you select characters and press SHIFT+F3, Word looks at the first two characters of each word in the selection to determine their current case. If no characters are selected, the key combination performs no action.

To change the case of characters

1   Select the characters you want to format.

2   Press SHIFT+F3 to change case as follows:

If characters are	Press SHIFT+F3 to get
All lowercase	All uppercase
First character lowercase	All uppercase
All uppercase	First character of each word to uppercase, all other characters to lowercase
First character uppercase	All lowercase

Changing the Default Formatting

The default Normal style in Word determines the formats—the font, point size, and other attributes—of the characters you type. You can change the formats using any of the methods presented in this chapter. However, if you frequently change to a specific format—a smaller point size, for example—you can save time and effort by changing the Normal style.

For more information on templates, see Chapter 37, "Document Templates."

In Word, each document is based on a template which provides a pattern for the final document. When you choose New from the File menu to start a new document, you can choose the template that you want to use. If you do not choose a template, Word uses the Normal template. When you change the default Normal style, you change it for the current document, the current template, and all new documents you create using that template. Changing the default Normal style does not affect existing documents and documents you create using a different template.

To change the default character formatting

1   From the Format menu, choose Character (ALT, T, C).

2   In the Font and Points boxes, type or select the font and point size you want to use for the current document and all new documents.

3   Select any other options that you want to include in the default Normal style.

4   Choose the Use As Default button.

Word displays a dialog box asking whether you want to change the Normal style for the current template.

5   Choose the OK button.

The new formatting takes effect immediately in the current document. When you exit Word or choose Save All from the File menu, Word asks whether you want to save changes to the template. Choose Yes to change the default Normal style for all new documents created with the current template.

Repeating and Copying Character Formats

For information on finding and replacing character formats, see Chapter 12, "Finding and Replacing Text or Formatting."

After applying formatting to a selection, you can quickly apply the same formatting to other text. You can repeat the formatting using the Repeat command on the Edit menu, or you can copy the formatting without the text, applying the formatting to another selection in the document or in another document.

You can copy formatting using the mouse or keyboard. The mouse procedure is explained in this chapter. To copy formats using the keyboard, you can add the CopyFormat command to a menu or assign a key combination to it. For more information, see Chapter 38, "Customizing Menus, the Keyboard, and the Toolbar."

To repeat character formats

1   Immediately after applying the original formatting, select the characters you want to format, or position the insertion point where you want to type characters in the new format.

2   From the Edit menu, choose Repeat Formatting (ALT, E, R) or press F4.

If you apply multiple formats using the Character dialog box, all the character formatting is repeated. However, if you apply multiple formats using the ribbon or the keyboard, the Repeat command repeats only the most recent character formatting.

To copy character formats

1   Select the text you want to format.

2   Position the insertion point on the character that has the formatting you want to copy.

3   Hold down CTRL+SHIFT and click the left mouse button.

Word applies character formatting to the selection; it does not copy and paste any text.

If you move the mouse pointer into the selection bar beside the paragraph, Word copies the paragraph formatting, such as tab settings and alignment, instead of the character formatting.

Inserting Special Characters

In addition to the letters, numbers, and punctuation marks shown on the keyboard, many fonts include bullets and symbols (sometimes called dingbats), such as •, §, ™, and ®. Most fonts also contain characters with diacritical marks (umlauts, tildes, and other accents) used in languages other than English; for example, ü, ñ, é, â, and ç.

The Symbol font consists entirely of symbols, including the Greek alphabet and a variety of mathematical symbols.

Word can display and print special characters if a screen font and a printer font that contain the characters have been installed. If you have only a printer font, the symbols print properly but may not display correctly.

Note Windows supplies a Symbol printer font that provides a standard set of symbols. When you run the Setup program to install Word, you automatically install a matching screen font. For more information on installing the standard Windows fonts, see your Windows documentation. If you purchase additional fonts, see the font documentation for installation information.

The Symbol Dialog Box

You can use the Symbol command on the Insert menu to insert symbols and special characters in your documents. In the Symbol dialog box, you can enlarge a character to see it better by pointing to it and holding down the left mouse button.

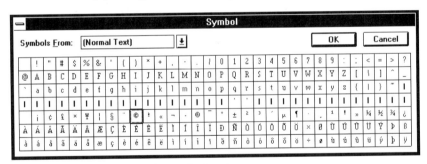

Symbol dialog box with an ANSI font displayed

The Symbol dialog box displays the characters available for the font or character group selected in the Symbols From list. All fonts in the ANSI character group are listed as one entry: Normal Text. Non-ANSI fonts are listed individually.

ANSI is a set of characters defined by the American National Standards Institute that includes 256 characters that are available from the keyboard. Many fonts, such as Times Roman and Courier, are based on the ANSI character set. Other fonts, such as Zapf Dingbats, are decorative fonts that don't match the ANSI character set.

To insert a special character

1   Position the insertion point where you want to insert the special character.

2   From the Insert menu, choose Symbol.

3   In the Symbols From box, select the font that contains the character.
    –or–
    Type the font name, and then click anywhere in the set of characters to display the font.

    The dialog box lists all ANSI fonts as Normal Text. If the document's current font is an ANSI font, Word displays characters in that font but shows Normal Text in the list box. To view a different ANSI font, type the font name in the Symbols From box.

4   Select the character in any of the following ways:

    ■   Click the character, and then choose OK.

    ■   Double-click the character.

    ■   Use the arrow keys to select the character, and then press ENTER.

    Word inserts the character in the current point size.

**For more information
on fields, see
Chapter 41, "Fields."**

If you choose a non-ANSI font and insert a character, Word protects the character by including it in a field. If the character weren't protected, font or style changes could cause Word to display a different character. If you have Field Codes selected on the View menu or in the View category of the Options dialog box (Tools menu), you can see these SYMBOL fields in your document.

When a character is protected by a field, you can't delete it using the BACKSPACE key, and you can't change the character's font using the ribbon or the Character dialog box. You delete a protected character by selecting it and then deleting it or inserting a new character. You can also change the font of a protected character by editing the field.

For a field-protected character, you can use the ribbon or the Character dialog box to change any character formatting except the font, as long as the font supports the character formatting. For example, you can change the size and color, or, if the font supports italic formatting, you can apply italic formatting. If you change character formatting for a protected character and then press the Update Field key (F9), you will lose any additional formatting you've applied.

Note   If you frequently create documents in languages other than English, you can change your keyboard driver to assign international characters to the keys on your keyboard. To change keyboard drivers, you choose International in the Control Panel. For more information, see your Windows documentation.

Inserting Special Characters with Codes

You can also insert ANSI characters, such as quotation marks, em dashes, and en dashes, by using the keys on the numeric keypad and typing the ANSI codes for the characters. For a list of the ANSI codes, see your Windows documentation.

To insert a special character with codes

1 Position the insertion point where you want to insert the special character.

2 With NUM LOCK on, hold down the ALT key. Then, using the keys on the numeric keypad, type **0** and the ANSI decimal code for the character you want to insert. For example, to insert the © symbol, with NUM LOCK on, you would hold down ALT and type **0169**

You must use the keys on the numeric keypad to type the ANSI code.

Character Formatting and Styles

For more information on styles, see Chapter 8, "Formatting with Styles."

You can change character formatting directly by choosing commands from the ribbon, choosing options in the Character dialog box, and typing key combinations.

If you have character formatting that you want to use consistently throughout a document or across different documents—for example, if you want to use a large, bold font for headings—you can create a style that contains the character formats you want.

You create a style by recording a group of formats that you have applied to one paragraph. Then you apply that style to all the paragraphs that you want to have the same formats. Once the paragraphs have the same style, you can quickly change formatting for all of the paragraphs by changing the formats for the style.

A paragraph can contain both direct formatting and a style. If the paragraph that contains the insertion point has both types of formatting, the Character dialog box shows the character formats of the style, plus any formats you applied directly.

If you apply direct formatting to all the text in a paragraph and then apply a style that includes character formats, the character formats for the style replace those that you applied directly. You can, however, add direct formatting to the text after you apply the style.

You can quickly strip a paragraph of its direct formatting, leaving only the character formats in its style, by using a key combination.

To remove direct character formatting

1 Select the text.

2 Press CTRL+SPACEBAR.

If you haven't changed the paragraph's style, pressing CTRL+SPACEBAR resets the text to the character formatting for the Normal style.

Troubleshooting

Occasionally, you may have problems displaying fonts correctly on the screen. This section lists some of the most common display problems, their probable causes, and some suggested solutions.

Only One Font Is Available

If only one font appears in the Font box, you may not have an active printer selected. You choose the active printer in the Windows Control Panel. For more information on selecting a printer, see your Windows documentation.

Text Is Not Displayed in the Chosen Font

If the Line Breaks And Fonts As Printed option is selected in the View category of the Options dialog box (Tools menu), Word displays only the fonts supported by the printer or cartridge selected in the Print Setup dialog box (File menu). If your document includes a font that is not supported, Word substitutes a font.

To view the correct font on the screen, clear the Line Breaks And Fonts As Printed option. When you print, however, Word will again substitute a font that your printer supports. If the font is not appropriate for your needs, you can do either of the following:

- Set up a printer and select a cartridge that provides the font. For more information, see your Windows documentation.

- Use the ribbon or the Character dialog box to change the font to one available on the selected printer or cartridge.

Note Word chooses the appropriate default font for your printer. If you want to, you can change the default font to another font. For more information, see "Changing the Default Formatting," earlier in this chapter.

Text Extends Beyond the Right Margin

If text extends beyond the right margin on the screen, this may mean that you formatted text with a printer font and you don't have a matching screen font.

To see all of your text without scrolling to the right, format the text in a different font or try clearing the Line Breaks And Fonts As Printed option in the View category of the Options dialog box (Tools menu). When you clear this option, the line breaks on the screen may not match the line breaks when you print the document.

If clearing the Line Breaks And Fonts As Printed option does not solve the problem, you may have installed the wrong screen fonts when you set up Windows. For example, you chose an EGA monitor when you set up Windows, and you installed VGA fonts. To fix the problem, reinstall the Windows screen fonts for the correct monitor. For more information, see your Windows documentation.

Installed Fonts Are Not Available

If you installed additional fonts after you installed Windows and the fonts aren't listed in the Font box, your printer may not be connected to a port. If this is the case, the Print and Print Preview commands will not be available from the File menu. For information about how to connect to a port, see your Windows documentation.

If your printer is connected to a port, you may need to choose your printer again to ensure that Word is aware of the printer's capabilities. Choose Print Setup from the File menu, select a different printer, and then reselect the original printer.

A font also may not be available if you didn't install it properly. For installation information, see the documentation that came with the font.

Word Can't Display Fonts Due to Low Memory

The font display in Word is limited by available memory, the sizes available in the printer driver you've selected in the Print Setup dialog box (File menu), and the type of font: fixed or proportional. (In a fixed-width font, every character is the same width. In a proportional font, character width varies; for example, the letter "i" takes up less space than the letter "w.")

Word may display a low-memory message if the Line Breaks And Fonts As Printed option is selected in the View category of the Options dialog box (Tools menu) and you type a size larger than the largest size in the Points list. You may also see this message if your open documents include many fonts and point sizes.

Save your documents and restart Word. Then do either of the following:

- Clear the Line Breaks And Fonts As Printed check box in the View category of the Options dialog box (Tools menu).

- Use fewer fonts and point sizes in your open documents. Note that if you do not resolve the problem, Word may substitute Windows fonts for some or all of the fonts installed for your printer.

Chapter . 7

Paragraph Formatting

In Word, the meaning of "paragraph" is somewhat different from its normal English usage. A paragraph is not necessarily a series of sentences. It is any amount of text and graphics plus the paragraph mark (shown as ¶) that follows it.

Just as you control the appearance of individual characters by applying character formatting, you can control the appearance of a paragraph with the paragraph formatting features in Word. For example, you can:

- Center a paragraph or align it with the left indent, the right indent, or both indents, which is called "justified text."

- Indent an entire paragraph from the left margin, the right margin, or both, or indent only the first line.

- Add custom tabs that are left-aligned, right-aligned, centered, or decimal-aligned.

- Adjust the line spacing within paragraphs or the spacing between paragraphs.

You change the formatting of a paragraph by first selecting the paragraph and then applying the formatting you want. Word stores the formatting instructions for the paragraph in the paragraph mark. When you start a new paragraph by pressing ENTER, Word copies the paragraph mark to the next paragraph, carrying with it the formatting instructions. If you delete, copy, or move a paragraph mark, you delete, copy, or move the formatting as well.

If you choose paragraph formatting before you start typing, the formatting is applied to the text as you type, and copied into the next paragraph when you press ENTER.

It's a good idea to display paragraph marks as you work, so that you don't accidentally delete the paragraph mark that contains the formatting for the paragraph.

To display paragraph marks

▶ Click the Show/Hide ¶ button on the ribbon.

–Or–

▶ Press CTRL+SHIFT+8.

–Or–

▶ From the Tools menu, choose Options (ALT, O, O). Select the View category. Under Nonprinting Characters, select Paragraph Marks.

Tip   When you delete a paragraph mark, the text before the paragraph mark becomes part of the next paragraph, taking on any formatting the paragraph has. If you accidentally delete a paragraph mark, immediately choose the Undo command from the Edit menu. Word restores the paragraph mark, and the paragraph mark restores the formatting.

Word offers a number of paragraph formatting options in addition to the ones discussed in this chapter. You can also use styles to quickly apply identical formatting to many paragraphs. A style is merely a group of paragraph formats, and optionally character formats, to which you give a name. For information about other paragraph formatting options and styles, see the following chapters.

For information about	See
Controlling page breaks in paragraphs	Chapter 23, "Pagination"
Applying borders and shading	Chapter 19, "Borders and Shading"
Positioning paragraphs	Chapter 21, "Positioning Text and Graphics on the Page"
Numbering paragraphs	Chapter 28, "Adding Bullets and Numbers"
Creating and using styles	Chapter 8, "Formatting with Styles"

Methods for Applying Paragraph Formats

When you create a document, Word automatically applies default, or preset, formats, so even if you only type and print, you produce a readable and presentable document. The default formats are:

- Paragraphs: left-aligned, single-spaced
- Tab stops: every 0.5 inch, left-aligned
- Margins: 1 inch top and bottom; 1.25 inches left and right

For information about setting margins, see Chapter 9, "Margins, Paper Size, and Page Orientation."

The margins are page setup options. They can be changed for the whole document or for a selected part of the document. The other formats are paragraph formats.

There are three ways to apply paragraph formats, each with its own advantages.

Method	Advantages
Ruler, ribbon, and Toolbar	Offer the quickest way to set indents, tab stops, and alignments by clicking buttons or dragging markers.
Paragraph and Tabs commands	The Paragraph dialog box gives you access to most paragraph formatting options. You can specify precise measurements for indents, line spacing, and spacing between paragraphs. The Tabs dialog box is used to set or reformat custom tab stops with various leader styles and alignments.
Key combinations	Provide quick ways to apply commonly used formats to paragraphs while keeping your hands on the keyboard.

Using the Toolbar, Ribbon, and Ruler

The Toolbar, ribbon, and ruler provide quick access to the most commonly used features in Word. For paragraph formatting, the following commands and options are available.

Toolbar   To quickly convert normal text paragraphs to a bulleted or numbered list, you can click one of two buttons. Word adds the bullets or numbers, and aligns the text to their right. By clicking another button, you can indent selected paragraphs incrementally to the default tab stops. Or click the button beside it to move the indent back out by the default tab stop interval.

Add bullets or numbers to the selected paragraphs

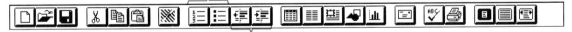

Indent or unindent paragraphs to the default tab stops

Ribbon   By clicking alignment buttons on the ribbon, you can change the alignment of paragraphs from left to centered, right, or justified (both left and right edges align). Tab buttons allow you to add tabs with one of four alignments, including decimal alignment, to selected paragraphs. The button at the right end of the ribbon displays or hides paragraph marks and other nonprinting characters.

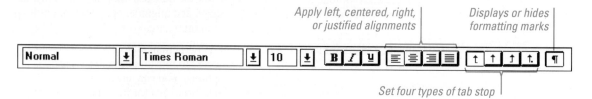

Apply left, centered, right, or justified alignments

Displays or hides formatting marks

Set four types of tab stop

Ruler   The tab buttons on the ribbon are used in conjunction with the ruler: Click the type of tab stop you want, and then, with the ruler in indent scale, indicate where you want the tab stop on the ruler. You also can drag an indent marker to change a paragraph's left, first-line, or right indent.

The ruler has three *scales*—indent scale, margin scale, and table scale—which display different markers for doing different types of work. For paragraph formatting, you use the *indent scale*, shown in the following illustration. The indent scale displays three triangular indent markers and also tab stop markers—upside-down T's that show the default tab stops in effect and up arrows that indicate where you have added a custom tab stop. If you don't see these markers, click the Ruler Scale symbol at the left end of the ruler to change the scale. The symbol changes to show the next scale you can select.

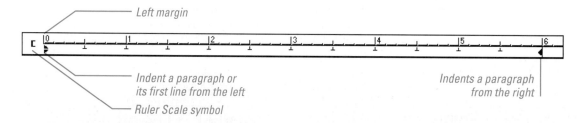

Left margin

Indent a paragraph or its first line from the left

Indents a paragraph from the right

Ruler Scale symbol

To set negative indents with the mouse, you need to scroll your document horizontally. If the horizontal scroll bar is not displayed across the bottom of the window, select the Horizontal Scroll Bars check box, a View option in the Options dialog box (Tools menu).

For information about creating and using templates, see Chapter 37, "Document Templates."

Word provides a ruler for each document window you open but only one ribbon and one Toolbar for all document windows. If you base your documents on different templates, the buttons on the Toolbar may change, depending on the template in use in the active window. You can use the ribbon and Toolbar regardless of which document window you work in.

The Toolbar, ribbon, and ruler are particularly useful if you like to work with the mouse, but you can still use the ruler to adjust paragraph indents and add tab stops even if you prefer to use the keyboard. To make the ruler active, press CTRL+SHIFT+F10. The ruler cursor—a black box—appears beneath the inch marker at the left end of the ruler. To switch back to the document, you press ENTER.

If you need more room on the screen to view a document, you can hide the Toolbar, ribbon, and ruler, and then display them again when you need them.

If you decide you want to use additional options, you can double-click anywhere in the numbers on the ruler to display the Paragraph dialog box, or double-click a tab stop marker to display the Tabs dialog box.

The ribbon and ruler show the formatting of the current paragraph—that is, the paragraph that contains the insertion point or the one that is selected. If you select more than one paragraph and the paragraphs have different formatting—for example, paragraphs with different indents—the settings shown on the ruler are for the first paragraph only, and appear shaded.

You can change the formatting of selected paragraphs, even if the paragraphs are formatted differently. For example, setting a left indent changes the left indent for all selected paragraphs. Word changes only the characteristics that you specify; all other formatting remains the same.

Tip   If you are formatting only one paragraph, place the insertion point anywhere in the paragraph and then choose the formatting that you want. Paragraph formatting affects the entire paragraph.

If you want to format more paragraphs than you can see on the screen at one time, click where you want the selection to start. Scroll to view the end of the text you want to select. Then hold down SHIFT and click after the last character you want to select. Word selects everything between the two locations you clicked. Any formatting you apply affects all selected paragraphs.

To display or hide the Toolbar, ribbon, or ruler

▶ From the View menu, choose one of the following commands:

- Toolbar (ALT, V, T)

- Ribbon (ALT, V, B)

- Ruler (ALT, V, R)

To change the scale on the ruler

▶ Click the Ruler Scale symbol on the ruler to cycle through the ruler's scales.

For information about table scale, see Chapter 17, "Tables."

In each scale, the Ruler Scale symbol changes to show the next scale that will be displayed. Table scale, displayed when you create a table, is only available when the insertion point or selection is in a table.

To make the ruler active using the keyboard

▶ Press CTRL+SHIFT+F10.

The ruler cursor appears beneath the number marker at the left end of the ruler. To return to your document, press ENTER.

Using the Paragraph and Tabs Commands

When you want to make fine adjustments to indents, set custom tab stops with leaders, or adjust the line spacing within paragraphs or the spacing between paragraphs, the Paragraph and Tabs commands on the Format menu give you the following formatting options. You can also change text alignment using the Paragraph command, though this can be done more quickly with buttons on the ribbon.

Paragraph dialog box   Use the Paragraph command to specify paragraph indents in very precise measurements, adjust line spacing within paragraphs and the spacing between paragraphs, automatically control page breaks in your documents, and show or hide the line numbers within a selection if they have been added using the Section Layout command on the Format menu. The Sample box shows the effects of indents and line spacing adjustments as you select options. The Tabs button opens the Tabs dialog box so that you can add custom tab stops to selected paragraphs.

For information about how to add automatic page break controls through paragraph formatting, see Chapter 23, "Pagination." For information about adding line numbers to the sections of your document, see Chapter 28, "Adding Bullets and Numbers."

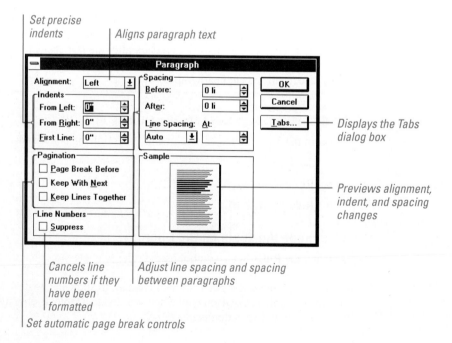

Set precise indents

Aligns paragraph text

Displays the Tabs dialog box

Previews alignment, indent, and spacing changes

Cancels line numbers if they have been formatted

Adjust line spacing and spacing between paragraphs

Set automatic page break controls

Tabs dialog box   Use the Tabs command to reformat tab stops, add custom tab stops with one of three types of leader, quickly clear all tab stops from a selection, or change the distance between default tab stops. The dialog box shows the settings for each tab stop you have added to the current paragraph. You can select any of the tab stops and change its alignment or leader character.

Tip   You can display the Paragraph dialog box by double-clicking the numbers on the ruler. To display the Tabs dialog box, double-click a tab marker on the ruler.

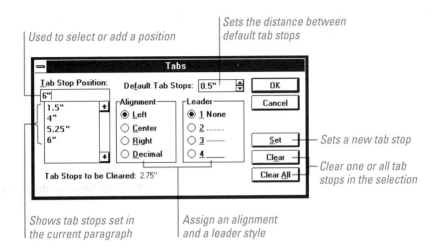

Used to select or add a position

Sets the distance between default tab stops

Sets a new tab stop

Clear one or all tab stops in the selection

Shows tab stops set in the current paragraph

Assign an alignment and a leader style

The settings in the dialog boxes reflect the formatting instructions for the current paragraph. If you select several paragraphs that have different formatting, the check boxes for these options are filled with gray, and boxes that should contain measurements are empty. If you type a measurement or select an option, all selected paragraphs change to match your new instructions when you choose the OK button.

You can type measurements in points (pt), picas (pi), centimeters (cm), inches (in), or lines (li). All measurements can be decimal fractions (for example, .5 in). You don't have to type a space between the measurement and the abbreviation. For example, you can type either **2 cm** or **2cm** to specify 2 centimeters.

When you choose the OK button, Word converts your measurement to the default unit of measurement—inches for U.S. version of Word, centimeters for non-U.S. versions. Spacing measurements are converted to lines. There are six lines per inch.

Changing the Default Unit of Measurement

If you often type measurements in units other than the default, consider changing the default unit of measurement to the one you most commonly use so that you won't have to type the unit. You'll have the added advantage of seeing the new unit of measurement on the ruler.

To change the default unit of measurement, choose Options from the Tools menu. From the Category list, select General. In the Measurement Units box, select the unit you want to use. Then choose the OK button.

Aligning and Indenting Paragraphs

When you align paragraphs, you specify where you want the lines of text to line up horizontally—on the left, center, or right, or justified. When you indent a paragraph, you specify how far in from the margin or how far out into it you want the text to print.

Note The margins can be set for the entire document or for selected areas of the document using the Page Setup command on the Format menu. Setting indents for paragraphs does not affect the margins.

Aligning Paragraphs

You can choose from four types of alignment:

Left Aligns each line of the paragraph on the left margin or paragraph indent, leaving a ragged right edge. This is the default alignment for Word.

Centered Aligns each line of the paragraph between the left and right margins or indents. This is useful for headings.

Right   Aligns each line of the paragraph on the right margin or paragraph indent, leaving a ragged left edge. This is useful for a right-aligned date and return address in a letter.

Justified   Adjusts spacing between words so that text aligns with both the left and right margins or indents. This creates a block of text with crisp left and right edges, like you see in newspaper columns. However, the extra word spacing may make the text harder to read.

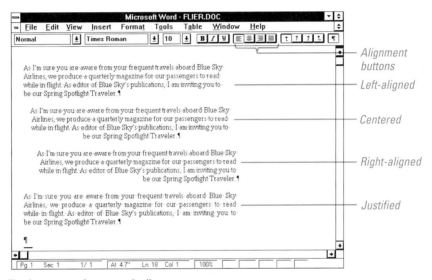

The four types of paragraph alignment

Note   The following procedure involves use of the ribbon. If the ribbon is not displayed, choose Ribbon from the View menu (ALT, V, B). For more information about using the Toolbar, ribbon, and ruler, see "Methods for Applying Paragraph Formats," earlier in this chapter.

To change paragraph alignment

Word automatically aligns paragraphs with the left margin or, if you have set a left indent for the paragraph, with the left indent. Use one of these procedures to change the alignment.

1   Select the paragraphs you want to align, or position the insertion point where you want the formatting to start as you type.

2   From the Format menu, choose Paragraph (ALT, T, P).

3   In the Alignment box, select the alignment you want.

4   Choose the OK button.

Shortcuts

1   Select the paragraphs you want to align, or position the insertion point where you want the formatting to start as you type.

2   On the ribbon, click one of the following buttons.

To align	Click
Left	Left-Aligned Text button
Centered	Centered Text button
Right	Right-Aligned Text button
Justified (left and right)	Justified Text button

1   Select the paragraphs you want to align, or position the insertion point where you want the formatting to start as you type.

2   Press one of the following key combinations.

To align	Press
Left	CTRL+L
Centered	CTRL+E
Right	CTRL+R
Justified (left and right)	CTRL+J

Indenting Paragraphs

You can quickly indent selected paragraphs by clicking a button on the Toolbar, or you can set an indent using the ruler or the Paragraph command. The Indent button on the Toolbar indents the paragraph to the next default tab stop. Indent markers on the ruler give you a quick and convenient way to set custom left, right, or first-line indents. The Paragraph command is useful when you know the exact measurement for an indent and you prefer to type the measurement.

Paragraph indents provide a variety of ways to emphasize elements in your document. You can create hanging indents to align the text in numbered or bulleted lists or to align the first line in bibliography entries with the margin, indenting the lines that follow. By creating a negative indent, you can print text such as headings in the document's margins. And you can nest paragraphs of subtext quickly by applying incremental indents. These three techniques are discussed after the basic indent procedures.

On the ruler, you set indents by dragging one of the three triangular indent markers which give you the flexibility to set left, right, and first-line indents in selected paragraphs. When you drag an indent marker, the text in the selected paragraphs aligns under the marker when you release the mouse.

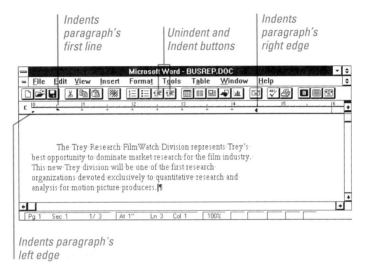

Indents paragraph's first line

Unindent and Indent buttons

Indents paragraph's right edge

Indents paragraph's left edge

A paragraph with three types of indent

The Right Indent marker affects all lines in the paragraph. The Left Indent marker (the bottom triangle on the left) gives you flexibility in your formatting. You can drag the marker to move all lines in the paragraph, or you can hold down SHIFT while dragging the marker to move all lines but the first.

Indents affect only paragraphs you select or the paragraph in which the insertion point is positioned. When you set an indent, the measurement is added to the margin. For example, if the margin is 1.0 inch and you indent a paragraph 0.5 inch, the paragraph prints 1.5 inches from the edge of the paper.

Note   The following procedures involve use of the Toolbar, ribbon, and ruler. If the Toolbar is not displayed, choose Toolbar from the View menu (ALT, V, T). If the ribbon is not displayed, choose Ribbon from the View menu (ALT, V, B). If the ruler is not displayed, choose Ruler from the View menu (ALT, V, R). For more information about using the Toolbar, ribbon, and ruler, see "Methods for Applying Paragraph Formats," earlier in this chapter.

To indent a paragraph to the next default tab stop

▶ With the selection or insertion point in the paragraph, click the Indent button on the Toolbar.

To move the paragraph back to the left, click the Unindent button on the Toolbar.

▶ Press CTRL+N.

To move a paragraph back to the left, press CTRL+M.

To set left, right, and first-line indents

1 Select the paragraphs you want to indent, or position the insertion point where you want the formatting to start as you type.

2 From the Format menu, choose Paragraph (ALT, T, P).

3 Under Indentation, do one or more of the following:

■ In the From Left box, type or select the distance from the left margin that you want to indent the paragraphs.

As you scroll through the list, the diagram in the Sample box changes shape as the measurements change. If you type a measurement, click in another box to see the change.

■ In the From Right box, type or select the distance from the right margin that you want to indent the paragraphs.

■ To indent each paragraph's first line differently from the rest of the paragraph, in the First Line box, type or select the distance from the left indent that you want the first line to begin. A negative number moves the first line to the left of the left indent.

The first-line indent is measured from the left indent setting, not the left margin.

4 Choose the OK button.

Shortcuts

1 Select the paragraphs you want to align, or position the insertion point where you want the formatting to start as you type.

2 On the ruler, do one or more of the following.

To indent	Do this
Entire left edge of the paragraph	Drag the Left Indent marker.
First line of the paragraph only	Drag the First-Line Indent marker.
Left edge of all lines but the first	Hold down SHIFT and drag the Left Indent marker.
Entire right edge of the paragraph	Drag the Right Indent marker.

1   Select the paragraphs you want to align, or position the insertion point where you want the formatting to start as you type.

2   To make the ruler active, press CTRL+SHIFT+F10.

3   Press the RIGHT ARROW or LEFT ARROW key to move the ruler cursor to where you want the indent.

4   Press one of the following letters.

To set	Press
Left indent	L
Right indent	R
First-line indent	F

5   To set other indents, repeat steps 3 and 4.

6   To return to the document and apply these changes, press ENTER.

Creating Hanging Indents

Hanging indents are useful for formatting numbered lists, bulleted lists, or bibliographies. With a hanging indent, the first line aligns on the left, and the rest of the paragraph "hangs," indented from the first line. You can create customized hanging indents by using the ruler or the Paragraph command, or you can create standard numbered or bulleted lists by clicking a button on the Toolbar.

If you use the Toolbar to create a numbered or bulleted list, Word adds an arabic numeral followed by a period (for example, 1.) or the default bullet (ALT+0183, Symbol font) to the left of each selected paragraph. If the paragraph that precedes the selection has been numbered or bulleted in this manner, Word resumes the previous numbering or applies the same bullet format.

You can renumber a list by selecting the numbered paragraphs along with any additional paragraphs you want numbered and then repeating the Toolbar procedure.

If your selection includes paragraphs that do not have numbers, and you want to leave them that way—for example, you have added indented comments beneath entries—use the command procedure and select the Replace Only Numbers option.

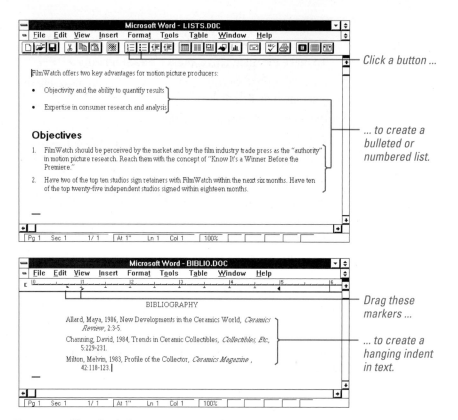

Two types of hanging indent

The techniques for formatting the indents differ, depending on whether you want to add bullets or numbers to the list or just change the indentation of the text. To create a hanging indent in text, you use standard paragraph formatting. If you want to add numbers or bullets, Word provides special commands that add the markers and reformat the text to their right in one step. In this section, procedures for indenting text paragraphs follow those for creating and updating numbered and bulleted lists.

To create a numbered or bulleted list

If you want a bullet style or numbering format other than the standard ones added using the Toolbar buttons, use this method.

1 Select the paragraphs you want to number or add bullets to.

2 From the Tools menu, choose Bullets And Numbering (ALT, O, B).

3 Select the Bullets option button or the Numbered List option button.

4 If you don't want the standard bullets or numbers, select the options you want under Bullet Character or under Number.

5 If you want to change the size of the indent from 0.25 inch, type or select a measurement in the Hanging Indent By box.

6 Choose the OK button.

Shortcut

To quickly add standard numbering or bullets to the paragraphs in a selection, use the Toolbar.

1 Select the paragraphs you want to number or add bullets to.

2 To create a numbered list, click the Numbered List button on the Toolbar.
 –or–
 To create a bulleted list, click the Bulleted List button on the Toolbar.

Word inserts a bullet or number and a tab character in front of each selected paragraph, adjusting the indents to align the text to the right of the bullet or number.

If you later decide to adjust the number format, the beginning number, or the size of the indent, you can select the paragraphs and choose the Bullets And Numbering command from the Tools menu.

To remove bullets or numbering

1 Select the numbered or bulleted paragraphs.

2 From the Tools menu, choose Bullets And Numbering (ALT, O, B).

3 Choose the Remove button.

To set a hanging indent for text only

Use this technique if you want to apply a hanging indent using a very precise measurement.

1 Select the paragraphs you want to indent, or position the insertion point where you want the formatting to start as you type.

2 From the Format menu, choose Paragraph (ALT, T, P).

3   In the From Left box under Indentation, type or select the distance from the left margin that you want to indent all lines but the first line.

4   In the First Line box under Indentation, type or select the negative measurement from the left indent by which you want to indent the first line.

For example, if you set a left indent of 0.5 inch, you would type **-.5** to align the first line with the margin.

The diagram in the Sample box changes when you select a measurement. If you type a measurement, click in any other box to view the change.

5   Choose the OK button.

Shortcuts

1   Select the paragraphs you want to indent, or position the insertion point where you want the formatting to start as you type.

2   On the ruler, hold down SHIFT and drag the Left Indent marker to where you want all lines but the first line.
–or–
Drag the First-Line Indent marker left to where you want the first line to begin.

1   Select the paragraphs you want to indent, or position the insertion point where you want the formatting to start as you type.

2   To make the ruler active, press CTRL+SHIFT+F10.

3   Press the RIGHT ARROW or LEFT ARROW key to move the ruler cursor to where you want to indent all lines but the first line, and then press L.

4   Press the RIGHT ARROW or LEFT ARROW key to move the ruler cursor to where you want the first-line indent, and then press F.

5   To return to the document and apply the changes, press ENTER.

Note that you can use the keyboard to move the first-line indent independently from the rest of the paragraph, but you cannot move the rest of the paragraph independently of the first line; when you set the indent by pressing L, the first-line indent moves to maintain the same position relative to the indent for the rest of the paragraph.

Tip   You can create a hanging indent quickly by selecting a paragraph or paragraphs and pressing CTRL+T. Word indents all lines but the first to the first default tab stop, or to the first custom tab stop you have set. You can extend the indent to the next tab stop by pressing CTRL+T again. To decrease the indent, press CTRL+G.

Setting a Negative Indent to Print Text in the Margin

You can set a negative indent, which causes a paragraph to extend into the the left or right margin of the page. For example, chapter titles are sometimes indented into the left margin to make them stand out.

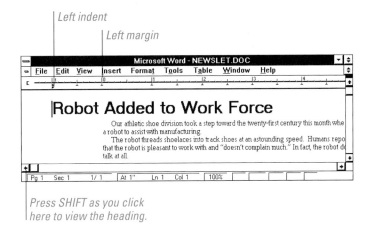

A heading with a negative left indent

To set a negative indent

1   Select the paragraphs you want to indent, or position the insertion point where you want the formatting to start as you type.

2   From the Format menu, choose Paragraph (ALT, T, P).

3   Under Indentation, type or select a negative number in the From Left or From Right box, depending on which indent you want to set.

   The diagram in the Sample box changes when you select a measurement. If you type a measurement, click in any other box to view the change.

4   Choose the OK button.

Shortcuts

1   Select the paragraphs you want to indent, or position the insertion point where you want the formatting to start as you type.

2   To view the left margin, hold down SHIFT and click the left scroll arrow to scroll to the left of zero.
   –or–
   To view the right margin, click the right scroll arrow to scroll to the right of the Right Margin marker.

3 To set the indents, do one or more of the following.

To indent	Do this
Entire left edge of the paragraph	Drag the Left Indent marker.
First line of the paragraph only	Drag the First-Line Indent marker.
Left edge of all lines but the first	Hold down SHIFT and drag the Left Indent marker.
Entire right edge of the paragraph	Drag the Right Indent marker.

1 Select the paragraphs you want to indent, or position the insertion point where you want the formatting to start as you type.

2 To make the ruler active, press CTRL+SHIFT+F10.

3 Press SHIFT+LEFT ARROW or press the RIGHT ARROW key to move the ruler cursor to where you want the indent.

4 To select an indent, press one of the following letters.

To indent	Press
Left edge of the paragraph	L
Right edge of the paragraph	R
First line of the paragraph	F

5 To apply the changes and return to the document, press ENTER.

Nesting Paragraphs

With Word you can quickly nest indents—that is, indent selected paragraphs from the left by incremental amounts. For example, you might want to indent several paragraphs of text that are quoted from another source. Or you might indent one bulleted list within another one.

Each time you click the Indent button on the Toolbar or press CTRL+N, Word moves the selected paragraphs to the next default tab stop on the right. To "unnest" an indent incrementally, click the Unindent button on the Toolbar or press CTRL+M. Each selected paragraph moves back to the left to the next default tab stop. These commands create an evenly staggered, or nested, appearance.

The default tab stops are preset at 0.5-inch intervals. You can change the default tab stops by using the Tabs command on the Format menu.

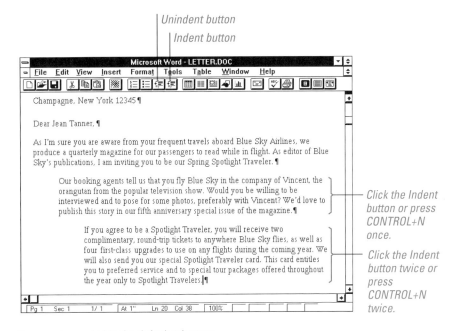

Paragraphs nested to the default tab stops

Setting Tabs

Working with tab stops in Word is like working with tabs on a typewriter. When you press the TAB key (or CTRL+TAB if the insertion point is in a table), the insertion point jumps to the next tab stop, and a tab character fills the space. The tab character does not print, and it is not visible unless you choose to display it.

Note If you want to produce columns and rows of text and numbers, it's easiest to make a table. You can insert a table grid and then fill in the rows and columns, or you can convert existing text to a table. With either method, you can easily change column widths, move around rows and columns, and add borders. For information about tables, see Chapter 17, "Tables."

Each paragraph in a new document has default tab stops, which are preset at half-inch intervals. You can use these tab stops, or you can:

- Change the interval of the default tab stops.

- Set custom tab stops at any position within selected paragraphs. You can specify how text aligns at custom tab stops (centered, for example). You can also add leader characters—solid, dotted, or dashed lines that fill the space taken by the tab character.

To add custom tab stops, you select the paragraph or paragraphs you want to set tab stops for and then set the tab stops. You can set the tab stops by using the ruler or by choosing the Tabs command on the Format menu. If you do not make a selection, tab stops are set for the paragraph that contains the insertion point. When you set a custom tab stop, Word clears all default tab stops to the left of the custom tab stop.

Word stores tab settings in the paragraph mark at the end of each paragraph. If you delete a paragraph mark, you delete the tab settings for that paragraph. The text of the paragraph becomes part of the paragraph that follows it. If you immediately choose Undo from the Edit menu, Word restores the paragraph mark, which restores the tab settings.

The space taken by a tab character is normally empty. You can fill the space for any tab stop with leader characters: a dotted line, a dashed line, or a solid line. This is useful for many kinds of lists, such as the cast of characters in a theater program. If you want to add a tab stop leader, use the Tabs command on the Format menu.

Hamlet................................Bruno Martin— *Dotted leader*

The Queen------------------Anne Caspare— *Dashed leader*

Director _____Maria Martin— *Solid leader*

Leader styles for custom tab stops

To display tab characters

▶ On the ribbon, click the Show/Hide ¶ button.

–Or–

1 From the Tools menu, choose Options (ALT, O, O).

2 Under Category, select View.

3 Under Nonprinting Characters, select Tabs.

4 Choose the OK button.

To change the default tab stops

The default tab stops initially are at 0.5-inch intervals for a document.

1 From the Format menu, choose Tabs (ALT, T, T).

2 In the Default Tab Stops box, type or select the distance you want between tabs.

3 Choose the OK button.

For information about creating and using templates, see Chapter 37, "Document Templates."

This changes the default tab stops for the document. You can change the default tab stops for a document template to have Word use that setting for all documents that you subsequently create using the template.

Setting Tab Stops with the Ribbon and Ruler

You can insert, remove, and move tab stops using the ribbon and ruler. You click a tab button on the ribbon to select an alignment. Then you click where you want the tab stop on the ruler. You can also set tab stops from the keyboard without using the ribbon.

If the selection includes paragraphs with different tab stops, the ruler displays the tab stops for the first paragraph, and the markers are shaded. If you remove a tab stop marker, all tab stops in the selected paragraphs that are within a few hundredths of an inch of the tab stop also are removed.

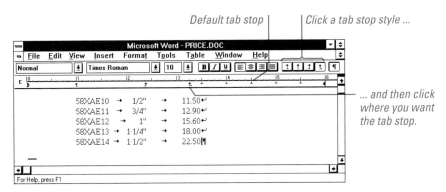

A paragraph with left-aligned, right-aligned, and decimal-aligned custom tab stops

Note The following procedures use the ribbon and ruler. If the ribbon is not displayed, choose Ribbon from the View menu (ALT, V, B). If the ruler is not displayed, choose Ruler from the View menu (ALT, V, R).

To set tab stops with the ribbon and ruler

1 Select the paragraphs you want to add tab stops to, or position the insertion point where you want the formatting to start as you type.

2 To change the tab stop alignment, click one of the following buttons on the ribbon.

To align	Click
Left	Left-Aligned Tab button
Center	Centered Tab button
Right	Right-Aligned Tab button
Decimal	Decimal Tab button

3 Click where you want the tab stop in the lower half of the ruler.

4 To add other tab stops, repeat steps 2 and 3.

1 Select the paragraphs you want to add tab stops to, or position the insertion point where you want the formatting to start as you type.

2 To make the ruler active, press CTRL+SHIFT+F10.

3 Press the LEFT ARROW or RIGHT ARROW key to move the ruler cursor to where you want the tab stop.

4 Select an alignment for the tab stop.

For this tab stop	Press
Left-aligned	1
Centered	2
Right-aligned	3
Decimal	4

5 To set a tab stop, press INS.

6 To add other tab stops, repeat steps 3 through 5.

7 To return to the document and apply the changes, press ENTER.

Note If you want to add a leader to a custom tab stop or change any other tab formatting, double-click the tab's marker on the ruler to display the Tabs dialog box.

To clear a custom tab stop with the ruler

1 Select the paragraphs that contain the tab stops you want to clear.

2 On the ruler, drag the marker for the tab stop you want to remove down out of the ruler.

1 Select the paragraphs that contain the tab stops you want to clear.

2 To make the ruler active, press CTRL+SHIFT+F10.

3 Press the LEFT ARROW or RIGHT ARROW key to move the ruler cursor to the tab stop you want to clear, and then press DEL.

4 To delete other tab stops, repeat step 3.

5 To return to the document and apply the changes, press ENTER.

Saving Time When Setting Tab Stops

If you know tab stop settings will be the same for several paragraphs, you can save time by setting the tab stops in the first paragraph that needs them before you start typing. When you press ENTER to start a new paragraph, Word copies the paragraph format-ting—including the tab stop settings—to the next paragraph.

When changing tab stop settings, make sure you select every paragraph you want the change to affect. Then you'll only have to change the settings once.

If you use the same tab stop settings often in your work, save the settings in a style. You can apply the style—and tab stop settings—quickly in other documents. For more information about styles, see Chapter 8, "Formatting with Styles."

Customizing Tab Stops with the Tabs Command

With the Tabs dialog box, you can:

- Position tab stops with more precision than you can using the ruler.

- Change the tab stop leader character—a solid, dotted, or dashed line that fills the space taken by the tab character.

- Quickly clear all the tab stops that you set for a paragraph (this restores the default tab stops).

You can display the Tabs dialog box by choosing Tabs from the Format menu or by double-clicking any tab stop marker on the ruler. You also can choose the Tabs button in the Paragraph dialog box.

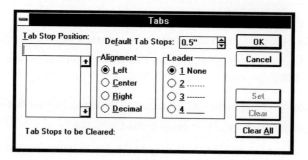

The Tab Stop Position box lists the positions of all tab stops you have set in the selected paragraph. You can select any tab stop and change its alignment and leader character, or you can delete the tab stop. If the selection includes paragraphs with different tab stop settings, no tab stops are listed. To remove or reformat a tab stop that is not shown, you can type the tab stop position in the Tab Stop Position box.

Tip To find the precise position of a tab stop, select the paragraph that contains the tab stop, and then display the Tabs dialog box.

To set tab stops with the Tabs command

Use this procedure when you want to set tab stops with leaders or with precise measurements you can't set using the ruler and ribbon.

1 Select the paragraphs you want to add the tab stops to, or position the insertion point where you want the formatting to start as you type.

2 From the Format menu, choose Tabs (ALT, T, T).

3 In the Tab Stop Position box, type the position where you want the tab (zero is the left margin).

You can type measurements in points (pt), picas (pi), centimeters (cm), inches (in), or lines (li). You don't have to type a space between the measurement and the abbreviation.

4 Under Alignment, select Left, Center, Right, or Decimal.

5   Under Leader, select one of the following options.

Option	Adds
None	No leader
. . .	Periods along the text's baseline
- - -	Hyphens
____	Underscore

6   Choose the Set button.

7   To set other tab stops, repeat steps 3 through 6.

8   Choose the OK button.

To reformat custom tab stops with the Tabs command

If the selection includes paragraphs that have different tab stops, the Tab Stop Position box does not show any tab stops. You can type a tab stop position to reformat all tab stops at that position within the selected paragraphs.

1   Select the paragraphs that contain the tab stops you want to reformat.

2   From the Format menu, choose Tabs (ALT, T, T).

3   In the Tab Stop Position box, select or type the position of the tab stop you want to reformat.

The Alignment and Leader options change to show the format of the selected tab stop.

4   Under Alignment, select Left, Right, Center, or Decimal.

5   Under Leader, select one of the three leader characters, or select None to remove a leader.

6   Choose the Set button.

7   To reformat other tab stops, repeat steps 3 through 6.

If you change your mind about the tab stop changes, you can select and reformat any of the tab stops, or choose the Cancel button to close the dialog box without making any of the tab stop changes.

8   Choose the OK button.

To clear tab stops with the Tabs command

If the selection includes paragraphs with different tab stops, the Tab Stop Position box does not show any tab stops. You can type a tab stop position to remove an individual tab stop.

1   Select the paragraphs that contain the tab stops you want to clear.

2   From the Format menu, choose Tabs (ALT, T, T).

3 To clear tab stops individually, select or type the first tab stop you want to clear in the Tab Stop Position box, and then choose the Clear button. Repeat this procedure to clear other tab stops.
   –or–
   To clear all tab stops, restoring the default tab stops, choose the Clear All button.

4 Choose the OK button.

Tip To remove all tab stops and other paragraph formatting (such as centered alignment), select the paragraph and press CTRL+Q. Any character formatting applied to the entire paragraph also is replaced by the character formatting in the style. All formatting is reset to the style applied to that paragraph. If no style has been applied, the formatting returns to Normal style.

Adjusting Spacing Between Lines and Paragraphs

You can adjust the space between lines of text in paragraphs, or between the paragraphs themselves. Custom spacing can improve the look of the document, and often makes the document more readable.

Adjusting Line Spacing Within Paragraphs

You can adjust the spacing between the lines in one, several, or all the paragraphs in your document. By default, Word single-spaces lines of text and automatically adjusts line height to accommodate graphics or larger or smaller font sizes. Word measures line spacing in points; there are 72 points in an inch.

You use the Paragraph command to adjust line spacing. You have the choice of using automatic line spacing, setting a minimum spacing that Word can make larger, or setting fixed spacing that Word cannot adjust. You can select single, double, or one-and-one-half line (the 1.5 Line option) spacing. Both Auto and Single spacing have about six lines per inch.

If you type a line spacing measurement in the At box, Word automatically selects the At Least option in the Line spacing box; your measurement sets a minimum spacing, which Word can adjust to accommodate larger fonts and graphics. If you don't want Word to adjust the line height, select the Exactly option in the Line spacing box. If you change your mind about the measurement, you can select Auto and return to the default line spacing.

The following illustration compares line spacing set with the Auto or At Least option, in the paragraph on the left, with line spacing set with the Exactly option. Notice that Word adjusts the line spacing of the paragraph on the left to accommodate a larger font and characters that have superscript and subscript formats but does not adjust the line spacing of the paragraph on the right.

To adjust line spacing

1 Select the paragraphs you want to adjust.

2 From the Format menu, choose Paragraph (ALT, T, P).

3 In the Line box under Spacing, select one of the following options.

To set	Select
Spacing that Word adjusts for the largest graphic or font size in a line	Auto
Single spacing that Word can increase	Single
One-and-a-half line spacing that Word can increase	1.5 Lines
Double spacing that Word can increase	Double
A minimum line spacing that Word can increase	At Least
Fixed line spacing that Word does not adjust	Exactly

4 In the At box under Spacing, type or select the amount of space you want between lines. You can specify a decimal fraction.

5 Choose the OK button.

Note   If you've chosen to superscript or subscript text more than the default 3 points, the display of the superscript or subscript may be cut off on the screen. It prints in the font size you specify but may overlap other text.

Adjusting Spacing Between Paragraphs

In addition to changing the line spacing within a paragraph, you can adjust the spacing between two or more paragraphs. For example, the title of a document often has additional spacing after it. Throughout a document, headings, lists, tables, and pictures usually have larger amounts of space before and after them than do regular paragraphs of text.

You can press ENTER to create blank lines just as you do on a typewriter, but using the Before and After options under Spacing in the Paragraph dialog box has several advantages:

- You can make fine adjustments to spacing, reducing or adding space to show relationships between elements in the document or to get better page breaks. You can indicate an exact amount of space before or after a paragraph, such as 5 centimeters or 0.7 inch.

- You can save spacing settings in styles. This speeds up your formatting and helps you maintain uniform spacing for items such as headings and bulleted lists.

- If you move a heading, graphic, or table formatted for extra space before or after, the space moves with it. If you insert extra space by pressing ENTER, you must move the extra paragraph marks.

- The spacing is uniform regardless of the font sizes used in surrounding paragraphs. If you press ENTER to create blank lines between paragraphs, Word adjusts the space between the paragraphs if you change font sizes.

- When you print the document, Word ignores the Before setting if the paragraph is at the top of a page. This keeps the top margin even with other top margins in the document.

Where to Add the Space

Because space can be added both before and after a paragraph, you may find the following guidelines helpful for deciding where to add space.

- For most paragraphs (with Normal style), add space before.

- For a single paragraph that is widely separated from its neighbors, add the extra space both before and after the middle paragraph so that you only have to format one paragraph.

- For headings, add space after to separate the heading slightly from the following text. Add more space before to set off the heading from the previous section.

- For signature spaces in letters, add space after the closing.

- For pictures (and tables), add space before and after the picture itself. Then, if you add text before and after the picture, the picture spacing isn't affected.

To adjust spacing between paragraphs

1 Select the paragraph or paragraphs for which you want to adjust space.

2 From the Format menu, choose Paragraph (ALT, T, P).

3 In the Before and After boxes under Spacing, type or select the measurements you want.

4 Choose the OK button.

Note If a paragraph has space added after it and the next paragraph has space added before it, the amount of space between them is the total of the two amounts.

If Normal for Word Isn't Normal for You

Do you usually press TAB when you begin a paragraph to indent the first line? Do you usually press ENTER to insert a blank line of space after each text paragraph? If so, save time by storing this formatting as your Normal style. Normal is the style Word applies to all new paragraphs unless you apply another style. If you save the style in a document template, you'll never need to press TAB to indent a paragraph's first line or press ENTER an extra time to add a blank line after a paragraph in documents based on the template. For more information, see Chapter 8, "Formatting with Styles," and Chapter 37, "Document Templates."

Removing, Repeating, and Copying Paragraph Formats

Word provides some shortcuts for working with paragraph formatting. You can quickly remove all formatting that you have applied manually. And you can repeat or copy paragraph formatting.

To remove all manual formatting from a paragraph

With this command, you can remove all paragraph formatting, including tab stop settings, that you have applied manually to selected paragraphs.

1 Select the paragraphs from which you want to remove manual paragraph formatting.

2 Press CTRL+Q.

The formatting is reset to the formats in the paragraph's style. Any character formatting that has been applied to the entire paragraph is replaced by the character formatting in the style. If no style has been applied, the selected paragraphs return to Normal style.

Tip   To replace *all* character formats in a paragraph with those in the paragraph's style, press CTRL+SPACEBAR. This cancels manual character formatting throughout the paragraph.

To repeat paragraph formats

After applying paragraph formatting, use this procedure to quickly apply the same formatting to other text. If you have done something else since applying the formatting, you can copy the paragraph formatting. See the procedure after this one.

1   Immediately after applying the original formatting, select the paragraph you want to format, or position the insertion point where you want the formatting to begin as you type.

2   Press F4.
    –or–
    From the Edit menu, choose Repeat Paragraph (ALT, E, R).

If you apply multiple formats using the Paragraph dialog box, the Repeat command repeats all of the paragraph formatting. However, if you apply formats individually using the Toolbar, ribbon, ruler, or keyboard, only the most recent paragraph format is applied.

To copy paragraph formats

1   Select the paragraph you want to format.

2   Position the pointer in the selection bar beside the paragraph with the formatting you want to copy.

3   Hold down CTRL+SHIFT and click the left mouse button.

Word applies the paragraph formatting to the selection; it does not copy and paste any text. Formatting applied directly, as well as the paragraph formatting in the paragraph's style, is applied.

Tip   To copy character formats, use the same procedure, but instead of positioning the mouse pointer in the selection bar by the paragraph you want to copy, point to a character with the formatting you want to copy.

Formatting with Styles

Suppose you've spent a few minutes formatting a paragraph to look the way you want. You've changed the font and point size, made the text italic, and indented the paragraph to set it off from the other text. Now you want several other paragraphs in your document to look the same. You could select the other paragraphs and apply the formatting to each. But that's extra work, and if you decide to change the formatting again later, you have to repeat the formatting steps for each paragraph.

Instead, you can save the formatting as a style. Just select the paragraph you formatted and assign that particular combination of formats a name. That's all a style is: a group of character and paragraph formats that you've given a name. Assigning the same named style to other paragraphs applies the same formats in one step—you don't have to choose each formatting command separately. Styles have these advantages as well:

- Styles save time formatting any type of document. You can quickly produce professional-looking memos, reports, and letters.

- Styles help ensure a consistent format. For long documents or projects involving many documents and writers, styles are virtually indispensable.

- Styles make design changes easy to incorporate, even at the last minute. Changing the format of a style reformats all paragraphs with that style throughout the document.

- Styles are easy to use. Just by choosing a few styles from a list, you can complete all the formatting for a document.

FilmWatch Division Marketing Plan

Introduction

The Trey Research FilmWatch Division represe[nts Trey's best opportunity to dominate]
market research for the film industry. This new [Trey division will be one of the first]
research organizations devoted exclusively to q[uantitative research and analysis for]
motion picture producers. We see two main targ[et markets:]

- Producers who want to test the appeal of a[ctors, actresses, locations, and so forth]
  prior to filming.

- Film companies who want to test the effec[t of different endings for films that have]
  already wrapped.

FilmWatch has already gained high visibility wi[th the hiring of Marla Jenkins as]
marketing director. (Marla's work in producing [the final ending used in a recent movie]
resulted in a revenue increase of about 42 perce[nt—an achievement written up in more]
than two dozen articles by the general business [and film industry trade press.) We intend]
to parlay the PR already won into contractual al[liances with several major film]
production companies.

FilmWatch offers two key advantages for motio[n picture producers:]

- Objectivity and the ability to quantify resu[lts]

- Expertise in consumer research and analys[is]

In the past, research on the Q factor for actors a[nd actresses was done primarily by]

FilmWatch Division Marketing Plan

Introduction

The Trey Research FilmWatch Division represents Trey's best opportunity to dominate
market research for the film industry. This new Trey division will be one of the first
research organizations devoted exclusively to quantitative research and analysis for
motion picture producers. We see two main target markets:

- Producers who want to test the appeal of actors, actresses, locations, and so forth
  prior to filming.

- Film companies who want to test the effect of different endings for films that have
  already wrapped.

FilmWatch has already gained high visibility with the hiring of Marla Jenkins as
marketing director. (Marla's work in producing the final ending used in a recent movie
resulted in a revenue increase of about 42 percent—an achievement written up in more
than two dozen articles by the general business and film industry trade press.) We intend
to parlay the PR already won into contractual alliances with several major film
production companies.

FilmWatch offers two key advantages for motion picture producers:

- Objectivity and the ability to quantify results

- Expertise in consumer research and analysis

In the past, research on the Q factor for actors and actresses was done primarily by

*Applying the same style
to several paragraphs
gives them exactly the
same format.*

*Changing a style's format reformats
any paragraphs with that style.*

Getting Started with Styles

If you've already formatted a few documents, most of the work to create a style is
behind you. Now all you have to do is name each combination of formats you want
to use again. This section explains how to:

- Create a style based on a formatted paragraph you select.

- Apply the style to other paragraphs that you want to format the same way.

- Change the format of a style. For example, you may want to change the style you
  used for all body text from justified to left-aligned.

Creating a Style

When you create a style based on a selected paragraph, Word defines the style as
having all of the paragraph formats applied to that paragraph, including borders,
shading, and the paragraph's frame position. The style also includes character formats
based on the format of most of the selected paragraph's text. For example, if most of
the text font is 10-point Times Roman and a few words are italic, Word defines the
style character format simply as 10-point Times Roman. If most or all of the text is
italic, however, Word includes italic as a character format for the style.

For information about character and paragraph formatting, see Chapter 6, "Character Formatting," and Chapter 7, "Paragraph Formatting."

In the following illustration, a new style is based on the indented paragraph and includes a 12-point font as its character format. Paragraph formats include left text alignment, spacing after the paragraph, and left and right indents.

A style based on this formatted paragraph would have 12-point Times Roman font, left and right indents, left text alignment, and spacing after the paragraph.

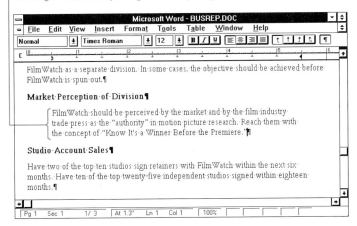

Styles you create for a document are saved when you save the document. You can create as many as 220 styles for a document. In addition, Word provides a number of standard styles that you can use to format many common elements in your document, such as headings. One standard style, Normal, is automatically applied to new paragraphs in a document. You can use the Normal style to control the default paragraph and character formats of your text.

The styles defined in a template appear in all new documents based on that template, so you only have to create a set of styles once. For more information about sharing styles among documents, see "Ensuring a Consistent Format Among Documents," later in this chapter.

To display the ribbon

In most cases, it is easiest to create and apply styles by using the ribbon. Before continuing with the instructions in this chapter, make sure the ribbon is displayed.

▶ From the View menu, choose Ribbon (ALT, V, B).

To create a style based on a formatted paragraph

1   Select a paragraph that has the formats you want to define as a style.

   The name of the style currently applied to the paragraph, in most cases Normal, is displayed in the Style box on the ribbon.

2   Use the mouse or press CTRL+S to select the name in the Style box on the ribbon.

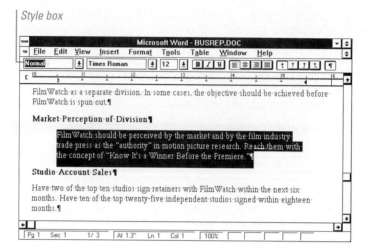

Style box

3   Type a new style name in the Style box, and press ENTER.

Rules for Style Names

Style names can contain up to 24 characters and can include any combination of characters and spaces, except the backslash character (\). Style names are not case-sensitive; Word treats "quote" and "Quote" as the same style.

The name you assign a style must be unique for a particular document. For example, a document can have only one style named "body text." Formatting with styles is more effective if you use a consistent set of style names for all your documents. The importance of consistent style names is discussed in "Working with Style Sheets," later in this chapter.

Applying a Style

Once a style is defined, you can apply it to any number of paragraphs in your document. Applying a style to a paragraph gives the paragraph the same formatting as the paragraph you used as the model for that style.

When selecting a paragraph to which you want to apply a style, you can place the insertion point anywhere in the paragraph or select any part of the text. Word considers the paragraph selected and uniformly applies the style formatting to the entire paragraph. All of the character formatting defined for the style is applied to all text in the selected paragraph, even though all of the paragraph text may not be highlighted on your screen.

*Choosing a style from the list applies
that style to the selected paragraph.*

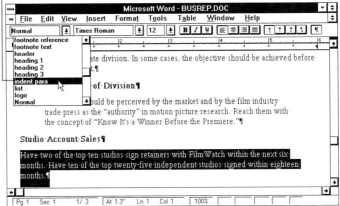

Now both paragraphs have identical formats.

To apply a style with the ribbon

1 Select the paragraph or paragraphs to which you want to apply the style.

2 Click the arrow next to the Style box on the ribbon, and then select the style you want.
–or–
Press CTRL+S, and then type the name of the style you want to apply, or use the UP ARROW and DOWN ARROW keys to select the style from the list of available styles, and then press ENTER.

Tip To apply the same style to other paragraphs in the document, select the paragraphs, and then choose the Repeat command from the Edit menu or press F4 as the next action after you apply the style. Continue selecting paragraphs and choosing Repeat until you've applied the style to all paragraphs you want to have the identical format.

Redefining the Format of a Style

Suppose you've indented the first line of all body text paragraphs in your document. You later want to change all body text to a block paragraph style and include a line of space before each paragraph. If you've used a style to format the body text, you need only redefine the style to have the new formats. Word immediately changes the format of all body text throughout the document.

Redefining the formats of a style updates that style only in the active document. To make the change in other documents that use the same style, see "Working with Style Sheets," later in this chapter.

To redefine the formatting of a style with the ribbon

1 Select any paragraph that has the style you want to redefine.

2 Make any changes to the formatting, using commands from the Format menu or the ribbon or ruler.

3 To select the name of the style in the Style box on the ribbon, use the mouse, or press CTRL+S, and then press ENTER.

4 Word displays a message that asks whether you want to redefine the style based on the selection. Choose the Yes button to redefine the style. If you choose the No button, the original style is reapplied to the selection. If you choose the Cancel button, the message box closes and no changes are made to the style. The formatting changes you made to the selection, however, remain in effect.

All paragraphs with the style you have redefined are updated with the new formatting.

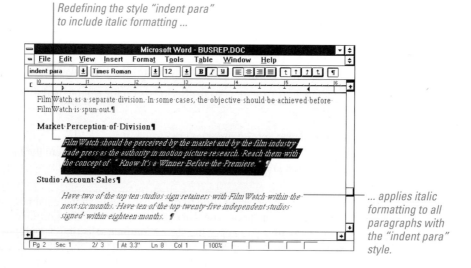

Redefining the style "indent para" to include italic formatting ...

... applies italic formatting to all paragraphs with the "indent para" style.

Using the Standard Styles in Word

For many elements in your documents—body text, headings, footnotes, headers, and footers, for example—Word provides a number of ready-to-use standard styles. Standard styles have preset formats designed for use in most types of documents. If you like, you can redefine their formats just as you redefine styles you create yourself.

In your day-to-day work, Normal style is the standard style you'll probably use most often. Normal style controls the document's default font, point size, line spacing, text alignment, and other text formats. In new documents, Normal is applied to the first empty paragraph. As you type, each new paragraph is formatted with Normal style until you apply a different style, such as a heading style.

Word applies standard styles to the appropriate document elements as you use them in your document. If you create an index, Word applies the standard styles Index 1 through Index 7 to the index entries. The text you type in the header of a document is automatically formatted using the standard style Header.

The following illustration shows some of the standard styles in Word and the elements in the document whose formatting they control.

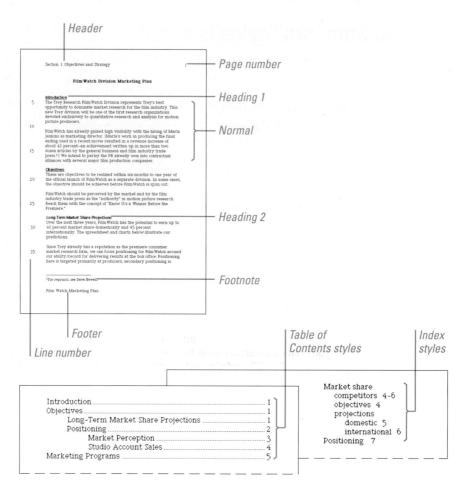

If you prefer different formats for main body text and other common document elements, you can redefine Normal and other standard styles to have any formats you want. The easiest way to change Normal character formats, including the font, is with the Use As Default button in the Character dialog box, which is displayed by choosing the Character command on the Format menu. To change other aspects of Normal style in addition to the character formats—to make text double-spaced and justified, for example—you redefine the formats of Normal as you would any other standard style.

Keep in mind that the formats of all standard styles are based on Normal style. This means that a standard style has all the formats defined for Normal style plus additional formats tailored for a particular element in the document. Therefore, redefining the formats of Normal style can also change some formats of other standard styles. Changing the font used by Normal to Helvetica, for example, changes the font used by most standard styles, thus ensuring a consistent text design.

You can define the standard styles differently for different templates. For example, you might define the heading styles for a business report template one way and define them a different way for a book manuscript template.

Tip The formatting you want ordinary body text to have may be unsuitable for other elements in a document—for example, you probably don't want headers, footers, and footnotes to have an indented first line and double line spacing. One way to avoid unwanted changes in the format of other standard styles is to create a new style for body text and use it instead of Normal. Any of the formatting you define for the new body text style won't affect the standard styles in the document.

Use Heading Styles to Produce a Table of Contents

If you're planning a table of contents for your document, make sure you format the headings in your document using the standard heading styles, Heading 1 through Heading 9. When you use the Table Of Contents command on the Insert menu, Word can automatically collect the headings to create the table of contents. If you manually format headings in your document or use your own styles for the headings, you need to mark each heading paragraph as a table of contents entry.

For instructions on applying the heading styles to paragraphs in your document, see the procedure "To apply a standard style with the Style command," later in this section. If you prefer a different format for the headings, you can redefine the heading styles; see the procedure "To redefine a standard style with the Style command," also later in this section.

In outline view, you can also drag paragraphs to the desired outline level to apply the appropriate heading style. For details on the use of heading styles with other Word features, see Chapter 29, "Indexes and Tables of Contents," and Chapter 27, "Outline View: Creating Outlines and Reorganizing Documents."

To change the default font and font size of Normal style

Use this procedure to change the default font, font size, and other character formats of Normal for the active document and all new documents based on the template currently attached to the active document. The character formatting of Normal style in existing documents other than the active one is not changed by this procedure.

1 From the Format menu, choose Character (ALT, T, C).

2 Select the character formatting you want for Normal style.

3 Choose the Use As Default button.

A message box asks you to confirm that you want to change the formatting for the Normal style. Choose the Yes button.

To apply a standard style with the Style command

Except for Normal and the first three heading styles, the standard styles do not appear in the Style dialog box or the Style box on the ribbon unless you have applied them in your document or have changed their default definitions. To see the complete list of standard styles, use this procedure.

1   Select the paragraph or paragraphs to which you want to apply the standard style.

2   From the Format menu, choose Style (ALT, T, Y).

3   Press CTRL+Y to list all standard styles, including those that are not currently used in your document.

4   From the Style Name box, select the one you want to apply.

5   Choose the Apply button, or press ENTER.

When you press CTRL+Y, the complete list of Word standard styles is displayed here.

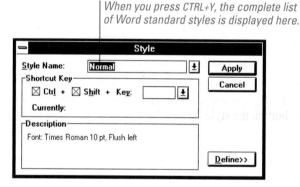

The Style dialog box

To redefine a standard style with the ribbon

Once you apply a standard style to text, the easiest way to redefine the style's format is to use the ribbon. The style format changes only in the current document. Standard styles in other existing documents or new documents you create are not affected.

1   If you have not already applied the standard style to a paragraph in your document, select the paragraph and apply the standard style you want to redefine. See the preceding procedure, "To apply a standard style with the Style command."

2   With the paragraph still selected, apply the formats you want to define for the standard style. Use the ribbon, ruler, or commands from the Format menu.

3   In the Style box on the ribbon, click the name of the style, and then press ENTER.

4   Word displays a message that asks whether you want to redefine the style. Choose the Yes button to redefine the style. If you choose the No button, the original style definition is applied to the selection. If you choose the Cancel button, the message box closes but no changes are made to the selection or to the style.

All paragraphs formatted using the standard style are updated with the new format.

To redefine a standard style with the Style command

Use this procedure to redefine the format of any standard style, including standard styles not currently used in your document. You can redefine the format for the standard styles not only for the active document but also for the attached template. When you redefine a template style, it becomes the default style for all new documents based on the template.

1   From the Format menu, choose Style (ALT, T, Y).

2   Choose the Define button.

3   Press CTRL+Y to list all the standard styles.

4   From the Style Name box, select the standard style you want to redefine.

   Word displays the formatting defined for the style in the Description box.

5   Use the buttons under Change Formatting to define the formats for the style just as you would format text in a document.

6   To use the redefined style in all new documents based on the template attached to the active document, select the Add To Template check box.

7   To redefine the style, choose the Change button.

   Word displays a message that asks you to confirm that you want to change the standard style. Choose the Yes button to change the standard style. If you choose the No button, the style formats listed under Description return to how they were when you opened the dialog box. If you choose the Cancel button, Word returns the Style dialog box to its former state without erasing or applying the formatting changes you defined.

8   Choose the Close button to close the dialog box and return to your document.

   If you choose the Apply button, Word applies the selected standard style only to the paragraph containing the insertion point or selection in your document.

Tip   If you've already redefined the format of a standard style using the ribbon and want to use that formatting as the default for the currently attached template, you can choose the Style command, select the standard style from the list, select the Add To Template check box, and then choose the Change button. Word uses the formatting defined for the standard style in all new documents you create based on the template currently attached to the document.

Working with Style Sheets

The styles available for a document—that is, the styles you define yourself and the standard styles supplied by Word—are referred to as a document's style sheet. A style sheet is an integral part of any Word document. You cannot detach a style sheet from a document. You can, however, change the document's style sheet in various ways. You do most of this work using the Style command on the Format menu. This section shows you how to do the following:

- Define and redefine styles
- Assign shortcut keys to styles
- Delete styles from a style sheet
- Rename styles
- Print the style sheet, showing you all styles defined for a document

To define a style with the Style command

In general, the easiest way to define a style is to select a formatted paragraph in your document and give the paragraph's formats a style name using the ribbon. On occasion, however, you may prefer to use the Style command, especially if you're defining a number of styles at once. You could be working from design specifications, for example, that identify the formats for each style in the document. Or you may have specific formats in mind for a style.

1   From the Format menu, choose Style (ALT, T, Y).

2   In the Style Name box, type a name for the style. Use any combination of up to 24 uppercase and lowercase characters and spaces except the backslash character (\).

3   Choose the Define button.

Word expands the dialog box to display additional options.

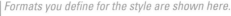

Formats you define for the style are shown here.

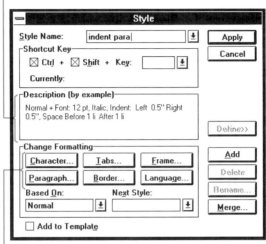

Choose these buttons to select the formats for the style.

4   Using the different buttons under Change Formatting, choose the formats you want to define for the new style.

For example, to define bold as a format for the new style, choose the Character button, select the Bold check box, and then choose the OK button. The style description in the Description box changes to show the formatting you have added to the style.

5   The formatting of the new style is initially based on the style applied to the selected paragraph in your document, which is indicated in the Based On box. Delete the style name shown in the Based On box unless you want the formatting of the new style to be based on the selected paragraph's format. For more information on this option, see "Using the Next Style and Based On Options," later in this chapter.

6   Choose the Add button to add the new style to your document's style sheet.

If you want to define another new style, repeat steps 2 through 6.

7   Choose the Close button to close the dialog box and return to your document.

If you choose the Apply button, Word applies the selected standard style only to the paragraph containing the insertion point or selection in your document.

To assign shortcut keys to a style

If you often use a style, you might want to assign a shortcut key or keys to it so that you can apply the style more easily. Style shortcut keys must be preceded by either the CTRL key or the key combination CTRL+SHIFT, except for shortcut keys consisting of the function keys (F2, F3, and so on) or the INS and DEL keys, which you can assign by themselves. For example, you can assign F2 as a shortcut key for a style, but you cannot assign A unless you precede it with either CTRL or CTRL+SHIFT.

1   From the Format menu, choose Style (ALT, T, Y).

2   In the Style Name box, select the style to which you want to assign a shortcut key or keys.

3   In the Key box, type the shortcut key or keys you want to assign to the style, or select a shortcut key or keys from the list of keys.

    If you do not you want the shortcut to include CTRL or SHIFT, clear those check boxes. Word displays a message if it does not accept the shortcut key or keys.

4   Choose the Apply button, or press ENTER.

To apply a style with shortcut keys

Once you assign a shortcut key or keys to a style, you can use the keys to apply the style quickly.

1   Select the paragraph or paragraphs to which you want to apply the style.

2   Press the shortcut keys assigned to the style you want to apply.

To redefine the format of a style with the Style command

1   From the Format menu, choose Style (ALT, T, Y).

2   In the Style Name box, select the style you want to redefine.

3   Choose the Define button.

4   Using the different buttons under Change Formatting, choose the formats you want to redefine for the style.

5   Choose the Change button to redefine the style.

    If you want to redefine another style, repeat steps 2 through 5.

6   Choose the Close button to close the dialog box and return to the document.

    If you chose the Apply button, Word applies the selected style only to the paragraph containing the insertion point or selection in your document.

To delete a style from a style sheet

When you no longer need a style for a document, you can delete the style from the document style sheet. Any paragraph in the document that was formatted with the deleted style changes to Normal. You cannot delete a standard style.

1   From the Format menu, choose Style (ALT, T, Y).

2   In the Style Name box, select the style you want to delete from the style sheet.

3   Choose the Define button.

4   Choose the Delete button.

Word displays a message that asks you to confirm that you want to delete the style. Choose the Yes button.

To delete another style, repeat steps 2 through 4.

5   Choose the Close button.

To add a style to the attached template

When you're working on a document based on a template, you may want to add a new style or redefine an existing one. You can modify the style sheet just for the active document, but to maintain consistent styles among your documents, you should also change the template's style sheet. The Add To Template check box referred to in this procedure can be used not only to add a new style to a template but also to redefine an existing style in the template.

1   From the Format menu, choose Style (ALT, T, Y).

2   Select the style that you want to add to the style sheet of the attached template or that you want to change.

3   Choose the Define button.

4   Select the Add To Template check box.

5   Choose the Change button.

6   Choose the Close button.

To rename a style

1   From the Format menu, choose Style (ALT, T, Y).

2   In the Style Name box, select the style you want to rename.

3   Choose the Define button.

4   Choose the Rename button.

5   Type a new name for the style, and choose the OK button.

6   Choose the Close button to close the Style dialog box.

Only the name of the style is changed; the formatting defined for the style is not changed.

To print a style sheet

Print a style sheet when you want to see the actual style names and definitions on paper; this is useful when you want to redefine styles or compare the style sheets of several documents. Word lists all the styles defined for the document and each style's formats.

1   From the File menu, choose Print (ALT, F, P).

2   In the Print box, select Styles.

3   Choose the OK button.

Finding and Replacing Styles

Using the Find and Replace commands on the Edit menu, you can:

■   Find all paragraphs formatted with a particular style in your document.

■   Find all paragraphs that have a certain combination of character and paragraph formats and apply a style to them.

■   Find paragraphs formatted with one style and apply a different style to them.

For more information, see Chapter 12, "Finding and Replacing Text or Formatting."

Ensuring a Consistent Format Among Documents

Suppose that you're working on a large project with numerous documents and that the formatting of each document must match strict design specifications. Or perhaps you want all your memos and letters to match your company's standard format. Styles help ensure a consistent format in all documents of a certain type, but they can do so only if you use them in a consistent way in your documents.

The style names you use in your documents are the key to consistent formatting. Using a common set of style names helps you remember which style to apply to the various elements in your documents and also allows you to easily update your documents' formatting as often as you like. If you create a style to format bulleted lists in one document, for example, use the same style to format bulleted lists in all other documents of that type.

Using Templates

Templates are special documents used as patterns to create other documents of the same type.

In Word, templates make it easy to create a consistent body of styles. You can create a template for each type of document you want to have a consistent format. In the template, you define the styles you plan to use for each type of document. For example, you might create one template for memos, another for letters, and another for reports.

The styles and other format settings for a particular type of document are ready for you to use as soon as you start a new document based on the template. Each new document has the same set of styles as the template.

For more information about templates, see Chapter 37, "Document Templates."

When you want to change the format of a style, make sure to redefine the format of the style in the template. The change in the template formatting is reflected in new documents you create from the template.

The benefits of this strategy are especially apparent if you later want to change the format of existing documents. For example, if a design change occurs late in a large project, you need only to redefine the styles once in the template, instead of redefining the styles in each document. Then, to update the styles in all of the related documents, you use the Style command to merge the template's style sheet with the style sheet of each document. Updating the style sheets in this way ensures that all documents in your project retain the identical formatting.

Merging Styles to or from a Template or Document

Merging style sheets combines the style sheet from a selected template or document with the style sheet of the active document. The formats defined for styles in the active document are updated to match the formats of styles of the same names from the incoming style sheet. This procedure updates the styles of the active document to reflect your latest document design. Styles from the incoming style sheet that are not defined in the active document are added to its style sheet.

If you have just made changes to the style sheet you want to merge, you must first save that template or document to record the changes in its style sheet. It's also a good idea to save the active document before you merge the style sheets. If you get results you don't want, you can close the document without saving the changes to its style sheet.

Just as it is sometimes useful to be able to update a document's style sheet by merging the style sheet from a template, it can be useful to update a template style sheet by merging a document's styles into it. For example, as you're working on a document based on a template, you may change several style definitions or add new styles. By merging the document style sheet into the template style sheet, you can update the template style sheet. When you merge a document style sheet into the style sheet of a template, the document's style definitions replace the template's style definitions for styles of the same name. Any styles in document style sheet that are not in the template style sheet are added to the template style sheet.

To merge styles from a template or document

1   Open the document that has the styles you want to update.

2   From the Format menu, choose Style (ALT, T, Y).

3   Choose the Define button.

4   Choose the Merge button.

5   If necessary, select the directory containing the template or document for merging from the Directories box.

6   In the File Name box, type or select the name of the template or document for merging, and then choose the From Template button.

Word displays a message that notifies you that it will change the formats of the styles in the active document to match the formats of styles with the same name from the style sheet of the selected template or document. Choose the Yes button to continue.

7   Choose the Close button to close the Style dialog box.

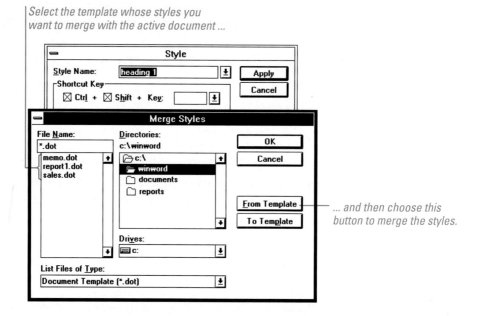

Select the template whose styles you want to merge with the active document ...

... and then choose this button to merge the styles.

As an example of what happens when you merge styles from a document or template—and to illustrate the importance of consistent style names—suppose you merge the styles from Template A into the style sheet of Document B. Both Template A and Document B include the styles Heading 1 and Normal, but the formatting defined for these styles is different. Template A also has the styles "note" for formatting notes and "list" for formatting bulleted lists. Document B has a style for formatting notes named "notice." After you merge the styles, Document B has a style sheet that includes the styles Heading 1, Normal, "note," and "list" formatted as in Template A, and the style "notice" formatted as in Document B.

The following list summarizes the rules Word observes in merging style sheets:

■ Styles that have identical style names are merged. The styles from the incoming style sheet override, or replace, the styles in the active document. In the preceding example, Heading 1 and Normal in the active document, Document B, take on the formatting of the incoming styles of Template A.

■ Styles in the active document that have unique style names are not changed. In Document B, the formatting of the style "notice" is not changed, because there is no style by that name in Template A. Its description becomes more explicit, however, since it no longer shares the same font as the Normal style.

■ Styles in the incoming style sheet that are not defined in the active document are added to the active document's style sheet. The "note" and "list" styles from Template A in the example are added to Document B's style sheet.

■ The case of the letters in the style names does not matter. For example, the styles "list" and "List" are considered the same style.

Tip If you want to merge a style sheet with a document having conflicting style names, first use the Style command on the Format menu to rename the styles in the active document to match the names in the incoming style sheet. Then, when you merge the style sheets, the appropriate styles are updated.

To merge styles to a template

You can merge a document's styles only to the template attached to the document.

1 Open the document that has the styles you want to merge to the template.

2 From the Format menu, choose Style (ALT, T, Y).

3 Choose the Define button.

4 Choose the Merge button.

5 In the File Name box, type or select the name of the template attached to the active document.

  Word displays a message that notifies you it will change the formats of the styles in the template to match the formats of styles with the same name from the style sheet of the active document. Choose the Yes button to continue.

6 Choose the Close button to close the Style dialog box.

What Happens When You Copy Text to Other Documents?

When you copy a paragraph (including the paragraph mark) from one document to another, the formatting of the paragraph sometimes changes after you paste it into the second document. For instance, if you copy a paragraph formatted with Normal style into a document that has Normal defined with a different font and font size, the format of the paragraph changes to match the formatting defined for Normal style in the second document. On the other hand, if the copied paragraph is formatted with a style that is not defined in the second document, Word adds the style to the second document's style sheet to retain the formatting of the paragraph.

Copying paragraphs formatted with styles is a convenient way to bring only a few styles you already created into another document. For example, if you create a style for notes in one document and want to use the same style in another document, you can simply copy a paragraph having the note style into the other document.

If you want only a few styles copied, make sure you copy fewer than 50 paragraphs at a time. That way, only the styles applied to the copied paragraphs are brought into the document into which you paste the paragraphs. If you copy more than 50 paragraphs or copy the entire document, all of the styles in that document's style sheet are merged with the style sheet of the document into which you paste the text. If styles in both documents have the same names, the style formats of the incoming document override the style formats of the document in which you pasted the text.

Other commands that insert text into a document, such as the Glossary and Paste Special commands on the Edit menu, can also bring styles into a document. If the text is formatted with a style that is also defined in the document into which the text is inserted, the text takes on the format defined for that style in the second document. If the inserted text is formatted with a style that is not defined in the document, the style is added to the document's style sheet.

Using the Next Style and Based On Options

The Next Style and Based On options in the Style dialog box can automate formatting a few steps further:

- Use the Next Style option in cases where a paragraph formatted with a particular style is routinely followed by another paragraph with a different style. For example, paragraphs of body text usually follow headings. Using the Next Style option, you can have Word automatically apply the appropriate style when you press ENTER to start a new paragraph.

- Use the Based On option to control the format of several related styles by basing them on a single master style. You can update the formatting of an entire group of styles just by redefining the formats of the style on which they are based.

Next Style: Applying Styles Automatically

To see the Next Style option at work, press ENTER to start a new paragraph. Without moving the insertion point, apply a heading style to the new paragraph by selecting Heading 1 from the list of styles in the Style box on the ribbon. Type some sample heading text, and then press ENTER again: Word automatically applies the Normal style to the new paragraph. If you look in the Style dialog box, you see that Normal is specified in the Next Style box for all standard heading styles. Normal style, on the other hand, is its own next style. You continue typing in Normal style until you apply a different style.

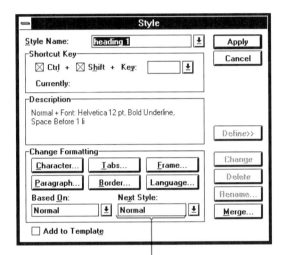

The style Heading 1 is defined
with Normal as the next style.

Business letters are good examples of documents in which the Next Style option can help automate formatting. In the following illustration, the heading, inside address, salutation, and other parts of the letter are formatted using styles. The style "heading" is defined to have "address 2" as the next style; the style "address 2" is defined to have "salutation" as the next style; and so on. Because you usually type several paragraphs in the body of a letter, the style "body" is its own next style. If you set up your letter styles this way, the letter practically formats itself as you type. Once you apply the style "heading" to the first paragraph, the only time you must apply a style is when you reach the closure.

Because the formats defined for the "heading" and "address 2" styles include space after the paragraph, SHIFT+RETURN is used to break the address lines to avoid adding space after each line.

Pressing ENTER here applies the style "address 2" to the next paragraph.

Press SHIFT+RETURN to type several lines without starting a new paragraph.

```
┌──────────────────────────────────────────────────────────┐
│ □                  Microsoft Word - LETTER.DOC        ▼ ▲ │
│ ▫  File   Edit   View   Insert   Format   Tools   Table   Window   Help   ▲ │
│                                    Blue·Sky·Airlines↵     │
│                                    555·Some·Street↵       │
│                                    Someplace,·USA·55555↵  │
│                                    December·5,·1991¶      │
│                                                          │
│        Ms.·Jean·Tanner↵                                  │
│        236·Promotion·Place↵                              │
│        Champagne,·New·York·12345¶                        │
│                                                          │
│        Dear·Ms.·Tanner,¶                                 │
│                                                          │
│           As·I'm·sure·you·are·aware·from·your·frequent·travels·aboard·Blue·Sky· │
│        Airlines,·we·produce·a·quarterly·magazine·for·our·passengers·to·read·while·in │
│        flight.·As·editor·of·Blue·Sky's·publications,·I·am·inviting·you·to·be·our·Spring· │
│        Spotlight·Traveler.¶                               │
│                                                          │
│           I·will·call·you·during·the·coming·week·to·discuss·the·details·with·you.·If·you· │
│        have·questions·before·then,·please·feel·free·to·call·me·at·(555)·555-6543.· │
│        Congratulations,·Jean!¶                           │
│                                                          │
│                                    Sincerely,¶           │
│                                                          │
│                                                          │
│                                    Julie·Gabor↵          │
│                                    Editor↵               │
│                                    Blue·Sky·Airlines¶    │
│                                                          │
│        JG/dmf¶                                           │
│        ──                                                │
│ ◄ □                                                    ► │
│ Pg 1   Sec 1   1/1   At 3.1"   Ln 5   Col 1   100%      │
└──────────────────────────────────────────────────────────┘
```

Pressing ENTER here applies the style "salutation" to the next paragraph.

After typing the body of the letter, apply the style "closure" and then continue.

Pressing ENTER here applies the style "paragraph" to the next paragraph.

Tip If you use a style other than Normal for the majority of the body text in your documents, you should specify that style as the next style for all of the standard heading styles.

To specify a next style

When you define a style using the ribbon, it's used as its own next style by default. You can specify a different next style by using the Style command. You must first create the style you want to specify as the next style, if it is not already available.

1 From the Format menu, choose Style (ALT, T, Y).

2 In the Style Name box, select the style for which you want to specify a next style.

3 Choose the Define button.

4 In the Next Style box, select the name of the style you want to follow the selected style.

   If you prefer, you can type the style name in the Next Style box.

5 Choose the Change button to redefine the style in the Style Name box.

6 Choose the Close button.

Based On: One Style Controls the Format of Many

Particularly in long documents, there may be many distinct elements—several different heading levels, bulleted lists, notes, step-by-step instructions, and several types of tables. Although each element is formatted with a different style, there are probably a number of formats you want certain elements to share, such as the font and text alignment.

To help ensure consistent formatting among related styles—and make working on large style sheets easier—you can base a number of related styles on a single master or base style. For example, you can control the font of all heading styles using one base style and control the font, font size, line spacing, and alignment of all other text using a different base style. By redefining only the two base styles, you can change the font of all headings from Helvetica to Times, for example, or change all body text from justified to left-aligned text.

In the following illustration, the heading styles are all based on the style "base headings," and all body text styles are based on the style "base text." Redefining the format of the two base styles changes the format of all styles based on them, giving the document a new look.

FilmWatch Division
Marketing Plan

Introduction

The Trey Research FilmWatch Division represents Trey's best opportunity to dominate market research for the film industry. This new Trey division will be one of the first research organizations devoted exclusively to quantitative research and analysis for motion picture producers. We see two main target markets:

- Producers who want to test the appeal of actors, actresses, locations, and so forth prior to filming.

- Film companies who want to test the effect of different endings for films that have already wrapped.

Objectives

These are objectives to be realized within six months to one year of the official launch of FilmWatch as a separate division. In some cases, the objective should be achieved before FilmWatch is spun out:

- Market Perception of the Division

  FilmWatch should be perceived by the market and by the film industry trade press as the "authority" in motion picture research.

- Studio Account Sales

  Have ten of the top twenty-five independent studios signed within eighteen months.

By default, all standard styles are based on Normal style. If you redefine Normal style to use a different font, for example, the font of many standard styles such as headers, footers, and footnotes is also changed to maintain a consistent look throughout your document. If you redefine a particular standard style to use a different font, the font does not change in other standard styles. To control the formatting of some standard styles without affecting others, as in the earlier example of the heading styles, you can base selected standard styles on a style other than Normal.

Keep in mind that when you define a style based on a selected paragraph in your document, the style currently applied to the paragraph—often Normal—is used as the the default base style. For example, suppose you used the style "body text" to format text in your document. To define a new style for quotations, you select a paragraph formatted with the "body text" style, indent the paragraph from the left and right margins, and define a new style, "quote." The style "body text" is the base style for "quote." All of the formatting for the style "quote" except for the left and right indents depends on the formatting of its base style, "body text."

If you later redefine the line spacing of "body text" to be double-spaced, for example, the line spacing of "quote" is also changed to match. If you do not want a style's formatting to be linked in this way to another style in your document, you can use the Style command to break the link to the base style.

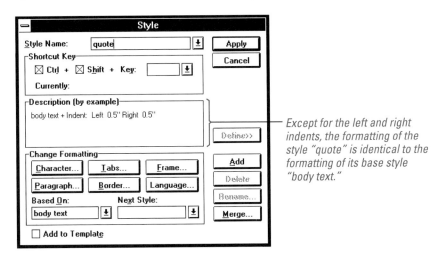

Except for the left and right indents, the formatting of the style "quote" is identical to the formatting of its base style "body text."

To create a base style

It's best to first create the base style, and then use the base style as a model to create the styles that you want to share some common formatting.

1   In your document, type a new paragraph of sample text, and then apply Normal style.

2   Apply to the paragraph the font and other formats that you want to control through the base style.

3   Use the mouse or press CTRL+S to select the style name (Normal) in the Style box on the ribbon.

4   Type a name for the new base style, and then press ENTER.

It's best to give the style a name that you can easily distinguish from the names of other styles in the document, such as "base headings style."

The new style is applied to the selected paragraph. Now you can model other styles on the base style you defined.

To base the formatting of a style on another style

Once you create a base style, you can use this procedure to create new styles that are modeled on the base style. You can also use this procedure to redefine a standard style to have a base style other than Normal.

1 In your document, select a paragraph, and then apply the style you want to use as a base style.

2 From the Format menu, choose Style (ALT, T, Y).

3 In the Style Name box, type a new name for the style.

   If you are redefining a standard style to have a base style other than Normal, type or select the name of the standard style in the Style Name box.

4 Choose the Define button.

   The new style you create will be based on the style specified in the Based On box, which is the style applied to the selected paragraph in your document.

5 Select any formats you want the new style to have in addition to the formatting it receives from the style specified in the Based On box.

6 Choose the Add button to define the style.

   Repeat steps 3 through 6 for each style you want to base on the style applied to the selected paragraph in your document.

7 Choose the Close button to close the dialog box and return to your document.

   If you choose the Apply button, Word applies the formatting of the new style only to the paragraph containing the insertion point or selection in the document.

To break the link of a style to its base style

You can break the link of a style to its base style if you don't want the style to contain the base style formatting and to be affected by changes made to the base style.

1 From the Format menu, choose Style (ALT, T, Y).

2 In the Style Name box, select the style you want disconnected from its base style.

3 Choose the Define button, and then delete the style name in the Based On box.

4 Choose the Change button to redefine the selected style.

5 Choose the Close button.

About Styles and Manual Formatting

Once you apply a style to a paragraph, you can apply additional formatting to the paragraph using the ruler, ribbon, and commands on the Format menu. To ensure consistent formatting, however, it's generally best to avoid manually changing a paragraph's format in this way. By making changes to a style instead of to an individual paragraph, you can ensure that all paragraphs to which you apply the style have the identical format. If formatting changes are needed for certain paragraphs, you can redefine the paragraphs' style or create a new style for them.

Occasionally, you may need to make minor adjustments to a few paragraphs and don't want to redefine the style or create a new style. It's helpful to understand the interaction of these extra formats with a paragraph's underlying style formatting. You can think of this additional formatting as another formatting layer applied on top of the style formatting.

Suppose you select a paragraph that is formatted using Normal style, which you have defined as 12-point Helvetica with a 0.5-inch first-line indent and double line spacing. You increase the point size to 14 points, apply bold, indent the paragraph from the left and right margins, add 10 points of space before and after, and add a border.

You later redefine Normal style as 10-point Times Roman with single line spacing, no indents, and 8 points of space after the paragraph. Changing the style has the following effects on the paragraph:

■ Formats you did not change—in this case, the font and line spacing—are still determined by the Normal style. Therefore, these formats are updated to match the new formats defined as Normal.

■ Formats that you changed from the style's formats are not updated. For example, the point size, indents, and paragraph spacing you manually applied to the paragraph override the indents, the point size, and spacing defined for the style. Additional formats you applied to the paragraph—the border and bold character format—also are not removed.

Paragraph with additional formatting

Paragraph formatted with Normal style

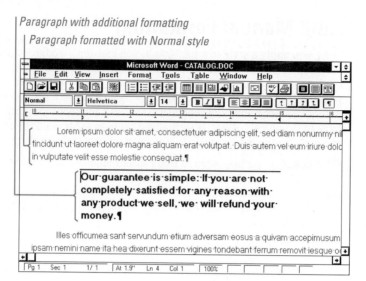

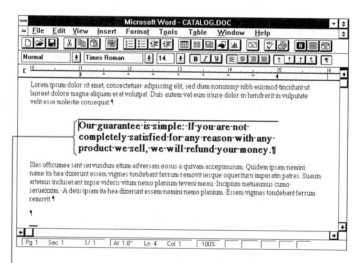

*After you redefine Normal, the font and line spacing
are updated, but other formatting isn't changed.*

To reapply a style to a paragraph

Reapplying a style to a paragraph returns all of its formatting to that defined for the style, removing any additional formats you applied using formatting commands or the ribbon or ruler.

1   Select the paragraph or paragraphs to which you want to reapply the style.

2   Use the mouse or press CTRL+S to select the style name in the Style box on the ribbon, and then press ENTER.

3   Word displays a message that asks whether you want to redefine the style based on the selection. Choose the No button.

–Or–

▶   Select the paragraph or paragraphs to which you want to reapply the style, and press CTRL+Q.

Word reapplies the original style formatting.

Styles and Character Formatting

Character formatting commands—bold, italic, strikethrough, hidden, small capital letters, and all capital letters—act like "toggle switches," turning a format on and off. For example, if you press CTRL+B to apply bold to nonbold text, you are in effect switching the option "on," making the text bold. If you then select the bold text and press CTRL+B again, you are switching the option "off," so the text is no longer bold.

Similarly, if you format a few words in a paragraph as bold, then apply a style to the paragraph that includes bold as part of its definition, all the nonbold text becomes bold, but the text that was already bold becomes nonbold. However, if you manually format most or all of the text in a paragraph as bold and then apply the style, all of the text becomes bold—the bold format defined for the style doesn't remove the bold formatting you applied manually.

Since Trey already has a reputation as the premiere consumer market research firm, we can focus positioning for **FilmWatch** around our ability/record for delivering results at the box office. Positioning here is targeted primarily at producers; secondary positioning is aimed at theater owners ("The **FilmWatch** name means box office success").

Since Trey already has a reputation as the premiere consumer market research firm, we can focus positioning for FilmWatch **around our ability/record for delivering results at the box office. Positioning here is targeted primarily at producers; secondary positioning is aimed at theater owners ("The** FilmWatch **name means box office success").**

To restore the character formatting defined by a style

When you apply a style whose definition includes the character formats described in this section, the style's character formatting may not remove the character formats that have been manually applied to text in the paragraph. Often that's desirable. When it isn't, you can use this procedure to remove manually applied character formats.

▶ Select the text, and press CTRL+SPACEBAR to remove any character formats not defined for the style of the selected paragraph.

Chapter 9

Margins, Paper Size, and Page Orientation

Word has default settings for margins, paper size, and page orientation so that you can produce attractive documents without having to change the settings. You can change the margins, paper size, or page orientation for any page of your document if you prefer different settings. To see the effect of your settings, choose the Page Layout command from the View menu.

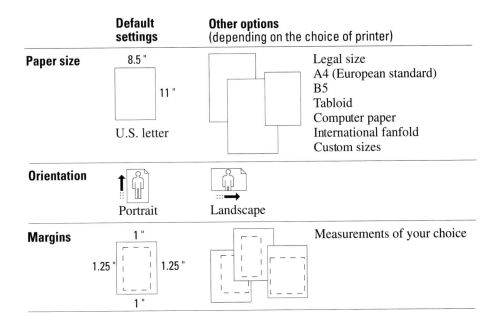

	Default settings	**Other options** (depending on the choice of printer)
Paper size	8.5" 11" U.S. letter	Legal size A4 (European standard) B5 Tabloid Computer paper International fanfold Custom sizes
Orientation	Portrait	Landscape
Margins	1" 1.25" 1.25" 1"	Measurements of your choice

Changing the Margins, Paper Size, or Page Orientation for Part of a Document

For more information on sections, see Chapter 10, "Sections: Formatting Parts of a Document."

You may want to change the margins, paper size, or page orientation for a portion of a document. For example, you may want 1-inch left and right margins for the first part of the document, 2-inch margins for the middle, and 1.5-inch margins for the end. With Word, you can divide your document into portions or *sections* and format the different sections the way you want. Sections that have a paper size or page orientation that is different from the preceding section begin on a new page.

Word stores the formatting instructions for margins, paper size, or page orientation in a section mark, which appears as a double-dotted line at the end of a section in normal view. In addition to storing formatting instructions, section marks indicate the location where formatting changes.

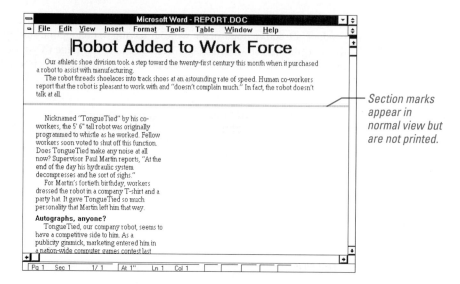

Section marks appear in normal view but are not printed.

You can use the Break command on the Insert menu to insert section breaks where you want to change the margins, paper size, or page orientation, or you can simply select the text and choose the Page Setup command from the Format menu to apply changes to the selection. Word inserts the section breaks before and after the selection for you.

Tip   If you delete a section mark, you delete the formatting instructions for the text that precedes the mark. The text becomes part of the next section and takes on the formatting of that section. If you accidentally delete a section mark, immediately choose Undo from the Edit menu. Word restores the section mark, and the section mark restores the formatting.

Working with Margins

Margins determine the distance between the text and the edges of the paper. Word prints text within the boundaries set by the margins.

Word sets margins 1 inch from the top and bottom of the page and 1.25 inches from the left and right edges of the page. You can adjust any of these settings.

There are several reasons you might want to adjust the margins in a document:

- To improve readability. Larger left and right margins create a narrower area for text. It's generally easier to read a short line of text than a long one.

- To change the length of a document. Smaller margins leave more room on each page for text and can reduce the number of pages in a long document.

- To allow room for binding. Depending on the binding method you choose, a portion of the margin is hidden by the binding. You may want to increase the margin width to compensate. Word provides an option called a gutter margin that you can set for the entire document or individual sections.

Margins vs. Indents

Margin settings affect every paragraph in a document or section, moving the text in from the edge of the page. If you want to emphasize certain paragraphs, you can indent them to set them off from the margins.

When you indent a paragraph, Word adds the indent measurement to the margin measurement. For example, if you have a 1-inch left margin and a 0.5-inch left indent, the paragraph begins 1.5 inches from the left edge of the paper. For details about setting indents, see Chapter 7, "Paragraph Formatting."

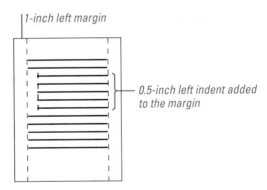

1-inch left margin

0.5-inch left indent added to the margin

Adjusting Margins

There are three ways to adjust margin settings. You may find it easiest to adjust margins in print preview, but each method has its own advantages.

This method	Affects	Advantages
Print preview	The section to which the page belongs	Drag each margin boundary where you want it, and view the effect on the entire page and document. View headers, footers, and page numbers as they appear in the margins when printed.
Ruler	The section that contains the insertion point or, if you have a selection, all selected sections	Drag the Left Margin and Right Margin markers, and continue editing text.
Page Setup command on the Format menu	Your choice of: The whole document Selected text All selected sections All text from the insertion point to the end of the document	Set precise measurements for all margins, add a gutter margin to allow extra space for binding, and create margins for facing pages.

Print preview, the ruler, and the Page Setup dialog box show the same margin settings. If you change the margins in any one of the three locations, all three reflect the change.

If your document contains tables, you may need to adjust the width of the table columns to fit within the new margins.

Adjusting Margins with the Print Preview Command

When you choose the Print Preview command, you can choose the Margins button to display margin boundary lines on the page you are previewing. Each margin boundary line ends with a square margin handle. To move a margin boundary line, drag the handle. You can drag all margin boundaries except the gutter—a special margin that reserves space for the document's binding—to the locations you want. When you drag a margin boundary line, you affect all pages in that section of the document. If you have not inserted any section breaks, your changes affect the entire document.

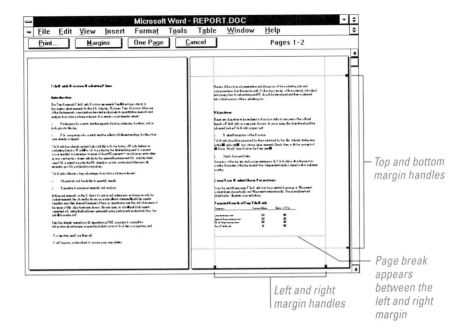

— Top and bottom margin handles

— Page break appears between the left and right margin

Left and right margin handles

To adjust margins with the Print Preview command

1   From the File menu, choose Print Preview (ALT, F, V).

2   Scroll to view the page whose margins you want to adjust.

3   Choose the Margins button to display the margins.

4   Position the mouse pointer over a margin handle. The pointer changes to cross hairs. Drag the margin handle to a new location on the page.
    –or–
    Press TAB repeatedly to move the pointer to the margin handle you want to move. Press an arrow key to move the margin, and then press ENTER.

    As you move the pointer, Word shows the margin position as a measurement in the upper-right corner of the window.

5   To view the effect of the changes, click anywhere off the page, or press ENTER.

    Word adjusts the layout to reflect the new settings.

6   Choose the Close button to exit print preview.

Tip   If you selected the Facing Pages option in the Page Setup dialog box and need to adjust the inside or outside margin, make sure you display two pages in print preview. Word displays even-numbered pages on the left and odd-numbered pages on the right, just as you would see them in a bound document. You can easily see and adjust the inside or outside margins.

You can adjust the margins with the mouse while viewing the document in print preview. You can also choose the Page Setup command from the Format menu, type the measurement you need, and then choose the OK button.

Adjusting Margins with the Ruler

You can adjust the left and right margin settings in normal or page layout view by dragging the margin markers, which appear on the ruler as brackets. Changes that you make affect the section that contains the insertion point or, if you have a selection, all sections that contain the selection.

To adjust the top or bottom margin, see "To adjust margins with the Print Preview command," earlier in this section, or "To adjust margins with the Page Setup command," later in this section.

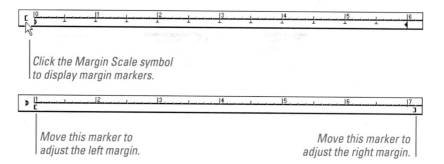

Click the Margin Scale symbol to display margin markers.

Move this marker to adjust the left margin.   *Move this marker to adjust the right margin.*

To adjust margins with the ruler

1   Position the insertion point in the section you want to change.

2   If the ruler is not displayed, choose Ruler from the View menu (ALT, V, R).

3   At the left end of the ruler, click the Margin Scale symbol to display the margin markers.

4   Drag the margin markers to change the margins the way you want.

   Word adjusts the layout of the section that contains the insertion point, or all sections that contain your selection, to reflect the new margin settings.

To display indent markers on the ruler once again, click the Indent Scale symbol at the left end of the ruler.

To see the effect your changes have on the look of the document, choose the Page Layout command from the View menu, or choose the Print Preview command from the File menu.

Changing the Margins of Multiple-Column Text

If the insertion point is in a multiple-column section of your document, the margin markers on the ruler reflect the column boundaries as well as the margins. The markers at the far left and right of the ruler control the margins. When you move the margin markers, Word adjusts the column boundaries to maintain equal-size columns and even column spacing. For more information about working with columns, see Chapter 18, "Columns."

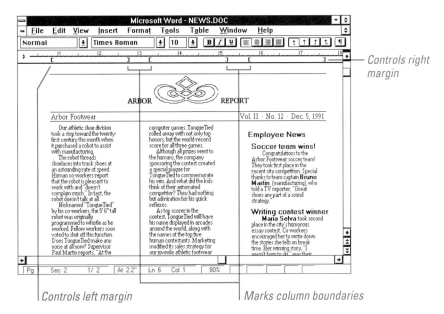

Controls right margin

Controls left margin

Marks column boundaries

Adjusting Margins with the Page Setup Command

If you want to specify the exact measurements of your margins, you can do so using the Page Setup command on the Format menu. You can select a portion of your document and change the margins, paper size, or page orientation for that portion of the document. If you have not already inserted section breaks in your document, Word inserts a section break before and after your selection. If you've already inserted section breaks, your formatting instructions affect the section that contains the insertion point or the sections that contain the selection. You can also choose to apply your formatting instructions to all text from the insertion point to the end of the document or to the entire document.

To adjust margins with the Page Setup command

1 Select the text whose margins you want to change, or position the insertion point at the point in the text where you want the margins to change.

2 From the Format menu, choose Page Setup (ALT, T, U).

3 Select the Margins option button if it's not already selected.

4 In the Top, Bottom, Left (or Inside), and Right (or Outside) boxes, type the measurements you want.

5 In the Apply To box, select one of the following. The options you see depend on the number of sections contained in the selection.

This option	Has this effect
Whole Document	Applies formatting to all sections in the document.
Selected Text	Inserts section breaks before and after the selection. The new sections always start on a new page.
This Section	Applies formatting to current section only.
Selected Sections	Applies formatting to all sections containing the selection.
This Point Forward	Inserts a section break at the location of the insertion point and applies the formatting to the new section. The new section always starts on a new page.

6 Choose the OK button.

To see the effect your changes have on the look of the document, choose the Page Layout command from the View menu, or choose the Print Preview command from the File menu.

Tip When you change the margins within a document, the text with the new margins begins on a new page. You can change the margins within a page if you prefer. To do this, position the insertion point in the section that has different margins, and choose the Section Layout command from the Format menu. In the Section Start box, select Continuous. On the page, Word sets the top and bottom margins based on the settings in the first section. The second section on the page can have different left and right margins.

Printing in the Margins

By default, Word prints page numbers and headers and footers in the margins. You can also print body text or graphics in the margins. You may need to adjust the margin setting to accommodate the text and graphics that you want to print in the margin. The following illustration shows items that you can print in the margins.

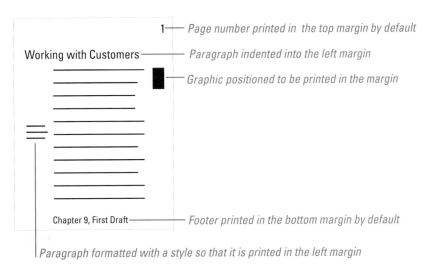

For information about printing this item in the margin	See
Text	Chapter 7, "Paragraph Formatting"
Graphics	Chapter 21, "Positioning Text and Graphics on the Page"

How Margin Settings Affect Headers and Footers

Word automatically adjusts the top and bottom margins to accommodate headers and footers that are several lines long. If you do not want Word to adjust your margin settings, type a minus sign in front of your top or bottom margin setting in the Page Setup dialog box. For example, in the Top or Bottom box, type **-1 in** to have the header or footer overlap the body text to create special effects such as watermarks.

Adjusting Margins for Facing Pages and Binding

Word provides two options that are useful when you are creating bound documents. Selecting the Facing Pages option in the Page Setup dialog box automatically changes your margin settings so that they are appropriate for two-page spreads that are held and read like a book. The Gutter option creates extra space in the margin to allow for binding.

Setting Up Facing Pages

If you select the Facing Pages check box in the Page Setup dialog box, the left and right margin labels change to read "Inside" and "Outside." The margins on odd and even pages mirror each other, as in the following illustration.

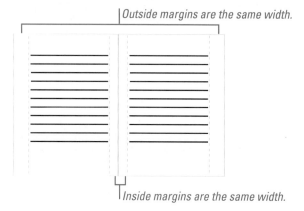

Outside margins are the same width.

Inside margins are the same width.

To set up facing pages

1   From the Format menu, choose Page Setup (ALT, T, U).

2   Select the Facing Pages check box.

3   Type the measurements you want for the margins.

    Note that Word changes the Left and Right margin options to Inside and Outside, respectively.

4   In the Apply To box, select the amount of text to which you want to apply the new page setup.

5   Choose the OK button.

To see the effect, choose the Print Preview command from the File menu.

Allowing Extra Space for Binding

If you bind pages, you may need to insert extra space in the margin to allow for the binding. This extra space is called a *gutter margin* and is hidden by the binding. Word provides a special option for creating gutter margins. You type the measurement required for the binding, and Word adds the measurement to the appropriate margins.

The following illustrations show the effect of gutter margins on single-sided and double-sided pages.

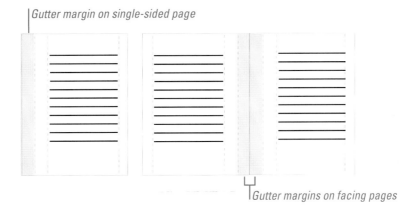

Gutter margin on single-sided page

Gutter margins on facing pages

To add gutter margins

1   From the Format menu, choose Page Setup (ALT, T, U).

2   In the Gutter box, type or select a measurement.

3   In the Apply To box, select the amount of text to which you want to add gutter margins.

4   Choose the OK button.

> Word adds the gutter measurement to the appropriate margins.

To see the effect your changes have on the look of the document, choose the Print Preview command from the File menu.

Changing the Paper Size

When you choose the Page Setup command and select the Size And Orientation option button, the dialog box lists the paper sizes that your printer provides. If you want a custom size, you can type the measurements you need. You can print all or part of a document on a particular paper size.

The paper sizes provided by your printer appear when you drop down this list.

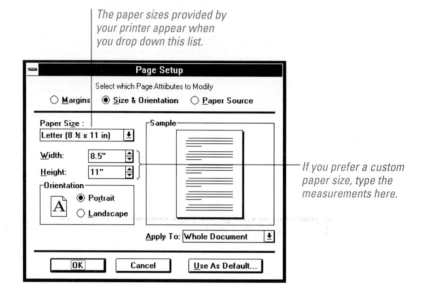

If you prefer a custom paper size, type the measurements here.

To select a paper size

1   Select the text you want to print on a particular paper size, or position the insertion point where you want to begin printing on a particular paper size.

2   From the Format menu, choose Page Setup (ALT, T, U).

3   Select the Size And Orientation option button.

4   In the Paper Size box, select the paper size on which you want to print.
    −or−
    In the Width and Height boxes, type or select the measurements you want.

    You can type **in** or **"** for inches, or **cm** for centimeters. If you do not type a unit of measurement, Word uses the default, which is inches unless you change it.

5   In the Apply To box, select how much of your document you want to print on this particular paper.

6   Choose the OK button.

To see the effect your changes have on the look of the document, choose the Page Layout command from the View menu, or choose the Print Preview command from the File menu.

Changing the Page Orientation

Word offers you a choice between *portrait* (vertical) and *landscape* (horizontal) page orientations. You can change the orientation within a document so that some pages are portrait and others are landscape.

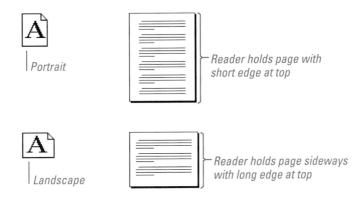

To change the page orientation

1   If you want to change the page orientation for a portion of your document, select the text, or position the insertion point in the section you want to change.

2   From the Format menu, choose Page Setup (ALT, T, U).

3   Select the Size And Orientation option button.

4   Under Orientation, select the Portrait or Landscape option button, and in the Apply To box, select the amount of text you want to print with the new orientation.

    The sample in the right of the dialog box reflects the change.

5   Choose the OK button.

To see the overall effect your changes have on the look of the document, choose the Print Preview command from the File menu.

When you change the page orientation, Word automatically transfers the default top and bottom margin measurements to the Left and Right margin boxes and vice versa as shown in the following illustration.

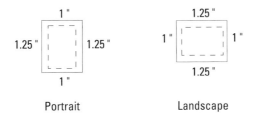

Portrait   Landscape

Changing the Default Margins, Paper Size, or Page Orientation

For more information about document templates, see Chapter 37, "Document Templates."

When you begin a document, Word assumes you will print on paper that is 8.5 by 11 inches in portrait orientation, with 1-inch top and bottom margins and 1.25-inch left and right margins. If you usually print on paper that is a different size, in landscape orientation, or with different margin settings, you can save time by changing the defaults. When you choose the Use As Default button in the following procedure, Word stores the default settings with the current template. If your current document is based on NORMAL.DOT template, each new document based on NORMAL.DOT automatically has the margins, paper size, and page orientation you prefer.

Note   The default values for margins and paper size may differ in non-U.S. versions of Word.

To change the default margins, paper size, or page orientation

1   From the File menu, choose New (ALT, F, N) to create a new document.

2   From the Format menu, choose Page Setup (ALT, T, U).

3   Select the appropriate option button under Select Which Page Attributes To Modify, and then type the measurements you want, or select any options you want.

4   Choose the Use As Default button.

5   Choose the Yes button.

New documents you create will have the default settings you specified. You can change any of these settings at any time by using the Page Setup command and typing or selecting the settings you prefer.

Sections: Formatting Parts of a Document

You can divide a document into any number of sections and format each section as you like. A section can be as short as a single paragraph—for example, a banner headline in a newsletter—or as long as an entire document. You decide where each section begins and ends.

When you begin a document, there are no section breaks. You create a new section when you want to change any of the following elements in part of a document:

- Margins, paper size, or page orientation
- Number of newspaper-style columns
- Format, position, and sequence of page numbers
- Contents and position of headers and footers
- Line numbering
- Location where footnotes are printed

Changing Formatting Within a Document

The following illustration shows a document with two sections. Each section is formatted with a different number of columns. The section break that divides the two sections is displayed on the screen in normal view but does not show when the document is printed.

For more information
about newspaper-
style columns, see
Chapter 18,
"Columns."

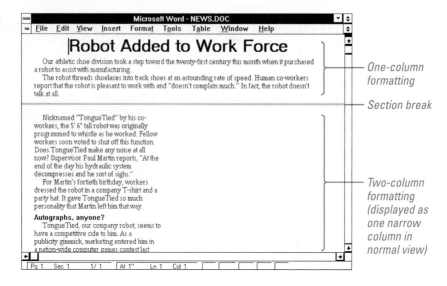

One-column
formatting

Section break

Two-column
formatting
(displayed as
one narrow
column in
normal view)

Tip To create side-by-side paragraphs (sometimes called parallel columns), you do
not need to create a new section. The table feature in Word is the easiest way to create
side-by-side paragraphs. For more information, see Chapter 17, "Tables."

To insert a section break

1   Position the insertion point where you want the new section to start.

2   From the Insert menu, choose Break (ALT, I, B).

3   Under Section Break, select where you want the new section to begin.

    For an explanation of the available options, see "Controlling Section Breaks," later
    in this chapter.

4   Choose the OK button.

In normal view, Word inserts a double-dotted line at the location of the insertion point
to mark the end of the previous section. If you insert the section break at the end of the
document, Word creates a new section beginning there. The insertion point moves into
the new section.

Tip   All section formatting is stored in the section mark. When you delete a section mark, you delete the section formatting for the text that *precedes* it. The text becomes part of the section that follows, and it assumes the formatting characteristics of that section.

If you accidentally delete a section mark, immediately choose the Undo command from the Edit menu. Word restores the section mark, and the section mark restores the section formatting. You must choose Undo before performing any other action.

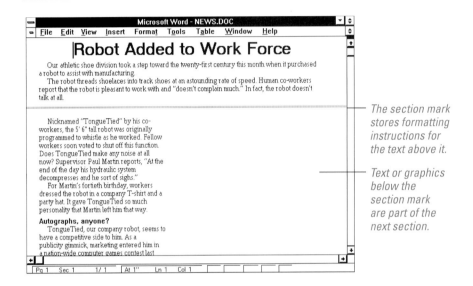

The section mark stores formatting instructions for the text above it.

Text or graphics below the section mark are part of the next section.

To remove a section break

1   Position the insertion point on the section mark.

2   Press DEL.

Tip You can copy section formatting by copying the section mark. When you paste the section mark in a new location, the text above the section mark takes on the formatting instructions contained in the section mark.

You can save the section mark and the formatting instructions it contains as a glossary entry for future use. For more information, see Chapter 13, "Glossaries: Storing Items for Reuse."

To format a section

1 Position the insertion point anywhere in the section you want to format.

2 Choose one or more of the following commands and set the options you want:

Menu	Command	Key sequence
Format	Page Setup	ALT, T, U
Format	Columns	ALT, T, O
Format	Section Layout	ALT, T, S
View	Header/Footer	ALT, V, H
Insert	Page Numbers	ALT, I, U

Tip You can display the Section Layout dialog box by double-clicking a section mark. The dialog box displays formatting instructions for text that precedes the section mark.

Controlling Section Breaks

You decide where you want a section to begin: on a new page, on the next odd or even page, or on the same page as the end of the preceding section. In the following illustrations, the dotted line indicates a section break.

This option	Has this effect	
Next Page	Word breaks the page at the section mark. The next section starts on the next page.	
Continuous	Word fills the last page of the previous section with text from the new section. If there are multiple columns in the previous section, Word balances the columns above the section mark and then fills out the page with the new section. If the previous section contains footnotes, the new section will start on a new page even if you have selected Continuous.	
Odd Page	Word starts printing the text of the section on the next odd-numbered page. This section break is often used for chapters that begin on odd-numbered pages. If the section break falls on an odd-numbered page, Word leaves the next even-numbered page blank.	

(continued)

This option	Has this effect
Even Page	Similar to Odd Page, but Word starts printing the text of the section on the next even-numbered page. If the section break falls on an even-numbered page, Word leaves the next odd-numbered page blank.

Shortcuts for Formatting Sections

When you begin a document, it is all one section. Any section formatting applies to the entire document. You can use this to your advantage to get a head start on formatting all sections.

Before you divide the document into sections, set the formatting options that apply to most of the sections. For example, if you want most of the sections to begin without page breaks, choose the Continuous option in the Section Layout dialog box. If you want most of the document to be two-column format, set that option. If you want to have the same header or footer for most of the sections, create it now.

Next, divide the document into sections. Each section will have the settings you just set. You can customize the formatting of each section as you need to, building on the basic section formatting.

If you know you'll be creating many documents similar to one you've already formatted, give yourself a head start by saving the formatting, along with any reusable text and graphics, as a template—a pattern for future documents. For more information, see Chapter 37, "Document Templates."

Examples of Section Formatting

The following examples show section formatting possibilities. (Section marks are shown here for example only; they do not show when the document is printed.)

For more information, see Chapter 9, "Margins, Paper Size, and Page Orientation."

Margins, paper size, and page orientation   You can change the margins, paper size, or page orientation for different sections of a document to allow for charts, graphics, or special layouts.

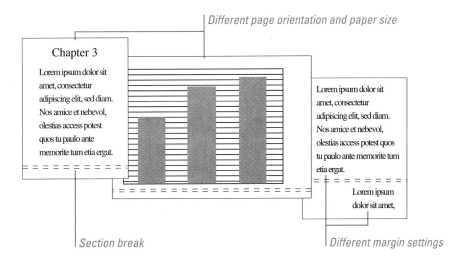

For more information, see Chapter 30, "Headers and Footers."

Headers and footers   A header (sometimes called a running head) is text that appears in the top margin area of every page of a section; a footer appears in the bottom margin area of every page of a section. You can create a different header and footer for each section in a document.

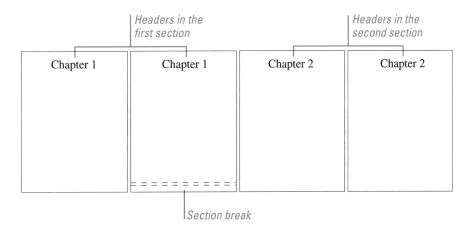

Tip   A header or footer can include the date and time of printing as well as the page number. Word automatically updates these for you. For information about these and other items you can include in headers and footers, see Chapter 30, "Headers and Footers."

For more information, see Chapter 28, "Adding Bullets and Numbers."

Line numbers   You can number lines for an entire document or for certain sections. This is useful for legal documents, scripts, and poems.

By default, Word restarts line numbers at 1 on every page. You can modify this setting to number lines continuously throughout a section or throughout the entire document.

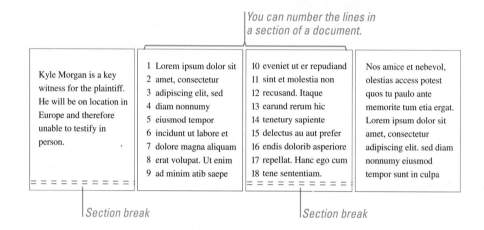

You can number the lines in a section of a document.

Section break

Section break

For more information, see Chapter 22, "Numbering Pages."

Page numbers   You control where page numbers appear on the page, which pages they appear on, the numbering format (arabic numbers, roman numerals, or letters), and the numbering sequence. You can vary the numbering format, position, and sequence from one section to another. For example, you can assign lowercase roman numerals to the front matter of a book (introduction, table of contents, and so on) and arabic numbers to the main text—as in the following illustration.

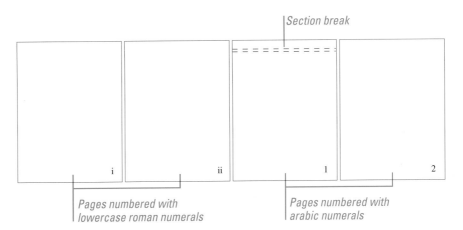

Section break

i   ii   1   2

Pages numbered with lowercase roman numerals

Pages numbered with arabic numerals

For more information, see Chapter 31, "Footnotes, Annotations, and Revision Marks."

Footnotes   You can choose between printing footnotes on the same page as their footnote reference marks and printing at the end of a section or document. (When printed at the end, they are sometimes called endnotes.) You can choose not to include footnotes in a particular section, and collect them and print them in a later section.

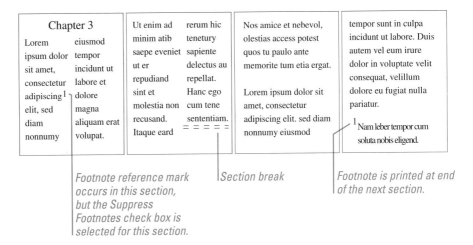

Footnote reference mark occurs in this section, but the Suppress Footnotes check box is selected for this section.

Section break

Footnote is printed at end of the next section.

Storing Section Formatting for Reuse

With the preset section formats, you can produce attractive documents without having to change any formats. However, if you always change the section formats for a particular type of document, you can save time by saving the section formatting in a template. New documents based on the template will automatically have the same section formats as the template.

The section defaults are as follows.

Section formatting option	Default
Page Setup	
Margins	1" top and bottom, 1.25" left and right
Paper Size	Letter (8.5" by 11")
Orientation	Portrait
Columns	
Number Of Columns	1
Space Between	0.5"
Section Layout	
Suppress Footnotes	Cleared
Add Line Numbering	Cleared
Count By (if Add Line Numbering is selected)	1
Header/Footer	
From Edge	0.5" for header, 0.5" for footer
Different First Page	Cleared
Different Odd And Even Pages	Cleared
Page Numbers	
Position	Bottom Of Page (Footer)
Alignment	Right
Number Format	1 2 3...

To store section formatting for reuse

1   Format each section of a document with settings you want in future documents.

2   Delete any text or graphics that you do not want to use in future documents, but do not delete the section marks (double-dotted lines in normal view).

3   From the File menu, choose Save As (ALT, F, A).

4   Type a name for the template.

5   In the Save File As Type box, select Document Template.

6   Choose the OK button.

When you want to create a document with these settings, you begin in the usual way, by choosing New from the File menu. In the Use Template box, select the name of your template. The new document has the same section formatting as the template.

Chapter 11

Setting Up Long Documents

You can create documents of any length with Word. If you are creating documents longer than 20 pages, it is helpful to do a little planning before you begin.

When you plan a long document, there are two main considerations: controlling the formatting throughout the document and increasing efficiency as you work. This chapter suggests ways to do both and refers you to chapters that provide specific procedures.

Controlling the Formatting of a Long Document

Word provides several methods to ensure consistent formatting in long documents while maintaining the flexibility you need. Consider these suggestions:

For more information, see Chapter 37, "Document Templates."

Create a template   If your document is longer than 20 pages, consider creating several smaller documents. Complete your work in the smaller documents. To ensure that all of the documents have the same formatting, create a template that has the formatting and options you want. When you create a new document in the series, base it on the template so the new document has the same formatting.

For more information, see Chapter 8, "Formatting with Styles."

Create styles   Format a paragraph of body text in your document to look exactly the way you want it. Then save the formatting as the Normal style for that template. Word applies the Normal style automatically as you type. Create your own styles for all elements of the document except the headings and subheadings. For these, it's better to customize the automatic styles.

Create all the styles you need, and save them in the template for the long document. If you must make substantial formatting changes to the document, change the styles and apply the changes to the template; then you can easily merge the template's styles into the documents that are based on the template.

For more information, see Chapter 29, "Indexes and Tables of Contents," and Chapter 27, "Outline View: Creating Outlines and Reorganizing Documents."

Use automatic heading styles   Word provides automatic heading styles—named Heading 1 through Heading 9—that you can change to match your design. Use automatic styles to:

- Create a table of contents.

- Display an outline of the document.

- Expand the outline to view the text below each heading.

- Reorganize the document by dragging a heading to a new location in the outline. The text below the heading moves with its heading.

For more information,
see Chapter 13,
"Glossaries: Storing
Items for Reuse."

Store text and graphics as glossary entries   You can store frequently used text and graphics (sometimes referred to as boilerplate text) so that you can quickly insert them into your document without having to retype them. You can store the formatting or style with the glossary entry.

Examples of glossary entries include proper names, copyright notices, addresses, and unusually formatted text that you use often. Glossaries save you time, reduce typographical errors, and help ensure consistency throughout a long document.

Saving a Long Document

It's especially important to save your work regularly when working on long documents. If you'd like Word to automatically save a document at regular intervals as you work, choose Options from the Tools menu. Select the Save category, and type or select the number of minutes you want between automatic saves.

Word normally performs a "fast save," which saves time as you work but may consume disk space. If you need to conserve disk space, choose the Options command from the Tools menu. Select the Save category, and then clear the Allow Fast Saves check box. You may notice that saving takes a moment longer, but your document takes up the smallest possible amount of disk space.

For more information,
see Chapter 10,
"Sections:
Formatting Parts of a
Document."

Long documents are often organized into chapters or other sections. If each major section or chapter of your document is approximately 20 pages long or longer, it's a good idea to divide the document into separate, smaller documents. However, if the sections or chapters are short and you prefer to keep them in one document, you can do so and still format each section as you like. A section is a part of a document in which page layout and other settings differ from those in other parts of the document.

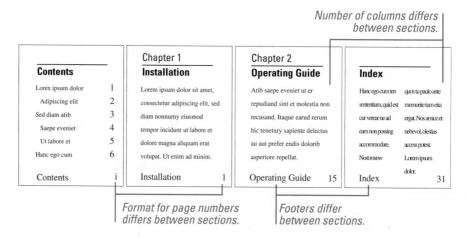

In this example, the table of contents, index, and each chapter are separate sections, formatted to begin on odd-numbered pages.

When you begin a document, there are no section breaks. You create a new section when you want to change the following elements in part of a document:

- The margins, paper size, or page orientation

- The number of newspaper-style columns

- The format, position, or sequence of page numbers

- The contents or position of headers or footers

- The line numbering

- The location where footnotes are printed

You insert a section break to indicate where new formatting or numbering should begin. Then, to change the formatting or numbering, you move the insertion point into the section you want to work with and make your changes.

Tip   If you want to print information about the current version of a draft on every page, you can create a header or footer that shows the name of the writer, the time and date printed, and other pertinent information. Format the header or footer text as hidden text. Print the drafts with hidden text displayed. When you are ready to print the final version, make sure you print it without hidden text displayed.

Improving Efficiency as You Work

You can work most efficiently if you keep your documents relatively short. The optimum length may be about 20 pages, or it may be as much as 50 pages—it depends on the memory in your computer and the complexity of your document. Generally, the more graphics, fields, bookmarks, and formatting you apply, the more you need to keep your file size to a minimum.

There are two methods for working with long documents. For either, you divide the long document into shorter documents. In one method, you combine the shorter documents before you print them. In the other method, you print them separately. Either way, you can create a table of contents and index. Whether you should combine the shorter documents or print them separately depends on the length of your finished document and your computer's memory. These are the two methods:

- Create a master document that contains INCLUDE fields. The fields refer to other documents you've created. When you are ready to print, the INCLUDE fields combine the text of the shorter documents. Page numbers, line numbers, and footnote numbers are automatically numbered sequentially. For details, see "Using INCLUDE to Assemble a Long Document," later in this chapter.

- Divide a very long document into several smaller documents, and then edit and print them separately. You can adjust the starting page numbers, line numbers, and footnote numbers in each of the shorter files so the finished document looks like one document. For details, see "Editing and Printing Portions of a Long Document," later in this chapter.

Tip It takes extra memory to display graphics as you work. Displaying graphics can also slow scrolling and slow some commands such as the Find command and the Spelling command. To work more efficiently, display placeholders instead of the real graphics. Choose the Options command from the Tools menu, and select the Picture Placeholders check box (View category). This option speeds up scrolling and does not affect the way graphics are printed.

Using INCLUDE to Assemble a Long Document

The INCLUDE field makes it possible to divide a long document into shorter pieces for editing but print them as though they were all one document. These shorter pieces are easier to handle because they make fewer demands on your computer's memory, and they are faster to open and save.

Once you divide a long document into separate files (for example, PART1.DOC, PART2.DOC, and PART3.DOC), you create a master document that contains only a list of INCLUDE fields. Each INCLUDE field contains the name of one of the pieces of your document. For example:

```
{include part1.doc}
{include part2.doc}
{include part3.doc}
```

The INCLUDE fields are special codes that instruct Word to insert into the document the item named in the code. In the master document, you can display either the field codes themselves or the results of the codes—the text and graphics that they insert—by choosing or clearing the Field Codes command from the View menu.

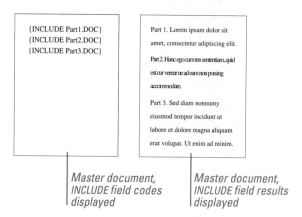

Master document,
INCLUDE field codes
displayed

Master document,
INCLUDE field results
displayed

When ready to print, you update each INCLUDE field to get the latest version of the document named by pressing the Update Field key (F9) while the insertion point is within the field.

Tip   For last-minute changes before you print, you can combine the shorter documents in the master document and then edit the text. Then you can select all text and press the Update Source key (CTRL+SHIFT+F7) to copy any editing changes you have made back to the original documents. For example, after editing part 1 of the master document, you display and select the field code {include part1.doc}. When you press CTRL+SHIFT+F7, Word copies the changes to the shorter PART1.DOC.

You can also use an INCLUDE field within a document as shown in the following illustration. With this method, you can store a portion of a document in a separate file. When you print, you instruct Word to include the separate file, and it is printed as an integral part of the document.

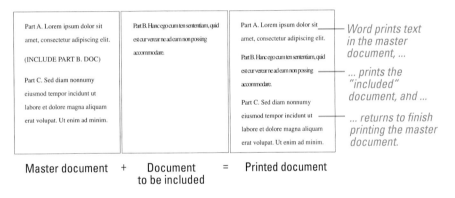

Master document   +   Document   =   Printed document
                       to be included

Tip   If you do not want to include all of a document in another document, you can mark the portion you want to include with a bookmark and use an INCLUDE field that specifies the file and the bookmark. For more information, see Chapter 40, "Bookmarks and Cross-references."

To set up a master document

1   Divide the large document into smaller files, and save each file with a new name.

For example, you might call them PART1.DOC, PART2.DOC, and PART3.DOC. These are called *source files*.

2   Open a new document.

This will be the master document.

3   From the Insert menu, choose Field (ALT, I, D).

4   In the Insert Field Type box, select Include.

5   In the Field Codes box, after the word "include," type the filename for the first of the documents.

For example, type **part1.doc** after "include."

6   Choose the OK button.

You can choose Field Codes from the View menu to display either the INCLUDE field or the results of the field code—the text and graphics from the shorter documents.

7   Press ENTER to begin a new paragraph.

8   Repeat steps 3 through 7 to include each of the shorter documents.

9   From the File menu, choose Save As (ALT, F, A), and type a name in the File Name box.

For example, type **MASTER.DOC**

10 Choose the OK button.

If Word displays the Summary Info dialog box, type any of the optional information you want to record, and then choose the OK button.

To print a master document

It does not matter if you have the field codes or the results displayed in the master document. Word prints the text.

1   From the File menu, choose Print (ALT, F, P).

2   Select the Options button.

3   Under Printing Options, select the Update Fields check box, and the master document incorporates all changes made to the shorter files.

4   Choose the OK button.

5   To print the master document, choose the OK button.

Tips for Working Efficiently

There are several things you can do to speed up your work on long documents. First, have a minimum of other applications running—especially applications that run in the background.

Next, consider working in draft mode. You can combine draft mode with normal view or outline view. Either combination displays text in the system font and point size. Formatting is indicated with underlines, and pictures are displayed as frames. For example, you can choose the Draft command from the View menu, type and edit without displaying character formatting or graphics, and then choose the Draft command again to see your formatting and graphics. Page layout view is the only view that you cannot combine with draft mode. Page layout view always displays formatting.

Finally, consider working without background repagination. You do not see accurate page breaks until you choose Repaginate Now from the Tools menu. To clear background repagination, choose Options from the Tools menu. In the General category, clear the Background Repagination check box.

Editing and Printing Portions of a Long Document

If your final document is very long—for example, an entire book—it's best to divide it into several smaller documents that you edit and print separately.

You can set a starting page number for each file in the series of documents so that the pages are numbered in proper sequence. You can then compile a table of contents and an index as if the series of documents is a whole document. Page references in the index and the table of contents are numbered as if the document were one long file. The index and table of contents are printed in their entirety; text files, however, must be printed individually.

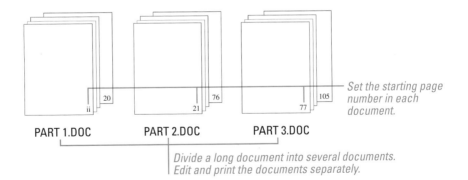

PART 1.DOC   PART 2.DOC   PART 3.DOC

Set the starting page number in each document.

*Divide a long document into several documents.
Edit and print the documents separately.*

Numbering Items Sequentially Across Documents

You can set starting numbers for pages, paragraphs, lines, and footnotes in each document so the items are numbered sequentially across several documents. You can also number tables, figures, photos, or any other sequence of items by using the SEQ field. To continue the numbering in the next document, you note the ending number in the first document and manually set the starting number in the second. You do the same for all remaining documents. Word does not adjust the starting numbers for these items. To save time, set these numbers after your editing is complete so you don't need to change any of the numbering.

Before setting your starting numbers, make sure your line breaks and page breaks are correct.

To ensure correct line breaks and page breaks

The following commands affect line breaks and page breaks. For each document in the series, set the options the way you want them for printing, and then set the starting page and line numbers. This ensures that the page numbers and line breaks you see on the screen match your printout.

▶   Do one or more of the following:

To confirm that	Use this command
The correct printer is selected	Print Setup (File menu).
Margins, paper size, and page orientation are set as you want them	Page Setup (Format menu).
The Hidden Text option is set as you want it	Print (File menu). Choose the Options button to check the setting for hidden text. Choose the Close or Cancel button to close the Print dialog box.
Field codes or their results are displayed as you want them printed	Field Codes (View menu).

Note   The two following procedures are unnecessary if you are creating a long document from a master document with INCLUDE fields. Use them only if you are printing separate documents.

To set starting numbers for a multiple-file document

Before beginning this procedure, make sure the status bar is displayed on the bottom of your screen. If it is not, choose Options from the Tools menu (ALT, O, O). Then choose the View category and, under Window, select the Status Bar check box. Choose the OK button to close the dialog box.

1   Open the first document in the series.

2   From the Tools menu, choose Repaginate Now (ALT, O, A).

3   When repagination is complete, do one or more of the following to ascertain the ending numbers in your first document.

If you are setting	Do this
Page or line numbers	Place the insertion point in the last line of the document, and note the page and line numbers in the status bar at the bottom of the screen.
Footnote numbers	Choose Footnotes from the View menu (ALT, V, F), and then scroll until you see the last footnote. Note the number.
Paragraph numbers	Note the last numbered paragraph in the document.
Numbers for photos, tables, or figures keyed to SEQ fields	From the View menu, choose Field Codes (if necessary) to display the numbers (field results) in the SEQ field. From the Edit menu, choose the Find command (ALT, E, F) to locate the last SEQ field of each type in the document. Note the last number in each sequence.

4   From the File menu, choose Save (ALT, F, S) to save the repagination.

5   Open the file for the next document in the series.

6   Choose the following commands as appropriate, and enter the starting numbers based on the ending numbers in the preceding document.

If you are setting	Follow these steps
Page numbers	This procedure assumes you've already inserted page numbers in each of the shorter documents.
	From the Insert menu, choose Page Numbers (ALT, I, U), and select the Format button. In the Start At box, type or select the page number following the last page number you observed in the status bar for the preceding file. Choose the OK button twice.
Footnote numbers	From the Insert menu, choose Footnote (ALT, I, N), and select the Options button. In the Start At box, type or select the footnote number following the last footnote number in the preceding file. Choose the OK button to close the Footnote Options dialog box, and then choose the Close button to close the Footnote dialog box.
Line numbers	This procedure assumes you've numbered lines in several documents in the series.
	From the Format menu, choose Section Layout (ALT, T, S), and select the Line Numbers button. In the Start At # box, type or select the line number following the number of the last line in the preceding file. Under Restart At, select the Continue option button. Choose the OK button twice.
Paragraph numbers	Select the first group of paragraphs you want to number or renumber. From the Tools menu, choose Bullets And Numbering (ALT, O, B), and select the Numbered List option button. In the Start At box, type the number following the number of the last numbered paragraph in the preceding file. Choose the OK button.
Numbers for sequences of items	If fields are not displayed in the document, choose Field Codes from the View menu (ALT, V, C). In the first SEQ field, type \r followed by the next number in the sequence. For example, to start a sequence of photos at number seven, edit the field {seq photos} to read {seq photos \r7} Set a starting number for each separate sequence in the document.

For more information, see Chapter 22, "Numbering Pages"

For details on numbering lines or paragraphs, see Chapter 28, "Adding Bullets and Numbers."

For more information about the SEQ field, see the SEQ field topic in online Help.

7   Open the next document in the series and repeat steps 2 through 6. Do this for all documents in the order in which you want to print them.

Tip   To save time as you set starting numbers, open the first and then the second document. Choose Arrange All from the Window menu. Word arranges the windows so you can see both documents at once. You can check the ending numbers in the first document and immediately set starting numbers in the second. When you're ready to set starting numbers in the third document, close the first file, open the third file, and choose the Arrange All command from the Window menu.

To print several documents at one time

You can use the Find File command to print several files.

1   From the File menu, choose Find File (ALT, F, F).

Word searches for documents in the path you last specified in the Search dialog box. If a document you want is not listed, choose the Search button, and type the correct path in the Path box. Then choose the Start Search button.

For more information about the Find File command, see Chapter 26, "Finding and Managing Files."

2   Click the first file you want to print; then hold down CTRL while clicking each additional file you want to print.

If you make a mistake, hold down CTRL and click any selected filename to remove the selection.

3   Choose the Print button.

4   Set the options as you want them, and then choose the OK button.

1   From the File menu, choose Find File (ALT, F, F).

Word searches for documents in the path you last specified in the Search dialog box. If a document you want is not listed, choose the Search button, and type the correct path in the Path box. Then choose the Start Search button.

2   Press the DOWN ARROW or UP ARROW key until the name of the first file you want to print is highlighted. Then press SHIFT+F8.

3   Press the DOWN ARROW or UP ARROW key to place a dotted frame around the next filename you want to print, and then press the SPACEBAR.

4   Repeat step 3 for each additional file you want to print.

If you make a mistake, press an arrow key to move to the filename again, and then press the SPACEBAR to remove the selection.

5   Choose the Print button.

6   Set the options as you want them, and then choose the OK button.

File Management

A long printed document—such as a book—may consist of more than one file, and several people may work on the same document. To help manage your documents, use the Summary Info command on the File menu to record important information about each document. You can use the Find File command to locate documents if you don't remember where they are stored. For more information, see Chapter 26, "Finding and Managing Files."

Creating an Index or Table of Contents

For more information, see Chapter 29, "Indexes and Tables of Contents."

There are several ways to create a table of contents or index. The method you choose depends on the length of the document, your computer's memory, and in the case of an index, the length of the index itself.

When you use INCLUDE fields to compile a long document, you can create a table of contents or index using the commands on the Insert menu. If you run into memory limitations, you can use the Referenced Document (RD) field to compile the table of contents or index separately from the text of the document.

For information on using the RD field, see the RD field topic in online Help.

If your document is very long—a book, for example—and you print it in shorter, separate documents, set a starting page number in each of the separate documents, and then use the RD field to compile the index and table of contents. Word searches each of the documents for entries and prints the index or table of contents as though the separate documents were one.

Indexes with more than 4,000 entries require considerable memory and should be compiled in several parts—for example, A through J, K through S, and T through Z.

Chapter 12

Finding and Replacing Text or Formatting

When you need to review or change text in your document, use the Find and Replace commands on the Edit menu. Use Find to quickly locate occurrences of the text you specify. To change a certain word or phrase used throughout your document, use Replace to make all the changes quickly and accurately. With Find and Replace, you can:

- Find all occurrences of a certain word, phrase, or sequence of characters.

- Find text that has a certain format, such as bold. You can replace the text with different text and also change the formatting. For example, you can replace Arbor Shoes Company with `Arbor Shoes, Inc.`

- Find and replace special characters such as tab characters, optional hyphens, and paragraph marks.

Finding and Replacing Text

When you use Find and Replace, you can have Word find only text that makes up a whole word or that has a certain pattern of capitalization. For example, you can find "and" but skip "candle" and "band" or find all occurrences of the name "Green" but skip the color "green."

Word normally searches the main text of the document that is displayed on the screen. To include hidden text in the search, make sure the hidden text is displayed. To display hidden text, select the Hidden Text check box under Nonprinting Characters, a View option in the Options dialog box (Tools menu).

To find text

Word searches for the specified text throughout the main text of the document unless you select the part of the document you want searched.

1   From the Edit menu, choose Find (ALT, E, F).

2   In the Find What box, type the text you're searching for.

If you used Find or Replace in your current work session, the text you last searched for is selected in the Find What box. Type over the text to find different text.

You can type up to 255 characters in the Find What box. Text scrolls horizontally in the box as you type.

If text formats are listed below the Find What box, choose the Clear button. Otherwise, Word finds only occurrences of the text having the listed formats.

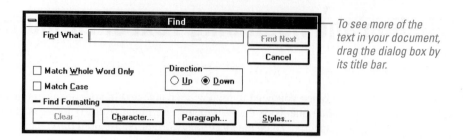

To see more of the text in your document, drag the dialog box by its title bar.

3   Select any options you want to control how Word searches through your document.

To	Select
Find only separate words, not characters embedded in other words. For example, select this option to find "act" but not "acting."	Match Whole Word Only
Find only words having a certain pattern of uppercase and lowercase letters. For example, select this option to find "Act" but not "act."	Match Case
Search up or down in the document from the current position of the insertion point.	Up or Down under Direction

4   Choose the Find Next button to begin searching.

Word selects the first occurrence of the text and scrolls to it in the document so you can see the text in your document. To find the next occurrence of the text, choose the Find Next button again.

To edit the found text, choose the Cancel button. To continue the search after editing the found text, press SHIFT+F4, or choose Find from the Edit menu again, and then choose the Find Next button.

If you began the search from the middle of the document, Word searches from the current position of the insertion point to either the end or to the beginning of the document and then asks if you want to continue the search. Choose the OK button to search through the remainder of the document, or choose the Cancel button to stop searching. When all text is searched, Word notifies you that it's reached the end of the document.

To replace text

Word replaces the specified text throughout the document unless you select a part of the document. If you're making major changes, it's a good idea to save your document before you start replacing. That way, if you don't like the results, you can close the document without saving the changes.

1   From the Edit menu, choose Replace (ALT, E, E).

2   In the Find What box, type the text you want to find.

If you used Find or Replace in your current work session, the text you last searched for is selected in the Find What box. Type over the text to find different text.

If text formats are listed below the Find What box, choose the Clear button unless you want to find only occurrences of the text that have that formatting.

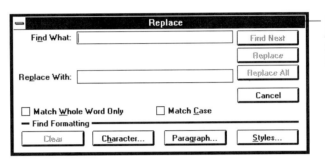

To see more of the text in your document, drag the dialog box by its title bar.

3   In the Replace With box, type the replacement characters.

If you used Replace in your current work session, the replacement characters you last specified are selected in the Replace With box. Type over the text to specify different replacement characters.

You can type up to 255 characters in the Replace With box. Text scrolls horizontally in the box as you type.

If text formats are listed below the Replace With box, choose the Clear button unless you want to change the formatting of the found text.

4   Select any options you want to control the changes Word makes in your document.

To	Select
Change only whole words, not the sequence of characters occurring in other words	Match Whole Word Only
Change only words having a certain pattern of uppercase and lowercase letters	Match Case

5   To begin searching, choose the Find Next or Replace All button.

To	Choose this button
Confirm each change	Find Next. When Word finds an occurrence of the search text, choose the Replace button to change the text or choose the Find Next button to continue without changing this occurrence.
Change all occurrences of the search text without confirmation	Replace All. If you selected a range of text, Word makes changes only in selected part of the document.

To cancel replacing

▶   To cancel replacing when you have chosen the Replace All button, press ESC. Choose Undo from the Edit menu (ALT, E, U) to reverse any changes made prior to pressing ESC.

To delete text with Replace

You should save your document before deleting text with the Replace command. That way, if you delete the wrong text, you can close the document without saving the changes.

1   From the Edit menu, choose Replace (ALT, E, E).

2   In the Find What box, type the text you want to find and delete.

3   Delete any text in the Replace With box.

4   If formats are shown below the Replace With box, choose the Clear button.

If formats are specified, Word changes the format of the found text instead of deleting it.

5   Choose the Find Next or Replace All button.

To search again for the same text

After using Find or Replace, you can continue searching for the same text.

▶   Press SHIFT+F4.

To undo changes completed with Replace

▶   To undo the effects of the Replace command, choose Undo from the Edit menu (ALT, E, U) as the first action after completing the changes.

Only the last change is reversed if you confirmed each change separately (that is, if you chose Find Next to start the search). All changes are reversed if you made the changes in one step (that is, if you chose the Replace All button).

Find and Replace Dialog Box Options

These options control the effects of the Find and Replace commands.

Match Whole Word Only   With this option selected, Word finds only whole words. If you're searching for the word "his," for example, select this option to avoid finding the characters "his" in such words as "this" and "whisper." Without this option selected, Word finds any sequence of characters matching the search text.

Match Case   With this option selected, Word observes the pattern of uppercase and lowercase letters exactly as you type the search and replacement characters in the Find What and Replace With boxes. If you type "Catering" as the search text, Word finds "Catering" but ignores "CATERING" and "catering." Without Match Case selected, Word finds all instances of the search characters, regardless of the case of the letters.

If you replace text with the Match Case option cleared, the case of the replacement characters matches the case of the found text occurrence. For example, if you replace "if" with "when," Word replaces "If" at the beginning of a sentence with "When." Select the Match Case check box, however, if you want the case of the replacement text to differ from the case of the found text—for example, if you're replacing the abbreviation "WHO" (all uppercase) with "World Health Organization" (initial capitals only).

Up and Down   These options appear under Direction in the Find dialog box. Unless you select the Up option button, Word begins searching from the insertion point to the end of the document (Down). If text is selected, Word searches from the beginning to the end of the selection (Down) unless you select the Up option button.

Use the Clipboard to Specify the Find and Replacement Text

If you've already typed the characters in your document that you want to find or use as replacement characters, you can avoid having to retype the characters in the Find or Replace dialog box. Before choosing Find or Replace, copy the characters onto the Clipboard. Then, in the Find or Replace dialog box, press SHIFT+INS to paste the contents of the Clipboard into the Find What or Replace With box.

You can paste up to 255 characters in the Find What and Replace With boxes. To specify larger amounts of replacement text, you can copy the text onto the Clipboard. To designate the Clipboard contents as the replacement text, type ^c in the Replace With box. You can also type ^c in the Replace With box to replace text with a graphic you've copied onto the Clipboard.

Finding and Replacing Formatting

If you use styles, you can replace formatting by redefining styles. For more information, see Chapter 8, "Formatting with Styles."

By specifying formats when searching for or replacing text, you can locate text that has a specific format, such as bold or underlining, and change the formatting as well as the text. For example, you can:

- Find text having a format such as bold or underlining and change the text, change its formatting, or both. For example, you can find **LitWare Company** and change it to **LitWare, Inc.**, LitWare Company, or **LitWare, Inc.**

- Find any text having a particular format and change only the formatting, leaving the text as is. For example, if you've underlined the titles of publications in your document and want to make them italic instead, you can find any underlined text and change the underlining to italic.

You can also find and replace paragraph formats and styles. For example, you can find all paragraphs having an indented first line and a 10-point Courier font and change the formatting by applying a style. Or you can find all paragraphs having the style Heading 1 and change the style to Heading 2. If you specify search text in the Find What box and also select a paragraph format or style, Word finds only occurrences of the find characters that appear in paragraphs having the indicated format or style.

For more information on formatting shortcut keys, see Chapter 6, "Character Formatting."

To indicate the format to find and to make formatting changes from the Find and Replace dialog boxes, you can use formatting shortcut keys such as CTRL+B for bold or CTRL+I for italic, or the Character, Paragraph, and Styles buttons.

Formats you are searching for are listed here.

Replace	
Fi_n_d What:	LitWare Company
Format:	Font: Helvetica, Bold Italic
Re_p_lace With:	LitWare, Inc
Format:	Font: Times Roman, Not Italic

Find Next   Replace   Replace All   Cancel

☐ Match Whole Word Only   ☐ Match Case

Replace with Format

Clear   Character...   Paragraph...   Styles...

Formats you are changing are listed here.

Choose formatting buttons or use formatting shortcut keys.

You need to select only enough formats to identify the text you want to find and to indicate the changes you want to make. In the Character and Paragraph dialog boxes, formats that you are not changing are indicated by check boxes filled with gray or empty text boxes. Clicking a check box selects the format; clicking twice clears the check box, indicating you want the format removed.

The following illustration shows how you would use the Find Character dialog box to specify the formats for characters in the Find What box.

Select Times Roman from the font list to find Times Roman text.

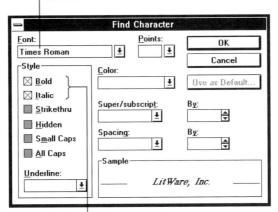

Select these check boxes to find bold and italic formats.

Dialog box showing specific formatting for the find text

When specifying the formatting for the replacement text, you need to select only the formats you want to be different. Formats you do not select are not changed.

Select Helvetica to change the font.

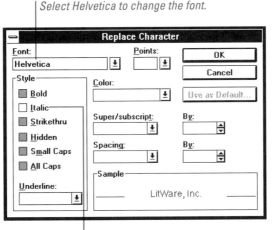

Clear this check box to remove the italic format.

Dialog box showing italic formatting removed from the replacement text

To find formatted text or just formatting

1 From the Edit menu, choose Find (ALT, E, F).

2 In the Find What box, do one of the following.

To	Do this
Find specific text having a specific format	Type the text you are searching for
Find all text having a specific format	Make sure the Find What box is empty, deleting any text in the box

3 With the insertion point or selection in the Find What box, specify the formats you are searching for by choosing the Character, Paragraph, or Styles button or by pressing formatting shortcut keys.

   To remove existing formats listed below the Find What box or to start over if you change your mind, choose the Clear button.

4 Select any other options you want, and choose the Find Next button.

   Word finds only occurrences of text having the selected formats.

To replace formatted text or just formatting

1 From the Edit menu, choose Replace (ALT, E, E).

2 In the Find What box, type the text you want to change.

3 With the insertion point or selection in the Find What box, specify the formats you are searching for by choosing the Character, Paragraph, or Styles button or by pressing formatting shortcut keys.

   To remove existing formats listed below the Find What box or to start over if you change your mind, choose the Clear button.

4 In the Replace With box, do one of the following.

To replace	Do this
Specific text but not its formatting	Type the replacement characters in the Replace With box. If replacement formats are listed below the box, choose the Clear button.
Specific text and its formatting	Type the replacement characters in the Replace With box. With the insertion point in the Replace With box, use formatting shortcut keys or the Character, Paragraph, and Styles buttons to specify the new formatting to apply.
Only the formatting of specific text	Make sure the Replace With box is empty, deleting any text in the box. With the insertion point in the Replace With box, use formatting shortcut keys or the Character, Paragraph, and Styles buttons to specify formatting.

5 Select any other options you want and choose the Find Next button.

Word finds only occurrences of the find characters having the selected formats.

In this example, Word replaces the found text occurrences with different text and also changes the formatting.

In this example, Word changes only the formatting of the found text occurrences.

To replace only formatting

1 From the Edit menu, choose Replace (ALT, E, E).

2 Make sure the Find What box is empty, deleting any text in the box.

3 With the insertion point or selection in the Find What box, specify the formats you are searching for by choosing the Character, Paragraph, or Styles button or by pressing formatting shortcut keys.

   Choose the Clear button to remove existing formats listed below the Find What box or to start over if you change your mind.

4 Make sure the Replace With box is empty, deleting any text in the box.

5 With the insertion point in the Replace With box, use formatting shortcut keys or the Character, Paragraph, and Styles buttons to change the format.

   Choose the Clear button to remove existing formats listed below the Replace With box or to start over if you change your mind.

6 Select any other options you want, and choose the Find Next or Replace All button.

   If you chose the Find Next button, Word finds any text having the selected formats. Choose Replace to change the formats.

   If you chose the Replace All button, Word automatically changes the formatting throughout the document.

Finding and Replacing Special Characters

You can type special codes in the Find and Replace dialog boxes to find characters other than ordinary text. To remove blank lines in your document, for example, you can find two consecutive paragraph marks and replace them with a single paragraph mark. If you're searching for similar words or are unsure how a word is spelled, you can use wildcards to represent any character in the search text. For example, you can search for "Gree??" to find all references to "Greece" or "Greek."

When searching for or replacing special characters, you may find it helpful to display paragraph marks, tab marks, and other nonprinting characters. If the nonprinting characters are not displayed, Word finds and selects the space these characters occupy. To display nonprinting characters, choose the Show/Hide ¶ button on the ribbon, or select the All option under Nonprinting Characters in the View category of the Options dialog box (Tools menu).

To specify a special character as search or replacement text

▶ With the insertion point in the Find What or Replace With box, type the special character combination.

If formats are listed below the Find What or Replace With box and you don't want the formats to influence the action of Find or Replace, choose the Clear button. Otherwise, Word finds only the special characters or combination of text and special characters having those formats.

The following table describes the codes you type to represent special characters in the Find What or Replace With box.

To find or replace	Type	Notes
Any character	?	For example, type **?nsure** in the Find What box to find "ensure" and "insure."
Tab character (→)	**^t**	For example, type **^t** in the Find What box and **^t^t** in the Replace With box to replace one tab character with two tab characters.
Paragraph mark (¶)	**^p**	For example, type **^p^p** in the Find What box and **^p** in the Replace With box to replace two paragraph marks with one paragraph mark.
Manual page break (dotted line across page)	**^d**	Finds manual page breaks, inserted by pressing CRTL+ENTER or by using the Break command from the Insert menu (ALT, I, B). Also finds section breaks.
Line break (↵)	**^n**	Finds line breaks inserted by pressing SHIFT+ENTER.
Column break (dotted line across a column)	**^14**	Finds column breaks, inserted by pressing CTRL+SHIFT+ENTER or by using the Break command on the Insert menu (ALT, I, B).
Section break (double-dotted line across page)	**^d**	Finds section breaks, inserted using the Break command on the Insert menu (ALT, I, B). Also finds manual page breaks.
Footnote reference mark	**^2**	Finds any automatic footnote reference mark in the document. Use this in the Find What box only.
Annotation mark	**^5**	Finds any annotation mark in the document. Use this in the Find What box only.

(continued)

To find or replace	Type	Notes
White space	^w	Finds any number and combination of spaces including normal and nonbreaking spaces, as well as tab characters.
Any graphic	^1	Finds any type of graphic.
Optional hyphen	^-	Finds optional hyphens (¬). If you specify search text without optional hyphens, Word finds all matching text, including text containing optional hyphens. If you specify optional hyphens in the search text, however, Word finds only words having optional hyphens in the indicated position. For instance, if your search text is "type^-writer," Word finds only "type¬writer"—that is, "type"(optional hyphen)"writer," but not "typewrit—er," or "type-writer" with a nonbreaking or normal hyphen.
Nonbreaking hyphen	^~	Nonbreaking hyphen (—)
Nonbreaking space	^s	Nonbreaking space (◊)
Any field	^19	Field codes must be displayed. To display field codes, choose Field Codes from the View menu (ALT, V, C).
Question mark (?)	^?	For example, the search text "Where^?" finds "Where?"
Caret character	^^	Finds or replaces the caret character (^).
Clipboard contents	^c	Replaces search text with the contents of the Clipboard. Use this in the Replace With box only. Use this if you want to replace the search text with a graphic or with more than 255 characters.
Any ANSI character	^0*nnn*	A character from the ANSI character set, where *nnn* is the ANSI code for the character.
Search text	^m	Uses the search text in the replacement. For example, typing **Schmidt** in the Find What box and **Dr. ^m** in the Replace With box replaces "Schmidt" with "Dr. Schmidt."

For more information about using special characters as search or replacement text, choose Help Index from the Help menu, and then use the Search button to locate the topic "Searching for tabs, paragraph marks, and other special characters."

Chapter 13

Glossaries: Storing Items for Reuse

A glossary stores frequently used text and graphics (commonly referred to as boilerplate) so that you can quickly insert them in your document with just a few keystrokes or a couple of mouse clicks.

You can store a long name such as Esmeralda Papathanasiou. Or if you frequently type, "If you have any questions, please feel free to contact me at my office, Room 227 of Building D," you can store that sentence as a glossary entry and never have to type it again.

Here are some other examples of what you might store in a glossary:

- Often-used mailing addresses
- Your company name or logo
- A common closing to a letter
- A long distribution list for memos
- Copyright notices
- Standard clauses in contracts
- Text with unusual formatting
- A signature scanned into your computer and copied to Word as a graphic

Most often, a glossary entry is a copy of a selected item. Occasionally you may prefer to delete text and graphics from several locations, collect them in one glossary entry, and store the collection for insertion in another location. For more information about storing several selections as one glossary entry, see "Using the Spike," later in this chapter.

For more information on templates, see Chapter 37, "Document Templates."

Glossary entries can be stored globally so that they are available to all documents. Items such as a company name or logo might be needed in many different types of documents. For other types of entries, you might find it more convenient to store them for use with specific documents. If your document is based on a template other than NORMAL.DOT, you can make glossary entries available to only those documents created from the same template. For example, you can save the complimentary closing of a business letter with your business letter template.

Glossary entries that are saved globally appear on the list of available glossary entries in all templates. Saving a glossary entry with its appropriate template means you do not have to scroll through unrelated glossary entries as you work.

Working with Glossary Entries

A glossary entry can include any amount (limited by available memory) of text, graphics, or a combination of text and graphics from one location in a document. To create a glossary entry, you type text or insert a graphic into a document, select the text or graphic, and then store the selection with a unique name—usually a brief, descriptive abbreviation that you can easily recall when you want to insert the entry.

If you need to create a glossary entry from several locations or from several documents, see "Using the Spike," later in this chapter.

A glossary entry name can be as many as 31 characters long and can contain spaces. You may want to keep the name as short as possible so it will be easy to use.

To store text or graphics as a glossary entry

1   Select the text or graphics for the glossary entry.

2   From the Edit menu, choose Glossary (ALT, E, O).

3   In the Glossary Name box, type a name for the glossary entry.

    You use this name whenever you insert the glossary entry into your document.

4   Choose the Define button.

    The Define button is unavailable if you have not made a selection in your document. If this is the case, close the dialog box, make a selection, and repeat steps 2 through 4.

When you quit Word, if you have created or edited glossary entries, Word may display a message asking if you want to save global glossary and command changes. Choose the Yes button to keep any changes for later use. If you choose the No button, changes to the glossary are discarded.

If your document is based on a template other than NORMAL.DOT and you have created or edited glossary entries, Word may display a message asking if you want to save changes to the template. The message appears when you close either the template or the last open document based on the template.

To specify a storage location for a glossary entry

If Word prompts you for a storage location, use the following procedure.

1   If you need the glossary entry for documents not based on the current template, select the As Global option button.
    –or–
    To make the glossary entry available only to documents based on the current template, select the In Template option button.

2   Choose the OK button.

You can store as many as 150 glossary entries in a document template.

Tip   If you are saving a phrase—for example, a company name—that you insert in sentences, select one blank space after the phrase when you create the glossary entry. Then, when you insert the phrase in a sentence, the blank space you normally insert after typing a word is already there.

Inserting a Glossary Entry into a Document

When you insert a glossary entry into a document, Word copies the contents of the entry to the location immediately following the insertion point.

To insert text or graphics from a glossary entry

1   Position the insertion point where you want to insert the glossary entry.

2   From the Edit menu, choose Glossary (ALT, E, O).

   The Glossary command is unavailable if there are no glossary entries and there is no selection.

3   Type or select a glossary entry name.

4   To insert the entry together with its formatting, choose the Insert button.
   –or–
   To insert the entry and apply to it the formatting of the surrounding text, choose the Insert As Plain Text button.

To insert a glossary entry with keys

If you know the name of the glossary entry, you may find this procedure a faster method of inserting it.

1   Position the insertion point where you want to insert the glossary entry.

   Make sure the insertion point is either at the beginning of a line or preceded by a space.

2   Type the name of the glossary entry.

   If you are typing the glossary name in front of text, make sure you type a space after the glossary name—unless you want the entry to run into the text following.

3   Press the F3 key.

   Your entry will be inserted; if the entry contains direct formatting, it is inserted with that formatting intact. You must change the formatting of the entry if you want it to be formatted like the surrounding text.

For more information
about using the
GLOSSARY field, see
the GLOSSARY topic
in online Help.

Tip   You can also use fields, a more complex feature of Word, with glossary entries. Using the GLOSSARY field, you can insert an entry in multiple locations within a document and then, if the contents of the entry change, update all entries automatically by pressing the F9 key.

Suppose, for example, you are creating a product catalog in which a telephone number for Customer Service appears many times. You can store the phone number as a glossary entry and then insert a GLOSSARY field containing the name of the glossary entry at each location you want the Customer Service number to appear. If the phone number changes, you simply update the instruction in the GLOSSARY field; then you select the entire document, and press the Update Fields key (F9). This corrects all listings of the phone number at one time.

Editing or Deleting a Glossary Entry

To keep glossary entries up to date, you can edit or delete them. You must first insert the glossary entry into the document.

To edit the text in a glossary entry

1   Insert the glossary entry into your document.

2   Make the changes you want.

3   Select the altered text or graphics.

4   From the Edit menu, choose Glossary (ALT, E, O).

5   In the Glossary Name box, type or select the original name of the glossary entry.

6   Choose the Define button.

   If Word prompts you for a storage location, select As Global to make the entry available for documents not based on the current template; or select In Template to make the entry available only for documents based on the current template.

7   When Word displays a message asking if you want to redefine the glossary entry, choose the Yes button.

To delete a glossary entry

1   From the Edit menu, choose Glossary (ALT, E, O).

The Glossary command is unavailable if there are no existing glossary entries and there is no selection.

2   In the Glossary Name box, select the glossary entry you want to delete.

3   Choose the Delete button.

4   Choose the Close button.

Tip   You cannot undo the deletion of a glossary entry until the end of a work session. Word asks whether you want to save glossary changes when you quit the current work session, close the template, or close the last document based on the template. To restore deleted glossary entries, choose the No button. Note, however, that by doing this you are also instructing Word not to save any glossary entries or macros you've created during the current working session.

To rename a glossary entry

1   Insert the glossary entry.

2   Select the text or graphics for the glossary entry.

3   From the Edit menu, choose Glossary (ALT, E, O).

4   Select the old name of the glossary entry and choose the Delete button.

5   In the Glossary Name box, type the new name for the glossary entry.

6   Choose the Define button.

Using the Spike

Word provides a special glossary entry called the Spike. Each item you store in the Spike is deleted from the document and added to the previous text or graphics stored in the Spike. The Spike is a convenient way to collect text and graphics from various locations when you want to remove items from a document and insert them as a group in another location.

You can insert the contents of the Spike as many times as you need, just like inserting a regular glossary entry. Alternatively, you can empty the Spike when you insert its contents in a document. This leaves the Spike ready to store the next collection of text and graphics.

To delete text and graphics and store them in the Spike

1   Select an item you want to send to the Spike.

2   Press the Spike key (CTRL+F3).

Word cuts the selected item and stores it in the Spike. Repeat this procedure to add text or graphics to the items currently stored in the Spike.

To insert the contents of the Spike more than once

This method does not empty the Spike. The contents of the Spike can be inserted again, just as you insert a regular glossary entry.

1   Position the insertion point where you want to insert the contents of the Spike.

2   Type **spike**

3   Press F3.

Word inserts a copy of the contents of the Spike.

To insert and empty the Spike

This method inserts the contents of the Spike into a document and empties the Spike, leaving it ready to store a new collection of text and graphics.

1   Position the insertion point where you want to insert the contents of the Spike.

2   Press the Unspike key (CTRL+SHIFT+F3).

Printing Glossary Entries

In the Glossary dialog box you see only the contents of one entry at a time—and, if the entry is too long to fit, only its first few words. However, you can print a list of glossary entries so that you can see all entries in their entirety. Moreover, since the font used in a dialog box cannot represent graphics or graphical fonts, printing the entries gives you a more accurate view of them.

Glossaries are printed separately from the document that is open. Entries are printed in alphabetical order with document template entries first, formatted as they would appear when inserted into a document.

To print a list of glossary entries

1   Open a document.

   If you want to print the glossary entries stored with a template other than NORMAL.DOT, you must open a document that is based on the other template.

2   From the File menu, choose Print (ALT, F, P).

3   In the Print box, select Glossary, and then choose the OK button.

Specifying a Location for Storing Glossary Entries

If your document is based on the NORMAL.DOT template, Word automatically stores glossary entries globally so that they are available to all documents. If your document is based on a different template, each time you create a new glossary entry you can choose to designate it for use with all documents or for use only with documents based on the current template.

If you do not want the prompt displayed, you can select a storage location for all future glossary entries. If you change your mind later, repeat the following procedure and select a different option.

To specify a location for storing glossary entries

1   From the File menu, choose Template (ALT, F, T).

2   Under Store New Macros And Glossaries As, select one of the following options:

Option	Effect
Global (Available To All Documents)	This makes glossary entries available to all documents.
With Document Template	This stores each entry with the current template.
Prompt For Each New	This is the default. This option displays a prompt each time you create or edit a glossary entry when the document you're working on is based on a template other than NORMAL.DOT.

3   Choose the OK button.

Chapter 14

Proofing a Document

The Word proofing commands can help you quickly find and correct many common errors. You can use the proofing commands to:

- Check spelling as a routine step in editing your documents.

- Check for grammatical and stylistic errors using the Grammar command. Word describes the error, suggests possible corrections, and makes the changes you select. The Grammar command also evaluates the readability of a document to help you ensure that your writing is suitable for your audience.

- Find a synonym or antonym for a particular word using the Thesaurus command.

- Hyphenate words at line breaks to reduce the raggedness at the margins and the extra spacing between words in justified text.

The Setup program you use to install Word on your computer gives you the option to install or not install the Word proofing commands. If you choose to install them, they appear on the Tools menu; otherwise, they do not. You can run the Setup program again and specify that you want to install the proofing commands only. For more information on the Setup program, see *Microsoft Word Getting Started*.

You can use the proofing commands with more than one language in a single document. You can also format text so that it is ignored by the proofing commands. For more information, see "Proofing Text in Different Languages," later in this chapter.

Checking Spelling

If you didn't install the Spelling command when you set up Word, see *Microsoft Word Getting Started*.

Word checks your document for spelling errors using a standard dictionary. If a word isn't found in the dictionary, the word is displayed in the Spelling dialog box so that you can correct the possible misspelling.

You often use words in your documents that are not likely to be in the Word dictionaries—for example, specialized terms, product codes, acronyms and abbreviations, and names of business associates. If you don't want Word to question such words during spelling checks, you can add them to a custom dictionary. You can use one or more custom dictionaries in addition to the standard main dictionary when you check your documents. Word can then check that the words entered in a custom dictionary are also correctly spelled. For more information on custom dictionaries, see "Using Custom Dictionaries," later in this chapter.

In addition to simple misspellings, Word also alerts you to repeated words—for example, "the the"—and words that have an unusual pattern of capitalization, such as "JUpiter." You can select additional options for checking spelling by choosing the Options button in the Spelling dialog box.

Unless text is selected when you choose the Spelling command, Word checks the entire document, including footnotes, annotations, and headers and footers. To check the spelling of hidden text, first select the Hidden Text check box, a View option in the Options dialog box (Tools menu).

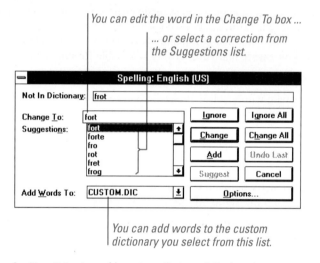

You can edit the word in the Change To box ...

... or select a correction from the Suggestions list.

You can add words to the custom dictionary you select from this list.

Spelling dialog box with a misspelled word displayed

To check spelling

Word normally checks all of your document beginning at the insertion point. To check only part of the document, select that part before choosing the Spelling command.

1   From the Tools menu, choose Spelling (ALT, O, S).
    –or–
    Click the Spelling button on the Toolbar

Spelling button

Word begins checking the document or the selected text. On finding a word that is not in any open dictionary, Word displays the word in the Spelling dialog box and selects the word in your document. Word scrolls through the document so you can see the word in its context. To see more text, drag the dialog box by its title bar.

2   Each time a word is displayed in the dialog box, you can do one of the following:

■   Correct the spelling.

    If you agree with the suggested correction in the Change To box, choose the Change button to correct the current instance of the word. To correct all instances of the same word subsequently found in your document, choose the Change All button.

    To specify a different correction, select a word from the Suggestions list and choose the Change button (or double-click the word) or the Change All button. If the Suggestions list is empty, choose the Suggest button to list possible spellings.

    If Word cannot suggest a correction, it inserts the questionable word in the Change To box. You can correct its spelling without retyping the whole word.

■   Leave the word unchanged and continue the spelling check.

    To skip only the current instance of the word, choose the Ignore button. To skip all instances of the word subsequently found in your document, choose the Ignore All button.

■   Add the word to a custom dictionary.

    To add the word to the custom dictionary shown in the Add Words To box, choose the Add button.

    To add the word to a different custom dictionary, select another dictionary from the list, and then choose the Add button.

    If the custom dictionary you want is not listed, choose the Options button and open the dictionary. For more instructions, see "To open or close a custom dictionary," later in this chapter.

■   Delete a repeated word.

    Choose the Delete button to remove the repeated word.

- Delete a misspelled word.

  Delete the word suggested in the Change To box, and then choose the Delete button. To delete all subsequent instances of the misspelling, choose the Delete All button.

- Undo previous spelling corrections.

  Choose the Undo Last button. You can undo the previous five corrections using the Undo Last button.

3 If the insertion point or selection was not at the beginning of your document when you began checking spelling, Word asks if you want to continue checking from the beginning of the document. Choose the Yes button to continue checking, or choose the No button to return to the document.

4 When Word has finished checking the spelling of a selection, it displays a message asking whether you want to check the spelling of the remainder of the document. Choose the Yes button to check the remainder of the document, or choose the No button to return to the document.

5 When Word displays a message indicating that it has checked all of the document, choose the OK button to return to the document.

Note If you choose the Change All button to correct all instances of a misspelled word, Word makes the specified change as subsequent instances of the word are found in the document. If you cancel the Spelling command before the entire document has been checked, some instances of the word may not have been changed.

To check the spelling of a selected word

▶ Select the word you want to check, and then choose Spelling from the Tools menu (ALT, O, S).

–Or–

▶ Select the word you want to check, and then press the Spelling key (F7).

–Or–

Spelling button

▶ Select the word you want to check, and then click the Spelling button on the Toolbar.

If the word is not in any open dictionary, Word displays the Spelling dialog box so you can correct the word or add it to a dictionary.

If the word is spelled correctly, Word displays a message indicating that it has finished checking the selection. Choose the Yes button to continue checking the remainder of the document or choose the No button to return to the document.

Tip Using the wildcard characters "?" and "*," you can type the part of the word you know in the Change To box and then choose the Suggest button, and Word will fill in the rest. The "?" wildcard is used to specify any single character. For example, if you're not sure whether it's "surprise" or "surprize," you can type **surpri?e**, and Word finds "surprise." The "*" wildcard is used to specify any multiple group of characters. For example, if you type **occur*** Word finds every word that begins with "occur."

To interrupt the spelling check to edit your document

While you are checking spelling, you can return to your document to make other changes and then continue checking.

1   Click in the document window, or press CTRL+TAB to switch to the document window.

    The document window becomes active. You can make changes to the document or scroll to see more text.

2   After editing the document, click the Start button in the Spelling dialog box to restart checking your document.

    Word begins checking from the current location of the insertion point or selection in your document.

To undo all spelling corrections

You can undo all of the spelling corrections made during the most recent spelling checking session.

▶   Immediately after you've finished checking spelling, choose Undo Spelling from the Edit menu (ALT, E, U).

Selecting Spelling Options and Dictionaries

You can control how Word checks spelling using the Options command on the Tools menu, or by choosing the Options button in the Spelling dialog box. With the Spelling options displayed in the Options dialog box, you can do the following:

■   Tell Word to ignore words that contain numbers or whose letters are all uppercase letters.

■   Select custom dictionaries to use in checking spelling.

When you next check spelling, Word uses the selected dictionaries and spelling options.

*Select categories of words
you want Word to ignore
during spelling checks.*

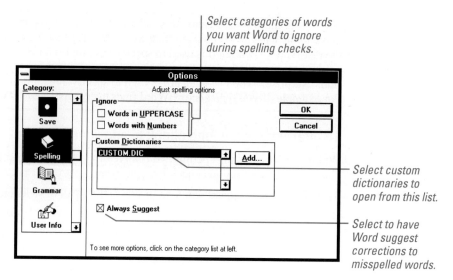

*Select custom
dictionaries to
open from this list.*

*Select to have
Word suggest
corrections to
misspelled words.*

Options dialog box showing the Spelling options

To select spelling options

To check which spelling options are selected, follow these steps before you choose the Spelling command. To change the options after you start checking spelling, choose the Options button in the Spelling dialog box.

1   From the Tools menu, choose Options (ALT, O, O), and then select the Spelling category to display the spelling options.

2   Under Ignore, select the class of words you want Word to skip during spelling checks.

Select this option	To ignore
Words In UPPERCASE	Words typed in all uppercase letters and any combination of uppercase letters and numbers; for example:
	UNESCO, NNW, T42D, FY90
	Word continues to check the spelling of words that are capitalized by means of the all caps or small caps character formats.
Words With Numbers	Any combination of characters that include numbers; for example:
	3cc, 20mg, 408tx1, ac501d4, TX102
	Even if this option is not selected, Word ignores combinations of numbers that contain only one letter, such as 3a or 40K.

3 Clear the Always Suggest check box if you do not want Word to suggest corrections to misspellings. Word can check spelling more quickly when this option is cleared.

4 Choose the OK button.

Word skips the indicated classes of words when you resume checking spelling.

Using Custom Dictionaries

You may often use words in your documents that are not in the standard dictionary Word uses—for example, specialized terms, acronyms and abbreviations, and names of clients and business associates. So that Word won't question the words during spelling checks, you can add them to a custom dictionary.

You can create as many new custom dictionaries as you like. For example, you can add client names to one dictionary for use in checking letters and memos, and add technical terms and product codes to another dictionary for checking specifications and operator manuals. You might need to use both dictionaries for checking reports and proposals. The first time you use the Spelling command, the dictionary CUSTOM.DIC appears in the Add Words To list. The dictionary is empty until you add words to it.

You can also purchase foreign dictionaries and dictionaries of specialized terms (medical and legal, for example). For information about how to purchase supplemental dictionaries, call the Microsoft Customer Service number on your Microsoft Word registration card.

When you add a word to a dictionary during a spelling check, the word is entered in the dictionary exactly as it appears in your document. If the word is in all lowercase letters, the word is recognized in subsequent spelling checks, regardless of the letter case used in a particular instance of the word in your document. If the word you add to a dictionary contains some uppercase letters, however, the word may not be recognized in your document if it has a different pattern of capitalization. The following table describes the results of adding to a custom dictionary words having all lowercase letters, initial capitals, all uppercase letters, and mixed capitalization.

If you add	Word recognizes	Word questions
ylem	ylem, Ylem, YLEM	yLem
Cambrian	Cambrian, CAMBRIAN	cambrian
UNESCO	UNESCO	Unesco, unesco
PostScript	PostScript	POSTSCRIPT, postscript

To add many words to a custom dictionary, first create a document that lists words you want in the dictionary. Open the custom dictionary or dictionaries you want to contain the words and then use the Spelling command to check the spelling of the list. As the words are displayed in the Spelling dialog box, you can add them to a custom dictionary.

Which Custom Dictionaries Are Open?

During a spelling check, Word consults only its standard dictionary and the custom dictionaries that are open. You can quickly see which dictionaries are open by checking the Add Words To list in the Spelling dialog box. Only the custom dictionaries included in this list are open. On the other hand, the Custom Dictionaries list in the Options command (Spelling category) includes all of your custom dictionaries. If, for example, you have ten different custom dictionaries, they are all listed in the Custom Dictionaries list. However, only the dictionaries that are selected (highlighted) are opened and consulted during a spelling check. You can have up to four custom dictionaries open at a time.

To open or close a custom dictionary

To have Word consult a custom dictionary when checking spelling, make sure that the dictionary is open before you choose the Spelling command. Word can check spelling more quickly if you close any custom dictionaries that are not needed to check a particular document.

1   From the Tools menu, choose Options (ALT, O, O), and then select the Spelling category.

2   Use the arrow keys to move through the Custom Dictionaries list, and then press the SPACEBAR to select or clear a dictionary.
    –or–
    Use the mouse to scroll through the list and click a dictionary name to select or clear it.

3   Choose the OK button.

Word uses the open dictionaries when you next choose the Spelling command.

To create a custom dictionary

1 From the Tools menu, choose Options (ALT, O, O), and then select the Spelling category.

2 Under Custom Dictionaries, choose the Add button.

   Word displays a dialog box asking you to name the dictionary.

3 Type a name for the new dictionary.

4 Choose the OK button.

The dictionary is listed in the Options dialog box and is selected, indicating it is open.

Using an Exclude Dictionary

An exclude dictionary is a dictionary you can create to specify spellings that you do not want the Spelling command to accept. For example, the Spelling command accepts the word "installment," but in some fields such as banking, it is commonly spelled "instalment," with one "l." In that case, you would like the Spelling command to accept "instalment" but flag "installment." You can accomplish this by adding "instalment" to a custom dictionary and adding "installment" to the exclude dictionary. Each language dictionary can have an exclude dictionary associated with it.

To create an exclude dictionary

1 In a new, empty document, type the words that you want to put in the dictionary, one word per line, ending each line with a paragraph mark.

2 From the File menu, choose Save As (ALT, F, A).

3 In the File Name box, type a name for the exclude dictionary.

   The exclude dictionary must have the same name as the main language dictionary with which it is associated, except that it must have the filename extension .EXC instead of .LEX. For example, the American English dictionary is called SP_AM.LEX, so the exclude dictionary associated with it must be named SP_AM.EXC.

4 In the Save File As Type box, select Text Only.

5 Choose the OK button.

Once you create an exclude dictionary, Word uses it automatically.

Checking Grammar

If you didn't install the Grammar command when you set up Word, see *Microsoft Word Getting Started*.

The Grammar command identifies sentences in your document that have possible grammatical errors or a weak writing style. For many types of errors, the Grammar command suggests ways to correct the sentence. You can choose the correction you want to make and have Word change the sentence in your document. You can also make changes directly in your document and then continue checking.

You can select the rules of style and grammar Word observes during grammar checks using the Options command on the Tools menu, or by choosing the Options button in the Grammar dialog box. For more information about the grammar options, see "Selecting Rules to Observe in Grammar Checks," later in this chapter.

While checking your document for grammatical errors, Word also checks spelling. If a questionable word is found, the Spelling dialog box is temporarily displayed over the Grammar dialog box so you can correct the word or add it to a custom dictionary. Word then continues the grammar check. You can have Word ignore misspelled words during grammar checks, if you prefer. For more information, see "To ignore spelling errors during grammar checking," later in this section.

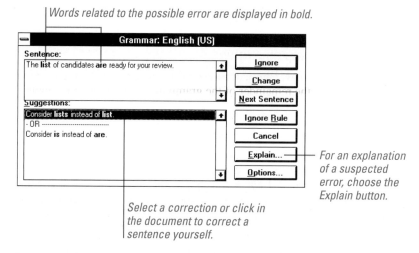

Words related to the possible error are displayed in bold.

For an explanation of a suspected error, choose the Explain button.

Select a correction or click in the document to correct a sentence yourself.

Grammar dialog box showing a possible error

To check grammar

Word normally checks all of your document beginning at the insertion point. To check only part of the document, select that part before choosing the Grammar command.

1   From the Tools menu, choose Grammar (ALT, O, G).

2   If Word finds a sentence with questionable grammar or style, it displays the sentence in the Grammar dialog box. Words related to the suspected error are displayed in bold. Do one of the following:

   ■   Make a suggested correction.

   Select a correction in the Suggestions box, and then choose the Change button, or double-click the suggestion. Word updates the sentence in your document.

   If the Change button is unavailable, the Grammar command is not able to make a correction. You can type a correction directly in the document.

   ■   Type a correction in the document.

   Click in the document window to make it active, or press CTRL+TAB. Edit the sentence, and then choose the Start button in the Grammar dialog box, or choose the Grammar command from the Tools menu, to restart checking from the insertion point.

   ■   Skip the questioned word or phrase without changing the sentence.

   Choose the Ignore button. To skip this and similar occurrences of the possible error, choose the Ignore Rule button. For example, to allow passive verbs for the remainder of the grammar check, choose the Ignore Rule button when Word questions the use of a passive verb.

   ■   Leave the current sentence unchanged, skipping all other possible errors in it.

   Choose the Next Sentence button. Word begins checking the next sentence.

   ■   Get more information about the error.

   Choose the Explain button. Word displays a dialog box describing the related rule of grammar or style. Press ESC to resume the grammar check.

   ■   Change the rules of style and grammar observed by Word in checking your document.

   Choose the Options button, and then select the option button for the rule group that you want observed for the remainder of the grammar check. You can use the Customize Settings button to observe or not observe individual rules. After you close the Options dialog box, Word continues checking the document.

3 When Word reaches the end of the document, it asks if you want to continue checking from the beginning. Choose the Yes button to continue checking or choose the No button to stop.

4 When Word displays a message that it has checked the entire document or the part you selected, choose the OK button to return to your document.

If the Show Readability Statistics After Proofing check box is selected in the Grammar category of the Options dialog box (Tools menu), Word displays information about the document in the Readability Statistics dialog box. Choose the OK button to return to your document. For more information about readability statistics, see "Evaluating the Readability of a Document," later in this chapter.

Selecting Rules to Observe in Grammar Checks

You may not want to observe all rules of style and grammar when you check a document. Rules of style are often subjective. Your subject and audience, among other things, influence the writing style that is appropriate for your documents. Rules of grammar, on the other hand, are less subject to choice. Circumstances may justify ignoring a grammar rule, however, when you are checking certain documents. Technical and legal documents, for example, may contain sentences in the passive voice or other sentence constructions that you do not want repeatedly questioned by the Grammar command. Also, the Grammar command may not recognize certain valid sentence constructions used in your documents.

When you select the Grammar category in the Options dialog box (Tools menu), you can select one of three predefined rule groups: Strictly (All Rules), For Business Writing, and For Casual Writing. The Strictly (All Rules) option applies every style and grammar rule; the For Business Writing option applies fewer of them; the For Casual Writing option applies fewer still. You can customize each of these rule groups by selecting or clearing options for individual grammar and style rules.

Select the rule group appropriate
for your document.

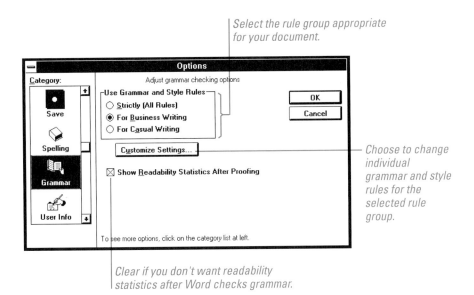

Choose to change
individual
grammar and style
rules for the
selected rule
group.

Clear if you don't want readability
statistics after Word checks grammar.

Options dialog box showing the grammar options

To change the grammar checking rule group

1   From the Tools menu, choose Options (ALT, O, O). In the Options dialog box, select the Grammar category to display the grammar options.

If you've already started checking grammar, choose the Options button in the Grammar dialog box.

2   Under Use Grammar And Style Rules, select the rule group you want Word to observe during grammar checks.

You can customize the selected rule group by choosing the Customize Settings button and selecting or clearing individual style or grammar rules. See the following procedure, "To customize a rule group."

3   Choose the OK button.

Word observes the selected rules the next time you choose the Grammar command.

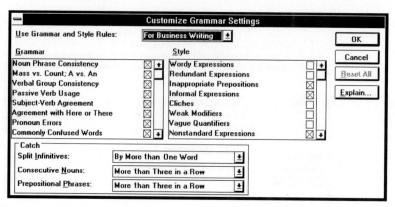

Customize Settings dialog box

To customize a rule group

1   From the Tools menu, choose Options (ALT, O, O). In the Options dialog box, select the Grammar category to display the grammar options.

If you've already started checking grammar, choose the Options button in the Grammar dialog box.

2   Under Use Grammar And Style Rules, select the rule group you want to customize.

3   Choose the Customize Settings button.

4   Select a rule check box to have Word observe a rule; clear the rule check box to have Word ignore a rule.

5   Under Catch, select options to control how Word checks for the following phrases.

For this type of phrase	Select an option to control
Split Infinitives	How many words can fall between the word "to" and an infinitive verb before Word questions the sentence.
	If you select the By More Than One Word option, Word questions an infinitive phrase split by more than one word, such as "to rather quickly get." Select Always to have Word question all split infinitives; select Never to have Word ignore split infinitives.
Consecutive Nouns	How many nouns can modify another noun before Word questions the sentence.
	If you select the More Than Three In A Row option, Word questions a long sequence of nouns such as "task resource management group," but does not question "task management group." Select Never to have Word ignore all instances of consecutive nouns.
Prepositional Phrases	How many prepositional phrases can fall consecutively before Word questions the sentence.
	If you select the More Than Three In A Row option, Word questions a sequence of prepositional phrases such as "the can of paint on the floor by the chair in the cor-ner," but does not question "the can of paint on the floor by the chair." Select Never to have Word ignore all instances of consecutive prepositional phrases.

6   Choose the OK button to close the Customize Grammar Settings dialog box.

7   Choose the OK button to close the Options dialog box.

Word observes the selected rules the next time you choose the Grammar command.

To ignore spelling errors during grammar checking

1   From the Tools menu, choose Options (ALT, O, O). In the Options dialog box, select the Grammar category to display the grammar options.

If you've already started checking grammar, choose the Options button in the Grammar dialog box.

2   Choose the Customize Settings button.

3   Under Grammar, clear the Spelling Errors check box.

4   Choose the OK button to close the Customize Grammar Settings dialog box.

5   Choose the OK button to close the Options dialog box.

Word ignores spelling errors when you resume checking grammar.

Evaluating the Readability of a Document

Word can provide information to help you evaluate how easily your writing can be understood by the average adult reader. You can display the Readability Statistics dialog box by selecting the Show Readability Statistics After Proofing check box, a Grammar option in the Options dialog box (Tools menu).

Most readability indexes assign a reading grade level. A Flesch Grade Level of 7, for example, indicates writing that can be understood by an average English-speaking reader who has completed seven years of education in the United States.

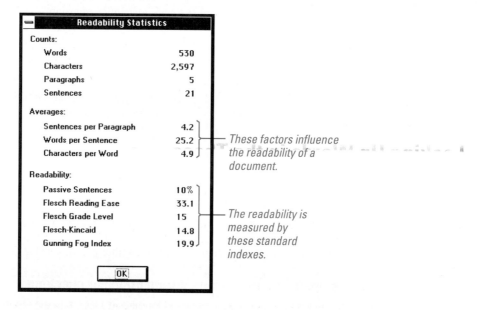

Readability Statistics	
Counts:	
Words	530
Characters	2,597
Paragraphs	5
Sentences	21
Averages:	
Sentences per Paragraph	4.2
Words per Sentence	25.2
Characters per Word	4.9
Readability:	
Passive Sentences	10%
Flesch Reading Ease	33.1
Flesch Grade Level	15
Flesch-Kincaid	14.8
Gunning Fog Index	19.9
OK	

These factors influence the readability of a document.

The readability is measured by these standard indexes.

Passive Sentences   This index reports the percentage of sentences that are passive ("The work was finished by Patrick.") instead of active ("Patrick finished the work."). Writing experts commonly advise you to avoid passive sentences unless the person or thing performing the action is unimportant or unknown.

Flesch Reading Ease and Flesch Grade Level   The Flesch Reading Ease and Flesch Grade Level indexes are based on the average number of words per sentence and the average number of syllables per 100 words. Standard writing averages approximately 17 words per sentence and 147 syllables per 100 words.

Flesch Reading Ease	Flesch Grade Level	Reading Ease
90–100	4	Very easy
80–90	5	Easy
70–80	6	Fairly easy
60–70	7–8	Standard
50–60	9–10	Fairly difficult
30–50	11–14	Difficult
0–30	15–16	Very difficult

Flesch-Kincaid   The Flesch-Kincaid index also assigns a grade level. A Flesch-Kincaid index of 7 or 8 is roughly equivalent to a Flesch Reading Ease Score of 60–70, the range for standard writing. A higher score indicates more difficult material.

Gunning Fog Index   This index is based on sentence length and the number of words per sentence with more than one syllable. Sentences with many multisyllable words are rated difficult to read—the higher the score, the more difficult.

Looking Up Words in the Thesaurus

If you didn't install the Thesaurus command when you set up Word, see *Microsoft Word Getting Started*.

You can use the thesaurus in Word to add interest and precision to your writing. You can quickly look up a synonym—a word with a similar meaning—for a selected word. Some words have several different meanings. For example, the word "work" is both a noun and a verb. You can select the meaning you want, and Word displays alternatives in the Thesaurus dialog box, shown in the following illustration.

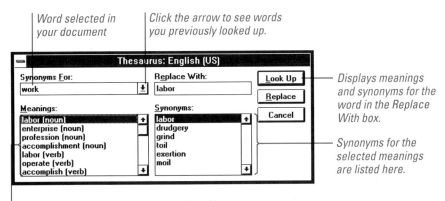

Word selected in your document

Click the arrow to see words you previously looked up.

Displays meanings and synonyms for the word in the Replace With box.

Synonyms for the selected meanings are listed here.

Different meanings for the word are listed here.

To look up words in the thesaurus

1   Select the word in your document you want to look up.

If you don't select a word, Word looks up the word containing or just before the insertion point.

2   From the Tools menu, choose Thesaurus (ALT, O, T).

Possible meanings for the selected word are listed in the Meanings box. Word inserts the first meaning from the list in the Replace With box and displays alternative words and phrases for it in the Synonyms box.

If a synonym can't be found, words close in alphabetical order to the selected word are listed instead of meanings. Make sure you spelled the word in your document correctly. If not, select a word from the alphabetical list or type the word in the Replace With box. Then choose the Look Up button.

3   Do one of the following.

To	Do this
Use a synonym from the Synonyms box	Select the synonym you want. Word displays the word in the Replace With box.
Find synonyms for a different meaning	Select a different meaning in the Meanings box. Word inserts the selected meaning in the Replace With box and lists synonyms for it in the Synonyms box.
Look up related words or antonyms	If the Related Words or Antonyms option appears in the Meanings box, select the option. The Synonyms box then becomes the Antonyms or Related Words box. You can then select a related word or antonym from the list Word displays.
Look up further meanings and synonyms for the word in the Replace With box	Choose the Look Up button. You can also type a word in the Replace With box, and then choose the Look Up button. Or you can select a word in the Meanings or Synonyms lists, and then choose the Look Up button or double click the word.

4   Choose the Replace button to replace the selected word in your document with the word or phrase in the Replace With box.
    –or–
    Choose the Cancel button to close the dialog box without changing the selected word in your document.

Note Word keeps track of the words you look up each time you use the Thesaurus command. To redisplay the meanings and synonyms for a word you previously looked up, click the down arrow next to the Synonyms For box, and then select the word from the list.

Hyphenating Words

If you didn't install the Hyphenation command when you set up Word, see *Microsoft Word Getting Started.*

Hyphenating words at line breaks improves the appearance of your document by reducing the raggedness of text at the margins. In justified text, hyphenation reduces the amount of space inserted between words to fill out each line. Hyphenation is especially useful for documents that have narrow text columns, such as newsletters and brochures.

When you choose the Hyphenation command on the Tools menu, Word scans your document and examines each line of a paragraph after the first line. If the first word in the line can be hyphenated, Word inserts a special hyphen called an optional hyphen and moves the first part of the word to the preceding line.

Optional hyphens, unlike the regular hyphen characters you type from the keyboard, are printed in your document only if they are needed to break a word at the end of a line. For more information about inserting hyphens, including optional and non-breaking hyphens, see Chapter 3, "Typing and Revising a Document." How optional hyphens are displayed on screen depends on settings in the View category of the Options dialog box (Tools menu). If, under Nonprinting Characters, the All check box or Optional Hyphens check box is selected, optional hyphens are displayed as the ¬ character in your document to distinguish them from the hyphen character. If the All check box or Optional Hyphens check box is cleared, only optional hyphens that will actually be printed—that is, those occurring at line breaks—are displayed. In this case, they are displayed like the hyphen character.

It's best to use the Hyphenation command after you complete writing and editing, but before you make final decisions about page breaks. That way, you'll only need to hyphenate your document once. If you edit your document extensively after using the Hyphenation command, line breaks may change. You'll then need to rehyphenate the document (or the parts that were edited) to ensure that words now appearing at line breaks are hyphenated where possible.

You can control the raggedness of line breaks using the Hot Zone box in the Hyphenation dialog box. The smaller the measurement, the less ragged the line breaks, or, if the lines are justified, the less space added between words.

Although Word hyphenates words correctly for breaking at the end of a line, you may want to hyphenate the word at a point other than the one Word proposes. When Word presents the word for hyphenation, you can select the hyphenation point.

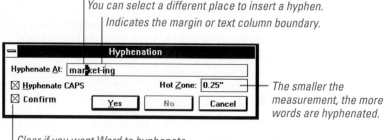

You can select a different place to insert a hyphen.
Indicates the margin or text column boundary.

The smaller the measurement, the more words are hyphenated.

Clear if you want Word to hyphenate your document automatically.

Hyphenation dialog box with a hyphenated word shown in a document

To hyphenate words automatically

Word normally hyphenates all text in your document beginning at the insertion point. To hyphenate text in only part of the document, select that part before choosing the Hyphenation command.

1   From the Tools menu, choose Hyphenation (ALT, O, H).

    Word displays the Hyphenation dialog box.

    To allow hyphenation of capitalized words, select the Hyphenate CAPS check box.

    Decrease the measurement in the Hot Zone box for less ragged margins and more hyphenation; increase it for less hyphenation and more ragged margins.

2   To confirm each hyphenated word, select the Confirm check box.

3   When you choose the OK button, Word begins hyphenating. If the Confirm option is selected, each word to be hyphenated is displayed in the Hyphenate At box. Do one of the following:

    ■ Hyphenate the word at the proposed location by choosing the Yes button.

    ■ Hyphenate the word at another point by moving the hyphenation point in the Hyphenate At box to where you want the word hyphenated and then choosing the Yes button.

    ■ Do not hyphenate the word by choosing the No button.

    ■ Stop hyphenating by choosing the Cancel button. Hyphens that Word inserted before you canceled hyphenation remain in your document.

4   When Word reaches the end of the document, it asks if you want to continue hyphenation from the beginning. Choose the Yes button to continue or choose the No button to stop.

To remove optional hyphens from a document

If you edit a document after using the Hyphenation command, the text may contain optional hyphens that no longer appear at line breaks. Although the extra hyphens won't be printed, you may find them distracting and want to remove them. If your document is very long, you may prefer to remove all optional hyphens at once. Then you can rehyphenate the document to insert hyphens only where they are needed at line breaks.

1   From the Edit menu, choose Replace (ALT, E, E).

2   Type ^- in the Find What box.

3   If the Replace With box is not empty, delete its contents.

4   Choose the Find Next button to find and replace each optional hyphen individually.
    –or–
    Choose the Replace All button to remove all optional hyphens at once.

5   To rehyphenate the document, choose Hyphenation from the Tools menu.

Proofing Text in Different Languages

The Word proofing commands are designed to work with more than one language. You can check the spelling, for example, of a document containing text in several different languages; Word can automatically check words using the appropriate dictionary for each language.

To prepare to proof text in more than one language, you must take the following two steps:

■   Install the appropriate language proofing files. For example, to check the spelling of German words, you must install a German spelling dictionary. For information on purchasing language proofing files, call the Microsoft Customer Service number on your Microsoft Word registration card.

■   Using the Language command on the Format menu, apply the appropriate language format to foreign words. German words, for example, must be formatted as German; otherwise Word assumes they are in the default language.

Once you have taken these steps, you can use the Word proofing tools to proof text in different languages in the same way that you proof text in the default language.

To apply language formatting

1   Select the text to which you want to apply language formatting.

2   From the Format menu, choose Language (ALT, T, L).

3 Select the appropriate language.

4 Choose the OK button.

You can now choose the proofing command you want to use if you have the appropriate proofing files.

Tip Using the Language command, you can apply a "no proofing" format to text. Text with this format is ignored by the Word proofing commands. You might want to apply this format to tables or technical material containing specialized terms that aren't in any of the standard spelling dictionaries, for example. The No Proofing option is the first item under Mark Selected Text As in the Language dialog box.

To change the default language

If you write most of your documents in a language other than the default one, it makes sense to change the default language to the one you use most often. For example, if you write your documents primarily in French, you can change the default language to French. The proofing tools will then automatically recognize the text in your documents as French—you won't have to apply the Language format to it.

1 From the Format menu, choose Language (ALT, T, L).

2 Select the language you want to make the default.

3 Choose the Use As Default button.

4 Choose the Yes button.

Chapter 15

Sorting

Using the Sorting command, you can quickly arrange text alphanumerically (by numbers first, then letters); by numbers only; or by date only. You can sort rows in tables, paragraphs, and tables created with tabs or commas. Word sorts your whole document or any portion that you select before choosing the Sorting command. You can choose to sort the text in ascending sequence (smallest to largest; for example, 0–9 or A–Z) or descending sequence (largest to smallest; for example, 9–0 or Z–A).

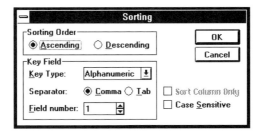

The Sorting dialog box is used to select options for sorting.

The Sorting command is also useful for organizing data documents prior to using the print merge feature. You can use the Sorting command to change the print order of data records by sorting, for example, the name or postal code column.

Note You should save your document before choosing the Sorting command. You can undo sorting, but you must choose the Undo command immediately after you sort. Saving your document before sorting provides an extra backup if the Sorting command does not produce the result you want. You can then close the document without saving changes and reopen it as it was before sorting.

Sorting Tables

Word changes the order of rows in a table based on the first column unless you specify a different column as the basis for sorting.

Archer	Michel	78
Brown	Paul	45
Rogers	John	396

— With the whole table selected, Word sorts the table based on the first column.

Brown	Paul	45
Archer	Michel	78
Rogers	John	396

— With one column selected, Word sorts the table based on that column.

To sort information in a table

1   Select the whole table or the column on which you want to base sorting.

To sort	Select
The whole table based on the first column	The whole table
The whole table based on other than the first column	The whole table, and then specify a column in the Field Number box
Only one column without changing the other columns	Only that column

2   From the Tools menu, choose Sorting (ALT, O, I).

If you have not made a selection, Word selects the whole document for sorting.

3   Under Sorting Order, select Ascending to sort from the beginning of the alphabet, the lowest number, or the earliest date.
–or–
Select Descending to sort from the end of the alphabet, the highest number, or the latest date.

4   Under Key Field, select the type of sorting you want in the Key Type box.

■   Select Alphanumeric to sort numbers, then text. Paragraphs that start with punctuation marks or other special characters are also sorted and placed before numbers and text. Dates are treated as numbers. The Case Sensitive option is only available for alphanumeric sorting. Select the Case Sensitive check box to give uppercase letters priority over lowercase letters.

■   Select Numeric to sort only numbers. All other characters are ignored. If the numbers you are sorting contain other characters, such as hyphens, select Alphanumeric so that Word does not ignore the other characters.

■   Select Date to sort by date. All characters not in recognizable date format are ignored. For more information, see "Date and Time Formats," later in this chapter.

5   Type or select a number other than 1 in the Field Number box if you want sorting to be based on a column other than the first (or selected one). For example, if you want to sort by the second column, type **2** in the Field Number box.

6   If you selected one column and want to sort that column only, leaving the other columns in the table unchanged, select the Sort Column Only check box. If you selected more than one column, this option is unavailable.

7   Choose the OK button.

If the results of the sort are not what you want, choose Undo from the Edit menu before taking any other action.

If you add borders to cells and then sort the cells, the borders stay with them. As a result, sorting a table may change its borders.

Date and Time Formats

When you sort using the Date option, Word sorts only those dates in recognizable date formats. The following are examples of the formats that Word recognizes as dates:

> 07/11/91
> 07-11-91
> July 11, 1991
> 11-Jul-91
> July-91
> 07/11/91 12:21 PM

Word does not recognize dates that are expressed as a month, day, or year by itself. In addition, Word does not recognize abbreviated month names with periods, such as Sept. 1, 1991. You can remove the period to make such a date one that Word can recognize.

To sort lists created with tabs

If you used tabs instead of a table to set up columns of text, you can specify which column to sort by, or you can sort one of the columns without changing the order of the others.

1   Select the portions of the list you want to sort.

To sort	Select
The whole list based on the first column	The whole list
The whole list based on other than the first column	The whole list, and then specify a column in the Field Number box
Only one column without changing the other columns	Only that column using column selection

2   From the Tools menu, choose Sorting (ALT, O, I).

    If you have not made a selection, Word selects the whole document for sorting.

3   Under Sorting Order, select Ascending to sort from the beginning of the alphabet, the lowest number, or the earliest date.
    −or−
    Select Descending to sort from the end of the alphabet, the highest number, or the latest date.

4 Under Key Field, select the type of sorting you want in the Key Type box.

- Select Alphanumeric to sort numbers, then text. Paragraphs that start with punctuation marks or other special characters are also sorted and placed before numbers and text. Dates are treated as numbers. The Case Sensitive option is only available for alphanumeric sorting. Select the Case Sensitive check box to give uppercase letters priority over lowercase letters.

- Select Numeric to sort only numbers. All other characters are ignored. If the numbers you are sorting contain other characters, such as hyphens, select Alphanumeric so that Word does not ignore the other characters.

- Select Date to sort by date. All characters not in recognizable date format are ignored. For more information, see "Date and Time Formats," earlier in this chapter.

5 Type or select a number other than 1 in the Field Number box if you want sorting to be based on a column in the list other than the first (or selected one). For example, if you want to sort by the second column, type **2** in the Field Number box.

6 Select the Tab option button to specify the tab character as the separator.

7 If you selected one column and want to sort that column only, leaving the other columns in the list unchanged, select the Sort Column Only check box. If you selected more than one column, this option is unavailable.

8 Choose the OK button.

If the results of the sort are not what you want, choose Undo from the Edit menu before taking any other action.

For more information about column selection, see Chapter 3, "Typing and Revising a Document."

Sorting Paragraphs

You can arrange paragraphs in alphanumeric, numeric, or date sequence by the first word or number in each paragraph. The paragraphs can be a list of items you want to sort alphabetically, numerically, or by date.

To sort paragraphs

1 Select the paragraphs you want to sort.

Word sorts the entire document unless you select specific paragraphs to sort.

2 From the Tools menu, choose Sorting (ALT, O, I).

If you have not made a selection, Word selects the whole document for sorting.

3 Under Sorting Order, select Ascending to sort from the beginning of the alphabet, the lowest number, or the earliest date.
   –or–
   Select Descending to sort from the end of the alphabet, the highest number, or the latest date.

4 Under Key Field, select the type of sorting you want in the Key Type box.

   ■ Select Alphanumeric to sort numbers, then text. Paragraphs that start with punctuation marks or other special characters are also sorted and placed before numbers and text. Dates are treated as numbers. The Case Sensitive option is only available for alphanumeric sorting. Select the Case Sensitive check box to give uppercase letters priority over lowercase letters.

   ■ Select Numeric to sort only numbers. All other characters are ignored. If the numbers you are sorting contain other characters, such as hyphens, select Alphanumeric so that Word does not ignore the other characters. Word does not sort numbers that are parts of words—for example, Alpha2; to sort numerically in such cases, set the number off by a space.

   ■ Select Date to sort by date. All characters not in recognizable date format are ignored. For more information, see "Date and Time Formats," earlier in this chapter.

5 Type or select a number other than 1 in the Field Number box if you want sorting to be based on something other than the first word in each paragraph.

To sort on other than the first word, the words in the paragraph must be separated by tab characters or commas.

6 Select the Comma option button to specify the comma as the separator.
   –or–
   Select the Tab option button to specify the tab character as the separator.

7 Choose the OK button.

If the results of the sort are not what you want, choose Undo from the Edit menu before taking any other action.

Note   If your document contains tables and you sort the entire document, Word treats each table as one unit and sorts tables within the document based on the contents of the first cell in each table.

Undoing Sorting

The Undo command on the Edit menu returns sorted text to its previous order. However, because the Undo command reverses only the most recent editing or formatting action, you should use it immediately after you sort.

To undo sorting

▶ From the Edit menu, choose Undo (ALT, E, U).

Sorting Order

If the text is a combination of letters, numbers, and special characters, Word sorts in ascending or descending alphanumeric order according to the following rules:

- Paragraphs or lines beginning with punctuation marks (such as ! ¡ « » # $ % or &) come before all others, those beginning with numbers come next, and those beginning with letters come last.

- Uppercase letters come before lowercase letters.

- If paragraphs or table rows begin with the same character, Word evaluates subsequent characters to determine which paragraph or table row should come first.

- Characters with diacritical marks (accents, umlauts, and so on) are sorted after the same character without the diacritical mark, and before the next character in the alphabet.

Chapter 16

Math Calculations

With the Calculate command, you can perform basic math calculations quickly and easily within a Word document. If you are working on a quarterly report, for example, or writing a cover letter for a financial statement, you can add rows of figures, multiply or divide numbers, or determine percentages and then insert the result anywhere in the document. You can perform the following operations: addition, subtraction, multiplication, division, calculating a power, calculating a root, and calculating a percentage.

You can calculate in Word either by using the Calculate command or by using expression fields. However, when you want to calculate using numbers in particular table cells or numbers that are spread throughout a document, or when you want to perform more complex calculations, you can use expression fields.

Adding with the Calculate Command

The math feature is especially useful if you want to add numbers in table columns, in table rows, or in columns created with tabs. Just select the row or column, and then choose Calculate from the Tools menu. Word calculates the result for you, and you can insert the result in a document.

Word ignores text and reads only numbers when calculating a selection. You don't need to type a plus sign (+), because Word automatically adds selected numbers separated by spaces unless you specify another mathematical operation.

To add numbers in columns or rows

1   Select the column or row of numbers you want to add.

To select	Do this
A column in a table	Click the right mouse button anywhere within the column.
A column created with tabs	Hold down the right mouse button, and drag from one corner of the column to the opposite corner.
A row in a table	Click to the left of the row. To select multiple rows, drag to the left of the row.

2   From the Tools menu, choose Calculate (ALT, O, C).

Word displays the calculation's result in the status bar for a few seconds. Word also copies the result to the Clipboard so you can paste it anywhere in your document.

To insert a calculation result into your document

1   Position the insertion point where you want the result to appear.

2   From the Edit menu, choose Paste (CTRL+V).

Other Operations with the Calculate Command

You can also use the Calculate command to subtract, divide, or multiply numbers or to calculate percentages, powers, and roots. When you perform calculations other than addition, you need to include mathematical operators. For example, if you want to multiply two numbers, type the first number, an asterisk (*), and the second number. Select the numbers and the asterisk, and then choose Calculate from the Tools menu. Word performs the calculation and displays the result for a few seconds in the status bar. The result is also automatically copied to the Clipboard.

The following table shows the operators to use for various calculations.

Use	To	Example	Expression	Result
- or ( )	Subtract	Budget for the rest of the month	1500-976 or 1500 (976)	524
/	Divide	Cost per month	$7000/12	$583.33
*	Multiply	Rent per year	12*$583	$6996.00
+ or space	Add	Joint income	19,000+16,500 or 19,000 16,500	35,500
%	Calculate percentage	Taxes due	$155.79*6%	$9.35
^	Calculate power	Six squared	$6\char94 2$	36
^	Calculate root	Cube root of eight	$8\char94(1/3)$	2

Note   As shown in the preceding table, you can specify that a number be subtracted by enclosing it in parentheses. This is standard practice for many financial statements where numbers are listed in columns. In the following example, Word subtracts 125 from 500, and then adds 250.

Month	Profit
January	500
February	(125)
March	250
Total	625

To perform math calculations

1 Type the numbers you want to calculate, along with the appropriate mathematical operators.

   Word can calculate numbers in a line, in a column or row in a table, or in a column separated from other columns with tabs. Word can also calculate numbers interspersed throughout the text in one or more paragraphs if you include a space on either side of each number.

2 Select the numbers and operators.

3 From the Tools menu, choose Calculate (ALT, O, C).

   Word calculates the result and displays it for a few seconds in the status bar. The result is stored on the Clipboard.

4 To insert the result into your document, position the insertion point and choose Paste from the Edit menu (CTRL+V) or click the Paste button on the Toolbar.

Guidelines for Calculation

Word uses the following guidelines when performing calculations:

- Word reads only numbers and operators when calculating a selection, ignoring text.

- Word uses ordered operations, meaning that certain calculations are performed before others.

   Percentage operations (%) take place before power and root (^) calculations. Power and root operations take place before multiplication and division (* and /). Multiplication and division take place before addition and subtraction (+ and −).

- Word calculates expressions in parentheses first.

   Enclosing numbers and an operator within parentheses tells Word to perform the enclosed operation first. However, enclosing a single number within parentheses tells Word to subtract it from the total. For example, if you select 25 (5*2), Word calculates a result of 35. But if you select 25 (5), Word calculates a result of 20.

- If one of the numbers in the selection contains a separator such as a comma or decimal point, the result also contains that separator. Make sure you have used the International category of the Control Panel to select the appropriate list separator before you use the Calculate command.

- If one of the numbers in the selection contains the currency symbol set in the Control Panel, the result contains that currency symbol. Make sure you have used the International category of the Control Panel to select the appropriate currency symbol before you use the Calculate command.

- If one of the numbers in the selection contains a decimal fraction, the result includes the same number of decimal places. Word automatically adds two decimal places to the result if any of the numbers contains the currency symbol set in the Control Panel, or if the result includes a fraction. For example, the result of £75–25 is £50.00. Word displays the result of 7000/6 as 1166.67.

Calculating Using Expression Fields

With expression fields, you can perform calculations in table cells or numbers spread throughout a document.

To calculate using numbers contained in table cells, you insert an expression field either inside or outside the table that refers to the appropriate cells.

To insert an expression field

▶ From the Insert menu, choose Field (ALT, I, D), and then in the Field Code box, type the expression.

–Or–

▶ Press the Insert Field key (CTRL+F9), and then type the expression.

Referring to Particular Cells

In an expression, you refer to cells with cell reference codes. Cell reference codes look like this: r*n*c*n*. The r stands for row; the c stands for column; and the *n* stands for a number, counted from the upper-left corner of the table. For example, [r1c1] refers to the cell at the intersection of the first row and column in a table.

You can refer to a range of cells by typing a colon between two cell reference codes. For example, the following procedure explains how to add the numbers in the second row of this table.

	c1	c2	c3	c4
r1	$4,865	$4,673	$3,685	$13,223.00
r2	$3,987	$2,385	$4,732	

1   Position the insertion point in the blank cell.

2   Press the Insert Field key (CTRL+F9) to insert a blank field.

Bold field characters ({}) appear, with the insertion point between them.

3   Type the expression **=sum([r2c1:r2c3])**

4   Press the Update Field key (F9) to update the field.

The number "$11,104.00" appears in place of the expression.

To edit an expression, highlight the result and press the Field Codes key (SHIFT+F9) or choose Field Codes from the View menu. The expression appears in place of the result, and you can make the necessary changes.

To refer to a whole row or column, you insert only the row or column reference. For example, [r2] refers to all cells in row 2, and [c3] refers to all cells in column 3. The r and c can be either uppercase or lowercase. In an expression, enclose each cell or range of cells in brackets and each function argument, such as **[r2c1:r2c3]** in the preceding procedure, in parentheses. For more information about function arguments, see Chapter 41, "Fields."

Creating a Simple Spreadsheet

You can create a simple spreadsheet in Word by inserting expression fields in table cells and then typing an expression that references the cells containing the numbers to be used in the calculation.

The following illustration shows the field expressions used to calculate three table totals.

	c1	c2	c3	c4
r1		**Last month**	**This month**	**Year to date**
r2	Doug	5434	2321	
r3	Steve	1234	2134	3368
r4	Kathy	5623	3412	9035
r5	**Total**	**12291**	**7867**	**20158**

— =sum([r2c2:r2c3])

=sum([r2c2:r4c2])   =sum([r2c4:r4c4])

For example, suppose you want Word to add Doug's sales from last month and this month and put the sum in the "Year to date" cell (the blank cell in the illustration). The following procedure explains how to do this.

To calculate within a table

1 Position the insertion point in the cell where you want the calculation result to appear.

You can also position the insertion point within text wherever you want to insert the result of the calculation.

2 Press the Insert Field key (CTRL+F9) to insert a blank field.

Bold field characters ({}) appear, with the insertion point between them.

3 Type an expression using the appropriate operators and the reference codes for the cells containing the numbers you want to include in the calculation.

In our example, the reference code for Doug's sales last month is r2c2 and the reference code for his sales this month is r2c3. Therefore, you would type **=sum([r2c2:r2c3])**. This expression means "Add all the numbers in the cells from row 2, column 2, to row 2, column 3."

You should not use the abbreviated form =sum([r2]) in this case. This expression adds all the cells in the row, including the cell containing the total, and therefore adds the result to the preview total each time the expression is updated.

4 Press the Update Field key (F9) to update the field.

To edit an expression, position the insertion point within the result and press the Field Codes key (SHIFT+F9) or choose Field Codes from the View menu. The expression appears, and you can make the necessary changes.

Calculating Cell Results from Outside a Table

If you insert an expression field in a table cell and use cell reference codes in the expression, Word assumes that these codes refer to cells in the same table as the field. But if you insert a field containing cell reference codes somewhere else in your text, you must add a bookmark name to the table so that Word can determine which cells the codes refer to.

To provide this information, insert a bookmark anywhere in the table, and then include the bookmark name in the field expression. Bookmark names can be from 1 to 20 characters long and must begin with a letter. They cannot contain spaces—only letters, numbers, and the underscore character (_).

For example, suppose you want Word to find the highest monthly sales amount from the previous table and then place that amount in a paragraph of text. The following procedure explains how to do this.

To calculate cell results from outside a table

1   Select the table that contains the numbers you want to use in the calculation.

2   From the Insert menu, choose Bookmark (ALT, I, M).

3   Type a bookmark name, and then choose the OK button.

The following example uses the name "sales."

4   Position the insertion point where you want the result of the calculation to appear.

For the list of functions such as "max," see the Expression (=) topic in online Help.

5   Press the Insert Field key (CTRL+F9) to insert a blank field.

Bold field characters ({}) appear, with the insertion point between them.

6   Type an expression containing both the bookmark name and the cell reference codes. For example:

```
{=max(sales[r2c2:r4c3])}
```

This expression means "From the table containing the bookmark called 'sales,' display the highest number listed in the cells from row 2, column 2, to row 4, column 3."

7   Press the Update Field key (F9) to update the field.

The number "5623" appears at the insertion point.

Calculating Numbers Spread Throughout a Document

You can easily calculate numbers located in different places throughout a document, whether they appear in table cells or in text. You can even have Word update the results of the calculation if you change any of the numbers later.

For example, suppose you want to subtract the total in one table from the total in another table and then refer to the result somewhere else in the document. To do this, you insert a bookmark for each number included in the calculation and insert a field where you want to display the result. If you later change any of the numbers included in the calculation, you can easily recalculate the result by updating the field. If you use a minus sign in the result field, make sure to include a space on either side of the minus sign.

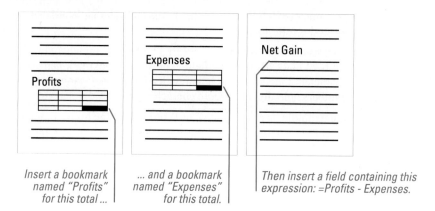

Insert a bookmark named "Profits" for this total ...   *... and a bookmark named "Expenses" for this total.*   *Then insert a field containing this expression: =Profits - Expenses.*

To calculate numbers spread throughout a document

1   Select the first number you want to include in the calculation. Be careful not to include the end-of-cell mark in the selection.

2   From the Insert menu, choose Bookmark (ALT, I, M).

3   Type a bookmark name, and then choose the OK button.

Bookmark names can be from 1 to 20 characters long and must begin with a letter. They cannot contain spaces—only letters, numbers, and the underscore character (_).

For more information about bookmarks, see Chapter 40, "Bookmarks and Cross-references."

4   Repeat steps 1 through 3 for each number you want to include in the calculation, typing a different bookmark for each number.

5   Position the insertion point in your text where you want the result of the calculation to appear.

6   To insert a blank field, press the Insert Field key (CTRL+F9).

Bold field characters ({}) appear, with the insertion point between them.

7   Type an expression using the bookmark names as the values to be calculated.

8   Press the Update Field key (F9) to update the field.

The result of the calculation appears in the field. If Word displays the field expression instead of the calculation result, position the cursor in the field and press the Field Codes key (SHIFT+F9).

To update calculation results

If you change any of the numbers included in a calculation that uses bookmarks and fields as described in the previous procedure, you can update the result in one of two ways. Make sure you reinsert the bookmark name for any number you change before you update the field.

For more information about updating fields, see Chapter 41, "Fields."

▶ To update the result in one field, position the cursor in the field and press the Update Field key (F9).

–Or–

▶ To update results in all the fields in a document, select the entire document and press the Update Field key (F9).

Tables

Word tables give you a quick and easy way to arrange and adjust columns of text and numbers—a much easier alternative than using tabs. And you can use tables for more than just tabular material. Tables give you a convenient way to group paragraphs side by side and to arrange text beside related graphics on a page. You can use tables to organize information in the data documents you merge to create form letters, mailing labels, and other merged documents. By adding borders and shading to a table, you can create many types of forms. For newsletters and brochures, you can create interesting page layouts with side-by-side columns of text and graphics.

If you have used Microsoft Excel, tables will seem very similar. In fact, if you insert a Microsoft Excel worksheet in your Word document, you can work with the spreadsheet data just as you would a Word table. All of the commands and techniques for working with tables can also be used on any worksheet in your Word document. For example, you can add borders and change the width of the worksheet columns. The reverse is also true: If you create a table in Word, you can insert the table in a Microsoft Excel worksheet and work with it as you would work with other spreadsheet data.

This chapter shows you how to set up and work with tables—rearranging the rows and columns, changing column widths, adding space between the rows, and making other changes to the table structure. With the few exceptions discussed here, you can edit and format text in a table just as you do in the rest of your document.

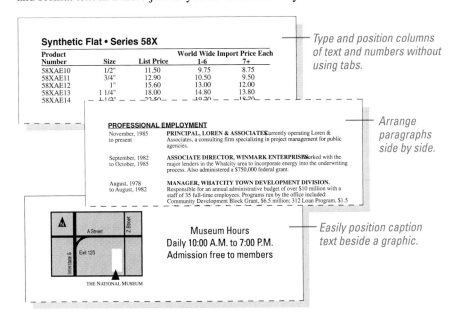

Type and position columns of text and numbers without using tabs.

Arrange paragraphs side by side.

Easily position caption text beside a graphic.

Setting Up a Table

You can think of a table as rows and columns of boxes, called *cells,* that you can fill with text and graphics. Within each cell, text wraps just as it does between the margins in other areas of your document. You can press ENTER to start new paragraphs, and you can easily add or delete text without affecting the columns of your table.

When you create a table, Word displays dotted gridlines between the cells to help you see which row and column of cells you're working in. An end-of-cell mark in each cell can be used to select the cell as you edit the table. Similar end-of-row marks at the end of each row of cells are used to position the insertion point for adding columns on the right. To reduce screen clutter, you can hide table gridlines as well as end-of-cell and end-of-row marks when you don't need to see them.

The following illustration shows the parts of a simple Word table.

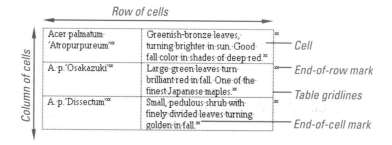

You can either insert a new table and fill in the empty cells, or you can convert existing paragraphs to a table. Word can convert tab-aligned columns of text to a table, making it easier for you to work with the text.

To display or hide table gridlines

▶   From the Table menu, choose Gridlines (ALT, A, G).

When table gridlines are displayed, a check mark appears next to the command on the menu.

–Or–

1   From the Tools menu, choose Options (ALT, O, O).

2   Under Category, select View.

3   Under Show Text With, select or clear the Table Gridlines check box.

4   Choose the OK button.

Note   Word does not print table gridlines. To add borders to the cells in a table, use the Border command on the Format menu. For more information, see Chapter 19, "Borders and Shading."

To display or hide end-of-cell marks

▶ Click the Show/Hide ¶ button on the ribbon.

–Or–

1 From the Tools menu, choose Options (ALT, O, O).

2 Under Category, select View.

3 Under Nonprinting Characters, select or clear the Paragraph Marks check box.

4 Choose the OK button.

Inserting a Table

Generally, the easiest way to insert a table is to use the Table button on the Toolbar. You can also use the Insert Table command on the Table menu. You might want to use this command if the Toolbar is not displayed, or if you want to specify the width of the table columns at the time you insert the table. You can also use the Column Width command on the Table menu to adjust column width after you insert a table.

To insert an empty table using the Toolbar

1 Position the insertion point where you want to insert the table.

2 Click the Table button on the Toolbar.

3 On the Table button grid, drag the mouse to select the number of columns and rows you want the new table to have.

   The number of columns and rows you select is indicated at the bottom of the grid. For example, if you select 2 rows and 3 columns, "2 × 3 Table" appears at the bottom of the grid.

4 Release the mouse button to insert the table.

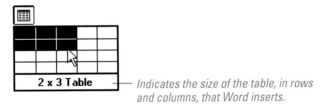

Indicates the size of the table, in rows and columns, that Word inserts.

To insert an empty table using the Insert Table command

1   Position the insertion point where you want to insert the table.

2   From the Table menu, choose Insert Table (ALT, A, I).

3   In the Number Of Columns box, type or select a number indicating how many columns you want.

   If you want to set the number of rows and the column widths now, you can do so in the appropriate boxes. If you're not sure what your requirements are, you can accept the default settings (one row with columns of equal widths). Later, you can add rows and adjust column widths to suit your needs.

4   Choose the OK button.

Word inserts an empty table with the insertion point in the first cell so that you can begin typing. Type the text for the first cell, pressing ENTER as needed to start new paragraphs in the cell. Then press TAB to move to the next cell. When you reach the rightmost cell, pressing TAB moves you to the first cell in the next row. When you reach the last cell in the table, you can press TAB to add another row of cells.

If you want to insert a tab character within a table, press CTRL+TAB. For more information about typing text in a table, see "Moving, Selecting, and Editing Within a Table," later in this chapter.

Note   If you're using a table to create a multiple-column layout, make sure you limit any one cell to less than the height of one page. If a cell doesn't fit on the current page, Word inserts a page break before the row containing that cell. Word cannot, however, insert a page break within a cell. If you insert more text in one row than will fit on the page, the text is displayed on your screen in normal view, but any text that exceeds the page boundary is not printed. To prevent this, insert an empty row right after where you want the page break to fall. Next, use the Cut command on the Edit menu to place the excess text from the original row onto the Clipboard, and then paste it into the new row.

Converting Text to a Table

You can easily convert text separated by paragraph marks, commas, and tab characters to a table. When you select text and choose the Convert Text To Table command from the Table menu, Word automatically creates a table using one of these characters to separate text into different cells. If more than one character could be used to separate the text, Word displays a dialog box so that you can select the one you want Word to use. Sometimes, you may need to remove extra paragraph marks, commas, and tab characters to get the table arrangement you want.

To convert existing text to a table

1   Select the lines of text or the paragraphs you want to convert to a table.

2   From the Table menu, choose Convert Text To Table (ALT, A, T).

Word converts the selected text into a table. If Word cannot determine how to convert the text, it displays a dialog box listing different conversion options.

3   If Word displays the Convert Text To Table dialog box, select the conversion options you want, and then choose the OK button.

If the resulting table is not what you want, choose Undo from the Edit menu before taking any other action.

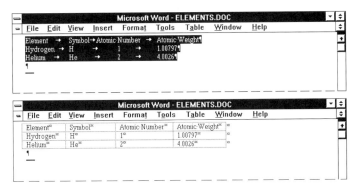

Tab-aligned columns converted to a Word table

Convert Text To Table Options

When you choose the Convert Text To Table command and Word cannot determine how to convert the text, it displays the following dialog box so that you can choose the most appropriate conversion option.

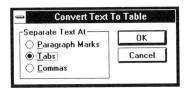

Paragraph Marks   When converting whole paragraphs, Word inserts one column and as many rows as there are paragraphs in the selection.

Tabs   If you select a tab character as the separating character, or delimiter, Word converts each paragraph and each line ending in a hard line break (inserted by pressing SHIFT+ENTER) to a row of cells. Word calculates the number of columns it inserts based on the greatest number of tab characters in any one paragraph or line.

Commas   If you select a comma as the separating character, or delimiter, Word converts each paragraph and each line ending in a hard line break (inserted by pressing SHIFT+ENTER) to a row of cells. Word calculates the number of columns it inserts based on the greatest number of commas in any one paragraph or line.

To split a table or insert text before a table

Use the following procedure to split a table and insert regular text between the two parts. If you started a table at the beginning of your document, you can also use this procedure to insert a heading or other text above the table.

1   Position the insertion point in the row beneath where you want the paragraph.
   –or–
   To add a text paragraph above the table, position the insertion point anywhere in the first row of cells.

2   From the Table menu, choose Split Table (ALT, A, S).
   –or–
   Press CTRL+SHIFT+ENTER.

   Word inserts a paragraph mark formatted with the Normal style above the row.

To convert a table to regular text paragraphs

If you decide to present information in the table in a different way, you can convert the table text to ordinary text paragraphs. You can separate the contents of cells with commas or tab characters, or convert the contents of each cell into one or more paragraphs. Paragraph conversion is the best choice if any of the cells have several paragraphs.

1   Select the rows of the table that you want to convert to text paragraphs.

2   From the Table menu, choose Convert Table To Text (ALT, A, T).

3   Select a Separate Text With option if you want to use one different from the one Word proposes.

4   Choose the OK button.

Moving, Selecting, and Editing Within a Table

For the most part, you move the insertion point and select and edit text in a table just as you do in the rest of your document. This section describes techniques that are unique to tables.

Moving the Insertion Point and Making Selections

Within a cell, you can move the insertion point and select text as you do in the rest of your document using the mouse or the arrow keys. For example, you can drag over text or double-click a word. The following keys and features have different uses in a table:

- Press TAB to move to the next cell in a row; press CTRL+TAB to insert a tab character. Use the arrow keys on the main keyboard and numeric keypad to move the insertion point through the text in the current cell before moving it to an adjacent cell. For example, pressing the RIGHT ARROW key moves through the current cell and then the next cell to the right.

- Use the selection bars to the left of each cell and at the top of each column to quickly select cells, rows, or columns. In the selection bar, the pointer changes to one of two styles of arrow.

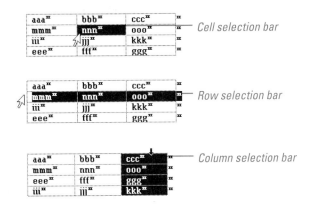

Cell selection bar

Row selection bar

Column selection bar

In the cell, row, and column selection bars, the pointer changes to an arrow.

To select within a table

▶ To select a table or part of a table, do one of the following.

To select	Do this
The next cell's contents	Press TAB
The previous cell's contents	Press SHIFT+TAB
An entire cell	Click in the cell selection bar or, with the insertion point in the leftmost position within the cell, press SHIFT+END.
	For some actions, such as adding or deleting cells, Word considers a cell selected if it contains the insertion point or selection.
A row of cells	Double-click in the selection bar of any cell in the row. Or click in the row selection bar to the left of the row. Or choose Select Row from the Table menu (ALT, A, R).
A column of cells	Click in the column selection bar at the top of the column. Or click anywhere in the column with the right mouse button. Or choose Select Column from the Table menu (ALT, A, C).
An entire table	From the Table menu, choose Select Table (ALT, A, A). Or press ALT+5 (numeric keypad).
Adjoining cells	Drag through the cells, or, while holding down SHIFT, press an arrow key repeatedly. When you cross cell boundaries, the selection automatically changes to include the entire cells.

Note   A table selection can include elements outside the table. A mixed selection affects the way deletions work. For more information, see "Deleting Text from Cells," which follows.

Deleting Text from Cells

Pressing BACKSPACE removes only the contents of the first cell in a selection. Press DEL to delete the contents of several cells, or use the Cut command on the Edit menu.

To delete text from cells

1 To delete text from several cells, select the text you want to delete.

2 From the Edit menu, choose Cut (ALT, E, T).

Word moves the selected cells and their contents to the Clipboard, leaving empty cells in their place. If the selection includes any text outside the table, no empty cells remain. Empty cells are also removed if the selection consists of an entire row or more than one entire row. For information about deleting cells from a table, see "Inserting, Deleting, and Moving Rows and Columns," later in this chapter.

Cutting, Copying, and Pasting Cells

You use the Cut, Copy, and Paste commands on the Edit menu to move and copy text and graphics within a table just as you do outside a table. If you select entire cells, including their end-of-cell marks, choosing Cut or Copy places the cells, as well as their contents, on the Clipboard. When you paste the cells back into the table using the Paste command, those cells replace entire cells. If you have copied one or more entire rows and select one or more entire rows, or position the insertion point in the first column, the rows are inserted and do not replace the selected cells. Use these techniques to copy or move cells within a table or to copy a table to another place in your document.

When you copy the entire cell ...

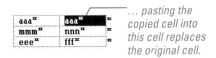

... pasting the copied cell into this cell replaces the original cell.

When you paste multiple cells into a table, position the insertion point in the upper-left cell of the area you want to paste into. Or select an area in the table that matches the pattern of cells on the Clipboard. When you choose Paste, Word replaces the cells in the paste area one for one with the cells from the Clipboard.

To copy or move text to new cells, first use the Insert Cells command to add empty cells where you want them. Then paste the cut or copied cells into the area. For instructions, see "Inserting Rows, Columns, and Cells," later in this chapter.

Element	Symbol	Atomic Number	Atomic Weight	
Hydrogen	H	1	1.00797	
Helium	He	2	4.0026	
Lithium	Li	3	6.939	

If you cut or copy these cells ...

... you can paste them here ...

... but not here.

To move or copy cells

1   Select the cells you want to move or copy.

2   From the Edit menu, choose Cut (ALT, E, T) or Copy (ALT, E, C).

Word places the cells and their contents on the Clipboard.

3   Position the insertion point in the upper-left cell of the area where you want to paste the cells, or select an area that matches the pattern of the cells you cut or copied.

4   From the Edit menu, choose Paste (ALT, E, P).

Formatting Text

When you insert a new table into your document, all cells in the table initially have the text format of the paragraph that contained the insertion point. You can use the ruler, ribbon, and commands on the Format menu to change the text formatting within the cells, just as you do in the paragraphs in the rest of your document. For example, to make column headings bold, simply select the row, and then click the Bold button on the ribbon.

The ruler has three available scales when you're working in a table: table scale, indent scale, and margin scale. When you first create a table, the ruler automatically switches to table scale. In table scale, Word displays column markers (**T**), which you can use to change column widths and indent rows of cells. For more information, see "Changing the Spacing of Columns and Rows," later in this chapter.

In margin scale, you can adjust margins, but this scale has no special use for tables. For information about changing margins with the ruler, see Chapter 9, "Margins, Paper Size, and Page Orientation."

The ruler can display indent scale both when the insertion point is in a regular paragraph and when it is in a paragraph within a table cell. In indent scale, the ruler displays paragraph indent markers. In a table, indents are set relative to the left and right cell boundaries instead of relative to the margins, which is the case when the insertion point is not within a table cell.

In indent scale, 0 marks the left boundary of the current cell or the first cell of the selection, and a solid vertical line marks the right cell boundary. If the indent settings for the text are too large in relation to the width of the cell, there is no room for the text in the cell, and the characters are displayed in a long vertical string. To fix this, align the left indent marker with the 0 mark and the right indent marker with the solid vertical line.

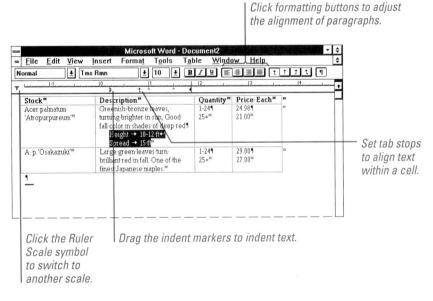

Click formatting buttons to adjust the alignment of paragraphs.

Set tab stops to align text within a cell.

Click the Ruler Scale symbol to switch to another scale.

Drag the indent markers to indent text.

Ruler in indent scale

To display different ruler scales

When the insertion point is within a table, the ruler displays table scale, unless you switch to a different scale.

▶ Click the Ruler Scale symbol at the far left of the ruler until the ruler displays the scale you want.

When the insertion point is within a table, clicking the Ruler Scale symbol switches between table scale, margin scale, and indent scale. When the insertion point is not within a table, clicking the Ruler Scale symbol switches between margin scale and indent scale only.

To insert a tab character in a table

In a table, the TAB key moves the insertion point or selection from cell to cell. Use the following technique to insert a tab character.

▶ Press CTRL+TAB.

If you set a decimal tab within a cell, Word automatically lines up numbers at the decimal tab position as you type them—you don't have to press CTRL+TAB to insert a tab character.

Inserting, Deleting, and Moving Rows and Columns

Using different commands on the Table menu, you can change the structure of a table in the following ways:

- Insert new rows, columns, and cells
- Delete selected rows, columns, and cells
- Merge cells to span several columns
- Move rows, columns, and cells

Inserting Rows, Columns, and Cells

If you're adding more than one row, column, or cell at a time, you first select the number of units that you want to insert. The selected cells indicate how many new cells to insert and where you want them inserted.

To insert a new row at the end of a table

▶ Position the insertion point in the table's last cell, and then press TAB.

Each cell in the new row has the text and cell formatting of the corresponding cell in the preceding row.

– Or –

▶ Position the insertion point in the line below the last row in the table, and then choose Insert Rows from the Table menu (ALT, A, I).

Word displays the Insert Rows dialog box, in which you can select the number of rows you want to insert.

To insert new rows within a table

1   To insert one row, select the row above which you want the new row.
    –or–
    To insert several rows, select as many rows as you want to add, directly beneath where you want them added.

2   From the Table menu, choose Insert Rows (ALT, A, I).

    The selected rows are shifted down to accommodate the new ones.

Element	Symbol	Atomic-Number	Atomic-Weight	
Hydrogen	H	1	1.00797	
Helium	He	2	4.0026	
Lithium	Li	3	6.939	

Select these two rows …

Element	Symbol	Atomic-Number	Atomic-Weight	
Hydrogen	H	1	1.00797	
Helium	He	2	4.0026	
Lithium	Li	3	6.939	

… to insert two new rows here.

To insert a single column to the right of a table

If table gridlines and end-of-cell marks aren't showing on your screen, choose Gridlines from the Table menu to display gridlines, and click the Show/Hide ¶ button on the ribbon to display end-of-cell marks.

1 Point to the right of the table and click the right mouse button to select all the end-of-row marks.

2 From the Table menu, choose Insert Columns (ALT, A, I).

If the new column extends past the document's right margin, you can resize the column. For information, see "Changing the Spacing of Columns and Rows," later in this chapter.

Tip If you're inserting more than one column to the right of the table, you can select the number of whole columns you want to add, and then choose Copy from the Edit menu. Next, position the insertion point immediately before the end-of-row mark of the first row, and then choose Paste from the Edit menu. You can also use this technique to paste one or more cells at the end of a particular row. To delete any text from the pasted cells, select the cells, and then choose Cut from the Edit menu.

To insert new columns within a table

1 To insert one column, select the column to the right of where you want to add the new column.
–or–
To insert several columns, select as many columns as you want to add, directly to the right of where you want to insert them.

2 From the Table menu, choose Insert Columns (ALT, A, I).

The selected columns are shifted to the right to accommodate the new ones.

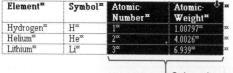

Select these two columns …

… to insert two new columns here.

To insert any number of cells into a table

You can use the following procedure to insert cells or entire rows and columns into a table.

1 Select as many cells as you want to add in the configuration in which you want to add them.

2 From the Table menu, choose Insert Cells (ALT, A, I).

3 Select one of the following options.

To	Select
Insert cells and shift the selected ones to the right	Shift Cells Right
Insert cells and shift the selected ones down	Shift Cells Down
Insert a row above the selected cells	Insert Entire Row
Insert a column to the left of the selected cells	Insert Entire Column

4 Choose the OK button.

Element"	Symbol"	Atomic-Number"	Atomic-Weight"	
Hydrogen"	H"	1"	1.00797"	
Helium"	He"	2"	4.0026"	
Lithium"	Li"	3"	6.939"	

Select these cells, and then choose the Insert Cells command.

Element"	Symbol"	Atomic-Number"	Atomic-Weight"	
Hydrogen"			H" 1"	1.00797"
Helium"			He" 2"	4.0026"
Lithium"	Li"	3"	6.939"	

The Shift Cells Right option moves cells to the right to accommodate the new ones.

Element"	Symbol"	Atomic-Number"	Atomic-Weight"	
Hydrogen"			1.00797"	
Helium"			4.0026"	
Lithium"	H"	1"	6.939"	
	He"	2"		
	Li"	3"		

The Shift Cells Down option adds new rows to contain the shifted cells.

Deleting Rows, Columns, and Cells

The commands on the Table menu for deleting different parts of a table change according to what part of the table is selected. If you select one or more rows, the menu contains the Delete Rows command. If you select one or more columns, the menu contains the Delete Columns command. If the selection includes part of a row or column, the menu contains the Delete Cells command.

To delete rows of cells

1   Select the rows you want to delete.

2   From the Table menu, choose Delete Rows (ALT, A, D).
    –or–
    From the Edit menu, choose Cut (ALT, E, T).

    You can only use the Cut command if entire rows are selected; if part of a row is selected, the Cut command removes the text, but not the cells.

To delete columns of cells

1   Select the columns you want to delete.

2   From the Table menu, choose Delete Columns (ALT, A, D).

To delete any number of cells

1   Select the cells you want to delete.

2   From the Table menu, choose Delete Cells (ALT, A, D).

3   In the Delete Cells dialog box, select the appropriate option to specify how you want Word to shift the remaining cells, or to delete the entire row or column that contains the selection.

4   Choose the OK button.

Merging Cells Within a Row

You may sometimes want to combine, or merge, two or more selected cells within a row to create a single cell. By merging cells, you can create a heading that spans several columns. The contents of each merged cell are converted to paragraphs within the combined cell, and the text retains its formatting.

To create the heading in the following illustration, type the heading text in the first cell of the table. Then select and merge the three cells in the first row. You can then delete the extra paragraph marks, center the text in the merged cell, and make it bold using the ribbon.

Select and merge these cells ...

... to create a single cell.

You can split a merged cell back into its constituent cells, but you cannot split cells that have not been merged.

To merge cells

You can only merge cells that are within the same row; you cannot merge cells from different rows.

1 Select the cells you want to merge.

Clicking the cell selection bar of one cell and then dragging across cell boundaries ensures that entire cells are selected.

2 From the Table menu, choose Merge Cells (ALT, A, M).

To split merged cells

1 Select the cell that has been merged.

2 From the Table menu, choose Split Cells (ALT, A, P).

If the Split Cells command is not available, it means that the selection does not consist of previously merged cells. You can get the effect you're looking for by adding a new cell to the left of the selected cell (using the Insert Cells command on the Tables menu), and then adjusting the widths of the cells.

Moving Rows, Columns, and Cells

You can move rows in a table by selecting them and dragging them to the desired
location, just as you can regular text. To move columns or a few individual cells, you
first need to insert new cells where you want the cells moved. Then you can copy the
cells you want to move to the new cells.

To move a row of cells

1 Select the row or rows you want to move, either by choosing Select Row from the
   Table menu (ALT, A, R) or by clicking in the selection bar next to the rows you
   want to select.

2 Drag the selected rows to the new location.

   Make sure you position the mouse pointer at the beginning of the first cell in the
   row before which you want to move the selected rows, and then release the left
   mouse button.

A dotted line indicates the row before which you want to move the selected row.

aaa	bbb	ccc	ddd
eee	fff	ggg	hhh
iii	jjj	kkk	lll
mmm	nnn	ooo	ppp

The pointer changes shape as you drag a selected row.

aaa	bbb	ccc	ddd
iii	jjj	kkk	lll
eee	fff	ggg	hhh
mmm	nnn	ooo	ppp

*Word moves the selected
row to the new location.*

Use the Sort Command to Reorder Rows in a Table

As with other text, you can sort entries in a table to arrange them in alphabetic or
numeric order. Suppose you've used a table to set up the membership list of your
organization. Each row of cells in the table contains the name, address, phone number,
and other information for one member. To list information in alphabetical order by each
person's last name, type the first name and last name in separate columns of the table.
Select the column containing the last names, and then choose the Sort command from
the Tools menu. Word orders each row alphabetically according to the name in the
selected column. To add new members to the list, enter their information in new rows at
the end of the table. Then sort the table again to place the new entries in their proper
order. For details about using the Sort command, see Chapter 15, "Sorting."

To move a column or individual cells

1 Before moving a column or individual cells, add new columns or cells where you want to move them.

   The number and arrangement of the inserted cells must match the number and arrangement of the cells you want to move. For instructions, see "Inserting Rows, Columns, and Cells," earlier in this chapter.

2 Select the columns or cells you want to move, and then choose Copy from the Edit menu (ALT, E, C).

3 Select the new cells you inserted, and then choose Paste from the Edit menu (ALT, E, P).

   You can now delete the moved cells from their original position using the Delete Cells command on the Table menu.

Changing the Spacing of Columns and Rows

You can change the width of selected cells and entire columns by dragging the column borders, by dragging the column markers (**T**) on the ruler, or by choosing the Column Width command from the Table menu. Using the Column Width and Row Height commands, you can:

- Adjust the spacing between the columns in each row

- Set a minimum or fixed height for each row

- Indent whole rows from the left margin to align the table rows with other text in your document

- Center a table or align the table left or right

Changing the Column Width and Column Spacing

For information about applying borders and shading to table cells, see Chapter 19, "Borders and Shading."

If you do not specify a column width when you insert a new table, Word bases the initial column width on the size of the main text area between the margins, with a small amount of spacing between the columns.

Unless your table design requires very precise column dimensions, it's easiest to change the column width by dragging the column borders or by dragging column markers on the ruler. The column markers are displayed when the insertion point or selection is within a table, unless you use the Ruler Scale symbol to switch to margin scale or indent scale.

When you drag a column border to resize a column, the columns to the right of it are shifted to the right or left, depending on whether you increase or decrease the column width. When you hold down the SHIFT key and drag a column border, the columns to the right are not shifted; instead, the width of the column immediately to the right increases or decreases as necessary to accommodate the column you are resizing. When you hold down the CTRL key and drag a column border, the column widths of all the columns to the right of the column you are resizing are equalized.

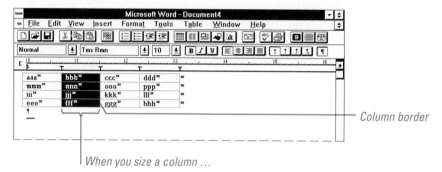

Column border

When you size a column ...

... by dragging a column border ...

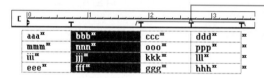

... columns to the right are shifted horizontally, but each column's width remains the same.

... by holding down SHIFT and dragging a column border ...

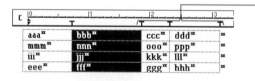

... columns are not shifted, but the column to the right is resized.

... by holding down CTRL and dragging a column border ...

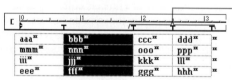

... columns to the right are resized proportionally.

To change column widths by dragging column borders

By dragging column borders, you can change the width of a column. If the column is selected, or if there is no selection, the width of the entire column is changed. If part of the column is selected, you can change the width of the selected cells by dragging the column border next to those cells. If you drag the column border above or below the selected cells, the width of the entire column changes.

▶ Use one of the following methods to change the width of a column by dragging.

To	Do this
Resize the column width, changing the overall table width	Drag the cell border on the right side of the column whose width you want to change.
Resize a column without changing the overall table width	Hold down SHIFT as you drag the cell border on the right side of the column.
Resize a column without changing the overall table width, and to divide equally the space between the column you are sizing and the end of the table	Hold down CTRL as you drag the cell border on the right side of the column.

To change column widths with the ruler

1 If the ruler is not displayed, choose Ruler from the View menu (ALT, V, R).

2 Select the rows in which you want the column widths to change.

3 If the ruler does not display column markers, click the Ruler Scale symbol to switch to table scale.

4 Do one of the following.

To	Do this
Resize the column width, changing the overall table width	Drag any of the column markers on the ruler. Column markers to the right of the marker that you drag also move to maintain the width of other columns in the table.
Resize a column without changing the overall table width	Hold down SHIFT as you drag the column marker. The markers to the right of the selected marker do not move.
Resize a column without changing the overall table width, and to divide equally the space between the column you are sizing and the end of the table	Hold down CTRL as you drag the column marker.

Ruler Scale symbol   *Column marker*

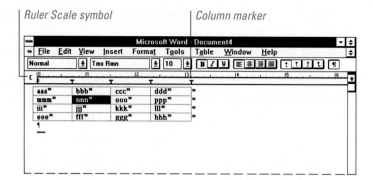

To change column widths with the Column Width command

Use the Column Width command if you want to specify the column width in a unit of measurement different from the ruler units. For example, you may want to specify the column width in picas, points, or centimeters when the ruler units are inches.

1 Select the column you want to adjust.

2 From the Table menu, choose Column Width (ALT, A, W).

3 In the Width Of Column(s) box, select or type a number to indicate how wide you want to make each column.

4 Choose the Next Column or Previous Column button to adjust the widths of additional columns.

5 Choose the OK button.

Note If you use the Next Column or Previous Column buttons to change the width of multiple columns and don't get the result you want, choosing the Undo command from the Edit menu reverses only the last change you made.

To change the space between columns

When changing the space between columns, keep in mind that the space affects the cell's usable column width. For example, in cells with a column width of 1.5 inches and a space between columns of 0.25 inch, the column area available for text and graphics is 1.25 inches.

The following procedure adjusts the standard spacing between columns in a table.

1 Select any column in the table.

2 From the Table menu, choose Column Width (ALT, A, W).

3 In the Space Between Cols box, type or select a number to specify how much spacing you want between the columns.

4 Choose the OK button.

Tip In some cases, you may want different amounts of space between the columns of a table. To vary the spacing, you can select each column and indent the text or graphics from the cell boundaries using the ruler or the Paragraph command on the Format menu.

Setting Row Height

Ordinarily, the height of each row depends on the contents of the cells in that row. The amount of paragraph spacing you add before or after text in a cell also affects the row height. You can override the automatic row adjustment by setting the row height in the Row Height dialog box. All cells within a row have the same height, but you can vary the height for each row.

In the following illustration, the row heights in the form have been adjusted to give the applicant room to write appropriate answers. The height of the first row is 5 lines. The height of the second row is 6 lines.

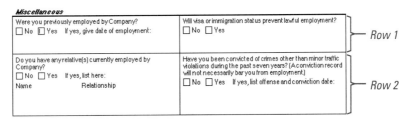

To set row heights

1 Select the rows you want to adjust.

2 From the Table menu, choose Row Height (ALT, A, H).

3 Select one of the following options from the Height Of Rows list. If you select At Least or Exactly, type the minimum or fixed height in the At box.

Option	Effect
Auto	Adjusts row height to accommodate any text or graphics in any cell in the row, up to the height of the page.
At Least	Sets a minimum row height of the size you specify in the At box. If a cell's text or graphics exceed the minimum height, Word adjusts the height to accommodate the material.
Exactly	Sets a fixed row height of the size you specify in the At box. If a cell's text or graphics exceed the fixed height, the contents of the cells may appear clipped on the screen and when you print the document.

4 Choose the Next Row or Previous Row button to adjust the heights of additional rows.

5 Choose the OK button.

Note If you use the Next Row or Previous Row button to make adjustments to multiple rows and don't get the result you want, choosing the Undo command from the Edit menu reverses only the last change you made.

Spacing Between Rows

To increase the spacing between rows of cells, you can use the Paragraph command on the Format menu to add space above or below the paragraphs in the selected rows.

In the following illustration, 3 points of space was added above each paragraph to increase the spacing between the rows of the table.

Synthetic Flat • Series 58X

Product Number	Size	List Price	World Wide Import Price Each	
			1-6	7+
58XAE10	1/2"	11.50	9.75	8.75
58XAE11	3/4"	12.90	10.50	9.50
58XAE12	1"	15.60	13.00	12.00
58XAE13	1 1/4"	18.00	14.80	13.80
58XAE14	1 1/2"	22.50	19.70	18.70

To add space between rows using the Paragraph command

1 Select the rows to which you want to add spacing.

2 From the Format menu, choose Paragraph (ALT, T, P).

3 Do one of the following.

To add space	Do this
Before the selected paragraphs	Type or select a measurement in the Before box.
After the selected paragraphs	Type or select a measurement in the After box.
Before and after the selected paragraphs	Type or select a measurement in the Before and After boxes.

Keep in mind that if you've selected the Exactly option in the Row Height dialog box, you should make sure the lines you're adding fit within the row height you've specified.

4 Choose the OK button.

Tip In the Before and After boxes, Word proposes measurements in lines. Word also recognizes the following units of measurement for spacing before and after: centimeters, points, and picas. For example, you can type **10 pt** to add 10 points of space before or after a paragraph.

Aligning and Indenting Rows

You may want to center a small table between the margins or indent a table so it aligns with other text in your document. You can control the horizontal placement of a table by changing the row alignment or the indentation of selected rows from the left margin. The row alignment and indentation do not affect the paragraph indents and the alignment of text within the table cells.

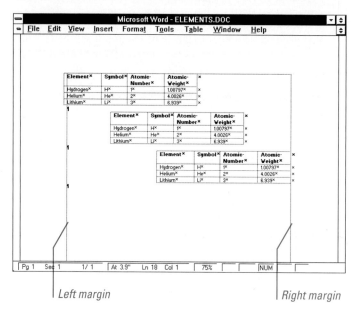

Tables with left, centered, and right row alignment

To change the row alignment

1 Select the rows whose alignment you want to change.

2 From the Table menu, choose Row Height (ALT, A, H).

3 Under Alignment, select the alignment you want.

4 Choose the OK button.

To indent rows using the ruler

If you need to indent a table row a precise distance from the left margin, you may prefer to specify a measurement in the Indent From Left box in the Row Height dialog box. Otherwise, it's more convenient to indent rows using the ruler.

1   If the ruler does not display column markers, click the Ruler Scale symbol to switch to table scale.

2   Select the rows you want to indent.

3   Drag the row indent marker to where you want the row indented.

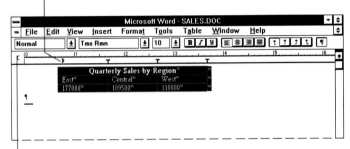

With the ruler in table scale, drag the row indent marker.

If the row indent marker is not shown, click the Ruler Scale symbol on the ruler.

Note   In table scale, the row indent marker (▶) is used to indent selected rows of a table. In indent scale, this marker is used to set the first-line indent and left indent of text within a cell.

Tricks and Tips for Working with Tables

This section includes some tips and techniques that can speed up your work and help you use tables to greatest advantage.

Saving a Table as a Glossary Entry

If you frequently use a certain type of table, you can store the table as a glossary entry. Then you can insert the ready-to-use table in any of your documents. You need to store only a few rows of the table. After you insert the table in a document, you can press the TAB key to add rows to the end of the table as you need them.

It saves time to format the table before you store it in the glossary. Format the first row the way you want your column headings and the remaining rows as table entries. You can include boilerplate text in the cells if you want. When you finish entering and formatting the rows, select them and use the Glossary command on the Edit menu to define the table as a glossary entry. For more information about glossaries, see Chapter 13, "Glossaries: Storing Items for Reuse."

Using a Table as a Simple Spreadsheet

To calculate within a column or row of numbers, select the cells containing the numbers and choose Calculate from the Tools menu. Word calculates the result, ignoring any text in the cells, displays it on the status bar, and stores it on the Clipboard. Note that Word adds the numbers unless you insert other mathematical operators (–, *, or /). You can then use the Paste command to insert the result into your document. For more information, see Chapter 16, "Math Calculations."

Using a Table to Create a Chart

Word makes it easy to convert data you have typed in a table into a chart. Simply select all or part of the table, and then click the Graph button on the Toolbar. Word opens Microsoft Graph, which uses the information in the table to create a chart. You can use any of the commands in Microsoft Graph to format the chart. When you are satisfied with the chart's appearance, choose Exit And Return from the File menu to insert the chart into your document immediately below the table you selected.

The chart that Microsoft Graph inserts into your Word document is an embedded object. To format or edit any of the information in the chart, you can double-click the chart to open Microsoft Graph. For more information about embedded objects, see Chapter 36, "Exchanging Information."

For more information about working with charts, see the *Microsoft Graph User's Guide.* You can easily get online Help in Microsoft Graph by pressing F1.

Using Styles to Format Your Tables

Using styles to format the text in a table ensures a consistent look for all tables in a document. In simple tables, you might create one style for the table column headings and another style for the table entries. To change the text format—for example, to change the text alignment of the column headings from centered to left alignment—you can redefine the table styles to update the formatting of all the tables in your document at once.

You can use the table styles to specify uniform paragraph spacing between rows of cells. In some tables, cells may contain several paragraphs, each differently formatted. You can define a style for each group of formats you use in the table. If the paragraphs follow each other in a predictable order, you can take advantage of the Next Style option of the Style dialog box to automatically apply the appropriate styles to each succeeding paragraph as you type.

In the following illustration, a style named Table Text is applied to all rows in the table after the row that contains the column headings. The formats defined for Table Text include 8 points of space before the paragraph to ensure that all of the rows are evenly spaced. In the second column, the second paragraph is formatted with the style Table Text 2, which includes a left indent, a tab stop, and 4 points of space before the paragraph. Word automatically applies the Table Text 2 style to the second paragraph as you type because Table Text 2 has been specified as the next style for the Table Text style. For more information, see Chapter 8, "Formatting with Styles."

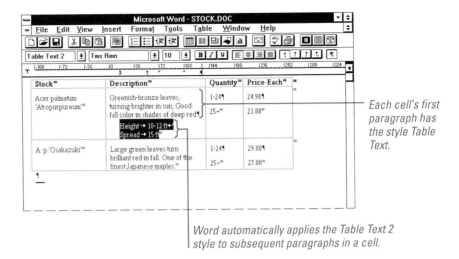

Each cell's first paragraph has the style Table Text.

Word automatically applies the Table Text 2 style to subsequent paragraphs in a cell.

Troubleshooting

This section describes some common problems you might encounter while working with tables and offers suggestions for overcoming them.

Table Text Is Cut Off at the Bottom of the Page

If you type more text in a cell than will fit on a single page, the text that exceeds the page is not printed. You can insert a new row immediately after where you want the page to break, and then move some of the text to the new row so that Word can insert a page break between the rows.

Text Is Not Visible or Is Displayed in One Long Vertical Column

Most likely the text indents are not in proportion to the width of the cell. For example, if the cells of the table are 2 inches wide and the text in the cells has 1-inch left and right indents, the cells have no room for the text. Use the following procedure to remove the indents from the text in all cells.

1   From the Table menu, choose Select Table (ALT, A, A) to select the entire table.

2   From the Format menu, choose Paragraph (ALT, T, P).

3   Under Indentation, type **0** (zero) in the From Left, From Right, and First Line boxes.

4   Choose the OK button.

Word realigns all indents with the cell boundaries, allowing the text to wrap properly in the cells.

Columns

Using Word, you can produce two general types of columns. The first are table columns (sometimes known as "parallel columns") created with the Table command, as explained in Chapter 17, "Tables." The second are "snaking" columns, in which text flows from the bottom of one column to the top of the next, as in newspaper columns. This chapter describes how you can format your entire document, or any section of it, in newspaper-style columns.

Product Number	Size	List Price
58XAE10	1/2"	11.50
58XAE11	3/4"	12.90
58XAE12	1"	15.60
58XAE13	1 1/4"	18.00
58XAE14	1 1/2"	22.50

The Table command organizes text into columns and rows. Column widths can vary.

Robot added to work force

Our athletic shoe division took a step toward the twenty-first century this month when it purchased a robot to assist with manufacturing.

The robot threads shoelaces into track shoes at an astounding rate of speed. Human co-workers report that the robot is pleasant to work with and "doesn't complain much." In fact, the robot doesn't talk at all.

Nicknamed "TongueTied" by his co-workers, the 5'6" tall robot was originally programmed to whistle as he worked. Fellow workers soon voted to shut off this function. Does TongueTied make any noise at all now? Supervisor Paul Martin reports, "At the end of the day his hydraulic

he worked. Fellow workers soon voted to shut off this function. Does TongueTied make any noise at all now? Supervisor Paul Martin reports, "At the end of the day his hydraulic system decompresses and he sort of sighs."

For Martin's fortieth birthday, workers dressed the robot in a company T-shirt and a party hat. It gave TongueTied so much personality that Martin left him that way.

Autographs, anyone?

TongueTied, our company robot, seems to have a competitive side to him. As a publicity gimmick, market-

scores on arcade-type computer games. TongueTied rolled away with not only top honors, but the world-record score for all three games.

Although all prizes went to the humans, the company sponsoring the contest created a special plaque for TongueTied to commemorate his win. And what did the kids think of their automated competitor? They had nothing but admiration for his quick reflexes.

As top scorer in the contest, TongueTied will have his name displayed in arcades around the world, along with the names of the top five human contestants. Market- ing modified its sales strategy for our

This chapter describes how to create newspaper-style columns such as these and others that are of equal width.

You can use the mouse and the Text Columns button on the Toolbar to format text in one column or multiple newspaper-style columns. With the Columns command on the Format menu, you can format text in up to 100 newspaper-style columns. You can also use the Columns command to:

- Change the space between columns.

- Add a vertical line between columns.

- Format the current section to start in a new column.

The total number of newspaper-style columns you can produce depends on the width of each column, the spacing between them, the width of the margins, the font size, the size and orientation of the paper on which you plan to print the document, and the default tab stop setting. You can format your document with a large number of columns each as narrow as the default tab stop, normally 0.5 inch. (For more information on margins, paper size, and page orientation, see Chapter 9, "Margins, Paper Size, and Page Orientation.")

Viewing Multiple-Column Documents

Word provides three views that are especially useful when working with multiple columns. Each view offers its own advantages.

View	Advantages
Normal (View menu)	Faster for text entry. Shows section marks. You can zoom in or out for a close-up look or an overview. Shows accurate column widths, but does not display columns side by side.
Page Layout (View menu)	Shows columns side by side with framed items such as graphics in the correct location. Good for final editing, manually inserting column breaks, and adjusting column width. You can zoom in or out.
Print Preview (File menu)	Shows overall page layout just as the document will print, including vertical lines between columns. Good for final adjustments to margins and page breaks. You can view two pages at once.

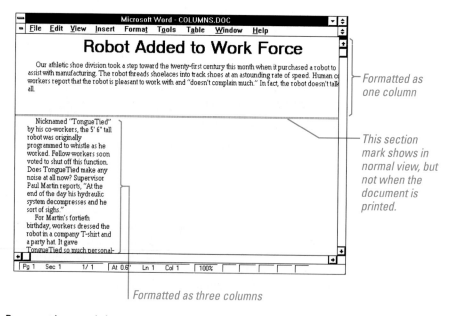

Document in normal view

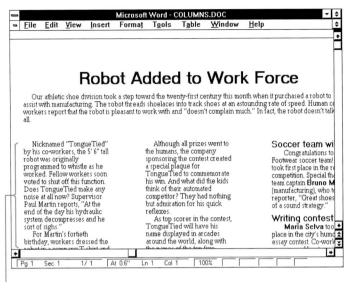

Displays multiple columns on the screen. You can type, edit, and use the ruler to adjust the column width.

Document in page layout view

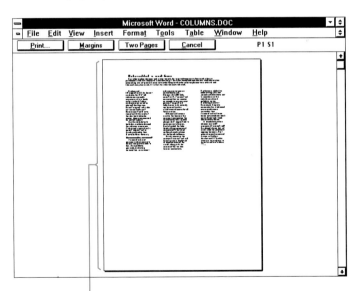

Shows how pages will look when printed. You cannot edit in print preview, but you can adjust margins and page breaks.

Document in print preview

Magnifying or Reducing the View of a Document

In page layout view and normal view you can zoom in to magnify the document for a close-up look or you can zoom out so the entire page shows on the screen at one time. Zooming in or out is for your convenience as you edit. Zooming in or out does not affect the way the document prints. You can use the Zoom command on the View menu to change the view from 25 percent to 200 percent, or if you are using a mouse, you can use the Toolbar.

The Toolbar provides three buttons that make it easy to magnify or reduce the view of the document. You can display the entire page and continue to edit it. Or you can reduce the size of a wide document so it fits margin to margin on the screen in page layout view. With the click of a button, you can return to 100 percent magnification in normal view.

To zoom with the mouse

1   If the Toolbar is not displayed, choose Toolbar from the View menu (ALT, V, T).

2   Do one of the following:

  ■ To view the entire page, click the Zoom Whole Page button.

  ■ To view the full width of the document, click the Zoom Page Width button.

  ■ To view the document at 100 percent magnification in normal view, click the Zoom 100 Percent button.

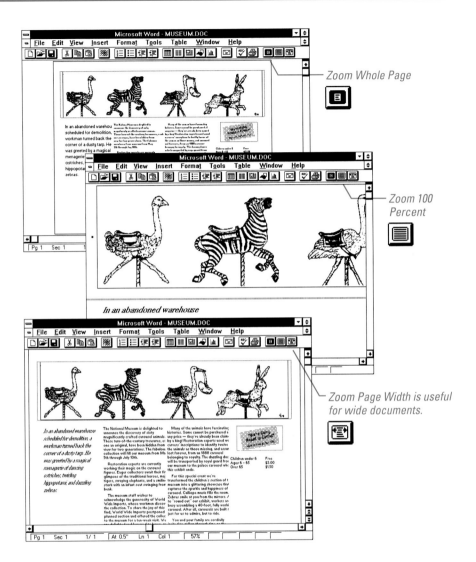

Zoom Whole Page

Zoom 100 Percent

Zoom Page Width is useful for wide documents.

To zoom with the keyboard

You can display the full page or, for wide documents, the page width. You can also choose from 25 percent to 200 percent magnification.

1   If you are not in page layout view, choose Page Layout from the View menu (ALT, V, P).

2   From the View menu, choose Zoom (ALT, V, Z).

3   Do one of the following:

- To display the entire page on the screen, choose the Whole Page button.

- To reduce a wide document enough to see the full width, choose the Page Width button.

- To reduce or magnify the display, under Magnification, select a percentage.

4   Choose the OK button.

Formatting a Document in Multiple Columns

For more information about sections, see Chapter 10, "Sections: Formatting Parts of a Document."

When you begin a Word document, it is all one section. Changing the number of columns affects the layout of the entire document. To change the number of columns in part of the document, you make that part a separate section. You insert a section break at the point where you want to start the new columns, and then specify the number of columns you want in the new section.

You can change the number of columns on a single page, or you can change the formatting between major parts of a document, such as the main text and the index. When you apply multiple column formatting, you choose how much of the document will be affectedñthe selected text, the section containing the insertion point, selected sections, or the whole document. If you do not make a selection, Word applies the formatting to the section that contains the insertion point. You can also choose to apply the formatting from the insertion point to the end of the document or to the whole document.

Tip   Sections of a document are divided by section marks, which appear as double-dotted lines in normal view. To search for section marks in a long document, choose the Find command from the Edit menu and type **^d** . This locates section marks and hard page breaks, which appear as single-dotted lines.

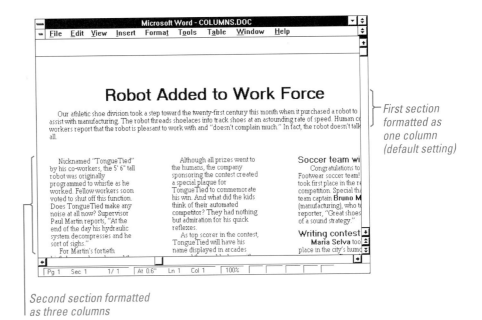

First section
formatted as
one column
(default setting)

Second section formatted
as three columns

Document in page layout view

Within each section, Word automatically adjusts the width of the columns to fit between the margins. If you adjust the margin settings or if you adjust the setting for the space between columns, Word changes the width of the columns so that they continue to fit within the margins. If you adjust the width of the columns, Word adjusts the space between the columns to create equal amounts of space.

For more information about sizing graphics, see Chapter 20, "Importing Graphics." For information about sizing tables, see Chapter 17, "Tables."

You can type, edit, and format text in multiple columns just as you edit any other text. If you change the number of columns in your document, you may want to adjust the size of graphics or tables to fit in the new columns.

Tip Word stores section formatting instructions for a section in the section mark. If you delete a section mark, any text in the section above it assumes the format of the section below it. If you accidentally delete a section mark, immediately choose Undo from the Edit menu. Word restores the section mark, and the mark restores the formatting.

To create a multiple-column layout

To see the columns side by side on the screen, choose Page Layout from the View menu before or after this procedure.

1   If the Toolbar is not displayed, choose Toolbar from the View menu (ALT, V, T).

2   Click in the section whose text you want to format.

3   On the Toolbar, click the Text Columns button.

4   Drag to the right to select the number of columns you want.

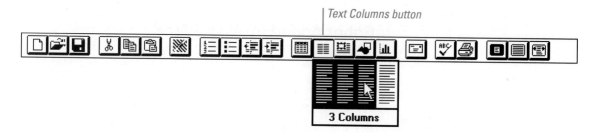

Text Columns button

When you release the mouse button, Word formats the section that contains the insertion point.

1   Select the text that you want to format in multiple columns or position the insertion point where you want to change the number of columns.

2   From the Format menu, choose Columns (ALT, T, O).

3   Type or select the number of columns you want.

4   In the Apply To box, select the amount of text you want to format.

5   Choose the OK button.

In normal view, one column appears at a time. In page layout view and in print preview, the columns appear side by side.

If one column is longer than another on the last page of a section or document, you can balance them to be the same length. For more information, see "Balancing the Length of Columns" later in this chapter.

Creating Banner Heads

You can create a full-width banner, or masthead, to call attention to the title of a multiple-column newsletter or report. (See the following illustration.) Position the insertion point below the banner text, and then choose the Columns command. Type the number of columns you want below the banner, and select This Point Forward in the Apply To box. Word places a section mark, which appears as a double-dotted line in normal view, between the banner and the multiple columns. This mark separates the section formatting of the banner from the section formatting of the text below it. The section mark does not print.

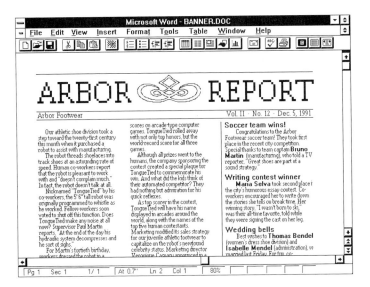

Document with a banner head in page layout view

Changing Column Width or Spacing Between Columns

To format columns with uneven widths, use the Insert Table command. For more information, see Chapter 17, "Tables."

When you create multiple columns, Word maintains the same column width and the same space between columns for all columns in the section. If you change the width of a column, Word changes the other columns to match. The same is true if you change the space between two columns; Word changes the other spaces to match.

To create columns with uneven widths, convert your text into a table with the Convert Text To Table command on the Table menu instead of using the following procedure.

To change column width

1   To view columns side by side, choose Page Layout from the View menu (ALT, V, P).

2   To display the ruler, choose Ruler from the View menu (ALT, V, R).

3   If the margin markers are not displayed above each column on the ruler, click the Margin Scale symbol at the left end of the ruler.

4   Drag a column marker ([or]) to adjust the width of the columns.

   Word automatically adjusts the width of the other columns and the corresponding space between the columns.

Click here if triangular indent markers show instead of margin markers.

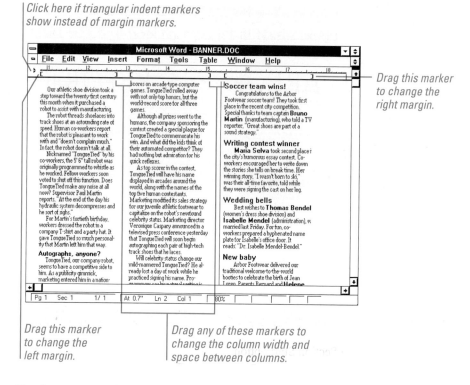

Drag this marker to change the right margin.

Drag this marker to change the left margin.

Drag any of these markers to change the column width and space between columns.

To change spacing between columns

1   To view columns side by side, choose Page Layout from the View menu (ALT, V, P).

2   Place the insertion point in any of the columns you want to format.

3   From the Format menu, choose Columns (ALT, T, O).

4   In the Space Between box, type or select the measurement you want.

The default spacing is 0.5 inch. You can also use centimeters (cm), points (pt), or picas (pi). For example, you can type **1.5 cm** to use centimeters.

5   Choose the OK button.

Word automatically adjusts the width of the other columns and the corresponding space between the columns.

If you've chosen a spacing too great for the number of columns and the width of the page, Word displays a message. Choose the OK button, type or select a smaller measurement in the Space Between box, and choose the OK button again.

To add vertical lines between columns

You can print vertical lines between columns. The lines are as long as the longest column on the page.

1 Position the insertion point in the section that you want to have lines.

2 From the Format menu, choose Columns (ALT, T, O).

3 Select the Line Between check box.

4 In the Apply To box, select how much of the document you want to add lines to.

5 Choose the OK button.

6 To see the vertical lines as they will print between the columns, choose Print Preview from the File menu (ALT, F, V).

Vertical lines are not displayed in normal view or page layout view. Paragraph borders that you apply with the Border command on the Format menu are displayed, however.

Tip You can select part of a section and format the selection to have vertical lines between columns. Word makes your selection into a separate section. The text following your selection is formatted to begin in a new column. If you want to adjust the section start for any of the sections, you can position the insertion point in the section you want to change, and then choose Section Layout from the Format menu and select a Section Start option.

Reading the Ruler in Multiple-Column Text

When you display indents and tab stop markers on the ruler and the insertion point is in multiple-column text, the ruler starts at zero for the column containing the insertion point. The following illustrations show the changes in the ruler's scale with a selection in the first column and with a selection in the second column.

Zero marks the boundary of the first column that contains the selection or the insertion point.

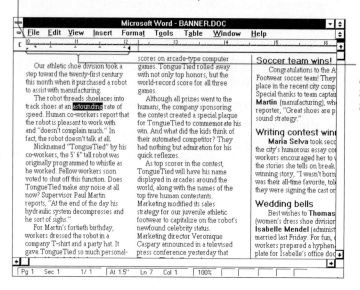

The indent markers reflect the settings in the first column.

Zero marks the boundary of the column that contains the selection or insertion point.

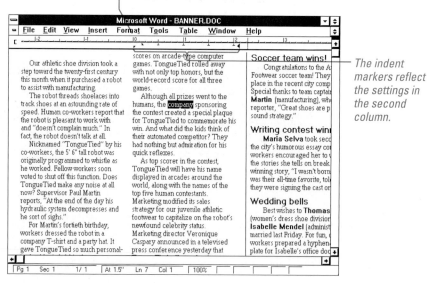

The indent markers reflect the settings in the second column.

To store a special layout for use in future documents

For more information about templates, see Chapter 37, "Document Templates."

New documents are formatted in a single column. If you always change the layout for a particular type of document, you can save time by formatting the document once and saving it as a template. New documents based on the template will automatically have the same layout as the template.

1 Format each section of a document with the number of columns and other options you want in future documents.

2 In normal view, delete any text or graphics that you do not want to appear in future documents, but do not delete the section marks (double-dotted lines).

Itís helpful to leave a few words that describe the formatting of the section. For example, you might type **two column** in a two-column section.

3 From the File menu, choose Save As (ALT, F, A).

4 Type a name for the template.

5 Under Save File As Type, select Document Template.

6 Choose the OK button.

7 If Word displays the Summary Info dialog box, type any of the optional information, and then choose the OK button.

When you want to create a document with these settings, choose the New command from the File menu. In the Use Template box, select the name of your template, and choose the OK button. The new document has the same number of columns and other section formatting as the template.

Paragraph Indents and Column Formatting

If you apply multiple-column formatting to your document after youíve applied paragraph indents, some or all of your columns may turn out narrower than you want them. (See the following illustration.) In this case, you need to adjust the paragraph indents. To do this, choose the Paragraph command from the Format menu and type zero in the From Left, From Right, and First Line boxes. If, after viewing the columns, you want to set indents, drag the indent markers on the ruler or use the Paragraph command.

To avoid the problem, make sure you format the multiple columns before you set any indents. For more information about indents, see Chapter 7, "Paragraph Formatting."

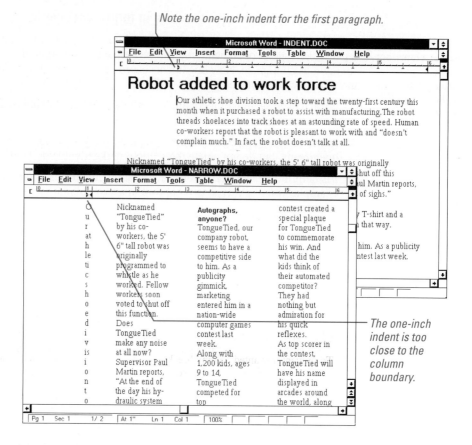

Note the one-inch indent for the first paragraph.

The one-inch indent is too close to the column boundary.

Controlling Column Breaks

Word automatically breaks columns so they fit on the page. If you'd like to change where the columns break, you can use the Break command on the Insert menu to indicate where you want a new column to start. Word inserts a *column break* at the location of the insertion point. For example, if you want to make sure a certain paragraph such as a heading appears at the top of a column, you insert a column break immediately before it. You can insert as many column breaks as you need to get the look you want.

You can create a new column at the start of a section by using the Columns command or the Section Layout command on the Format menu. If you select the New Column option in either dialog box, the section that you are formatting begins in a new column.

To break a column manually

1   To display the columns side by side, choose Page Layout from the View menu (ALT, V, P).

2   Place the insertion point where you want to start a new column.

3   From the Insert menu, choose Break (ALT, I, B), select Column Break, and then choose the OK button.
    −or−
    Press CTRL+SHIFT+ENTER.

To insert a page break in a multiple-column section

1   Place the insertion point where you want to break the page.

2   From the Insert menu, choose Break (ALT, I, B), and then choose the OK button.
    −or−
    Press CTRL+ENTER.

Controlling Unwanted Column Breaks

You can use the Paragraph command on the Format menu to keep two paragraphs together in the same column. For example, you could keep a graphic and its caption together, or keep a heading with the text it describes.

To prevent unwanted column breaks, you select the first of the two paragraphs you want to keep together, and then choose the Paragraph command from the Format menu. Select the Keep With Next check box; this ensures that the paragraphs will print in the same column. If a column break should naturally fall between the paragraphs, Word moves both paragraphs into the next column instead of separating them. The Paragraph command has a similar option that keeps all lines in a paragraph together. For more information, see Chapter 7, "Paragraph Formatting."

Balancing the Length of Columns

The last page of a section or document often isnít a full page of text. In a multiple-column layout, Word fills each column to the length of the page and leaves the last column empty or partially filled. This gives the columns an uneven appearance. To balance the length of the columns, you can insert an extra section break after the text and specify Continuous as the Section Start option.

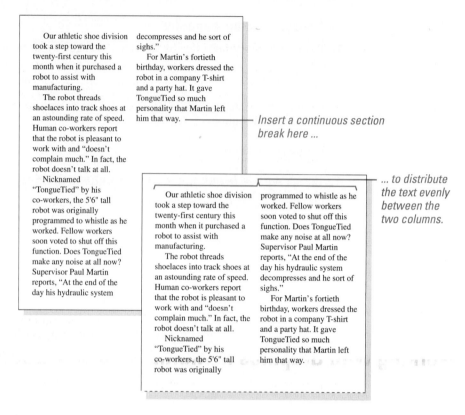

Insert a continuous section break here ...

... to distribute the text evenly between the two columns.

To balance the length of columns

Use this technique at the end of a document or at the end of a section when columns end unevenly.

1   Place the insertion point at the end of the text in the columns you want to balance.

   If the columns are already followed by a section mark, make sure you place the insertion point before the existing section mark.

2   From the Insert menu, choose Break (ALT, I, B).

3   Under Section Break, select Continuous.

4   Choose the OK button.

5   To see the columns side by side, choose the Print Preview command from the File menu (ALT, F, V), or choose the Page Layout command from the View menu (ALT, V, P).

Balancing Columns Before a Section Title

If a new section has a title, use the Break command on the Insert menu to insert a continuous section break before and after the title. This balances the columns above the title and keeps the title from interfering with the balanced look of the columns below it.

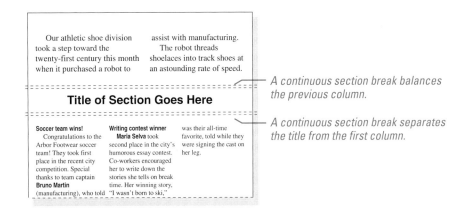

Our athletic shoe division took a step toward the twenty-first century this month when it purchased a robot to assist with manufacturing. The robot threads shoelaces into track shoes at an astounding rate of speed.

A continuous section break balances the previous column.

Title of Section Goes Here

A continuous section break separates the title from the first column.

Soccer team wins!
Congratulations to the Arbor Footwear soccer team! They took first place in the recent city competition. Special thanks to team captain **Bruno Martin** (manufacturing), who told

Writing contest winner
Maria Selva took second place in the city's humorous essay contest. Co-workers encouraged her to write down the stories she tells on break time. Her winning story, "I wasn't born to ski,"

was their all-time favorite, told while they were signing the cast on her leg.

Working with Graphics in Multiple-Column Documents

You can position graphics so that they span one or more newspaper-style columns. If you want the graphic to span two columns, as in the following illustration, and you are using a mouse, you can drag a sizing handle on the graphic until it is the size you want. For more precision, you can measure the width of each column and add to that measurement the space between the columns. Use the Picture command on the Format menu to make the total measurement equal to the width of the graphic. You'll also need to adjust the height of the graphic.

If there is more than an inch of space between the graphic and the column boundary, the margin, or another positioned item, you can flow text around the graphic. For more information about positioning graphics on the page, see Chapter 21, "Positioning Text and Graphics on the Page."

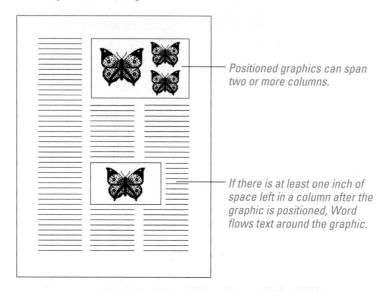

Positioned graphics can span two or more columns.

If there is at least one inch of space left in a column after the graphic is positioned, Word flows text around the graphic.

Chapter 19

Borders and Shading

With the Border command on the Format menu, you can add lines and boxes to paragraphs of text, graphics, or the cells in a table. You can also shade paragraphs and tables. If you have a color printer, you can print colored borders and shading. The following illustrations show a few of the effects you can achieve using the Border command.

A box can give a graphic a finished look ...

... or emphasize a text paragraph.

Shading can call attention to a paragraph ...

... or highlight a column in a table.

Borders can separate sections of your layout ...

... or make table headings and entries easy to scan.

This chapter presents the basic procedures for applying borders, followed by specific techniques for working with paragraphs, tables, and graphics. Then the chapter presents procedures for shading text and tables.

Applying Borders

Whether you're applying borders to graphics, to paragraphs, to the outer edges of a table, or to individual cells in a table, you use essentially the same technique:

- Select the paragraphs, table cells, or graphic in your document.

- Use the Border command to select options for the borders you want to apply.

When you choose the Border command, Word displays a dialog box similar to the one in the following illustration. The title of the dialog box changes, depending on what you have selected in your document when you choose the command. If you select a paragraph, the title bar of the dialog box reads "Border Paragraphs." If you select a table cell or cells, the title bar reads "Border Cells." If you select a graphic, the title bar reads "Border Picture." Throughout the remainder of this chapter, however, the dialog box is always referred to as "the Border dialog box."

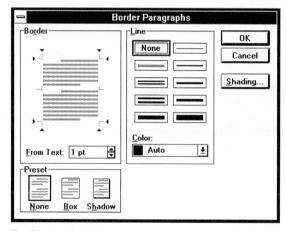

The Border dialog box

The sample diagram under Border changes to reflect the type of selection you made in your document. When you select a part of the border sample, border markers indicate the border that is affected when you carry out the command.

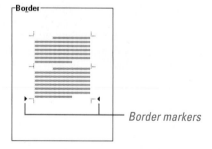

Border markers

Border markers show where a border will be applied.

Clicking a side of the diagram selects that side. You can also click between the units in the border sample to apply borders between items. With the keyboard, you can press ALT+R to move the border sample and then press the DOWN ARROW key to select one side at a time, all sides, or the border between items.

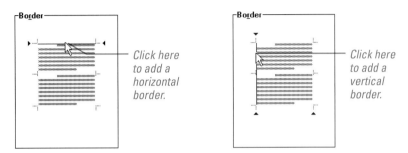

The border sample shows each border as you add it.

When a selection is very large or includes items that have different types of borders applied, the borders that represent items with more than one format appear dimmed in the border sample. You can select a dimmed border if you want to apply a line style to that side of all the selected items or to remove all borders on that side.

Word applies borders to the selected area in your document. If no area is selected and the insertion point is in regular text, the border is applied to the paragraph that contains the insertion point. If there is no selection in a table, the border is applied to the cell that contains the insertion point.

To apply borders

To apply borders, first select the item or items to which you want to apply a border. Methods for selecting graphics or selecting parts of a table follow this procedure.

1 Select the graphic, paragraphs, or table cells to which you want to apply borders.

2 From the Format menu, choose Border.

3 To apply a box, click an option under Preset, and then click a line style under Line. If you want to change the color of the border, select a color in the Color box.
   −or−
   To create a custom border or to add lines within a box, click the border sample where you want to apply a border, and then click a line style under Line.

4 Choose the OK button.

1   Select the graphic, paragraphs, or table cells to which you want to apply borders.

2   From the Format menu, choose Border (ALT, T, B).

3   To apply a box, select an option under Preset, move to the Line box (ALT+L), and then press the DOWN ARROW key to select a line style. If you want to change the color of the border, move to the Color box (ALT+C), and then press the DOWN ARROW key to select a color.

   –or–

   To create a custom border or to add lines within a box, move to the border sample, and then press the DOWN ARROW key (ALT+R) to select a border. Move to the Line box (ALT+L), and then press the DOWN ARROW key to select a line style.

4   Repeat step 3 for each border you want to add.

5   Choose the OK button.

The border extends between the indents of text paragraphs. For instructions on changing the border length, see "Indents and Paragraph Borders," later in this chapter.

Tip   Occasionally, a page break may fall within items that have a box border around them. For example, if two paragraphs have a box around them, the first paragraph and the top of the box may be printed at the bottom of one page, while the second paragraph and the bottom of the box are printed at the top of the next page. If you want items to stay together on a page, you can select all but the last paragraph or table row within the border, then choose the Paragraph command from the Format menu. Under Pagination, select the Keep With Next check box. If a page break should fall between the bordered items, Word moves all the items to the next page. You can also select the Keep Lines Together check box to prevent a page break within a single paragraph.

To select graphics and items within tables

▶ Do one of the following:

To select	With the mouse	With the keyboard
A graphic	Click the graphic. Small sizing handles indicate that the graphic is selected.	Position the insertion point before the graphic, and then press SHIFT+RIGHT ARROW.
A cell in a table	Click inside the cell.	Position the insertion point inside the cell.
A row of cells	Click to the left of the first cell in the row.	Position the insertion point in the row and, from the Table menu, choose Select Row (ALT, A, R).
A column of cells	Point anywhere in the column, and then click the right mouse button.	Position the insertion point in the column and, from the Table menu, choose Select Column (ALT, A, C).
The entire table	Hold down either mouse button, and then drag across all columns.	From the Table menu, choose Select Table (ALT, A, A), or press ALT+5 on the numeric keypad with NUM LOCK off.

A Shortcut for Applying Borders

You can use styles to apply borders. The borders you apply to a paragraph are part of the paragraph's formatting. Therefore, you can include border effects when you define styles. Just apply the border along with the other paragraph formatting you want to define as the style. For more information, see Chapter 8, "Formatting with Styles."

To remove borders

After you apply borders to a paragraph, table, or picture, you may want to remove one or more of the borders. For example, you may decide to remove the border between paragraphs in a series and just keep the box around them.

1 Select the item that has the border you want to remove.

2 From the Format menu, choose Border.

3 If you want to remove all borders, click None under Preset.
   –or–
   If you want to remove one border at a time, click the border you want to remove on the border sample, and then click None under Line.

4 Choose the OK button.

1   Select the item that has the border you want to remove.

2   From the Format menu, choose Border (ALT, T, B).

3   If you want to remove all borders, select None under Preset.
    –or–
    If you want to remove one border at a time, press ALT+R to move to the border sample, and then press the DOWN ARROW key to select the border you want to remove. Move to the Line box (ALT+L), and then press the DOWN ARROW key to select None.

4   Choose the OK button.

To change the line style of borders

After you apply a border to a paragraph, table, or picture, you can change the line style of the border. For example, you might want to change a thick border to a double border.

1   Select the item that has the border you want to change.

2   From the Format menu, choose Border (ALT, T, B).

3   Do any of the following:

   - Under Preset, select a different option.

   - In the Color box, select a color.

   - To change the line style of a box border, select a different style under Line.

   - To change any part of the border sample, select the border you want to change, and then select a different style under Line. Repeat for each part of the border sample you want to change.

4   Choose the OK button.

To adjust the spacing between a paragraph's text and its borders

You indicate the distance between a paragraph's text and its border in points—a standard unit of measurement in publishing. There are 72 points in an inch, 36 points in a half-inch, and 18 points in a quarter-inch.

1   Select the paragraph whose spacing you want to adjust.

2   From the Format menu, choose Border (ALT, T, B).

3   In the From Text box, type or select a measurement up to 31 points.

4   Choose the OK button.

To place a border around every page in a section

You can apply a border to an empty paragraph in the header, and then adjust the size of the empty paragraph so the border surrounds the page. The following procedure places a border around an 8.5-inch-by-11-inch page with a portrait orientation. Adjust the measurements if you are using landscape orientation or a different paper size.

1 From the Format menu, choose Page Setup (ALT, T, U).

2 Select the Margins option button, type a minus sign before the measurement in the Top box, and then choose the OK button.

3 From the View menu, choose Header/Footer (ALT, V, H).

4 In the Header/Footer box, select Header, and then choose the OK button.

5 If the insertion point is not in an empty paragraph, press ENTER, and then move the insertion point into the new empty paragraph.

6 From the Format menu, choose Border (ALT, T, B). Select a preset border or specify a custom border, and then choose the OK button.

7 From the Format menu, choose Paragraph (ALT, T, P). In the At box under Spacing, type **60 li** (for lines).

8 If you want the border to be printed outside the left and right margins, in the From Left and From Right boxes under Indentation, type a negative number to specify how far outside the margin you want Word to print the border.

For example, to print one-half inch outside the left or right margin, type **-0.5 in**

9 Choose the OK button.

10 If you are working in normal view, choose the Close button to close the header pane.

To see the border, choose Print Preview from the File menu.

You can experiment to adjust the position of the border on the page. You can adjust the width of the border by using the Paragraph command on the Format menu to change the left and right indents. To adjust the bottom margin, change the measurement in the At box under Spacing in the Paragraph dialog box. To adjust the top margin, choose the Header/Footer command from the View menu. Under From Edge, type or select a measurement in the Header box.

Border Options

You can set the following options in the Border dialog box.

Preset   The Box option applies a plain box border to the selection in your document. The Shadow option applies a shadow box border to the selection. The None option removes any border currently applied to the selection. If the selection includes several cells in a table, the Shadow option becomes the Grid option and places a box around each selected cell.

Line   The line style you select is applied to the currently selected border or borders. The following illustration shows the line styles that you can apply. The exact measurement for each line type depends on your printer; the measurements shown are approximate.

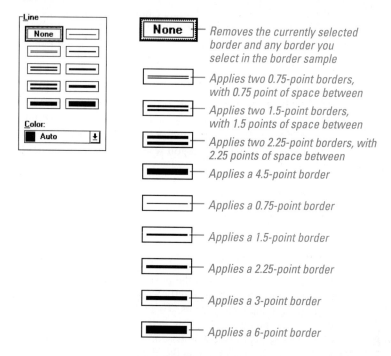

From Text   By default, Word places at least 1 point of space between a paragraph's text and its borders. To increase the spacing, type or select a measurement up to 31 points.

Color   Borders can be any one of the 16 colors displayed in this box. The default color for borders is the same as the default color for the text on your screen, usually black. If you select items in your document that have borders of different colors, the box appears blank indicating the mixture of settings. To change the color or line style of items with different border settings, it is best to select each item individually and use the Border command to change its border settings.

More About Borders for Paragraphs

The borders that you apply to a paragraph become part of its paragraph formatting. As with other paragraph formats, if you apply a border to a paragraph and then continue typing, each new paragraph you start by pressing ENTER also has the border. If this is not what you want, move the insertion point into a paragraph that does not have borders before you continue typing, or use the Border command to remove the borders from the next paragraph that you type.

Paragraph formatting instructions, including information about borders, are stored in the paragraph mark at the end of each paragraph. If you delete the paragraph mark, you delete the formatting. If you accidentally delete a paragraph mark, immediately choose Undo from the Edit menu, or click the Undo button on the Toolbar. Word restores the paragraph mark and, with it, the formatting.

If you regularly apply borders to certain types of paragraphs, you can define a style that includes the border formatting. For example, if you want headings to have a thick top border, you can define the heading styles to apply the border along with the other paragraph formats.

Note If you apply a box around a paragraph and text extends beyond the right border of the box on the screen, it may be because there isn't a screen font available that corresponds to the printer font for the printer selected in the Print Setup dialog box. The text and border are printed correctly, however. To change the screen display, try clearing the Line Breaks And Fonts As Printed check box in the View category of the Options dialog box (Tools menu). You can also try switching to print preview to verify that the text and border will be printed correctly.

Indents and Paragraph Borders

For more information about indents, see Chapter 7, "Paragraph Formatting."

Adjusting border length A top or bottom border extends margin to margin unless you have adjusted the paragraph indents. For the most precise adjustment, choose Options from the Tools menu. In the View category, select the Line Breaks And Fonts As Printed check box under Show Text With. To control the length of the paragraph border, you can then change the measurements for indents in the Paragraph dialog box, or you can drag the indent markers on the ruler, as shown in the following illustrations. In the first illustration, the border above the heading extends to the right indent of the paragraph. By dragging the Right Indent marker, you can shorten the border to the length of the heading.

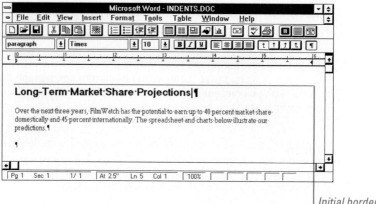

Initial border length

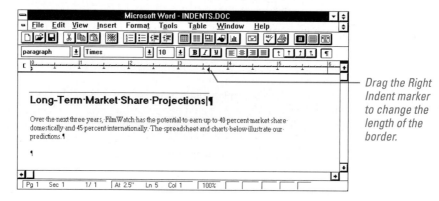

Drag the Right Indent marker to change the length of the border.

Working with varying indents   If you want to apply the same border to a group of paragraphs—for example, if you want to place several paragraphs in a single box—all the paragraphs must have the same indents. Otherwise, Word places the paragraphs in separate boxes. To get around this, you can convert the paragraphs to a one-column table.

For example, in the first part of the following illustration, the paragraphs in the checklist on the left are indented further than the heading above the checklist. To enclose the heading and the checklist in one box, you first select the paragraphs and remove the paragraph borders. Then convert the paragraphs to a table by selecting them and choosing Convert Text To Table from the Table menu. You can then apply a box around the table, as shown in the second part of the illustration. Word does not print the table gridlines.

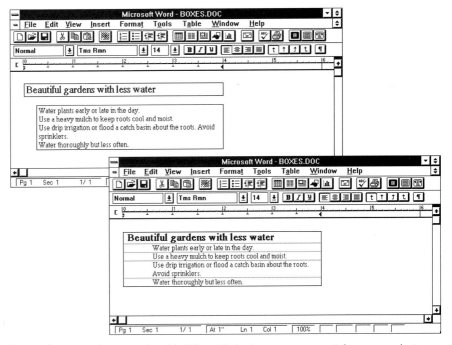

To put a box around paragraphs with different indents, you can convert the paragraphs to a single-column table.

Aligning Paragraph Borders with the Margins

If you print a document that includes borders or choose Print Preview from the File menu and then choose the Margins button, you can see that the left and right borders are placed just outside the margins unless you have indented the paragraph with the border. If you want borders even with the margins, you can adjust the paragraph's indents.

The amount you need to indent the paragraph depends on the line style of the border and the amount of space you specify with the From Text option, both of which are set in the Border dialog box. You can adjust the left and right indents on the ruler using the mouse, or, for more precision, you can use the Paragraph command on the Format menu. You may need to adjust the measurements slightly for your printer.

For a narrow border, start by adding 0.04 inch to the indent, and then adjust the measurement as necessary. For a wide border, add 0.13 inch, and adjust as necessary. For more information about adjusting indents, see Chapter 7, "Paragraph Formatting."

Drawing a Box Around Paragraphs

Selecting an option under Preset in the Border dialog box draws a box around the selected paragraphs. Once you select a preset border, you can select a line style under Line, and Word applies the style to the box. For a line between paragraphs, select the area between the paragraphs in the border sample and then select the line you want.

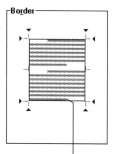

Choose a preset border to enclose paragraphs in a box.

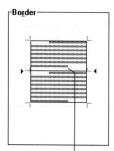

Select the middle of the border sample to add lines between paragraphs.

Note   If the paragraphs in your selection have different indents, you must set the same indent for all paragraphs or convert the paragraphs to a table to apply a box to the group. For more information, see "Indents and Paragraph Borders," earlier in this chapter.

Drawing Lines Above, Below, and Between Paragraphs

If you apply a top or bottom border to a selected group of paragraphs, Word displays one border above or below the paragraphs as though they were a single block of text. If you want borders between the paragraphs, click the space between the paragraphs in the border sample. In the following illustration, thick borders have been applied above and below the paragraphs, with a single line between paragraphs.

Click here to apply a border above the first paragraph.

Click here to apply borders between paragraphs.

Click here to apply a border below the last paragraph.

On the move — Facilities reports that our new administration wing is almost complete. The sound of hammering has finally given way to the dull thumps of the carpet layers. By the first of next month, departments should be relocated as indicated on the map.

Soccer team wins! — Congratulations to the Arbor Footwear soccer team! They took first place in the recent city competition. Special thanks to team captain Bruno Martin (manufacturing), who told a TV reporter, "Great shoes are part of a sound strategy."

Writing contest winner — Maria Selva took second place in the city's humorous essay contest. Co-workers encouraged her to write down the stories she tells on break time. Her winning story, "I wasn't born to ski," was their all-time favorite, told while they were signing the cast on her leg.

If you select several paragraphs and apply a top or bottom border, all the paragraphs in the stack have the formatting instructions for the border, even though the border is displayed only for the top or bottom paragraph. Deleting the first or last paragraph doesn't disturb the border layout.

Note   If the selected paragraphs have different indents, Word inserts a border above and below each paragraph. If you want to maintain the different indents and have a line at the beginning and at the end of the list, you need to convert the paragraphs to a table. For more information, see "Indents and Paragraph Borders," earlier in this chapter.

More About Borders for Tables

Word can display table gridlines around all the cells in a table to make it easier for you to work. Word does not print the table gridlines. You can apply borders on top of any of the gridlines to make a table easier to read. If you want to display a table's gridlines, choose Gridlines from the Table menu.

For more information about working with tables, see Chapter 17, "Tables."

When you select cells in a table and choose the Border command, the border sample and the options under Preset reflect the arrangement of the selected cells. A different sample is shown if you select a single cell, cells in a column or row, or cells in multiple columns and rows. The border sample changes so that it reflects that type of selection. The following illustration shows the four possible border samples and the Preset options for selections within a table.

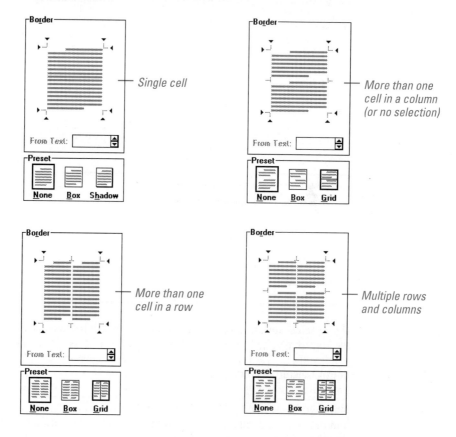

You can apply borders to paragraphs and graphics within a table cell in addition to the borders you apply to the cell itself. The second part of the following illustration shows three types of borders applied to two cells within a table. The entire table row was given top and bottom borders. The graphic in the left cell was given a box border. A border was applied to the left side of the text paragraph in the right cell. To apply a border or shading to a paragraph within a cell, you must select at least one character of text and then apply the formatting.

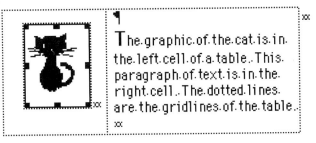

Table before applying borders

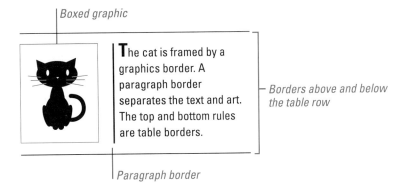

Boxed graphic

Borders above and below the table row

Paragraph border

Table with borders applied

You can use different line styles for any borders you apply to table cells. For example, to add a double border to separate the column headings from the table entries as shown in the table in the following illustration, first apply single borders on all sides of the cells—select the table, choose Border from the Format menu, under Preset select Grid, and then choose the OK button. Then select the first row of the table, and change the line style of the border below the row.

Element	Symbol	Atomic Number	Atomic Weight
Silver	Ag	47	107.870
Platinum	Pt	78	195.09
Gold	Au	79	196.967
Lead	Pb	82	207.19

You can apply a box to a selection in a table by selecting Box under Preset. You can select Shadow when a single cell is selected. If more than one cell is selected, the Shadow option changes to a Grid option that places borders on each side of selected cells.

Tip   You can adjust the spacing between borders and the contents of the table cells. To change the vertical spacing, use the Paragraph command on the Format menu. To change the horizontal spacing, use the Column Width command on the Table menu. (Note that changing the column width also changes the total width of the table.) For details, see Chapter 17, "Tables."

Aligning Table Borders with the Margins

If you print a document that includes borders or choose the Print Preview command from the File menu and then choose the Margins button, you can see that the left and right borders are placed just outside the margins unless you have adjusted the position of the table. If you want the borders even with the margins, you can adjust the column boundaries of the first and last columns in the table.

The amount you need to adjust the columns depends on the line style of the border and the amount of space you specify with the From Text option, both of which are set in the Border dialog box. You can adjust the column boundaries on the ruler using the mouse. For more precision, you can adjust the boundary of the first column by choosing the Row Height command from the Table menu and then typing or selecting a measurement in the Indent From Left box. The boundary of the last column shifts accordingly; you can adjust it by selecting the column, choosing the Column Width command from the Table menu, and then typing or selecting a measurement in the Width Of Column box. You may need to adjust the measurements slightly for your printer.

For more information about working with table columns, see Chapter 17, "Tables."

More About Borders for Graphics

For more information about working with graphics, see Chapter 20, "Importing Graphics."

Word applies borders to the edges of a selected graphic. If you've cropped very close to the image, you may want to allow more space between the border and the image. Select the graphic to display its sizing handles. Then press SHIFT, and drag the center handles on each side of the graphic to increase the space between the edge of the graphic and the image. You can also use the Picture command on the Format menu to increase the space between the border and the image by typing or selecting negative measurements in the Left, Right, Top, and Bottom boxes under Crop From.

You can select and apply borders to a group of graphics. For special effects, place the graphics in a table, and then apply the borders you want to the table cells. For more information, see "More About Borders for Tables," earlier in this chapter.

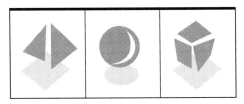

Three graphics in a table, with borders applied to the table cells

Shading Paragraphs and Tables

You can shade paragraphs, and you can shade the cells in a table. Word does not apply shading to graphics. As are borders, shading is another paragraph format that you can include in a style. If you have a color printer, you can shade tables and paragraphs with colors. If you choose a color and then print using a black and white printer, the color is converted to a shade of gray, or a pattern on some printers.

Shading can be used effectively in a variety of ways. You might, for instance, shade a short feature story in a newsletter or an important column of numbers within a table. In the office form in the following illustration, a paragraph with 30 percent shading creates a wide border at the top of the page. Lighter shading (10 percent) within a cell distinguishes an area for office use from entries that the applicant must supply.

When applied to paragraphs, shading begins at the left indent for the selected paragraphs and extends to the right indent. Shading within table cells fills the cells.

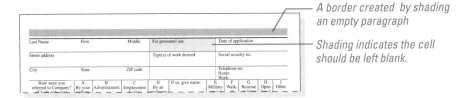

A border created by shading an empty paragraph

Shading indicates the cell should be left blank.

The shading patterns that look best in your documents depend on the resolution of your printer, which is measured by the number of dots per inch (dpi) your printer can produce. The higher the resolution, the finer the shading.

You can experiment with the Pattern, Foreground, and Background options in the Shading dialog box to get the effect you want.

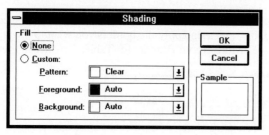

Shading dialog box

When you choose the Shading button in the Border dialog box, Word displays the preceding dialog box.

None   Removes shading from the selection.

Custom   This option button is automatically selected when you change the pattern, foreground, or background.

Pattern   Displays percentages of gray shading from 5 percent to 90 percent, as well as several patterns including clear and solid.

Foreground   The default foreground color, Auto, is the same color used to display text on the screen, usually black. You can choose from a list of 16 colors. Combining a color from this box with a color from the Background box creates special effects.

Background   The default background color, Auto, is the same color that is used to display the background of windows, usually white. You can choose from a list of 16 colors. Combining a color from this box with a color from the Foreground box creates special effects.

To apply shading to paragraphs or table cells

1   Select the paragraphs or table cells you want to shade.

 If you want to apply shading to a paragraph within a table cell, you must select at least one character in the paragraph.

2   From the Format menu, choose Border (ALT, T, B).

3   Choose the Shading button.

4   In the Pattern box, select a shading percentage or pattern.

 If you want to display and print the shading in color, you can select a color in the Foreground box or the Background box, or both.

5   Choose the OK button to close the Shading dialog box.

6   Choose the OK button again to close the Border dialog box and apply the shading.

Tip   Shading affects the legibility of text. Generally speaking, the smaller the font size, the lighter the shading should be. You might begin experimenting by choosing 20% in the Pattern box, Black in the Foreground box, and White in the Background box and adjusting the shading percentage as needed. Sans serif text is often easier to read in shaded areas than serif text. Applying bold to text may also increase legibility.

Chapter 20

Importing Graphics

You can add graphics to a document either by using Microsoft Draw, the built-in drawing application included with Word or by importing graphics that were created with other applications such as PC Paintbrush.

For more information about using Microsoft Draw to create line drawings and other simple graphics, see the *Microsoft Draw User's Guide*

When you want to use a graphic created with another application in a Word document, you must first import it into Word. Next, you can scale or crop the graphic to suit your document. Finally, you can position it precisely on the page. This chapter explains how to import, scale, and crop graphics. To learn about positioning graphics and other objects on the page, see Chapter 21, "Positioning Text and Graphics on the Page."

You can import a graphic by using the Picture command on the Insert menu or by pasting it from the Clipboard. If the application used to create the graphic is open, it's usually easier to copy the graphic from the application to the Clipboard and then paste it into a document. If you just have access to the graphic file itself, you need to use the Picture command on the Insert menu.

You can import graphics into a Word document from many different applications and in a variety of graphic formats, including the following:

- Windows Metafile (*.WMF)
- Encapsulated PostScript (*.EPS)
- TIFF (tagged image file format) (*.TIF)
- Computer Graphics Metafile (*.CGM)
- HP Graphic Language (*.HGL)
- DrawPerfect (*.WPG)
- Micrografx Designer 3.0/Draw Plus (*.DRW)
- PC Paintbrush (*.PCX)
- Windows Bitmaps (*.BMP)
- AutoCAD 2-Dimensional (*.DXF)
- AutoCAD Plotter Format (*. PLT)
- AutoCAD Binary ADI (*. PLT)
- Lotus 1-2-3 Graphics (*.PIC)

Support for additional graphic formats may have become available after this guide went to press. For more information about the graphic formats you can import, see README.DOC, a file that came with your Word package.

Graphic Import Filters

To import graphics, you must have the appropriate graphic import filter installed on your system. If you select the Complete Setup option during installation, Word installs all available filters.

To see which graphic import filters are installed

1 From the Tools menu, choose Options (ALT, O, O).

2 Under Category, select WIN.INI.

3 In the Application box, select MS Graphic Import Filters.

All installed filters appear in the Startup Options box. For information about installing additional graphic import filters, see *Microsoft Word Getting Started.*

Importing Graphics with the Picture Command

When you choose the Picture command from the Insert menu, Word displays a dialog box, in which you can find, select, and preview a file before importing it.

To import a graphic using the Picture command

1 Position the insertion point where you want the graphic to appear.

2 From the Insert menu, choose Picture (ALT, I, P).

3 In the File Name box, select a graphic file to import.

   If you want to look at the graphic before you import it, choose the Preview button. The graphic appears in the Preview Picture box.

   If you want to link the inserted picture to its original file, select the Link To File check box. Word then inserts the picture in an IMPORT field, so that you can later automatically update the picture if you modify the original file in the source application.

4 Choose the OK button.

Tip   If only the lower portion of an imported graphic appears on the screen, it may be because the line spacing for the paragraph containing the graphic is too small for Word to display the entire graphic. To view the entire graphic, click the graphic to select it, and then choose Paragraph from the Format menu. Under Spacing, select Auto in the Line Spacing box.

To update a linked graphic

Sometimes you will want to modify a graphic in the source application after you have imported the graphic into Word. If the Link To File option was selected when you first imported the graphic, you can update it automatically in Word to reflect the changes.

1   Save the modified graphic in the source application.

2   In Word, choose Links from the Edit menu (ALT, E, L).

3   In the Links box, select the name of the graphic you want to update.

4   Choose the Update Now button.

Word updates the graphic in your document to match the modified version in the source application.

Importing Graphics with the Clipboard

In addition to importing graphics with the Picture command, you can copy a graphic from the source application onto the Clipboard and then paste it into your Word document.

For information about linking graphic files so that you can automatically update them later, see Chapter 36, "Exchanging Information."

To import a graphic with the Clipboard

1   Select the graphic in the drawing application, and then copy it onto the Clipboard.

2   In your Word document, position the insertion point where you want to insert the graphic.

If you've used an empty frame for a placeholder, click the frame so that the handles are visible.

3   From the Edit menu, choose Paste (ALT, E, P).

The Clipboard contents are inserted at the insertion point or within the selected frame.

Adding Callouts and Captions to Graphics

An easy way to add callout text to graphics is by using a table. Create a table with rows or columns where you want the callouts to appear, and then paste the graphic into one cell, and type the callouts wherever you want them. For more information about tables, see Chapter 17, "Tables."

If you insert a frame around a graphic, you can select the frame, press ENTER, and then type your caption text in the new paragraph you created beneath the graphic. This text stays with the graphic even if you move the graphic to another location in your document.

Importing and Editing Graphics Using Microsoft Draw

You can import graphics into your Word document using Microsoft Draw. When you choose Import Picture from the File menu in the Microsoft Draw window, you can select additional options for importing graphics in certain graphic file formats. For more information, see the *Microsoft Draw User's Guide*.

In the Microsoft Draw window, you can edit graphics in most file formats. You can modify individual elements in the graphic, add different colors, and add callouts and other text.

To edit a graphic using Microsoft Draw

1 Double-click the graphic to open Microsoft Draw.
 –or–
 Select the graphic, and then choose Microsoft Drawing Object from the Edit menu (ALT, E, B).

2 Using the Microsoft Draw tools, modify the graphic or add text.

 For information about how to use Microsoft Draw, either choose How To from the Help menu in the Microsoft Draw window, or see the *Microsoft Draw User's Guide*.

 If you want to see what the modified graphic looks like in your document before you close the Microsoft Draw window, choose Update from the File menu. Drag the title bar of the Microsoft Draw window out of the way if it hides the graphic in your document.

3 When you are finished modifying the graphic, choose Exit And Return from the File menu (ALT, F, X).

 When Word asks whether you want to update the graphic, choose the Yes button to update the graphic in your Word document, choose the No button to discard the changes and return to your document, or choose the Cancel button to continue editing in Microsoft Draw.

Note In the Microsoft Draw window, you can modify the individual elements of graphics in most formats except those with the following filename extensions: .BMP, .EPS, .PCX, and .TIF.

Scaling, Cropping, and Adding Borders to Graphics

You can easily scale (resize) and crop (trim) graphics in Word. By scaling a graphic, you can enlarge or reduce the size of the actual image. By cropping, you can leave the actual image in its original size, while hiding the portions you don't want to display or print. Word "remembers" the way a graphic looked when you first imported it so that you can later restore it to its original size.

Clicking a graphic selects it and displays sizing handles. Simply drag one of these handles to scale a selected graphic. To crop a selected graphic, hold down SHIFT while you drag one of the handles.

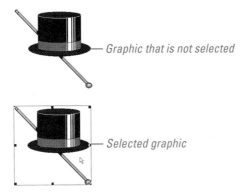

— *Graphic that is not selected*

— *Selected graphic*

As you drag a handle, Word displays the percentage of the graphic's original size in the status bar. If you want to check the current size of the graphic, you can choose the Picture command from the Format menu.

To scale a graphic

1 Click the graphic to select it.

2 Drag one of the handles.

Dragging a corner handle scales the graphic proportionally.

This graphic is scaled to 75 percent of its original size.

Dragging a top, bottom, or side handle stretches the graphic.

To crop a graphic

1 Click the graphic to select it.

2 Hold down SHIFT and drag one of the handles.

Holding down SHIFT and dragging a top, bottom, or side handle ...

... changes the width or height of the frame.

Holding down SHIFT and dragging a corner handle ...

... maintains the proportional width and height of the frame.

To restore a scaled graphic to its original size

1 Click the graphic to select it.

2 From the Format menu, choose Picture (ALT, T, R).

3 Choose the Reset button.

4 Choose the OK button.

The graphic returns to its original size.

Applying Borders to Graphics

You can set off a graphic from the surrounding text by applying a border to it with the Border command on the Format menu.

For more information about applying borders to graphics, see Chapter 19, "Borders and Shading."

To apply a border to a graphic

1 Click the graphic to select it.

2 From the Format menu, choose Border (ALT, T, B).

3 Under Preset, select Box or Shadow.
–or–
Holding down SHIFT, click the border sample to place or remove arrows from the sides on which you want a border.

4 Under Line, select a line style.

5 Choose the OK button.

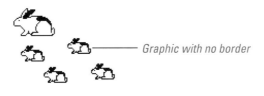

Graphic with no border

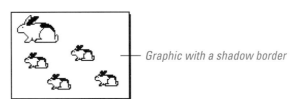

Graphic with a shadow border

Chapter 21

Positioning Text and Graphics on the Page

As you work in your document, the text, graphics, tables, and other items you insert are normally displayed and printed one after the other. On occasion, you may want an item to appear elsewhere in the page layout. For example, you might want to print headings in the left margin, or center a table or a graphic on the page with text flowing around it.

To position an item, you first enclose it within a *frame*. When you move the frame, the contents of the frame move with it. You can easily position a frame vertically at the top, center, or bottom of a page. You can also position a frame horizontally at the left, center, or right edge of a page. If you want to position an item more precisely—for example, 2 inches from the top margin and 4 inches from the left margin—you can specify those measurements. You can position virtually any item in your document other than footnotes or annotations. You can also insert and size an empty frame as a placeholder.

The following illustrations suggest some ways you can position text and graphics on a page. In the document on the left, text is positioned in the left margin. In the document on the right, a chart is centered on the page.

A chart centered on the page

Text positioned in the margin

Frame Basics

When you insert a frame, Word automatically applies a box border to the frame. If you do not want to print a box around the framed item, you can remove the border without affecting the frame. You can also change the line style of the border if you want something other than a single-line box border around the framed item.

It's best to work with frames in page layout view. This view displays the frame's actual location on the page, and, using a mouse, you can easily size a framed item and drag it to a new location on the page. Normal and outline views indicate that an item is framed but do not display the framed item in its assigned position. Neither can you drag a framed item to a new location in either of these views. For details about how frames are displayed in other views, see "Displaying Frames in Different Views," later in this chapter.

It's easiest to use a mouse when you are working with frames. You size frames by dragging the sizing handles that surround the frame. You move frames by dragging the frame itself. If you need more precision in the placement of the frame, you can type specific measurements in the Frame dialog box. You can type the measurements in centimeters (cm), inches (in or "), points (pt), lines (li), or picas (pi). Word converts your measurement to the default unit of measurement when you choose the OK button.

Positioning a frame anchors it in a particular location on the page such as the center or the top. The frame may shift to a different page as you add or delete text that precedes it, or as you change the number of columns in the document. The frame retains its assigned position in the page layout—the top or center, for example—on whichever page it happens to fall.

Information about the frame is stored in the paragraph mark at the end of each framed paragraph. It's a good idea to work with paragraph marks displayed. Selecting and deleting a paragraph mark can delete the frame that surrounds it.

Positioning Graphics and Charts

When you insert a frame around a graphic or chart, Word automatically makes the frame the same size as the selected item. If you insert a graphic in an empty frame, Word sizes the graphic to match the frame.

You can easily add text to a frame that contains a graphic. This is useful when you want to position a caption with the graphic. If you select the graphic and then press ENTER, Word adds a blank paragraph below the graphic, but within the frame. When you type, the text wraps within the frame.

Positioning Tables and Spreadsheets

You can position an entire table or spreadsheet, or position any selected rows. The frame is as wide as the selected item. If you've framed a table or spreadsheet that is linked to another document or application, you can continually update the information without disturbing the placement of the frame on the page.

Positioning Text and Equations

When you insert a frame around text, the frame is by default as wide as the text area between the left and right indents of the paragraph. You may want to specify a different width for the frame to get the effect you want. For example, if you're positioning a note in the left margin, you need to make the frame width smaller than the margin. The text wraps within the frame. You can frame any text other than footnotes or annotations.

You can frame a single character, a word, or an equation in a paragraph. Word makes the selection into its own paragraph, frames the selection, and inserts it preceding the original paragraph. This is most often used for creating dropped capital letters. For more information, see "Setting Up a Dropped Capital Letter," later in this chapter.

Note When you insert a frame around a paragraph, the paragraph retains all of its current formatting, including indents. If the indents are too large in relation to the frame width, the text in the frame may be displayed in a vertical string of characters. The problem is easy to correct by making the indents smaller. For more information, see "Troubleshooting," later in this chapter.

Formatting Text Within a Frame

Working with text in a frame is similar to working with any other text. As you type, text wraps in the frame just as it does between the margins of your document. To apply formatting, you first select text within the frame and then apply formatting using the ruler, ribbon, Toolbar, or any formatting commands. In page layout view, you can move the insertion point into a frame with the mouse. You click once to select the frame and click a second time to position the insertion point in the frame.

You can format any amount of text within the frame—from several characters to one or more paragraphs. To change the formatting of all the paragraphs in the frame, select the frame itself and then apply formatting.

If you are applying formatting using styles, it's a good idea to apply styles first and then insert frames. In this way you can add the frame and the positioning to the formatting that the style applies. If you do this the other way around, by inserting a frame and then applying a style to the framed item, the style may remove the frame or change the frame's position on the page according to the definition of the style. You can include a frame and positioning in a style to format and position items quickly and consistently. For example, you can create a style that formats headings and positions them in the left margin, or you can create a style that centers tables horizontally on the page.

Positioning instructions for the frame are stored in each paragraph mark within the frame. When you delete the last paragraph mark in the frame, you delete the frame itself. If you accidentally delete a paragraph mark, immediately select the Undo command from the Edit menu, or click the Undo button on the Toolbar. This restores the paragraph mark, and the paragraph mark restores positioning.

For more information about indents, see Chapter 7, "Paragraph Formatting."

When the insertion point or selection is within a frame, the 0 (zero) mark on the ruler aligns with the left edge of the frame. You can indent the text within the frame by dragging the indent markers on the ruler, or you can use the Paragraph command on the Format menu.

Adding a Caption to a Graphic or Chart

Word makes it easy to add a caption to a framed graphic or chart. The text you want to use as a caption can stay with the item even if you later move the item to another location in your document.

When you select a framed graphic or chart and then press ENTER, Word inserts a paragraph mark underneath the item within the frame. You can add a caption before the paragraph mark. If you later move the graphic or chart to a new location, the caption text stays with the framed item.

Paragraph Alignment vs. Moving a Frame

You have tremendous flexibility in how you place text and graphics on the page. Not only can you position a frame on the page, but you can also align items within the frame. You use the Frame command on the Format menu to move the frame. You use the Paragraph command on the Format menu, or the ribbon, ruler, or Toolbar, to align or indent items within the frame.

Paragraph alignment—left, right, centered, or justified—applied with the ribbon or with the Paragraph command does not affect the position of the frame. For example, if you format a framed paragraph as centered, it is centered within its frame. You can position the frame anywhere on the page, and the text remains centered within the frame. The same is true of paragraph indents. The paragraph is indented from the boundaries of its frame regardless of where on the page you position the frame.

Working with Frames with the Mouse

Word displays two different mouse pointers when you are working with frames. You can use the two-headed arrow to size a frame. You can use the four-headed arrow to select or move a frame.

To insert a frame around selected items

You can use the Frame command on the Insert menu or the Frame button on the Toolbar to insert a frame.

1 If you are not working in page layout view, choose Page Layout from the View menu.

2 Select the item or items that you want to frame.

To frame a paragraph, make sure you select the entire paragraph, including the paragraph mark.

Frame button

3 On the Toolbar, click the Frame button.
–or–
From the Insert menu, choose Frame.

Word inserts a frame with eight sizing handles around the selection. The framed item remains selected.

To select a frame

▶ If the insertion point is outside the frame, click anywhere within the frame.

–Or–

▶ If the insertion point is within the frame, click any side of the frame.

The four-headed arrow both selects and moves the frame. Make sure you do not drag the mouse when you select the frame.

To size a frame

1   If you are not working in page layout view, choose Page Layout from the View menu.

2   Select the frame that you want to resize.

Eight sizing handles appear.

3   Position the mouse pointer over any of the sizing handles until the pointer becomes a two-headed arrow.

Note that a four-headed arrow moves the frame instead of sizing it.

4   With the two-headed arrow, drag the handles to resize the frame.

To move a frame

1   If you are not working in page layout view, choose Page Layout from the View menu.

2   Position the mouse pointer over the frame until the pointer becomes a four-headed arrow.

Note that a two-headed arrow changes the size of the frame instead of moving it.

3   With the four-headed arrow, drag the frame to a new position.

A dotted frame indicates the position of the frame as you drag it. The contents of the frame move when you release the mouse button.

Tip   You can zoom out to view an entire page before you drag a frame to a new location on the page. To do this, click the Zoom Whole Page button on the Toolbar. To return to page layout display at full magnification, choose Zoom from the View menu, and then select the 100% option button.

To insert, size, and position an empty frame

To insert an empty frame, you do not make a selection in your document.

1   If you are not working in page layout view, choose Page Layout from the View menu.

2   On the Toolbar, click the Frame button.
    –or–
    From the Insert menu, choose Frame.

The pointer changes to cross hairs.

3   Position the cross hairs where you want the upper-left corner of the frame, hold down the left mouse button while you drag the frame to the size you want, and then release the mouse button.

Word positions the insertion point within the frame, ready for you to type.

To remove a border from a frame

If you do not want to print a frame's border, you can remove the border without removing the frame.

1   Select the frame.

2   From the Format menu, choose Border.

3   Under Preset, select None.

4   Choose the OK button.

Within the frame, bordered graphics and tables retain their borders; bordered paragraphs, however, lose their borders.

Tip   Occasionally, you may want to print a top, bottom, left, or right border but not print an entire box. After step 3 of the preceding procedure, you can click the side of the border sample where you want a border and then click a line style. For example, if you want a top and bottom border, click the top of the border sample, and then click a line style. Click the bottom of the border sample, and then click a line style.

Working with Frames with the Keyboard

If you have a mouse, it may be easier to use the procedures under "Working with Frames with the Mouse," earlier in this chapter.

To insert a frame around selected items

1   If you are not working in page layout view, choose Page Layout from the View menu (ALT, V, P).

2   Select the item or items that you want to frame.

   To frame a paragraph, make sure you select the entire paragraph, including the paragraph mark.

3   From the Insert menu, choose Frame (ALT, I, F).

   Word inserts a frame with eight sizing handles around the selection. The framed item remains selected.

To move the insertion point into a frame

Before you can size or move a frame, you must position the insertion point within the frame. Before you can apply borders to a frame, you must select the entire contents of the frame.

1   If you are not working in normal view, choose Normal from the View menu (ALT, V, N).

Framed items have small squares, or nonprinting bullets, called frame markers to the left of them in normal view.

2   Press an arrow key to move the insertion point into the frame.

3   From the View menu, choose Page Layout (ALT, V, P).

By switching back to page layout view, you can see the results on the screen as you size and move the frame.

To size a frame

1   In normal view, use the arrow keys to position the insertion point within the frame you want to size.

In normal view, framed items are indicated with a small square to the left of the paragraph.

2   From the View menu, choose Page Layout (ALT, V, P).

3   From the Format menu, choose Frame (ALT, T, F).

4   Under Size, select one of the following options in the Width box:

- To have Word adjust the width of the frame as you increase or decrease the width of the selected table, graphic, or text, select Auto.

- To specify a fixed width for the frame, select Exactly.

5   If you selected Exactly in the Width box, type or select the width you want in the At box.

6   Under Size, select one of the following options in the Height box:

- To make the height of the frame the same as the selected text, table, or graphic, select Auto.

- To set a minimum height that Word can increase if you add text or enlarge the contents of the frame in some other way, select At Least.

- To specify a fixed height for the selected frame, select Exactly. Word does not display text or portions of a graphic that exceed the size of the frame.

7   If you selected At Least or Exactly in the Height box, type or select the height you want in the At box.

8   Choose the OK button.

To insert and size an empty frame

To insert an empty frame, you do not make a selection in your document.

1   If you are not working in page layout view, choose Page Layout from the View menu (ALT, V, P).

2   From the Insert menu, choose Frame (ALT, I, F).

The pointer changes to cross hairs.

3   Use the arrow keys to position the cross hairs where you want the upper-left corner of the frame.

4   To anchor the upper-left corner of the frame, press ENTER.

If you change your mind and do not want to insert the frame, press ESC.

5   To size the frame in small increments, press the RIGHT ARROW key or the DOWN ARROW key.
–or–
To size the frame in larger increments, press SHIFT+RIGHT ARROW or SHIFT+DOWN ARROW.

6   When the frame is the size you want, press ENTER.

You can move the insertion point out of the frame by pressing one of the arrow keys.

Moving a Frame with the Keyboard

You use the Frame command on the Format menu to position a frame using the keyboard. This method allows you to type precise measurements and to position frames relative to a margin, page, or column. For the complete procedure, see "To position a frame relative to a page, margin, or column," later in this chapter.

To remove a border from a frame

Removing the box border from a frame does not affect the frame's size or position. Within the frame, bordered graphics and tables retain their borders; bordered paragraphs, however, lose their borders.

1   Select the entire contents of the frame.

2   From the Format menu, choose Border (ALT, T, B).

3   Under Preset, select None.

4   Choose the OK button.

Tip   Occasionally, you may want to print a top, bottom, left, or right border but not print an entire box around a frame. After step 3 of the preceding procedure, you can press ALT+R to move to the border sample and then press the DOWN ARROW key to select the side of the border sample where you want a border. Press ALT+L to move to the Line options, and then press the DOWN ARROW key to select a line style.

Flowing Text Around Framed Items

You can wrap text around a framed paragraph, table, or graphic if there is at least 1 inch between the frame and the margin, column boundary, or another framed item. You can control the space between the frame and the text that surrounds it. The following illustration demonstrates the text wrapping options in the Frame dialog box.

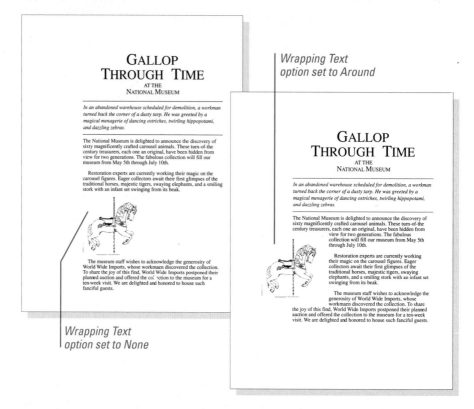

To wrap text around a frame

1   If you are not working in page layout view, choose Page Layout from the View menu (ALT, V, P).

2   Position the insertion point within the frame.

3   From the Format menu, choose Frame (ALT, T, F).

4   Under Text Wrapping, select Around.

5   Choose the OK button.

If you do not want text to flow around a frame, select None under Text Wrapping in step 4.

To set the distance between text and a frame

1 If you are not working in page layout view, choose Page Layout from the View menu (ALT, V, P).

2 Position the insertion point within the frame.

3 From the Format menu, choose Frame (ALT, T, F).

4 If you are wrapping text around the frame, under Horizontal, type a measurement for the space to the left and right of the frame in the Distance From Text box.

5 Under Vertical, type a measurement for the space above and below the frame in the Distance From Text box.

6 Choose the OK button.

Tip If you insert a frame at the beginning of your document and later want to add text above it, position the insertion point anywhere within the frame, and then press CTRL+SHIFT+ENTER. Word inserts a paragraph with Normal style above the frame.

Removing a Frame

When you remove a frame, the contents remain in line with the text that precedes and follows them. If you delete all the contents of a frame, Word automatically deletes the frame as well.

To remove a frame

1 If you are not working in page layout view, choose Page Layout from the View menu.

2 Click anywhere within the frame.

3 From the Format menu, choose Frame.

4 Choose the Remove Frame button.

1 If you are not working in normal view, choose Normal from the View menu (ALT, V, N).

2 Position the insertion point in the text or table or select the graphic from which you want to remove the frame.

Frame markers appear to the left of the item to indicate that it is framed.

3 From the Format menu, choose Frame (ALT, T, F).

4 Choose the Remove Frame button.

The frame markers are removed, indicating that the frame has been removed. If you've applied borders, the borders remain. To see the effect on the layout, switch to page layout view or print preview.

Displaying Frames in Different Views

For more information about different views, see Chapter 24, "Viewing Documents."

It's best to insert, size, and move frames in page layout view. You can, however, switch to another view if you need to work on other elements in your document. Regardless of how you view the document, the framed item is always printed in its assigned position.

Here's how Word displays framed items in different views.

Page layout   In this view, Word displays the framed item in its assigned position on the page. You should use page layout view when you are inserting, moving, and sizing frames. You can drag frames to new locations. You can use the Zoom command on the View menu to zoom in and get a closer look at the frame in relation to its surrounding text. Or you can zoom out using buttons on the Toolbar or the Zoom command to see more of the page. You can edit and format text within a frame, size and scale graphics, and make other changes to the contents of the frame and the surrounding text. For example, you may want to change the Distance From Text options in the Frame dialog box to improve the spacing between the frame and the surrounding text.

Normal view   In this view, Word displays the framed item on the page on which it will be printed, but not in its assigned location on the page. Normal view is often the best view for entering and editing text. Instead of displaying the frame, Word displays a small square to the left of each line in a framed paragraph when you are working in normal view. Word does not print these frame markers.

It's a good idea to display paragraph marks when you are working with frames in normal view. Positioning instructions for the frame are stored in the paragraph marks. If you select and delete the last paragraph mark in a group of framed paragraphs, you also delete the frame and the positioning.

Outline view   In this view, Word displays a small square to the left of each line in a framed paragraph. The frame marker is not printed.

Note   In both normal and outline views, Word displays small, solid, nonprinting bullets called "frame markers" to the left of framed items. You should not promote, demote, or move a framed item up or down in outline view because you may inadvertently change the position of the framed item.

Print preview   In this view, Word displays framed items in their assigned positions. Although you cannot change the position of frames in this view, Word can display two pages at a time. If you have selected the Facing Pages check box, a Margin option in the Page Setup dialog box (Format menu),Word displays the document in two-page spreads, just as the pages will appear in a bound document. You can choose the Margins button to display margins and page breaks.

Aligning Frames with a Reference Point

Dragging a frame on the page generally positions the frame a fixed distance from the left and top edges of the page. As you edit your document, the frame remains fixed to that spot on the page. This is often exactly what you want. For some effects, however, you'll get better results by selecting options in the Frame dialog box. With these options, you can select a point of reference on the page and then position the frame in relation to that reference. For example, you can align a graphic with the left margin by selecting Left and Margin as the Horizontal options. If you later change the margin, the graphic remains aligned with the margin.

The following procedure provides basic guidelines for using the Frame dialog box. For information about the effects that each combination of options yields, see "Aligning Frames Horizontally" and "Aligning Frames Vertically," later in this chapter.

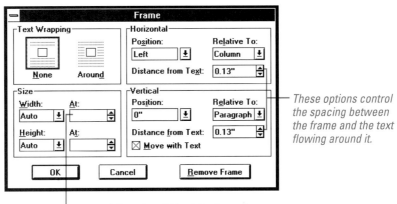

These options control the spacing between the frame and the text flowing around it.

Type or select the width of the frame here.

To position a frame relative to a page, margin, or column

1 If you are not working in page layout view, choose Page Layout from the View menu (ALT, V, P).

2 Position the insertion point within the frame.

3 From the Format menu, choose Frame (ALT, T, F).

4 Under Horizontal, type a measurement or select the horizontal location you want for the frame in the Position box.

5 Under Horizontal, select a reference point in the Relative To box.

6 Under Vertical, type a measurement or select the vertical position you want for the frame in the Position box.

7 Under Vertical, select a reference point in the Relative To box.

8 Choose the OK button.

Aligning Frames Horizontally

You can center a frame horizontally or align it flush with the right or left margins or edges of the page. If you're using newspaper-style columns, you can also align the frame in relation to the column boundaries. Under Horizontal in the Frame dialog box, you select the frame alignment—left, right, or centered, for example—in the Position box and select the part of the page you want to use as the reference point in the Relative To box. To position the frame at a specific distance from the left edge of the page, margin, or column, you can type a measurement in the Position box.

The following table shows the horizontal alignment options available in the Frame dialog box. Combine any alignment option from the left column with any option from the right column. For information about the Inside and Outside options, see "Positioning a Frame in a Facing-Page Layout," later in this chapter.

Select an alignment	Relative to a reference point
Left	Margin
Center	Page
Right	Column
Inside	
Outside	

Centering a Frame Horizontally

You can center a frame between the edges of the page, the left and right margins, or the left and right edges of the text column that contains the frame by selecting the following options in the Frame dialog box.

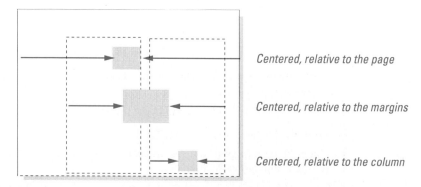

Centered, relative to the page

Centered, relative to the margins

Centered, relative to the column

Aligning a Frame Left or Right in the Text Column

You can align a frame with the left or right edge of the text column or page margin by selecting the Left or Right option and using Column or Margin as the reference point.

If the page has one text column, you get the same results whether you use the Margin or the Column option as the reference. If you are using multiple newspaper-style text columns, however, you get a different result with each option.

To illustrate this, assume you have a page with two text columns. You insert one frame (A) in the left column and another frame (B) in the right column and then position the two frames. Selecting Column as the reference point aligns the frames on the right or left edge of their respective columns. Selecting Margin as the reference point, however, aligns the frames on the left or right edge of the page margins, possibly moving the frames into a different text column. This situation is shown in the following illustration.

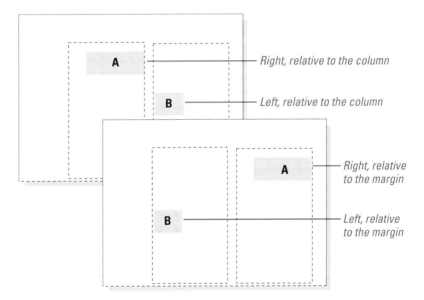

The following table summarizes the effects you can achieve by selecting various combinations of left or right alignment options.

Select these options	To align a frame
Position Left and Relative To Column	With the left side of the text column that contains the frame
Position Left and Relative To Margin	With the left page margin
Position Right and Relative To Column	With the right side of the text column that contains the frame
Position Right and Relative To Margin	With the right page margin

Positioning a Frame in the Left or Right Margin

The easiest way to place headings, notes, and other items in the margin is to select the Left or Right option in the Position box under Horizontal relative to the page. If you want the frame to stay with its related text, even if the text moves up or down on the page, leave the Move With Text check box selected, which is the default.

If you want the frame to fit entirely within the margin, make sure you set the frame width so that it is smaller than the margin. If the frame is wider than the margin, the frame extends from the edge of the page into the main text area. Word uses the measurement in the Distance From Text box under Horizontal to determine the frame's distance from the main text area.

The following illustration shows the effects of selecting various combinations of Horizontal options.

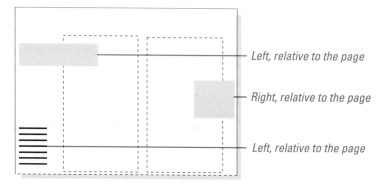

Left, relative to the page

Right, relative to the page

Left, relative to the page

To position a frame in the margin

If you are not sure of the margin setting, you can check before you begin this procedure by choosing Page Setup from the Format menu. Select the Margins option button to check the settings.

1   If you are not working in page layout view, choose Page Layout from the View menu (ALT, V, P).

2   Position the insertion point within the frame you want to position.

3   From the Format menu, choose Frame (ALT, T, F).

4   Under Horizontal, do the following.

In this box	Do this
Position	Select either the Left or Right option, depending on the margin in which you want to position the frame.
Relative To	Select Page.
Distance From Text	Type or select the amount of space you want between the frame and the text to the left or right of the frame.

5   Under Size, type or select the dimensions you want for the frame.

If you want a text frame to fit entirely within the margin, make sure you type a measurement that is narrower than the margin.

6   Choose the OK button.

If the frame is wider than the margin, the frame extends from the edge of the page into the main text area.

Note   Many printers do not print within approximately 0.5 inch of the page edge. The minimum printer margin varies according to your printer and paper size. When you position a frame near the edge of the page, it's a good idea to check the frame in print preview to make sure it lies within the printable area of the page.

Positioning a Frame in a Facing-Page Layout

For more information about facing-page layouts, see Chapter 9, "Margins, Paper Size, and Page Orientation."

In the Position box under Horizontal, use the Inside and Outside options to position frames on pages that will be bound in two-page spreads, with even-numbered pages on the left and odd-numbered pages on the right. For example, suppose you want to position notes in the outside margins of facing-page layouts. Select Outside and Relative To Page. Word places the notes in the right margin if the frame falls on an odd-numbered page and in the left margin if the frame falls on an even-numbered page.

In the following illustration, the page on the left shows how frames positioned with the Outside and Inside options would print on an even-numbered page. The page on the right shows how the same items would print on an odd-numbered page.

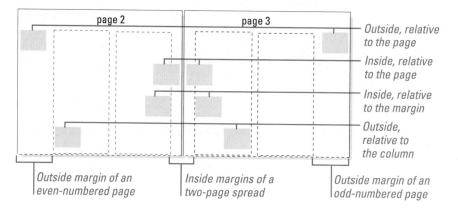

The following table summarizes the effects of using the Inside and Outside options to position frames on facing pages.

Select these options	To position a frame
Position Inside and Relative To Column	Aligned with the right side of the text column on even-numbered pages and with the left side of the text column on odd-numbered pages
Position Inside and Relative To Margin	Aligned with the right margin on even-numbered pages and with the left margin on odd-numbered pages
Position Inside and Relative To Page	In the right margin on even-numbered pages and in the left margin on odd-numbered pages
Position Outside and Relative To Column	Aligned with the left side of the text column on even-numbered pages and with the right side of the text column on odd-numbered pages
Position Outside and Relative To Margin	Aligned with the left margin on even-numbered pages and with the right margin on odd-numbered pages
Position Outside and Relative To Page	In the left margin on even-numbered pages and in the right margin on odd-numbered pages

Positioning a Frame a Fixed Distance from the Column, Margin, or Page

Typing a measurement in the Position box under Horizontal positions the frame the specified distance from the left edge of the text column containing the frame, the left margin, or the left edge of the page. You can specify the measurement in inches (in or "), points (pt), picas (pi), or centimeters (cm). For example, to position a frame 13.5 points from the left margin, type **13.5 pt** in the Position box and select Margin under Relative To as the reference point.

Aligning Frames Vertically

Using the Vertical options in the Frame dialog box, you can center a frame vertically on a page or between top and bottom margins; you can align a frame flush with the top or bottom margin or edge of the page; or you can align it relative to a paragraph. Under Vertical, select or type a measurement in the Position box, and then select the part of the page to use as a reference point in the Relative To box.

The following table shows the vertical alignment options available in the Frame dialog box. Combine the Top, Center, or Bottom alignment option from the left column with an option from the right. The Paragraph option and the Move With Text option position a frame relative to other text; these are described in the next section.

Select an alignment	Relative to a reference point
Top	Margin
Center	Page
Bottom	

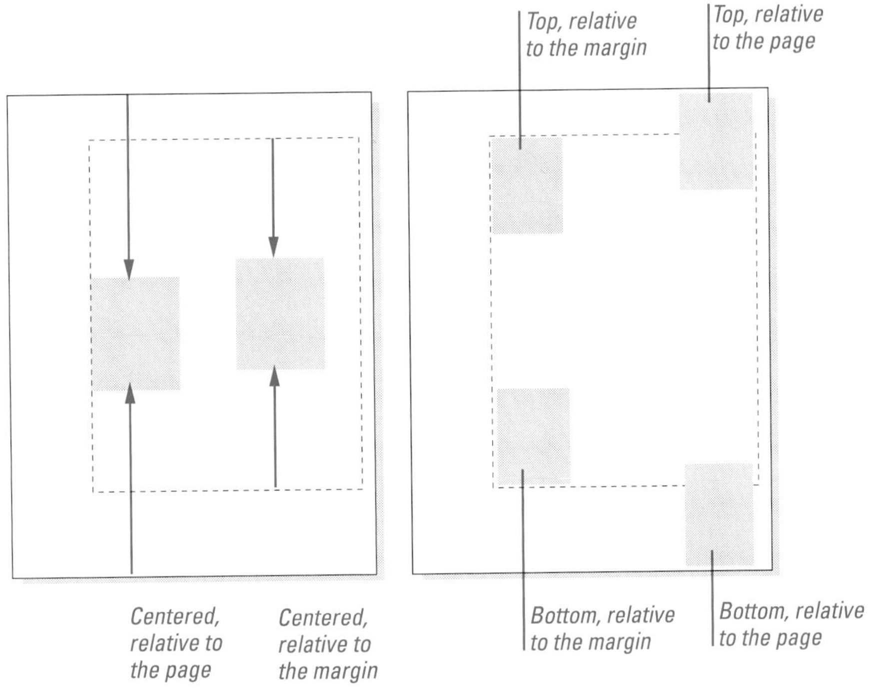

Top, relative to the margin

Top, relative to the page

Centered, relative to the page

Centered, relative to the margin

Bottom, relative to the margin

Bottom, relative to the page

Positioning a Frame Relative to Text

When you want a frame to remain close to the text that originally preceded and followed it, select the Move With Text check box under Vertical. Regardless of the frame's horizontal position, Word automatically adjusts the vertical position, moving the framed item with its related text.

For example, assume you inserted a graphic between two text paragraphs, framed the graphic, and then used Horizontal options to position the graphic in the margin. If you select Move With Text as the Vertical option, the graphic keeps its position in relation to the text paragraphs that originally preceded and followed it, even if the paragraphs move up or down on the page as you add and delete text.

In the following illustration, the page on the left shows the graphic in the position it was inserted in the document. The middle page shows the graphic positioned in the left margin, with Move With Text selected under Vertical. The graphic maintains its position relative to the text paragraphs that originally preceded and followed it, even if the paragraphs move up or down on the page.

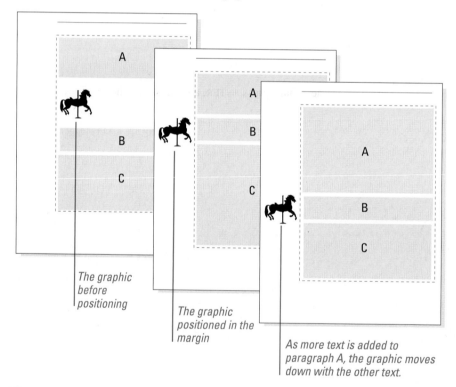

The graphic before positioning

The graphic positioned in the margin

As more text is added to paragraph A, the graphic moves down with the other text.

You can also specify that a frame be positioned a certain distance down from a particular paragraph. By default, frames are anchored to a paragraph near them. Selecting the frame displays a short dotted line at the beginning of the paragraph that the frame is anchored to. When you move the frame, the dotted line indicates the new anchor paragraph. Under Vertical, typing or selecting a measurement in the Position box and selecting Paragraph in the Relative To box indicates that you want the frame to remain a specified distance from the paragraph to which it is anchored. If you add text above the paragraph, the paragraph moves down on the page. The frame also moves down to maintain its distance from the paragraph.

Ideas and Examples

You can use the following examples as starting points for your own documents. To get similar results, follow the instructions in the procedure "To position a frame relative to a page, margin, or column," earlier in this chapter, using the Frame dialog box settings suggested in the following examples.

Centering a Chart in a Two-Column Page Layout

If you're centering the chart by itself, with no accompanying text, leave the Width box set to Auto as in this example—Word sets the width to match the width of the chart. If you want to include a caption below the chart but within the frame, you select the framed chart, press ENTER, and then type the text for the caption.

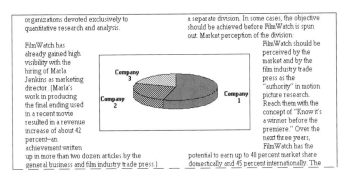

Text Wrapping: Around
Horizontal
   Position: Center
   Relative To: Margin
   Distance From Text: 0.25"
Vertical
   Position: Center
   Relative To: Margin
   Distance From Text: 0.25"
   Width: Auto

Printing Sideheads in the Left Margin or on Facing Pages

First, set a large left margin for your document—in the following example, the left margin is set at 2.5 inches. Set the frame width so that the frame fits within the printable area of the margin and allows sufficient space between the sidehead and the main text. In this example, the Width and Distance From Text settings allow a printer margin of 0.5 inch from the edge of the page. Using the Paragraph command on the Format menu, the text in the heading is aligned right. The Space Before settings are the same for the sidehead and the text paragraph on its right, so the top of the sidehead aligns with the top of the text. If you do not want to print a box around the sidehead, choose Border from the Format menu, and then select None under Preset.

Long-Term Market Projections

These are objectives to be realized within six months to one year of the of launch of FilmWatch as a separate division. In some cases, the objective sh achieved before FilmWatch is spun out.

Over the next three years, FilmWatch has the potential to earn up to 40 pe market share domestically and 45 percent internationally. The spreadsheet charts below illustrate our predictions.

Since Trey already has a reputation as the premier consumer market resea we can focus positioning for FilmWatch around our ability/record for deliv results at the box office. Positioning here is targeted primarily at producers secondary positioning is aimed at theater owners ("The FilmWatch name m box office success").

Horizontal
    Position: Left
    Relative To: Page
    Distance From Text: 0.25"
Vertical
    Position: 0"
    Relative To: Paragraph
    Move with Text: Selected
    Width: Exactly At 1.75"

You can use similar settings to print notes, small graphics, and other items in the outside margin of each page. Using the Margins option in the Page Setup dialog box (Format menu), select the Facing Pages check box, and then set the Outside margin to 2.5 inches. In the Frame dialog box (Format menu), under Horizontal, select Outside in the Position box and Page in the Relative To box. Notes are printed in the left margin on even-numbered pages and in the right margin on odd-numbered pages. To see the overall effect, choose Print Preview from the File menu and display two pages.

Positioning Several Paragraphs as a Single Block

The small form shown in the following illustration is positioned 1 inch from the left edge of the page. The following lines for the name and address were created with tab leaders. The right-aligned tabs were set at the 2.5-inch mark on the ruler. One check box was created with Microsoft Draw and then pasted into each location. The illustration shows the graphic displayed in page layout view with paragraph marks displayed.

When you insert a frame around two or more paragraphs together, as in this example, make sure you select all of the paragraphs before you insert the frame.

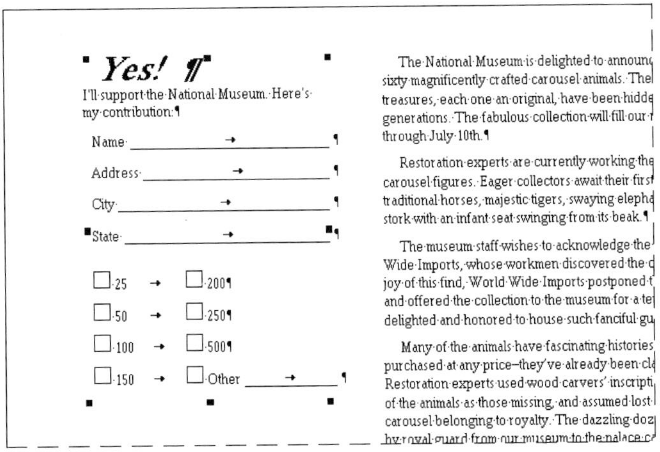

Text Wrapping: Around
Horizontal
    Position: 1"
    Relative To: Page
    Distance From Text: 0.5"
Vertical
    Position: Top
    Relative To: Margin
    Distance From Text: 0.5"
    Width: Exactly At 2.5"

Positioning a Graphic with Its Caption

The graphic shown in the following illustration is positioned along with its caption on the right side of the text column. A box border has been applied to the graphic. The text paragraphs that followed the graphic now flow up beside it. The frame is automatically as wide as the graphic, so that the caption wraps beneath it. The spacing from the text is specified in points; Word converts these dimensions to the default unit of measure after the Frame dialog box is closed.

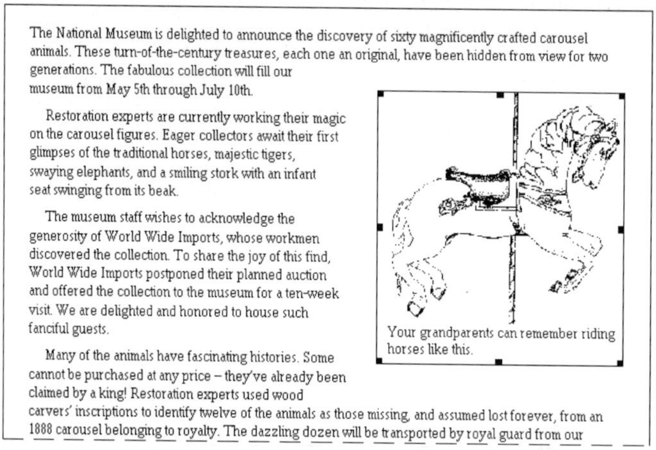

Text Wrapping: Around
Horizontal
   Position: Right
   Relative To: Column
   Distance From Text: 18 pt
Vertical
   Position: Top
   Distance From Text: 18 pt
   Move With Text: Selected

Positioning a Table with Its Title at the Bottom of the Page

The table and its title in the following illustration are aligned with the right and bottom margins of the page. Make sure you select the entire table as well as its title before you insert the frame. The frame width is set at 4 inches, the width of the table. If you're positioning a table without accompanying text, leave the Width option set to Auto—Word sets the width of the frame to match the width of the table. You can position spreadsheet data in the same way.

Projected Growth of Trey FilmWatch

Company	Current Share	Share in 3 Yrs
Largest competitor	55%	30%
Second largest competitor	25%	20%
Third largest competitor	20%	10%
Trey FilmWatch	0%	40%

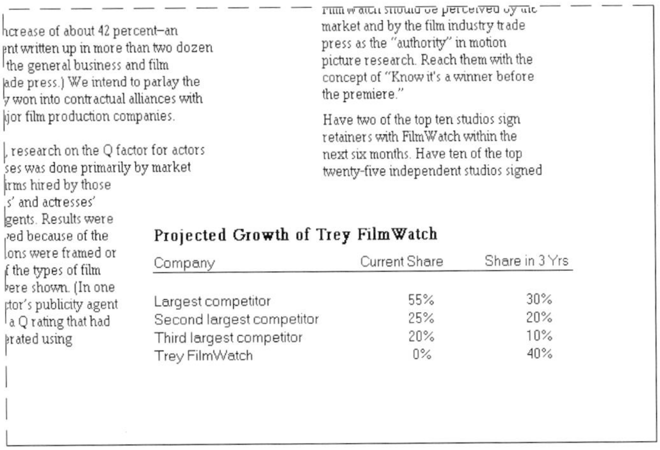

Text Wrapping: Around
Horizontal
  Position: Right
  Relative To: Margin
  Distance From Text: 0.65 cm
Vertical
  Position: Bottom
  Relative To: Margin
  Distance From Text: 0.65 cm
  Width: Exactly At 10 cm

Repeating the Contents of a Frame on Every Page

The following illustration shows a sample press release. You use the Header/Footer command on the View menu to insert traditional headers and footers if you want.

To repeat the graphic in the left margin of each page, use the Page Setup command on the Format menu to specify a left margin to accommodate the graphic. In this example, the left margin was set at 3 inches, and the right margin was set at 1 inch.

Next, switch to normal view, and then choose Header/Footer from the View menu. In the Header/Footer box, select Header, and then choose the OK button. In the header pane, type the text you want for a header, if you want one. Press ENTER to create a new paragraph. Insert a graphic with the Picture command on the Insert menu or by pasting a graphic you have created in another application from the Clipboard into your document.

Crop and scale the graphic with the mouse or by using the Picture command on the Format menu until it looks the way you want. Use the Frame button on the Toolbar or the Frame command on the Insert menu to place a frame around the graphic. If necessary, adjust the size of the frame with the mouse or by using the Frame command on the Format menu. Choose the Close button to close the header pane.

Switch to page layout view, and then scroll until you see the graphic that is part of the header. Select the framed graphic and when the insertion point becomes a four-headed arrow, drag the graphic to the position where you want the graphic to appear on every page.

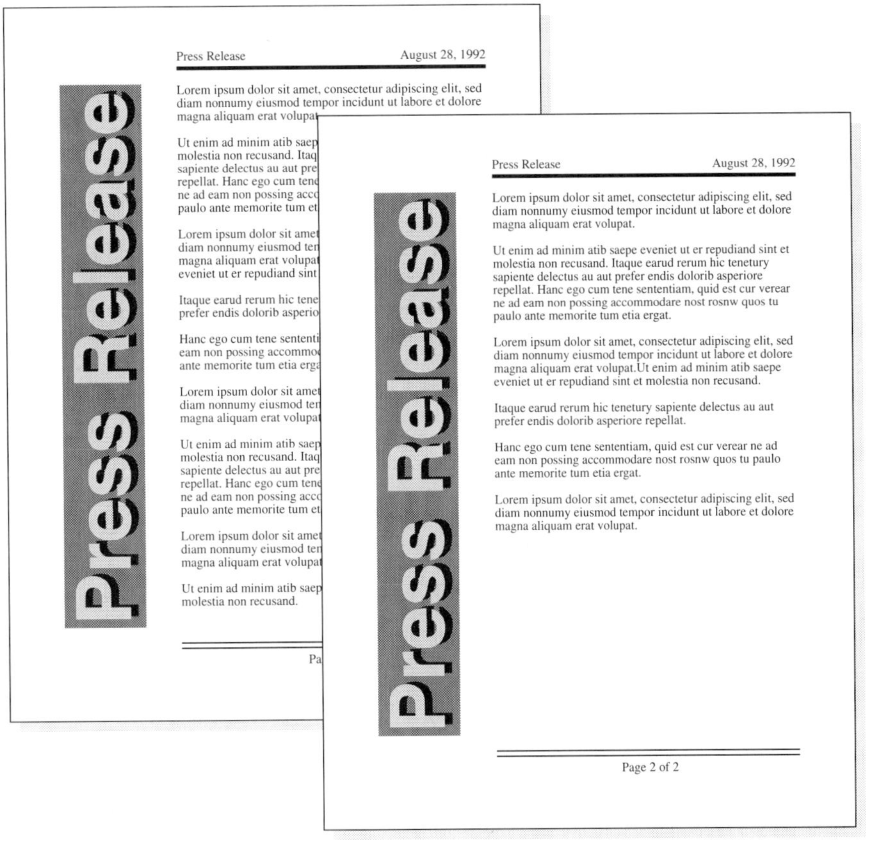

Text Wrapping: Around
Horizontal
    Position: 1"
    Relative To: Page
    Distance From Text: 0"
Vertical
    Position: 1.5"
    Relative To: Page
    Distance From Text: 0"
    Width: Exactly 1.75"
    Height: Exactly 8.25"

Creating Special Effects with Text

You can use a special feature called Microsoft WordArt to rotate or flip text characters. You can print text in a circle or half circle, print text in a vertical line, or create other special effects.

Text items you insert into your document with Microsoft WordArt, like drawings you create with Microsoft Draw or charts you create with Microsoft Graph, are embedded objects.

To create a WordArt object, choose Object from the Insert menu. In the Object Type box, select MS WordArt, and then choose the OK button. In the Microsoft WordArt dialog box that appears, you can choose the Help button for more information on adding WordArt to your document.

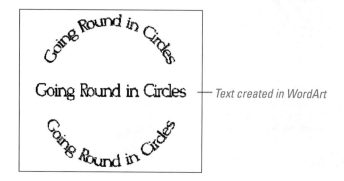

— Text created in WordArt

Setting Up a Dropped Capital Letter

You can use Microsoft WordArt to set off the first letter in a text paragraph by creating a dropped capital letter, sometimes called a display capital letter. In the following illustration, the first letter in the paragraph was replaced with a WordArt object. For more information, see "Creating Special Effects with Text," directly preceding.

You can crop and scale the WordArt object with the mouse or by using the Picture command on the Format menu until the letter looks the way you want. Use the Frame button on the Toolbar or the Frame command on the Insert menu to place a frame around the WordArt object.

> **I** PSEM LOREM QUO VADIM LOQUAS IPSEM. Non fecit
> in terris dolorem. Ipsem lorem quo vadim loquas ipsem. Non
> fecit in terris dolorem. Ipsem lorem quo vadim loquas ipsem.
> Non fecit in terris dolorem. Ipsem lorem quo vadim loquas
> ipsem. Non fecit in terris dolorem. Ipsem non lorem quo
> vadim loquas ipsem. Non fecit in terris non dolorem. Ipsem non lorem
> quo vadim loquas ipsem. Ipsem lorem quo vadim loquas ipsem. Non
> fecit in terris dolorem. Ipsem lorem quo vadim loquas ipsem.

Text Wrapping: Around
Horizontal
    Position: Left
    Relative To: Column
    Distance From Text: 0.05"
Vertical
    Position: 0"
    Relative To: Paragraph
    Distance From Text: 0"
    Move With Text: Selected
    Width: Exactly 0.45"
    Height: Exactly 0.7"

Troubleshooting

If you're not getting the results you want, this section may help you identify the problem.

Frame Is Not Printed on the Page You Want

The frame moved to another page as you added or deleted text above it. In normal view, select the contents of the frame and, using the Cut and Paste commands on the Edit menu, move the framed items to the page on which you want Word to print them. Choose Page Layout from the View menu to check the position.

Text Does Not Flow Around Frame

Make sure you selected the Around option under Text Wrapping in the Frame dialog box. Make sure there is slightly more than 1 inch of space available for text between the frame and another text boundary such as a margin, column, or other frame. You can make the frame width smaller to make more room for text by selecting the frame and dragging a sizing handle or using the Frame command on the Format menu and then typing a smaller measurement in the Width box.

Text Does Not Wrap Within Frame

If the text appears to be cut off at the right edge of the frame, the printer and screen fonts do not match. Word will print the text correctly, however. For information about installing screen and printer fonts, see your Windows documentation or printer documentation.

Items Are No Longer Framed

Either the final paragraph mark in the frame was deleted or a style that did not contain a frame as part of its definition was applied to the framed item. To restore the frame, click the Undo button on the Toolbar or choose Undo from the Edit menu. Word restores the frame if the last action you took removed it. If this does not restore the frame, select the items you want framed, and then insert and position the frame again.

Framed Items Are No Longer Linked

If a group of paragraphs or a table is linked to other text or another application, framing one of the paragraphs or part of the table and moving it out of the group breaks the link for the item you moved. This is also true if you have a group of items marked as a bookmark. Framing and moving an item out of the bookmark group removes it from the bookmark. To remove a frame, choose Frame from the Format menu, and then choose the Remove Frame button.

Framed Text Is Displayed in a Long Vertical String

If the text is displayed in long vertical strings of characters or is not visible in the frame, the paragraph probably has left and right indents that are too large in relation to the frame width. To adjust the indents, choose the Paragraph command from the Format menu, and then set the First Line, From Left, and From Right boxes to 0 (zero). If after checking the result of this procedure you'd like to indent the paragraphs, use the Paragraph command or the ruler to set indents.

In the following illustration, the text in the frame has left and right indents that are too large for the frame. Resetting the indents to zero allows the positioned text to wrap within the frame.

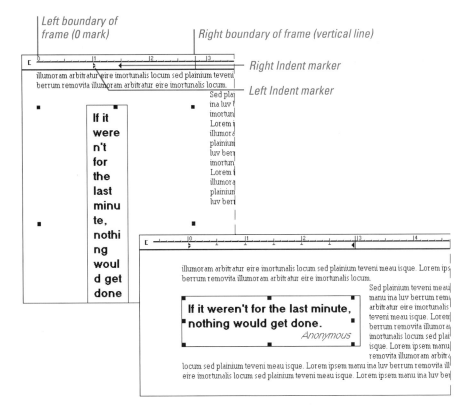

Word Does Not Display All or Part of a Framed Item

If you drag a framed item so that it overlaps another framed item, Word may not display both items in their entirety. Depending on your printer, Word prints both framed items in their entirety or as they are displayed on your screen.

Chapter 22

Numbering Pages

With Word, you can number pages quickly and easily using the Page Numbers command on the Insert menu. Just choose the command, and Word inserts page numbers on every page after the first. Word updates page numbers automatically so they're always current for your document.

There are also several ways to customize page numbering in your document or in different sections of your document. You can skip numbering the first page of the document or section and have Word begin numbering with 1 on the second page. You may find this useful for documents that begin with a title page or abstract. You can number each page in your document, and you can include the chapter number with the page number. You can also select a different number format (arabic or roman numerals, or letters) or a different starting page number for the document or for each individual section.

This chapter explains the two basic techniques for adding page numbers and then tells how to customize page numbering schemes for your document by working with sections, numbering formats, and starting numbers.

Two Ways to Add Page Numbers

You can choose to have Word number your documents in one of two basic ways.

Method	Use it when
Page Numbers command (Insert menu)	You want to print a standard, stand-alone page number on all pages but the first in a document or section.
Header/Footer command (View menu)	You want any of the following:
	■ A page number on the first page.
	■ Additional text, such as a date or chapter name, in the header or footer with the page number.
	■ Different page number headers or footers for the odd and even pages in your document—for example, to always print the page numbers in a bound document in the pages' outer margin.

When you add page numbers, the page numbers are always inserted in your document as part of either a header or footer that prints within the top or bottom margin of the pages. Headers and footers often include other information as well, such as the author's name or the document title, the section or chapter title, or the date.

For more information on headers and footers, see Chapter 30, "Headers and Footers."

With either method, you can position the page numbers at the top or bottom of the page, and you can change the number format from arabic numerals (1, 2, 3, and so forth) or change the starting number.

By dividing your document into sections, you can treat page numbering differently in different sections. For example, you can exclude a title page from the page numbering, or you can number an introduction in lowercase roman numerals (i, ii, iii, and so forth), restarting numbering of the main body of the document with page 1. For information about working with sections and procedures for making this type of adjustment, see "Variations for Customizing Page Numbers," later in this chapter.

To view the position of page numbers in relation to the rest of the text on the page, choose Print Preview from the File menu, or choose Page Layout from the View menu. You can change the position of the page numbers by changing the position of the header or footer that includes them.

Page numbers are formatted with the standard style Header or Footer. To change the formatting of the page numbers, you change the definition for the standard style or apply character formatting directly to the page number in the header or footer pane. For more information on standard styles, see Chapter 8, "Formatting with Styles."

To number all pages except page 1

You can have Word automatically skip numbering on the first page of your document and begin numbering the second page as page 2. This option is useful when writing letters, reports, and many other types of documents.

1   If your document has multiple sections:

- Position the insertion point in the section in which you want to insert page numbers.

- To number all sections, position the insertion point in the first section.

2   From the Insert menu, choose Page Numbers (ALT, I, U).

3   To print the page numbers in the top margin, select Top Of Page (Header) under Position.
    –or–
    To print the page numbers in the bottom margin, select Bottom Of Page (Footer) under position.

4   Under Alignment, select the option that you want.

5   Choose the OK button.

Word may display a message asking if you want to replace the existing header or footer with page numbers. Choose the Yes button to add the page numbers. The page numbers replace any existing header or footer in that position.

If you want to keep your current header or footer, choose the No button. You can add the page numbers to the header or footer by following the next procedure. Or repeat this procedure, but position the numbers opposite (at the top or bottom) of the existing header or footer.

Word inserts page numbers on every page of your document except the first. As a result, your document now contains a different header and footer on the first page than on other pages. When you choose Header/Footer from the View menu, the Different First Page check box is selected, and First Header and First Footer are added in the Header/Footer box.

Note   If you don't want a page number on your first page and you want your second page to be page 1—if your first page is a title page or an abstract, for instance—use the procedure "To begin numbering with 1 after the first page," later in this chapter.

To insert page numbers directly in headers or footers

If your document has a header or footer on the first page that is different from those on other pages or the headers or footers on odd pages are different from those on even pages, you see several choices in the Header/Footer dialog box. To insert page numbers in each header or footer, you can select each one individually and follow the procedure below.

Make sure your document is in normal view before starting this procedure. To switch to normal view, choose Normal from the View menu.

1   From the View menu, choose Header/Footer (ALT, V, H).

2   If you don't want a different header or footer for the first page, make sure the Different First Page check box is clear.

3   In the Header/Footer box, select a header or footer that you want to contain a page number. Then choose the OK button.

   Word opens the pane for the header or footer, with the insertion point positioned to insert a right-aligned page number.

4   Position the insertion point where you want the page number.

   Word provides preset tab stops that you can use to center or right align the page number. You can use any other combination of tab stops, alignment options, and spaces to position the page number.

5   To insert a page number, click the Page Number button.

6   Add any other text or formatting that you want in the header or footer.

7   To close the header or footer pane, choose the Close button.

Repeat this procedure for each header or footer that you want to include a page number.

This button ...   *... inserts a page number.*

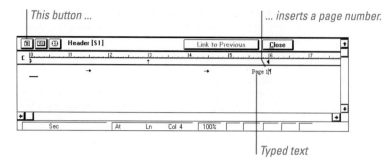

Typed text

A header pane with a right-aligned page number

Variations for Customizing Page Numbers

By dividing your document into sections, you can use a different page numbering scheme in each section. For example, you might use one of the following variations:

- Begin numbering later in your document, after a title page or abstract.

- Number an introduction with lowercase roman numerals, restarting page numbering in the main body of the document with 1.

- Start page numbering for the document or section at a particular number.

- If your document contains several chapters, have Word automatically add the appropriate chapter number along with the page numbers.

The following procedures tell how to add section breaks and how to format the sections to get each of these effects.

Section Breaks and Page Numbering

When you are working with a document that has several sections, you probably will want to number pages in one of two ways:

- Each page in every section of the document is numbered in the same way.

- Some sections are numbered differently from others—for example, an introduction is numbered using roman numerals, followed by the main body of the document numbered with arabic numerals.

If you want to number each page in the same way throughout all sections, it's easiest to add page numbers before adding section breaks. If you've already added section breaks and now you want to add page numbers, position the insertion point in the first section of the document and then insert page numbers. Word numbers each following section exactly like the first, with the page numbers continuing sequentially throughout.

If you want different page numbering schemes in your document, add the section breaks first, and then position the insertion point in each section and number the sections individually.

As you work with the page numbers for sections of a document, keep in mind the following basic rules about headers and footers:

For more information on adding headers and footers to sections, see Chapter 30, "Headers and Footers."

- All headers and footers start out linked to the ones in the previous section. Unless you unlink the headers or footers, changes made in a preceding header or footer are reflected in all headers or footers that follow.

- To keep your headers and footers the same in different sections, always work with the one closest to the beginning of the document. That way, all of the following ones remain linked and change in the same ways.

- When you make a change to a header or footer, this breaks the link with the one in the preceding section. You can link the header or footer with the previous one again by clicking the Link To Previous button in the header/footer pane. This cancels any changes made to the current header or footer.

To add a section break

1 Position the insertion point where you want the new section to begin.

2 From the Insert menu, choose Break (ALT, I, B).

3 To start the section on a new page, select the Next Page option button under Section Break.

4 Choose the OK button.

To add page numbers to a section, position the insertion point anywhere in the section and use either method described earlier in the section "Two Ways to Add Page Numbers."

Delaying the Start of Page Numbering

If your document begins with an abstract, an introduction, or a title page, you may not want to begin page numbering on the first page. To start page numbering later in the document, you can divide the document into two sections and begin your page numbering in the second section.

To begin numbering with 1 after the first page

Make sure your document is in normal view before beginning this procedure. To switch to normal view, choose Normal from the View menu.

1 Position the insertion point at the beginning of the paragraph that you want to begin page 1.

2 To add a section break that starts a new page, choose Break from the Insert menu (ALT, I, B), and then select Next Page under Section Break, and choose the OK button.

3   To add page numbers, position the insertion point in the new section, and then choose Header/Footer from the View menu (ALT, V, H).

4   Do one of the following:

■   If you want the page number for page 1 to be printed, clear the Different First Page check box. Then, in the Header/Footer box, select a header or footer, and choose the OK button.

■   If you don't want the page number for page 1 to be printed, select the Different First Page check box. Then, in the Header/Footer box, select a header or footer, and choose the OK button.

5   In the header/footer pane, position the insertion point where you want the page number, and then click the Page Number button.

6   Add any other text or formatting you want in the header or footer.

7   To close the header/footer pane, choose the Close button.

Changing the Starting Page Number

Word numbers the pages of your document continually through all sections unless you set a different starting page number. The numbering continues even if you choose not to print the numbers on all pages or you change the number format.

You can change the starting page number for your document or for any section in your document. For instance, if your first section is an introduction, you can number that section from i through v using roman numerals. Then in the second section, which begins the main body of your document, you can restart numbering with 1.

You might want to start numbering on the first page of a document or section with a number other than 1—for example, if you're working with a long document that you've divided into several files. If your first file includes pages 1 through 24, you'll want to start numbering in the second file with page 25.

When you are working with several documents, use the following procedure after you've completely finished editing your documents. Otherwise, if you make any changes that alter the number of pages, you will need to repaginate and renumber the pages in the documents that follow.

You can change the starting page number while you are adding page numbers, or you can use either the Page Numbers command on the Insert menu or the Header/Footer command on the View menu to change it later.

To change the starting page number

Make sure your document is in normal view before beginning this procedure.

1 If your document has multiple sections, position the insertion point in the section in which you want to change the starting page number.

2 To display the Page Number Format dialog box, do one of the following:

- From the Insert menu, choose Page Numbers (ALT, I, U). Then choose the Format button. Note that if you take this approach, your starting page number will not be printed.

- From the View menu, choose Header/Footer (ALT, V, H). Then choose the Page Numbers button.

3 Under Page Numbering, type or select the page number you want to start with in the Start At box.

4 If you want to change the number format, select one in the Number Format box.

5 Choose the OK button.

Word closes the Page Number Format dialog box.

6 Choose the Close button.

If the sections that follow the one you just renumbered have the Continue From Previous Section option button selected in the Page Number Format dialog box, the sections are renumbered automatically.

Changing the Number Format

By default, Word adds arabic numbers when you insert page numbers. You can select any of the following number formats:

- Arabic numerals (1, 2, 3 ...)
- Lowercase or uppercase letters (a, b, c ... or A, B, C ...)
- Lowercase or uppercase roman numerals (i, ii, iiii ... or I, II, III ...)

You can change the number format while you are adding page numbers, or you can use either the Page Numbers command on the Insert menu or the Header/Footer command on the View menu to change it later.

To change the number format

1 If your document has multiple sections, position the insertion point in the section that you want to change.

2 To display the Page Number Format dialog box, do one of the following:

- From the Insert menu, choose Page Numbers (ALT, I, U). Then choose the Format button.

- From the View menu, choose Header/Footer (ALT, V, H). Then choose the Page Numbers button.

3   Select a format in the Number Format box.

4   If you want to change the starting page number, type or select the page number that you want to start with in the Start At box under Page Numbering. If you selected an alphabetic format, type 1 to start with a or A.

5   Choose the OK button.

Word closes the Page Number Format dialog box.

6   In the initial dialog box, choose the Close button.

Changing the Character Formatting of Page Numbers

To change the character formatting of page numbers, select the page number in the header or footer and use the Character command on the Format menu. You can also change the formatting by changing the automatic style Header or Footer. For more information on automatic styles, see Chapter 8, "Formatting with Styles."

Including Chapter Numbers with the Page Numbers

You can have Word include the chapter number with the page number in your document—for example, 5-67, which would be printed on page 67 in Chapter 5. This numbering format is frequently used in manuals. To include the chapter number, you create a SEQ field that adds it to the header or footer that contains the page number.

For more information on using fields, see Chapter 41, "Fields."

A SEQ field simply inserts a number in a sequence. You give each sequence a name. Each time that Word encounters the field name, it prints the next number in the sequence. Using SEQ fields, you can have Word number the chapters within a document. In addition, you can number the figures and tables within a chapter, the steps within each procedure in the chapter, and so forth. If you rearrange any items in a numbered sequence, Word automatically renumbers them.

You can give the sequence any name that you like as long as you use the name consistently. To have Word apply character formatting to the numbers, format the field name in the formats that you want. If you want Word to use a numbering format other than arabic numerals—for example, if you want your appendixes labeled A, B, and so forth—you can use a general switch within the SEQ field to change the format.

Adding the chapter numbers involves three tasks, which are described in the following procedures:

■   Define the SEQ field that inserts the chapter numbers.

■   Add a SEQ field to each header or footer that contains your page numbers.

■   If your document contains more than one chapter, add a section break and a hidden SEQ field definition for each chapter after the first one. The headers or footers that you created earlier are repeated in each new section, with the next chapter number.

For more information on creating and assembling long documents, see Chapter 11, "Setting Up Long Documents."

These procedures are useful if you are working with a single document that contains all of the chapters in a book or manual. They are necessary if you want chapter-page numbers in an index or table of contents.

To define a SEQ field for the chapter numbers

1 Choose Field Codes from the View menu (ALT, V, C) so that you can see the field codes you insert.

2 Position the insertion point at the beginning of the first chapter, and press the Insert Field key (CTRL+F9).

   Word inserts the field characters { } and positions the insertion point between them.

3 Type **seq** followed by the name you want to give the sequence and then **\h**. For example:

   seq chapter \h

   In this example, chapter is the field sequence name. The \h switch hides the result of the field so it is not printed.

4 Press the Update Field key (F9).

To add the SEQ field to your headers or footers

1 Make sure you are in normal view, and then, from the View menu, choose Header/Footer (ALT, V, H).

2 In the Header/Footer box, select the header or footer that you want to contain a chapter and page number, and choose the OK button.

3 In the header or footer pane that opens, position the insertion point where you want the chapter number, and press the Insert Field key (CTRL+F9).

4 Between the field characters { } that Word inserts, type **seq chapter \c** (or whatever sequence name you used).

5 If you want Word to apply character formatting to the chapter numbers, select the sequence name and format it the way you want the numbers.

6 Press the Update Field key (F9).

7 Outside of the field characters, type any other text that you want in the header or footer—for example, a hyphen to separate chapter numbers from page numbers. Click the Page Number button in the upper-left corner of the pane to insert page numbers. Your finished text might look like this:

   `{seq chapter \c}-{PAGE}`

   This instruction prints the chapter and page number in the format 1-34. With field codes displayed, you see the {PAGE} field instead of the page number for the current page.

8 Click the Close button.

9 Repeat steps 1 through 8 for each header or footer that you want to have a chapter and page number.

If your document contains only one chapter, you can skip the following procedure.

To format a section for each chapter

If your document contains more than one chapter, use this technique to insert a section break for each chapter and add a hidden SEQ field definition at the beginning of the section. Each new section has the headers or footers that you created for the document as a whole. The SEQ field at the beginning of the section tells Word to print the next number in the chapter sequence in each of the headers or footers.

1 Position the insertion point at the beginning of the second chapter in your document.

2 To insert a section break, choose Break from the Insert menu (ALT, I, B). Under Section Break, select Next Page, and choose the OK button.

3 Press the Insert Field key (CTRL+F9).

4 Between the field characters { } that Word inserts, type the sequence field definition in the format you used for the first chapter, including the \h switch to hide the field in the printed document. For example, type:

seq chapter \h

5 Press the Update Field key (F9).

6 Repeat steps 1 through 5 for each of the other chapters in your document.

Tip When you finish, you may want to check the page numbering for each chapter. First, hide the field codes again by choosing Field Codes from the View menu. Then choose Page Layout from the View menu to show each page number. To quickly move to any page, use the Go To command on the Edit menu. By typing **s** followed by the section number in the Go To box, you can move to the first page in any section.

Removing Page Numbers

You can remove page numbers from an individual section or from your entire document.

To remove page numbers

Make sure your document is in normal view.

1   If your document has multiple sections, do one of the following:

- Position the insertion point in the section from which you want to remove the page numbers.

- To remove the page numbers from the entire document, position the insertion point in the first section.

2   From the View menu, choose Header/Footer (ALT, V, H).

3   In the Header/Footer box, select a header or footer that contains page numbers. Then choose the OK button.

4   In the header or footer pane, select the page number and press BACKSPACE.

5   To close the header or footer pane, choose the Close button.

6   Repeat steps 2 through 5 for each header or footer that contains a page number.

Related Topics

You can find information about the following topics related to page numbering in this manual.

For information on	See
Numbering pages in long documents	Chapter 11, "Setting Up Long Documents"
Using and formatting sections of a document	Chapter 10, "Sections: Formatting Parts of a Document"
Using headers and footers	Chapter 30, "Headers and Footers"
Positioning parts of a document on the page	Chapter 21, "Positioning Text and Graphics on the Page"
Redefining standard styles	Chapter 8, "Formatting with Styles"
Changing the character formatting of page numbers	Chapter 6, "Character Formatting"
Using fields	Chapter 41, "Fields"

Chapter 23

Pagination

As you are working on a document, Word breaks pages automatically every time you add a pageful of text or graphics. These breaks are called automatic, or *soft*, page breaks. As you edit and reformat, Word continually recalculates the amount of text on the page and adjusts soft page breaks accordingly.

You can insert page breaks manually whenever you want to force a page break at a particular spot—before a large graphic, for example. Page breaks that you insert yourself are called *hard* page breaks. When you insert a hard page break, Word automatically adjusts the soft page breaks that follow. Word cannot move hard page breaks; you must adjust them yourself.

There are a number of options you can select to indicate how you want pages to break around certain elements within your document. For example, you may want a certain heading at the top of each new page; you can instruct Word to insert a page break before that heading. As you edit your document, Word will always break pages according to that instruction.

Breaking Pages

Word is a document-oriented word processor; it treats your document as one continuous stream of text. Word inserts soft page breaks according to the page size, margin settings, font size, line spacing, and other formatting within your document. The number of lines of text on a page can vary throughout a document depending on the formatting of each page.

How Background Repagination Works with Page Breaks

By default, Word updates page breaks whenever you pause while editing or typing. This is called *background repagination*. You can cancel this function by clearing the Background Repagination check box in the General category of the Options dialog box; doing so may provide additional memory and speed.

Even if background pagination is off, Word repaginates automatically whenever you do the following:

- Print your document
- Choose Page Layout from the View menu or Print Preview from the File menu
- Choose Repaginate Now from the Tools menu
- Compile an index or table of contents

To change background repagination

1 From the Tools menu, select Options (ALT, O, O).

2 Under Category, choose General.

3 Under Settings, select or clear the Background Repagination check box.

4 Choose the OK button.

To update pagination and page numbering when background repagination is off, you must use the Repaginate Now command.

To repaginate a document

▶ From the Tools menu, choose Repaginate Now (ALT, O, A).

Inserting and Removing Page Breaks

You can insert hard page breaks anywhere in a document. On your screen in normal view, they are displayed as dotted lines, and you can select and delete, move, or copy them as you can any other characters. For information about adjusting page breaks in print preview, see "Adjusting Page Breaks," later in this chapter.

To insert a hard page break

1 Position the insertion point where you want the page break.

2 From the Insert menu, choose Break (ALT, I, B).

3 Under Insert, select the Page Break option button.

4 Choose the OK button.

Word inserts the page break immediately before the insertion point.

▶ Press CTRL+ENTER to insert a page break.

You can delete a hard page break as you can any other character; however, you cannot delete a soft page break. You must be in normal view to perform this procedure.

To remove a hard page break

1 Select the hard page break you want to delete.

2 From the Edit menu, choose Cut (CTRL+X).
   –or–
   Press the DEL key.

You can also delete hard page breaks and move soft page breaks in print preview. For more information, see "Adjusting Page Breaks," later in this chapter.

Tip   You can search for page breaks using the Find command on the Edit menu. In the Find dialog box, type **^d** in the Find What box.

You can search for and delete hard page breaks using the Replace command on the Edit menu. In the Replace dialog box, type **^d** in the Find What box, and then leave the Replace With box empty.

Word finds section breaks as well when you type ^d. If you have section breaks in your document, make sure not to remove them.

Adjusting Page Breaks

In normal view and print preview, Word displays soft page breaks as thinly dotted lines. You cannot delete or move soft breaks; however, you can prevent them from occurring in places where they would be awkward.

There are several ways to adjust page breaks before you print your document:

- In normal view, you can scroll through your document and look at page breaks, editing and reformatting as you go.

- In page layout view, you see the current page, complete with headers, footers, and footnotes, as it looks when printed. You can edit and format the page and immediately see the effects on pagination.

- Print preview shows you entire pages at a reduced size. You can see one or two pages at a time. You cannot edit or format text. You can check and change page breaks and adjust the margins.

For more information about page layout and using page layout view and print preview, see Chapter 21, "Positioning Text and Graphics on the Page," and Chapter 24, "Viewing Documents."

Note   Whenever you choose Page Layout or Print Preview, Word repaginates the document automatically. When you choose Page Layout, Word repaginates up through the page that contains the insertion point or selection.

To adjust page breaks in print preview

1   From the File menu, choose Print Preview (ALT, F, V).

2   Choose the Margins button.

3   With the mouse, drag the page break to the position you want. Word adjusts subsequent soft page breaks.

- Drag a soft page break—shown as a thin dotted line—up the page to make the page shorter.

- Drag a hard page—shown as a darker dotted line—up or down the page. To delete a hard page break, drag it down the page or off the page.

4   When you're finished, choose the Close button.

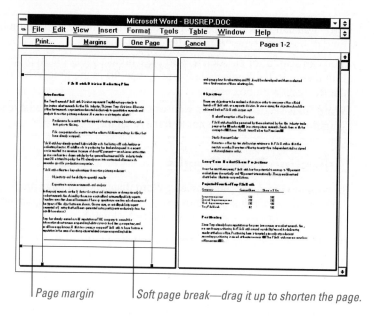

Page margin | Soft page break—drag it up to shorten the page.

To adjust page breaks in page layout view

To see how changes to your text affect page breaks in page layout view, make sure background repagination is on.

1 From the View menu, choose Page Layout (ALT, V, P).

2 Use the scroll bar or the UP ARROW or DOWN ARROW key to scroll to the tops or bottoms of pages.

3 Edit or reformat text to adjust page breaks.

Tip To view a specific page, exit print preview and then use the Go To command on the Edit menu. If your document has multiple sections, type the page number first followed by the section number. For example, to go to page 6 in section 4, type **6s4**

Controlling Pagination

In Word, automatic pagination may sometimes produce page breaks where you don't want them—for example, in the middle of a list or between a graphic and the text that refers to it.

Some of the things that affect pagination are:

- When hidden text and field codes are displayed, they affect page breaks. It's a good idea to hide hidden text and field codes before compiling a table of contents or index and final repagination or printing. For information on hidden text, see Chapter 6, "Character Formatting."

- Hyphenation can affect page breaks by changing line breaks. Hyphenate your document before compiling an index or table of contents or before final repagination and printing.

- You can print footnotes at the bottom of the page, just below the last text on the page, or at the end of the document or section. If you print them at the bottom of the page or beneath text, Word leaves space for them and paginates accordingly.

- Graphics are treated as indivisible objects. If necessary, Word breaks a page just before a graphic rather than dividing the graphic.

- If you have framed an item and then positioned it, pagination does not affect its position on the page. It remains in the position you specify.

- If a row in a table has multiple lines of text, Word does not break the row; instead, it breaks the page just above the row.

You can specify that certain lines or paragraphs be kept together or that certain paragraphs start a page. You can also control whether or not Word permits widow and orphan lines—single lines at the top and bottom of a page.

To keep lines together on a page

You can specify that Word keep lines within a paragraph together to prevent an unwanted page break.

1 Select the lines you want to keep together.

2 From the Format menu, choose Paragraph (ALT, T, P).

3 Under Pagination, select the Keep Lines Together check box.

4 Choose the OK button.

To keep paragraphs together on a page

This procedure is useful when you want to keep two paragraphs together—for example, to keep a heading on the same page as the paragraph that follows it, to keep all the items of a list together, or to keep introductory text with a graphic.

1   Position the insertion point in the paragraph you want to keep with the next paragraph.

2   From the Format menu, choose Paragraph (ALT, T, P).

3   Under Pagination, select the Keep With Next check box.

4   Choose the OK button.

Tip   Word treats rows in a table as separate paragraphs. If you want to keep all the rows of a table together, use the Keep With Next check box in the Paragraph dialog box.

Also, to make sure that a heading is never left at the bottom of a page, you can make Keep With Next part of a heading style.

To print a paragraph at the top of a page

For more details on formatting with the Paragraph command, see Chapter 7, "Paragraph Formatting."

You may have a paragraph that you always want at the top of a page—for example, you may have a chapter heading that should always start a page.

1   Position the insertion point in the paragraph you want to start the page.

2   From the Format menu, choose Paragraph (ALT, T, P).

3   Under Pagination, select the Page Break Before check box.

4   Choose the OK button.

Tip   You can include Page Break Before as one of the formats in the style definition for heading paragraphs.

To allow widow and orphan lines

A widow is a single line at the top of a page; an orphan is a single line at the bottom of a page. Word automatically checks to prevent widows and orphans, but you can change this setting. You might permit widows and orphans, for example, if you want to print a specific number of lines on a page, or if you need to minimize page count.

1   From the Tools menu, choose Options (ALT, O, O).

2   Under Category, select Print.

3   Clear the Widow/Orphan Control check box.

4   Choose the OK button.

How Section Breaks Affect Pagination

You use sections to vary page formatting within a document—for example, you may want to format part of your document as two-column text. You separate a document into sections so that you can have a distinctive format in each section.

For more details on formatting sections, see Chapter 10, "Sections: Formatting Parts of a Document."

Section breaks affect pagination because they vary the format of pages and because you can choose to insert page breaks at section breaks. For example, you may want each section of your document to begin on a new page, or on a new odd-numbered page. Use the options in the Break command on the Insert menu to control these section break options:

- Next Page breaks the page at the section mark and starts the new section on the next page.

- Continuous starts the next section with no page break.

- Even Page starts printing the next section on the next even-numbered page, leaving a blank page if the last page was even-numbered.

- Odd Page starts printing the next section on the next odd-numbered page, leaving a blank page if the last page was odd-numbered.

To insert a section break

1 Position the insertion point where you want the new section to start.

2 From the Insert menu, choose Break (ALT, I, B).

3 Under Section Break, select the option button whose title describes where you want the text in the new section to start printing: Next Page, Continuous, Even Page, or Odd Page.

4 Choose the OK button.

Note All section formatting is stored in the section mark. You can select the section mark as you can any other character and copy, move, or delete it. If you delete it, all the section formatting is lost—column formatting, line numbering, page numbering, headers and footers, and so on. If you delete the section mark by accident, choose Undo from the Edit menu immediately.

Troubleshooting

The way your document has been formatted can complicate pagination. This section describes some common problems and offers suggestions for overcoming them.

Unwanted Page Breaks in Midpage

Automatic page breaks that occur in the middle of a page can be caused by any of several feature settings. The following table lists some common causes of the problem and suggests solutions.

Cause	Solution
A special paragraph format, such as Page Break Before, Keep With Next, or Keep Lines Together, may have been applied.	Check the paragraph just after the unwanted page break for paragraph formats such as these. From the Format menu, choose Paragraph, and then clear the unwanted options.
Section breaks may have been applied with the Next Page option button selected under Section Break.	If you don't want a page break at the section break, choose Section Layout from the Format menu. Under Section Start, select Continuous.
Word does not break a page in the middle of a table cell. (Remember that tables formatted as hidden text still take up space and affect pagination.)	If you want to break the page in the middle of a cell, split the cell manually into two cells at the point where you want the page to break: Use the Insert Cells command on the Table menu to insert a new row above the cell you want to split. Then copy some of the text into a cell in the empty row. To insert the page break, position the insertion point before the text in the second cell, choose Break from the Insert menu, and then, under Insert, select the Page Break option button.

Page Break Is Ignored

If you inadvertently format a hard page break as hidden text—this is easy to do if your break is immediately before an index entry or table of contents entry—and then specify in the Print dialog box that hidden text does not print, your page break is ignored.

This problem can also be caused by an entire paragraph of hidden text following a hard page break. When you show hidden text, you might get extra pages when printing your document.

To solve this problem, select the page break, and then choose the Character command from the Format menu; then clear the Hidden check box. Make sure that some portion of the paragraph immediately following the hard page break is not hidden.

Pictures or text inserted in a frame and positioned outside the margins can cause a page break to be ignored.

Break Command Is Unavailable When Selection Is Positioned

If you frame an item and then specify a position for it, you cannot insert a page or section break in the middle of the item. The Break command is not available when the insertion point is in a positioned item.

Chapter 24

Viewing Documents

Word provides four ways to view your document on the screen: normal view, page layout view, print preview, and outline view. Each view shows you different aspects of your work. When you switch from one view to another, the insertion point remains in the same location in the document to mark your place. The insertion point changes to a pointer in print preview, the only view in which you cannot edit text.

In all views except print preview, you can enlarge or reduce the size of the document on the screen to get an overview of an entire page or to get a closer look at text that's formatted in a small font size. Regardless of the display size, you can edit as you normally do. The display size does not affect the printed document.

- Normal view is the best all-purpose working view. You will probably do most of your typing, editing, and formatting in this view. You can make normal view even faster by choosing the Draft command on the View menu. This command hides character formatting and all graphics, representing them instead with underlining and frames.

- Page layout view displays the layout of each page in your document as it looks when printed. You can see multiple-column layout, headers and footers, and footnotes in place on the page, as well as the accurate position of any item you put in a frame. Use this view to work with frames or multiple columns or to check the final appearance of your document and make last-minute changes to the text, formatting, and layout. You can move framed items on the page by dragging with the mouse.

- Print preview shows a miniature version of your document exactly as it is printed, reduced in size to display one or two pages on the screen. Although you can't edit text in this view, it provides a quick and convenient way to review the final page layout and adjust page breaks and margins.

- Outline view is useful even if you don't write your documents from an outline. This view makes it easy to move and copy text, to reorganize long documents, and to move quickly to a different location within the document.

Normal view, page layout view, and print preview are described in this chapter. For information about outline view, see Chapter 27, "Outline View: Creating Outlines and Reorganizing Documents."

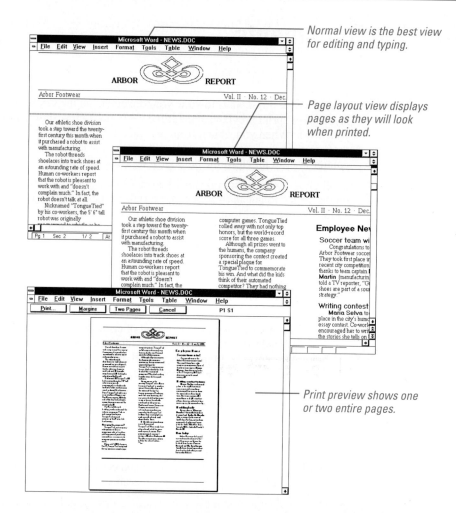

Normal view is the best view for editing and typing.

Page layout view displays pages as they will look when printed.

Print preview shows one or two entire pages.

Normal View: For Most of Your Work, Most of the Time

Normal view, the default view in Word, is best for the everyday work of entering and formatting text and graphics. You can see most text formatting—the font, point size, line spacing, indents, and so forth—as it looks when printed, but the arrangement of text and graphics on the page is simplified. Multiple columns, though shown in their actual width, are displayed as one continuous column, instead of as columns arranged side by side on the page. Text and graphics you positioned using the Frame command on the Format menu appear in the order you inserted them in your document, not in the position where they are printed.

Normal view makes it easy to edit text across page breaks, shown as dotted lines, and section breaks, shown as double dotted lines. To work with headers, footers, and footnotes, you open a separate pane. For example, to insert or edit a header (the text printed in the top margin of each page), open the header pane using the Header/Footer command on the View menu. You can switch to print preview or page layout view to see the page as it looks when printed.

To display a document in normal view

▶ From the View menu, choose Normal (ALT, V, N).

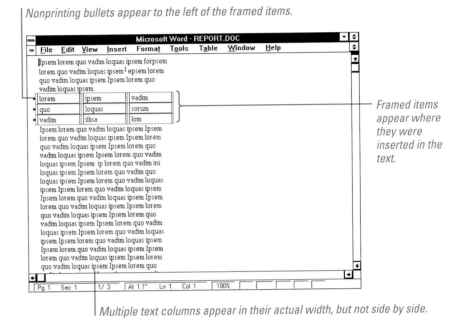

Nonprinting bullets appear to the left of the framed items.

Framed items appear where they were inserted in the text.

Multiple text columns appear in their actual width, but not side by side.

Document displayed in normal view

Using Draft Mode in Normal View

Word provides the power to create, edit, display, and print very complex documents. Draft mode can increase the display speed of some documents by reducing the amount of computation needed to display a document. Draft mode displays text in one font and size, regardless of the fonts and sizes you have applied. Character formatting appears as underlining, and pictures appear as empty frames.

To display a document in draft mode

▶ From the View menu, choose Draft (ALT, V, D).

Page Layout View: See and Edit the "Printed" Page

After you type text and insert graphics into your document, switch to page layout view. You can see how page elements such as multiple text columns, graphics, headers, footers, and footnotes are positioned on the printed page. You can also continue to type, edit, and format text in this view. The only page elements that are not visible are line numbers and lines between columns, which are displayed only in print preview. The only formatting not visible is justified vertical alignment.

To display a document in page layout view

▶ From the View menu, choose Page Layout (ALT, V, P).

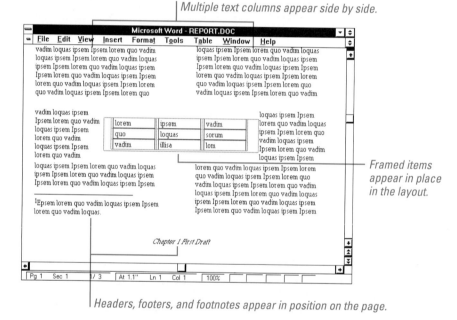

Multiple text columns appear side by side.

Framed items appear in place in the layout.

Headers, footers, and footnotes appear in position on the page.

Document displayed in page layout view

Note   By default, Word displays line breaks and fonts as they are printed. If the Line Breaks And Fonts As Printed check box has been cleared in the View category of the Options dialog box (Tools menu), the screen display is slightly different from the printed document.

Working in Page Layout View

With a few exceptions, you can edit and format your document in page layout view exactly as you do in normal view. Here are some differences you'll notice:

- You can drag framed items to adjust their position on the page.

- You can move, type, and edit headers, footers, and footnotes without opening a separate pane.

- The 0 (zero) mark on the ruler doesn't always line up with the left margin when Word displays indents and tab stop markers on the ruler. Instead, the 0 mark aligns with the left boundary of the paragraph containing the insertion point or selection, which may be in the right column of a two-column page. This alignment gives you precise measurements when you set tab stops or indents in a column.

- You can scroll one page at a time. When you reach the bottom of a page, scrolling down changes the screen to show the top of the next page. You cannot see the bottom of one page and the top of another at the same time.

- You can display dotted lines to mark the boundaries of the individual blocks of text and graphics on the page—each text column, the headers and footers, footnotes, and so forth. To display the boundaries, you choose the Options command from the Tools menu. Select the View category, and then select the Text Boundaries check box under Show Text With. Word displays boundaries around the page elements in the active window and any new window you open until you clear this option.

For more information on background repagination, see Chapter 23, "Pagination."

By default, Word updates page breaks whenever you pause while editing or typing. This is called *background repagination*. You can cancel this function by clearing the Background Repagination check box in the General category of the Options dialog box (Tools menu); doing so may provide additional memory and speed as you work.

Word repaginates the document when you choose the Page Layout command, whether the Background Repagination option is selected or cleared. After that, if the option is cleared, Word does not reformat the page until you choose to repaginate, as long as editing or formatting does not cause a text area to exceed the current page. If a text area exceeds the page limit, Word repaginates the affected pages automatically. To repaginate the document, choose the Repaginate Now command from the Tools menu.

Moving the Insertion Point and Selecting Text

You select text in page layout view the same way you select it in normal view. In page layout view, note that paragraph selection bars are active at the left of each paragraph as they are in other views. In page layout view, selection bars are active for paragraphs in multiple columns and frames containing text or graphics.

For the most part, you use the scroll bars and move the insertion point in page layout view just as you do in normal view. When you work in page layout view, you can also move quickly to the previous or next page by clicking the Page Forward or Page Back button at the bottom of the vertical scroll bar. After you click the Page Forward or Page Back button, click in the document window so that the status bar displays information about the page you are viewing.

Note   After scrolling to a new page with the mouse, make sure you position the insertion point on the current page before you begin typing or editing. If you type without positioning the insertion point at the new location, Word jumps back to the original location of the insertion point and displays your typing there.

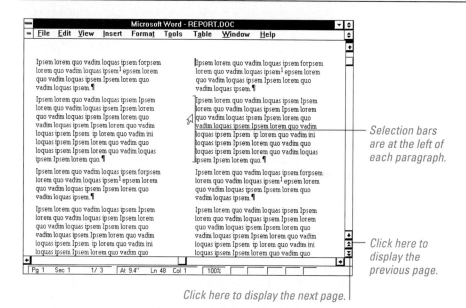

Selection bars are at the left of each paragraph.

Click here to display the previous page.

Click here to display the next page.

When you use arrow keys to move the insertion point in page layout view, the insertion point first moves through the current page element—that is, through the text column, header or footer, footnotes, framed paragraph, table, or graphic—before it proceeds to the adjacent element. For example, if you have multiple columns in your document, pressing the RIGHT ARROW key moves the insertion point to the end of the current text column before moving it into the next column. To move directly to an adjacent page element, press ALT+UP ARROW or ALT+DOWN ARROW.

Positioning Objects on the Page

With the Frame command on the Format menu and the Frame command on the Insert menu, you can place a paragraph containing text or graphics in any location within the printable area of the page. You can specify the position of the item relative to the margins, edges of the page, or the column boundaries of newspaper-style, or snaking, text columns.

You can also insert frames around tables that you create using the Insert Table command on the Table menu. You can position the entire table as a whole or position one or more framed rows independent of the rest of the table.

In page layout view, you can fine-tune the location of any framed item by dragging it on the page. For more information about framed items, see Chapter 21, "Positioning Text and Graphics on the Page."

Working with Headers, Footers, and Footnotes

In page layout view, choosing the Header/Footer command from the View menu moves the insertion point into the appropriate header or footer area instead of opening the header or footer pane. You also can use the arrow keys or the mouse to move the insertion point directly to existing header or footer text. When you type, edit, or format header or footer text, the changes are reflected on all pages of that section of the document.

You can also type footnotes in the document without opening a separate window. Choosing the Footnote command from the Insert menu inserts the selected reference mark in the text. Word then moves the insertion point to the area in your document where the footnote text is printed, whether it's the bottom of the page, end of the section, or end of the document.

Tip　After typing or editing the header, footer, or footnote text, use the Go Back key (SHIFT+F5) to return the insertion point to where you were previously working.

Print Preview: See Results Before You Print

Print preview shows you how your document looks when you print it. You can see whole pages one or two at a time and see elements of the document that aren't shown in normal view or page layout view. If you decide you're ready to print after checking the pages, choose the Print button to open the Print dialog box.

All page elements that appear within the printable area of the page are shown in print preview. Some printers, including most laser printers, cannot print all the way to the edge of the page. If you've placed page elements in the margins, you can use print preview to make sure that they lie within the printable area.

If your document contains hidden text that you want to print, choose the Options button in the Print dialog box, then select the Hidden Text check box under Include With Document. Word then displays page breaks and text layout allowing for the hidden text.

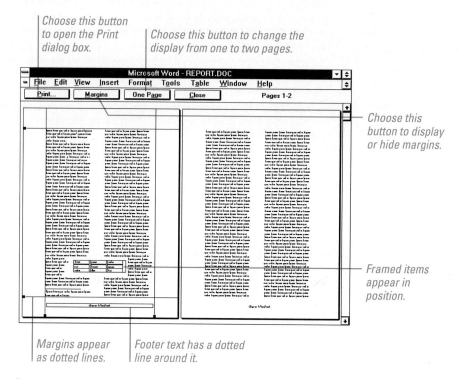

Choose this button to open the Print dialog box.

Choose this button to change the display from one to two pages.

Choose this button to display or hide margins.

Framed items appear in position.

Margins appear as dotted lines.

Footer text has a dotted line around it.

Document displayed in print preview

Tip If the Print Preview command is unavailable, Word cannot determine the type of printer you want to use. Either no printers have been installed on your system, a default printer has not been selected in the Control Panel, or the default printer is not connected to a port. Refer to your Windows and printer documentation for instructions on connecting a printer.

To display a document in print preview

1   From the File menu, choose Print Preview (ALT, F, V).

Word displays the page visible at the top of the document window and the following page, if two-page display is selected.

2   Do any of the following to see more of the document.

To	Do this
Display the next page or set of facing pages	Click the down scroll arrow, or press the PAGE DOWN key.
Display the previous page or set of facing pages	Click the up scroll arrow, or press the PAGE UP key.
Scroll forward or backward several pages at a time	Drag the scroll box down to scroll forward or up to scroll back.

3   After viewing the document, you can do one of the following.

To	Do This
Print the document	Choose the Print button to open the Print dialog box.
Return to the previous view of the document	Choose the Close or Cancel button.
Display the document in page layout view	Double-click anywhere off the page or set of facing pages.

Tip   Even though the document is displayed in print preview, you can still type precise measurements for margins, add a gutter margin, set up facing pages, or change the paper size or page orientation. Choose the Page Setup command from the Format menu to do any of these.

Viewing One or Two Pages

You can view one or two pages at a time in print preview. Single-page display is useful if you're working with a wide document. With two-page display, adjacent pages are shown side by side. As you scroll through the document, the right page shifts to the left, and the next page is displayed on the right.

If you specified facing pages with the Page Setup command on the Format menu, Word can display your document in two-page spreads. Even-numbered pages are on the left, and odd-numbered pages are on the right. These two-page spreads scroll two pages at a time, as though you are turning the pages of a book. Specifying different headers or footers on odd-numbered and even-numbered pages by choosing the Header/Footer command on the View menu has the same effect.

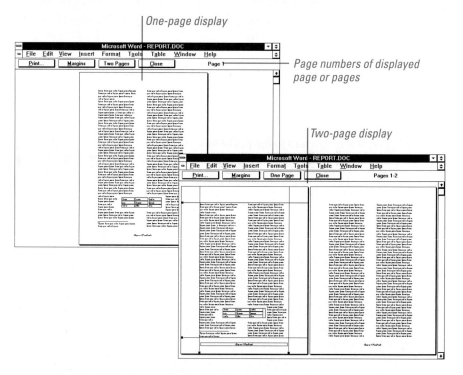

One-page display

Page numbers of displayed page or pages

Two-page display

To switch between one-page and two-page display

▶ Choose the One Page or Two Pages button.

Adjusting the Layout in Print Preview

Although you can't type or format text in print preview, you can adjust the layout of pages. When you choose the Margins button, dotted lines mark document margins and the boundaries of certain page elements. By dragging the boundaries, you can:

- Adjust the margins for the current section.

- Adjust the positions of headers and footers for the current section.

- Insert, move, and delete page breaks.

As you drag a margin, page break, header, or footer, the measurements in the top of the window change to show the position of the item relative to the edges of the page. Once you change the placement of an element, Word updates the settings in the appropriate dialog box. For example, when you change the margins, Word updates the margin settings in the Page Setup dialog box.

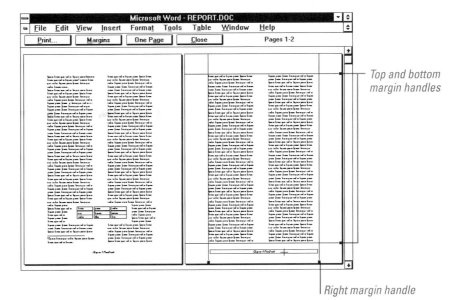

Top and bottom margin handles

Right margin handle

Print preview makes it easy to adjust page breaks and to see the effects immediately. For example, you can adjust a page break so that a heading appears at the top of the next page. Adjusting page breaks in print preview helps you avoid having to reprint your document.

For more information about breaking pages, see Chapter 23, "Pagination."

When you choose the Margins button, Word displays the document's page breaks. Unlike the lines marking the top and bottom document margins, which extend across the page and end with handles, page break lines extend only between the left and right margins. You can adjust the page breaks with a mouse or with the keyboard.

To adjust margins, headers, and footers

Adjusting the margins or header or footer for any page affects all pages in that section.

1   In print preview, display the margins by choosing the Margins button.

2   If you are displaying two pages, click the page for which you want the margins displayed.

3   Point to a margin handle or to the item you want to move.

The pointer changes to cross hairs over any item that can be moved.

4   Drag the margin handle or item to its new position, and then release the mouse button.

As you drag, Word displays the distance from the item to the edge of the page in the upper-right corner of the window.

5   To update the display, click anywhere off the page.

6   To return to the previous view of your document, choose the Close button.
–or–
To display the document in page layout view, double-click anywhere off the page.

1   In print preview, choose the Margins button.

2   Press TAB until the item you want to move is selected.

The margin line or boundaries disappear for the selected item.

3   Use the direction keys to move the item, and press ENTER to set the new location.

4   To update the page layout, press ENTER.

5   To return to the previous view of your document, choose the Close button.

To move page breaks

1 In print preview, choose the Margins button to display boundaries.

2 If you are displaying two pages, click the page for which you want to adjust the page break.

3 Point to the page break, or press TAB to select the page break.

The pointer changes to cross hairs.

4 Do one of the following.

To	Do This
Insert a manual page break	Drag the automatic page break—usually located near the bottom margin—up to where you want the page to break. You cannot insert a page break within a table.
Move a manual page break	Drag the page break up or down. If Word needs to insert an automatic page break before the new manual page break, it does so and deletes the manual break.
Delete a manual page break	Drag the page break into the bottom margin. Word fills the page with text from the next page. You cannot set a page break below the bottom margin.

Magnifying or Reducing the Display Size

If you are using a small font size and want a closer look at the text in normal view, page layout view, or outline view, you can magnify, or zoom in on, the page you want to see and continue typing or editing in the magnified version. You can also zoom out to see an entire page at once, giving you an overview as you rearrange the headings of an outline or drag framed items such as pictures or tables to a new location on the page.

If you are editing a document that is larger than 8.5 by 11 inches, or one that is printed with a landscape orientation—with the wider side at the top—you can reduce the display size to see the full width of the page, eliminating the need to scroll horizontally. The spacing of the tick marks on the ruler adjusts to accurately reflect the size of the display as you magnify or reduce.

You can change the magnification for any document window. If you open a new window, it has the level of magnification you last chose. The level of magnification is for your convenience as you edit. It affects only the screen display. It does not change the look or size of the printed document. You can use the Zoom command on the View menu to change the display size in a range from 25 percent through 200 percent of the original. Or, if you are using a mouse, you can change the magnification using buttons on the Toolbar.

The Toolbar provides three buttons that make it easy to magnify or reduce the size of the document in the active window. You can display the entire document on the page in page layout view and continue editing. Or you can reduce the size of a wide document so that the entire page width fits on the screen in page layout view. You can return to 100 percent magnification and normal view with the click of a button.

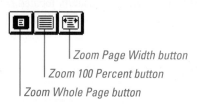

                   │ *Zoom Page Width button*

             │ *Zoom 100 Percent button*

     │ *Zoom Whole Page button*

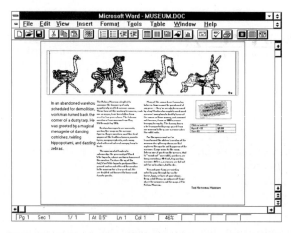

Zoom Whole Page

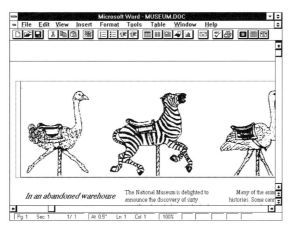

Zoom 100 Percent

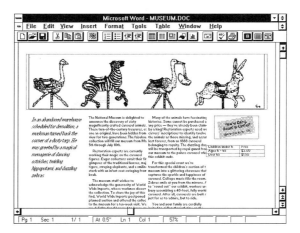

Zoom Page Width

To magnify or reduce the display size of a page

1   If the Toolbar is not displayed, choose Toolbar from the View menu (ALT, V, T).

2   Do one of the following.

To view	Click
The entire page	The Zoom Whole Page button
The document at 100 percent magnification and in normal view	The Zoom 100 Percent button
The full width of the page	The Zoom Page Width button

1 From the View menu, choose Zoom (ALT, V, Z).

2 Select the magnification or reduction you want.

To display	Do This
The widest line on the page	Choose the Page Width button.
The entire page at once	Choose the Whole Page button.
The page at twice the original size	Select the 200% option button.
The page at the original size	Select the 100% option button.
The page at 75 percent of the original size	Select the 75% option button.
The page at half the original size	Select the 50% option button.
The page at a size you specify	In the Custom box, type or select a size from 25 percent through 200 percent.

3 Choose the OK button.

To customize the Zoom 100 Percent button

By default, the Toolbar buttons provide the three most often used levels of magnification. If you customize the Zoom 100 Percent button, you can use it with a mouse to quickly select any size level, in 5 percent increments, from 25 percent through 200 percent of the original.

1 Create a new document based on the NORMAL template.

2 From the Tools menu, choose Options (ALT, O, O).

3 Under Category, select Toolbar.

4 In the Tool To Change box, select ViewZoom100.

5 In the Commands box, select ViewZoom.

6 Choose the Change button.

7 Choose the Close button.

Now when you click the Zoom 100 Percent button on the Toolbar, Word displays a graphical arrow. As you drag downward along the arrow with the mouse, Word displays percentages from 25 percent through 200 percent in the box below the arrow. Release the mouse button to display your document at the percentage you want.

You can change the Zoom 100 Percent button permanently. When you quit Word, a message asks if you want to save global glossary and command changes. Choose the Yes button.

The Difference Between Print Preview and Zooming Out

You use the Print Preview command on the File menu to switch to print preview, which is the only view in which you cannot zoom in or out. Print preview displays the document in a reduced size that you cannot change. You cannot edit text in print preview, but you can easily adjust the location of margins, headers, footers, and page breaks.

Print preview offers another advantage—you can view two pages at a time. The two-page display is especially useful if you've chosen the facing pages option in the Page Setup dialog box. Word displays the pages of your document as though you were turning the pages of a book. Even-numbered pages always appear on the left; odd-numbered pages always appear on the right.

The ability to zoom in or out adds power to the views in which you edit text—all views except print preview. You choose how much to reduce or enlarge the page to get the size you want. You can type or edit text as you usually do, regardless of the display size.

Forms

By combining some of the powerful features available in Word, you can quickly produce professional-looking printed and online forms. Using tables, borders, shading, and tabs, you can create customized forms for messages, employment applications, invoices, purchase orders, or whatever you need.

Forms that are filled in online can have their own set of custom dialog boxes to prompt the user for information. The user can move automatically through all fields, typing information at each prompt. To further automate the process, you can create an AutoNew macro that begins prompting automatically when the user starts a new document based on the form template and then chooses the Save command when all information has been entered.

The following sample shows how Word features can be used to create a printed form.

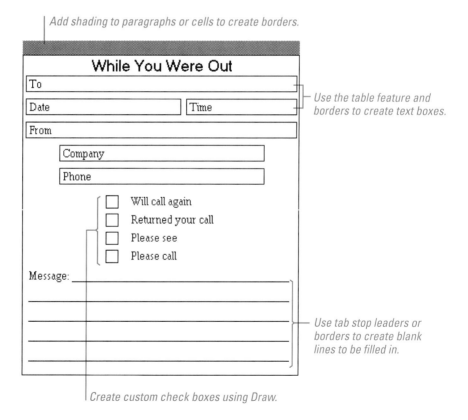

Add shading to paragraphs or cells to create borders.

Use the table feature and borders to create text boxes.

Use tab stop leaders or borders to create blank lines to be filled in.

Create custom check boxes using Draw.

The first section in this chapter summarizes techniques for creating both printed and online forms—using tables, applying boxes and borders, and adding blank lines and check boxes. The second section gives special techniques for creating, filling in, and automating online forms that prompt for information. The chapter concludes with two sample forms—a medical form and a legal document—that demonstrate some advanced uses of fields.

Creating Printed and Online Forms

Before you create a form in Word, sketch it on paper. This helps you decide which sections to include in a Word table and which to create using tabs or graphics. Then use the techniques described in this section to tailor the form to your needs.

If you're creating an online form, consider adding fields that prompt the user for information. For instructions, see "Special Techniques for Online Forms," later in this chapter.

Note The procedures in this chapter briefly introduce features such as tables, borders, and Microsoft Draw graphics, which you may want to use in creating forms. The quickest approach—often using the Toolbar and mouse—is presented. For detailed information and alternate methods, including keyboard procedures, see the related chapter.

Using Tables in a Form

For more information about working with tables, see Chapter 17, "Tables."

Tables are especially useful in forms if you want to position text elements side by side or create a framework in which to fill in information. The table gridlines you see on the screen do not print. You can add borders to set off areas of your form.

To prepare to work with tables

In a table, you can show gridlines to indicate where the cell boundaries are and end-of-cell marks (¤) to help you position the insertion point and select areas of the table. If you're working with the mouse, you should display the Toolbar, ribbon, and ruler.

1   From the Table menu, choose Gridlines (ALT, A, G).

2   To display the Toolbar, ribbon, and ruler, choose the commands with those names from the View menu.

3   To display the end-of-cell marks, click the Show/Hide ¶ button on the ribbon.

To create a table using the Toolbar

The quickest way to insert a table is to click the Table button on the Toolbar. You can then quickly drag through a grid to select the number of columns and rows to insert. The columns are spaced evenly between the document's margins.

Table button

1   Position the insertion point where you want to insert the table.

2   On the Toolbar, click the Table button.

3   Drag over the grid that drops down to select the number of columns and rows you want in the table.

    You can drag down or to the right to add rows and columns to the initial grid. The label at the bottom tells how many rows and columns your table will have. For example, if you select 2 rows with 3 columns, the label reads "2 × 3 Table."

4   Release the mouse button to insert the table.

Note   You can also create a table using the Insert Table command on the Table menu. With this command, you can assign a precise column width as you insert the table.

To change the width of a column or cell

When you position the insertion point on a vertical gridline, the pointer shape changes to a bar with arrows pointing left and right. This pointer is used to drag the column boundary. Unless you select the cell or cells with boundaries that you want to move, this pointer moves the boundaries of all cells in the column.

▶   To move a column boundary, position the insertion point anywhere on the column boundary you want to move. Then drag it to where you want it.

–Or–

▶   To adjust the width of one or more cells in a column, select the cell(s), including the end-of-cell mark. Then drag the cell boundary.

–Or–

▶   To resize a column or cells without changing the table width, hold down SHIFT as you drag using either of the methods above.

Note   If you want to use precise measurements, you can use the Column Width command on the Table menu to specify an exact width for each column and the space between the columns.

To insert one or more rows

▶ To insert a row at the bottom of the table, position the insertion point at the end of the final cell in the last row, and press TAB.

–Or–

▶ To insert a row within the table, select the entire row beneath where you want the new one, and then choose Insert Rows from the Table menu. To insert more than one row, select the number of rows that you want to insert. Word adds the number of rows that you select.

To insert a column

1   Select the column to the right of where you want to insert the column.
    –or–
    To insert a column at the right end of the table, select the column of end-of-row marks at the right end.

2   From the Table menu, choose Insert Columns.

To merge cells in a row

To add a heading that spans more than one column or to give one item more space than those above or below it, you can merge two or more cells within a row. You cannot merge cells within a column.

1   Select the cells you want to merge.

    To make sure that you select entire cells, click the cell selection bar to the left of one cell and then drag across cell boundaries. In the cell selection bar, the pointer shape changes to an arrow, as shown in the following illustration.

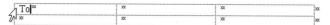

2   From the Table menu, choose Merge Cells (ALT, A, M).

In the merged cell, a paragraph mark replaces each end-of-cell mark from the deleted cells. You can delete the paragraph marks.

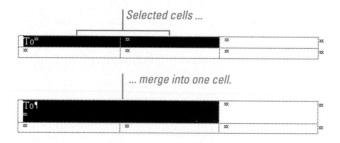

Selected cells ...

... merge into one cell.

To add a cell to a row

You may want some rows in your table to have more columns than others. For example, you may want to add boxes that serve as check boxes. You can add one or more cells to a row and then adjust the column widths.

1. Select as many cells as you want to add to the row.

   Word adds as many cells as you select, moving the selected cells to the right.

2. From the Table menu, choose Insert Cells (ALT, A, I).

3. Select the Shift Cells Right option button.

4. Choose the OK button.

Once you insert the cells, you can adjust their widths. Make sure you select the entire cell—including the end-of-cell mark—before dragging its cell boundary so that you adjust the width of the cell and not the entire column.

Adding Boxes and Borders

For more information about borders, see Chapter 19, "Borders and Shading."

To create boxes or lines within your forms, you can use the Border command on the Format menu to apply borders to a paragraph, a table, or any selection of cells within a table. For a paragraph in a table, you have a choice of applying a border to the cell or to the paragraph within the cell, depending on the effect you want.

The cell borders form a continuous grid; the paragraph borders box each entry individually. The following illustration shows both types of borders. You can adjust the length of a top or bottom paragraph border by setting a left or right indent.

While You Were Out

To	
Date	Time
From	
Company	
Phone	

Borders applied to table cells

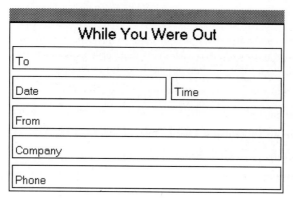

Borders applied to paragraphs

In an online form, the gridlines provide natural partitions between cells. You can add borders to distinguish areas of the form. If the form will be used on color monitors, you may want to add color borders; you do not need a color printer to do this.

Note To add horizontal lines after text labels in a printed form ("blanks" to be filled in), use a custom tab stop instead of a border. For instructions, see "Creating Blank Lines to Be Filled In," later in this chapter.

For a summary of methods for selecting columns, rows, and cells in a table, see Chapter 17, "Tables."

What you select before choosing the Border command determines whether you add cell borders or paragraph borders:

- To add a paragraph border within a cell, you must select at least one character in the paragraph. If you position the insertion point in the paragraph without making a selection, Word applies cell borders.

- If a selection within a cell does not include the end-of-cell mark, Word applies paragraph borders.

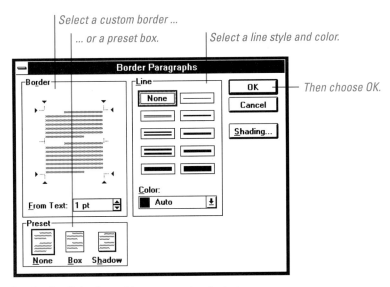

Select a custom border ...

... or a preset box.   *Select a line style and color.*

Then choose OK.

The Border dialog box with a paragraph selected

To apply a preset box

1 Select the paragraphs or cells you want to apply the border to.

2 From the Format menu, choose Border (ALT, T, B).

3 Under Preset, click a box type.

   Word applies the box to the border sample.

4 Under Line, select a line style.

5 If you want to change the border's color, select an option from the Color list.

6 Choose the OK button.

To apply custom borders or add lines within a preset box

1 Select the paragraphs or cells you want to apply the border to.

2 From the Format menu, choose Border.

3 On the border sample, select the border you want to add by clicking in it.

   Small triangles (border markers) mark the beginning and end of a selected border.

4 Under Line, select a line style.

   Word adds a border in the selected line style to the sample.

5 If you want to change the border's color, select an option from the Color list.

6 To apply other borders with the same style and color, select each border on the border sample.

7   Repeat steps 3 through 5 to apply other styles of borders.

8   Choose the OK button.

Adding Shading

Using the Border command, you also can add shading to paragraphs or to table cells. When applied to cells, shading fills the entire area within the gridlines. When applied to paragraphs, the shading fills the area between the paragraph's left and right indents.

To add shading to cells or paragraphs

1   Select the paragraphs or cells you want to shade.

2   From the Format menu, choose Border.

3   Choose the Shading button.

4   In the Pattern box, select a percentage of shading that you want.

In the sample form at the beginning of this chapter, 50 percent shading was used.

5   Choose the OK button to close the Shading dialog box.

6   Choose OK again to close the Border dialog box.

Creating Blank Lines to Be Filled In

If a printed form requires several lengths of lines or lines that follow text labels, the best way to add the lines is to use tab stops. This method does not work in online forms; the user's response would replace the line. In the following form, tab stops were used to add all of the lines.

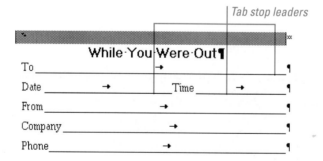

To create a horizontal line using a tab leader

If the ribbon and ruler are not displayed, display them before beginning this procedure by choosing the Ribbon and Ruler commands from the View menu (ALT, V, B and ALT, V, R).

1　Position the insertion point where you want the line to begin.

2　On the ribbon, click the Right-Aligned Tab button.

3　On the ruler, add a tab stop by clicking where you want the line to end.

4　To open the Tabs dialog box, double-click the tab stop marker you just inserted.

5　Under Leader, select the solid-line option (4).

6　Choose the OK button.

7　Press TAB to create the line.
　　–or–
　　Within a table cell, press CTRL+TAB.

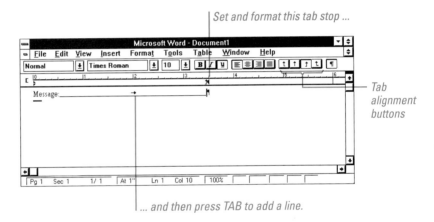

Set and format this tab stop ...

Tab alignment buttons

... and then press TAB to add a line.

Note　You can also add tabs using the Tabs command on the Format menu. For information, see Chapter 7, "Paragraph Formatting."

Creating Check Boxes

If a form will be filled in after it is printed, you can use Microsoft Draw to create different styles of check boxes. For online forms, you can create a check box by applying a border to a table cell.

Check Boxes for Printed Documents

In a printed form, you can use Draw to create check boxes that are round, square, oval, or rectangular. The following illustration shows two styles of check boxes created using Draw.

ProseWare Corporation

How were you introduced to our product?

- A friend recommended us.
- You were satisfied with other products in the ProseWare line.
- Through advertisements. If so, please check one or more below:
  - Yellow Pages
  - Newspaper ads
  - Television ads
  - Radio ads
- Other. Please specify:

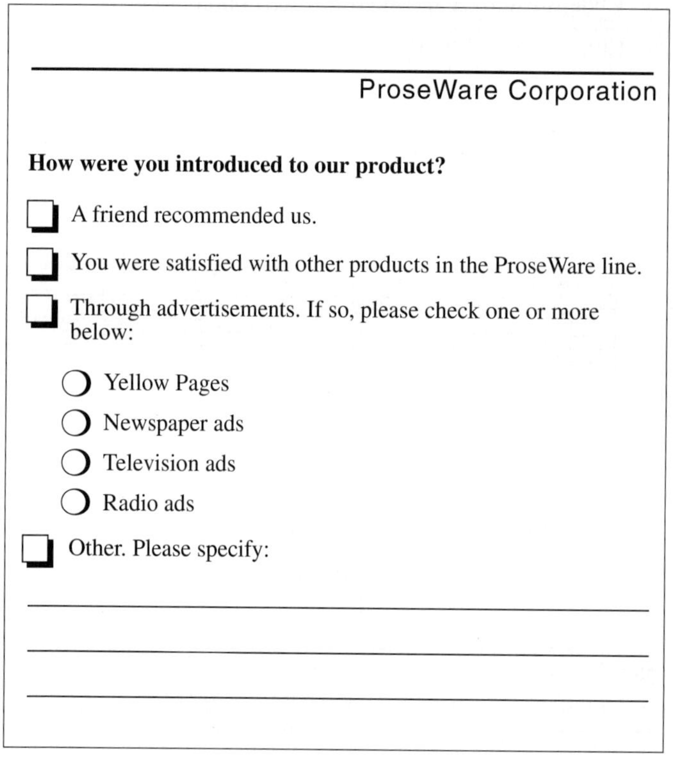

To create a check box in Draw

This procedure displays the Draw window, which has its own menu bar. When you choose a command, make sure you choose it from the Draw menus.

1   Position the insertion point where you want the check box.

2   Click the Draw button on the Toolbar.
    –or–
    From the Insert menu, choose Object. Then double-click Microsoft Drawing in the Object Type list.

    In the Draw window, drawing tools are located along the left side. When you select a tool, the pointer shape changes to cross hairs. Click where you want the shape and drag to create it.

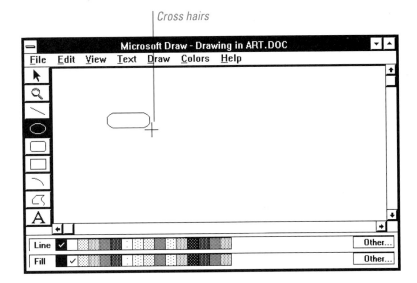

Cross hairs

Draw offers many other drawing and formatting options. For information, see the *Microsoft Draw User's Guide*.

3   To insert a shape, do one of the following:

To insert	Do this
Square	Select the rectangle tool. Then hold down SHIFT and drag.
Rectangle	Select the rectangle tool and drag.
Circle	Select the oval tool. Then hold down SHIFT and drag.
Oval	Select the oval tool and drag.

4 To change the style of the line, choose Line Style from the Draw menu. Then select the option you want.

A diamond identifies the current style.

You may want to experiment with several styles of check boxes. When you finish, select and delete all drawings except the one you want to use.

5 From the File menu, choose Exit And Return.

A dialog box asks whether you want to update your document.

6 Choose the Yes button to insert the new check box as a graphic.

Note If field codes are displayed, an "EMBED MSDraw" field appears instead of the check box. To see the check box, choose Field Codes from the View menu.

To enlarge or reduce the check box

The check box is entered in your document as a graphic. You can size it as you would any other graphic.

1 Click the check box to select it.

2 Drag the handle in the lower-right corner to size the check box.

To adjust the spacing above or below the check box, use the Paragraph command on the Format menu. Under Spacing, type a measurement in the Before box, the After box, or both.

Tip To keep your check boxes standard and avoid repeating the formatting each time, use the Glossary command on the Edit menu to store the check box for repeated use in the current form or in other forms. For information about making and using glossary entries, see Chapter 13, "Glossaries: Storing Items for Reuse."

Check Boxes for Online Forms

To create a check box for a form to be filled in online, you can add a table cell, adjust the cell's width and row height, and add a box using the Border command on the Format menu. Procedures for each of these tasks are included earlier in this section.

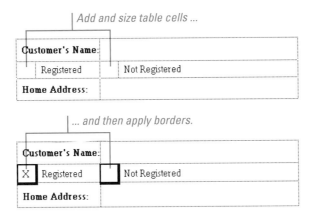

Adjusting the Spacing in Forms

To adjust horizontal spacing, you can adjust tab stops, or you can adjust the column or cell width in a table. To adjust vertical spacing, you can adjust the space before or after a paragraph, or you can adjust the row height in a table.

Experiment with the options listed below to get the look you want.

To adjust	Choose this command	Set this option
Height of one or more rows in a table	Row Height (Table menu)	Height Of Row At
Space between paragraphs	Paragraph (Format menu)	Spacing Before Spacing After
Horizontal distance between text that is separated with tabs	Tabs (Format menu)	Tab Stop Position
Column width of a table	Column Width (Table menu)	Width Of Column

(continued)

To adjust	Choose this command	Set this option
Distance between a paragraph and the left and right table cell boundaries	Paragraph (Format menu) -or- Column Width (Table menu)	Indentation Space Between Columns
Distance between a paragraph and the top and bottom table cell boundaries	Paragraph (Format menu)	Spacing Before Spacing After

Special Techniques for Online Forms

Online forms provide labeled areas that can be filled in using Word. If you set up a form as a table, it's best to give each label and each area to be filled in its own cell.

To have Word prompt for the information, you can add a field at each place where information is needed. The user can automatically move from field to field. You can create a macro that begins this process when a user starts a new form.

To protect the original form, save it as a template. Each time a person opens a new document based on a template, Word makes a copy of the template. The person fills out the copy and saves it with a document name.

Creating a Form That Prompts the User

For more information about fields, see Chapter 41, "Fields."

This section tells how to insert two types of fields that prompt for information—a FILLIN field that inserts the information at the field location and a REF field that stores information to be inserted in other places. You can use other fields as well in your online forms. The techniques for inserting the fields are similar.

Prompting for Information

By inserting a FILLIN field at each place where you need information, you can eliminate the need for scrolling and moving the insertion point. As a person responds to the prompts for information, Word inserts the information in the field location.

A FILLIN field code looks like this:

```
{fillin "What is the company's name?"}
```

You insert the field characters, { }, which mark the beginning and end of the field, by pressing the Insert Field key (CTRL+F9). The text within the quotation marks, which follows the field name, is the prompt that Word will display.

The following illustration shows how a FILLIN field works. When the user types a response and chooses the OK button, Word inserts the response—the *field result*—at the field location. The result is not visible until field codes are hidden.

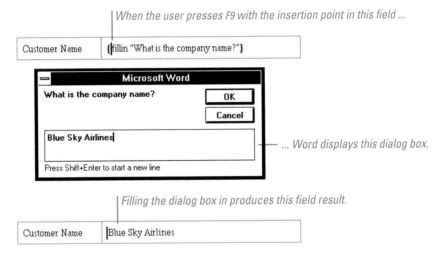

You can view either the field codes or the field results. When field codes are in view, embedded objects such as equations and graphics also appear as codes.

You should display the field codes as you create the fields. If you change your mind about the wording of a prompt, you can edit the text in the field as you would edit any other text. While the form is in use, hide the field codes so that users can see the responses as they fill them in.

To view or hide field codes

▶ From the View menu, choose Field Codes (ALT, V, C).

Note   The procedures in this section use the Insert Field key (CTRL+F9) to enter fields in a document. You can also insert a field by using the Field command on the Insert menu.

To create a FILLIN field

This field prompts the user for information by displaying a dialog box that contains the text you type. Word inserts the user's response at the location of the field code.

1   Position the insertion point where you want the information.

2   Press the Insert Field key (CTRL+F9).

Word inserts field characters, positioning the insertion point between them.

3   Type **fillin** followed by the prompt text you want to use. Enclose the prompt text in quotation marks.

For example, to prompt for a customer's name, you might create this field:

{fillin "What is the customer's name?"}

Make sure you include both opening and closing quotation marks around the prompt text.

4   Press an arrow key to leave the field.

Tip   To apply character formatting to field results, apply the formatting that you want to the field name. The field results are displayed and printed with those formats.

Common Typing Errors

If a field code contains typos, the field won't produce the expected results. The field's behavior when you press F9 to update it often indicates the type of error you made.

If this happens	Check this
You see an error message instead of a prompt.	Make sure the word "fillin" is spelled correctly.
Only the first word of a prompt appears.	The prompt text probably is missing an opening or closing quotation mark.
Word ignores a field.	The braces that enclose the field code may not have been inserted by pressing CTRL+F9. If you can select one of the braces without selecting the entire field, you need to replace the braces with field characters. Position the insertion point where you want the field, and press CTRL+F9. Copy the text from the old field into the new one. Then delete the old field code.

Repeating Information

Using ASK and REF fields, you can have the user type information once, and then automatically insert the information in several locations in the form.

An ASK field prompts for information. You can set up as many ASK fields as you like to prompt for different types of information. To identify each ASK field, you assign it a unique bookmark.

The ASK fields store information; they don't display it. Add a REF (Reference) field wherever you want the information inserted. The REF field includes the field name followed by the bookmark for the information you want to insert. When the REF field is updated, Word inserts the referenced information.

In the following employment application form, ASK and REF fields are set up to repeat a person's work telephone number in two places.

ASK field prompts for the "workphone" information.

REF fields insert the information here ...

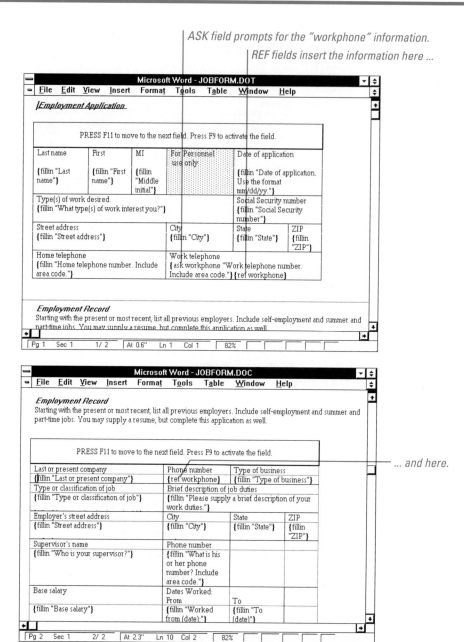

... and here.

An online form that uses ASK and REF fields

The following illustration shows the user's view of the form, with fields, gridlines, and paragraph marks hidden.

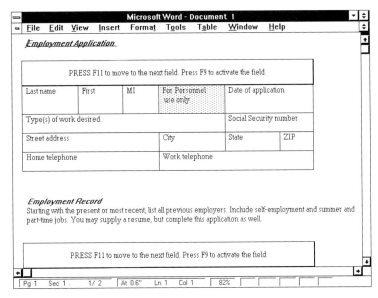

The user's view of the online form

To create an ASK field

The ASK field stores information to be inserted by a REF field. It must precede any REF field that references it.

1 Position the insertion point where you want the ASK field.

2 Press the Insert Field key (CTRL+F9).

3 In the field characters that Word inserts, type **ask** followed by the bookmark you want to assign and then the prompt text. Enclose the prompt text in quotation marks.

For example, you might create the following ASK field, named "address," which prompts for the customer's address:

{ask address "What is the customer's address?"}

Make sure you type both the opening and closing quotation marks around the prompt text.

4 Press an arrow key to move out of the field.

To reference an ASK field

At each place where you want to enter the information from an ASK field, insert a REF field that references the field. The ASK field must precede any REF field that references it.

1 Position the insertion point where you want to insert the ASK information.

2 Press the Insert Field key (CTRL+F9).

3 In the field characters that Word inserts, type **ref** followed by the bookmark for the ASK field. The "ref" label is optional unless the bookmark is also a field name.

  For example, to reference the ASK field created in the preceding procedure, you could type **ref address** or just **address**

4 Press an arrow key to move out of the field.

Other Useful Fields

Word provides several other fields that you may find useful as you create forms. The following table lists a few.

Field	Inserts
AUTHOR	Author's name, taken from the Summary Info dialog box.
CREATEDATE	Date when the document was created.
DATE	Date when the field was most recently updated.
TIME	Time when the field was most recently updated.
Expression(=)	Result of a calculation. For example, you can calculate the sum of a column of numbers or multiply an item's price by the quantity ordered.
IF	Allows you to change the order in which fields are processed by defining conditions. For example, if a customer plans to pay cash for an order, you can set up an IF field that skips fields requesting credit card information.

To see examples of how the IF field and other fields can be used in an online form, see "Advanced Examples," later in this chapter.

Saving the Form As a Template

For information about creating and using templates, see Chapter 37, "Document Templates."

It's best to save any online form that you create as a template, letting users fill in a document based on the template. This protects the original form.

You can save a macro with the template to move the user from field to field automatically. For instructions, see "Automating the Process," later in this section.

To save a form as a template

1 From the File menu, choose Save As (ALT, F, A), or press F12.

2 In the File Name box, type a name for the form.

3 In the Save File As Type box, select Document Template.

4 Choose the OK button.

5 Choose the OK button again to close the Summary Info dialog box.

To fill in the form, a user will open a new document based on the template by choosing New from the File menu. If you want to update the form template, choose Open from the File menu, and select the template.

Filling in an Online Form

If each area that requires information is set up as a field, a person can move automatically through the fields to fill in the form.

To fill in an online form that has fields

If you haven't saved your form as a template, follow the steps in "To save a form as a template," earlier in this section, before beginning this procedure.

1 From the File menu, choose New (ALT, F, N).

2 In the Use Template box, select the form, and choose the OK button.

3 From the Edit menu, choose Select All to select the entire form.

4 Press the Update Fields key (F9).

Word displays a dialog box similar to the following one, with the prompt text from the first FILLIN or ASK field.

5   Type the information that is requested, and choose the OK button.

Word displays the dialog box for the next FILLIN or ASK field.

6   Repeat step 5 until you complete the form.

Word updates each REF field automatically with the information you supply in the FILLIN and ASK fields.

7   Choose Save from the File menu.

Word displays the Save As dialog box, set for saving a Word document.

8   Type a name for the document in the File Name box, and choose the OK button.

Tip   If you don't want to update all of the fields in a form, you can press the Next Field (F11) and Previous Field (CTRL+F11) keys to move from field to field. Or you can use any other method for positioning the insertion point. Within a field, press the Update Field key (F9) to display the prompt dialog box or, in a REF field, to insert the ASK information.

Automating the Process

For more information about macros, see Chapter 42, "Using Macros."

To automate the process of filling in an online form, you can create an AutoNew macro that records your keystrokes as you update the fields. If you store the macro with the form template, the macro starts automatically each time a user opens a new document based on the template.

When the document opens, Word immediately displays the information prompts. After all information has been entered, Word opens the Save As dialog box so the user can save the form.

Note   Using the macro language in Word, you can create a macro that includes conditional prompts that determine the order in which prompts are displayed and information is inserted in the form based on the user's responses. For an example of this type of form, see "Advanced Examples," later in this chapter.

Before you begin the macro

If you haven't saved your form as a template, follow the steps in "To save a form as a template," earlier in this section, before beginning this procedure.

1 From the File menu, choose New. In the Use Template box, select the form, and choose the OK button.

2 From the File menu, choose Save (ALT, F, S). Type a name for the new document, and choose the OK button twice. (You don't need to fill in summary information.)

The name you give the document doesn't matter. This step is included to enable you to choose the Save command later as part of the macro.

To start the macro

1 From the Tools menu, choose Record Macro (ALT, O, R).

2 Under Record Macro Name, type **autonew**

Any macro that you assign the "autonew" name starts automatically when a user opens a new document based on the template.

3 Under Description, type a brief description of what the macro will do.

4 Choose the OK button.

To record your keystrokes

1 From the Edit menu, choose Select All to select the entire form.

2 Press the Update Fields key (F9) to instruct Word to update all fields.

Word displays the dialog box for the first ASK or REF field.

3 Without typing any information, choose the OK or Cancel button.

4 Repeat step 3 until you complete the form.

5 From the File menu, choose Save (ALT, F, S).

To stop the macro

▶ From the Tools menu, choose Stop Record (ALT, O, R).

You save the macro with the form template when you close the document. When a user opens a new document based on the template, the macro starts automatically.

To save the macro in the form template

1 From the File menu, choose Close (ALT, F, C).

   Word asks whether you want to save the changes to the template (the template has a .DOT filename extension).

2 Choose the Yes button.

Advanced Examples

This section provides two examples of more advanced forms: an online form with conditional prompts and a legal document assembled with the help of field instructions.

An Online Form with Conditional Prompts

Many forms include sections that are filled in only if a person has responded in a particular way to an earlier part of the form. The sample document described in this section is an employee health insurance form in which the last part is filled out only if the patient is an employee's family member rather than the employee.

For information about writing macros in Word, see Chapter 42, "Using Macros." Using the macro language in Word, you can automate this form so that it displays a prompt for the last part of the form *conditionally*—only if the patient is a family member. This kind of conditional prompt is especially useful for complex forms in which a particular response may require a series of different prompts.

The sample online form has two main elements:

- The form template, which contains the text and borders that make up the form, as well as the bookmarks labeled in the following illustration.

- An AutoNew macro that automatically displays a series of prompts for the information the form requires when a form is started. In this respect, the AutoNew macro works like a series of ASK fields, discussed earlier in this chapter. Unlike the ASK fields, the macro can test responses and display prompts conditionally. The macro is saved with the template.

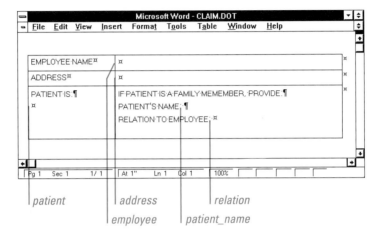

The form template with bookmarks labeled

The following illustration shows each part of the AutoNew macro.

```
Sub MAIN

employee$ = InputBox$("Enter the employee's name:")
address$ = InputBox$("Employee's address:")                                    } A
patient$ = InputBox$("Enter 1 if patient is an employee; 2 if patient is family member:")
If patient$ = "2" Then
     patient_name$ = InputBox$("Enter the patient's name:")
     relation$ = InputBox$(" What is patient's relation to employee?:")        } B
End If
EditGoTo "employee"
Insert employee$
EditGoTo "address"                                                             } C
Insert address$
EditGoTo "patient"
If patient$ = "2" Then
     Insert "Family member"
     EditGoTo "patient_name"
     Insert patient_name$
     EditGoTo "relation"                                                       } D
     Insert relation$
Else
     Insert "Employee"
End If

End Sub
```

A   The three macro statements at the top are similar to ASK fields. Each prompts for information when the macro runs. The user's response to each prompt is stored in a variable—employee$, for example. The third prompt ("Enter 1 if patient is an employee; 2 if patient is a family member") enables the macro to test whether the patient is an employee or a family member.

B   This If...End If conditional statement tests the response given to the previous prompt. If the response was "2"—to indicate that the patient is a family member—then the macro prompts for additional information about the patient.

C   After prompting for all needed information, the macro begins to insert that information in the form. The form template includes several bookmarks, shown in the earlier illustration, which mark the locations where information should be inserted. The EditGoto statements in this section of the macro are equivalent to Go To commands on the Edit menu: they move the insertion point to bookmarks such as employee and address. The Insert statement that follows each EditGoto statement then inserts the contents of a variable such as employee$ or address$. These variables store the responses to the earlier prompts. For clarity, the bookmark names and variable names in this example match; this isn't necessary.

D   Like the earlier If...End If conditional statement, this If...Else...End If conditional tests whether the patient is a family member. The Else statement determines what action the macro takes if the patient is not. If the patient is a family member, then the macro inserts the words "Family member" at the appropriate place, and then inserts other relevant information about the family member. If the patient is not a family member, then the macro inserts "Employee."

A Legal Document

You can automate much of the routine work of preparing legal briefs, contracts, wills, and other legal documents. The sample document in this section is a legal brief assembled using ASK and INCLUDE fields. The initial ASK fields prompt for information used to prepare the brief. The INCLUDE fields bring in the text of three other documents when the brief is printed.

Tip   This use of ASK fields to prompt for information is appropriate for documents such as a brief, which you typically prepare one document at a time. If you want to prepare many versions of a document at once, each with different case information, it may be easier to use the Print Merge feature. For information about Print Merge, see Chapter 32, "Print Merge Basics."

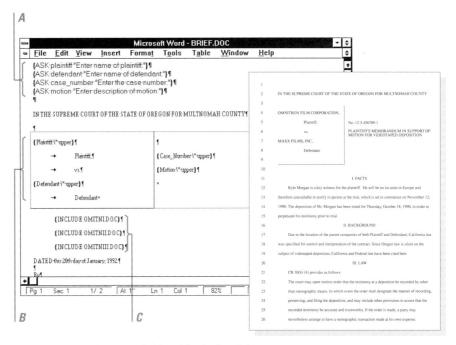

Legal brief main document (left) and final printed document

A These ASK fields define bookmarks describing the plaintiff, the defendant, the case number, and the motion. When you update the document's fields, Word displays a series of dialog boxes prompting for the information for each of the fields. To prevent blank lines in the printed document, the ending paragraph marks have the hidden character format.

B Each bookmark that the ASK fields defined is inserted in the standard text of the brief where you want the case information printed. To ensure that the information is printed in uppercase letters, regardless of the case in which it is typed, each field includes an uppercase format switch (* upper).

C Sections of the document are prepared separately and then incorporated using these INCLUDE fields. This is particularly useful if, for example, several people are working on a large contract, each responsible for a different section.

Other Features for Legal Documents

Word has many other features that can further automate your work with legal documents. Be sure to investigate the features described in the following chapters:

Chapter 13, "Glossaries: Storing Items for Reuse"

Chapter 28, "Adding Bullets and Numbers"

Chapter 36, "Exchanging Information"

Chapter 37, "Document Templates"

Chapter 38, "Customizing Menus, the Keyboard, and the Toolbar"

Chapter 26

Finding and Managing Files

Over time, you will probably create many documents that contain information you want to reference or reuse. With Word, if you want to locate a quotation, reuse a graphic, review a document's contents, or compare information with a co-worker, you can quickly locate the information you need from any drive or directory to which you have access.

With the Find File command, you can locate a document by searching for almost any information you can remember—or guess—about the document. For example, if you remember the name, or even part of the name, of the file that contains the information, you can search by filename. If you want to find all files that contain a phrase, such as "annual income," you can search specifically for that phrase. If you need to recall information from a memo that a colleague wrote last May, you can search for files on that subject created by your colleague during the month of May.

Using Summary Information

When you save a file for the first time, Word by default displays the Summary Info dialog box. Although you don't have to provide summary information, taking a minute to type information about the document—such as its title and subject—will help you locate the document more quickly when you need it later. This is useful if you work with many documents over a network or on a project involving many people.

You can also provide summary information for a new document by choosing the Summary button in the New dialog box. You can review, fill in, or edit summary information for the active document at any time by choosing the Summary Info command from the File menu or selecting the Summary button in the Find File dialog box (File menu). If you fill in the summary information before saving a document for the first time, Word does not display the Summary Info dialog box when you save.

If you don't want Word to display the Summary Info dialog box when you save documents, choose the Options command from the Tools menu, select the Save category, and then clear the Prompt For Summary Info check box.

In the Summary Info dialog box, you can do any of the following:

- Fill in the information you want.

- Choose OK without filling in any information. If you are saving, Word saves the document and does not prompt you for summary information the next time you save the document.

- Choose Cancel without filling in information. If you are saving, Word saves the document and displays the Summary Info dialog box again the next time you save.

- View statistics about the document, such as the creation date, the date the document was last saved, and the number of words and pages in the document.

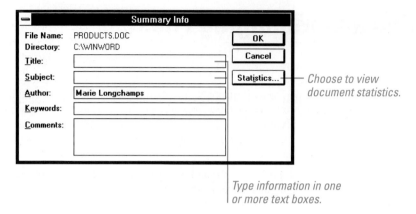

Choose to view document statistics.

Type information in one or more text boxes.

Summary Info dialog box

File Name   The filename of the active document.

Directory   The location of the active document.

Title   The title of the the active document. The title can be longer and more descriptive than the filename.

Subject   A description of the document's contents.

Author   By default, the name assigned to your copy of the Word program during setup. Change the author for the active document by typing a new name. Change the author for all future documents by choosing Options from the Tools menu, selecting the User Info category, and then typing a new name in the Name box.

Keywords   General topics in the document or other important information, such as client names and account numbers.

Comments   Any remarks you want to keep with the document for future reference.

Statistics   Additional information about the document. Choose the Statistics button to display the Document Statistics dialog box.

To fill in and edit summary information

1   If the Summary Info dialog box is not already displayed, choose Summary Info from the File menu (ALT, F, I).

2   Fill in the information you want for the document. You can type as many as 255 characters, including spaces and punctuation, for each category of information.

Use the same procedures for editing that you use for document text. Use the mouse or the TAB key to move from box to box.

3   Choose the OK button.

Note When you save a document to a file format other than Word Document or Rich Text Format (RTF), Word does not display the Summary Info dialog box. If you choose Summary Info from the File menu and fill in summary information for the document, Word automatically changes the file format to Word Document format and records the summary information so you can use it in a search. If you save the file again in a file format that does not include summary information, the summary information is deleted from the document.

To view additional information about a document

1 If the Summary Info dialog box is not already displayed, choose Summary Info from the File menu (ALT, F, I).

2 Choose the Statistics button.

3 If you made changes to the document since you last saved it, choose the Update button to update the statistics.

4 To close the Document Statistics dialog box, choose the OK button.

5 To close the Summary Info dialog box, choose the OK button.

Although most of the information in the Document Statistics dialog box is self-explanatory, a few items may require clarification.

Revision Number The number of times the document has been saved.

Total Editing Time The number of minutes the document has been open during all editing sessions since it was created. This does not include time when the document was open with read-only access. However, if you save the read-only file to a different name, the read-only time is added to the editing time for the new document.

For more information on templates, see Chapter 37, "Document Templates."

Template The template on which the document is based. If you haven't changed templates, this is the template you chose in the New dialog box when you created the document.

Tip If you are viewing statistics and you want to update them, you must choose Summary Info directly from the File menu and then choose the Statistics and Update buttons. You cannot update statistics if you entered the Summary Info and Document Statistics dialog boxes through the Find File dialog box.

To print summary information and statistics with your document

1 From the File menu, choose Print (ALT, F, P).

2 Make sure that Document is selected in the Print box.

3 Choose the Options button.

4 Under Include With Document, select the Summary Info check box.

5 Choose the OK button.

6 In the Print dialog box, select any other options you want.

7 Choose the OK button.

Summary information is combined with the document statistics and printed in the default font. The summary information is printed on a separate page following the document text; if you are printing annotations, summary information follows the annotations. If you print hidden text, the statistics for pages, words, and characters will include the hidden text.

To print only summary information and statistics

1 From the File menu, choose Print (ALT, F, P).

2 In the Print box, select Summary Info.

3 Select any other options you want.

4 Choose the OK button.

Summary information is combined with the document statistics and printed in the default font.

Note You can choose to print summary information with all of your documents by choosing Options from the Tools menu, selecting the Print category, and then selecting the Summary Info check box.

Using Fields to Insert Summary Information in Your Document

You can use fields to insert information from the Summary Info dialog box and the Document Statistics dialog box directly into the text of a document. If information changes, you can quickly update it throughout the document by selecting the fields and pressing the Update Field key (F9).

For example, you can insert the TITLE field in the document's header. The text you type in the Title box in the Summary Info dialog box will be printed at the top of each page when you print the document. If you change the title in the Summary Info dialog box and update the TITLE field, the new title will be inserted.

You can insert any of the following fields: AUTHOR, COMMENTS, FILENAME, KEYWORDS, SUBJECT, and TITLE; the date the file was created (CREATEDATE), the name of the person who last saved the document (LASTSAVEDBY), the number of minutes the document has been open (EDITTIME), the number of characters in the document (NUMCHARS), the number of pages (NUMPAGES), the number of words (NUMWORDS), the revision number (REVNUM), the date last printed (PRINTDATE), the date last saved (SAVEDATE), and the name of the document's template (TEMPLATE).

You can also use the INFO field to insert information from the Summary Info dialog box and to automatically change the information in the Author, Comments, Keywords, Subject, and Title boxes in the Summary Info dialog box. For more information about using fields, see Chapter 41, "Fields."

Retrieving Documents with the Find File Command

The first time you choose Find File from the File menu, Word searches the current directory for all Word (*.DOC) files and then lists the files in the Find File dialog box. From the Find File dialog box you can learn a file's location, display its contents, and view other information about the file without opening it. You can also perform file-management tasks such as opening, printing, copying, and deleting one or more files.

The categories of information you use to locate a document—filename, author, subject, and so on—are called the search criteria. You can choose the Search button in the Find File dialog box to specify the search criteria that you want Word to use in determining the files it lists. Each time you change the search criteria, files are listed according to your new criteria, which remain operative until you change them again.

Note   Word cannot carry out file-management tasks on files with read-only access. Read-only files are not listed in the Find File dialog box.

In the Find File dialog box, Word lists the drives and directories that were searched to create the File Name list. The File Name list shows the location of the files by displaying the path through the directory hierarchy. By default, Word displays files with the filenames in alphabetical order and previews the content of the file selected.

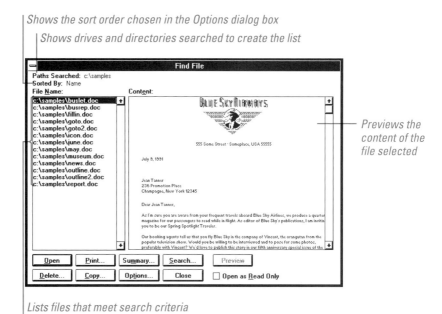

Find File dialog box

Viewing Information About a File

In the Find File dialog box, you can choose the Options button to specify whether you want to display the filename and title of a document, view summary information, view document statistics, or preview the content of a file without opening it.

You can choose to preview the content of a file by choosing the Options button and selecting Content (if it's not already selected) in the List File Names With box. If you preview the content of a Word for Windows file, Word displays all of the text as it would appear in Normal view with formatting. If the file includes both text and graphics, you can see both in the file. If the selected file is in Microsoft Word for the Macintosh, Microsoft Word for DOS, Microsoft Works, or Microsoft Write format, the text is displayed without formatting and without graphics unless you select the Preview button.

For more information on graphics files, see Chapter 20, "Importing Graphics."

If the file you select is a graphics file, you must choose the Preview button to display it. It may take some time to convert the contents of a graphics file for display. If the file is not in a format Word recognizes, it cannot be displayed.

Note that the Preview button is available only when you're previewing the content of a file. It has no effect on a nongraphics file.

To view information about a file

1 In the Find File box, select the file you want to preview.

2 Choose the Options button.

3 Under List File Names With, select one of the following:

To view filenames plus	Select
The title of the document (as typed in the Summary Info dialog box) and the sorting criteria	Title
The content of the file	Content
Information from the Summary Info dialog box: title, subject, author, keywords, and comments	Summary Info
The template used, title, creation date, date last saved, name of the person who last saved the file, revision number, editing time, and document size	Statistics

4 Choose the OK button.

If you selected more than one file, Word displays the information for the first file in the selection.

Sorting the File List

The Find File dialog box lists the files that match your criteria in alphabetical order by path and filename.

You can use the Options button in the Find File dialog box to sort the list of files in the order you find most convenient. You can sort by the file's author, the date the file was created, the name of the person who last saved the file, the date the file was last saved, the filename, or the size of the file.

To sort a list of files

1   In the Find File dialog box, choose the Options button.

2   Under Sort Files By, select the criterion for sorting.

To sort files	Select
Alphabetically by author name	Author
Chronologically by date created	Creation Date
Alphabetically by name of the person who last saved	Last Saved By
Chronologically by date of last save	Last Saved Date
Alphabetically by filename	Name
By size, from smallest to largest file	Size

3   Under List File Names With, select the option you prefer.

4   Choose the OK button.

The second line of text in the upper-left corner of the Find File dialog box displays the sorting criterion currently applied to the File Name list.

Note If you sort the files more than once and use different criteria, the File Name list shows all of the results. For example, if you sort first by author and again by creation date, all of the files created on any given date are sorted alphabetically by author, and the oldest files (those created first) are listed first.

It's important to note that only documents having Microsoft Word for Windows format contain summary information capable of being sorted. Documents in other formats may be listed in the Find File dialog box, but they cannot be sorted. If you instruct Word to sort them by author, for example, the dialog box indicates they are sorted by Author, but no such sorting actually takes place.

Specifying the Search Criteria

By default, the Find File dialog box lists all Word (*.DOC) files in the current directory. You can choose the Search button to specify criteria for a list of files that have similar filenames, contain specific text, or were created or modified during a specific period or by a specific person.

You can also locate files that contain any summary information—title, subject, author, keywords, and comments. You can further modify your search by specifying all drives, or a specific drive, on your computer or a network. You can search for files with a specific filename extension, such as graphics files with the filename extension .BMP.

After you create a list in the Find File dialog box, you can return to the Search dialog box, change the search criteria, and use the search options to create a new list or revise the existing list.

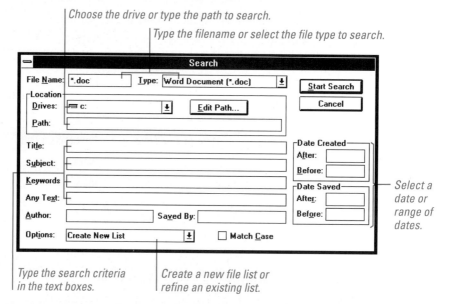

Choose the drive or type the path to search.

Type the filename or select the file type to search.

Type the search criteria in the text boxes.

Create a new file list or refine an existing list.

Select a date or range of dates.

Search dialog box

File Name   The name of the file to locate. You can use wildcards if you don't know the filename or you want to search for multiple files. Type * for any number of un-specified characters and ? for any one character. For example, type ***.DOC** to search for all Word documents, or **Chapt?.DOC** to search for the Word documents Chapt1.DOC through Chapt9.DOC.

Type   The filename extensions to be considered in the search. This option provides a convenient alternative to inserting a filename extension in the File Name box. If there is a conflict between the information in the File Name and Type boxes, Word uses the information in the File Name box as the search criterion.

The choices in the Type box differ depending on how you open the Search dialog box. If you choose the Find File command from the File menu, the Type box contains a short list of text and graphics file types. If you open Find File from within the Open dialog box (File menu), it contains a short list of text file types. If you open Find File from within the File or Picture dialog box (Insert menu), the Type box contains a more complete list of text file types or graphics file types, respectively. No matter how you open the Find File dialog box, however, you can type any filename extension in the File Name box or choose All Files from the Type box.

Drives   The drive or drives you want to search. Note that the Path Only option, displayed by default after every search, limits your next search to the directories containing files that match the search criteria you last specified. If the Drives box displays the Path Only option and the Path box is blank, Word searches the current directory.

Note that the All Drives and All Local Drives options do not include floppy disk drives; to search a floppy disk drive, you must select that drive individually.

Path   The path to search. If there is no entry, Word searches the current directory. When Word finds files that match the criteria in the Search dialog box, the names of the directories containing those files are displayed in the Path box, overwriting any existing path. The search path is retained between Word sessions.

The Drives box overrides the Path box. If there is any contradiction between the two boxes, Word uses the information in the Drives box as the search criterion.

If the Path box contains more than 255 characters, you must use the Edit Path button to modify the search path.

Edit Path   An easy alternative to typing the path in the Path box. For more information, see the procedure "To change the search path," later in this section.

Title, Subject, Keywords, Author   Text recorded in a document's Summary Info dialog box. These fields are considered only when searching for Word for Windows documents.

Any Text   Text that appears in the documents you want to locate. Word searches the entire content of each document for matching text. (Applies only to Word for Windows documents.)

Match Case   An option that restricts the search to text that exactly matches the case (uppercase and lowercase) of the search text in the Any Text box.

Date Saved, Date Created   The date when the file was last saved and (Word for Windows documents only) the date when the file was created. Type the dates in the format you set in the Control Panel. If you haven't changed the date format, the format is day/month/year; you can type, for example, **5/12/91** or **05/12/1991**

Saved By   The name of the person who last saved the file. (Applies only to Word for Windows documents.)

Options   Further search options. Create New List replaces the current list in the Find File dialog box. Add Matches To List applies another set of criteria and adds files to the current list. Search Only In List applies another set of criteria to the files in the current list. For more information, see "Changing the Search Options," later in this chapter.

Note If you are using the Any Text box to search for specific text, Word may not find files that were saved using the fast save option. If you use the Any Text box in searches, you should always save your documents with full save. Choose Options from the Tools menu, select the Save category, and then clear the Allow Fast Saves check box.

To search for a file

1   From the File menu, choose Find File (ALT, F, F).

    Word displays all files that match the current search criteria.

2   If the filename you want is not listed under File Name, choose the Search button.

3   In the File Name box, type the filename. You can use wildcards: type * to indicate any number of unspecified characters and ? to indicate any one character.
    –or–
    From the Type box, select the type of file you want to find. In the File Name box, Word inserts an asterisk (*) followed by a period and the filename extension.

4   Under Drives, select the drive you want to search.
    –or–
    Under Path, type the paths that you want to include in the search (maximum 255 characters). Separate the paths with semicolons or commas—for example
    c:\winword; c:\winword\reports
    –or–
    Choose the Edit Path button to add locations to, delete locations from, or include more than 255 characters in the search path. For more information, see the procedure "To change the search path," later in this section.

5   If you want to specify additional search criteria, type the information in the remaining text boxes (maximum 255 characters per box).

    If you type characters in the Any Text box and want to match uppercase and lowercase letters, select the Match Case check box.

6   If you want to specify a date or range of dates created or saved, fill in the appropriate boxes under Date Created or Date Saved.

    To set a range of dates, type the earlier date (the date after which Word is to search) in the After box and the later date in the Before box. To see files from only one date, type the same date in the After and Before boxes.

7   To create a new list in the Find File dialog box, make sure the Create New List option is selected in the Options box. To revise an existing list, select another option from the Options box. For more information, see "Changing the Search Options," later in this chapter.

8   Choose the Start Search button.

    Word closes the Search dialog box, locates the files that match the criteria you specified in steps 3 through 7, and lists them in the Find File dialog box.

To cancel a search in progress, choose the Cancel button or press ESC. If you cancel a search while Word is building the search path, the search stops, and displays the previous search path. If you cancel your search while the dialog box displays "Building File List," your new search path is retained, and the next time you choose Find File, Word continues the search.

Tip   In the Find File dialog box, Word lists all files that match the search criteria specified in the Search dialog box. If you make changes to your files, such as adding and deleting text or changing their filenames or locations, the files listed may no longer match the search criteria. To ensure accurate matches when you choose Find File, choose the Search button, check the search criteria, and redo the search.

To change the search path

1   In the Search dialog box, choose the Edit Path button.

2   Do any of the following:

To	Do this
List the directories on another drive	In the Drives box, select the drive.
Add a directory to the search path	In the Directories box, select the directory, and then choose the Add button.
Remove a directory from the search path	In the Search Path box, select the directory, and then choose the Delete button.
Delete all directories in the search path	Choose the Delete All button.

3   Choose the Close button.

Tips for Specifying Search Criteria

Pinpointing a file   The more criteria you specify, the more you narrow the list in the Find File dialog box and the faster you can locate the exact file you want. For example, when you search for Any Text, Word searches the entire content of each file, including headers, footers, footnotes, and hidden text. If you have a lot of files and Any Text is the only criterion you specify, the search may take a long time.

Although it's often a good idea to include more than a single criterion for a search, you should include only the search criteria you need to locate a file. For example, if you want a list of all the document templates on the current drive, the only criteria you should specify are the current drive and the file type. Make sure all of the text boxes are empty, and select the following options: the current drive in the Drives box, Create New List in the Options box, and Document Template (.DOT) in the Type box.

Searching more than one file type or drive If you want to search a combination of file types but don't want to search all file types, first search one type, and then select the Search button in the Find File dialog box. Select another file type, and then select Add Matches To List in the Options box in the Search dialog box. You can also use this method to search multiple drives quickly.

Allowable characters in the File Name box You can type as many as 12 characters in the File Name box—8 characters for the filename, a period, and a three-character filename extension. If you don't know the filename, or if you want to search for multiple files, you can use wildcards. Type * for any number of unspecified characters and ? for any one character. For example, ***.DOC** searches for all documents with the filename extension .DOC, and **Chapter?.DOC** searches for the documents Chapter1.DOC through Chapter9.DOC.

Allowable characters in a text box You can type as many as 255 characters in any text box in the Search dialog box. An exception to this is the File Name box, which allows only 12 characters. You can also use wildcards in text boxes. For example, you can type **?** to search for any one character. Typing **th?n** would find *than, thin,* and *then,* but not *thorn.* Typing **th??n** would find *thorn.* Note that typing **the** would find both *the* and *theater.* To find only *the,* type a space after **the** and enclose the word in quotation marks: **"the "**

You can type partial words and any combination of uppercase and lowercase letters. For example, you can type **sa** or **SA** or **Sa** in the Title box to list the files with titles *1992 Sales Figures* and *Salesmanship.*

Whenever the text you type includes spaces or punctuation, enclose the text in quotation marks. For example, to find the phrase *modern dance* in your documents, type **"modern dance"**

You can use any of the following characters in a text box.

Character	Meaning
? (question mark)	Match any single character.
* (asterisk)	Match any number of characters.
" " (quotation marks)	Treat the enclosed character (space, asterisk, question mark, comma, ampersand, or tilde) as a normal character. For example, to indicate a question mark, type "**?**"
, (comma)	Logical OR. The information may match any or all items, but it must match at least one item. For example, if you type **dance, modern** in the Keywords box, Word searches for any document containing either **dance** or **modern.**
& (ampersand) (space)	Logical AND. The information must match all of the items in the list. For example, if you type **dance & modern** or **dance modern** Word searches for any document that contains both words.
~ (tilde)	Logical NOT. The information must not match this item. For example, if you type **~modern** Word does not include any files that contain the word *modern* in the Find File list.

Note that spaces preceding and following commas and ampersands are ignored. For example, both **dance, modern** and **dance,modern** find documents containing either the word *dance* or the word *modern*, or both words.

Changing the Search Options

After you create a list in the Find File dialog box, you can select the Search button to return to the Search dialog box. Then you can change the search criteria and use the search options to create a new list or revise the existing list.

Options box in the Search dialog box

If you select Create New List, Word revises the list in the Find File dialog box to include only those files that meet the new set of criteria. The new list replaces the list previously created. Create New List is the default setting.

If you select Add Matches To List, Word adds files that meet the new set of criteria to the current list. This option usually increases the number of files in the list, because it includes files that meet one set of criteria plus files that meet another set of criteria. The Add Matches To List option is especially useful if you want to search a different drive or search for a different file type using the same set of criteria.

If you select Search Only In List, Word adds to the list files that meet both the previous criteria and the new criteria. This option usually decreases the number of files in the File Name list, because Word applies the new search criteria only to the files already listed in the Find File dialog box.

For example, if you search your files for the word *banana,* Find File lists the files that contain the word *banana.* If you search again, this time for *orange,* the result in the File Name list is based on the selection in the Options box:

If you select	Word lists
Create New List	Only files that contain *orange*
Add Matches To List	Files that contain *banana,* files that contain *orange,* and files that contain both *banana* and *orange*
Search Only In List	Only files that contain both *banana* and *orange*

Tip   The search path remains intact, even between Word sessions, until you specify new criteria and search again. If you have changed a file so that it no longer matches your search criteria, or you've changed the file's location, you can redo the search using the existing criteria to remove the file from the list.

Managing Files with the Find File Command

In addition to locating and viewing files, you can perform any of the following actions from the Find File dialog box:

- Opening files
- Printing files
- Copying files
- Deleting files
- Making changes to a document's summary information

If you already know the file's name and location, the Find File command may not be the simplest method for opening, printing, or saving the file. The simplest way to open a file is to click the Open button on the Toolbar or choose Open from the File menu. To print or copy a file, you can open the file and then print or save it by clicking the appropriate button on the Toolbar or choosing the appropriate command from the File menu.

However, if you choose one of these commands, you can work with only one file at a time. If you want to open, print, or copy more than one file at a time, or if you need to locate a file before you work with it, you can do so from the Find File dialog box.

Note   If nine documents are already open, you must close a document before you can choose the Open button in the Find File dialog box. This button is also unavailable if the File Name list is empty. The Print, Delete, and Copy buttons are also unavailable when the File Name list is empty.

To select multiple files in the Find File dialog box

▶ Hold down CTRL while you click each filename.

If you select a file by mistake, hold down CTRL and click the filename again.

If you want to select two or more files in sequence, you can click the first filename and then hold down the SHIFT key and click the last filename in the series.

1   Press SHIFT+F8.

2   Press the UP ARROW or DOWN ARROW key to move to the filename you want.

3   Press the SPACEBAR.

If you select a file by mistake, press the SPACEBAR again.

4   Repeat steps 2 and 3 until all the files you want are selected.

If you want to select two or more files in sequence, hold down SHIFT while you press the arrow keys.

5   Press SHIFT+F8.

Note   If you choose the Find File button in the File or Picture dialog box (Insert menu), you can select only one file. The Open button is replaced by the Insert button. When you choose Insert, Word returns you to the File or Picture dialog box so that you can choose additional options before inserting the file.

To open, print, and delete files from the Find File dialog box

1   Use the Find File command to locate and list the files, as described earlier in this chapter.

2   Select the files you want.

3 Do any of the following.

To	Do this
Open the files	Choose the Open button, or open a single file by double-clicking the filename.
Open the files and prevent changes	Select the Open As Read Only check box, and then choose the Open button.
Print the files	Choose the Print button.
Delete the files	Choose the Delete button.

If you select several files at once, the action you choose affects the files in the order they are listed in the File Name box.

4 If you are opening files that are not in Word format, you may be asked to verify the file type from which you are converting. Word proposes the file type; choose OK. For more information, see Chapter 35, "Converting File Formats."

5 If you are printing files, select any options you want, and then choose the OK button.

If you choose to print only a range of pages, that same range will be printed for all of the files selected.

6 If you are deleting files, Word asks if you want to delete the files. Choose the Yes button to delete all of the files selected.

You cannot delete an open document, or a document from which you cut or copied information during the current session, without first quitting Word.

Note If you attempt to open a read-only document, or if you are connected to a network and attempt to open a document in use by someone else, Word displays a message to let you know that the file is in use. You can read or print the document, but you can't save any changes unless you save the document under a different name, on a different drive, or in a different directory.

To copy and move files from the Find File dialog box

1   Use the Find File command to locate and list the files, as described earlier in this chapter.

2   Select the files you want to copy or move.

3   Choose the Copy button.

4   Specify where you want the files by typing a path in the Path box or selecting a location in the Drives and Directories boxes.

    You cannot copy files to the current directory; you must type or select a different directory for the files.

5   Choose the OK button.

If you try to copy a file to a directory that already contains a file with the same name, Word asks you to confirm that you want to overwrite the file. If you have selected multiple files and there is more than one duplicate filename, Word asks you to confirm only once, but if you choose to overwrite the file, it will overwrite all of the duplicate files.

Tip   If you want to rename a file, use the Save As command from the File menu. You can also use the Save As command to save the file to a different directory or drive. If you want to delete the original version of the file, use the Find File command to locate and then delete it.

To view and edit summary information from the Find File dialog box

1   Use the Find File command to locate and list the file, as described earlier in this chapter.

2   Select the file you want.

3   Choose the Summary button.

    If you have selected more than one file in the Find File dialog box, Word displays the Summary Info dialog box for the first document selected.

4   Edit the summary information, and choose the OK button.

    For more information on editing summary information, see "Using Summary Information," earlier in this chapter.

Recovering Lost Work

For details on saving and backing up your documents, see Chapter 2, "Opening, Saving, and Deleting Documents."

While you work in Word, problems with your power source, operating system, or software may occasionally cause you to lose your work. The most important precaution against losing work is to save it frequently. If a file is especially important, save an extra copy on a floppy disk or a network server.

Word contains two features to help you prevent or minimize loss: the backup option and the automatic save option. The backup option automatically creates a backup file every time you save a document. The automatic save option automatically saves your document at regular intervals as you work.

If you use these options, you can usually recover most of your work if a document is accidentally deleted, changed, or damaged.

Outline View: Creating Outlines and Reorganizing Documents

Most people are familiar with outlining as it's taught in school—you create headings for key ideas and organize them in relation to one another until you work out a structure for the document you want to write. Outline view in Word includes features to ease the task of compiling this sort of traditional outline. Beyond this, and equally important, outline view is a powerful tool that you can use to reorganize a document—as you draft it or even afterwards, when the document already exists.

With outline view, you don't have to develop an outline independently and then refer to it as you do your "real" work. This is because outline view is, as its name suggests, just a view of a document, a different perspective you can switch to when you want to create, review, and rearrange headings. The work you do in outline view directly affects your whole document. If you type text, the text becomes part of the document. If you reorganize, which you can do quite handily in outline view by moving headings and their associated subtext, the whole document is reorganized.

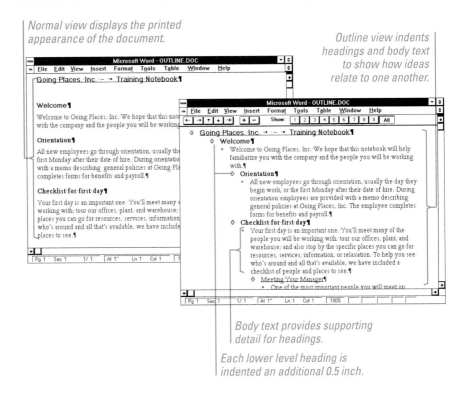

Normal view displays the printed appearance of the document.

Outline view indents headings and body text to show how ideas relate to one another.

Body text provides supporting detail for headings.

Each lower level heading is indented an additional 0.5 inch.

In outline view, you can *expand* and *collapse* the headings in an outline. You expand headings to see more of the outline—main headings, subordinate headings, and any body text associated with a heading. You collapse headings to focus more on higher-level structure and less on the detail. You might, for example, look only at the main headings and one or two subordinate headings.

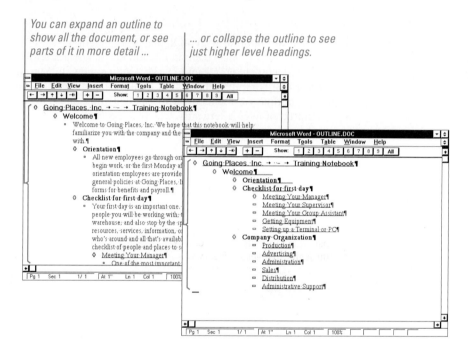

You can expand an outline to show all the document, or see parts of it in more detail ...

... or collapse the outline to see just higher level headings.

In addition to using the collapse and expand feature to view documents at different levels of detail, you can use it to move large chunks of material efficiently and accurately. Just collapse a heading and move it; all subordinate text moves with the heading.

Creating an Outline

If you are creating a document from scratch and want to outline it, you can type and arrange headings in outline view. If a supporting thought occurs to you while you work, you can add it as a body text paragraph. The headings and body text you add are part of your document; you'll see them when you switch to normal view or page layout view to flesh out your ideas, adding more detail, tables, formatting, or anything else that you are more comfortable adding when you see your document in a more standard form.

When you build an outline, you are both creating and organizing the headings. You can work in outline view and assign levels to headings as you type, "demoting," or moving, subordinate headings to lower levels and creating paragraphs of body text. Or you can type headings and text first and organize them into an outline with various heading levels later. This section explains how to type in outline view and assign levels to headings as you type. For more information about promoting and demoting headings, as well as information about collapsing and expanding outlines and rearranging outline text, see the next section, "Organizing in Outline View." You'll probably want to move between these two sections as you work on your first outline.

Styles in Outlines

Word uses styles—stored groups of formats—to define how each heading level in an outline looks. When you promote or demote a heading to a given level, Word automatically applies that level's style and displays the defined character formats. The paragraph formats for the style are not shown because they could disrupt the ordered arrangement of indents that an outline requires.

Because heading styles are automatically applied, you can simultaneously develop the structure of a document and format its headings. The advantage comes when you switch back to normal or page layout view: The document will be arranged the way you want and every heading in your document will be formatted (with all formats, including paragraph formats, displayed). Word comes with default styles for heading levels 1 through 9. To get the look you want for a document, you may need to change the formats for these styles. For information about styles, see Chapter 8, "Formatting with Styles."

To switch to and from outline view

▶ From the View menu, choose Outline (ALT, V, O).

To return from outline view, choose Normal or Page Layout from the View menu.

To type an outline

Promote Heading Level

Demote Heading Level

Demote To Body Text

1 From the View menu, choose Outline (ALT, V, O).

2 Type the text for the heading, and then press ENTER.

A first-level heading is inserted and the insertion point moves to the next line, where you can type the next heading.

3 Do one of the following for each subsequent heading, pressing ENTER after typing each one.

To type	Do this
A heading that is the same level as the one preceding it	Type the text for the new heading.
A heading that is subordinate to the one preceding it	Click the Demote Heading Level button on the outline bar and then type the heading. –or– Press ALT+SHIFT+RIGHT ARROW.
A heading that is superior to the one preceding it	Click the Promote Heading Level button on the outline bar and then type the heading. –or– Press ALT+SHIFT+LEFT ARROW.
Body text	Click the Demote To Body Text button on the outline bar and then type the body text. –or– Press ALT+SHIFT+5 on the numeric keypad (NUM LOCK off).

Selecting Text for Editing in Outline View

You select text in outline view just as you do in normal view—double-click a word, click in the selection bar next to a heading or body text paragraph, hold down the CTRL key and click in a sentence, drag across text, and so on.

When you drag to select text, make sure that you drag across the actual text you want to select. If the pointer changes to a ⊕, you have positioned the pointer over one of the outline selection symbols adjacent to a heading or body text paragraph. If you drag at this time, you will reposition the heading or body text paragraph.

Organizing in Outline View

Whether you're building a new outline or rearranging an existing document, you need to see the current order of your ideas and then move the ideas into new arrangements. Word helps you with both tasks.

When you switch to outline view, Word displays the outline bar in place of the ruler, indents paragraphs to reflect their respective heading levels, and displays a selection symbol next to each heading and each paragraph of body text. The ✚ selection symbol indicates that subtext—subordinate headings and body text—follows the heading; the ☐ symbol indicates that no subtext follows the heading; and the ▫ symbol indicates the paragraph is body text. By clicking buttons on the outline bar, you can demote or promote headings, move selected text to a new location, and collapse or expand the outline.

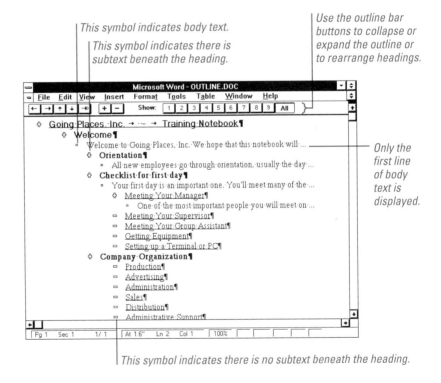

This symbol indicates body text.

This symbol indicates there is subtext beneath the heading.

Use the outline bar buttons to collapse or expand the outline or to rearrange headings.

Only the first line of body text is displayed.

This symbol indicates there is no subtext beneath the heading.

Methods for Working in Outline View

There are three methods you can use to control your view of an outline or arrange headings, each of which has its advantages.

Method	Advantages
The outline bar	Displays buttons for all the viewing and organizational actions you can take in outline view. You just click a button to perform an action.
Heading and body text selection symbols	Allow you to simultaneously select and drag headings or body text to a new location. All subtext for a heading is included in the selection.
Key combinations	Allow you to perform outline actions without taking your hands off the keyboard.

You can click the buttons on the outline bar at the top of the screen to perform the following actions in outline view.

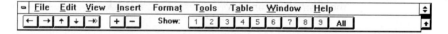

To	Click		Or press ALT+SHIFT+
Demote a selection down one level	→	Demote Heading Level	RIGHT ARROW
Promote a selection up one level	←	Promote Heading Level	LEFT ARROW
Move a selection above the preceding heading	↑	Move Paragraph Up	UP ARROW
Move a selection below the preceding heading	↓	Move Paragraph Down	DOWN ARROW
Convert a heading to body text	→»	Demote To Body Text	5 (on numeric keypad)
Expand subheadings or body text beneath a heading	+	Show Subtext	PLUS SIGN
Collapse subheadings or body text beneath a heading	−	Hide Subtext	MINUS SIGN
Expand an outline to display the desired heading levels, showing first-level, second-level, and so forth, up to ninth-level headings	1 2 3 4 5 6 7 8 9		a number from 1 through 9
Expand an entire outline to show all heading levels and body text	All	Show All Headings And Text	A

To select headings or body text

Before you promote or demote headings or move them to a new location, you need to first select the text.

▶ To select headings or body text, do one of the following.

To select	Do this
A single heading at a time or a paragraph of body text	Click in the selection bar to the left of the heading or paragraph.
A heading, including any subtext it may have, or a paragraph of body text	Click the selection symbol next to the heading or paragraph.
Several consecutive headings or body text paragraphs	Drag across them or drag down through the selection bar. Do not point to a selection symbol and drag—this drags the single heading with the selection symbol to a new position; it does not select.

To split a window and display another view

Except for moments of inspiration, it's likely that you'll do most outline-related work, such as adding headings or making major organizational changes, in outline view and most detail work in normal or page layout view. If you split the document window, you can show a different view of the same document in each pane, enabling you to move easily between the two views and to see immediately how changes you make in one view affect the other.

1 Double-click the split box on the vertical scroll bar.

2 From the View menu, choose the view you want for the lower pane of the window.

    To move the insertion point between the upper and lower panes of the window, click within the pane you want.

1 From the Document Control menu, choose Split (ALT, HYPHEN, T).

    Word displays a two-headed arrow.

2 Press the UP ARROW or DOWN ARROW key to position the split bar.

3 Press ENTER to set the split.

4 From the View menu, choose the view you want for the lower pane of the window.

    To move between the upper and lower panes of the window, press F6.

Work in outline view in this part of the window ...

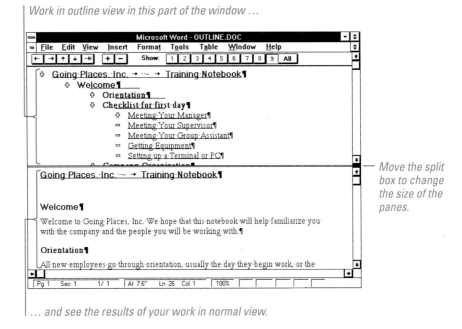

— Move the split box to change the size of the panes.

... and see the results of your work in normal view.

To restore the whole window

▶ Double-click the split box on the vertical scroll bar.

−Or−

1 From the Document Control menu, choose Split (ALT, HYPHEN, T).

   Word displays a two-headed arrow.

2 Press the DOWN ARROW key to move the split bar to the bottom of the window.

3 Press ENTER to remove the split.

Expanding and Collapsing an Outline

To see your ideas clearly and at a level of detail that's useful, you can expand and collapse headings. You can focus on a specific area in the outline or pull back for a view of only the main ideas. When you expand headings, you open out subtext under higher level headings, and when you collapse headings, you fold away the subtext. In addition to expanding and collapsing, you can also change the body text display, showing just the first line of body text paragraphs or complete paragraphs.

To expand or collapse headings and body text

There are several ways to expand and collapse text. Choose the one best suited to your intention and preferred method.

▶   To expand or collapse headings and body text, do one of the following.

To	Do this
Expand or collapse all subheadings and body text below a heading	Double-click the selection symbol next to the heading. –or– Select the heading and click the Show Subtext or Hide Subtext button on the outline bar. –or– Select the heading and press the PLUS SIGN (+) or MINUS SIGN (-) key on the numeric keypad.
Expand subheadings and body text below a heading, one level at a time, starting at the highest level	Position the insertion point in the heading and click the Show Subtext button on the outline bar. –or– Position the insertion point in the heading and press the PLUS SIGN (+) key on the numeric keypad.
Collapse subheadings and body text below a heading, one level at a time, starting at the lowest level	Position the insertion point in the heading and click the Hide Subtext button on the outline bar. –or– Position the insertion point in the heading and press the MINUS SIGN (-) key on the numeric keypad.
Expand or collapse several headings at once	Select the headings you want to expand or collapse and click the Show Subtext or Hide Subtext button on the outline bar. –or– Select the headings and press the PLUS SIGN (+) or MINUS SIGN (-) key on the numeric keypad.
Expand or collapse the entire outline to a specified level	On the outline bar, click the number for the heading level you want displayed. –or– Press ALT+SHIFT+a number from 1 to 9 on the main keyboard.
Expand all headings and body text, or collapse all body text	Click the Show All Headings And Text button on the outline bar. –or– Press the ASTERISK (*) key on the numeric keypad. –or– Press ALT+SHIFT+A.

Tip   Word displays character formatting even in outline view. However, some character formats, such as very large fonts or italic, can make it difficult to view the structure. You can hide character formatting by choosing the Draft command from the View menu. The Draft command displays all headings and body text in one font and point size, so you can view more of a document at once. Remember to choose Draft from the View menu again when returning to normal view so you can see character formatting again.

To display complete body text paragraphs or first lines only

To make it easier to concentrate on headings when you work in outline view, you can collapse text paragraphs so that only the first line, instead of the whole paragraph, is displayed. Word inserts an ellipsis (…) after the first line to indicate there is more body text.

▶   To switch back and forth between first line only and complete paragraph display, press ALT+SHIFT+F.

Reorganizing Headings and Body Text

You rearrange headings in outline view for either of two purposes. To change the order in which you present ideas, you can move a heading up and down in the outline without changing the heading level. To establish which ideas are superior and which subordinate, you can promote and demote headings to different levels.

Whether moving headings to a new place or to a new level in the outline, you can easily bring along subordinate headings and body text. If subtext is collapsed beneath a heading, it automatically moves with the heading. If subtext is expanded, it moves with the heading if you include it in the selection.

To promote and demote headings and body text

1   In outline view, select a heading you want to promote or demote, or the body text paragraph(s) you want to promote to a heading.

If the heading is collapsed, or if you click a ✚ selection symbol, Word includes all subtext in the selection and promotes or demotes the subtext with the heading. If the heading is expanded, Word promotes or demotes the heading and selected subheadings only. Body text always travels with its corresponding heading.

2   Do one of the following, repeating the action where appropriate to promote or demote by more than one level:

■   Click the Promote Heading Level, Demote Heading Level, or Demote To Body Text button on the outline bar.

■   Drag the selection symbol next to the heading left to promote or right to demote. Any subtext for that heading is also selected and promoted or demoted.

■   Press ALT+SHIFT+LEFT ARROW to promote or ALT+SHIFT+RIGHT ARROW to demote.

To move headings and body text

Outline view provides a convenient and accurate way to reorganize material in a document. If you collapse the subtext under a heading, you only have to look at and move the single heading to potentially move a great deal of information. All changes you make in outline view affect the entire document.

1   In outline view, select the heading(s) or body text paragraph(s) you want to move.

    If a heading is collapsed, or if you click a ✚ selection symbol, Word includes all subtext in the selection and moves the subtext along with the heading. If a heading is expanded, Word moves the heading and selected subtext.

2   Do one of the following:

    ▪ Click the Move Paragraph Up or Move Paragraph Down button on the outline bar.

    ▪ Drag the selection symbol next to the heading up or down. Any subtext for that heading is also selected and moves with the heading.

    ▪ Press ALT+SHIFT+UP ARROW to move the selection up or ALT+SHIFT+DOWN ARROW to move the selection down.

To change the indent distance for heading levels

Usually, the indent distance for each lower level heading matches the settings for default tab stop intervals. If the intervals are 0.5 inch, each lower level heading is indented an additional 0.5 inch.

1   From the View menu, choose Normal to switch back to normal view (ALT, V, N).

2   From the Format menu, choose Tabs (ALT, T, T).

3   In the Default Tab Stops box, type a measurement for default tab stop intervals, and then choose the OK button.

    The indents for different heading levels match these intervals.

4   From the View menu, choose Outline to return to outline view (ALT, V, O).

Working with an Existing Document

You can use the advantages of outline view with an existing document, moving headings to reorganize the document or collapsing headings to help you navigate through the document more quickly. For information on reorganizing, see "Organizing in Outline View," earlier in this chapter.

If the headings in a document were formatted with the Word standard heading styles, you don't have to convert the headings when you switch to outline view. However, if the headings were formatted any other way, you'll have to convert them to standard outline view headings.

To outline an existing document

1   From the View menu, choose Outline (ALT, V, O).

All the text in your document that is not formatted with a standard heading style is initially formatted as paragraphs of body text.

2   Use any of the methods for promoting and demoting to set up the outline structure you want.

To navigate through a long document

An outline displays a condensed view of a document, and so it's easier to move through the document to a desired spot.

1   To display just the number of heading levels you need for quick navigation, click the appropriate number on the outline bar.

2   Move to the heading you want or the heading above the body text you want.

3   If you want to see body text, double-click the ✛ selection symbol next to the heading above the body text.

Once you've located the text you want, you can work on it in outline view. To work on the text in normal or page view, use the scroll bar to position the text at the top of the window in outline view, and then change views. Or split the window to see both views at once. For more information, see "To split a window and display another view," earlier in this chapter.

Generating a Table of Contents

The headings in a document often correspond to the entries that appear in a table of contents. Rather than retype these entries or manually add table of contents codes to each heading, you can use the Table Of Contents command on the Insert menu to read an outline's headings and collect them in a table of contents that's inserted at the beginning of the document. You can specify how many heading levels to include in the table of contents.

It's a good idea to wait until you are ready to print your final document before compiling the table of contents. Page numbers can vary if you add or delete text or change formatting.

For more information about creating and controlling the appearance of tables of contents, see Chapter 29, "Indexes and Tables of Contents."

Numbering an Outline

You can number the headings in an outline using one of several formats. The following procedure describes how to number an outline with a traditional outline numbering format. For more information on numbering outlines and numbering in general, see Chapter 28, "Adding Bullets and Numbers."

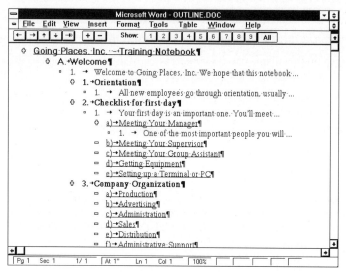

A numbered outline

To number an outline in traditional outline format

Word numbers only visible headings. If there are headings you don't want to number—for example, lower level headings—collapse them before numbering.

1   Select the part of the outline that contains the headings you want to number.

    Usually, you will want to exclude the title of a document if it's a first-level heading.

2   From the Tools menu, choose Bullets And Numbering (ALT, O, B).

3   Make sure that the Outline option button is selected.

4   Select the Auto Update check box if you want Word to automatically update numbers if you later change the order of the headings.

5   In the Format box, select the numbering scheme you want to use.

    Word inserts a tab character between the numbering character (I, A, and so on) and the first character of a heading.

6   Choose the OK button.

Printing an Outline

For more information
about printing, see
Chapter 4, "Printing a
Document."

You print a document while in outline view just as you would in normal view—with one significant difference. With outline view, you can control how detailed the printed document will be. Word prints the outline as it appears on the screen, so you can collapse or expand headings and body text to print the entire outline or only selected heading levels.

To print an outline

1 Display as much of the outline as you want to print.

2 From the File menu, choose Print (ALT, F, P).

3 Choose the OK button.

Adding Bullets and Numbers

Bulleted or numbered lists, numbered headings, and line numbers are common requirements for many documents. To meet these needs, Word provides bullets and three different types of numbering:

- List numbering, with which you can turn a series of paragraphs into a bulleted or numbered list, choosing from different bullet types and numeric formats.

- Outline numbering, which provides different ways to number a hierarchy of headings.

- Line numbering, which is used in documents, such as legal documents or scripts, in which the ability to refer to specific lines within a document is important.

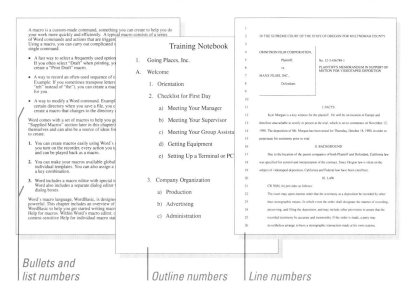

Bullets and
list numbers   Outline numbers   Line numbers

Bullets and List Numbers

Using the Bullets And Numbering command, you can turn a series of paragraphs into a bulleted or numbered list. For bulleted lists, you can choose from several predefined bullets or specify different bullet characters. For numbered lists, you can select different numeric formats and separator characters or type separator characters of your own choice.

An easy way to add bullets and numbers is to first type the paragraphs you want to make into a list, select them, and then add bullets or numbers. Sometimes, though, you may want to add bullets or numbers as you create a list. That is, each time you create a new item for the list, you may want to add a bullet or number to it. You can easily do so using buttons on the Toolbar. For more information, see "Using the Toolbar to Add Bullets and Numbers," later in this chapter.

When you add bullets or numbers to paragraphs, Word automatically formats the paragraphs with hanging indents, unless you clear the Hanging Indent By check box in the Bullets And Numbering dialog box. In a paragraph with a hanging indent, the first line extends to the left of the rest of the paragraph, as shown in the following illustration.

A macro is a custom-made command, something you can create to help you do your work more quickly and efficiently. A typical macro consists of a series of Word commands and actions that are triggered when you run the macro. Using a macro, you can carry out complicated word-processing tasks with a single command.

- A way to record an often-used sequence of commands and actions. Example: If you sometimes transpose letters when you're typing (type "teh" instead of "the"), you can create a macro to fix the transposition for you.

Word comes with a set of macros to help you get started (described in the "Supplied Macros" section later in this chapter). These macros are useful in themselves and can also be a source of ideas for macros you yourself may wish

Paragraph formatted with a hanging indent

Hanging indents and bullets or numbers are a good combination because the hanging indent separates the bullets or numbers from the text of the paragraphs, which makes the list easier to read. For more information on indents, see Chapter 7, "Paragraph Formatting."

When you use the Bullets And Numbering command to add a bullet, Word actually inserts a SYMBOL field, which displays a bullet. You can treat this field just as you would a regular character. The only difference is that when the Field Codes command on the View menu is preceded by a check mark, you see the SYMBOL field instead of the bullet. To see the bullet, choose the Field Codes command again to display the result of the field rather than its code.

Word normally inserts a tab character between the bullets or numbers it adds and the following text. However, if you clear the Hanging Indent By check box, Word inserts a space instead.

You can also use the Bullets And Numbering command to replace existing bullets with new ones or to update list numbers.

The Bullets Option

The following illustration shows the Bullets And Numbering dialog box with the Bullets option button selected.

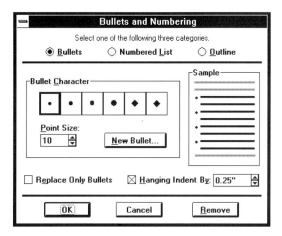

Bullet Character   You can select one of the predefined bullets or define a new bullet using the New Bullet button. The new bullet replaces the bullet selected under Bullet Character.

Point Size   Select or type a size to change the point size of the bullet selected under Bullet Character.

New Bullet   This button displays the Symbol dialog box, in which you can select from any of the available characters to define a new bullet.

Replace Only Bullets   When this check box is selected, Word changes the bullets for those paragraphs that already have bullets and does not add bullets to any unbulleted paragraphs within your selection.

Hanging Indent By   This check box, selected by default, formats the selected paragraphs with hanging indents. You can control the amount of the indent. The default is 0.25 inch. If a paragraph is already formatted with a hanging indent with a different indent setting, Word does not change the existing formatting. When this option is selected, Word inserts a tab character between the bullets it adds and the text; otherwise, Word inserts a space.

The Numbered List Option

The following illustration shows the Bullets And Numbering dialog box with the Numbered List option button selected.

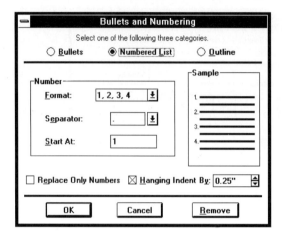

Format   Lists the different numeric formats available. Select a format to see an illustration of it in the Sample box.

Separator   Lists available separator characters and an option for no separator character. Select a character to see an illustration of it in the Sample box. You can also type the character you want if the list does not include it. Word inserts a tab character between the separator and the text of a paragraph if the paragraph is formatted with a hanging indent; otherwise, Word inserts a space.

Start At   You can enter a starting number in this box for the numbers Word inserts. If you select part of a numbered list, this box shows the number of the first paragraph in the selection.

Replace Only Numbers   When this check box is selected, Word changes only those paragraphs that already have numbers. This is useful if you want to renumber a document in which numbered paragraphs are mixed with unnumbered paragraphs.

Hanging Indent By   This check box, selected by default, formats the selected paragraphs with hanging indents. You can control the amount of the indent. The default is 0.25 inch. If a paragraph is already formatted with a hanging indent with a different indent setting, Word does not change the existing formatting. When this option is selected, Word inserts a tab character between the numbers it adds and the text; otherwise, Word inserts a space.

To add bullets to a list

1   Select the paragraphs to which you want to add bullets.

2   From the Tools menu, choose Bullets And Numbering (ALT, O, B).

3   Select the Bullets option button.

4   Under Bullet Character, select the bullet you want to use.

You can make the bullet larger or smaller by typing or selecting a different size in the Point Size box. You can also choose a different bullet using the New Bullet button, which displays the Symbol dialog box. In the Symbols From box, you can select any available symbol set.

5   If you do not want the paragraphs you have selected to be formatted with hanging indents, clear the Hanging Indent By check box.

6   Choose the OK button.

To add numbers to a list

1   Select the paragraphs to which you want to add numbers.

2   From the Tools menu, choose Bullets And Numbering (ALT, O, B).

3   Select the Numbered List option button.

4   In the Format and Separator boxes, select the numeric format and the separator character you want to use.

If you want to use a separator character not included in the list of separator characters, you can type it in the Separator box.

5   If the number in the Start At box is not the number you want to start the list numbers you are applying, type the one you want in the Start At box.

6   If you do not want the paragraphs you have selected to be formatted with hanging indents, clear the Hanging Indent By check box.

7   Choose the OK button.

To change bullets or update list numbers

If the paragraphs you select include some paragraphs that are bulleted or numbered and some that are not, select the Replace Only Bullets or Replace Only Numbers check box. With one of these options selected, Word either changes the bullets or updates the numbering only for paragraphs with bullets or numbers.

1   Select the paragraphs you want to change.

2   From the Tools menu, choose Bullets And Numbering (ALT, O, B).

3   Select the Bullets option button to change bullets.
    –or–
    Select the Numbered List option button to update numbers.

4   If you want to change only previously bulleted paragraphs, select the Replace Only Bullets check box.
    –or–
    If you want to update only previously numbered paragraphs, select the Replace Only Numbers check box.

5   Choose the OK button.

To remove bullets or list numbers

1   Select the paragraphs from which you want to remove bullets or numbers.

2   From the Tools menu, choose Bullets And Numbering (ALT, O, B).

3   Select the Bullets option button to remove bullets.
    –or–
    Select the Numbered List option button to remove numbers.

4   Clear the Hanging Indent By check box if you want to remove hanging indent formatting from the selected paragraphs.

5   Choose the Remove button.

Tip   Immediately after using the Bullets And Numbering command to add bullets or numbers, you can choose Undo from the Edit menu to remove them.

To convert a bulleted or numbered list

You can use the following procedure to convert a bulleted list to a numbered list or a numbered list to a bulleted list.

1   Select the paragraphs you want to convert.

2   From the Tools menu, choose Bullets And Numbering (ALT, O, B).

3   To convert to a numbered list, select the Numbered List option button.
    –or–
    To convert to a bulleted list, select the Bullets option button.

4   Clear the Replace Only Bullets or the Replace Only Numbers check box if it is selected.

5   Choose the OK button.

    Word asks you to confirm that you want to convert the list. Choose the Yes button.

Using the Toolbar to Add Bullets and Numbers

The Toolbar includes a Bulleted List button for adding bullets and a Numbered List button for adding list numbers or outline numbers. The Toolbar buttons are especially useful for adding bullets or numbers to one paragraph at a time as you're typing a list or outline.

Numbered List button

Bulleted List button

For example, when you click the Bulleted List button, Word adds bullets to the selected paragraphs, or, if you have no paragraphs selected, Word adds a bullet to the paragraph that contains the insertion point. Each time you want to add an item to a bulleted list, you can create a new paragraph and then press the Bulleted List button. Word inserts a bullet and formats the current paragraph with a hanging indent, unless the paragraph is already formatted with a hanging indent.

The Bulleted List button inserts a bullet of the default type or the type that you have previously selected in the Bullets And Numbering dialog box.

When you use the Numbered List button, Word checks the paragraph just before the paragraphs you have selected to see if it is numbered. If it is, Word adds the same kind of numbering to the selected paragraphs. For example, if the paragraph just before the selected paragraphs has outline numbering applied to it, Word applies outline numbering to the selected paragraphs.

Likewise, if the previous paragraph includes a list number, Word adds list numbers to the selected paragraphs, using the same number format and separator characters as in the previous paragraph. For example, if the previous paragraph looks like this,

a)   Lorem ipsum dolor sit amet, consectetur adipiscing elit, sed diam nonnumy eiusmod tempor incidunt ut labore et dolore magna aliquam erat volupat.

and you click the Numbered List button, Word adds "b)" and a tab character to the next paragraph,

a)   Lorem ipsum dolor sit amet, consectetur adipiscing elit, sed diam nonnumy eiusmod tempor incidunt ut labore et dolore magna aliquam erat volupat.

b)

and you're ready to begin typing the next item in the list. As shown in this example, Word looks at the list number of the previous paragraph to decide which number to begin numbering with.

Even if the previous paragraph isn't numbered, Word uses the number format and separator character you previously selected in the Bullets And Numbering dialog box. If you haven't selected a number format or separator character, Word uses the defaults.

If the first paragraph in the selection is formatted with a heading style, Word applies outline numbers to the selection. In outline view, Word applies traditional outline numbers; in normal view, Word applies legal outline numbers.

To add bullets to an existing list with the Toolbar

1   Select the paragraphs to which you want to add bullets.

2   Click the Bulleted List button on the Toolbar.

To add outline or list numbers to an existing list with the Toolbar

1   Select the paragraphs to which you want to add numbers.

2   Click the Numbered List button on the Toolbar.

Outline Numbers

When Word applies outline numbering, it recognizes different heading or indent levels and applies numbering that reflects the hierarchy of headings. Four different outline numbering formats are available: traditional, all-level, legal, and sequential.

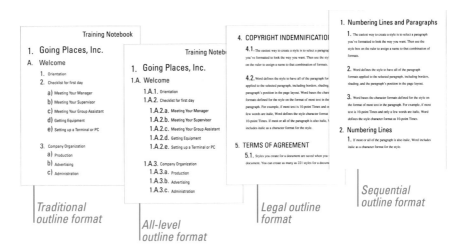

Traditional outline format

All-level outline format

Legal outline format

Sequential outline format

The traditional outline format numbers paragraphs as described in *The Chicago Manual of Style*, 13th ed. (University of Chicago Press). The traditional outline format uses different separator characters—a period, or single or double parentheses—for different heading levels. The all-level format has the same appearance but includes the number of each superior level with the current level.

The legal format includes the number of each superior level with the number of the current level. The legal format is like the all-level format, except that it uses arabic numerals. Legal documents and technical manuals often use this type of numbering.

The sequential outline format is like the legal format—it uses arabic numerals and periods—but it doesn't include the numbers of superior levels with the number of the current level.

You can create your own variations on these outline formats and then have Word "learn by example" to apply the formats to the entire document. For example, suppose you want to change the separator character used for some levels in the traditional outline format. Instead of:

I.
   A.
      1.
         and so on,

perhaps you want:

I)
   A)
      1)
         and so on.

You can format the first instance of each heading level in a selection, and Word can pattern its formatting for the rest of the selection after your example. For more information, see "To number an outline by example," later in this chapter.

Word assigns different outline number levels to paragraphs that are either formatted with automatic heading styles or formatted with different indent levels. Word does not recognize paragraphs indented with tab characters or spaces as having different levels.

Word numbers every paragraph that you select, except empty paragraphs—paragraph marks without text.

You may have had the experience of creating a numbered outline, rearranging it, and then having to retype the outline numbers. In Word, you can have outline numbers updated for you, either automatically, whenever the outline changes, or each time you choose the Bullets And Numbering command.

If you choose to apply numbering that is updated automatically using the Auto Update option, Word inserts a field at the beginning of each numbered paragraph. When Word applies automatic outline numbering, it uses three different field types: AUTONUM for sequential outline numbers, AUTONUMOUT for traditional outline numbers, and AUTONUMLGL for legal outline numbers. Note that automatic updating is not available for the all-level format. For more information on these fields, see online Help.

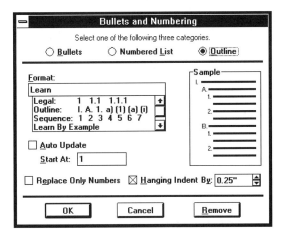

Format Lists the different outline formats available. Select a format to see an illustration of it in the Sample box. You can also type your own number format. The Outline All and Learn By Example formats are not available if the Auto Update check box is selected.

Auto Update Applies outline numbering by inserting fields that Word updates automatically. When this option is selected, the Start At box is unavailable, because automatic numbering always starts at 1.

Start At You can enter a starting number in this box. The number should be in the same format as the format selected in the Format box. For example, if you're using the legal outline format, and you want to set the starting number to 1.1.2 for example, you must type that number in the Start At box. The Start At box is not available when Auto Update is selected.

Replace Only Numbers When this option is selected, Word changes only those paragraphs that already have numbering. This is useful if you want to renumber a document containing both numbered and unnumbered paragraphs.

Hanging Indent By Select this option to format the selected paragraphs with hanging indents. You can control the amount of the indent. The default is 0.25 inch. If a paragraph is already formatted with a hanging indent with a different indent setting, Word does not change the existing formatting.

To apply outline numbering

1 Select the paragraphs to which you want to apply outline numbering.

If you don't make a selection, Word numbers only the paragraph that contains the insertion point.

2 From the Tools menu, choose Bullets And Numbering (ALT, O, B).

3 Select the Outline option button.

4 Select the options you want.

5 Choose the OK button.

To update outline numbers

If you selected the Auto Update check box when you applied outline numbering, Word updates the outline numbers automatically as you edit your document. If you did not select the Auto Update check box, use the following procedure to update outline numbers.

1 Select the paragraphs whose outline numbers you want to update.

2 From the Tools menu, choose Bullets And Numbering (ALT, O, B).

3 Select the Outline option button.

4 If you want to update only previously numbered paragraphs, select the Replace Only Numbers check box.

5 Choose the OK button.

To remove outline numbers

1 Select the paragraphs from which you want to remove outline numbers.

2 From the Tools menu, choose Bullets And Numbering (ALT, O, B).

3 Select the Outline option button.

4 Choose the Remove button.

Tip If you have just numbered some paragraphs and want to remove the numbers, choose the Undo command from the Edit menu immediately after numbering.

To number an outline by example

You can use this procedure to create your own outline numbering formats.

1 In front of the first instance of each level you want to number, type an example of the format you want to apply.

2 Select the paragraphs to which you want to apply outline numbering, including the example paragraphs.

3 From the Tools menu, choose Bullets And Numbering (ALT, O, B).

4 Select the Outline option button.

5 Clear the Auto Update check box, if it is selected.

6 In the Format box, select Learn By Example, and then select any other options you want.

7 Choose the OK button.

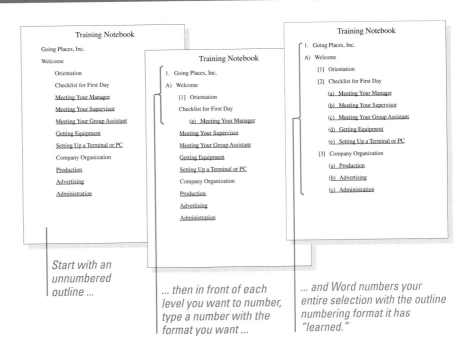

Start with an unnumbered outline ...

... then in front of each level you want to number, type a number with the format you want ...

... and Word numbers your entire selection with the outline numbering format it has "learned."

Tip   Rather than adding example numbers to the headings to which you want to apply numbers, you can type the numbers right in the Format box. For example, to apply the traditional outline format using different separator characters, you can type **I) A) 1) a)**, where I) is applied to the first level, A) is applied to the second level, and so on. Add a space at the end of each heading level you type to separate it from the following heading.

Numbering Headings Only

If your headings are formatted with the standard heading styles in Word (Heading 1, Heading 2, and so on), you can use outline view to apply outline numbering to headings only. Also, by displaying or not displaying different levels of headings, you can apply numbers to certain levels of headings only.

To number only the headings in a document

1 From the View menu, choose Outline (ALT, V, O).

2 On the outline bar, click the buttons with the numbers corresponding to the heading levels you want to number.

3 Select the headings you want numbered.

4 From the Tools menu, choose Bullets And Numbering (ALT, O, B).

5 Select the Outline option button.

6 In the Format box, select the numbering format you want.

7 Choose the OK button.

8 To return to normal view, choose Normal from the View menu (ALT, V, N).

Tip   You can also apply outline numbers to headings but not to other text paragraphs when you are working in normal view—you do not have to switch to outline view.

First, select the paragraphs you want Word to number, making sure that the first paragraph in the selection is formatted with a standard heading style, such as Heading 1. When you choose the Bullets And Numbering command, clear the Auto Update check box to have Word apply outline numbering to headings but not to other text.

Line Numbers

Line numbers do not appear on screen, except in print preview, and are printed in the margin or between columns. You can set line numbers to appear on every line, on every fifth line, or at any increment you want.

You can set the line number count to restart at the top of each page, at the beginning of each section, or to continue from the beginning to the end of a document.

Because line numbering is a section format, applied using the Section Layout command on the Format menu, you can choose to add or not add line numbers to different sections of your document. If your document contains only one section, Word applies line numbers to the entire document. For more information on sections and section formatting, see Chapter 10, "Sections: Formatting Parts of a Document."

Word normally counts every line in a section except lines in footnotes, tables, headers, and footers. If there are other lines that you do not want Word to include in its count, you can suppress line numbering for selected paragraphs.

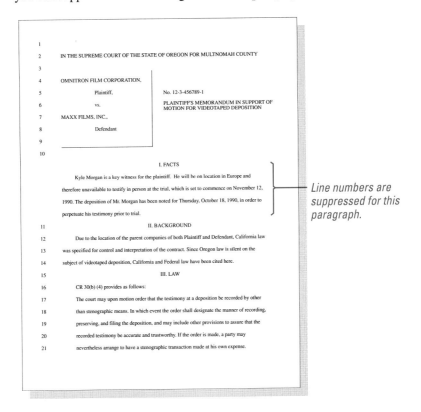

Line numbers are suppressed for this paragraph.

To add line numbers

1   Position the insertion point in the section in which you want to number lines.

2   From the Format menu, choose Section Layout (ALT, T, S).

3   Choose the Line Numbers button.

4   Select the Add Line Numbering check box.

5 Do one or more of the following.

If you want	Do this
To begin line numbering with a number other than 1	In the Start At # box, type or select the line number you want.
To specify a distance between the line number and the text	In the From Text box, type or select the measurement you want. The default option, Auto, is 0.25 inch for a single column and 0.13 inch for multiple columns.
Line numbers to be printed only at specific intervals	In the Count By box, type or select the number you want. For example, type **5** to display a line number at every fifth line.

6 To specify where line numbering restarts, select one of the following options under Restart At.

Option	Result
Every New Page	Restarts numbering at the top of each page
Every New Section	Restarts numbering at the beginning of each section
Continue	Numbers lines consecutively from one section to the next

7 Choose the OK button to close the Line Numbers dialog box.

8 Choose the OK button to add line numbers to the section.

To remove line numbers

1 Position the insertion point in the section from which you want to remove line numbers.

2 From the Format menu, choose Section Layout (ALT, T, S).

3 Choose the Line Numbers button.

4 Clear the Add Line Numbering check box.

5 Choose the OK button to close the Line Numbers dialog box.

6 Choose the OK button to remove line numbers from the section.

To suppress line numbering for selected paragraphs

You can suppress line numbering for paragraphs such as titles, headings, or empty paragraphs whose lines you don't want numbered. Line numbers do not appear next to the lines in the paragraphs for which you suppress line numbering, and those lines are not included in the line count.

1   Select the paragraphs in which you want to suppress line numbers.

2   From the Format menu, choose Paragraph (ALT, T, P).

3   Under Line Numbers, select the Suppress check box.

4   Choose the OK button.

Indexes and Tables of Contents

A Word document can include an index, a table of contents, and other lists, such as lists of figures and tables of illustrations.

You can create a simple index, with a single level of entries or with multiple levels of entries. You can include entries that match the exact text in the document and entries that are synonyms for text, even if the synonym itself doesn't appear in the document. You can divide the index into alphabetic sections separated by letters or blank lines and make your page numbers bold or italic (or both).

Using heading styles, you can create a simple table of contents or another similar list in a document.

You may prefer to use fields to create more complex indexes and tables of contents. Fields are sets of codes that instruct Word to insert information into a document. For example, you can use fields to create an index that includes text instead of page numbers and that shows a page range for a topic that spans several pages. You can use fields to include a table of contents and multiple lists in the same document and to create a table of contents for part of a document. You can also create an index and table of contents that include both chapter and page numbers.

If you are creating a complex index or table of contents, you need to understand some basic concepts about fields. This information is included in "Background on Fields," "How the Indexing Fields Work," and "How the Table of Contents Fields Work," later in this chapter.

Tip   If you plan to include an index, table of contents, and other lists in your document, you may want to create the index and other lists before you create your table of contents. That way, the table of contents can include page numbers for the index and the other lists.

For more information on long documents, see Chapter 11, "Setting Up Long Documents."

If you are working with very long documents, you can often work more efficiently by dividing the document into several files and connecting the files later. When the files are connected, you can compile the index, table of contents, and other lists for the whole document. For information on generating a table of contents and index for a series of connected documents, see "Creating Indexes and Lists for Long Documents," later in this chapter.

Background on Fields

Fields provide information and give instructions to Word. Some fields, like the XE (Index Entry) and TC (Table of Contents Entry) fields, identify information for Word to collect. Other fields, like the INDEX and TOC (Table of Contents) fields, collect information and display a result (text and page numbers) at the location of the field.

A field is composed of the following:

- Field characters, a pair of braces that surround a field code
- The field type, which is the name of the field
- Additional instructions, if any. These instructions may include switches (optional commands).

The following is an example of the INDEX field code:

```
{index \e " — "}
```

The braces { and } are the field characters inserted by pressing CTRL+F9; index is the field type; \e is a switch instructing Word to use the following character, or characters, to separate index text from page references; and the dash, enclosed in quotation marks, is the separator character.

For more information on working with fields, see Chapter 41, "Fields."

To view an XE or TC field, select the Hidden Text or All option in the View category of the Options dialog box (Tools menu), or click the Show/Hide ¶ button on the ribbon. To view an INDEX or TOC field, choose Field Codes from the View menu, or select the Field Codes check box in the View category of the Options dialog box.

Creating an Index

You can create a simple index or a complex index in Word. A simple index can have single-level or multiple-level entries. In a simple index, text is separated from page numbers by a comma and a single space.

```
sand flea, 14
sanderling, 12, 33, 35
sandpiper, 45
```

An index with a single
level of entries

```
Bodies of water
    Lakes
        Dallas, 14
        Travis, 8-9
```

An index with subentries

A more complex index can include the following elements:

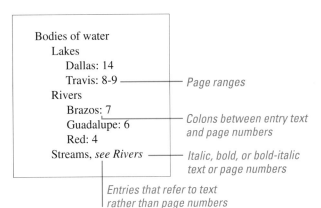

What to Include in an Index

The real value of an index is determined by the entries you include. Some topics you might want to include as index entries are:

- The main ideas in a document
- The main subject of a chapter
- Variations of headings and subheadings
- Any special terms
- Abbreviations and acronyms
- Synonyms: other words that could describe topics
- Inverted phrases: for example, "Vacation policies" and "Policies, vacation"

For more information on how to plan and organize your index, refer to a book on indexing or *The Chicago Manual of Style,* 13th ed. (University of Chicago Press).

Creating a Basic Index

You create an index in two basic steps: First, you identify the text you want in the index. Then, after you identify all of the entries you want to include, you compile the index.

Identifying Index Entries

You can identify the text you want in the index by selecting text in the document and choosing the Index Entry command from the Insert menu, or by choosing the Index Entry command and typing text in the Index Entry dialog box. You edit text in the dialog box just as you edit text in a document.

When you choose the Index Entry command from the Insert menu, Word displays the
Index Entry dialog box:

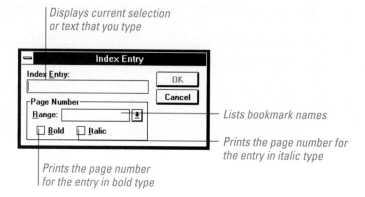

*Displays current selection
or text that you type*

Lists bookmark names

*Prints the page number for
the entry in italic type*

*Prints the page number
for the entry in bold type*

Index Entry dialog box

When you choose the OK button, Word inserts the index entry at the insertion point,
encloses it in a field, and formats the entire entry as hidden text. The field is displayed
on the screen if you have Hidden Text selected in the View category of the Options
dialog box (Tools menu), or if you click the Show/Hide ¶ button on the ribbon, but it
will not appear in the document when you print it. The text does appear in the index
when the index is compiled.

To insert an index entry

1   Select the text in the document (maximum 64 characters) that you want to be an
    entry in the index, or position the insertion point where you want to type the index
    entry.

2   From the Insert menu, choose Index Entry (ALT, I, E).

3   Type the index entry, or edit the existing index entry.

4   If you want the page number for the entry to be bold or italic in the index, select
    Bold or Italic. You can select both.

5   If you want to specify a range of pages for the index entry, type or select a
    bookmark name. For more information, see "To indicate a range of pages in an
    index entry," later in this chapter.

6   Choose the OK button.

Tip   If you type the index entry, make sure your page numbers are correct by positioning the insertion point at the end of the text you want to index. If you insert the index
entry before the text you want to index, Word may insert a page break between the
entry and the text during pagination.

To create index subentries

By typing text, you can also create an index with more than one level of index entry. Although two or three subentry levels is most common, an index can contain as many as seven subentries, each separated by a colon. To create a subentry:

1   Position the insertion point where you want to type the index entry.

2   From the Insert menu, choose Index Entry (ALT, I, E).

3   Type the main entry text, followed by a colon. For example, type the entry text **Tuxedo:**

4   Type text for each subentry, up to seven levels, with each level separated by a colon in the index entry. For example, you could type text with one subentry like this:

   Tuxedo:jacket style

5   Choose the OK button.

When you compile the index, Word automatically lists subentries in alphabetical order under the main entry.

For these index entries	You type
Tuxedo	
jacket style 69	**Tuxedo:jacket style**
morning coat 71	**Tuxedo:jacket style:morning coat**
tails style 46	**Tuxedo:tails style**

To create a main entry without a page number, don't create an index entry for the main entry, but do include the main entry with any subentries. For example, don't type **Tuxedo** as an index entry, but do use **Tuxedo:jacket style** and **Tuxedo:tails style** as index entries.

If you select text in your document that contains a colon (:), Word inserts a backslash (\) in front of the colon. This means that the colon will be printed as part of the index entry. If you want the colon to indicate a subentry instead, delete the backslash in front of the colon.

Note   To create an entry that uses text instead of a page number, you must type the text in the index entry field. For more information, see "To follow an index entry with text," later in this chapter.

Compiling the Index

When you are ready to collect the index entries, you place the insertion point where you want to insert the index and choose the Index command from the Insert menu. You can create a normal or run-in index, and divide the index into sections with blank lines or letters of the alphabet.

Displays entries and subentries on the same line

Displays subentries below the main entry (on separate lines)

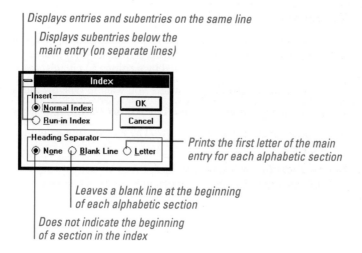

Prints the first letter of the main entry for each alphabetic section

Leaves a blank line at the beginning of each alphabetic section

Does not indicate the beginning of a section in the index

Index dialog box

In a normal index, subentries are indented and placed below the main entry; in a run-in index, the entries are on one line. In a run-in index, text wraps to the next line, if necessary. A run-in index can save space, but it may not be as easy to read as a normal index. To create a run-in index, your index entries must include subentries.

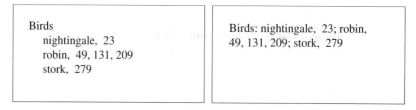

A normal index entry indents subentries.

A run-in index entry runs subentries onto the same line.

By default, Word creates indexes without blank lines or alphabet-letter designators between alphabetic sections. You can add either of these options. See the following procedure, "To compile a complete index."

Word indexes do not include text from headers, footers, footnotes, annotations, or embedded objects.

Note If you create an index and then add or delete text in your document, the page numbers may no longer be accurate. If you make changes, update your index before you print the document. For more information, see "Updating an Index," later in this chapter.

To compile a complete index

1 Insert index entries into your document and position the insertion point where you want the index to begin.

2 To ensure accurate pagination of the document, clear hidden text and field codes:

- If hidden text is displayed, click the Show/Hide ¶ button on the ribbon, or clear the All and Hidden Text check boxes in the View category of the Options dialog box (Tools menu).

- If field codes are displayed, choose the Field Codes command from the View menu (ALT, V, C) to display field results.

3 From the Insert menu, choose Index (ALT, I, I).

4 Select a format:

- If you want subentries displayed below the main entry, select the Normal Index option button.

- If you want subentries on the same line as the main entry, select the Run-In Index option button.

5 If you want a blank line or a letter separating alphabetic sections of your index, in the Heading Separator box, choose Blank Line or Letter.

6 Choose the OK button.

   If you want to cancel the compilation in progress, press ESC.

An index field is inserted after the insertion point. You can view the INDEX code by choosing Field Codes from the View menu, or by selecting the Field Codes check box in the View category of the Options dialog box. To view the index text and page numbers, choose the Field Codes command (ALT, V, C) to remove the check mark beside the command on the menu.

Tip   You can divide your index into alphabetic sections and include both a blank line and a letter of the alphabet by using fields. For more information, see "Using Fields to Format an Index," later in this chapter.

How the Indexing Fields Work

When you select text and choose the Index Entry command, you are actually inserting an Index Entry (XE) field immediately following the selection. When you type an entry in the Index Entry dialog box and choose the OK button, you insert an XE field at the insertion point. An XE field specifies each entry you want to appear in the index and indicates its location so that a page number can be automatically assigned. The XE field is formatted as hidden text.

When you choose Index from the Insert menu, you insert an INDEX field in your document, beginning at the insertion point. The INDEX field acts as the mechanism for compiling the index entries into an index. If you choose to create a run-in index, Word automatically includes the \r switch in the field code to place all subentries on the same line. If Field Codes is chosen on the View menu or selected in the Options dialog box, you can see the INDEX field in your document; if it is not selected, you see the text and page numbers in the index (the field results).

If you make additional changes to the document, you must update the INDEX field to generate an up-to-date version of the index. You can update the index by choosing the Index command again, or you can place the insertion point anywhere in the INDEX field and press the Update Field key (F9). If you choose the Index command, Word asks if you want to replace the existing index. If you press the Update Field key, Word replaces the existing index without prompting you.

Using Other Indexing Features

You can use fields and bookmarks to create more complex indexes and better control how indexes are displayed. For example:

- You can use fields to follow an entry with text, rather than a page number, to create an entry like this:

  Streams, *See Rivers*.

- When a topic extends over several pages, you can indicate a range of pages for the topic by using bookmarks. If an entry covers information on pages 3, 4, and 5, you can create an entry like this:

  Texas rivers, 3-5.

- You can use fields to include chapter and page numbers in your index. The index might include the following entry for page 1 in Chapter 9:

  Conflict negotiation   9-1

The following procedures give basic information on how to use fields and bookmarks in indexes. For more detailed information, see Chapter 41, "Fields." For complete information on using bookmarks, see Chapter 40, "Bookmarks and Cross-references."

Tip If you want to use an index entry in more than one place, you don't have to retype it. Just copy the field and insert it in a new location. If you want to make changes to the entry, you can edit it just as you edit any field.

You can also select an index entry and define it as a glossary entry for automatic insertion in your document. For more information on glossaries, see Chapter 13, "Glossaries: Storing Items for Reuse."

To follow an index entry with text

This procedure is useful when you want to make a cross-reference in your index.

1 Select the text you want to index, or position the insertion point where you want to create the index entry.

2 From the Insert menu, choose Field (ALT, I, D).

3 In the Insert Field Type box, select Index Entry.

4 In the Field Code box, following the field name **xe** (automatically typed there for you), type the following in the order indicated:

- The index entry, enclosed in quotation marks

- The switch **\t**, preceded and followed by a space

- The text you want to include, enclosed in quotation marks

5 Choose the OK button (ENTER).

The following is an example.

For this index entry	You type
Lavaliere, see Microphone	**"Lavaliere" \t "see Microphone"**

The field code looks like this:

```
{xe "Lavaliere" \t "see Microphone"}
```

Tip You can add the \i switch to make the referenced text italic:

```
{xe "Lavaliere" \t "see Microphone" \i}
```

For a list of all available switches, see the Index Entry (XE) field topic in online Help.

To indicate a range of pages in an index entry

This procedure describes how you designate an index entry for a topic that ranges over several pages—for example, a topic that begins on page 2 and continues to page 4.

1   Select the text you want covered by the index entry.

2   From the Insert menu, choose Bookmark (ALT, I, M).

3   Type a name for the bookmark. The name can contain as many as 20 characters, cannot include spaces, and must begin with a letter.

4   Choose the OK button.

5   From the Insert menu, choose Index Entry (ALT, I, E).

6   Type a name for the index entry you want to reference, or accept the proposed index entry.

7   In the Range box under Page Number, type or select the name of the bookmark.

8   Choose the OK button.

To index a document with chapter-page numbers

This procedure uses the SEQ (Sequence) field to create chapter-page numbers in the index; it does not insert page numbers in the document. To insert chapter-page numbers in a document, see Chapter 22, "Numbering Pages."

1   Insert index entries in your document.

2   For each chapter, position the insertion point at the end of the chapter and, from the Insert menu, choose Break (ALT, I, B). Under Section Break, select the option you want and choose the OK button.

3   From the Insert menu, choose Page Numbers (ALT, I, U); choose the Format button, select the Start At option button, and type **1**

4   Choose the OK button twice to close both dialog boxes.

    If you have headers or footers in your document, Word asks if you want to replace the existing header or footer with page numbers. Choose the No button.

5   Position the insertion point at the beginning of the first chapter and press the Insert Field key (CTRL+F9).

6   Between the field characters, type **seq** followed by a space, a sequence name, another space, and **\h**

    For example, type **seq chapter \h**

    The \h switch hides the result of the field so it is not displayed in the document text.

7   With the insertion point in the field, press the Update Field key (F9).

When you update the SEQ field, it is no longer displayed on the screen. You can choose Field Codes from the View menu to view SEQ fields.

8   Repeat steps 5 through 7 for each chapter.
–or–
Copy the field and insert it at the beginning of each chapter.

9   Position the insertion point at the end of the text in the document and press the Insert Field key (CTRL+F9).

10   Between the field characters, type **index** followed by **\s** *SequenceName*

For example, type **index \s chapter**

11   Position the insertion point within the INDEX field.

12   To ensure accurate pagination of the document, make sure the Field Codes are not displayed.

If hidden text is displayed, click the Show/Hide ¶ button on the ribbon or clear the All and Hidden Text check boxes in the View category of the Options dialog box (Tools menu).

13   With the insertion point in the INDEX field, press the Update Field key (F9).

Any page on which an index entry (*seq chapter* in the example given) appears will be referenced in the index by both chapter and page numbers.

Updating an Index

Ordinarily, you compile an index after you have finished the document. However, if you make changes to the document that affect how pages break (for example, adding or deleting text), you can compile the index again by choosing the Index command from the Insert menu.

To ensure the accuracy of the page numbers in the index, clear field codes and hidden text immediately before you update the index.

When you choose the Index command, Word asks if you want to replace the existing index. Choose Yes to replace the index; if you choose No, you cancel the command without changing the index.

Choosing Yes replaces the existing index with a simple index. If you used fields to create your index, update the INDEX field by using the Update Field key (F9).

If you move the index to another location in the document and choose to update it, Word replaces the index at its current location. If you have more than one index and create a new index, Word replaces the first index in the document. If you want to update more than one index, select the entire document and use the Update Field key (F9).

Formatting an Index

When you compile an index, Word formats it for you. If you want a different look for the index, or for specific entries in the index, you can change the format:

- When you compile the index, by using the Bold and Italic check boxes in the Index Entry dialog box.

- At any time by redefining the index styles.

- After you compile the index, by using formatting commands.

- When you compile the index, by using fields with special switches.

For more information about redefining styles, see Chapter 8, "Formatting with Styles."

When you compile an index, it is automatically based on the Index 1 through Index 7 styles. This means that, no matter what formatting or style you have applied to text in the document, the text in the index has an index style. The index styles are like the Normal paragraph style, except that each succeeding index-entry level is indented 0.25 inch. You can redefine these standard styles if you want a different look for your document.

You can specify separator characters for the different sections of an index with the {INDEX \h " "} field. The separator characters are indicated inside the quotes. For example, the field {INDEX \h "-A-"} separates each section with the appropriate letter surrounded by dashes. You can define the Index Heading style to format the separator characters.

You can also change character formatting directly by using the ribbon or the Character command on the Format menu. You can change paragraphs and sections by using the Paragraph and Section Layout commands. However, if you recompile the index after making direct formatting changes, Word discards the changes along with the old index. For this reason, it is usually better to redefine the index styles than to make direct formatting changes.

Using Fields to Format an Index

In the Index dialog box, you can choose whether or not you want to divide the index into alphabetic sections and whether or not you want to designate the sections by letters. If you use fields, you can use any characters or a combination of an empty line and characters to divide the index. If you use letters to divide sections, Word automatically advances through the alphabet when the first letter of the main entries in a section changes.

Word automatically inserts a comma and one space between an index entry and a page number or text reference. If you want, you can change this spacing and use another character, such as a colon, after the entry text. You can also make page numbers or a text reference bold, italic, or both.

To separate the sections in an index using fields

1   If field codes are not displayed, from the View menu, choose Field Codes
    (ALT, V, C).

2   Position the insertion point at the end of the text in the document.

3   Press the Insert Field key (CTRL+F9).

4   Type any of the following field information:

To	Use this field code
Use an alphabetic character to separate sections	`{index \h "A"}`
Use any characters to separate sections (for example, **--AA--**)	`{index \h "characters"}`
Use an empty line between sections	`{index \h " "}`
Use an empty line plus a letter between sections	`{index \h "¶ A"}`

Note that, in the last example, ¶ stands for pressing the ENTER key.

5   Position the insertion point in the INDEX field.

6   To ensure accurate pagination of the document, choose the Field Codes command
    from the View menu so the field results are displayed.

    If hidden text is displayed, click the Show/Hide ¶ button on the ribbon, or clear the
    All and Hidden Text check boxes in the View category of the Options dialog box
    (Tools menu).

7   With the insertion point in the INDEX field, press the Update Field key (F9) to
    compile the index.

To format the characters between index text and page numbers

Word provides defaults for the separator character between page numbers, and
between items and page numbers. The defaults for the separator characters are the
following: a comma plus a space to separate index text from page numbers; a comma
between page numbers; and a hyphen between page numbers in a range and between
chapter and page numbers.

▶   To replace any of the default characters with one to three characters of your choice,
    use the following syntax for the INDEX field in your document:

    {index *Switch [SequenceName]* *"characters"***}**

Note the following examples. In the field code of the first example, the → symbol represents a tab character (visible as such if you select the Show/Hide ¶ button).

To	Example	Use this field code
Separate index text from page numbers by tabs	Topic 24	{index \e "→"}
Insert a semicolon and a space between page numbers	Topic 24; 32	{index \l "; "}
Insert a colon between page numbers in a page range	Topic 18:24	{index \g ":"}
Separate chapter and page numbers by a dash	Topic 18–24	{index \s chapter \d "–"}

If You Have Problems with Page Numbers

If the page numbers in your index don't match the page numbers in your document, make sure that hidden text and field codes are not displayed when you compile or update the index.

If you still have problems with page numbers, you may have page or section breaks in your document that are formatted as hidden text. If you have a hidden page or section break in the middle of a field, this may insert a break in the index itself.

To find all page and section breaks formatted as hidden text and clear the hidden text formatting, use the Replace command from the Edit menu. For more information on the Replace command, see Chapter 12, "Finding and Replacing Text or Formatting."

Creating a Table of Contents and Other Similar Lists

You can create a table of contents with several levels of headings, and you can include other lists in a document—for example, tables of figures, tables of photographs, and tables of tables.

Unless otherwise noted, wherever you see references to a table of contents in this chapter, assume that the information also applies to other similar lists.

You create a table of contents in two basic steps:

- Identify the text you want to include in the table of contents.
- Compile the table of contents.

You can identify table of contents entries in two different ways. The faster and easier way is to use heading styles.

The second way is to use fields. Fields are especially useful if you want to create different kinds of lists for one document, or if you want special effects, such as entries that are different from the headings in your document. For example, you might have photographs and charts sequentially labeled "Figure 1," "Figure 2," and so on. If you want to make separate lists for the photographs and charts, you can create entries for the list of photos and for the list of charts that include a description of the figure but don't include the word "Figure" and its accompanying number.

When you are ready to create the table of contents, you place the insertion point where you want to insert the table and choose the Table Of Contents command from the Insert menu or insert a TOC field.

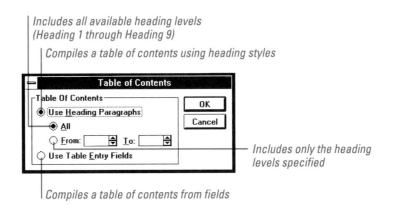

Includes all available heading levels (Heading 1 through Heading 9)

Compiles a table of contents using heading styles

Includes only the heading levels specified

Compiles a table of contents from fields

In the Table Of Contents dialog box, you indicate whether you are collecting the table of contents from heading-style entries or field entries. If you are using heading styles, you can include all of the entries or only a subset of the entries. For example, you may have six heading levels in your document but you may want to include only the first three in the table of contents.

When you choose the OK button in the Table Of Contents dialog box, Word paginates the document, compiles the table of contents, and inserts a table of contents field at the insertion point. Each table of contents entry is placed on a separate line, as shown in the following illustration.

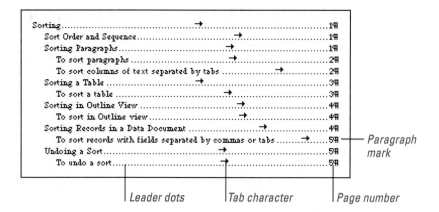

Paragraph mark

Leader dots   Tab character   Page number

For each entry, Word inserts a tab character with leader dots, a page number, and a paragraph mark. This is according to the standard table of contents style, but you can change this. For more information, see "Formatting a Table of Contents," later in this chapter.

Note   Word tables of contents do not include text in headers, footers, footnotes, annotations, or embedded objects.

If you create a table of contents and then add or delete text in your document, the page numbers may no longer be accurate. If you make changes, you should update the table of contents before you print the document. For more information, see "Updating a Table of Contents," later in this chapter.

Creating a Table of Contents Using Heading Styles

This section gives basic information on using styles to create a table of contents. For details on styles, see Chapter 8, "Formatting With Styles."

The simplest way to create a table of contents is by applying a heading style for each heading, subheading, caption, or other text you want in the table of contents. You apply a standard heading style to each table of contents entry. When you compile the table of contents, each paragraph is displayed at the level determined by its heading style. For example, a paragraph with a Heading 1 style will be aligned with the left margin and a paragraph with a Heading 2 style will be indented one-half inch from the left margin.

If you've already applied standard heading styles to the headings and subheadings in your document, you're ready to compile the table of contents. If you haven't applied styles, refer to the following procedure, "To apply heading styles."

Heading Styles Basics

You can apply a group of formats to a paragraph and give the group of formats a style name. You then apply the name to all paragraphs that you want to have the same formats. This is a quick way to ensure consistent formatting in your document or across different documents. Using styles also makes it very easy to change formatting for a number of paragraphs. You just change the formatting for the style, and all paragraphs with that style name change automatically.

Word provides standard styles that are already formatted specifically. For example, you can use Heading 1 through Heading 9 to create consistent headings in your document, to create an outline, and to create tables of contents and other similar lists. You can also change the formatting of a standard style to adjust the appearance of all paragraphs containing that style.

To apply heading styles

1 Select a paragraph in your document that you want to be an entry in the table of contents.

2 In the Style box on the ribbon, select the appropriate heading level for the paragraph. For example, for a first-level heading, select Heading 1.

If the style is not listed in the Style box, follow steps 2 through 4 of the keyboard procedure (immediately following this procedure) to select from a list of all heading levels.

3 Repeat steps 1 and 2 for each paragraph you want to include as an entry in the table of contents.

The name of the style applied to the selected paragraph is displayed in the Style box at the far left end of the ribbon.

1 Select a paragraph in your document that you want to be an entry in the table of contents.

2 From the Format menu, choose Style (ALT, T, Y).

3 Choose the appropriate heading level from the list. If the style is not listed, press CTRL+Y to view all available styles.

4 Press the ENTER key.

The name of the style applied to the selected paragraph is displayed in the Style box at the far left end of the ribbon.

To compile a table of contents using heading styles

With this procedure, you create a complete table of contents—that is, one that includes all available heading styles.

1 Apply heading styles throughout your document.

2 Position the insertion point where you want the table of contents.

For example, if you want the table of contents to be placed immediately before the first page of your document text, position the insertion point at the very beginning of your document.

3 To ensure accurate pagination of the document, clear hidden text and field codes:

- If hidden text is displayed, click the Show/Hide ¶ button on the ribbon, or clear the All and Hidden Text check boxes in the View category of the Options dialog box (Tools menu).

- If field codes are displayed, choose the Field Codes command from the View menu (ALT, V, C) to display the field results.

4 From the Insert menu, choose Table Of Contents (ALT, I, C).

5 Select the Use Heading Paragraphs option button and the All option button.

6 Choose the OK button.

If you want to cancel a compilation in progress, press ESC.

A Table of Contents (TOC) field is inserted at the insertion point. If you choose Field Codes from the View menu or select the Field Codes check box in the View category of the Options dialog box (Tools menu), you can see the TOC code. To view the table of contents, choose the Field Codes command again to clear the codes and show the field results.

To compile a partial table of contents

With this procedure, you create a table of contents using a subset of the available headings. You can, for example, compile a table consisting of entries from only the first three heading levels.

1   Follow steps 1 through 4 of the foregoing procedure, "To compile a table of contents using heading styles."

2   Select the Use Heading Paragraphs option button and the From option button.

3   In the From and To boxes, type or select a number from 1 through 9 for the highest heading level (the heading style with the smallest number) and the lowest heading level (the style with the largest number) you want to include. For example, to compile entries from levels 1 through 3, type **1** in the From box and **3** in the To box.

If you want to collect entries from only one level, type the same number in both the From and To boxes.

4   Choose the OK button.

If you want to cancel a compilation in progress, press ESC.

Note   If you want to include both a table of contents and another list in the same document, you must insert fields in your document. For more information, see "Creating a Table of Contents Using Fields," later in this chapter.

How the Table of Contents Fields Work

When you choose the Table Of Contents command and select the Use Heading Paragraphs option, you are instructing Word to treat outline headings as if they included Table of Contents Entry (TC) fields. A TC field specifies each item you want to appear in the table of contents and indicates its location so that a page number can be assigned to each heading.

You insert TC fields by choosing Field from the Insert menu and selecting TC, or typing **tc** followed by the text for the table of contents entry surrounded by quotation marks. A TC field is formatted as hidden text.

When you choose Table Of Contents from the Insert menu, you insert a TOC field in your document at the insertion point. The TOC field acts as the mechanism for compiling the outline headings or TC fields into a table of contents. If Field Codes is chosen on the View menu or selected in the Options dialog box, Word displays the TOC field; if not, you see the text and page numbers in the table of contents (the field results).

If you make additional changes to the document, you must update the TOC field to generate an up-to-date version of the table of contents. You can update the table of contents by choosing the Table Of Contents command again, or you can place the insertion point anywhere in the TOC field and press the Update Field key (F9). If you choose the Table Of Contents command, Word asks if you want to replace the existing table of contents. If you press the Update Field key, Word replaces the existing table of contents without prompting you.

Creating a Table of Contents Using Fields

This section gives basic information on using fields in tables of contents. For more details, see the TOC field and TC field topics in online Help.

You can use fields to identify text as table of contents entries, and to create other similar lists, such as tables of illustrations and tables of tables. Fields are especially useful if you want to include multiple lists in your document. They are also useful if your document does not have obvious headings for every entry you want to include in the table of contents.

You can use fields to create simple or complex tables of contents. You can:

- Create a simple table of contents or other list with a single level of entry or multiple levels of entry.

- Create a table of contents and other lists for the same document.

- Include chapter and page numbers in your table of contents. For example, the table of contents might include this entry for page 1 in Chapter 7:

  The Effect of Exercise on Mental Health................7-1

- Consecutively number items in a table of contents or other list and automatically renumber the items if you change their order in the document.

To create a table of contents using fields

1 Do one of the following to make hidden text visible:

- On the ribbon, click the Show/Hide ¶ button.

- From the Tools menu, choose Options (ALT, O, O), and, in the View category, select the Hidden Text check box. Then choose the OK button.

2 Position the insertion point just after the text you want to include in the table of contents.

3 Press the Insert Field key (CTRL+F9).

4 Type **tc** "*text*" where *text* is what you want to insert as a table entry.

5 Repeat steps 2 through 4 for each table of contents entry.

6 Position the insertion point where you want the table of contents.

7 To ensure accurate pagination of the document, clear hidden text and field codes:

- If hidden text is displayed, click the Show/Hide ¶ button on the ribbon, or clear the All and Hidden Text check boxes in the View category of the Options dialog box (Tools menu).

- If field codes are displayed, choose the Field Codes command from the View menu (ALT, V, C) to display the field results.

8 From the Insert menu, choose Table Of Contents (ALT, I, C).

9 Select the Use Table Entry Fields option button.

10 Choose the OK button.

For this entry in the TOC	Your field code should be
Summary of Research	`{tc "Summary of Research"}`

Make sure you enclose your entry text in quotation marks and include a space between the field type (TC) and the first set of quotation marks.

Note   Instead of choosing the Table Of Contents command to compile the table of contents, you can press the Insert Field key (CTRL+F9) and type **toc** followed by **\f** to indicate that you are using fields instead of heading styles. Then, with the insertion point in the TOC field, press the Update Field key (F9). To ensure accurate pagination of the document, remember to clear the display of field codes and hidden text before pressing F9.

You can use fields to create a table of contents from outline headings by typing **toc \o** *level-level* in the TOC field. For example, to create a table of contents with outline headings of levels 1 through 3, press the Insert Field key (CTRL+F9) and type **toc \o 1-3**

To create sublevels using fields

When you use heading styles to create a table of contents, the headings automatically create sublevels. Heading 2 is a sublevel for Heading 1, Heading 3 is a sublevel for Heading 2, and so on. If you are using fields, you indicate the level by adding a number from 1 through 8 to the TC field. Word automatically creates the appropriate sublevel.

▶ Follow the foregoing procedure, "To create a table of contents using fields," and in step 4 type **\l** and a number from 1 through 8 following the text in the TC field.

For these entries in the TOC	Your field code should be
In The Rose Garden	`{tc "In The Rose Garden"}`
Songs of a Wild Rose	`{tc "Songs of a Wild Rose" \l 2}`
The Rose in Autumn	`{tc "The Rose in Autumn" \l 3}`

You can use any of the following to indicate a first level entry: \l or \l 1 or no switch.

To create a table of figures, photos, tables, or another list using fields

1   Follow steps 1 through 7 in the procedure "To create a table of contents using fields." At step 4, follow the text in the TC field with **\f** plus a list identifier.

   Your list identifier should be a one-character instruction in the field code. For suggestions, see the table following this procedure.

2   Insert a TOC field by pressing the Insert Field key (CTRL+F9) and typing **toc** followed by **\f** and the list identifier you used in step 1.

3   Position the insertion point in the TOC field.

4 To ensure accurate pagination of the document, clear hidden text and field codes:

- If hidden text is displayed, click the Show/Hide ¶ button on the ribbon, or clear the All and Hidden Text check boxes in the View category of the Options dialog box (Tools menu).

- If field codes are displayed, choose the Field Codes command from the View menu (ALT, V, C) to display the field results.

5 With the insertion point in the TOC field, press the Update Field key (F9).

For this entry in a table of graphs	Your TC and TOC field codes should be
Rate of Growth	`{tc "Rate of Growth" \f g}`
	`{toc \f g}`

You can use any character for a list identifier; however, if you use *c*, you will create an ordinary table of contents (*c* is the default). The following table lists suggested identifiers.

Type of list	Character suggested
Authorities	a
Contents	c
Illustrations	i
Figures	f
Charts or graphs	g
Photographs	p
Tables	t
Lists	l

To create multiple lists using fields, choose a different list identifier for the entries you want to include in each table. For example, use *i* for a list of illustrations and *g* for a list of graphs, and include two TOC fields: `{toc \f i}` and `{toc \f g}`.

Note If you are using the \l switch to indicate a specific level of entry, type it after the \f switch and the list identifier. For example, if you want the Figure title "Melodrama" to be a second-level entry in a table of figures, your field code should look like this:

`tc "Melodrama" \f f \l 2`

Tip When you are creating both a table of contents and one or more other lists, compile the table of contents last. Other tables can then be entries in the table of contents.

To create a table of contents with chapter-page numbers

This procedure creates chapter-page numbers in the table of contents but not in the document. To insert chapter-page numbers in a document, see Chapter 22, "Numbering Pages."

1   Insert table of contents entries in your document, using heading styles or fields.

2   For each chapter, position the insertion point at the end of the chapter and, from the Insert menu, choose Break (ALT, I, B). Under Section Break, select the options you want and choose the OK button.

3   For each chapter, from the Insert menu, choose Page Numbers (ALT, I, U); choose the Format button, select the Start At option, and type or select **1**. Choose the OK button twice to close both dialog boxes.

   If you have headers or footers in your document, Word asks if you want to replace the existing header or footer with page numbers. Choose the No button.

4   Position the insertion point at the beginning of the first chapter, and then press the Insert Field key (CTRL+F9).

5   Between the field characters, type **seq** followed by a space, a sequence name, another space, and **\h**

   For example, type: **seq chapter \h**

   The \h switch hides the result of the field.

6   With the insertion point in the field, press the Update Field key (F9).

   When you update the SEQ field, it is no longer displayed on the screen. You can choose Field Codes from the View menu to view SEQ fields.

7   Repeat steps 4 through 6 for each chapter.
   –or–
   Copy the field and insert it at the beginning of each chapter.

8   Position the insertion point where you want to locate the table of contents and press the Insert Field key (CTRL+F9).

9   Do one of the following:

If you created entries using	Type
Heading styles	**toc \s** *SequenceName* Example: **toc \s chapter**
Fields	**toc \f \s** *SequenceName* Example: **toc \f \s chapter**

10   Position the insertion point in the TOC field.

11 To ensure accurate pagination of the document, clear hidden text and field codes:

- If hidden text is displayed, click the Show/Hide ¶ button on the ribbon, or clear the All and Hidden Text check boxes in the View category of the Options dialog box (Tools menu).

- If field codes are displayed, choose the Field Codes command from the View menu (ALT, V, C) to display the field results.

12 With the insertion point in the TOC field, press the Update Field key (F9).

Any page where a table of contents entry appears will be referenced in the table of contents by both chapter and page numbers.

Note The default separator character between chapter and page numbers is a hyphen. You can change this to any separator character or characters you prefer (maximum three) by adding a \d switch to the TOC field, followed by the character(s) of your choice enclosed in quotation marks. For example, if your sequence name is chapter and you want to separate the chapter and page numbers with a colon and a space, your field code would look like this:

```
{toc \s chapter \d ": "}
```

Numbering Items and Creating a List of Figures

Special items in your document—photographs, tables, charts, and other illustrations—can be numbered consecutively by typing a caption that includes a SEQ (Sequence) field. When you update an item, Word numbers the items in sequence. If you change the order of the items, Word renumbers them when you update the SEQ fields.

To sequence captions and create a list of figures using heading styles

1 From the View menu, choose Field Codes (ALT, V, C).

2 For each caption you want to number, position the insertion point in the caption, press the Insert Field key (CTRL+F9), and type **seq** *SequenceName*

For example:

To include a caption like this	Use the following in your document
Figure 1. Roses	Figure {seq figure}. Roses
Figure 2. Daisies	Figure {seq figure}. Daisies

3 For each field, position the insertion point in the field, and press the Update Field key (F9).

4 If you want to create table of contents entries, apply heading styles to the captions as explained in "Creating a Table of Contents Using Heading Styles," earlier in this chapter. Make sure to apply a heading style you're not using elsewhere in the document, and type the same number in the From and To boxes in the Table Of Contents dialog box.

To sequence captions and create a list of figures using fields

1 Follow steps 1 through 3 in the foregoing procedure, "To sequence captions and create a list of figures using heading styles."

2 Use fields to create table of contents entries, as explained in "Creating a Table of Contents Using Fields," earlier in this chapter. Include a sequence field that contains the \r switch.

The \r switch begins the sequence with the number you specify; for example, \r 1 begins figure numbers at 1.

As an example, after the first caption, you could insert this field:

```
{tc "Figure {seq figure \r 1}. Roses" \f f}
```

The first caption now looks like this:

```
Figure {seq figure}. Roses {tc "Figure {seq figure \r 1}. Roses" \f f}
```

For the second figure and any figures following, you maintain the correct numbering by using the \c switch. The \c switch prevents the SEQ field from incrementing by 1. For example, the second figure caption would look like this:

```
Figure {seq figure}. Daisies {tc "Figure {seq figure \c}. Daisies" \f f}
```

3 Select the entire document and press the Update Field key (F9).

4 Position the insertion point where you want the list to appear, and press the Insert Field key (CTRL+F9).

5 Type **toc \f** and the list indicator. If your list indicator is *f,* for example, your TOC field code looks like this:

```
{toc \f f}
```

6 To ensure accurate pagination of the document, clear hidden text and field codes:

- Click the Show/Hide ¶ button on the ribbon, or clear the All and Hidden Text check boxes in the View category of the Options dialog box (Tools menu).

- To display the field results, choose the Field Codes command from the View menu (ALT, V, C).

7 With the insertion point in the TOC field, press the Update Field key (F9).

To use chapter-page numbers in this scenario, first you create a section for each chapter by choosing Break from the Insert menu. Start the page numbering at one in each section by choosing Page Numbers from the Insert menu, choosing the Format button, and typing **1** in the Start At box. Insert a SEQ field containing an identifier— for example, {seq chapter}—for each section. Use the following caption and TC fields for figure 1:

```
Figure {seq chapter \c}-{seq figure \r 1}. Roses {tc "Figure {seq
chapter \c}-{seq figure \c}. Roses" \f f}
```

For any figures other than figure 1, use the following caption:

```
Figure {seq chapter \c}-{seq figure}. Daisies {tc "Figure {seq chapter
\c}-{seq figure \c}. Daisies"  \f f}
```

Use the following TOC field to create the list of figures:

```
{toc \f f \s chapter}
```

The items will be automatically renumbered if you change their order in the document.

Updating a Table of Contents

Ordinarily, you compile a table of contents after you have finished a document. However, if you then make changes to the document that affect how pages break (for example, adding or deleting text), you can compile the table of contents again by choosing the Table Of Contents command from the Insert menu or by positioning the insertion point in the TOC field and pressing the Update Field key (F9).

To ensure the accuracy of the page numbers in the table of contents, clear field codes and hidden text before you update the table of contents.

When you choose the Table Of Contents command, Word asks if you want to replace the existing table of contents. Choose Yes to replace the table of contents, or choose No to cancel the command without changing the table of contents.

Choosing the Table Of Contents command replaces the table of contents with a simple table of contents. If you used fields to create your table of contents, make sure you update the TOC field by pressing the Update Field key (F9).

If you move the table of contents to another location in the document and update it, Word rebuilds the table of contents in its new location. If you have more than one list in a document and use the Table Of Contents command, Word replaces the first list. To maintain multiple lists, update the lists with the Update Field key (F9).

Formatting a Table of Contents

When you compile a table of contents, Word formats it for you. If you want a different look for the table of contents, you can change the format:

- At any time by redefining the table of contents' standard styles.

- After you compile the table of contents, by using formatting commands.

For more information about styles, see Chapter 8, "Formatting with Styles."

When you compile a table of contents, it is automatically based on the TOC 1 through TOC 8 styles. This means that, no matter what formatting or style you have applied to text in the document, the text in the table of contents will have a TOC style. The TOC styles are based on the Normal paragraph style, plus a 0.5-inch right indent, a left-aligned tab at 5.75 inches, dot leaders, and a right-aligned tab at 6 inches. These styles are standard styles that you can redefine if you want a different look for your table of contents.

You can also change character formatting directly by using the ribbon or the Character command on the Format menu; you can change paragraphs and sections by using the Paragraph and Section Layout commands. However, if you update the table of contents after making direct formatting changes, Word discards the changes along with the old table of contents. For this reason, it is usually better to redefine the table of contents styles than to make direct formatting changes.

Special Formatting Tips

If the spacing or leader characters in your table of contents are not formatted the way you want them—whether you are using standard styles, your own styles, or manual formatting—the following information may assist you.

Spacing Between Dots

When you print a table of contents, the spacing of the dots in a leader may differ from line to line when the tab character is formatted with a proportional-space font or if you are using expanded character formatting. You can make the space between dots equal by formatting the tab characters in the table of contents with a monospace font, such as Courier and use normal character spacing. The space between the dots may be larger than the space between characters in the proportionally spaced text, but the distance between each dot on each line will be the same.

Word Spacing

Words on some lines in a table of contents may be spaced farther apart than you would like. For example, your text may look like this when printed:

B. Social   Science,   semester   hour................ 2

when you want this:

B. Social Science, semester hour............................ 2

This occurs if you are using a proportional-space font or justified alignment for the TOC style. The spacing between characters varies when you use a proportional-space font, and justified alignment adds extra space between words to make the right end of a line even with the right paragraph boundary.

This situation is also likely to occur if you number paragraphs manually (without using the automatic numbering feature in Word) and use spaces to separate the line number from the text. To correct the situation, use tabs to separate the number from the text.

Note that tabs line up the beginning of text properly, but letter spacing within an entry may still be inconsistent. You may encounter the problem discussed under "Tabs and Leaders," next.

Tabs and Leaders

For more information on tabs and leader characters, see Chapter 7, "Paragraph Formatting."

TOC styles include tab leaders, producing dots between the text and page number, as in the following example:

II. The Seven Keys 10

If you prefer, you can change or omit the leader character by changing the tabs using the Style command on the Format menu. If you select the None option button under Leader in the Tabs dialog box, for example, the preceding entry appears in your table of contents like the following:

II. The Seven Keys   10

If You Have Problems with Page Numbers

If the page numbers in your table of contents don't match the page numbers in your document, make sure hidden text and field codes are not displayed when you compile or update the table of contents.

If your table of contents is more than one page long, you may need to update it. See "Updating a Table of Contents," earlier in this chapter.

If you still have problems with page numbers, you may have page or section breaks that are formatted as hidden text. To find them and clear the hidden text formatting, use the Replace command from the Edit menu. For information on the Replace command, see Chapter 12, "Finding and Replacing Text or Formatting."

Creating Indexes and Lists for Long Documents

For more information about connecting documents, see Chapter 11, "Setting Up Long Documents."

Generating a long index or creating a table of contents for a lengthy document may require lots of memory and take considerable time. Word provides several ways of making your work with long documents faster and easier. You can:

- Create partial indexes for a document that is especially long or complex (approximately 4000 entries or more) and combine them later. For example, you can compile an index for the letters A through L and another for M through Z, or you can compile an index for a range of pages you specify.

- Create a table of contents for part of a document—for example, a separate table of contents for each chapter in a multiple-chapter document.

- Divide your document into smaller documents and use the INCLUDE field to recombine the document.

- Create a table of contents and index in a separate document using the Referenced Document (RD) field.

- Set starting numbers for pages, footnotes, lines, and sequences in each file in a multiple-file document. This ensures that each item has the correct number.

For more information on the INCLUDE field, see the appropriate topic in online Help.

The INCLUDE field is most useful for documents of less than about 80 pages. INCLUDE can require a lot of memory, because it builds the entire document as a single file and then builds the index and table of contents.

If you have a long document with an index or table of contents, using RD is more appropriate. Because RD creates the table of contents and index without building the document as a single file, it requires less memory and can be faster to use.

If, however, you have a document with a very large index, you should use the \p (partial) switch to create an index for a range of letters, as described in the following procedure.

To create an index for a range of letters

1   Insert index entries in your document.

2   Position the insertion point in the document where you want to create the index.

3   To ensure accurate pagination of the document, clear hidden text and field codes:

- Click the Show/Hide ¶ button on the ribbon, or clear the All and Hidden Text check boxes in the View category of the Options dialog box (Tools menu).

- If field codes are displayed, choose the Field Codes command from the View menu (ALT, V, C) to display fields results.

4   From the Insert menu, choose Field (ALT, I, D).

5   In the Field Code box, delete the equal sign and type **index \p** *letter-range*

For example, for letters A through L, type **index \p A-L**

6   Choose the OK button.

Word displays all main entries that begin with the letters you specify, and all subentries under these main entries.

7   From the View menu, choose Field Codes (ALT, V, C).

8   Position the insertion point to the right of the closing field character in the INDEX field and press ENTER.

9   Choose the Field Codes command to display the field results, and repeat steps 4 through 6 for another range of letters—for example, M through Z.

10 If you are building your index in more than two letter ranges, repeat step 8 and steps 4 through 6 for each additional index section.

Note   If Field Codes is chosen on the View menu, or the Field Codes check box is selected in the View category of the Options dialog box, you see the INDEX code rather than the index text. To view the field results (index text and page numbers), choose the Field Codes command again.

To compile an index for a range of pages

1   Insert index entries.

To view the index entries, click the Show/Hide ¶ button on the ribbon.

2   Select the pages you want to include in the index.

3   From the Insert menu, choose Bookmark (ALT, I, M).

4   Type a name for the bookmark. The name can contain as many as 20 characters, cannot include spaces, and must begin with a letter. For example, type **range1**

5   Choose the OK button.

6   Position the insertion point in the document where you want the partial index to begin.

7   Press the Insert Field key (CTRL+F9).

8   Type **index \b** *BookmarkName*

9   Position the insertion point in the INDEX field.

10 To ensure accurate pagination of the document, clear hidden text and field codes:

■   Click the Show/Hide ¶ button on the ribbon or clear the All and Hidden Text check boxes in the View category of the Options dialog box (Tools menu).

■   If the field codes are displayed, choose the Field Codes command from the View menu (ALT, V, C) to display field results.

11 With the insertion point in the INDEX field, press the Update Field key (F9).

The index includes only those entries that appear on the pages indicated by the bookmark.

To create a table of contents for part of a document

1   Insert table of contents entries using heading styles or fields.

   If you use fields to insert the entries, you can click the Show/Hide ¶ button on the ribbon to view them.

2   Select the pages you want to include in the table of contents.

3   From the Insert menu, choose Bookmark (ALT, I, M).

4   Type a name for the bookmark. The name can contain as many as 20 characters, cannot include spaces, and must begin with a letter. For example, type **chapter1**

5   Choose the OK button.

6   Position the insertion point in the document where you want to insert the partial table of contents.

7   Press the Insert Field key (CTRL+F9).

8   Do one of the following:

If you created entries using	Type
Heading styles	**toc \b** *BookmarkName* Example: **toc \b chapter1**
Fields	**toc \f \b** *BookmarkName* Example: **toc \f \b chapter1**

9   Position the insertion point in the TOC field.

10   To ensure accurate pagination of the document, clear hidden text and field codes:

   ■   Click the Show/Hide ¶ button on the ribbon, or clear the All and Hidden Text check boxes in the View category of the Options dialog box (Tools menu).

   ■   If field codes are displayed, choose the Field Codes command from the View menu (ALT, V, C) to display the field results.

11   With the insertion point in the TOC field, press the Update Field key (F9).

   The table of contents includes only those entries that appear on the pages indicated by the bookmark.

Using the RD Field

To use the RD field, you divide a long document into separate files. Then you create a master document for the table of contents and index, including an RD field in the master document for each of the smaller files. For example, if you name your smaller files CHAPT1.DOC and CHAPT2.DOC, you can create a master document with the following RD fields:

```
{rd chapt1}
{rd chapt2}
```

When you update the fields in the master document, Word refers to each of the smaller files in turn, collects the index or table of contents entries, and compiles all the entries into a single table of contents and a single index.

If you have outline headings in the RD master document and create a table of contents from the outline, Word collects the outline headings from the master document first and then from the referenced documents.

To create a table of contents and index using the RD field

This procedure creates only the table of contents and the index. You print the document text separately.

1   Create and save a new document for each part of the larger document that includes table of contents and index entries.

2   Create a new document to contain the RD fields for the table of contents and index.

3   Press the Insert Field key (CTRL+F9).

4   Type **rd** *filename*

    For example, type **rd chapt1**

5   Repeat steps 3 and 4 for each file that makes up the larger document.

6   Position the insertion point where you want to insert the table of contents; choose Table Of Contents from the Insert menu (ALT, I, C), set the options you want in the Table Of Contents dialog box, and choose the OK button.

7   Position the insertion point where you want to insert the index; choose Index from the Insert menu (ALT, I, I), set the options you want in the Index dialog box, and then choose the OK button.

In a document with RD fields, you set the page numbers only for the table of contents and index because those are all that will be printed. When you print the document itself, the first file in the sequence will automatically be correct; you set the starting numbers for the second through the last file.

Setting Starting Numbers for a Multiple-File Document

For details on setting starting numbers, see Chapter 11, "Setting Up Long Documents."

To ensure that each part of the document has the correct page, line, footnote, and sequence numbers, you need to set the starting number for each of these in each document before you print. You then update the TOC and INDEX fields in the document that contains the RD fields.

Headers and Footers

A header or footer is descriptive text to be printed at the top or bottom of every page in your document. Headers and footers can be simple, consisting of the document name and the page number. However, you can create headers and footers that contain a variety of information, multiple paragraphs, and even graphics. For example, you can include the date and author's name in a header or footer for a report. In a brochure or promotional piece, you might include the company logo. Headers and footers for books often have the book title on the left page and the chapter title on the right.

Header text is printed in the top margin of each page of a document or section. Footer text is printed in the bottom margin. Word automatically adjusts the size of the margins to accommodate the text or graphics in the header or footer.

Creating headers or footers is easy. You open the header or footer pane and type the text you want. Word inserts and positions the header or footer on every page.

If you want to change the way headers and footers are printed on the page, you have a great deal of flexibility. For example, you can:

- Put a unique header or footer on the first page of the document or on the first page of each section—or have no header or footer on the first page.

- Position the header or footer anywhere on the page.

- Use different headers or footers on odd and even pages.

- Format the header or footer text, using options such as bold or italic.

- Specify different headers and footers for each section within a document.

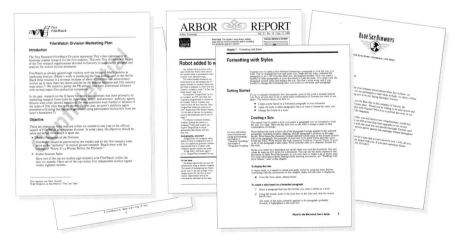

Examples of headers and footers

Adding Headers and Footers

You create a header or footer using the Header/Footer command on the View menu. Unless you create a header or footer, Word does not insert one into the document. When you work with them in normal view, headers and footers appear in separate panes. To see headers and footers as they appear when printed, you can view them in print preview or page layout view.

Creating Headers and Footers

To create or make changes to a header or footer, you work within a header or footer pane. This pane is similar to the document window, with scroll bars, an option bar, and a text area. You can use the ribbon, ruler, and Toolbar in the header or footer pane as well.

Using the buttons in the pane, you can insert the page number, date, or time into the header or footer. Word updates these entries automatically for you.

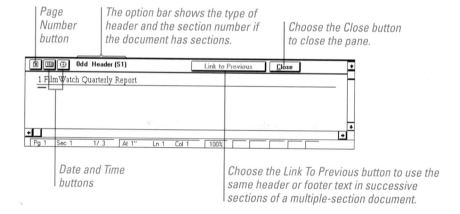

Page Number button

The option bar shows the type of header and the section number if the document has sections.

Choose the Close button to close the pane.

Date and Time buttons

Choose the Link To Previous button to use the same header or footer text in successive sections of a multiple-section document.

To create a header or footer

For more information on numbering pages of your document in a variety of ways, see Chapter 22, "Numbering Pages."

Make sure that you are in normal view before beginning this procedure.

1 From the View menu, choose Header/Footer (ALT, V, H).

2 In the Header/Footer box, select a header or footer.

You may have several choices, including First Header, First Footer, Even Header, Odd Header, and the like, depending on which check boxes (Different First Page and Different Odd And Even Pages) are selected.

3 Choose the OK button.

Word opens the header or footer pane.

4 Type the header or footer text in the pane.

You can press the TAB key to align the text. The header and footer panes have two default tab stops: the first centers the text, and the second aligns text on the right.

5 If you want, you can insert any of the following into the header or footer.

To insert	Click this button	Or press these keys
The page number	[#]	ALT+SHIFT+P
The current date	[📅]	ALT+SHIFT+D
The current time	[🕐]	ALT+SHIFT+T

6 To close the pane, choose the Close button (ALT+SHIFT+C).

If you don't want a header or footer on the first page of your document, you can follow the procedure "To add a different first-page header or footer" in the section "Varying Headers and Footers," later in this chapter.

Note Page layout view displays the headers and footers as part of the document, exactly as they are printed. If you choose the Header/Footer command while you're in page layout view, Word scrolls and positions the insertion point in the header or footer. If you haven't created the header or footer yet, Word creates an empty header or footer in the margin and places the insertion point there.

Word uses the following default settings for headers and footers:

■ The same header or footer is used for all subsequent sections in the document.

■ The top of the header prints 0.5 inch from the top edge of the page.

■ The bottom of the footer prints 0.5 inch from the bottom edge of the page.

Adding Fields to Headers and Footers

For more information about fields, see Chapter 41, "Fields."

You can add the name of the author, title of the document, filename, chapter number or name, section name, total number of pages, or the contents of any other field to the header or footer.

To add fields to a header or footer

Make sure you are in normal view before beginning this procedure.

1   From the View menu, choose Header/Footer (ALT, V, H).

2   In the Header/Footer box, select a header or footer.

3   Choose the OK button.

4   Move the insertion point to where you want the field, and press the Insert Field key (CTRL+F9) to insert the field characters ({ }).

   Word places the insertion point between the field characters.

5   Type one of the following field codes.

To insert	Type this code
Author's name	author
Title of document	title
Filename of document	filename
Chapter number	seq *sequence name*
Total pages in document	numpages

   To include the chapter number, you must insert the correct field codes at the beginning of the chapter. For information on how to do this, see Chapter 22, "Numbering Pages."

6   With the insertion point between the field characters, press the Update Field key, (F9).

7   To close the pane, choose the Close button.

Viewing Headers and Footers

Word does not show header or footer text in normal view. To view headers and footers, use one of the following methods:

- Open the header or footer pane by choosing Header/Footer from the View menu and selecting a header or footer.

- Choose Page Layout from the View menu, and scroll up to see headers or down to see footers. You can also edit and format headers and footers in this view.

- Choose Print Preview from the File menu to see the entire page (or both facing pages) in reduced size. You can reposition headers and footers in print preview, but you cannot edit or format the text.

Editing and Formatting Headers and Footers

For more information about formatting characters, see Chapter 6, "Character Formatting."

You edit header or footer text as you do any other text. To apply such formatting as bold or italic, or to use a different font, use the ribbon or the Character command on the Format menu.

You can also indent headers and footers or change their alignment with the ruler, the ribbon, the Toolbar, or the Paragraph command on the Format menu. For more information about controlling where headers and footers are printed, see "Positioning Headers and Footers," later in this chapter.

For more information on using styles, see Chapter 8, "Formatting with Styles."

For header or footer text, Word uses standard header or footer styles based on the Normal style. If you want to make header or footer text smaller, larger, or different in some other way, you can modify the header or footer style using the Style command on the Format menu.

Page numbers, dates, and times can be formatted as well. Page numbers are in the number format specified for the current section in the Page Numbers dialog box (Insert menu).

To edit or format a header or footer

Make sure you are in normal view before beginning this procedure.

1   From the View menu, choose Header/Footer (ALT, V, H).

2   In the Header/Footer box, select a header or footer.

3   Choose the OK button.

4   In the header or footer pane, edit and format the text as you would any other text.

    If you want to delete the page number, date, or time, first select it, and then press DEL.

5   To close the pane, choose the Close button.

Tip   You can also use page layout view to edit or format header and footer text. Choose Page Layout from the View menu, and then scroll up to the header or down to the footer. Edit or format the text as you usually do.

To delete a header or footer

Make sure you are in normal view before beginning this procedure.

1   From the View menu, choose Header/Footer (ALT, V, H).

2   In the Header/Footer box, select a header or footer.

3   Choose the OK button.

4   Delete all the text within the pane.

5   To close the pane, choose the Close button.

You cannot delete the last paragraph mark in the header or footer pane. This paragraph mark may contain formatting information, such as that for a border. If the header or footer contains formatting after you have deleted the text, select the paragraph mark and remove the formatting by pressing CTRL+Q.

Note   If the document has several sections and you want to change or delete the header or footer for a specific section, make sure the insertion point is in that section before you choose the Header/Footer command. For information about revising, deleting, and formatting headers and footers in a multiple-section document, see "Headers and Footers in Multiple-Section Documents," later in this chapter.

Positioning Headers and Footers

In some cases, you may want to change the default position of headers or footers. You can change the vertical position, increasing or decreasing the distance from the top or bottom edge of the page. Or you can change the horizontal position, centering the header or footer on the page or moving it into the page margin. You can also adjust the space between the header or footer text and the document text.

The Header/Footer command gives you the greatest control over the vertical position of the header or footer. You can also change the vertical position by dragging the header or footer in print preview or by pressing the ENTER key in page layout view to add extra space above or below.

For information on formatting and indenting paragraphs, see Chapter 7, "Paragraph Formatting."

With the paragraph formatting options on the ruler and Toolbar or in the Paragraph dialog box, you can change the horizontal position of the header or footer. For example, you can center the header or footer on the page, align it with the right or left margin, or extend it beyond the document text to print in the margin.

The following examples illustrate various ways to position headers and footers on the page.

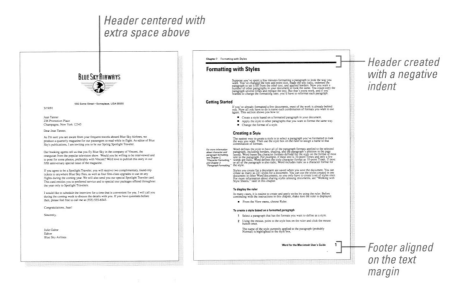

Header centered with extra space above

Header created with a negative indent

Footer aligned on the text margin

To position headers or footers vertically with the Header/Footer command

If you have more than one section in your document, you can change the header or footer position for each section. If you want headers or footers for all sections in the same position, it's easiest to position the header or footer before dividing the document into sections.

1   From the View menu, choose Header/Footer (ALT, V, H).

2   Under From Edge, type the distance from the edge of the page, or select one of the measurements listed.

- For a header, type or select the distance from the top of the page in the Header box.

- For a footer, type or select the distance from the bottom of the page in the Footer box.

3   Choose the OK button.

Tip   To add space between the header or footer and the document text, you can increase the size of the top and bottom margins using the Page Setup command on the Format menu.

To position headers and footers vertically using print preview

You can change the vertical position of headers and footers in print preview, but you cannot edit the text.

1   From the File menu, choose Print Preview (ALT, F, V).

2   Choose the Margins button.

Headers and footers are shown with a gray line around them.

3   Point to the header or footer. When the mouse pointer changes to cross hairs, drag the header or footer vertically to a new position.

If you want to override the margins and move the header or footer into the text area, hold down the SHIFT key while you drag the header or footer.

4   Click outside the page to update the display.

Margins button

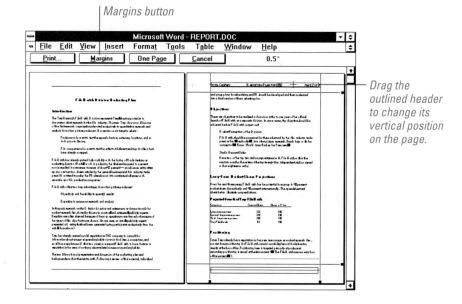

Drag the outlined header to change its vertical position on the page.

To position headers or footers horizontally

Make sure you are in normal view before beginning this procedure.

1 From the View menu, choose Header/Footer (ALT, V, H).

2 In the Header/Footer box, select a header or footer.

3 Choose the OK button.

   Word opens a header or footer pane.

4 Select the header or footer text.

5 Use tab stops or paragraph formatting buttons on the ruler, ribbon, or Toolbar to change the horizontal position of the header or footer.
   −or−
   Choose Paragraph from the Format menu (ALT, T, P), and then select the paragraph formatting options you want.

Note If you want headers or footers printed in the side margins of the page, set negative indents using the ruler or the Paragraph command on the Format menu. For example, you can type **-1** in the From Left box in the Paragraph dialog box to create a negative indent of 1 inch. For more information, see Chapter 7, "Paragraph Formatting."

Varying Headers and Footers

By default, Word prints the same header or footer on every page in the same position. For some documents, you may want to change this. For example, you can print different headers on even and odd pages, with the even headers displaying the document title and the odd headers displaying the section or chapter name. Or you may want the even and odd pages to mirror each other, so you can bind them with even pages on the left and odd pages on the right. In this case, you can print the headers or footers aligned with the outside page margins.

You can also add a different header or footer to the first page of a document. For example, you may want to use a logo on the first page of a presentation, or you may want to omit the header or footer on the first page of a business letter.

To add a different first-page header or footer

Make sure you are in normal view before beginning this procedure.

1 From the View menu, choose Header/Footer (ALT, V, H).

2 Select the Different First Page check box.

3 If you don't want a header or footer on the first page, choose the OK button, and then choose the Close button in the header or footer pane.
 –or–
 If you want to create a special header or footer for the first page, in the Header/Footer box, select First Header or First Footer, and then choose the OK button.

4 Type the text you want for the header or footer on the first page.

5 To close the pane, choose the Close button.

To add separate headers or footers for even and odd pages

Make sure you are in normal view before beginning this procedure.

1 From the View menu, choose Header/Footer (ALT, V, H).

2 Select the Different Odd And Even Pages check box.

3 In the Header/Footer box, select a header or footer and then choose the OK button.

4 Type the header or footer text.

5 To close the pane, choose the Close button.

6 From the View menu, choose Header/Footer (ALT, V, H).

7 Repeat steps 3 through 5 for each of the alternating headers and footers you want to add.

Note If you subsequently clear the Different Odd And Even Pages option in the Header/Footer dialog box, Word uses the contents of the odd header or footer for all pages of the document.

Varying Headers and Footers on Facing Pages

When documents are printed on both sides of the paper and bound with facing pages —sometimes called mirrored pages—the header and footer text is usually different on odd and even pages. Each header or footer is typically positioned on the outside edge of the page.

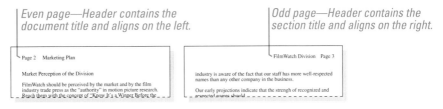

Even page—Header contains the document title and aligns on the left.

Odd page—Header contains the section title and aligns on the right.

Headers on facing pages

Note   If you're planning to use facing page headers or footers that include both text and page numbers, as shown in the preceding examples, use the Page Number button in the header or footer pane to insert the page numbers.

To vary headers and footers on facing pages

For more information on setting margins for your document, see Chapter 9, "Margins, Paper Size, and Page Orientation."

Make sure you are in normal view before beginning this procedure.

1   From the Format menu, choose Page Setup (ALT, T, U).

2   Select the Margins option button at the top of the dialog box.

3   Select the Facing Pages check box.

4   In the Gutter box, you can type or select a measurement for a gutter margin.

   The gutter margin is applied to the right edge of the left-hand page and the left edge of the right-hand page. It's useful when you want to bind the document.

5   In the Apply To box, select the option you want, and then choose the OK button.

6   From the View menu, choose Header/Footer (ALT, V, H).

7   If you want to vary the text of the header or footer for odd and even pages, select the Different Odd And Even Pages check box. If you use the same text in both odd and even headers or footers, you do not need to select this check box.

8   In the Header/Footer box, select a header or footer, and then choose the OK button.

9   Type the text and, if you want, insert the page number, date, or time.

You can change the alignment of the header or footer text using the buttons on the ribbon or the Paragraph command on the Format menu.

10   To close the pane, choose the Close button.

11   Repeat steps 6 through 10 until you have finished creating even and odd headers or footers for your document.

Headers and Footers in Multiple-Section Documents

For more information on multiple-section documents, see Chapter 11, "Setting Up Long Documents."

When you use headers and footers in documents with more than one section, keep the following in mind:

- If you want to add a header or footer for a specific section, place the insertion point in the appropriate section before choosing Header/Footer from the View menu.

- Once you add a header or footer to a section, Word proposes the same header or footer for every subsequent section when you open the header or footer pane—unless, of course, you've already assigned a header or footer to another section. If you want different headers or footers for each section, you need to supply new header or footer text for each section.

- If Word encounters a section with an empty header or footer, it inserts the header or footer text from the preceding section. To print a section without a header or footer, open the header or footer pane for that section, and delete all the text. If the header or footer contains formatting after you delete the text, select the paragraph mark and remove the formatting by pressing CTRL+Q.

Making Headers and Footers Consistent

If you want the header or footer text in one section to be the same as the header or footer text in the previous section, choose the Link To Previous button in the header or footer pane. Word asks if you want to delete any existing header or footer that may exist in the current section and link to the header or footer in the previous section. Choose the Yes button. Word then searches for a header or footer in the previous section and copies that into the pane. If there are both odd- and even-page headers or footers, Word copies the odd-page header or footer. If there is no header or footer in the previous section, the current section loses any it had.

If the header or footer is already the same as the one in the previous section, the Link To Previous button is not available.

Troubleshooting

This section describes some common problems associated with headers and footers and offers suggestions for overcoming them.

Page Number in Header or Footer Does Not Match Actual Page Number

If the page number in the header or footer doesn't match the page number displayed in the status bar, do the following:

- Check the first line of text at the top of the document window. Word displays the page number for the first line of text in the window, and you may be looking at portions of two pages. For example, the first line in the window may be on page 3, with the page break just below it and the rest of the text on page 4.

- Update page numbering by choosing Repaginate Now from the Tools menu.

- Select the page number in the header or footer, and press the Update Field key (F9).

Header or Footer Doesn't Appear on First Page of Section

If a document has two or more sections with different headers or footers, the new header or footer may not appear until the page following the page that contains the section break. This occurs when the Continuous option button is selected under Section Break in the Break dialog box. Any changes in the header or footer text and formatting do not take effect until after a page break.

You can have the new header or footer appear on the same page as the beginning of the new section by moving the section break. Position the insertion point at the top of the page that includes the section break. Choose Break from the Insert menu (ALT, I, B) and, under Section Break, select the Next Page option button. Make sure the insertion point is within this section when the header or footer is defined. Finally, delete the old section break. Note, however, that by doing this, you in effect move the entire page into the new section; all of the formatting that you apply to the new section also applies to the text on this page that precedes the former section break.

Another possible cause of the problem is that, intentionally or not, you may have instructed Word not to print the header or footer on the first page of a section. To fix this, make sure the insertion point is within the new section and clear the Different First Page check box in the Header/Footer dialog box. Choose the OK button and, before closing the Header/Footer pane, verify the header or footer information.

Header or Footer Pane Doesn't Open

The header or footer pane opens only when you are working in normal view. If you don't see the header or footer pane, you may be in page layout view. To switch to normal view, choose Normal from the View menu.

Dialog Box Doesn't List All Header or Footer Types

If the Header/Footer box doesn't list all of the header or footer types you've added to your document—Even Header, Odd Footer, and others—you may not be in normal view. Choose the Cancel button to close the dialog box, and choose Normal from the View menu (ALT, V, N). Then open the Header/Footer dialog box again.

Can't Print Headers or Footers in the Text Area

Unless you specify otherwise, Word prints headers and footers in the margin and adjusts the margin to accommodate them. If you want to print the header or footer to overlap the text area, you need to set the margin so Word won't adjust it. There are two ways to do this.

To print headers or footers in the text area

▶ Choose Print Preview from the File menu (ALT, F, V). Choose the Margins button, and then hold down SHIFT while you drag the header or footer into the text area.

–Or–

1 From the Format menu, choose Page Setup (ALT, T, U).

   Note that the Page Setup command is not available if your insertion point is in the Header/Footer pane.

2 Make sure the Margins option button is selected, and insert a minus sign in front of the measurements in the Top and Bottom boxes.

3 Choose the OK button.

4 From the View menu, choose Header/Footer (ALT, V, H).

5 Under From Edge, type or select a measurement for the header or footer from the edge of the page.

6 Choose the OK button.

7 Choose the Close button.

Chapter 31

Footnotes, Annotations, and Revision Marks

With Word, it is easy to add footnotes to your document. You can type footnote text of any length, with as many paragraphs as you want. You can format footnote text just as you would other text. You can also include graphics in footnotes.

When you add footnotes to your document in normal view, Word opens a footnote pane below the main document window for displaying and editing footnote text. Word gives you full control over footnotes. You can choose where to print footnotes, and you can customize the footnote reference marks and footnote separators that Word inserts into your document.

Word also provides two special features that make it easy to revise documents and incorporate comments from reviewers: annotations and revision marks.

Annotations are initialed, numbered comments that reviewers can attach to a document. They are a special form of footnotes. The annotation text appears in a separate pane, so it doesn't interfere with your text and graphics. Each reviewer can use up to five characters to identify his or her comments, and the annotation mark is formatted as hidden text, so that you can locate annotations when you need them and hide them when you don't. Annotations are numbered separately from footnotes and are printed on a separate page at the end of the document. When you finish revising your document, you can remove the annotations.

In Word, revision marks can help readers see at a glance where changes have been made to a document. You can mark a document as you edit it to show where you've inserted, deleted, or moved text. There are a variety of ways to mark revisions—you can insert revision bars beside the changed text, strike through deleted text, or specify that added text be bold, italic, or underlined.

Working with Footnotes

Word automatically reserves space at the bottom of each page for footnote text. Word also adjusts text on the page so that the footnote text and its reference mark—the corresponding superscript character in the body of the document—are on the same page. If you use numbered footnotes, Word automatically renumbers footnotes and reference marks whenever you add, delete, or move footnotes.

You can use the automatic, or default, settings in Word to add footnotes quickly and easily. If you want to customize footnotes, you have a great deal of control and flexibility in how you format and print footnotes:

- You can use any character as a reference mark instead of having Word automatically number footnotes.

- You can change the formatting of the reference mark and the footnote text.

- You can print footnotes at the bottom of the current page, at the end of sections, or at the end of the document. If the document text does not fill a page, you can print footnotes just below the last line of text.

- You can customize the line that separates footnote text from document text on a page.

- You can add a continuation notice for footnotes that continue from one page to another.

Adding Footnotes

To add a footnote to your document, you use the Footnote command on the Insert menu. Word displays the Footnote dialog box, in which you can select the type of reference mark you want Word to use. You can then choose the Options button to select other footnote options such as footnote position, numbering, and separators.

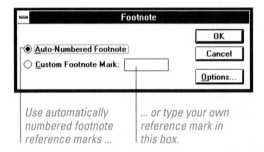

Use automatically numbered footnote reference marks ...

... or type your own reference mark in this box.

When you close the Footnote dialog box by choosing the OK button, Word inserts a footnote reference mark at the insertion point or preceding the selection in the document. Word also opens the footnote pane, where you type the footnote text.

Normal View vs. Page Layout View

When you choose the Footnote command while you are working in normal view, Word opens the footnote pane, in which you can type or edit the text for footnotes. When you have finished typing or editing in the footnote pane, you can choose the Close button to return to your document.

If you are working in page layout view when you choose the Footnote command, Word does not open the footnote pane but moves the insertion point to the location you have selected for footnotes to be printed, whether it is the bottom of the page, immediately below the text, or the end of the section or document. To return to the location of the insertion point before you chose the Footnote command, you can press the Go Back key (SHIFT+F5).

The procedures in the remainder of this section assume that you are working in normal view.

With the Word default settings, you can insert footnotes into your documents quickly and easily.

- Word automatically numbers the footnotes sequentially and renumbers them automatically when you add, delete, copy, or move footnotes.

- Word formats the footnote as 10-point text and the reference mark as 8-point superscript, using the font defined in Normal style.

- The footnotes are printed at the bottom of the page, with a line separating the footnote text from the document text.

Note Do not insert index or table of contents entries into footnotes. Word does not include page references in indexes or tables of contents to entries contained in footnotes.

To add a footnote

1 Position the insertion point in your document where you want the footnote reference mark to appear.

   If you have a block of text selected, Word inserts the reference mark immediately before the selection.

2 From the Insert menu, choose Footnote (ALT, I, N).

3 To have Word automatically number the footnote, use the default setting, Auto-Numbered Footnote.
   –or–
   To use a different type of reference mark, such as a dagger, an asterisk, or other characters, type up to 10 characters in the Custom Footnote Mark box.

4 Choose the OK button.

   Word inserts a footnote reference mark at the insertion point or before the selection and opens the footnote pane at the bottom of the document window.

5 Type your footnote text in the footnote pane.

6 Choose the Close button (ALT+SHIFT+C) to close the footnote pane and return to your place in the document.

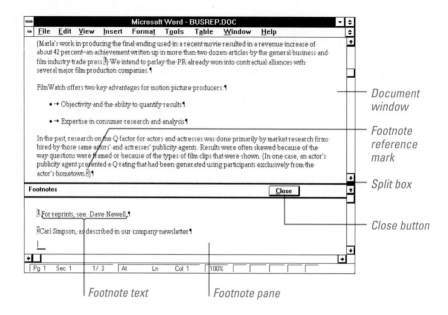

Document window

Footnote reference mark

Split box

Close button

Footnote text

Footnote pane

Tip   If you prefer to leave the footnote pane open while you work in your document, you can switch back and forth between the document window and the footnote pane by pressing F6. Or you can use the mouse to click in either the document window or the footnote pane.

Viewing Footnotes

You can open the footnote pane at any time while you work on your document to view or edit existing footnotes. The footnote pane has a title bar and a text area, and it can display scroll bars. You can use the ribbon, the ruler, and commands on the Format menu to apply formatting to text in the footnote pane.

When the footnote pane is open, it shows the footnotes corresponding to the reference marks in the document window. As you scroll through your document window, the footnote pane scrolls automatically as well. You can change the size of the footnote pane by dragging the split box up or down.

There are several ways to open the footnote pane and edit the text without adding a new footnote.

To view footnotes

▶ Do any of the following to view footnotes.

Do this	For this result
Double-click a footnote reference mark.	Word opens the footnote pane and displays the footnote text that corresponds to the reference mark.
From the View menu, choose Footnotes (ALT, V, F).	Word opens the footnote pane and displays footnote text.
In normal view, press the SHIFT key while you drag the split box down from the top of the vertical scroll bar.	Word opens the footnote pane and displays footnote text.
From the View menu, choose Page Layout (ALT, V, P), and then scroll to the location you have specified for footnotes.	Word displays footnote text, available for editing, in place in your document.

Note You can double-click an automatically numbered footnote reference mark to open the footnote pane in normal view or jump to the footnote in page layout view. Double-clicking a custom footnote mark has no effect. To jump to a footnote with a custom footnote mark, use one of the methods in the preceding procedure to open the footnote pane.

Revising and Customizing Footnotes

Word makes it easy to edit, revise, and customize your footnotes. You can:

- Edit the footnote text and apply formatting.
- Add or delete footnotes.
- Copy the text of a footnote you use repeatedly and insert it elsewhere in the document.
- Change the reference mark of an existing footnote.
- Redefine the style used for the footnote text or reference marks.
- Change the separators Word inserts between the document text and footnotes.
- Add a continuation notice for long footnotes that continue to the next page.

You type and edit text in the footnote pane the same way you do in a document window. You can also apply formatting, using the ribbon, ruler, and commands on the Format menu.

As you work in your document, you may need to revise the existing footnotes. In Word, you can add a footnote anywhere in the document, including between existing footnotes. You can also delete a footnote by simply deleting its reference mark. If you use the text of one footnote repeatedly, you can copy that footnote and insert it elsewhere in the document to avoid retyping it. Word adjusts automatically numbered reference marks each time you add, delete, or copy a footnote, or when you change a footnote reference mark.

The font, font size, and formatting of the footnote text and reference mark are predefined as standard styles in Word. To change the font or formatting of these elements, you must redefine the standard styles, using the Styles command on the Format menu.

To locate a footnote

1   From the Edit menu, choose Go To (ALT, E, G).

2   In the Go To box, type one of the following:

To go	Type
To the next footnote	**f**
To the previous footnote	**f-**
To a specific footnote	**f** n (where n is the nth footnote)
Forward a number of footnotes	**f+**n (where n is the number of footnotes after the current one)
Back a number of footnotes	**f-**n (where n is the number of footnotes before the current one)

3   Choose the OK button.

Tip   Instead of using the Go To command, you can press F5. Word displays "Go to:" in the status bar. To go to the footnote you want, type your destination as shown in the preceding table, and then press ENTER.

To delete a footnote

1 In the document window, select the reference mark for the footnote you want to delete.

2 From the Edit menu, choose Cut (ALT, E, T).
  −or−
  Press the DEL key.

Word deletes the footnote reference mark from the document window and the text associated with the mark from the footnote pane. If you are using automatically numbered footnotes, Word renumbers the footnotes.

Note You cannot delete a footnote by merely deleting the text in the footnote pane. Although the text disappears, the last paragraph mark for the footnote is not deleted, and the footnote reference mark remains in the document.

If you accidentally delete a footnote reference mark, you can restore it by immediately choosing the Undo command from the Edit menu.

Tip You can delete all automatically numbered footnotes quickly with the Replace command on the Edit menu. In the Find What box, type ^2 and leave the Replace With box empty. Choose the Replace All button.

To copy a footnote

1 In the document window, select the reference mark of the footnote you want to copy.

2 From the Edit menu, choose Copy (ALT, E, C).

3 Position the insertion point where you want the new reference mark.

4 From the Edit menu, choose Paste (ALT, E, P).

Word inserts the reference mark in the document window and copies the corresponding footnote text to the appropriate position in the footnote pane. If you are using automatically numbered footnotes, Word also inserts the correct reference number in the appropriate positions in document and footnote text, and automatically updates all subsequent numbers.

Cross-references Within Footnotes

If you want to include within footnotes cross-references to other footnotes, you can use bookmarks and the FTNREF field.

For example, you might want to create a footnote that looks like the following:

[16]See note 2 *supra.*

If you deleted the first footnote in the document, you would want this footnote to read:

[16]See note 1 *supra.*

By selecting the footnote reference mark of the footnote to which you want to refer, inserting a bookmark, and then inserting a FTNREF field, you can create within a footnote a cross-reference to another footnote that Word automatically renumbers if you add or delete footnotes.

With field codes displayed, the footnote might look like the following:

[16]See note {FTNREF *bookmark_name*} *supra.*

If you add or delete footnotes, you can update the FTNREF field in the footnote to ensure that the cross-reference is up-to-date.

For more information about the FTNREF field, see online Help.

To change a footnote reference mark

You can use the following procedure to change the type of reference mark (automatically numbered versus custom) or to replace one custom reference mark with another.

1   Select the reference mark in the document window.

2   From the Insert menu, choose Footnote (ALT, I, N).

3   In the Custom Footnote Mark box, type a new reference mark.
    −or−
    If you want to change a custom reference mark to an automatically numbered mark, select the Auto-Numbered Footnote option button.

4   Choose the OK button.

Word changes the reference mark in both the footnote pane and the document window and adjusts any automatically numbered footnotes.

To change the style of the footnote text or footnote reference mark

1 From the Format menu, choose Style (ALT, T, Y).

2 In the Style Name box, select either Footnote Text or Footnote Reference.

3 Choose the Define button.

4 Under Change Formatting, choose the command button for the kind of formatting you want to change.

5 In the dialog box Word displays, select the formatting options you want, and then choose the OK button.

6 Choose the Change button.

   When Word asks you to confirm the change, choose the Yes button.

7 Choose the Close button.

   Make sure you choose the Close button. If you choose the Apply button instead, Word reformats the entire paragraph that contains the insertion point or the selection.

Tip If you'd like to use a modified footnote style with other documents, you can select the Add To Template check box in the Style dialog box after you choose the Define button.

Changing Separators and Adding Continuation Notices

By default, Word prints a separator—that is, a short line separating the document text from the footnote text. For long footnote text that continues to the next page, Word prints a continuation separator—a margin-to-margin line between the text and the remainder of the footnote on the next page. You can replace either of these separators with other characters or graphics. For example, you could use a double line as the separator.

You can also tell Word to include a continuation notice for footnotes that continue to the next page.

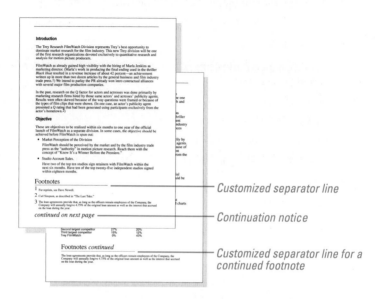

Customized separator line

Continuation notice

Customized separator line for a continued footnote

To change the footnote separator

1   From the Insert menu, choose Footnote (ALT, I, N).

2   Choose the Options button.

3   Under Footnote Separators, choose either the Separator or the Cont. Separator button.

   A separate pane appears in which you can edit the footnote separator or the continuation separator.

4   Select the existing separator characters, and then type the characters or insert the graphics you want to use.
   −or−
   Choose the Reset button (ALT+SHIFT+R) to restore the original separator.

5   Choose the Close button (ALT+SHIFT+C) to close the pane.

To add a continuation notice

1 From the Insert menu, choose Footnote (ALT, I, N).

2 Choose the Options button.

3 Under Footnote Separators, choose the Cont. Notice button.

   A separate pane appears in which you can type or edit the footnote continuation notice.

4 Type the text you want to use as a continuation notice.

5 Choose the Close button (ALT+SHIFT+C) to close the pane.

Controlling the Position of Footnotes

With Word you can control where footnotes are printed—on the same page as the footnote reference marks, at the end of a section, or at the end of the document. Footnotes that are on the same page as their reference marks can be printed at the bottom of the page or, if the document text does not fill the page, just below the last line of text.

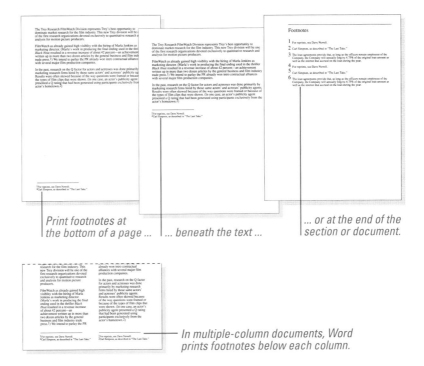

Print footnotes at the bottom of a page ... ... beneath the text ... ... or at the end of the section or document.

In multiple-column documents, Word prints footnotes below each column.

To change the position of footnotes

1   From the Insert menu, choose Footnote (ALT, I, N).

2   Choose the Options button.

3   In the Place At box, select one of the following options.

To have footnotes printed	Select this option
Flush with the bottom margin	Bottom Of Each Page
Just below where text ends on the page	Beneath Text
At the end of the section	End Of Section
At the end of the document	End Of Document

4   Choose the OK button.

Note If you print footnotes at the end of each section, Word automatically clears the Suppress Footnotes check box in the Section Layout dialog box. If you do not want Word to print footnotes for a certain section, you can choose the Section Layout command from the Format menu and then select the Suppress Footnotes check box to tell Word not to print footnotes for that section.

Controlling the Numbering of Footnotes

You can change the default numbering scheme for footnotes. For example, if you have a very long document composed of several connected documents, you may need to start footnotes in some of the documents at a number other than 1. Or you may want to restart numbering footnotes on each page or at the beginning of each section, instead of numbering footnotes sequentially throughout the document.

To change the numbering of footnotes

1   From the Insert menu, choose Footnote (ALT, I, N).

2   Choose the Options button.

3   Do one of the following:

   ■ To have the first footnote number for the document be any number other than 1, type or select the appropriate number in the Start At box.

   ■ To restart footnote numbering at 1 on each page, select the Restart Each Section check box.

   Word restarts the numbering at 1 according to the Place At option that is selected—on each page, each section, or each document.

4   Choose the OK button.

To number footnotes in long documents

For more information on working with long documents, see Chapter 11, "Setting Up Long Documents."

For a long document composed of several connected documents, you must indicate with which number footnotes start for each connected document. For example, the second document may start with footnote 9, the third document with footnote 16, and so on.

1   Open the first document in the sequence.

2   From the Insert menu, choose Footnote (ALT, I, N).

3   Choose the Options button.

4   In the Start At box, type or select the number you want for the first footnote in the document.

5   Choose the OK button.

6   Repeat steps 2 through 5 for each document in the sequence.

Note   To maintain automatic footnote numbering in sequence across connected documents, make sure the Restart Each Section check box in the Footnote Options dialog box is cleared.

If you use an INCLUDE field to connect two or more documents that include footnotes, Word automatically adjusts the footnote numbers. For more information on using INCLUDE fields, see online Help and Chapter 11, "Setting Up Long Documents."

Troubleshooting for Footnotes

If you experience any difficulties working with footnotes, read the following section. It describes some common problems and explains how to address them.

Can't Delete Paragraph Mark in Footnote Pane

In the footnote pane, you can delete the text but not the final paragraph mark of a footnote. The text disappears, but the paragraph mark remains. Also, deleting footnote text does not remove the corresponding reference marks from the document window.

To remove the final paragraph mark of a footnote from the footnote pane, delete the corresponding footnote reference mark in the document window.

Can't Print Separator on Letter-Quality Printer

By default, Word uses line graphics for the footnote separators. However, some letter-quality printers (daisy-wheel printers, for example) cannot print line graphics. To print the separators, choose Footnote from the Insert menu, choose the Options button, and then choose the Separator button. In the footnote separator pane, replace the line graphic by selecting it and then typing characters that your printer can print.

Bookmark Is No Longer Defined

Word displays this message when you've used the FTNREF field to cross-reference a footnote, but the original footnote with its bookmark has been deleted. You must delete all FTNREF fields that refer to the deleted footnote.

Using Annotations

Annotations are comments that reviewers insert into a Word document. They are useful for documents that you want to distribute for others to review and add comments to.

Annotations make online reviewing easier for both the reviewer and the author incorporating all the comments. Reviewers can enter comments in a separate annotations pane so that the comments do not disrupt the original text and you can see both text and comments at once. Reviewers can also include graphics in annotations. Once the author has reviewed the comments, they can be deleted or pasted into the document.

Reviewers can identify their comments with their initials, so it's easy to locate a particular reviewer's comments. The initials appear in the document and are formatted as hidden text.

You can insert and review annotations just as you would footnotes. Annotations are numbered separately and are printed on a separate page at the end of the document.

If you are circulating an online Word document for review, you may also want to lock the document for annotations so that reviewers can add comments but cannot actually modify the document text.

Inserting Annotations

You insert annotations using the Annotation command on the Insert menu. When you choose this command, Word opens a separate annotation pane in which you can type your comments.

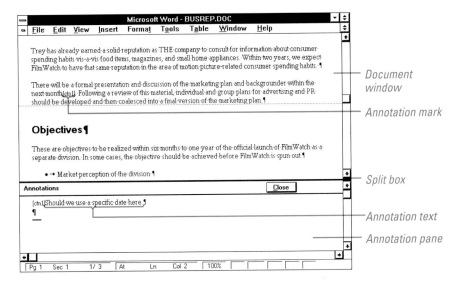

- Document window
- Annotation mark
- Split box
- Annotation text
- Annotation pane

To insert an annotation

1   Position the insertion point next to the text on which you want to comment.

2   From the Insert menu, choose Annotation (ALT, I, A).

Word inserts in your document an annotation mark—your initials with a number—formatted as hidden text, and then Word opens the annotation pane in the lower part of the document window.

3   In the annotation pane, type your comments, and then format them the way you want, using the ribbon and ruler or commands on the Format menu.

4   Choose the Close button (ALT+SHIFT+C) to close the annotation pane and return to your place in the document.

Tip   If you prefer to leave the annotation pane open while you work in your document, you can switch back and forth between the document window and the annotation pane by pressing F6. Or you can use the mouse to click in either the document window or the annotation pane.

Viewing Annotations

The annotation pane has a title bar and a text area, and it can display scroll bars. You can use the ribbon, the ruler, and commands on the Format menu to apply formatting to text in the annotation pane.

When the annotation pane is open, it shows the annotations corresponding to the annotation marks in the document window. As you scroll through the document window, the annotation pane scrolls automatically as well. You can change the size of the annotation pane by dragging the split box on the vertical scroll bar up or down.

To view annotations

1   If you want to view a particular annotation, select its annotation mark in your document.

2   From the View menu, choose Annotations (ALT, V, A).
    –or–
    In the document window, double-click the annotation mark.

3   When you're finished viewing annotations, choose the Close button (ALT+SHIFT+C) to return to your document.
    –or–
    Press F6 to return to the document window without closing the annotation pane.

To view or hide annotation marks in your document

1   From the Tools menu, choose Options (ALT, O, O).

2   Under Category, select View.

3   Under Nonprinting Characters, select or clear the Hidden Text check box.

4   Choose the OK button.

Tip   To view or hide annotation marks in document text without using the Options dialog box, you can click the Show/Hide ¶ button on the ribbon. To use this shortcut, you must first clear the Hidden Text check box, a View option in the Options dialog box (Tools menu).

Revising and Customizing Annotations

Word makes it easy to revise and customize your annotations. You can:

- Edit the text and apply formatting.

- Incorporate annotations into your document.

- Copy the text of an annotation you use repeatedly and insert it elsewhere in the document.

- Delete annotations.

You can delete an annotation simply by deleting its annotation mark in the document. If you use the text of one annotation repeatedly, you can copy and insert it elsewhere in the document to avoid retyping it. Word automatically renumbers annotation marks each time you add, delete, or copy an annotation.

To locate an annotation

1   From the Edit menu, choose Go To (ALT, E, G).

2   In the Go To box, type one of the following.

To go	Type
To the next annotation	**a**
To the previous annotation	**a-**
To a specific annotation	**a** n (where n is the nth annotation)
Forward a number of annotations	**a+**n (where n is the number of annotations after the current one)
Back a number of annotations	**a-**n (where n is the number of annotations before the current one)
Annotation mark on a page	**p**x**a**n (where x is a page and n is an annotation on that page)
Annotation mark within a section	**s**x**a**n (where s is a section and n is an annotation within that section)

3   Choose the OK button.

Tip   Instead of using the Go To command, you can press F5. Word displays "Go to:" in the status bar. To go to the annotation you want, type your destination as shown in the preceding table, and then press ENTER.

To incorporate an annotation into your document

1   From the View menu, choose Annotations (ALT, V, A).

2   In the annotation pane, select the annotation text only; do not select the annotation mark or the final paragraph mark of the annotation.

3   From the Edit menu, choose Cut (ALT, E, T) to place the annotation text onto the Clipboard.

4   In the document window, position the insertion point where you want to insert the text.

5   From the Edit menu, choose Paste (ALT, E, P).

    The text you insert is formatted with the Normal style. You may want to reformat it, depending on where you insert it in your document.

6   In the document window, select the annotation mark for the comment you inserted, and then press the DEL key.

To delete an annotation

1   In the document window, select the mark for the annotation you want to delete.

2   From the Edit menu, choose Cut (ALT, E, T).
    –or–
    Press the DEL key.

Word deletes the annotation mark from the document window and the text associated with the mark from the annotation pane and automatically renumbers subsequent annotations. If you accidentally delete an annotation, you can restore it by immediately choosing the Undo command from the Edit menu.

Note   You cannot delete an annotation by merely deleting the text in the annotation pane. Although the text disappears, the final paragraph mark for the annotation isn't deleted, and the annotation mark remains in the document.

To copy an annotation

1   In the document window, select the mark of the annotation you want to copy.

2   From the Edit menu, choose Copy (ALT, E, C).

3   Position the insertion point where you want the new annotation mark.

4   From the Edit menu, choose Paste (ALT, E, P).

Word inserts the annotation mark in the document window and copies the corresponding annotation text to the appropriate position in the annotation pane. Word automatically updates the numbering of the copied annotation and all subsequent annotations.

To change the initials Word uses for annotation marks

Normally, Word uses your initials as the annotation mark. You can change this mark to any other characters.

1   From the Tools menu, choose Options (ALT, O, O).

2   Under Category, select User Info.

3   In the Initials box, type the characters you want to use for annotation marks.

4   Choose the OK button.

Printing Annotations

You can choose to print annotations with or without the rest of the document.

If you print annotations alone, Word prints the page number of the annotation mark, the annotator's initials, the annotation number, and then the annotation text.

If you print annotations with document text, Word prints annotations on a separate page after the document text. Word also prints hidden text within the document text, including annotation marks. The printed annotations are preceded by the page number of the annotation mark, the annotator's initials, and the annotation number.

To print a document with annotations

1   From the File menu, choose Print (ALT, F, P).

2   Choose the Options button.

3   Under Include With Document, select the Annotations check box.

4   Choose the OK button to close the Options dialog box.

5   Set any other printing options you want, and then choose the OK button.

To print annotations only

1   From the File menu, choose Print (ALT, F, P).

2   In the Print box, select Annotations.

3   Choose the OK button.

Locking Documents for Annotations

When you're sending documents out for comments, you may find it helpful to lock the document so that you can control revisions to the document. This ensures that reviewers use annotations for making their comments, rather than inserting their comments directly into the document. Only the author can lock or unlock a document.

To lock or unlock a document

1   From the File menu, choose Save As (ALT, F, A).

2   Choose the File Sharing button.

3   Select or clear the Lock File For Annotations check box.

4   Choose the OK button to close the File Sharing dialog box.

5   Choose the OK button to lock or unlock the document for annotations.

Using Revision Marks

Revision marks are useful for helping readers see what changes have been made to a document since the last version. Revision marks make it easy to see additions, deletions, replacements, and moved text because Word marks only those paragraphs that have changed.

There are two basic ways you can have Word mark revisions. You can choose to mark revisions as you make them and then search for revision marks later to review all your changes. You can also mark revisions later by comparing two versions of the document.

Marking Revisions

You use the Revision Marks command on the Tools menu to add revision marks as you work. Deletions are always marked with strikethrough character formatting. In the Revision Marks dialog box, you can specify whether you want revision bars and where they should appear. You can also specify the character formatting Word uses to mark added text.

You use the Compare Versions command on the Tools menu to compare two versions of a document. When you use this command to compare documents, Word adds revision bars next to modified paragraphs in the newer document.

To start or stop revision marking

1 Open the document you want to edit.

2 From the Tools menu, choose Revision Marks (ALT, O, K).

3 Select or clear the Mark Revisions check box.

4 Under Revision Bars, select an option for positioning revision bars:

- None displays and prints no revision bars.

- Left displays and prints revision bars in the left margin.

- Right prints revision bars in the right margin. On the screen in normal view, the bars always appear on the left.

- Outside prints revision bars in the outside margin of facing pages—in the left margin of even pages and in the right margin of odd pages. On the screen in normal view, the bars always appear at the left.

5 Under Mark New Text With, select an option for formatting added text.

6 Choose the OK button.

When you edit your document, Word starts or stops marking changes with the formatting you specified. When Word is marking revisions, MRK is displayed in the status bar.

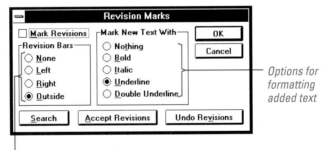

Options for formatting added text

Options for revision bars

To compare two versions of a document

1 Open the newer version of the document.

2 From the Tools menu, choose Compare Versions (ALT, O, V).

3 In the File Name box, type the name of the older version of the document or select it from the list of documents.

4 Choose the OK button.

To search for revision marks

1 Open the document in which you want to search for revision marks.

2 From the Tools menu, choose Revision Marks (ALT, O, K).

3 Choose the Search button.

Word locates the first occurrence of revision marks.

4 Continue choosing the Search button to review the revisions one at a time.

If the search reaches the end of the document, Word displays a message. Choose the Yes button to continue searching at the beginning of the document, or choose the No button to return to your document.

5 When you're finished searching for revision marks, choose the OK button.

Incorporating Revisions

After you've reviewed a document with revisions, you can choose to accept or undo the changes and remove the revision marks from the document.

When you accept revisions, you remove deletion marks and deleted text, the specified formatting for added text is removed, and the added text takes on the formatting of the paragraph in which it's located. The revision bars are no longer displayed. If you decide you want to keep text you marked for deletion, you can undo revisions—Word removes the strikethrough formatting, and the text remains in the document.

You can remove revision marks from the entire document or just from a selected area of the document.

To accept revisions

1   Select the text for which you want to accept revisions.

   If there is no selection, Word accepts revisions for the whole document.

2   From the Tools menu, choose Revision Marks (ALT, O, K).

3   Choose the Accept Revisions button.

   If no text was selected, Word asks you to confirm that you want to accept all revisions.

   Word deletes any text that was marked for deletion and removes all revision marks from the document or the selection.

To undo revisions

1   Select the text for which you want to undo revisions.

   If there is no selection, Word undoes the revisions for the whole document.

2   From the Tools menu, choose Revision Marks (ALT, O, K).

3   Choose the Undo Revisions button.

   If no text was selected, Word asks you to confirm that you want to undo all revisions. Word removes all revision marks from the document or the selection and undoes any marked revisions that were made.

Chapter 32

Print Merge Basics

Using the Print Merge command, you can combine, or merge, lists of variable information in one file with a Word document to print mailing labels, individualize form letters, assemble legal documents, and create other types of merged documents.

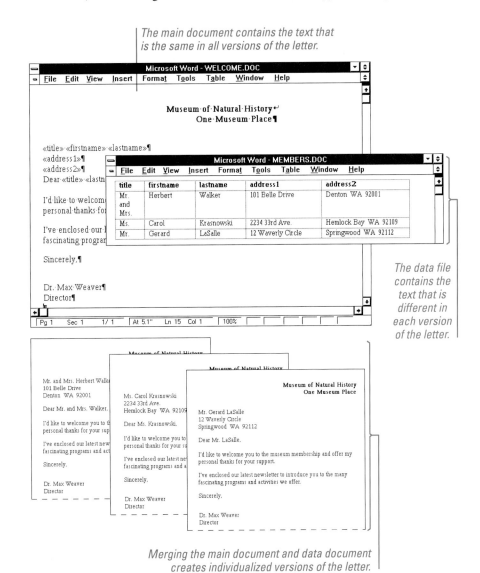

The main document contains the text that is the same in all versions of the letter.

The data file contains the text that is different in each version of the letter.

Merging the main document and data document creates individualized versions of the letter.

Preparing any type of merged document typically involves two files, a *main document* and a *data file*. The main document contains the standardized text, punctuation, spaces, graphics, and other information you want to be identical in each version of the merged document. The data file contains the information that varies with each version—for example, names, addresses, account numbers, and product codes. You insert special instructions called *merge fields* to indicate where you want the variable information printed from the data file.

When you merge the data file and the main document, Word inserts the appropriate information from the data file in the main document's standard text.

Merging Documents: Basic Techniques

Whether you're printing mailing labels or personalizing a form letter, you use the same basic techniques. The Print Merge command on the File menu guides you through the steps:

- Select the data file containing the variable information you want to merge.

  If you're creating a new data file, Word organizes the data for you in a Word table. You can also use a data file that you created in an earlier version of Word for Windows, in Microsoft Excel, in a database application, or in a word processor other than Word for Windows. For step-by-step instructions and some tips on what information to include in a data file, see "Creating and Attaching a Data File," later in this chapter.

- Insert the merge field names from the data file into your main document.

  The main document can be any Word document that contains the text or graphics that you want to print in each merged document. Once you've attached the data file, you're ready to insert the merge field names in the main document. For instructions on inserting the merge fields, see "Inserting Merge Fields in the Main Document," later in this chapter.

- Merge the main document with the data file, as described in "Merging and Printing the Documents," later in this chapter.

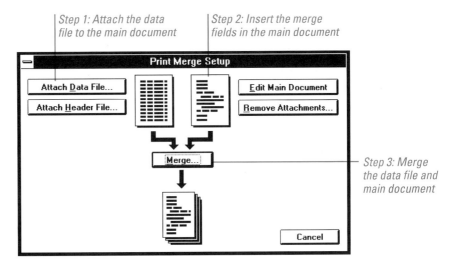

The Print Merge command guides you through each step.

About Data Files

If you've used Microsoft Excel or another spreadsheet or database application, you're probably familiar with data files. If the terms *records* and *fields* are unfamiliar to you, or if you have never used the print merge feature, read this section before you continue.

The data file contains the text and graphics that vary with each version of a merged document. Each set of related information makes up one *record* in the data file. One record in a customer mailing list, for example, contains all the information for one customer. The different types of information—customer name, mailing address, account number, and so on—are called *fields*. Each field in the data file must have a unique name. In most cases, you list the field names in the first record of the data file, called the *header record*. The remaining records in the data file, the *data records,* contain the field information corresponding to each field name in the header record.

When you merge the data file and the main document, the variable information from each data record is combined with the main document to produce a unique merged document—one form letter, for example, or one printed mailing label.

When you use the Print Merge command to create the data file, Word organizes the data records in a table. The following illustration shows a data file for a mailing list set up as a table. The field names in the first row of cells, the header record, act as column headings for the address information. For example, the town in which each addressee lives is in the column of cells labeled "town." Each of the remaining rows of cells, the data records, contains a set of information for one addressee.

name	company	house	road	town	county	postcode	
Mr C Evans	Evans Ltd	Evans House	10 Willow Road	Newtown	Berks	RG5 6GH	
Mrs Groves		The Red House	Bridge Road	Middletown	Berks	RG7 4BP	
Miss Gardener	Wheeler Bicycles Ltd	Wheeler House	2 Field Road	Lowtown	Berks		

Data file for a mailing list

Tip In some cases, you may find it convenient to place the header record in a separate document called a header file. Suppose you have several data files containing account information for the various sales divisions of your company. You can create a single header file and use it to merge any of the data files. Using a header file ensures that the merge field names you insert in the main document always match the merge field names in the header record regardless of the data file you are merging. For more information about header files, see "Creating a Header Record for an Existing Data File," later in this chapter.

Creating and Attaching a Data File

Attaching a data file identifies the name and location of the file containing the variable information that you want to merge with the active document. When you attach a data file, the active document becomes a print merge main document. Within the print merge main document, Word keeps track of the attached data file to ensure that the merge field names in the data file's header record match those inserted in the main document; this prevents errors when you merge the documents.

You can merge the same data file with any number of main documents. For example, you can use the same data file to produce a form letter and also to print the mailing labels for the letters. However, a main document can have only one data file attached to it at a time.

With a few exceptions, the data file can contain any text and graphics that you can insert in an ordinary Word document. However, a data file cannot contain the following:

- Items positioned in a frame
- A Word table within a data record field
- Fields that display items in a document as their result:

AUTONUM	INCLUDE
DDE and DDEAUTO	LINK
EMBED	QUOTE
FORMULA	SYMBOL
IMPORT	

If your data file contains one of these fields, you must unlink the field in your data file before merging. To unlink the field, position the insertion point in the field, and press CONTROL+SHIFT+F9. The "result" of the field is displayed in the data file as ordinary text or a graphic, which can then be merged.

Creating a New Data File

The first step in creating a new data file is to decide which information you want to vary in each version of the merged document. For each type of variable information, you define a merge field in the data file.

To decide which merge fields you need to define, you may find it helpful first to type the standard text in the main document. If you're creating a form letter, for example, type the text that you want to include in each version of the letter, inserting blanks or X's where the text will change with each letter. After creating the data file, you can go back and insert the merge field names at the appropriate points in the standard text.

On the other hand, if you have a good idea of the merge fields you need to define, it's easier to create the data file first. That way, you can insert the field names as you type the main document.

If you have a great deal of information to merge, you may prefer to organize the data as ordinary paragraphs instead of a table, with different types of information separated by tabs. For details, see "Other Ways of Organizing the Data File," later in this chapter.

Planning the Data File

Taking a few minutes to plan the information you want to include in the data file can save you time and work in the long run. Here are a few questions to ask yourself when you're preparing the data file.

Will some records have more information than others?   Some entries in a mailing list might have a business name, a department title, and up to three lines for the address. Other entries might have only a name, a one-line street address, and the city, state, and postal code. In the data file, however, each record must have the same number of fields. Make sure to plan enough fields to accommodate the records with the most information. If a record doesn't have a particular type of information, you can leave the field blank for that record in the data file.

Do you plan to sort the data?   For example, the city, state, and postal code are almost always printed on the same line of a mailing label, so you could include this information in one field. However, if you want to sort the records by the postal code, state, or city, you must divide the information into separate fields. The same is true if you want to sort your mailing list by the addressee's last name—the last name and first name must be in separate fields.

Will you use information in a particular field in different ways?   In the form letter shown at the beginning of this chapter, the first line of the address contains a title and the recipient's complete name—in this case, Mr. Gerard LaSalle. The salutation, on the other hand, contains only the title and last name: Dear Mr. LaSalle. By placing the title, first name, and last name in separate fields, you can use the same field to print the last name in both the address and salutation.

Will you use the data for several types of documents?   Consider the types of main documents you will be merging with the data. For example, you can use the same data file for printing both an invoice and a shipping label. In the case of a form letter, plan the addressee information so you can use the same data file for the inside address, and the salutation, and the address on the mailing label or envelope.

The following two procedures take you through the steps for creating and attaching a data file.

To set up a new data file

1   Do one of the following:

- If you need to create a new main document, choose New from the File menu (ALT, F, N) to open a new document. Use this as the main document.

- If you've already typed the standard text you want repeated in each merged document, open the document containing your standard text, and use it as the main document.

2   From the File menu, choose Print Merge (ALT, F, M).

3   In the Print Merge Setup dialog box, choose the Attach Data File button.

4   In the Attach Data File dialog box, choose the Create Data File button.

Word displays the Create Data File dialog box.

5   In the Field Name box, type the name of the first field; then choose the Add button or press ENTER. Repeat this for each field you want to add.

Each field name must be unique and can have as many as 32 characters. You can use letters, numbers, and underscore characters, but not spaces. The first character must be a letter.

You can list the fields in any order. The order of fields in the data file does not affect the order in which you can insert the fields in your main document.

To delete a field name from the list, select the field name and choose the Delete button.

6   When you've typed all the fields you want to define in the data file, choose the OK button.

Word displays a dialog box for you to save the data file.

7   Type a name for the data file in the File Name box, and then select the drive and directory where you want the data file stored. Then choose the OK button.

Word opens a new document window and inserts a table in the new data file. The field names you specified in the Create Data File dialog box are listed in the first row of the table, which is the header record of the data file. The second row becomes the first of your data records. You can now fill in the data records and save the data file.

name	company	address1	address2	city	state	postcode

Header record in the new data file

To fill in and save the data file

1   Beginning with the first cell of the empty data record, type information that corresponds to the field name at the top of the column. Press the TAB key to move to the next cell.

If a record does not have information for a particular field, press TAB to leave the cell for that field empty. Make sure you don't type spaces in the empty cells. Otherwise, empty spaces will appear in your merged documents.

2   When you reach the end of a data record (a row of cells), press TAB to insert a new row for the next record. You can add as many records as you like, and you can later add more records as you need them.

Field information can wrap within a cell without affecting how the text is printed when merged with the main document. If you want the field text to be printed on more than one line, insert a paragraph mark (by pressing the ENTER key) or line break (SHIFT+ENTER) where you want to break the line.

3   From the File menu, choose Save (ALT, F, S) to save the data records. Add any summary information you want, and then choose the OK button.

The table of data records should look similar to the following illustration.

For more information about working with tables, see Chapter 17, "Tables."

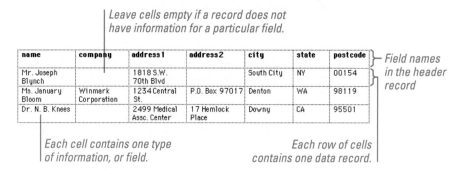

Leave cells empty if a record does not have information for a particular field.

name	company	address 1	address 2	city	state	postcode
Mr. Joseph Blynch		1818 S.W. 70th Blvd		South City	NY	00154
Ms. January Bloom	Winmark Corporation	1234 Central St.	P.O. Box 97017	Denton	WA	98119
Dr. N. B. Knees		2499 Medical Assc. Center	17 Hemlock Place	Downy	CA	95501

Field names in the header record

Each cell contains one type of information, or field.

Each row of cells contains one data record.

Data file

Note If you need to use more than 31 fields in the data file, you must organize your data records as paragraphs, using tabs or commas to separate the fields. See "Other Ways of Organizing the Data File," later in this chapter.

The main document you opened in the procedure to set up the data file remains open and is listed on the Window menu. You can now switch to the main document and insert the merge field names you've defined in the data file. For instructions on inserting the merge field names, see "Inserting Merge Fields in the Main Document," later in this chapter.

To switch to the main document

▶ From the Window menu, choose the main document name (ALT, W, *n*).

–Or–

▶ From the File menu, choose Print Merge (ALT, F, M), and then choose the Edit Main Document button.

Editing a Data File

When you create a new data file, Word bases the data file on the template DATAFILE.DOT. This template includes several ready-to-use macros to help you work with the data file. For example, you can add a new record, edit or delete a record, or link data to an external database.

Using the DataFile Macros

When the data file is the active document, the commands Record Management Tools and Database Management Tools are added to the Tools menu. Choosing either of these commands activates the macros stored in DATAFILE.DOT.

Record Management Tools

The Record Management Tools command provides the following options:

Use this option	To do this
Add New Record	Insert new data records. Word prompts you to type information for each field and adds the completed record to the data file.
Edit Record	Change the field information for selected records.
Delete Record	Delete specified records.
Go To	Locate a record based on its record number or specified field information.

Database Management Tools

The Database Management Tools command provides the following options:

Use this option	To do this
Add New Field	Insert a new field in the data file. After inserting the new field, you can use the Edit Record tool to add the new field information for each record.
Sort Record	Sort the data file. You can select one to three fields to use as sort keys.
Number Records	Insert a new field containing the record number of each record in the data file.
Clean Up Database	Scan a data file converted from another application to ensure that the data records are in the correct format.
Link to Ext. Database	Link information in the data file to its original application. When the original data file is modified in its source application—for example, Microsoft Excel—your Word data file is automatically updated.

The DATAFILE.DOT template is placed in your Word program directory when you install Word using Setup. If you store your templates in another directory, make sure you indicate its location in your WIN.INI file. To do this, choose the the the Options command on the Tools menu; select the WIN.INI category, and set the correct directory path for .DOT files. For information about updating the WIN.INI file, see Appendix B, "Modifying the WIN.INI File."

Adding a New Field to a Data File

The following procedure is an alternate way to add a field to a data file. It is particularly useful if you are working with a data file created in another application or in a version of Word prior to version 2.0.

To add a new field in a data file

Use this procedure to insert a new column of cells in the data file to contain a new field.

1   In the data file, click anywhere in the column of cells to the right of where you want the new column inserted. To add the column at the extreme right of the cells, click at the end of a row of cells, just outside the table gridline.

The order in which you insert the new field in your data file is not important. You can insert the fields in any order in your main document.

2   From the Table menu, choose Insert Cells (ALT, A, I).

3   In the Insert Cells dialog box, select the Insert Entire Column option button.

4   Choose the OK button.

Word inserts a column of cells to the left of the column containing the insertion point. You can now fill in the text for both the header record (the field name) and each data record.

If You Create the Data File Yourself

If you're merging documents for the first time, it's best to use the Print Merge command to create the data file. If you set up the table for the data yourself, it's a good idea to base the new data file on the template DATAFILE.DOT. That way, you can use the Record Management Tools and the Database Management Tools commands on the Tools menu when working in the data file.

Make sure you observe the following rules when setting up the records:

- Use the Insert Table command on the Table menu to insert a table that has one column for each type of field information you want to define in the data file.

- Type the name of each field in the first row of the table, the header record. You can think of the field names as "column headings" for the table. Delete any text or blank lines (paragraph marks, ¶) before the table.

- Each record (row of the table) must have the same number of fields (columns) as there are merge field names in the header record.

- Information you enter in the subsequent rows of the table must be in the same order, left to right, as the corresponding field names in the header record. However, the order in which you list the field names in the header record is not important.

- If a record doesn't have information for a certain field, leave the cell for that field blank.

If you have more than 31 merge fields, you must organize the data records in paragraphs, with each field separated by tabs or commas. For more information, see "Other Ways of Organizing the Data File," later in this chapter.

Attaching an Existing Data File

You can use a data file created in any version of Microsoft Word for Windows, in Microsoft Excel, in a database application, or in a word processor other than Word for Windows.

Using a Data File Created in Microsoft Word

If your data file and main document were created in a version of Word for Windows earlier than version 2.0, you can simply open the main document. Word interprets the DATA field in your main document and automatically attaches the specified data file. Word also attaches the specified header file if a header file is specified in the DATA field. Word then deletes the DATA field from the main document.

If you created the data file in Word for Windows (any version) but have not yet created a main document to merge with the data, open a new file. This becomes the main document to which you attach the data file.

See the procedure "To attach an existing data file to the main document," later in this chapter.

Using a Data File from Another Application

The variable information you want to merge may be in a Microsoft Excel worksheet, a dBASE file, or a file created in some other application. If you included the appropriate conversion filter when you installed Word, you can simply attach the data file as usual, and Word automatically converts a copy of the file to Word format.

For a complete list of conversion filters provided with Word, see Chapter 35, "Converting File Formats."

If you installed Word completely, the proper conversion filters should be in place for your use of files from Microsoft Excel, dBASE, Lotus 1-2-3, or WordPerfect versions 4 and 5. If you're in doubt, check your Word program directory for the following files.

File format to convert	Conversion filter
Microsoft Excel	XLBIFF.CNV
dBASE	DBASE.CNV
Lotus 1-2-3	LOTUS123.CNV
WordPerfect 4, 5	WPFT4.CNV, WPFT5.CNV

When you convert a Microsoft Excel worksheet or a dBASE file to Word format, the data is formatted as a Word table. If the data file contains more than 31 fields, however, the data records are formatted as paragraphs, with the fields separated by tabs. (There can be at most 31 columns in a Word table.) Data records converted from other applications are also converted to paragraphs or to comma- or tab-delimited files.

After converting a data file from another format, you must ensure that the records are in the proper format. For example, if the text in a data field contains a tab, comma, quotation marks, a line break, or a paragraph mark, make sure the field is enclosed in quotation marks (" "). Requirements for data records organized in paragraphs are discussed in "Other Ways of Organizing the Data File," later in this chapter.

If the data file does not define the data field names in a header record, you need to add a header record to the data file or attach a separate header file to the main document before you attach the data file. For instructions, see "Creating a Header Record for an Existing Data File," later in this chapter.

To attach an existing data file to the main document

1 Do one of the following:

- If you need to create a new main document, choose New from the File menu (ALT, F, N) to open a new document. Use this as the main document.

- If you've already typed the standard text you want repeated in each merged document, open the document containing your standard text, and use it as the main document.

2 From the File menu, choose Print Merge (ALT, F, M).

3 In the Print Merge Setup dialog box, choose the Attach Data File button.

   Word displays the Attach Data File dialog box.

4 In the Directories box, select the directory containing the data file.

5 In the List Files Of Type box, select All Files (*.*).

6 Under File Name, select the file containing the data, and then choose the OK button.

7 If you select a data file in a format other than that of Word for Windows, Word displays a dialog box asking you to select the file format you are converting from. Select the appropriate file format, and choose the OK button.

   If you are converting a Microsoft Excel worksheet, Word asks you to select the entire worksheet or specify the range of cells. If the data you want is in a named range of cells in the worksheet—for example, a range you've set as a database—select or type the name of the range. If the data is not in a named range, specify the row and column. For example, type **A1:H58** to specify the range of cells from column A, row 1, to column H, row 58.

Word opens a copy of the file in Word format and attaches the converted copy to the main document.

As you work with the main document, Word continually refers to the attached data file to ensure that the merge fields you insert in the main document match the names in the header record (or attached header file). If you have converted the data file from another file format and don't expect the data to change, it's best to save the converted copy of the file to disk. That way, Word can refer to the information in the data file more quickly. If you do not save the converted file, Word automatically reconverts the file from its original format each time you open the main document to which the file is attached. This may cause delays in the case of very large data files. However, you may want to do this if the data changes frequently and you always want to merge the latest data.

Use Database Management Tools to Link the Data File

If you expect the information in your data file to change frequently, you can link a copy of the file to its source application. When the original data changes, your copy in Word is automatically updated. However, to use the data file for merging documents in Word, you cannot use the Paste Special command on the Edit menu—the usual method of linking.

To link the data file, you first create a new data file based on the DATAFILE.DOT template. Basing your data file on the template makes the Database Management Tools command available on the Tools menu. From the File menu, choose the New command; select the DATAFILE template, and choose the OK button. In the dialog box, choose the Link to Ext. Database button. Word displays a series of dialog boxes that guide you through linking the selected data file. For more information about the DATAFILE.DOT template, see "Editing a Data File," earlier in this chapter.

Creating a Header Record for an Existing Data File

If the data file you convert to Word doesn't contain a header record, you must add a header record to the data file or create a separate header file that contains the header record.

If you use a separate header file, you can use the same header record and field names for merging data from various sources without having to repeat or change the header record in each data file. For example, you may frequently use data converted from a database. Although you can reference the database for use as your print merge data file, you may not be able to make changes to it to define a header record with the field names you want to use. You can create a header file to define the field names to correspond with the information in the database.

The header record must contain the same number of field names as there are fields in the data file. Therefore, all data files used with a particular header file must contain the same number of fields.

If you've already inserted merge field names in the main document to which you attached the header file, the field names in the header record must match the merge field names in the main document. Make sure you delete any empty paragraphs before the header record and after the data records.

You also can use a data file that contains a header record as a header file. For example, if you've broken up your data into several documents, you can define the field names in a header record in the first data file. When you're merging from other data files that don't have a header record, attach the first data file as the header file. Then attach each of the remaining data files in turn. Word uses only the header record of the first data file, ignoring all of the data records in the file.

Note When using a header file to define the merge field names, make sure you attach the header file to the main document *before* you attach the data file. Otherwise, Word interprets the first record in the data file as the header record. The field information in the data record most likely does not qualify as valid merge field names. If you get a message to that effect after attaching the data file without a header record, choose Print Merge from the File menu, and choose the Remove Attachments button. Attach the header file to the main document, and then reattach the data file.

To create and attach a new header file

1 Make sure the main document is the active document.

2 From the File menu, choose Print Merge (ALT, F, M).

3 In the Print Merge Setup dialog box, choose the Attach Header File button.

4 In the Attach Header File dialog box, choose the Create Header File button.

5 In the Create Header File dialog box, type the name of each field in the Field Name box, and then choose the Add button.

   Field names can have as many as 32 letters, numbers, and underscore characters. The first character must be a letter. You can list the fields in any order. The order of fields in the header file does not affect the order in which you can insert the merge fields in your main document.

   To delete a field name from the list, select the field name and choose the Delete button.

6 When you've typed all the fields you want to define in the header file, choose the OK button.

   Word displays a dialog box for you to save the header file.

7 Type a name for the header file in the File Name box, and select the drive and directory where you want the header file stored. Then choose the OK button.

   Word opens a new document window and inserts a table containing one row of cells in the new data file. The field names you specified in the Create Header File dialog box are listed in the cells.

The main document you opened in step 1 remains open and is listed on the Window menu. You can now switch to the main document and insert the merge field names you've defined in the header file. For instructions on inserting the merge field names, see "Inserting Merge Fields in the Main Document," later in this chapter.

To attach an existing header file to the main document

Use these instructions if you have already created the header file.

1   Make sure the main document is the active document.

2   From the File menu, choose Print Merge (ALT, F, M).

3   In the Print Merge Setup dialog box, choose the Attach Header File button.

4   In the Attach Header File dialog box, select the name of the header file and then choose the OK button.

Word displays the print merge bar at the top of the main document window and adds the name of the new header file on the right end of the bar. You can now insert the field names you've defined in the data file into your main document. For instructions, see "Inserting Merge Fields in the Main Document," later in this chapter.

To add a header record to an existing data file

If the data file is set up as paragraphs, you can insert a new paragraph at the beginning of the data file and type the field names, using tabs or commas to separate the fields. Use the following procedure to insert a header record in a data file set up as a Word table. Make sure you add the header record before you attach the data file to the main document.

1   Position the insertion point in the first row of cells in the data file.

2   From the Table menu, choose Insert Cells (ALT, A, I), select the Insert Entire Row option button, and then choose the OK button.

Word inserts a new row of cells at the beginning of the table.

3   Beginning with the first cell in the row, type a field name for each field in the data file. Press TAB to move to the next cell.

4   From the File menu, choose Save (ALT, F, S) to save the data file with its new header record.

Note   If you've already inserted field names in the main document, make sure that the field names you type in the header record exactly match the field names in the main document. If the merge field names don't match the fields, Word displays a message. In the message box, choose the Use Fields In Header File button. Word then lists the merge field names from the new header record in the Insert Merge Field dialog box. In your main document, select each of the existing merge field names, including the enclosing { } or « » characters, and replace it with the appropriate merge field name from the header file.

Inserting Merge Fields in the Main Document

The main document contains the standard text, spaces, and punctuation you want printed in all versions of the merged document. To tell Word where you want variable information printed, you insert the merge field names defined in the attached data file. When you merge the main document with the data file, Word replaces the merge field names with the corresponding field information from each record in the data file. Each data record produces a unique version of the main document.

You can type the main document from scratch or use an existing document that is similar to what you want. For instance, you may have typed a letter to one of your clients and want to send the same letter to other clients. You can use the existing letter and simply attach a data file that contains your client information. Then you can replace the name, address, and other information for the first client with the appropriate merge field names from the data file.

Inserting the Merge Fields

Inserting the field names in your main document is easiest if you first create and attach your data file. You can insert the field names in the main document by selecting them in the Insert Merge Field dialog box.

If you are viewing the main document with field codes showing, merge fields are displayed as field characters enclosing the keyword MERGEFIELD, followed by a merge field name; for example, {MERGEFIELD address1}. The MERGEFIELD keyword indicates that the instruction address1 is a merge field name defined in a data file. If field results are displayed, the merge field name is enclosed in the characters « »—for example, «address1» How you view the main document doesn't affect how it's merged with the data file.

The following illustration shows the main document for a simple form letter.

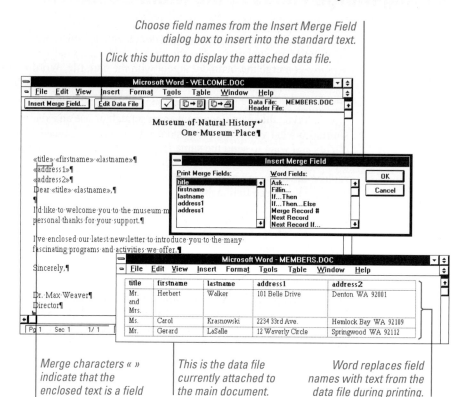

Choose field names from the Insert Merge Field dialog box to insert into the standard text.

Click this button to display the attached data file.

Merge characters « » indicate that the enclosed text is a field name, not ordinary text.

This is the data file currently attached to the main document.

Word replaces field names with text from the data file during printing.

In addition to merge field names, you can use other Word fields such as IF, ASK, and SET to control how the variable text is merged with the main document. For information about these fields, see "Using Fields in Merged Documents," later in this chapter.

Note The field characters {} begin and end any type of field you insert in a main document. These are not the regular braces on the keyboard. Word inserts the field characters for you if you insert the merge field names and other fields using the Insert Merge Field button on the print merge bar or the Field command on the Insert menu. If you type the merge field manually, you must use the Insert Field key (CTRL+F9) to insert field characters. Similarly, the merge characters « » are not characters you can insert as you do other ANSI characters; they are displayed only as the "result" of a MERGEFIELD when field codes are hidden. Selecting one field character or one merge character automatically selects the entire merge field. Therefore, you cannot delete or edit a single field character or merge character.

To insert field names in the main document

Before inserting field names in the main document, attach the data file to the main document using the Print Merge command on the File menu, as described earlier in this chapter.

1 If you haven't typed the text of the main document, type and format the standard text as you would in any Word document.

Type only the text, spaces, punctuation marks, and other information that you want printed in each version of the document.

2 Position the insertion point where you want variable information printed from the data file.

3 On the print merge bar, choose the Insert Merge Field button.

Word displays the Insert Merge Field dialog box.

4 In the Print Merge Fields box, select the merge field name, and then choose the OK button.

5 Repeat steps 2 through 4 at each location where you want information printed from the data file.

You can insert the merge field names in any order and insert the same field name more than once.

You're now ready to merge the main document and the data file. For instructions, see "Merging and Printing the Documents," later in this chapter.

To display or hide field codes

▶ From the View menu, choose Field Codes (ALT, V, C).

To insert a merge field name manually

1 From the Insert menu, choose Field (ALT, I, D).

2 In the Insert Field Type box, select Merge Field.

In the Instructions box, Word displays the merge field names defined in the data file or header file attached to the main document.

3 Select the name of the merge field that you want to insert.

4 Choose the Add button.

5 Choose the OK button.

To replace a merge field with a different merge field

1   In the main document, select the merge field name you want to replace.

Make sure you select the entire field, including the enclosing field characters {} or merge characters « », depending on whether field codes or results are displayed.

2   On the print merge bar, choose the Insert Merge Field button.

3   In the Print Merge Fields box, select the merge field you want.

4   Choose the OK button.

Tip   With field codes displayed, you can manually replace a merge field by changing the merge field name between the field characters { }. You must then update the field by pressing the Update Fields key (F9).

Formatting the Merged Information

Text merged from the data file or inserted using other Word fields takes on the formatting you apply to the corresponding field in the main document. If you want each addressee's name in a form letter to be bold, for example, just apply bold character formatting to the MERGEFIELD keyword in the merge field for the addressee in your main document. The format of the data file has no effect. You can also use general formatting switches in the merge field and other Word fields you've inserted.

To format the merged information

1   If field codes are not displayed, choose Field Codes from the View menu (ALT, V, C).

2   In the main document, select the entire field corresponding to the information you want to format.

3   Apply formatting using the ribbon, the Character command on the Format menu, or formatting key combinations.

When the main document is merged, Word formats the merged information to match the format of the first character in the field following the opening field character {.

Note   In the data file, you can type several paragraphs within a single field. When you merge the data file, the last paragraph in the field takes the style of the paragraph containing the merge field name in the main document. All other paragraphs in the field take Normal style; however, Word automatically changes the formatting of these paragraphs—"on top" of their Normal style, so to speak—so that they match the appearance of the last paragraph.

Switching Data Files

You can attach a different data file to a main document. However, if the newly attached data file contains field names different from those inserted in the main document, you must either change the field names in the header record to match the field names in the main document or replace the field names in the main document.

To attach a different data file to the main document

1 In the main document, double-click the Data File: *DOCUMENT NAME* label toward the right end of the print merge bar.
   –or–
   From the File menu, choose Print Merge (ALT, F, M).

2 Choose the Attach Data File button.

3 Do one of the following:

   ■ Under File Name, select the data file you want to attach, and then choose the OK button.

   ■ Choose the Create Data File button to create and attach a new data file. For instructions on creating the data file, see "Creating and Attaching a Data File," earlier in this chapter.

4 If the merge field names in the new data file do not match those already inserted in the main document, Word displays a message. Do one of the following:

To	Do this
Replace the merge fields in the main document with new merge fields from the selected data file	Choose the Use Fields In Data File button. In the main document, select each merge field and replace it with a field from the new data file using the Insert Merge Fields dialog box.
Change the merge field names in the header record of the data file to match those used in the main document	Choose the Cancel button. On the print merge bar, choose the Edit Data File button to display the attached data file.
Select a different data file	Choose the Switch/Locate Data File button. Then select a different data file.

Removing the Attached Data File or Header File

If you no longer want to use a document as a main document, you can remove the attached data or header file to make it an ordinary Word document. You might also want to remove the existing data or header file so that you can attach a different one.

Note that removing the data or header file doesn't remove the merge field names you've inserted in the main document. If you plan to attach a different data or header file, make sure that the merge field names in the main document match those in the new data or header file.

To remove the attached data or header file

Make sure the main document is active.

1 From the File menu, choose Print Merge (ALT, F, M).

2 Choose the Remove Attachments button.

Word displays a message asking if you want to make your main document a normal document.

To do this	Choose this button
Remove the currently specified data and header file, making the main document an ordinary Word document	Yes
Close the message box and leave the data and header files attached	No
Display Help	Help

Merging and Printing the Documents

Once you've attached the data file to the main document and inserted the merge field names, you can do one of the following:

- Merge the main document and data file, and print each resulting merged document.

- Merge the main document and data file, and store the resulting documents in a new document called Form Letters1. You can view each version of the merged document on-screen and check formatting, spacing, and other details. You can save the Form Letters1 document and print it later, using the Print command on the File menu.

- Have Word check the main document and data file and alert you to errors. For example, Word notifies you if the main document contains a merge field name that is not defined in the attached data file.

You can merge the documents by choosing the Print Merge command on the File menu or clicking the appropriate button on the print merge bar.

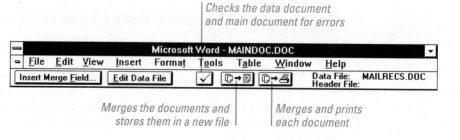

Checks the data document and main document for errors

Merges the documents and stores them in a new file

Merges and prints each document

The print merge bar

The first time you merge the main document with the data file, it's best to use the Print Merge command. You can select options to prevent blank lines in the merged documents caused by empty fields in the data file. You can also select the records you want to merge with the main document. For example, you can choose to merge only the data records having the value "NY" specified in the state merge field.

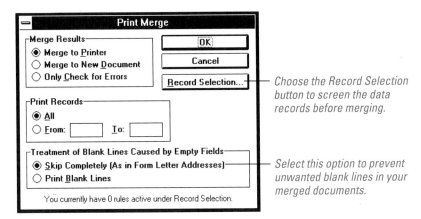

— *Choose the Record Selection button to screen the data records before merging.*

— *Select this option to prevent unwanted blank lines in your merged documents.*

The Print Merge dialog box is displayed when you choose the Merge button in the Print Merge Setup dialog box.

The merge options you select are stored with your main document. Until you select new options, Word continues using the current options when merging that main document with any data file, whether you choose the Print Merge command or click a button on the print merge bar.

Tip If you prefer, you can merge only one type of data record. First, sort the data records to group them according to selected field information, such as postal code or last name. You can then merge only the range of records having the information you want. This technique is useful if you want to merge the records in a particular order. For instructions on sorting entries in a table, see Chapter 15, "Sorting."

To merge the main document and data file

Unless you choose otherwise, Word merges each record in the data file with the main document. The records are merged in the order in which they occur in the data file. Before merging, close all files you are not using. This ensures that Word has enough memory for merging your documents.

1 Make sure the main document is the active document and the data file is attached to it.

   You don't need to open the data file.

2 From the File menu, choose Print Merge (ALT, F, M).

   Word displays the first Print Merge Setup dialog box.

3 Choose the Merge button to display the Print Merge dialog box.

4 Under Print Records, select the All option button to print all records, or specify the range of record numbers in the From and To boxes.
   –or–
   To select the criteria that each data record must meet to be merged, choose the Record Selection button. For instructions on selecting the criteria, see "Selecting Data Records to Merge," later in this chapter.

5 By default, Word deletes any blank lines in the merged documents caused by empty fields in the data records. If you want blank lines in your document, select the Print Blank Lines option button. For more information, see "Controlling Blank Lines," later in this chapter.

6 Under Merge Results, select the merge option you want.

To	Select this option button
Send the merge results directly to the printer	Merge To Printer
Merge the data file and the main document into a new document without printing	Merge To New Document
Check for errors without merging the data file and the main document	Only Check For Errors

7 Choose the OK button.

Controlling Blank Lines

Unless you clear the Skip Completely option button in the Print Merge dialog box, Word deletes blank lines in your merged documents that are caused by empty merge fields. Deleting the blank lines is useful when you are merging documents such as form letters and mailing labels and the amount of address information varies from letter to letter. For example, in addition to a street number and name, some records may include a post office box or building name and suite number.

The following illustration on the left shows merge field names inserted in a main document for a form letter. The illustration on the right shows a letter printed from a data record that has no company name specified in the «company» field, only one line for the street address in the «address1» field, and nothing in the «address2» field.

```
«title» «firstname» «lastname»
«company»
«address1»
«address2»
«city» «state» «postcode»

Dear «title» «lastname»,
```

```
Mr. Joseph Berger
1818 S. W. 70th Blvd.
South City NY 00154

Dear Mr. Berger,
```

Treatment of empty fields with the Skip Completely option button selected

Word deletes lines caused by empty merge fields if the merge field name in the main document is in a paragraph containing no other printable text. Word also omits a paragraph if the only other text in the paragraph is a space or punctuation mark. For example, if in the above example the «city», «state», and «postcode» fields are empty, Word omits the paragraph containing the comma and spaces between the field names.

If the empty merge field is contained in a table in the main document, Word deletes the paragraph in the cell containing the merge field but does not delete the cell itself.

In certain cases, you may want to allow blank lines. To do so, you insert the merge field name in a paragraph with other text. Instead of pressing ENTER to start new lines in the paragraph, use line breaks (SHIFT+ENTER). As long as the other lines of the paragraph contain text—not just punctuation or spaces—Word leaves the blank line in the paragraph.

To leave all blank lines wherever they occur, select the Print Blank Lines option button. If a merge field for a particular data record is empty, no information is printed in place of the merge field name you insert in the main document. However, if the merge field name is in a paragraph by itself followed by no other printable text in the paragraph, the paragraph mark is still inserted in each version of the merged document, causing a blank line.

Selecting Data Records to Merge

In addition to specifying the range of records to merge, you can select the data records that meet the criteria you specify. For example, you can merge only data records having "98100" in the «postcode» field. All data records not meeting the criteria, or rules, you set are skipped.

When setting a record selection rule, you specify the following information:

- A merge field name corresponding to a merge field in the attached data file

- A comparison phrase, such as "Equal To" or "Not Blank"

- A value with which the information in the merge field is compared

The record selection rules are stored with the main document. Word follows these rules each time it merges the main document. You can delete rules or select new rules to merge a different set of data records.

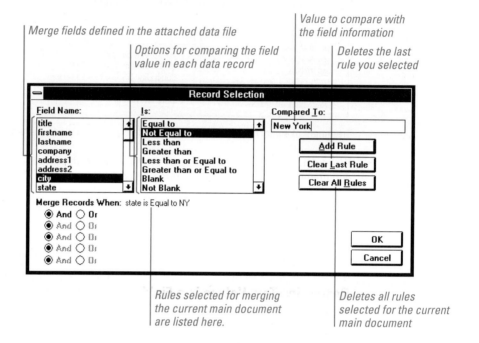

Merge fields defined in the attached data file

Value to compare with the field information

Options for comparing the field value in each data record

Deletes the last rule you selected

Rules selected for merging the current main document are listed here.

Deletes all rules selected for the current main document

To select criteria for merging data records

1   From the File menu, choose Print Merge (ALT, F, M).

2   Choose the Merge button, and select the merge options as described in the procedure "To merge the main document and data file," earlier in this chapter.

3   Choose the Record Selection button.

Word displays the Record Selection dialog box.

4   In the Field Name box, select the field name you want Word to examine.

5   In the Is box, select the rule that indicates how you want the value for the field compared in each data record.

6   In the Compared To box, type the text or number that you want compared with the field value.

The value can be text or numbers, including numbers with decimal points. If you type text, use uppercase and lowercase letters as appropriate.

The Compared To box is unavailable if you've selected Blank or Not Blank in step 5.

7 Choose the Add Rule button.

Word displays the selected field and compared value in the list following Merge Records When. The Compared To box is cleared so you can type different information for the next rule.

8 If you want to select additional rules, first select the next available And or Or option button.

For instructions on using And and Or, see "Selecting Multiple Rules," later in this chapter.

9 Repeat steps 4 through 8 for each rule you want to select.

You can select the same merge field more than once to compare it with different values. If you want to select additional rules later, open the Record Selection dialog box and repeat steps 8 and 9.

To delete selection rules

▶ In the Record Selection dialog box, choose the Clear Last Rule button to delete the last rule specified in the Merge Records When list.

–Or–

▶ Choose the Clear All Rules button to delete all selection rules.

Comparing Text Values in a Field

When evaluating a field that contains text, Word compares the sort order of the sequence of characters based on the ANSI International sorting order. The text "apple" is considered less than the word "berry" because, alphabetically, "apple" precedes "berry."

If you want, for example, to send a form letter only to members of your organization whose last names begin with "A" through "L," select the field containing the last name from the Field Name box in the Record Selection dialog box. (The last name must be contained in a separate field, or else it must precede the first name in the field.) Select Less Than in the Is box, and then type the letter **M** in the Compared To box. Any name beginning with "A" through "L" is considered less than "M," and so the data records containing those names are selected for merging.

Selecting Multiple Rules

You can use the And and Or options to link together up to six selection rules, enabling you to zero in on the records you want to merge.

- Select And to link multiple rules that must all be met. When you use And between two selection rules, Word selects only those records that satisfy both rules. Each additional rule you link using And eliminates more of the records from the data file, enabling you to select the particular records you need.

- Select Or to choose from among several selection rules. When you use Or between two selection rules, Word selects any record that satisfies at least one of the rules. If a record doesn't satisfy the first rule you select, it may satisfy the second or third.

You can use And and Or separately or in combination. Because the And operator takes precedence over Or, Word evaluates the rules or series of rules you connect using And before the rules connected using Or. How you connect the rules with And or Or affects which data records are merged.

Suppose you want to send a form letter to all residents of Tucson and Phoenix, Arizona. You select the following rules:

state Is Equal To AZ
And city Is Equal To Tucson
Or state Is Equal To AZ
And city Is Equal To Phoenix

With these rules, Word determines if the addressee in the current data record lives in Tucson, Arizona. Word then evaluates the next set of rules connected by And and, last, the set of rules connected by Or. Letters are sent only to residents of Arizona who live in Tucson or Phoenix.

Notice that the following set of rules would not produce the same result:

state Is Equal To AZ
And city Is Equal To Tucson
Or city Is Equal To Phoenix

Because And takes precedence, the first set of rules connected by And selects records for addressees who live in Tucson, Arizona. However, the rule following Or also selects records for residents in any city named Phoenix—including those in cities named Phoenix not in Arizona.

You can also use And and Or operators to compare the selected merge field with a range of values rather than a single value. For example, if you select the following rules, Word merges all data records having a value of 98001 through 98500 in the «postcode» field.

postcode Is Greater Than Or Equal To 98001
And postcode Is Less Than Or Equal To 98500

Use a Main Document Template to Store Rules

If you frequently create similar types of merged documents, you can save time and work by creating a template. New main documents you base on the template will contain the standard text, merge field names, and other information you specify in the template, and you can use the glossaries and macros you define for the template. In addition, record selection rules you specify for the template will be used in all new main documents you create from the template—you don't have to select new rules for each document. The template also stores the option you select to control blank lines. You can change the selection rules for a particular main document without affecting the standard rules stored with the template.

For more information about creating and using templates, see Chapter 37, "Document Templates."

Using Fields in Merged Documents

In addition to the merge field names from the attached data file or header file, you can insert other types of fields in the main document. These fields act as special commands that tell Word how you want a particular main document merged with the variable text from the data file.

- Use IF fields to print additional text in a merged document only if one or more conditions you specify are met. For example, in letters to clients who live in a certain postal code area, you can include information about special fire insurance rates.

- Use ASK, FILLIN, QUOTE, and SET fields to print variable information that is not defined in a data file. The ASK and FILLIN fields instruct Word to prompt you for text you want to be different in each merged document. Use SET and QUOTE fields to repeat the same text in each document.

- MERGEREC inserts the record number of the data record that is merged to produce a particular version of a merged document.

- Use NEXT fields to print information from different data records in the same merged document. For example, you can print several addresses on one sheet of mailing labels.

- Use SKIPIF fields to skip merging a data record if it does not meet the criteria you specify. Use NEXTIF fields to merge both the current record and the next record if the current record does meet the conditions.

This section describes how to use these fields to personalize the text in a merged document. For general information on the use of fields, see Chapter 41, "Fields." For information on specific fields and the switches available for modifying them, see the topic for each field in online Help.

The easiest way to insert the fields is to select the appropriate option from the Word Fields box in the Insert Merge Field dialog box. In some fields, you must replace the sample text with your own information.

Important

The following fields used in merging documents are listed differently in the Insert Merge Field dialog box (which you open from the print merge bar) and the Field dialog box (which you open from the Insert menu).

To select this field	In the Insert Merge Field dialog box, select this option	In the Field dialog box, select this option
IF	If...Then *or* If...Then...Else	If
MERGEREC	Merge Record #	Merge Rec.
NEXT	Next Record	Next
NEXTIF	Next Record If	Next If
SET	Set Bookmark	Set
SKIPIF	Skip Record If	Skip If

Select the field options from this list.

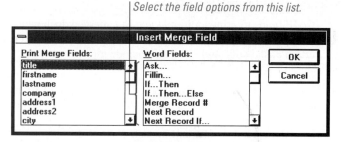

Insert Merge Field dialog box

To insert a field

If field codes are not displayed, choose Field Codes from the View menu (ALT, V, C). With field codes displayed, you can see the complete field information in your main document. When you merge the main document, Word carries out the field instructions. The fields themselves are printed.

1   In the main document, position the insertion point where you want to insert the field.

2   On the print merge bar, choose the Insert Merge Field button.

3   In the Word Fields box, select the option designating the field you want inserted, and then choose the OK button.

4   If the field contains sample text, select each word of sample text and replace it with the indicated information.

If sample text is enclosed in quotation marks, make sure you leave the quotation marks around your own information. Use spaces between the information as indicated in the sample field.

If you insert a FILLIN field, for example, Word inserts the field in the following form:

`{FILLIN "Prompt"}`

To complete the field, select the word `Prompt` and then type your own prompt text between the quotation marks.

`{FILLIN "Please enter the name of the policyholder:"}`

For more information about fields, see Chapter 41, "Fields."

For details on replacing the sample text for each field, see the descriptions and examples of the fields later in this chapter.

Note   SET, ASK, NEXT, and other fields are not printed in the main document; however, inserting a field on a line by itself can produce a blank line in the resulting merged documents. For ways to prevent blank lines, see Chapter 34, "Form Letters and Other Merged Documents."

Using the IF Field: If...Then and IF...Then...Else

The statement "If the weather is sunny, we'll go to the park" identifies a condition that must be met (the weather being sunny) for a certain action to take place (going to the park). You can use an IF field in a similar way to control how text is printed in a particular version of a merged document.

An example of an IF field is shown in the following illustration. As each record from the data file is merged with the main document, Word examines the value of the amount merge field in the record. If the value is greater than 50, additional text is printed in the merged document. If the value is 50 or less, the text is omitted.

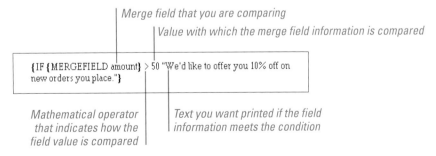

Elements of an IF field

You can also specify the text you want to print if the condition is not met. In the statement "If the weather is sunny, we'll go to the park; if not, we'll go to a movie," an alternative activity is proposed in case the weather isn't sunny. From the preceding illustration, suppose that you want to print different text if the amount field value is 50 or less. You can specify the alternative text to be printed as shown in the following illustration.

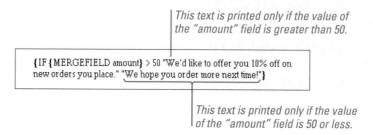

This text is printed only if the value of the "amount" field is greater than 50.

{IF {MERGEFIELD amount} > 50 "We'd like to offer you 10% off on new orders you place." "We hope you order more next time!"}

This text is printed only if the value of the "amount" field is 50 or less.

IF field with alternative text specified if condition is not met

To specify a condition, you can use Expression (=) fields, bookmarks, and other fields within the IF field.

To specify a condition in an IF field

1 In the main document, position the insertion point where you want to print the text you specify in the IF field.

2 On the print merge bar, choose the Insert Merge Field button. Select one of the following options from the Word Fields box, and then choose the OK button.

Select this option	To insert the IF field in the following form
If…Then	{IF Exp Op Exp "TextIfTrue"}
If…Then…Else	{IF Exp Op Exp "TextIfTrue" "TextIfFalse"}

3 In the IF field, select the first Exp, and then do one of the following:

- Insert a merge field that you want to evaluate. To insert the merge field, choose the Insert Merge Field button on the print merge bar; then, in the Print Merge Fields box, select the merge field, and choose the OK button.

- Insert a bookmark that you want to evaluate. The bookmark can be one you defined by choosing Bookmark from the Insert menu or in an ASK or SET field inserted earlier in the main document. To insert the bookmark field, delete Exp, press CTRL+F9, and then type the name of the bookmark between the field characters {}.

- Insert an Expression (=) field to compute a numeric value.

4 To specify the mathematical operator, select Op, and type one of the following operators.

Operator	Function
=	Equals a specified number or exactly matches a sequence of text characters
<	Is less than
<=	Is less than or equal to
>	Is greater than
>=	Is greater than or equal to
<>	Is not equal to a number or does not match a sequence of characters

If you use the operators >, =>, <, or <= when evaluating a merge field that contains text, Word compares the sort order of the sequence of characters, based on the ANSI International sorting order. For example, the text "apple" is considered less than the word "berry" because, alphabetically, "apple" precedes "berry."

5 Select the second Exp, and do one of the following:

- Type a number or sequence of text characters you want to compare with the value of the merge field specified in step 3. Make sure you enclose the text or numbers in quotation marks. Type empty quotation marks "" to indicate a null or "blank" value.

  If you are comparing text, make sure there are no extra spaces between the quotation marks; otherwise, the spaces are considered part of the text compared with the field value.

- Insert a merge field or bookmark as described in step 3. Word compares the value of this field with the value of the item you specified in step 3.

6 Select the sample text "TextIfTrue" and type the text you want to print if the condition is met. Make sure you do not delete the quotation marks enclosing the text.

If you inserted an If...Then...Else field, select "TextIfFalse" and type the text you want printed if the condition is not met. Make sure you don't delete the quotation marks.

You can also insert another field in place of the sample text to specify the text you want to be printed.

The following examples illustrate some uses of IF instructions. The examples are shown as they appear with field codes displayed.

```
{IF {rate} <= "10%" "We'll offer you a larger discount."}
```

If the value of the rate bookmark is 10 percent or less, the specified text ("We'll offer you a larger discount.") is printed. The bookmark must be one you defined using the Bookmark command on the Insert menu or in an ASK or SET field inserted earlier in the main document.

```
{IF {MERGEFIELD rate} = {MERGEFIELD discount} "We'll offer you a larger discount."}
```

This example compares the value of the rate merge field with the value of the discount merge field. If the values are identical, the specified text is printed.

```
{IF {MERGEFIELD company} <>"" "{MERGEFIELD company_address}"
"{MERGEFIELD home_address}"}
```

If the company merge field for a data record contains any information—that is, the field is not empty—text from the company_address merge field is printed. Otherwise, if the company merge field is empty, then text from the home_address merge field is printed. To test that a merge field is not blank, use the <> operator and the empty quotation marks "" as shown.

```
{IF {MERGEFIELD business_address} = "" "{MERGEFIELD home_address}"}
```

If the business_address merge field is empty, indicated by the = operator and empty quotation marks "", text from the home_address merge field is printed.

```
{IF {= {MERGEFIELD balance}-{MERGEFIELD payment}}> 0 "Your current
balance is {= {MERGEFIELD balance}-{MERGEFIELD payment}}." "Your account
is paid in full. Thank you."}
```

An Expression field, indicated by the = within the second opening field character, is used to compute the current balance of each account. The value of the payment merge field is subtracted from the value of the balance merge field. If the result is greater than zero, a balance remains, and the expression field is repeated in the text that reports the current balance. If the computed balance is 0 or less, the second set of text ("Your account is paid in full.") is printed.

```
{IF {MERGEFIELD loan_rate} >= {= {current_rate}+ 2.0} "You may want to
consider refinancing your loan."}
```

In the preceding example, the IF field determines whether a customer's interest rate on a loan is significantly higher than the current interest rate. The expression field adds two interest points to the value assigned to the bookmark current_rate. If the value of the loan_rate merge field is greater than or equal to the resulting sum, the specified text ("You may want to consider refinancing your loan.") is printed.

Comparing the Contents of a Merge Field with Text

When you compare the value of a merge field or bookmark with text, the pattern of uppercase and lowercase letters in the text is significant.

For example, suppose the `product_code` field of a record in your data file contained the code 2301xl. If you compare the field with 2301XL, as shown in the following example, Word doesn't consider the code a match, and the text specified in the IF field isn't printed.

```
{IF {MERGEFIELD product_code} = "2301XL" "We regret we are out of stock
for this item."}
```

You may not know how text in a particular field was typed in the data file. To make sure that a text comparison is valid, you can use switches in the IF field to compare the text using a specific pattern of capitalization. In the following example, the general format switch * caps is used to evaluate the value in the country field as though each word in the field has an initial capital letter:

```
{IF \* caps {mergefield country} = "United Kingdom" "We can offer
special rates on travel to the British Isles."}
```

Use this switch	To evaluate the field information as
* upper	All uppercase letters (UNITED KINGDOM)
* lower	All lowercase letters (united kingdom)
* firstcap	First word having an initial capital letter (United kingdom)
* caps	All words having initial capital letters (United Kingdom)

Using Fields to Specify the Text to Be Printed

Instead of typing the text you want to be printed, you can replace the sample text "TextIfTrue" and "TextIfFalse" in the IF field with other fields to insert various types of information.

In the following example, an INCLUDE field is used to insert the contents of the indicated document if the condition is met.

```
{IF {MERGEFIELD state} = "NY" "{INCLUDE c:\\worddocs\\contract.doc}"}
```

Note If the document you specify in the INCLUDE field contains a table created using the Insert Table command on the Table menu, the table will not be displayed in the resulting merged documents.

You can also use GLOSSARY fields to insert text assigned to glossary entries. The glossary entry must be defined in the global document template or in the template used to create the main document.

Before merging the main document, make sure you update the GLOSSARY field. Position the insertion point in the GLOSSARY field anywhere between the field characters { }, and then press the Update Fields key (F9).

In the following example, a GLOSSARY field is used to print the text assigned to the glossary entry copyrt1 if the condition is met. If the condition is not met, text assigned to the glossary entry copyrt2 is printed.

```
{IF {MERGEFIELD state}= "NY" "{GLOSSARY copyrt1}" "{GLOSSARY copyrt2}"}
```

Setting Multiple Conditions in an IF Field

In an IF instruction, you can specify multiple conditions by nesting IF fields. You can require that all conditions or any one condition that you specify be met in order for the text you specify to be printed.

In the following example, both conditions specified in the IF fields must be met. The second IF field is inserted in place of the "TextIfTrue" sample text of the first IF field. If the condition specified in the first IF field is met, the second IF field is carried out. If this second condition is also met, Word prints the text specified in the second IF field. Therefore, the text is printed only in reply to orders for the specified item in the color red. Note that each IF field must end with a closing field character }.

```
{IF {MERGEFIELD item_number} = "2301XL" {IF {MERGEFIELD color}= "RED"
"We regret we are out of stock for this item."}}
```

In the next example, the text is printed only in letters sent to residents of New York state who do not live in New York City.

```
{IF {MERGEFIELD state} = "NY" {IF {MERGEFIELD city} <> "New York" "Have
you ever visited New York City?"}}
```

If only one of two or more conditions must be met, insert an IF field (If...Then...) specifying the first condition. Replace the "TextIfTrue" sample text in the first IF field. Then insert a second If...Then... clause just before the field character } closing the first IF field. In the following example, if any one of the conditions is met, the text in the appropriate IF field is printed. Otherwise, if the state field specifies a state other than California, Oregon, or Washington, no text is printed.

```
{IF {MERGEFIELD state} = "CA" "For California residents, we offer
special rates to the Near East and Japan." {IF {MERGEFIELD state} = "OR"
"For Oregon residents, we offer special rates to the Near East and
Japan." {IF {MERGEFIELD state}= "WA" "For Washington residents, we offer
special rates to the Near East and Japan."}}}
```

Using IF Fields to Prevent Blank Lines

If you insert a field such as a bookmark on a line by itself in the main document and no information is printed to replace the field, a blank line will appear in the resulting merged document. In cases like this, you can use IF fields to prevent the blank lines. Note that IF fields aren't necessary in the case of empty merge fields in the data file. You can simply select the Skip Completely option button in the Print Merge dialog box when you merge the main document.

Suppose you are sending a form letter to a number of people whom you don't plan to contact again. Instead of storing the names and addresses in a data file, you can use ASK fields to prompt you to enter the names and addresses as each copy of the letter is merged and printed. (For more information about ASK fields, see "Using the ASK, FILLIN, QUOTE, and SET fields," later in this chapter.) In the inside address and salutation of the main document, you insert the appropriate bookmarks where you want the name and address information printed. For some addresses, you may not have information to assign to a particular bookmark—for example, all addresses may not include a business name or second line of street address information. To prevent blank lines in the letter caused by the empty bookmarks, you can insert the bookmarks in an IF field, as shown in the following illustration.

The closing quotation marks and field character ending the IF field are placed on the next line.

```
{name}¶
 {IF·{company}·<>·""·"{company}¶
{"}{address1}¶
 {IF·{address2}·<>·""·"{address2}¶
{"}{city}···{state}···{postcode}¶
```

These paragraph marks are skipped if the "company" and "address2" fields are empty.

When you press ENTER following the bookmark fields {company} and {street2}, paragraph marks are inserted in your main document within the quotation marks of the IF field. They will start new lines in the resulting letter only if you've assigned information to the company and street2 bookmarks for that version of the letter. If you didn't assign information to the bookmarks, Word skips to the next field following the field character for each IF field.

You can also include line breaks, page breaks, and section breaks in the text you specify in the IF field. As with ordinary text, the break character is inserted only if the condition is met.

Using the ASK, FILLIN, QUOTE, and SET Fields

You can use ASK, FILLIN, QUOTE, and SET fields to print variable information that is not defined in a data file.

- Use ASK and FILLIN to print different information in each version of the merged document. In ASK and FILLIN fields, you specify the prompt text that you want displayed. As each data record is merged with the main document, Word displays the prompt in a dialog box so you can enter the information you want in a particular version of the merged document.

- Use SET and QUOTE fields to print the same information in all versions of the merged document. You specify the text to be printed within the field.

ASK and SET fields define bookmarks. Bookmarks are simply names that stand for any text, number, or graphic that you assign to them. To print in each merged document the information you assign to the bookmark, you insert a bookmark field in the standard text of the main document. You can insert the bookmark field as many times as you like. The SET or ASK field defining a bookmark must be placed before the first bookmark field in the main document.

Using SET and ASK, you can refer to the value you assign the bookmark by inserting the bookmark field within other fields. In the following example, the IF field compares the value assigned to the bookmark `current_rate` with the value of the merge field `interest`.

```
{SET current_rate "9.8"}

{IF {MERGEFIELD interest} > {current_rate} "You may want to consider
refinancing your loan."}
```

Unlike SET and ASK, FILLIN and QUOTE fields do not define a bookmark. You insert FILLIN and QUOTE fields in the main document text where you want the information you specify to be printed. Use FILLIN or QUOTE fields when you want to print information only once in the document.

Consider the following illustration. In the main document, an ASK field defines the bookmark `contact`. A SET field is used to specify the text of the current month's special promotion. When you merge this main document with the data file, Word displays a prompt asking for the name of the contact before merging each data record. The name you enter in response to each prompt is printed in the appropriate letter wherever you've inserted the bookmark contact. The text you assign the bookmark special in the SET field is repeated in each letter. The FILLIN field allows you to add different remarks in each letter.

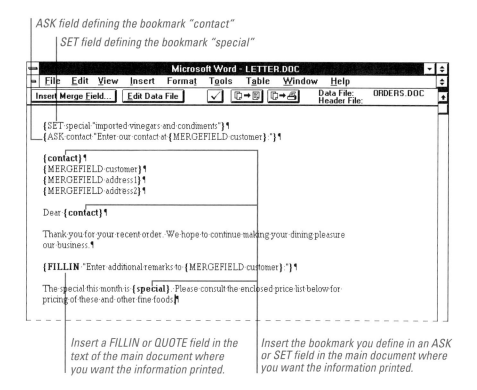

Main document with ASK, SET, and FILLIN fields (field codes showing)

The following illustration shows the resulting text printed in each version of the letter.

*A different name replaces the {contact}
bookmark in each version of the letter.*

Mr Lemond
First Restaurant Group
121 Column St.
Seattle WA 98111

Dear **Mr Lemond**:

Thank you for your recent order. We hope to continue making your dining pleasure our business.

You'll be happy to know we've lowered our prices on our entire line of pasta products. We offer only premium 100% semolina pasta.

The special this month is **imported vinegars and condiments**. Please consult the enclosed price list below for pricing of these and other fine foods.

Ms. Waites
Alice's Restaurants
95 38th St.
San Jose CA 95112

Dear **Ms. Waites**:

Thank you for your recent order. We hope to continue making your dining pleasure our business.

Did you know we now supply organically grown herbs, wheat grass, and other produce? We can promise delivery in your area the next business day.

The special this month is **imported vinegars and condiments**. Please consult the enclosed price list below for pricing of these and other fine foods.

Mr Perri
Francie's, Inc
123 Main St.
Portland OR 97405

Dear **Mr. Perri**:

Thank you for your recent order. We hope to continue making your dining pleasure our business.

In your order, you asked about Middle Eastern foods. We now have suppliers for an expanded line of products from Italy, Greece, and the Middle East.

The special this month is **imported vinegars and condiments**. Please consult the enclosed price list below for pricing of these and other fine foods.

*Text you type in response
to the FILLIN prompt
personalizes each letter.*

*The same product special is printed in place of the
{special} bookmark, which was defined using SET.*

To insert a bookmark field

After you define a bookmark in an ASK or SET field, use this procedure to insert the bookmark name in the text of your main document. You can insert the bookmark field anywhere in the main document following the ASK or SET field defining the bookmark.

1   Position the insertion point where you want to print the information you assign to the bookmark.

2   Press CTRL+F9 to insert a pair of field characters to enclose the bookmark name.

3   Between the field characters, type the name of the bookmark you defined in the SET or ASK field.

    To ensure that the bookmark name matches the name in the ASK or SET field, you can copy the bookmark name and paste it between the field characters.

Inserting ASK and FILLIN Fields

Selecting Ask or Fillin from the Insert Merge Field dialog box inserts an ASK or FILLIN field in the following form:

```
{ASK Bookmark "Prompt"}
{FILLIN "Prompt"}
```

In an ASK field, you replace `Bookmark` with a bookmark name. In both ASK and FILLIN fields, you replace `Prompt` with the prompt text you want displayed as each record of the data file is merged with the main document. Make sure you don't delete the quotation marks enclosing the prompt text. When you merge the data file with the main document, Word displays the prompt in a dialog box so you can type your response.

Type your response to the prompt here and press ENTER.

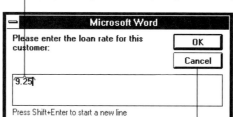

Choose the Cancel button if you don't want any information printed for the current version of the merged document.

In the case of an ASK field, the information you type in response to the prompt is assigned to a bookmark. Make sure to insert the bookmark field where you want to print the information in each merged document. In the case of FILLIN fields, your response is printed where you inserted the FILLIN field in your main document.

The following are examples of ASK and FILLIN fields.

```
{ASK client_name "Please enter the client's name:"}
```

When you merge the main document with the data file, the specified prompt is displayed before each data record is merged with the main document. The name you type in response to the prompt—maximum 255 characters—is assigned to the bookmark `client_name`. You can specify a different name for each version of the merged document.

```
{FILLIN "Please enter the client's name:"}
```

The text you type in response to each prompt replaces the FILLIN field in the current version of the merged document.

```
{ASK rate "Enter the current interest rate:" \o}
```

By specifying the \o switch in the field, you can have Word display the specified prompt once before the first document in the series is merged. The information you type in response to the prompt is printed in place of the bookmark rate in all versions of the merged document. You can also use the \o switch in a FILLIN field.

```
{ASK time "Please enter the appointment date and time for {MERGEFIELD
patient_name}:"}
```

In the preceding example, a merge field name is included in the prompt text to iden-tify the person for whom the date is specified. The merge field is from the data file attached to the main document. When the prompt is displayed, the name of the patient is displayed in place of the merge field patient_name. You can also include a book-mark field in the prompt text. You must have previously defined the bookmark name using the Bookmark command on the Insert menu or in an ASK or SET field inserted in the main document.

Inserting SET and QUOTE Fields

Selecting Set Bookmark or Quote in the Insert Merge Field dialog box inserts the selected field in the following form:

```
{SET Bookmark "Data"}
{QUOTE "Data"}
```

In a SET field, you replace Bookmark with a bookmark name. In both SET and QUOTE fields, you replace Data with the text or numbers you want printed in all versions of the merged document. Make sure you don't delete the quotation marks enclosing your data.

In the case of a SET field, the information you specify in place of Data is assigned to the bookmark. Make sure you insert the bookmark field where you want to print the information in each merged document. In the case of a QUOTE field, the information is printed where you insert the QUOTE field in your main document.

The following are examples of SET and QUOTE fields.

```
{SET bonus_offer "10% off your next order"}
```

The preceding example sets the bonus_offer bookmark to the specified text.

```
{SET rate "25.3"}
```

The preceding example sets the rate bookmark to the specified number.

```
{SET rate "{= {cost} * 10%}"}
```

This example assigns to the `rate` bookmark a value that is 10 percent of the value of the `cost` bookmark. The value is calculated using an Expression (=) field. The `cost` bookmark must be defined using the Bookmark command on the Insert menu or in an ASK or SET field inserted before the SET field defining `rate`.

```
{QUOTE "The current fee for accounts of this type is {={rate} *
{account_typeA}}"}
```

An Expression (=) field is used in the QUOTE field to compute the value that is printed with the other information in quotation marks. `Rate` and `account_typeA` are bookmarks.

Using the NEXT Field: Next Record If

The NEXT field tells Word to print information from the next data record without starting a new version of the merged document.

Suppose you want to print a list of the names, addresses, and phone numbers of the members in your organization. You've stored the membership information in a data file. In the main document, you fill one page with sets of the merge field names from the data file. You insert a NEXT field before each set of field names, beginning with the second set. When you merge the main document, Word prints the information from each successive data record on the same page instead of producing a separate merged document from each data record.

```
{MERGEFIELD name}          {MERGEFIELD address}      {MERGEFIELD phone}
{NEXT}{MERGEFIELD name}    {MERGEFIELD address}      {MERGEFIELD phone}
{NEXT}{MERGEFIELD name}    {MERGEFIELD address}      {MERGEFIELD phone}
```

Tip By inserting a NEXT field at the end of the main document, you can print all even- or odd-numbered records in your data file. When you merge the documents, Word merges the next record in the data file. However, because no merge field names follow the NEXT field, every other record in the data file, in effect, is skipped. By default, Word prints odd-numbered records beginning with the first. If you want to print only even-numbered records, type **2** in the From box of the Print Merge dialog box; Word will print all even-numbered records. You can also specify a starting record number to print; for example, if you type **3** in the From box, Word will print all odd-numbered records beginning with the third record.

Using SKIPIF (Skip Record If) and NEXTIF (Next Record If)

You can use SKIPIF and NEXTIF fields to control which records from the data file are merged with the main document. You can continue to use these fields in main documents that you created in earlier versions of Word. However, in many cases you can select the desired records more easily by choosing the Record Selection button in the Print Merge dialog box and specifying criteria.

SKIPIF Fields

Selecting Skip Record If from the Insert Merge Field dialog box inserts a SKIPIF field in the following form:

```
{SKIPIF Expression}
```

In place of the sample text Expression, you specify a condition that Word evaluates. If the condition you specify is met, Word does not merge the information from that data record. Word proceeds to the next data record and again evaluates the condition. Only the data records meeting the condition you specify are skipped. All other records in the data file—that is, records *not* meeting the condition—are merged.

The following is an example of how you might use the SKIPIF field.

```
{SKIPIF {MERGEFIELD rate} <= "10%"}
```

If the value of the rate merge field in the current data record is 10 percent or less, the data record is not merged. Data records with a rate value greater than 10 percent are merged.

Note   SKIPIF cannot be used in conjunction with a NEXT field. Therefore, you shouldn't use SKIPIF fields in main documents used to print mailing labels.

NEXTIF Fields

You specify a condition in a NEXTIF field just as you do in SKIPIF. With NEXTIF, however, if the current data record meets the condition you specify, Word merges information from the current data record *and* the next record in the data file. For example, if record number 34 meets your condition, Word merges the information from that record and also the information in record number 35.

Using the MERGEREC Field: Merge Record

Selecting the Merge Record # option inserts a MERGEREC field. When the main document is merged with the data file, the record number of each merged data record is printed in the merged document containing that record's information.

Other Ways of Organizing the Data File

You can have at most 31 columns in a table. If you have more than 31 fields in your data records, you need to make each record a separate paragraph, using tabs or commas to separate the fields. Your data file may already be in this format if you created it in another application and converted it to Word format.

As with any data file, you must organize the data so that Word can correctly merge the data with the main document. Check that the data file is organized as follows:

- Each record has the same number of fields as there are field names in the header record.

- Each record ends in a paragraph mark (¶), and there are no extra paragraph marks between or following the data records. Word interprets any empty lines as incorrect records.

- The same character, either a tab or comma, is used to separate the fields in all records of the data file. For example, you can't use tabs in the header record and commas in the data records. Since the text in many fields may contain commas, it's better to use tabs to separate the fields.

- If text in a field contains a tab, comma, line break, paragraph mark, or quotation marks (single or double), you must enclose the entire field in double quotation marks. If you've specified a different list separator character in the International category of the Control Panel to separate the fields, you must also include quotation marks around any fields that contain that character.

The following illustration shows a data file set up as paragraphs. To see the tabs and paragraph marks on your screen as shown in the illustration, click the Show/Hide ¶ button on the ribbon.

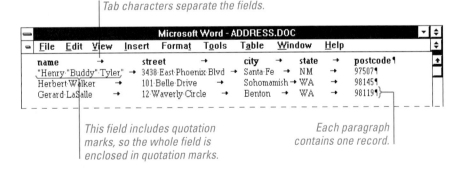

Tab characters separate the fields.

This field includes quotation marks, so the whole field is enclosed in quotation marks.

Each paragraph contains one record.

Tip If your data is in paragraphs, consider converting the paragraphs to a table. Fields without information are easier to see as empty cells in the table, and you don't have to use quotation marks to set off fields containing line breaks, quotation marks, commas, tabs, or paragraph marks. The records are also easier to sort using the Sort command. For information about converting paragraphs to tables and working with tables, see Chapter 17, "Tables."

However, if you've used commas to separate fields and some fields also contain commas, Word can't tell how many columns the table should have. In this case, use the Replace command on the Edit menu to replace the commas separating the fields with tabs before converting the paragraphs.

Troubleshooting

This section describes some messages you may encounter when merging documents and the steps you can take to remedy the problem.

Word Can't Open Attached Data File or Header File

When you open a main document, Word also opens the attached data file and header file, if there is one, for its own use. The documents are not displayed in a window. If Word cannot locate the files, a message is displayed with the following options.

Option	Action
Switch/Locate Data File	Word displays the Open dialog box so you can search for and open the data file. You don't see the data file in a window unless you choose the Edit Data File button on the print merge bar. Word remembers the location of the data file the next time you open the main document.
Open Main For Edit Only	Word opens the main document without the data file. You can edit the main document, but you cannot insert merge field names or merge the main document with the data file. The print merge bar is not displayed.
Remove Attachments	Word detaches the data file and header file, making the main document an ordinary Word document.
Help	Word displays information on the merge process.

Word Can't Open the Data File or Header File Specified in a DATA Field

In main documents created in Word for Windows earlier than version 2.0, a DATA field is used to specify the data file to be merged with the main document. When you open the main document in Word for Windows version 2.0, Word automatically attaches the specified data file to the main document and deletes the DATA field. If Word cannot locate the data file, a message is displayed with these options:

Option	Action
Switch/Locate Data File	Word displays the Open dialog box so you can search for and open the data file. Word then deletes the DATA field from the main document. You won't see the data file in a window unless you choose the Edit Data File button on the print merge toolbar. Word remembers the location of the data file the next time you open the main document.
Leave Data Statement	Opens the main document without attaching the data file specified in the DATA field. You can edit the main document but not insert merge field names or merge it with the data file. The print merge toolbar is not displayed. The DATA field is left unchanged in the main document.
Remove Data Statement	Opens the main document and removes the DATA field, making the main document an ordinary Word document.
Help	Displays information on the merge process.

Merge Field Names Do Not Match

Word compares the merge field names in the main document with the merge field names defined in the header record of the attached data file or header file. If one or more of the merge field names do not match, Word displays a message with the following options.

Option	Action
Use Fields In Data File	In the Insert Merge Field dialog box, Word lists the merge fields defined in the header record of the attached data or header file. You must replace the unmatched merge field names in your main document with the appropriate merge field from the header record.
Switch Data File	Word displays the Attach Data File dialog box. Attach the data file or header file containing the merge field names that match those in the main document.
Cancel	Word closes the message box and halts whatever action you were attempting—for example, merging or checking the main document for errors. You can edit the merge field names in either the main document or the header record to make sure they match.
Help	Word displays information on the merge process.

If you are using a header file, make sure you attach the header file first; otherwise, Word interprets the first record of your data file as the header record.

Merge Field Name Is Not Valid

Merge field names can have as many as 32 characters. You can use letters, numbers, and underscore characters—but not spaces. The first character must be a letter. If a field name in the header record is not valid, Word displays a message with the following options.

Option	Action
Fix Error Now	Word opens the file containing the header record and selects the invalid field name so you can correct it.
Fix Error Later	Word closes the message box and displays the main document. No merge fields are listed in the Insert Merge Field dialog box until you correct the name. Word alerts you to the error each time you activate the main document or when you merge or check for errors.
Help	Word displays information on the merge process.

No Data File Is Attached

You can insert the merge field names and work in the main document with only the header file attached. However, if you attempt to merge the main document before attaching the data file, Word displays a message with the following options.

Option	Action
Continue	Word merges the field names from the header record to produce one merged document.
Cancel	Word closes the message box and halts the merge. To attach the data file, choose Print Merge from the File menu, and choose the Attach Data File button.

Error! Unknown Op Code for Conditional

You inserted an IF field from the Insert Merge Field dialog box and did not replace the Op sample text. This message is displayed in a merged document in place of the IF field. Return to the main document and replace Op with one of the following valid mathematical operators: =, <>, >, >=, <, or <=.

Mailing Labels

Word uses a macro (a custom command) to help you print mailing labels. The mailing label macro is stored in the MAILLABL.DOT template and starts running as soon as you create a new document based on the template. The macro prompts you to answer several questions and uses the information you provide to print mailing labels according to your needs. You can:

- Set up a new data file to store names and addresses for mailing labels, and print multiple labels using the Print Merge command.

- Print multiple mailing labels from an existing data file.

- Print a single mailing label.

For any of these activities, you specify the type of printer you're using and the type of mailing label sheet on which you intend to print the labels. In asking you to specify the type of mailing label sheet, Word assumes you are using Avery mailing labels and prompts you for the product number of the sheet type. If you're using another brand, you may find an equivalent Avery product number printed on the mailing label sheet; this is the number you should use.

If you print multiple mailing labels, Word uses the Print Merge command to automate your printing. Much of the preparation for print merge is controlled by the mailing label macro; however, it's still important to understand the basics of merging a main document and data file and to be familiar with such terms as *field* and *record.* For an overview of these topics, see the first few pages in Chapter 32, "Print Merge Basics."

Tip After you identify the kind of printer and mailing label sheet you're using, the mailing label macro is designed to print the names and addresses squarely on each label. However, since the paper position is adjustable on a printer, the paper may not exactly match the position the mailing label macro assumes. It's a good idea, therefore, to print names and addresses on a plain sheet of paper before printing them on your label sheets. You can then hold the printed sheet of paper up to an empty mailing label sheet to see if you need to reposition the mailing label sheets. For information about adjusting a table, see Chapter 17, "Tables."

Setting Up and Printing Multiple Mailing Labels

When you want to create a new data file for mailing labels, the mailing label macro opens a new data file and sets up its structure. The macro also sets up a corresponding main document. All that remains for you to do is to add name and address information to the data file and instruct Word to print the labels.

Once you've used the mailing label macro to set up, you don't have to go through the process again to print mailing labels; you just open the main document the macro creates and choose the Print Merge command.

To set up a main document and data file for mailing labels, and then print the labels, you need to carry out the three following procedures in sequence. For subsequent mailing labels printings, when the main document and data file are already set up, you only need to use the third procedure, "To print mailing labels."

Note You can use the mailing label template to print labels on a dot-matrix or laser printer if you are running Windows version 3.1 or later. If you are using Windows 3.0 you can use the template to print labels on a laser printer.

To use MAILLABL.DOT and run the mailing label macro

1 From the File menu, choose New (ALT, F, N).

Do not use the Toolbar to open the new file, because you need to use the Templates option.

2 In the Use Template box, select MAILLABL.DOT.

3 Choose the OK button.

Word opens a new document based on MAILLABL.DOT and starts running the mailing label macro.

4 Respond to the prompts for the following information, and choose the OK button after indicating your choice. Each prompt appears in a separate dialog box.

- If you are using Windows 3.1 or later, the type of printer you use (laser or dot matrix).

- The product number for the type of Avery mailing labels you use—or the equivalent number for another brand.

- The number of labels you want to print: one label (you add the information yourself) or multiple labels (you use Print Merge to provide mailing label information).

After you've answered the final prompt, Word displays the Attach Data File dialog box.

5 In the Attach Data File dialog box, choose the Create Data File button.

To fill in information in a data file

After you choose the Create Data File button, Word builds the main document you need to print mailing labels, prompts you to save the main document, and then displays a data file that looks similar to the following example. The first row in a table is the header record that lists field names and guides you when adding specific information to subsequent records in the data file.

Honorific	FirstName	SecondName	LastName	CompanyName	Address1	Address2	City	State	PostalCode

1 Beginning with the first field, type the information for each field in the record. Press TAB to move to each subsequent cell.

   If a record does not have information for a field, press TAB to leave the cell for that field empty. Make sure you don't type spaces in the empty cells. Otherwise, empty spaces will appear in the printed mailing labels.

   If you need to add information for which there is no separate field—for example a person's job title—you can include this information by adding a second line within a field, as shown in the example for Ms. Ella Rose Martin, Managing Editor, in the illustration following this procedure.

2 When you reach the end of a row, press TAB to insert a new row of cells for the next record.

   You can add as many records as you like, and you can later add more records as you need them.

3 From the File menu, choose Save (ALT, F, S) to save the data file. Give the file a name, and then choose the OK button.

   Add any summary information you want.

4 Choose the OK button.

Tip If you want to print mailing labels in a particular sequence—for example, by postal code—you can sort the records in a data file table. The mailing labels are printed in the order of the sorted records. For information about sorting in a table, see Chapter 15, "Sorting."

Two lines of information are included in this field.

Honorific	FirstName	SecondName	LastName	CompanyName	Address1	Address2	City	State	PostalCode
Mr.	Dave	S.	Newell	Encyclopedia International	6767 A Street		Pecos	TX	70345
Ms.	Ella	Rose	Martin Managing Editor	Blue Sky Airlines	7248 Abbey Place	P.O. Box 97017	Koshen	CA	80254
Mr.	Carl		Simpson		88 Ohio Street	Townhouse 31	Aloha	MN	41246
Ms.	Claudia		Loren		236 Promotion Place		Kent	WA	97555

These records include no second name, so the cells in the "SecondName" field are left blank.

Data records for mailing labels

To print mailing labels

To print mailing labels, you choose the Print Merge command when the main document is active. Word provides options to control where the merge results are sent (to a file or the printer) and also which records in the data file to merge. These options are described in Chapter 32, "Print Merge Basics."

1   Make sure the mailing label main document is the active document.

2   From the File menu, choose Print Merge (ALT, F, M).

3   In the Print Merge Setup dialog box, choose the Merge button.

Word displays the Print Merge dialog box.

4   In the Merge Results box, select the option you want.

To	Select this option button
Send the merge results directly to the printer	Merge To Printer
Merge the data file and the mailing label main document into a new document without printing	Merge To New Document
Check for errors without merging the data file and the main document	Only Check For Errors

Note that only the first option (Merge To Printer) actually prints the mailing labels. The second option (Merge To New Document) is useful if you need to transfer your merged file elsewhere—for example, to another computer—to connect to a printer.

5   Specify which data records you want to print by doing one of the following.

To	Do this
Print all of the records in the data file	Under Print Records, select the All option button.
Print a range of records	Under Print Records, type, in the From and To boxes, the beginning and ending numbers of the records you want to print.
Set more specific rules for Word to follow in screening records to use for printing the mailing labels	Choose the Record Selection button, and, in the Record Selection dialog box, specify as many as six rules. Then choose the OK button.

6   At the bottom of the Print Merge dialog box, select either the Skip Completely option or the Print Blank Lines option, depending on how you want Word to treat empty cells in the data file. (In most cases, you will probably want to select Skip Completely.)

7   Choose the OK button.

If you've selected the Merge To Printer option, Word now opens the Print dialog box. Set all options as you want them, and then choose the OK button. Word prints your mailing labels.

Printing Multiple Mailing Labels from an Existing Data File

If you already use print merge for mailings to a client base, you may have a data file that stores the information needed to print mailing labels. Rather than retype all the mailing label information into a new data file, you can use the existing data file.

The first time you print mailing labels from your existing data file, you need to attach the data file to a main document and set up the main document to work with this data file. You can then print the labels. For subsequent printings, you only need to open the main document and print.

To start the mailing label macro and attach your data file

1 From the File menu, choose New (ALT, F, N).

Do not click the New button on the Toolbar to open the new document.

2 In the Use Template box, select MAILLABL.DOT, and then choose the OK button.

3 Answer the four mailing label prompts.

After you answer the final prompt, Word displays the Attach Data File dialog box.

4 Select the name of the data file you want to use for printing mailing labels, and then choose the OK button.

Word displays the Layout Mailing Labels dialog box.

You use the Layout Mailing Labels dialog box to select field names and special characters that indicate the content and layout of your mailing labels.

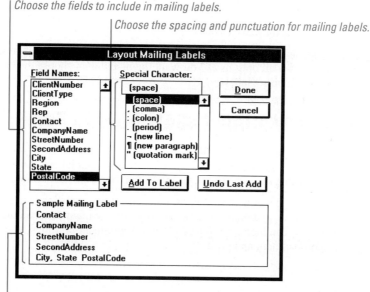

Choose the fields to include in mailing labels.

Choose the spacing and punctuation for mailing labels.

Shows the fields and layout you've set up for mailing labels

To set up the mailing labels for printing

1   In the Layout Mailing Labels dialog box, select the name of a field to use in the mailing labels, and then choose the Add To Label button.

Word displays what you add in the Sample Mailing Label box.

2   If you want to add a space, punctuation mark, or line break, select the appropriate special character in the Special Character box, and then choose the Add To Label button.

If you add a wrong field name or special character, choose the Undo Last Add button to remove what you added. You can choose this field repeatedly to remove more than one item.

3   Repeat steps 1 and 2 for each field name to be included in the mailing labels.

4   When you have field names and special characters laid out the way you want them, choose the Done button.

Word returns to the main document, where it adds the field names as indicated and prompts you to save the main document.

To print mailing labels using an existing data file

1   Make sure the mailing label main document is active.

2   From the File menu, choose Print Merge (ALT, F, M).

3   In the Print Merge Setup dialog box, choose the Merge button.

Word displays the Print Merge dialog box.

For more information, see Chapter 32, "Print Merge Basics."

4   In the Merge Results box, select the option you want.

To	Select this option button
Send the merge results directly to the printer	Merge To Printer
Merge the data file and the mailing label main document into a new document without printing	Merge To New Document
Check for errors without merging the data file and the main document	Only Check For Errors

Note that only the first option (Merge To Printer) actually prints the mailing labels. The second option (Merge To New Document) is useful if you need to transfer your merged file elsewhere—for example, to another computer—to connect to a printer.

5   Specify which data records you want to print by doing one of the following.

To	Do this
Print all of the records in the data file	Under Print Records, select the All option button.
Print a range of records	Under Print Records, type, in the From and To boxes, the beginning and ending numbers of the records you want to print.
Set more specific rules for Word to follow in screening records to use for printing the mailing labels	Choose the Record Selection button, and, in the Record Selection dialog box, specify the rules of your choice. Then choose the OK button.

6   At the bottom of the Print Merge dialog box, select either the Skip Completely option or the Print Blank Lines option, depending on how you want Word to treat empty cells in the data file. (In most cases, you will probably want to select Skip Completely.)

7   Choose the OK button.

If you've selected the Merge To Printer option, Word now opens the Print dialog box. Set all options as you want them, and then choose the OK button. Word now prints your mailing labels.

Printing a Single Mailing Label

When you print a single mailing label, the mailing label macro prompts you for information about your type of printer, the type of mailing label sheet you're using, and which label on the sheet you want to print the address on. Because you directly type the information, there is no need to set up a main document and data file.

To use all of the labels on a sheet, you can direct Word to print on the first label the first time you print, the second label the second time you print, and so on.

For more information about letter templates, see Chapter 37, "Document Templates."

If you use the letter templates for assistance in creating letters, you can open MAILLABL.DOT while one of the letter templates is active and print a mailing label for the addressee.

To print a single mailing label

1 From the File menu, choose New (ALT, F, N).

2 In the Use Template box, select MAILLABL.DOT, and then choose the OK button.

3 Answer the mailing label prompts.

After you've answered all prompts, Word displays the Layout Mailing Labels dialog box.

4 Under Field Names, select the information you want on the mailing label, line by line.

5 To end a line or insert special characters, select the special character in the Special Character box.

6 When the mailing label has the content and layout you want, choose the Done button.

7 After the mailing label appears in a new document, choose Print from the File menu (ALT, F, P).

To print a single mailing label from one of the supplied letter templates

1 From the File menu, choose Open (ALT, F, O).

2 In the File Name box, select or type MAILLABL.DOT, and then choose the OK button.

3 Answer the mailing label prompts.

4 In the Mailing Labels dialog box, verify or type the correct mailing label information. Make sure to include the correct information in the Row and Column boxes.

5 Choose the Done button.

6 After the mailing label appears in a new document, choose Print from the File menu (ALT, F, P).

Chapter 34

Form Letters and Other Merged Documents

This chapter uses a typical form letter and data file to show specific examples of how to use the general print merge procedures described in Chapter 32, "Print Merge Basics." The sample form letter and data file illustrate several common print merge tasks, including:

- Selecting records in the data file that meet certain criteria.

- Using IF fields to customize the text printed in each version of a document.

- Using SET and ASK fields to fill in information not defined in a data file.

- Using INCLUDE fields and bookmarks to insert text from another document into a merge document.

Information in this chapter assumes that you're familiar with the fundamentals of creating a data file and that you know how to insert field names and merge instructions in the main document. For step-by-step instructions for a particular task, see Chapter 32, "Print Merge Basics."

Sample Form Letter

When merging form letters, you must consider which records to merge and how to customize the text of each letter.

The following illustrations show the data records and main document that are merged to produce individualized versions of a form letter. The merge instructions inserted in the main document text and the results are described in detail later in this chapter.

customer	contact	address1	address2	code	quantity	unit_cost
Pierre's	Mr. LeBrun	456 Seventh	New York, NY 10027	3109	20	17.00
First Restaurant Group		121 Column St.	Seattle, WA 98111	1067	24	29.99
Alice's Restaurants	Ms. Waites	95 38th St.	San Jose, CA 95112			
Fancie's Inc.	Mr. Lawencia	123 Main St.	Portland, OR 97405	2189	10	10.99

Data file for a form letter

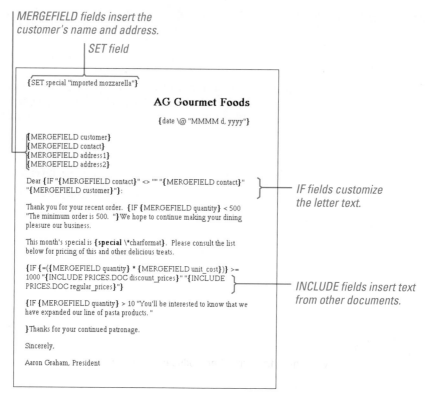

*MERGEFIELD fields insert the
customer's name and address.*

SET field

{SET special "imported mozzarella"}

AG Gourmet Foods

{date \@ "MMMM d, yyyy"}

{MERGEFIELD customer}
{MERGEFIELD contact}
{MERGEFIELD address1}
{MERGEFIELD address2}

Dear {IF "{MERGEFIELD contact}" <> "" "{MERGEFIELD contact}"
"{MERGEFIELD customer}"}:

*IF fields customize
the letter text.*

Thank you for your recent order. {IF {MERGEFIELD quantity} < 500
"The minimum order is 500. "}We hope to continue making your dining
pleasure our business.

This month's special is {**special** *charformat}. Please consult the list
below for pricing of this and other delicious treats.

{IF {=({MERGEFIELD quantity} * {MERGEFIELD unit_cost})} >=
1000 "{INCLUDE PRICES.DOC discount_prices}" "{INCLUDE
PRICES.DOC regular_prices}"}

*INCLUDE fields insert text
from other documents.*

{IF {MERGEFIELD quantity} > 10 "You'll be interested to know that we
have expanded our line of pasta products. "

}Thanks for your continued patronage.

Sincerely,

Aaron Graham, President

Main document for a form letter

In the sample main document, merge fields are used to create the letter's address. They
are also used with IF fields to determine which text is inserted in the documents
produced by the print merge.

Merging the sample main document with the sample data file produces the letters shown in the following illustration. Although there are four records in the data document, only three merged documents are created. A rule set in the Record Selection dialog box specifies to use only records in the data document in which the `quantity` data field is not empty. Because the `quantity` data field is empty in one record, that record is not used to produce a merged document. For a detailed explanation of the Record Selection dialog box, see "Selecting Records to Be Merged," next.

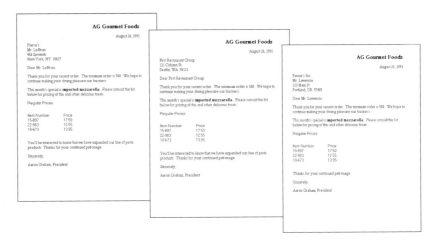

Versions of the form letter produced by merging the main document and data file

Selecting Records to Be Merged

Suppose you want to send a letter to certain clients on your mailing list. There are two approaches you can take.

You can send the letter to clients living in a certain city, state, or postal code by sorting the mailing list according to the selected data field. Then you can use the Print Merge command on the File menu to merge only the range of records with the specified information in the selected data field.

In other cases, you may want to send the letter only if specific conditions are met. The sample document in this chapter is a form letter that confirms an order from a customer. If the customer hasn't ordered anything, a letter should not be sent. In the sample data file, the `quantity` data field indicates the size of the customer's order. Therefore, to send letters just to the customers who have placed orders, you should merge all of the customer records except the ones in which the `quantity` data field is empty. You can use the Record Selection button in the Print Merge dialog box to set rules that Word uses to select which records to print. In the following illustration, the "quantity is Not Blank" rule instructs Word to merge all records in which the `quantity` data field is not blank.

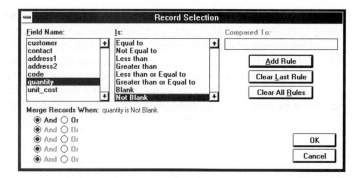

Preventing Blank Lines in Merged Documents

By default, Word does not print blank lines caused by empty merge fields. In the sample main document, the address includes a merge field for a contact. But in some records in the data file, the `contact` data field is empty, and so in some merged documents, a contact name will not be included in the address. When that is the case, Word omits the line containing the empty `contact` merge field.

While Word omits unintentional blank lines caused by empty MERGEFIELD fields, merge instructions, such as those of the IF, SET, and ASK fields, can also cause unwanted blank lines. Following are two techniques for avoiding these blank lines.

Format a paragraph mark as hidden text   Select the paragraph mark at the end of each field and apply the hidden text character format using the Character command on the Format menu or by pressing CTRL+H. You could also format the entire field as hidden text. To view or edit the fields, select the Hidden Text check box in the View category of the Options dialog box (Tools menu).

When you merge and print the letters, make sure the Hidden Text option in the Print category of the Options dialog box is cleared.

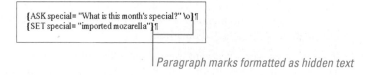

Paragraph marks formatted as hidden text

Embed merge instructions within the standard text In other cases, the simplest solution is to insert the instructions within the standard text. For example, the last IF field in the sample main document inserts additional text if the item code is within a certain range. If the text is inserted, the paragraph mark within the conditional text—that is, the paragraph mark before the closing field character—is inserted to place the conditional text in a separate paragraph. If the item code is not within the specified range, the additional text and the paragraph mark are not inserted.

```
{IF {MERGEFIELD quantity > 10} "You'll be interested to know that we
have expanded our line of pasta products.¶
"}¶
```

Printing Variable Text

In the main document, you can use IF fields to customize each letter by evaluat-ing the contents of one or more fields in the data file. Also, you can use SET or ASK fields to define the text of one or more bookmarks before a print merge or as each letter is being printed.

Using IF Fields

In the examples that follow, IF instructions are used to customize each merged letter based on information from the data file.

```
Dear {IF "{MERGEFIELD contact}" <> " " "{MERGEFIELD contact}"
"{MERGEFIELD customer}"}:¶
```

The salutation includes an IF field that checks if the `contact` merge field contains an entry for the current record. If so, the contact's name is printed. Otherwise, the customer's name is printed.

```
{IF {(={MERGEFIELD quantity} * {MERGEFIELD unit_cost})}
>= 1000 {INCLUDE PRICES.DOC discount_prices}
{INCLUDE PRICES.DOC regular_prices}}¶
```

The preceding example shows how you can calculate a result from data fields and use the result to control what text is printed in the merged document. The values of the `quantity` and `unit_cost` data fields are multiplied using the * operator. Then the IF instruction evaluates the result. If the result is equal to or greater than 1000, the customer is eligible for the discount price list. The discount price list is stored in the separate document PRICES.DOC and is marked by the bookmark `discount_prices`. An INCLUDE field inserts the price list from the document into the letter. If the result of the calculation is less than 1000, the alternative INCLUDE field inserts the regular price list from PRICES.DOC, marked by the bookmark `regular_prices`.

```
{IF {MERGEFIELD quantity > 10} "You'll be interested to know that we
have expanded our line of pasta products.¶
"}¶
```

In the final example, the IF field tests whether the quantity is greater than 10. If so, the text about the expanded line of pasta products is printed. To prevent a blank line in letters to customers who did not order pasta, the paragraph mark is placed before the closing quotation mark at the end of the optional text.

Using SET and ASK Fields

You often use the same standard text in a form letter for a number of different mailings. With each mailing, you can change particular types of information printed for each set of letters.

In the sample main document, the SET field defines a bookmark, special. Text you define as the bookmark special is printed in each letter at the point where you insert the bookmark field {special} in the standard text. In the following example, the bookmark field is formatted in bold. You can apply any character formatting to the bookmark field.

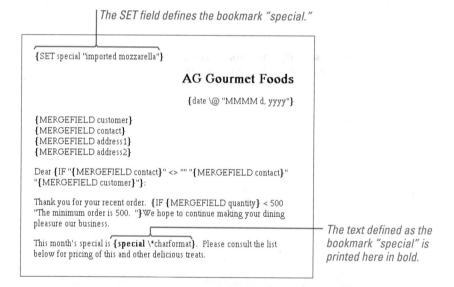

The SET field defines the bookmark "special."

The text defined as the bookmark "special" is printed here in bold.

Variable information you want to include in a form letter may change frequently or be used only once. Rather than set up a data file, you can use ASK fields and type the variable information as each document is merged.

The following illustration shows how you might set up the sample main document using ASK fields instead of a data file to provide the variable information. As each new letter is merged, Word asks you to enter the information for the fields you've defined in each ASK instruction.

ASK fields define each field instead of a data document.

```
{SET special "imported mozzarella"}¶
{ASK customer "Type the customer name:"}¶
{ASK contact "Who is our contact at {customer}? (If none, type 'x'.)"}¶
{ASK address1 "Type the street address for {customer}:"}¶
{ASK address2 "Type the city, state, and postal code for {customer}:"}¶
{ASK code "Type the product code:"}¶
{ASK quantity "Type the quantity ordered:"}¶
{ASK unit_cost "Type the cost of {code}:"}¶

                                            AG Gourmet Foods¶
                                                            ¶
                                        {date \@ "MMMM d, yyyy"}¶

¶
{customer}¶
{IF {contact} = "x" "" "{contact}¶"}
{address1}¶
{address2}¶
```

Text you type in response to the prompts is
printed where you insert the field names.

You must insert the bookmark name defined in the ASK instruction in the main document text where you want the text defined as the bookmark to print. You can insert the bookmark name at any point following the ASK field in which it is defined, including in other ASK fields. In this example, the `customer` bookmark name is inserted in the prompt text for the next ASK instruction. The customer name typed in response to the first prompt is displayed in the prompt asking for the contact. Inserting bookmark fields in the prompt text helps identify the version of the letter for which you are specifying information.

Because there is no data file attached to the main document, there cannot be any MERGEFIELD fields in the document; MERGEFIELD statements always refer to fields in a data file. Thus the sample letter's address, which is composed of MERGEFIELD fields when a data file is used, is now composed of bookmark fields instead.

Also, because there is no data file attached to the main document, you can no longer use the Print Merge command to print the document. Without a data file attached to it, the main print merge document becomes a normal document, so you use the Print command and select the Update Fields check box in the Options dialog box. As Word prints the document, it updates the fields, which causes the ASK fields to prompt you for the information required.

Because the document is no longer a print merge document, you must choose the Print command for each version of the letter you want to print. However, if you want to print many versions of the letter at once, you can attach a data file—it doesn't matter that there are no merge fields from the data file in the main document—and then choose the Print Merge command. Word creates as many merged documents as there are records in the data file.

Converting File Formats

You can open documents created by many other applications directly in Word. Word recognizes the file formats of popular word processors, spreadsheets, and other applications, and converts their files into Word format, preserving the content and formatting of the original documents. You can also save documents you create in Word for use with popular word processing applications.

Word also converts to and from plain text formats, which allows you to move files between applications when a specific conversion isn't available or necessary. These text options are described under "Text File Formats," later in this chapter.

Word provides conversions for the following file formats:

- Word for Windows 1.*x*; Word for DOS 4.0, 5.0, and 5.5; and Word for the Macintosh, 4.0 and 5.0

- WordPerfect 5.0, and 5.1

- RFT-DCA (for DisplayWrite and IBM 5520)

- Works for Windows and Works 2.0 for DOS (word processing documents only)

- WordStar 3.3, 3.45, 4.0, 5.0, and 5.5

- Lotus 1-2-3 2.*x* and 3.0 (convert to Word format only, not from Word format)

- Microsoft Excel BIFF 2.*x* and 3.0 (convert to Word format only)

- Multiplan 3.0 and 4.2

- dBASE (II, III, III PLUS, and IV)

- Text (with options for Text only, Text only with line breaks, and Text with layout)

- DOS Text (with options for DOS Text only, DOS Text only with line breaks, and DOS Text with layout)

- Rich Text Format (RTF)

For more information on installing converters, see *Microsoft Word Getting Started.*

Word uses separate programs, called *converters,* to convert the text and formatting within a document to a different file format. When converting *to* Word format from Word for DOS and WordPerfect formats, Word uses additional programs, called *graphic filters,* to convert the graphics that are within a file or linked to a file to the Windows Metafile graphic format (WMF). For WordPerfect documents, Word converts graphics to or from WordPerfect's graphic format (WPG). For a complete list of the graphic file formats Word converts, see Chapter 20, "Importing Graphics."

Note You install converters and graphic filters with the Setup program, using either the Complete Installation or Custom Installation option. If you have not installed the converter you need, see *Microsoft Word Getting Started* for information on running Setup.

For comprehensive information about each converter, see the file CONVINFO.DOC, included in the Word package.

Text File Formats

A file saved in a word processing application usually includes the text in the file as well as additional information such as formatting codes. If you open the file in another application without converting it, you're likely to see unrecognizable characters mixed with the document text. By using text file formats, you can save just the text portion of a file, which most other applications can recognize correctly.

Word can open or save text files in three file formats: Text, DOS Text, or Rich Text Format. The Text file format is used to share files among Windows applications, and the DOS Text file format is for sharing files between Word, a Windows application, and other applications that run in DOS but are not designed specifically for Windows. Technically, the Text format uses the ANSI character set, the Windows standard, and the DOS Text format uses the extended ASCII character set, the standard for character-based applications.

When you save a document using the Text or DOS Text format, you can choose variations that control how much of the formatting in the document is converted. RTF adds the option to convert all formatting. The differences and potential uses for text options are described in the following paragraphs.

Text only and DOS Text only   Saves the text without the formatting. Newline characters, section breaks, and page breaks are all converted to paragraph marks. Use this basic text file format only if the application to which you're converting the document is unable to read any of the other available file formats.

Text only with line breaks and DOS Text only with line breaks   Saves all of the text in a document without the formatting, but places a paragraph mark at the end of every line, and replaces section breaks and page breaks with paragraph marks. This format is useful when you want to keep your lines at a certain length, for example, when transferring files to an electronic mail system.

Text with layout and DOS Text with layout   Preserves line breaks and also preserves indents, tables, line spacing, paragraph spacing, and tab stop positions by inserting spaces in the file. Section breaks and page breaks are replaced by single paragraph marks. This is useful for converting a document in text file format and maintaining the page layout. You can reformat the document in the new application, using the converted layout as a guideline.

Rich Text Format (RTF)   Saves all of the formatting in the file. Formatting is converted to instructions that other applications can read and interpret. Where there isn't a specific conversion, RTF is useful for converting files from one Microsoft application to another and for transferring files between a Macintosh and a DOS system. You can also use RTF to transfer fully formatted documents using communications software that accepts only text files.

Opening Files Created in Other Applications

With the appropriate converter, you can open files from other applications that have been saved in a non-Word file format. For a list of file formats Word converts, see the introduction to this chapter.

You open files from other applications as you would a Word document, by choosing Open from the File menu. You can then use the List Files Of Type box to have Word list the group of files that may contain the one that interests you. Word lists documents according to the three-character filename extension. Word documents, for example, usually end with .DOC, and text files with .TXT.

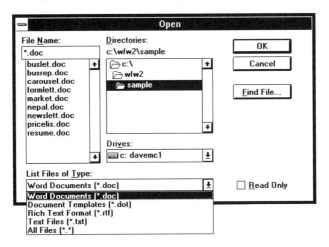

Select this type	To display
Word Documents	All Word and other documents that end with the .DOC filename extension.
Document Templates	Word templates that end with the .DOT filename extension.
Rich Text Format	Files that end with the .RTF filename extension.
Text Files	All files with the .TXT filename extension. Includes files saved as Text or DOS Text, whether text only, text with line breaks, or text with layout.
All Files	All files in the selected directory of any file format.

If you're looking for a file with a filename extension that's not listed, you can type the extension in the File Name box, and then press ENTER. For example, type ***.xls** to list Microsoft Excel files or ***.wps** to list word processing files from Microsoft Works. If you don't know the extension of the file you're looking for, or if it doesn't have an extension, choose All Files in the List Files Of Type box.

To open a file created by another application

You must have the appropriate converter installed to convert files from a particular application. For more information on installing converters, see *Microsoft Word Getting Started*.

1 From the File menu, choose Open (ALT, F, O).

2 In the List Files Of Type box, select the type of files you want to display.

   If you want to see files of a type not listed in the List Files Of Type box, in the File Name box, type an asterisk followed by the filename extension of the types of files you want to display, and then press ENTER. For example, type ***.xls** or ***.wps**

   Word will continue to use the file type you select until you select a new one or quit Word.

3 In the File Name box, type or select the name of the document you want to open.

   If you do not see the name of the file you want, you can change the file type, the current directory, or the current drive, or you can choose the Find File button to help you locate the file.

4 Choose the OK button.

   Word looks at the file to determine as best it can the file format of the document you want to open, and displays the Convert File dialog box.

5 If the suggested file format in the Convert File dialog box is not accurate, select another file format to convert from.

6 Choose the OK button.

After you've converted a document, you may notice that some things have changed. For example, formatting is not always retained exactly when converted from one program to another. For more information about the details of converting from a specific file format, see CONVINFO.DOC, included in the Word package.

Saving Word Documents in Another File Format

You can create documents using Word and then save them in file formats that can be used by many other applications. You can then work on the documents using other applications or share them with people who don't have Word.

To save a Word document in another file format

When you save a Word document in another file format, you give it a new name and then save it. The Word document that is the base for your save remains open after the save. You may want to save the Word document in Word format in case you need it later.

1 From the File menu, choose Save As (ALT, F, A).

2 In the Save File As Type box, select the file format you want.

The file format is displayed only if the corresponding converter is installed.

3 In the File Name box, type a new name for the document. Word does not allow you to save a file in a different file format with the same name.

If you don't type a filename extension, Word adds the filename extension that's characteristic for the file format you selected in the Save File As Type box. Word adds the .TXT filename extension to all Text and DOS Text formats. Word adds the .DOC filename extension to documents saved in WordPerfect format.

4 Choose the OK button.

Tip To make it easier to identify files you've converted to a different file format, you can change the default filename extension for a particular converter. For example, for WordPerfect documents, you might change the extension from .DOC to .WPF to distinguish these documents from Word documents, which also have a .DOC extension.

To change a converter's default filename extension, choose Options from the Tools menu, and then select the WIN.INI category. In the Application box, select MSWord Text Converters, and in the Startup Options box, select the converter whose extension you want to change. Finally, in the Setting box, scroll to the end of the string of characters and change the three-letter extension that appears there.

Saving Word Documents in Another File Format

Exchanging Information

As software and software users become more sophisticated, individual applications provide even more powerful ways to manipulate specific kinds of information. Applications are now available that help you create graphs, drawings, worksheets, text documents, slides, electronic mail, and charts—to name only a few. With the linking and embedding features in Word, you can now draw all of these separate kinds of information together into an integrated document. And you can keep the information current and correct with very little effort.

Linking and embedding are both based on the standard method of exchanging information using the Clipboard. First, you select information in the source document or application and use the Copy command to place it on the Clipboard. Then, in the destination document, you position the insertion point at the desired location and use the Paste Special command from the Edit menu to link or embed the information.

Once you have linked information from another document or application, Word can automatically update the information with any changes that occur in the original. For instance, if you link sales data from a worksheet to a report written in Word, the Word document can automatically reflect changes to the data in the worksheet. You can also link Word documents to other applications or documents so that changes in the Word documents are reflected in the other applications or documents.

Alternatively, you can embed information from another application or document. This means the information actually becomes part of your Word document; there are no links to other files. For example, you can create a logo in a drawing application and embed it in a Word document. If you decide to change the design of the logo, you can just double-click it, and Word opens a window from the drawing application. When you've finished making changes, you save the logo, close the drawing window, and return to Word; the logo is updated in your Word document. You can also embed Word documents or text in other applications or documents and edit them in the same way.

The primary difference between linking and embedding is the location where the actual data is stored. The information in a link is stored outside of the active document in the source application or document. Embedded information, however, is stored right in the active document. Keep this difference in mind when deciding whether to link or embed information. If you want to use the information in one document only, it's better to embed; in most other cases, it's better to link.

Linking

By creating links in Word, you save time and ensure consistency in your documents. You can share information from one document with several others, and you only need to maintain the original; the others are updated automatically. For example, if you store sales figures in a worksheet, you can use that data in several different reports written in Word. As long as you update the worksheet, Word updates the reports.

Creating links is as easy as copying and pasting. You copy a selection from an application or document called the *source* and paste it at another point called the *destination*. You can create links between two Word documents or between a Word document and a file created by another application.

Once you've established links, you can check for new data and retrieve it with a single keystroke. Or you can specify that new data is sent as soon as it is available.

You can link information in a variety of presentation formats—for example, as unformatted or formatted text.

You can create links between Word and other applications that support linking, such as Microsoft Excel.

Creating Links

To create links, you use the Paste Special command on the Edit menu.

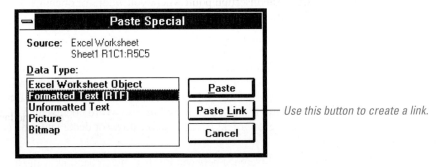

Paste Special dialog box

Source   The application containing the source of the information on the Clipboard. For some source applications such as Microsoft Excel, more information—for example, the range of cells selected—is given.

Data Type   The presentation formats available for the information on the Clipboard. These vary from application to application. Those that support embedding provide a format whose name ends with the word "object," as in Excel Worksheet Object, shown in the preceding illustration. Do not select this format when linking; it's used only to embed information.

Switching Between Applications

When you are linking, you need to switch between applications. You can do this quickly using one of two shortcuts. You can switch from the current application to the one you were using just previously by pressing ALT+TAB.

If you're working with several applications, it's sometimes easier to use the Task List dialog box. Press CTRL+ESC to open the dialog box. Select the application you want to use from the task list, and then choose the Switch To button. If you prefer to display both documents at once, you can choose the Cascade or the Tile button instead of the Switch To button.

To create a link from a source file in another application

Use this procedure when the source information for the link is in an application other than Word—for example, to link cells from a worksheet to a report in Word. Make sure you save the file you're copying from before beginning this procedure.

1 In the application containing the information you want to use in your document, select the information and, from the Edit menu of the application, choose Copy.

The selected information is copied onto the Clipboard, ready for you to link.

2 Switch to Word, and open the document in which you want to create the link.

3 Position the insertion point where you want the upper-left corner of the copied information to be displayed.

4 From the Edit menu, choose Paste Special (ALT, E, S).

Word selects a default presentation format.

5 If you want Word to display the linked information in one of the other presentation formats available, select the format you want from the Data Type box.

If you select the presentation format that has "object" as the last word, Word embeds the information instead of linking it.

6 Choose the Paste Link button.

If the Paste Link button is not available, the application from which you copied the information does not support linking or embedding. You can choose the Paste button, and the information is inserted into your document just as if you had chosen Paste from the Edit menu.

For more information on fields, see Chapter 41, "Fields." Linked information in Word is contained in a field. If you are working with field codes on, you don't see the full text of the linked information (the field result); you see the code Word uses to maintain the link. For example, in a link from Microsoft Excel, you might see the following:

```
{LINK ExcelWorksheet C:\\EXCEL\\SALES.XLS R1C1:R9C5 \* mergeformat \r
\a}
```

If you are linking to an application that predates Word for Windows version 2.0, the field displayed in your code may be DDE or DDEAUTO instead of LINK. For more information on the DDE and DDEAUTO fields, see the appropriate topics in online Help.

To display the field result

▶   Position the insertion point within the field, and then press the Field Codes key (SHIFT+F9).

–Or–

▶   From the View menu, choose Field Codes (ALT, V, C). This replaces all field codes in your document with field results, and Word removes the check mark next to the command on the menu.

Tip   After you've linked information into your Word document, any changes you make to it are replaced the next time you update the information. In a Word document that contains both linked and unlinked information, you may want to mark the linked information to distinguish it. This can be particularly helpful if other people work with the document. Here are three possible approaches:

■   Display field codes so that the linked information is not fully visible.

■   Use the Annotation command on the Insert menu to place an identifying annotation near the linked information.

■   Use the Character command on the Format menu to change the color of the linked information so that it stands out from the rest of your text.

To create a link with a chart embedded in a Microsoft Excel worksheet (version 3.0 or later)

Linking with a chart that is embedded in a worksheet of Microsoft Excel version 3.0 or later presents a special situation, and you should follow this procedure. Before you begin, make sure you save the worksheet containing the embedded chart.

1   In Excel, double-click the chart to place it in a chart window.

2   From the File menu of Excel, choose the Save command (ALT, F, S), type a name for the chart, and choose the OK button.

3   From the File menu of Excel, choose Open (ALT, F, O). In the Files box, select the chart you just named, and then choose the OK button.

4   Select the chart you just opened, and, from the Edit menu, choose Copy (ALT, E, C).

5   Switch to Word.

6   From the Edit menu, choose Paste Special (ALT, E, S).

7   In the Data Type box, select Picture.

8   Choose the Paste Link button, and then choose the OK button.

The chart is now displayed in Word. The data in this Word chart is automatically updated to reflect new data in the source if the chart in Excel that you named and saved is open. If that chart is not open, you can manually update the Word chart by selecting the LINK field and pressing the Update Field key (F9).

Naming Data You Link from Microsoft Excel

When you link information from Microsoft Excel to Word, Word uses a cell reference to locate the linked cells in the field definition—for example:

```
{LINK ExcelWorksheet C:\\EXCEL\\SALESRPT.XLS R1C1:R1C4 \* mergeformat \r}
```

In this example, R1C1:R1C4 represents the range of the linked cells. This is fine as long as you don't insert or delete rows within this range. If you do, Word still receives the range described in the field, but that may not contain the data you want. To make sure you receive the data you want, you can name the cell range in Microsoft Excel using the Define Name command on the Formula menu. If you do this before you link the information, Word automatically uses the correct information, even if you later insert or delete rows within the cell range.

For more information on naming ranges of cells, see the *Microsoft Excel User's Guide*.

If you name the cell range after you link the information, you need to change the item entry for the link. To do this, choose Links from the Edit menu in Word, select the link you want to change, and choose the Change Link button. In the Item box, delete the cell range and type in the name you defined in Microsoft Excel. Choose the OK button twice.

To create a link from a source document in Word to another application or document

Use this procedure when the source information for the link is in Word—for example, when you're linking text from one Word document to another. Make sure you save the Word document you're copying from before beginning this procedure.

1   In Word, select the information you want to link and, from the Edit menu, choose Copy (ALT, E, C).

The selected information is copied onto the Clipboard.

2   Switch to the other document window or destination application, and open the file in which you want to create the link.

3   Position the insertion point where you want to insert the information.

4   From the Edit menu, choose Paste Special (ALT, E, S).

Some applications may have the Paste Link command instead of Paste Special.

If the Paste Link or Paste Special command is not available, check the application's documentation for more information on how to link.

Updating Links

Links can be updated either automatically or only when you request it. For example, if you link a worksheet to a Word document, you can control whether the information in the Word document changes every time the worksheet changes or only when you want the Word document to change. Use the Links command on the Edit menu to change the update option.

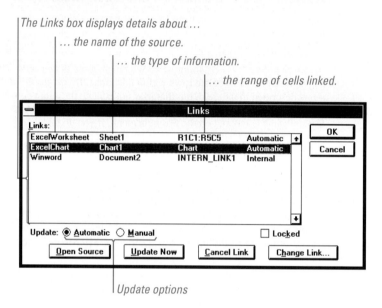

Links dialog box

Automatic   Whenever a change is made in the source file, that change is shown immediately in each destination document. You don't have to request updates, and you always have the most recent information.

Manual   You request changes from the source file when you want them. This option gives you more control over your document.

Locked   The information in the link is frozen when you select this check box. Use this option when you've reached the final version of the linked information and want to stop updating without canceling the link.

Note   Links between two Word documents or within the same Word document are *internal* links. Internal links are always updated manually. The Winword (Word for Windows) link in the preceding illustration is an internal link.

To change the update option of a link

You can determine whether each separate link in your document is automatically updated or not. This is useful if you are linking to several different sources. Some links may need to be updated frequently and others only when you ask for changes.

1 In the destination document, choose Links from the Edit menu (ALT, E, L).

Remember that the destination document is the one containing the result of the link.

2 In the Links box, select the link for which you want to change the update option.

You can select more than one link. To do this, hold down the CTRL key as you click each link you want. Alternatively, you can press SHIFT+F8, use the UP ARROW or DOWN ARROW key, and press the SPACEBAR to make each selection.

3 If you want automatic updates, select the Automatic option button.
–or–
If you want to request updates, select the Manual option button.

4 Choose the OK button.

To update a link manually

1 In the destination document, choose Links from the Edit menu (ALT, E, L).

2 In the Links box, select the links you want to update.

You can select more than one link and update them all at the same time. To do this, hold down CTRL as you click each link you want to update.

3 Choose the Update Now button.

1 In the destination document, position the insertion point anywhere within the field (the link) you want to update.

2 Press the Update Field key (F9).

If the source file and application are not open, the destination document opens them. Any changes that have been made to the source since the last update are now reflected in your document.

Tip   You can update all of the links in a document at once by first pressing CTRL+5 on the numeric keypad to select the entire document, and then pressing F9.

To print the Word document with updated links

1   Open or switch to the Word document you want to print.

2   From the File menu, choose Print (ALT, F, P).

3   Choose the Options button.

4   Under Printing Options, select the Update Fields check box.

5   Choose the OK button.

6   Change other options in the Print dialog box as you prefer, and then choose the OK button.

To reconnect a broken link

If you move or change the name of the source after you create the link, Word cannot update the information. When this happens, you can tell Word the new name or location using the Links dialog box.

1   In the destination document, choose Links from the Edit menu (ALT, E, L).

2   In the Links box, select the link you want to change.

3   Double-click the link.
    –or–
    Choose the Change Link button.

    Word displays the Change Link dialog box.

4   In the File Name box, type the new name or new path for the link.

    You can also change the information in the Item box, if necessary.

5   Choose the OK button.

6   In the Links dialog box, choose the Update Now button to update the link.
    –or–
    Choose the OK button.

There may be some information in your document that you don't want to update. For example, if you link monthly sales data from a worksheet to a status report in Word that contains descriptions of the data, you would not want to update until the following month. You can lock links to prevent their being updated until you unlock them.

To lock a link

1   In the destination document, choose Links from the Edit menu (ALT, E, L).

2   In the Links box, select the links you want to lock.

    You can select more than one link.

3   Select the Locked check box.

4   Choose the OK button.

To unlock the link, follow the same procedure, clearing the Locked check box.

Tip   You can quickly lock a LINK or INCLUDE field in a document by selecting it and pressing CTRL+F11. To unlock the field, select it, and press CTRL+SHIFT+F11.

Editing Linked Information

In general, if you need to change the contents or the formatting of linked information, it's best to make the changes at its source. It's easy to move directly from the destination to the source of a link using the Links command.

To switch from a destination to its source

1   In the destination document, choose Links from the Edit menu (ALT, E, L).

2   In the Links box, select the link whose source you want to view or edit.

    For editing purposes, you can select only one link at a time.

3   Choose the Open Source button.

    Word opens the source. If that source application is not running, Word starts the application and then opens the source.

When you finish making changes to the source, save it as you usually would. The changes are reflected in the destination according to the update options you have selected.

Note   With most applications, you can edit the linked information at the destination; however, most of your changes are lost when the destination receives an update. If the * mergeformat switch is in the field definition, Word does try to maintain any formatting you've applied to the linked information in the destination document. Depending on the type of formatting, it may not be maintained exactly after an update. Word automatically includes the * mergeformat switch in LINK field definitions.

Canceling a Link

When you cancel a link, the linked information remains in your document, but it can no longer be updated.

To cancel a link

1 In the destination document, choose Links from the Edit menu (ALT, E, L).

2 In the Links box, select the link you want to cancel.

You can select more than one link by holding down CTRL as you click each link you want to cancel.

3 Choose the Cancel Link button.

Word displays a message asking you to confirm the you want to cancel the link.

4 Choose the Yes button.

1 In the destination document, select the field for the link you want to cancel.

If you want to cancel all of the links in your destination document, you can select the entire document.

2 Press CTRL+SHIFT+F9.

Note   You can keep the link in your document but prevent updating by choosing Links from the Edit menu and selecting the Locked check box. You may want to do this instead of canceling the link unless you are sure you won't need to update the destination again. For more information, see "Updating Links," earlier in this chapter.

Embedding

By embedding information, you gain fast access to the functionality of another application without having to return to that application each time you want to make a change.

The technique of embedding is simple: You copy a selection from one document and then insert it into another. The information you insert is called an *object*.

When you embed an object, all of the instructions used to create the object are encapsulated and inserted along with it. The instructions include the object's file format, which application created the object, and all of the information about how to display it. You don't see this information, but the application uses it to display and edit the object.

Embedding makes editing and updating the object quick and simple. You can just double-click the object to open it in its source application. Then you make your changes and close the file or choose the Update command from the application's File menu, and the object you embedded is updated automatically.

You may also want to use the Object command on the Insert menu to create new objects in Word. For example, if you are writing a report and need to include some data, you can choose the Object command and select an object type from the Object Type box—for example, Microsoft Excel Worksheet. Word opens a Microsoft Excel window in which you can create the object. When you've finished, you just close the window, and the object is inserted into your document automatically. You never have to leave Word or save a separate file.

You may want to use embedding instead of linking if you're creating information to use in one Word document only. Because the information is actually added to your Word documents, it's not as easy to share it with other people or use it again in other documents, but it is easier to manage.

You can embed objects created using applications that support embedding such as Microsoft Excel, Microsoft Draw, Microsoft Graph, and the Microsoft Equation Editor.

Embedding Objects

Using the Copy and Paste Special commands on the Edit menu, you can embed information created in different documents or applications. Using the Object command on the Insert menu, you can insert new blank objects and create the information right in your document.

Embedding Existing Objects

You use the Paste Special command to embed an object that has already been created.

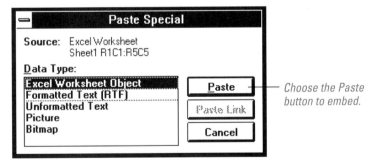

Paste Special dialog box

Source The source application. For some source applications such as Microsoft Excel, more information—for example, the range of cells selected—is given.

Data Type Lists the presentation formats available for the information on the Clipboard. These vary from application to application. Make sure you select the data type ending with the word "object," as in Excel Worksheet Object, shown in the preceding illustration.

To embed an existing object created in another application

Use this procedure when the information you want to embed has already been created in an application other than Word—for example, when you're embedding a worksheet created in Microsoft Excel.

1 In the application containing the information you want to embed in your document, select the information and, from the Edit menu of the application, choose Copy.

   The selected information is copied onto the Clipboard.

2 Switch to Word and, if you haven't already done so, open the document in which you want to embed the object.

3 Position the insertion point where you want to embed the copied object.

4 From the Edit menu, choose Paste Special (ALT, E, S).

5 In the Data Type box, select the type that includes the word "object."

   This is usually the first or second entry in the list. If this presentation format is not in the list, the source application does not support embedding. For more information, check the documentation for the source application.

6 Choose the Paste button.

Note Some applications automatically embed when you copy information from them and paste it into Word using the regular Paste command on the Edit menu. This means you can easily edit anything you paste into Word from those applications. Applications that embed automatically include, among others, Microsoft Excel (charts only), Draw, Graph, and the Equation Editor.

For more information on fields, see Chapter 41, "Fields."

Embedded information in Word is contained in a field. If you are working with field codes on, you see the information Word uses to identify the object instead of the result of the field. For example, for an object from Microsoft Excel, you might see the following:

```
{EMBED ExcelWorksheet \s \* mergeformat}
```

To display the field result

▶ Position the insertion point within the field, and then press the Field Codes key (SHIFT+F9).

–Or–

▶ From the View menu, choose Field Codes (ALT, V, C). This replaces all field codes in your document with field results, and Word removes the check mark next to the command on the menu.

To embed a Word document as an object in another application

Use this procedure when the information you want to embed has already been created in Word—for example, you might want to include the contents of a Word document in a message created by an electronic mail application.

1   Select the information, and choose Copy from the Edit menu (ALT, E, C).

   The selected information is copied onto the Clipboard.

2   Switch to the application and file in which you want to embed the information.

3   Position the insertion point where you want to embed the information.

4   From the Edit menu, choose Paste Special.

   If the Paste Special command is not available, check the destination application's documentation for information on embedding.

5   In the Data Type box, select the type that includes the word "object."

6   Choose the Paste button.

The object is displayed in your document as a representation. To view or edit the text of the object, double-click it. For more information on editing objects, see "Editing an Object," later in this chapter.

Creating and Embedding Objects

You can use the Object command on the Insert menu to create a new object and embed it in your document in one step.

You can choose to embed information from any application on your computer that supports embedding. These applications are listed in the Object Type box in the Object dialog box.

Note that if you want to embed a Microsoft Excel chart, you may find it easier to create the chart in Microsoft Excel and then use the procedure described earlier, "To embed an existing object created in another application."

Important   The applications that support embedding must be installed using their appropriate setup programs, or else they are not listed in the Object dialog box.

To embed a new object

1   Position the insertion point where you want to embed the new object.

2   From the Insert menu, choose Object (ALT, I, O).

3   In the Object Type box, select the type of object you want to create, and then choose the OK button.

Word opens the application with which you can create that type of object and a window in which you can create the object. The window is given the name of the document you are working in and an object identifier—for example, Drawing in SALES.DOC. The exact name depends on the application.

4   In the object window, create the object.

5   From the File menu of the object window, choose Update.

The Update command is in different locations on the File menus of different applications.

6   Close the object window, and return to Word.

Some applications—for example, Microsoft Draw—have an Exit And Return command on the File menu; you can use this to update your Word document and close the object window in one step.

Editing an Object

When you want to change or update an object you have embedded, you can double-click it, and Word opens an object window and application you can use to edit the object.

To edit an object

1   Double-click the object you want to edit.

Word opens an object window and the application you used to create the object.

2   Make the changes you want to the object.

3   From the File menu of the application, choose Exit and Return or Update. Close the object window if necessary.

Note   Some objects perform an action when you double-click them. For example, Sound Recorder objects play a sound. To edit this type of object, you can hold down the ALT key while double-clicking the object, or you can select it in your document and choose the command at the bottom of the Edit menu that includes the word "object"—for example, Sound Recorder Waveform Audio Object.

Canceling Embedding

Because the objects you embed include the information necessary to create them, embedding can increase the size of your files. You can reduce your file size by changing the object to a picture. The object remains in your document, but you can no longer edit it by double-clicking it. However, you can still scale, crop, or format it using Word commands.

To cancel embedding

1   Select the object in your Word document.

2   Press the Unlink Field key (CTRL+SHIFT+F9).

Troubleshooting

This section contains information that may help you work through problems you encounter.

Remember that each message on the screen contains a Help button. You can choose the Help button for an explanation of the message. This doesn't cancel your work. When you've finished reading the Help information, you can quit Help, and Word returns you to the message.

Row and Column Numbers Appear in Links from Microsoft Excel

If you copy cells from a Microsoft Excel worksheet and link them to Word using the bitmap presentation format, the row and column numbers are included in the Word document even if you do not select them in Microsoft Excel. If you don't want these numbers in your Word document, do the following before you copy the object in Microsoft Excel:

1   From the Microsoft Excel Options menu, choose Display.

2   Under Cells, clear the Row & Column Headings check box.

3   Choose the OK button.

Now you can copy and link without including the row and column numbers.

Word Cannot Link to an Object

If you're having trouble updating a link in Word and the field information shows both "LINK" and "object" in the description, you may have linked to an embedded object. For example, the field might show the following:

```
{LINK ExcelWorksheet "/WordDocument%SALES.DOC%Word Object #018"
R1C1:R1C4\* mergeformat \r \a}
```

Because Word cannot update links to objects, you should delete the LINK field. Then you can save the object in the source application as a file. Now you can create in Word a link to the information in the file.

Word Cannot Update a Link

There are several reasons why Word might be unable to update a link. Most commonly, it is because the source document for the link has been renamed, moved, or deleted. If the source document has been deleted, you won't be able to update the link again. You can figure out if the source has been renamed or moved by checking the information in the Change Link dialog box. Follow this procedure:

1   In your document, choose Links from the Edit menu (ALT, E, L).

2   In the Links box, select the link you want to update, and then choose the Change Link button.

3   Edit the filename and path as they appear in the File Name box so that they reflect the current filename and path of the linked information.

4   Choose the OK button.

5   In the Links dialog box, choose the Update Now button to update the link.

6   If Word asks whether you want to reestablish remote links, choose the Yes button.

Note   Microsoft Excel contains an Ignore Remote Requests option. If this is selected, all links from Microsoft Excel are broken, and you cannot update any information you've linked from Microsoft Excel to Word. To remove this restriction, switch to Microsoft Excel and choose the Workspace command from the Options menu (ALT, O, W); then clear the Ignore Remote Requests check box, and choose the OK button.

Document Templates

A document template is a special document you can use as a pattern to create other documents of the same type. For example, you can create a document template for letters that makes it easy to produce letters that follow the same format. The idea behind templates is that while you may create dozens of documents, you generally create only a few different *types* of documents. A college student may write nothing but term papers and the occasional letter home. A business executive may use Word primarily for writing memos. By providing a storage place for formatting and "boilerplate" text that can be used in every document, templates reduce the work necessary to set up a document. When you use a template, you no longer have to start from scratch each time you create a document. Tasks such as setting the margins, choosing a font, and creating headers and footers have already been taken care of.

But document templates are more than a convenient way to generate certain types of documents. Templates can affect not only the content and formatting of a new document, but even which commands are available on the menus, which buttons appear on the Toolbar, and which key combinations are assigned to commands. In other words, templates can shape not only documents but Word itself. With Word document templates, you can design a work environment customized for the kinds of documents you produce.

Word comes with predefined templates for the most common types of documents. These templates are described under "Using the Document Templates That Come with Word," later in this chapter. You can use these document templates as they are, or you can customize them to your own specifications.

Following is a closer look at how templates function both as patterns for new documents and as working environments.

A Template as a Pattern for Documents

Documents based on a template inherit the following elements:

Formatting   A template can store information about margin settings, the number of columns, page orientation, and other document and section formatting. Like a document, a template can contain more than one section, with different formatting for each section.

Boilerplate text   A template can store text that is the same in every document for which it is a pattern. Every memo, for example, may have the same memo heading. This text appears in every document based on a template.

Styles   A template can provide a way to store and easily apply many different character, paragraph, and section formats. Since documents based on a template inherit the template's styles, you can use templates and styles to maintain consistent formatting among a body of documents.

For example, consider a template for a business letter. A business letter format specifies elements such as margin settings, the appropriate font, and how paragraphs should be indented. A letter template could also include boilerplate text that is used in every letter. For example, each letter may begin with the current date and end with a closing such as "Sincerely" or "Yours truly," followed by your name. These elements, then, are common to every letter and can be saved as part of a template. Once these elements are stored in the template, you do not have to recreate them for each letter you write.

A Template as a Working Environment

In addition to serving as a pattern for new documents, a template can also shape Word itself. You can use templates to customize Word in various ways to make it more suitable for the kind of document you're using the template to create. A template, then, can create an "environment" in Word for working on a specific type of document. A template's working environment can include:

- Glossary entries
- Menu, keyboard, and Toolbar assignments
- Macros

Glossary entries may be the first element you add to a template. Suppose you use several different closings in your business letters—"Sincerely," "Yours truly," and so on—depending on the letter's recipient. You can store each closing as a glossary entry. Another use of glossary entries in a letter template might be to store addresses, as the letter templates supplied with Word do.

Customizing menu, keyboard, and Toolbar assignments is a matter of adding commands or removing them. You can simplify a menu by removing commands you're not likely to use for the type of document produced by the template. For example, you might want to remove the Index Entry and Index commands from the Insert menu of a letter template—you're not likely to create an index for a letter. Similarly, you can add commands appropriate for the kinds of documents the template produces. These new commands might be macros or existing Word commands that are not normally included on a menu.

The NORMAL Template's Special Role

By default, new documents are based on a file called NORMAL.DOT—the NORMAL template. That is, when you use the New command on the File menu to create a new document, Word bases the new document on the NORMAL template unless you select a different one. The NORMAL template is also where Word stores items that are "globally" available. Globally available items are available for every document, regardless of which template the document is based on. These items include glossary entries, macros, menu assignments, Toolbar button assignments, and keyboard assignments. If you were to delete the NORMAL template, you would lose these glossary entries and macros, as well as any changes you have made to customize Word.

Template Management

Template filenames end with the extension .DOT rather than .DOC, which Word uses for documents. When you name a new template, Word automatically adds the .DOT extension, unless you type a different one. If you type a different extension, however, the new template does not appear in the Use Template box when you choose the New command from the File menu to create a new document. For this reason, it is easier to base new documents on a template that has the .DOT extension that Word expects.

By default, Word stores all template files in the same directory as the one in which Word is stored. However, if you have a large number of templates, you may be able to manage them more easily by storing them in a separate directory. You can accomplish this by adding a DOT-PATH entry to the [Microsoft Word 2.0] section of your WIN.INI file. For example, if you added the following line:

```
DOT-PATH=C:\WINWORD\DOTFILES
```

Word would look in the C:\WINWORD\DOTFILES directory for templates.

Using a Template to Create a New Document

Every Word document is based on a document template. In fact, it's impossible to create a new document that is *not* based on a template. If you don't select a template when you create a new document, Word bases the new document on the NORMAL template.

When you choose the New command from the File menu, Word displays a dialog box that lists the document templates that are available.

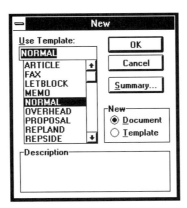

To create a new document based on a document template

1   From the File menu, choose New (ALT, F, N).

2   In the Use Template box, type or select the template on which you want to base the new document.

3   Choose the OK button.

Assign a Document Template to a Menu

If you use a certain document template frequently, consider assigning it to the File menu so that you can choose it more easily when you want to create a document based on it. To assign a template to the File menu, you create a macro that records the process of creating a new document based on that template, and then assign the macro to the File menu. You could call the command that appears on the menu "Letter," for example, or "Memo," corresponding to the kind of new document it produces. When you choose this command, Word creates a new document based on the template you chose when you recorded the macro. For information on recording a macro and assigning it to a menu, see Chapter 42, "Using Macros."

Changing the Template Attached to a Document

Once a new document is created, the template on which it is based remains attached to the document. You can check to see which template is attached to a document by choosing the Template command from the File menu. The template that is attached to the document determines the working environment for that document. That is, the template attached to the document can make available template-specific glossary entries and macros, as well as assignments for menus, keys, and the Toolbar.

You can use the Template command to change the template attached to a document. Suppose you are working on a document based on the NORMAL template, and you realize that you'd like to use a glossary entry or a macro available in a different template. To do so, you attach the template in which the glossary or macro is stored.

Although the template working environment—the menu commands and keyboard assignments, for example—can change when you change the template attached, the document itself does not change. That is, the document's styles do not change, for example, even if the newly attached template has different styles. If the template you attach contains boilerplate text, that text does not appear in your document, nor do any differences in its margins or other options you set with the Page Setup command on the Format menu.

To change the template attached to a document

1 From the File menu, choose Template (ALT, F, T).

2 In the Attach Document To box, type or select the template you want to attach to the document.

3 Choose the OK button.

Although any new document inherits the formatting and any text or graphics contained in the template on which it is based, the new document's formatting, styles, and text are not changed automatically if those elements are subsequently changed in the template. If you change the margins of the new document, the margins of the template attached to it do not change. Likewise, if you change the margins of the template, the margins of documents previously created with the template do not change. Subsequent documents based on the template have the new margins, however.

Creating a New Template

There are three ways to create a new template:

- Convert the document you're working on into a template.

- Choose the New command from the File menu, and then select the Template option button under New.

- Modify an existing template, and then save it with a new name.

The most appropriate method depends on your situation. If you're working on a document and decide you want to use the document as a template, you can easily save the document as a template. Or you might want to plan a template in the early stages of a project before you begin work. This could also be appropriate if you're creating a complex template, such as the form in the following illustration.

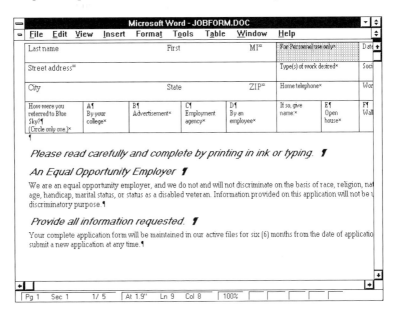

Or you might want to create a variation on an existing template—a fax template, for example, that you customize for someone with whom you correspond frequently. To do so, you make the changes to the current template as necessary, and then save the template under a new name.

To create a document template by modifying an existing document or template

1   From the File menu, choose Open (ALT, F, O).

2   In the File Name box, type or select the name of the document or template on which you want to base the new template.

    To see a list of document templates, select Document Templates under List Files Of Type.

3   Choose the OK button.

4   Change the document or existing template any way you want.

5   From the File menu, choose Save As (ALT, F, A).

6   In the File Name box, type a name for the new template.

    If you are creating a template from a document, select Document Template under Save File As Type.

7   Choose the OK button.

To create a new document template

1   From the File menu, choose New (ALT, F, N).

2   Under New, select the Template option button.

3   In the Use Template box, type or select the name of the template, or type the name of the document, on which you want to base the new template, and then choose the OK button.

4   Insert any text you want and create styles, macros, and glossary entries as you would for any document.

    You can store macros and glossary entries as part of the new template or as part of the NORMAL template so that they are available to all documents. For more information, see "Specifying How Macros and Glossary Entries Are Stored," later in this chapter.

5   From the File menu, choose Save As (ALT, F, A).

6   Type a name for the new template.

7   Choose the OK button.

Modifying a Template

Once you have created a template and have begun to use it, you may want to fine-tune it in various ways. Perhaps you'd like to change the formatting of text in the header or footer or change the definitions of some of the styles. You may want to add a glossary entry or a new macro. You can modify many aspects of a template as you're working on a document based on it. For example, you can change the definition of template styles or change the margins. There is often no need to open a template and work with it directly, but it's probably easiest to do so if you want to make a large number of changes to it. You can open a template just as you would a regular document and then edit it.

Note If you change the formatting or any boilerplate text or graphics of a template, those elements of documents previously created with the template do not change. Subsequent documents based on the template inherit any modified elements.

To modify a document template directly

1   From the File menu, choose Open (ALT, F, O).

2   Under List Files Of Type, select Document Templates.

3   Type or select the name of the template you want to edit, and then choose the OK button.

4   Edit and format the template as you would a document. Any text in the template will be inserted into every new document created from the template.

5   From the File menu, choose Save (ALT, F, S) to save the changes to the template.

To change a template's formatting with the Use As Default button

Some formatting commands—the Character, Language, and Page Setup commands—include Use As Default buttons in their dialog boxes. When you choose a Use As Default button, the settings in the dialog box are applied not only to the active document but also to the attached template. The following procedure assumes that the active document is based on the template whose formatting you want to change.

1   From the Format menu, choose one of the following commands:

   ■ Character (ALT, T, C)

   ■ Language (ALT, T, L)

   ■ Page Setup (ALT, T, U)

2   Change the settings you want.

3   Choose the Use As Default button.

4   When Word asks whether you want to save the changes to the attached template, choose the Yes button.

To change a template's menu, key, or Toolbar assignments

1 From the Tools menu, choose Options (ALT, O, O).

2 Under Category, select Menus, Keyboard, or Toolbar.

3 Change the menu, keyboard, or Toolbar assignments the way you want.

4 Under Context, select the Template option button.

5 Choose the OK button.

Changing Template Styles

There are three different ways to change a template's styles, each of which is appropriate in different situations. You can open the template itself and add, delete, or redefine styles just as you would in a regular document. This is the most efficient method if you have a large number of changes to make.

A second technique is to merge styles into the template from another template or from a document. You might want to do this if you've made changes to the styles of a document based on the template and want to update the template's styles so that they're consistent.

The third technique is to update a template's styles one style at a time. For example, if you are working on a document based on a template and make a change to a style, you can update the template so that it reflects the style change you made in the document. This is similar to merging styles into a template, except that instead of merging all the styles from a document, you merge a single selected style. To do so, you can choose the Style command on the Format menu and then select the Add To Template check box.

The Merge Styles dialog box has two buttons for merging styles, From Template and To Template. The To Template button merges the styles of the active document into the template attached to the document. The From Template button merges styles from the attached template into the active document. In the case of styles with the same name, including standard styles such as Normal, the style definitions of the template you are merging from replace the style definitions of the document or template you are merging to. So, for example, if you have changed a style definition in the active document and you choose the To Template button, the changed style overwrites the existing style in the template. If you choose the From Template button, the template's style definition overwrites the changed style in the active document.

To merge styles to and from a template

1 Open all of the documents and templates from or to which you want to merge styles.

2 From the Format menu, choose Style (ALT, T, Y).

3 Choose the Define button, and then choose the Merge button.

4 Select the template you want to merge styles from, and then choose the From Template button or the OK button to merge the styles in the selected template into the active document.
–or–
Select the template you want to merge styles to, and then choose the To Template button to merge the styles of the active document or active template into the attached template. You can only merge styles to the attached template.

Note Changes to the styles of a template do not automatically become part of existing documents that are based on the template. To update the styles of existing documents, you must merge the styles from the template.

Specifying How Macros and Glossary Entries Are Stored

By default, new macros and glossary entries are stored in the NORMAL template and are available to all of your documents. However, you may want to make some macros and glossary entries available for certain documents only. For example, if you are writing a series of documents for a particular project, you may want to create macros and glossary entries specifically for that project.

If you don't often use macros or glossary entries, you don't need to worry about different templates; you can store everything globally. Being able to store glossaries in different templates is most useful if you have many glossary entries. You can organize them by storing them in different templates.

Using the Template command on the File menu, you can select one of three options.

Global (Available To All Documents)   This is the default setting. Each new glossary entry and macro that you create is automatically stored in the NORMAL template.

With Document Template   With this option selected, new glossary entries and macros are automatically stored in the template attached to the document.

Prompt For Each New   With this option selected, Word prompts you each time you create a new glossary entry or record a macro and asks whether you want to make it available to all documents or only to documents based on the attached template.

To specify how macros and glossary entries are stored

1 From the File menu, choose Template (ALT, F, T).

2 Under Store New Macros And Glossaries As, select the option you want.

3 Choose the OK button.

Note If you create a macro using the Macro command on the Tools menu, you can specify how the macro is stored. Under Show, select the Template Macros option button to store the macro as part of the attached template, or select the Global Macros option button to make the macro available to all documents. If the NORMAL template is attached to the document, the Template Macros option button is unavailable.

Using the Document Templates That Come with Word

Word comes with templates for creating many of the most common kinds of documents. Where possible, these templates are based on widely used, standard formats. The letter templates, for example, are based on letter formats described in *Webster's Secretarial Handbook,* 2nd ed. (Merriam-Webster, Inc., 1984). You can use any of these templates as they are or as starting points for formats of your own design. You can easily modify the appearance of documents based on these templates by redefining the styles used to format different document elements.

Installing the Supplied Templates

When you run the Setup program to install Word, you can choose to install or not install the supplied templates. If you choose not to install them when you set up Word, you can run Setup at any time to install them later. For more information about the Word Setup program, see *Microsoft Word Getting Started.*

Creating a New Document Based on the Supplied Templates

Once you have installed the templates in your Word directory, you can use them to create new documents. When you choose the New command from the File menu, Word lists all available templates in the Use Template box.

To create a new document based on a supplied template

1 From the File menu, choose New (ALT, F, N).

2 Select the supplied template you want to base a new document on.

3 Choose the OK button.

Working with Documents Based on the Supplied Templates

Virtually all of the supplied templates share common elements, so once you're comfortable using one template, you'll have a good understanding of how the other ones work as well. Following are some of the elements you can expect to find in the supplied templates.

An Initial Dialog Box

Most of the supplied templates display a dialog box immediately after you create a new document based on them. For example, when you base a new document on the PROPOSAL template, Word displays the following dialog box:

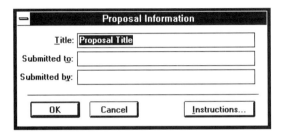

The information you type in the dialog box is inserted in the appropriate places in your document. If you're not ready to provide the information the dialog box requests—for example, you may not be sure of the title of your proposal yet—you can choose the OK button or the Cancel button to close the dialog box. Later, when you're ready to include the information in your document, you can choose a specialized command from the Format menu to open the dialog box.

Predefined Styles

All of the supplied templates include styles appropriate for their formats. The names of these styles correspond closely to the elements of the document for which they are intended. For example, the styles defined for the business letter templates include Date, InsideAddress, SubjectLine, CompClose, and Signature. By applying these styles to the elements for which they're intended, you can easily create a document with the format for which the template is designed.

Specialized Commands

Most of the templates include specialized commands to help you accomplish tasks specific to the type of document you create with the template. In each template, these additional, specialized commands, created with the WordBasic macro language, are listed at the bottom of the Format menu.

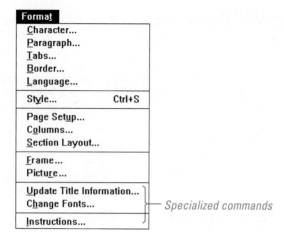

Specialized commands

Commands for Customizing the Templates

Many templates include a command that provides an easy way to customize basic template settings. For example, the letter templates include a command called Set Letter Options with which you can change the first page header, margins, fonts used in different styles, salutation, and other aspects of the letter. These settings are changed not just for the current document, but for the template on which it is based, so that the new settings affect all new documents based on the template.

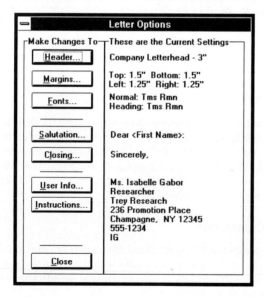

Instructions Command

Most templates include an Instructions command that provides an overview of how to use the template.

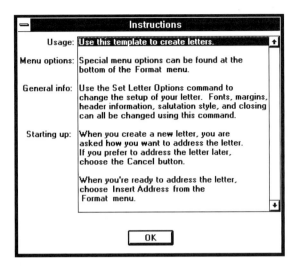

A Gallery of Supplied Templates

The templates presented in this section are organized into four categories:

- Letters
- Memos
- Reports
- Other documents

The "other documents" category includes templates for facsimile cover sheets, business proposals, overhead transparencies, articles, dissertations, mailing labels, and press releases.

Letter Templates

Word comes with four business letter templates based on the formats described in *Webster's Secretarial Handbook*. Each template provides ways to handle addresses and includes a command for creating a facsimile cover sheet for the letter.

Addresses

When you create a new document based on one of the letter templates, Word prompts you to create a new address, select an existing address that has been stored as a glossary entry, or create a mail merge document.

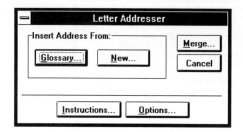

If you choose the New button, Word displays a dialog box with places to enter each component of the address.

This address is inserted in your letter as the inside address and can be used to create a mailing label using the Create Mailing Label command on the Format menu. Each new address you create can be stored as a glossary entry. Once you have added an address to the glossary, you can retrieve it by choosing the Insert Address command from the Format menu.

Block letter   You can use the LETBLOCK template to produce a letter in a standard block letter format. As shown in the following illustration, each element of a block letter begins flush with the left margin; the first line of each paragraph within the body of the letter is not indented.

Modified block letter   You can use the LETMODBK template to produce a modified block letter as shown in the following illustration. The modified block letter differs from a block letter in the placement of the date, closing, and second-page header.

Modified semi-block letter   You can use the LETMDSEM template to produce a letter in the modified semi-block format as shown in the following illustration. In a semi-block letter, the date and closing are aligned slightly to the right of center, and paragraphs in the letter are indented 0.5 inch.

Personal letter   You can use the LETPERSN template to produce a modified block letter. A personal letter does not include the letter writer's title or special notations after the closing.

Memo Template

Word comes with a *template* you can use to produce a memo in the traditional format described in *Webster's Secretarial Handbook*. When you create a new document based on the MEMO2 template, Word prompts you to type the memo subject and to type or select the names of the recipients of the memo. You can use the memo template to store recipient names either individually or in groups.

Standard memo   You can use the MEMO2 template to produce a memo using a simple format as described in *Webster's Secretarial Handbook*.

Report Templates

Word comes with three report templates, one using a standard portrait format, one using a landscape format, and one using a format with side headings.

When you create a new document based on one of these templates, Word prompts you for the report title, subtitle, byline, and other information used to set up the report.

Standard report   You can use the REPSTAND template to produce a standard report as shown in the following illustration. The footer for each page after the first page includes the document title, page number, and the text of the nearest heading with the Heading 1 style.

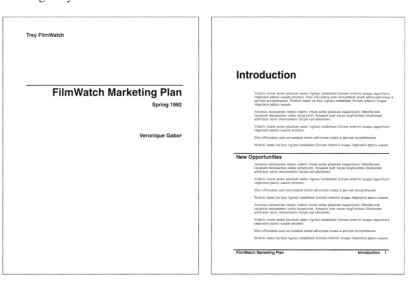

Standard landscape report   You can use the REPLAND template to produce a standard report in landscape format. A report based on the REPLAND template is the same as one based on the REPSTAND template, except that it is in landscape orientation.

Report with side headings   You can use the REPSIDE template to produce a report with side headings as shown in the following illustration.

Templates for Other Documents

This section describes templates for creating the following types of documents: facsimile cover sheets, business proposals, overhead transparencies, magazine articles, press releases, dissertations, and mailing labels.

Facsimile cover sheet   You can use the FAX template to produce a cover sheet that includes addresses and phone numbers for recipient and sender, and the number of pages transmitted.

Business proposal You can use the PROPOSAL template to produce a business proposal as shown in the following illustration.

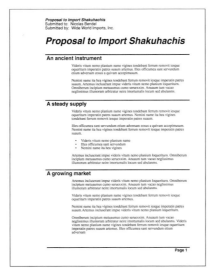

Overhead transparency You can use the OVERHEAD template to produce an overhead transparency as shown in the following illustration.

Article　You can use the ARTICLE2 template to produce a magazine article according to the specifications described in *Writer's Market 1991* (Writers Digest, 1990).

Press release　You can use the PRESS template to produce a press release in the format described in the *Associated Press Stylebook* (Dell, 1990).

Term Paper　You can use the TERM2 template to produce a term paper according to the specifications described in the authoritative guide, *A Manual for Writers of Term Papers, Theses, and Dissertations,* 5th ed. (Chicago, 1987) by Kate L. Turabian, revised and expanded by Bonnie Birtwistle Honigsblum.

Dissertation　You can use the DISSERT2 template to produce a dissertation according to the specifications described in the authoritative guide, *A Manual for Writers of Term Papers, Theses, and Dissertations,* 5th ed. (Chicago, 1987) by Kate L. Turabian, revised and expanded by Bonnie Birtwistle Honigsblum.

Mailing labels　You can use the MAILLABL template to create mailing labels. You can also use the letter templates described earlier in this chapter to create a mailing label for a single address. For more information about how to use the MAILLABL template, see Chapter 33, "Mailing Labels."

Customizing Menus, the Keyboard, and the Toolbar

By customizing menus, shortcut keys, and the Toolbar, you can change Word to better suit your writing and editing needs. You can add features you use regularly, such as commands and dialog box options, to menus and the Toolbar and remove the features you rarely use. You can customize key assignments by creating the shortcut keys handiest for you.

To customize Word, choose the Options command from the Tools menu. Word displays the Options dialog box.

Select the category you want to view.

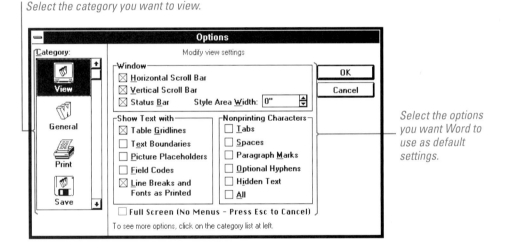

Select the options you want Word to use as default settings.

The Options dialog box is divided into two parts: the list of categories on the left and the options panel on the right. When you select a category from the list, the panel changes to display the available options for that category. You determine the default settings—the ones Word automatically uses each time you open a new document—for any category by selecting or clearing the options in the panel. To change the options for several categories, select a category, select or clear the options, and then select the next category from the list. The new default settings take effect when you choose another category or close the dialog box.

The individual options for each category are described in Chapter 39, "Setting Preferences."

Tip If you want to create different configurations of Word, you can preserve original menu settings, key assignments, and defaults in one template and then create separate templates for customized settings.

Making Changes Globally or in a Template

For more information about templates, see Chapter 37, "Document Templates."

Changes you make in most of the Options categories are saved globally in the NORMAL.DOT or WINWORD.INI files and apply to any document you open, regardless of which template you are using. Changes you make in the Menus, Keyboard, and Toolbar categories, however, can be saved globally, so that they are available to all documents, or with the attached template, so that they are available only to documents based on that template.

If you want to save changes made in these three categories in a particular template, you must attach that template by using the Template command on the File menu. If you want to save changes made to these categories globally, so they are available in all templates, attach the NORMAL.DOT template.

By using different templates, you can create the most suitable work environment for each kind of document you produce. For example, if you frequently use tables when you write reports, you can add the commands you use most often to the Table menu and save these menu settings in a template. Then when you write a report, you can attach this template to the Word document, and the commands will be right where you want them.

To attach a different template

1 From the File menu, choose Template (ALT, F, T).

2 Under Attach Document To, type or select a template name.

3 Choose the OK button.

Customizing Menus

You can easily customize menus so that they contain the commands and macros you use most often.

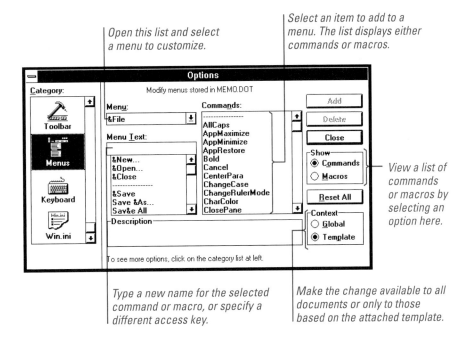

Open this list and select a menu to customize.

Select an item to add to a menu. The list displays either commands or macros.

View a list of commands or macros by selecting an option here.

Type a new name for the selected command or macro, or specify a different access key.

Make the change available to all documents or only to those based on the attached template.

To add a command or macro to a menu

1   From the Tools menu, choose Options (ALT, O, O).

2   Under Category, select Menus.

3   Under Context, select the Template option button if you want to make the command or macro available only to documents based on the attached template.

The Template option button is unavailable if the template attached to your document is NORMAL.DOT.
    –or–
Under Context, select the Global option button if you want to make the command or macro available to all documents, including those based on the attached template.

4   Under Show, select either Commands or Macros.

5   In the Menu box, select the menu to which you want to add the command or macro.

6   Do one or more of the following:

   ▪ To add an item to the menu, select the command or macro you want to add in the Commands/Macros box.

   ▪ To add a separator line to the menu, select the dotted line at the top of the Commands/Macros box.

   ▪ To rename a command or macro, select the original name in either the Commands/Macros box or in the list below the Menu Text box. Then type the new name in the Menu Text box.

7   Choose the Add button.

8   Repeat steps 3 through 7 for each command or macro you want to add.

9   Choose the Close button.

Note If you want to use a letter of the command name as an access key, type an ampersand (&) before the letter in the Menu Text box. If a particular access key is used twice on the same menu, you will need to press the key once and then press ENTER to choose the first command or press the key twice and then press ENTER to choose the second command.

To remove a command or macro from a menu

1   From the Tools menu, choose Options (ALT, O, O).

2   Under Category, select Menus.

3   In the Menu box, select the menu containing the command or macro you want to remove.

4   In the list under the Menu Text box, select the command or macro you want to remove.

5   Choose the Delete button, and then choose the Close button.

To reset menus to the Microsoft standard

You can reset the menus to the default arrangement originally set by Microsoft.

1   From the Tools menu, choose Options (ALT, O, O).

2   Under Category, select Menus.

3   Choose the Reset All button, and then choose the Close button.

To save the new menu assignments

▶ To save the new menu assignments, do one of the following:

- To save the new assignments immediately, choose Save All from the File menu (ALT, F, E). When Word prompts you to save global glossary and command changes, or changes to the attached template, choose the Yes button.

- To save the new assignments when you exit Word, choose the Yes button when Word prompts you to save global glossary and command changes, or changes to the attached template.

Customizing Shortcut Key Assignments

In the Keyboard category of the Options dialog box, you can change the shortcut keys that choose commands or start macros.

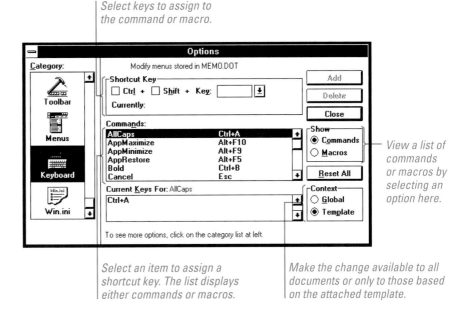

Select keys to assign to the command or macro.

View a list of commands or macros by selecting an option here.

Select an item to assign a shortcut key. The list displays either commands or macros.

Make the change available to all documents or only to those based on the attached template.

To assign a shortcut key to a command or macro

You can make commands, dialog box options, and other items more accessible by assigning key combinations to them.

1 From the Tools menu, choose Options (ALT, O, O).

2 Under Category, select Keyboard.

3 Under Context, select the Template option button if you want to make the key assignment available only to documents based on the attached template.

The Template option button is unavailable if the template attached to your document is NORMAL.DOT.

–or–

Under Context, select the Global option button if you want to make the key assignment available to all documents, including those based on the attached template.

4 Under Show, select either Commands or Macros.

5 In the Commands/Macros box, select the command or macro to which you want to assign a key combination.

In the Current Keys For box, Word lists the keys currently assigned to the selected command or macro.

6 Under Shortcut Key, select the keys you want to assign, or press the key combination you want.

For keys other than the function keys (F1, F2, F3, and so on), you must include either or both the CTRL and SHIFT keys in the key combination.

If the key combination you select is already assigned, the name of the command or macro it's assigned to appears next to Currently. To reassign the combination to the item now selected, proceed to the next step. If you want the key combination to remain assigned to its current command or macro, press or select a different key combination before proceeding.

7 Choose the Add button.

8 Repeat steps 3 through 7 for every shortcut key you want to assign.

9 Choose the Close button.

To remove a shortcut key assignment

You can remove key assignments from commands, dialog box options, and other items, freeing those key combinations for other assignments.

1 From the Tools menu, choose Options (ALT, O, O).

2 Under Category, select Keyboard.

3 Under Show, select either Commands or Macros.

4 In the Commands/Macros box, select the command or macro from which you want to remove the shortcut key.

5 In the Current Keys For box, select the shortcut key assignment you want to remove.

6 Choose the Delete button, and then choose the Close button.

To reset key assignments to the Microsoft standard

You can reset shortcut keys to the assignments originally set by Microsoft.

1   From the Tools menu, choose Options (ALT, O, O).

2   Under Category, select Keyboard.

3   Choose the Reset All button, and then choose the Close button.

To save the new key assignments

▶   To save the new key assignments, do one of the following:

■   To save the new assignments immediately, choose Save All from the File menu
(ALT, F, E). When Word prompts you to save global glossary and command
changes, or changes to the attached template, choose the Yes button.

■   To save the new assignments when you exit Word, choose the Yes button when
Word prompts you to save global glossary and command changes, or changes
to the attached template.

Customizing the Toolbar

In the Options dialog box, you can customize the Toolbar so that it contains buttons
for the commands or macros you use most often.

*Add, remove, or change
existing buttons.*

*Select an item to add to the Toolbar. The
list displays either commands or macros.*

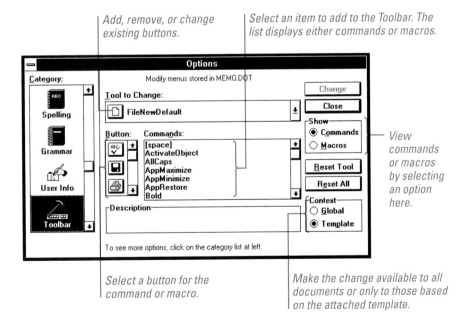

*View
commands
or macros
by selecting
an option
here.*

*Select a button for the
command or macro.*

*Make the change available to all
documents or only to those based
on the attached template.*

To add a command or macro to the Toolbar

When you add a new command or macro, you select both the command or macro and a button. Then on the Toolbar, you select the space that you want to replace with the new button.

1 From the Tools menu, choose Options (ALT, O, O).

2 Under Category, select Toolbar.

3 Under Context, select the Template option button if you want to make the Toolbar change available only to documents based on the attached template.

   The Template option button is unavailable if the template attached to your document is NORMAL.DOT.
   –or–
   Under Context, select the Global option button if you want to make the Toolbar change available to all documents, including those based on the attached template.

4 Under Show, select either Commands or Macros.

5 In the Commands/Macros box, select the command or macro you want to add to the Toolbar.

6 In the Button box, select a button for the command or macro.

7 In the Tool To Change box, select the space where you want the button to appear.

8 Choose the Change button.

9 Repeat steps 3 through 8 for each command or macro you want to add.

10 Choose the Close button.

To remove a button from the Toolbar

To remove a button from the Toolbar, you replace the button with a space.

1 From the Tools menu, choose Options (ALT, O, O).

2 Under Category, select Toolbar.

3 In the Tool To Change box, select the button you want to remove.

4 In the Commands/Macros box, select the first entry, [space].

5 Choose the Change button.

6 Repeat steps 3 through 5 for each button you want to remove.

7 Choose the Close button.

To change the command or macro assigned to a button

1   From the Tools menu, choose Options (ALT, O, O).

2   Under Category, select Toolbar.

3   Under Show, select Commands or Macros.

4   In the Commands/Macros box, select the command or macro you want to add to the Toolbar.

5   In the Tool To Change box, select the button you want to assign to the new command or macro.

6   Choose the Change button, and then choose the Close button.

To reset a Toolbar button to the Microsoft standard

You can return an individual button to the default assignment originally set by Microsoft, leaving other buttons customized.

1   From the Tools menu, choose Options (ALT, O, O).

2   Under Category, select Toolbar.

3   In the Tool To Change box, select the button you want to return to the Microsoft standard.

4   Choose the Reset Tool button, and then choose the Close button.

To reset the entire Toolbar to the Microsoft standard

For a complete listing of the default Toolbar assignments originally set by Microsoft, see Chapter 1, "The Word Workplace."

You can return the entire Toolbar to the default assignments originally set by Microsoft.

1   From the Tools menu, choose Options (ALT, O, O).

2   Under Category, select Toolbar.

3   Choose the Reset All button, and then choose the Close button.

To save the new Toolbar assignments

▶   To save the new Toolbar assignments, do one of the following:

   ■   To save the new assignments immediately, choose Save All from the File menu (ALT, F, E). When Word prompts you to save global glossary and command changes, or changes to the attached template, choose the Yes button.

   ■   To save the new assignments when you exit Word, choose the Yes button when Word prompts you to save global glossary and command changes, or changes to the attached template.

Chapter 39

Setting Preferences

Imagine designing your own word processor with menu commands, key assignments, dialog box defaults, and other screen elements set up precisely the way you want. Versatile customizing features in Word make it possible for you to do just that.

You can accept the default option settings that come with Word, or you can change them to suit your own preferences. For example, you might want to:

- Open documents with hidden text, such as index entries, visible.
- Have Word update all fields in a document before printing.
- Have backup copies of your documents made automatically.
- Have Word automatically save your documents at a specified time interval.
- Specify which rules the Spelling and Grammar commands apply.

You can change eleven categories of options by choosing the Options command from the Tools menu. The individual options for each category are described in "Options in Detail," later in this chapter.

Use this category	To set these options
View	Defaults such as showing hidden text, table gridlines, or nonprinting characters.
General	Defaults concerning general editing features and preferred unit of measure.
Print	Printing defaults, such as whether or not to update fields when you print, and whether or not to print field codes, annotations, and hidden text.
Save	Defaults such as whether or not to make backup copies, allow fast saves, or automatically save your work at an interval you specify.
Spelling	Spelling rules and the dictionaries used by the Spelling command.
Grammar	Style and grammar rules used by the Grammar command.
User Info	Your name, initials, and mailing address.
Toolbar	Buttons assigned to the Toolbar and which command or macro is assigned to each one.
Menus	Commands and macros assigned to menus.
Keyboard	Shortcut keys assigned to commands and macros.
WIN.INI	Startup options for converters, filters, and proofing tools.

Changing Default Options

When you choose the Options command from the Tools menu, Word displays the Options dialog box.

Select the category you want to view.

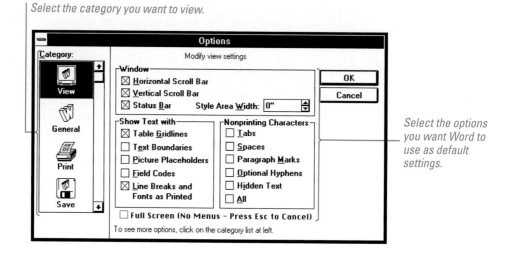

Select the options you want Word to use as default settings.

The Options dialog box is divided into two parts: the Category box on the left and the options panel on the right. When you select a category, the panel changes to display the options and default settings in that category. You determine the default settings for any category by selecting or clearing the options in the panel. To change the options for several categories, select a category, select the options, and then select the next category. The new default settings take effect when you choose another category or close the dialog box.

To set options

1 From the Tools menu, choose Options (ALT, O, O).

2 In the Category box, select the category containing the default options you want to change.

3 In the panel on the right, select or clear options to specify the default settings you want Word to use.

For information about each option in a particular category, see "Options in Detail," later in this chapter.

4 Select another category or close the dialog box by choosing the OK or Close button.

Making Changes Globally or in a Template

For more information about templates, see Chapter 37, "Document Templates."

Changes you make in most of the Options categories are saved in the NORMAL.DOT or WINWORD.INI files and apply to any document you open, regardless of which template you are using. However, changes you make in the Menus, Keyboard, and Toolbar categories can be saved globally, so that they are available to all documents, or with the attached template, so that they are available only to documents based on that template.

If you want to save changes made to these three categories in a different template, you need to attach that template by using the Template command on the File menu. To save changes made to these categories globally, so they are available in all templates, attach the NORMAL.DOT template.

By using different templates, you can create the most suitable work environment for each kind of document you produce. For example, if you frequently use tables when you write reports, you can add the commands you use most often to the Table menu and save these menu settings in a template. Then when you create a report, attach this template to the Word document, and the commands will be right where you need them.

Options in Detail

This section describes the preferences you can set using the Options command.

View

Select the View category to specify how Word displays your documents. For example, if you frequently use tables, you could select the Table Gridlines check box. Then each time you open a document, table gridlines will be visible. Once the document is open, you can change the display at any time by changing the appropriate options.

Window

Use options under Window to determine which window elements Word displays when you open a new document.

Horizontal Scroll Bar Select this option to have a scroll bar automatically displayed along the bottom of the Word window each time you open a new document.

Vertical Scroll Bar Select this option to have a scroll bar automatically displayed along the right side of the Word window each time you open a new document.

Status Bar Select this option to have the status bar automatically displayed at the bottom of the Word window each time you open a new document. The status bar provides information about the active document, such as the current page number and the total number of pages, and information about Toolbar buttons and typing modes.

Style Area Width Word opens the style name area on the left side of the document window to display style names. Type a value or click the arrows to set the width of the style name area.

Show Text With

Use these options to determine what text guidelines and information Word displays.

Table Gridlines   With this option selected, Word displays dotted lines between rows and columns in tables. These gridlines can help you determine the boundaries of cells when working with tables. Word does not print table gridlines.

Text Boundaries   Use this option to display dotted rectangles around elements such as text areas, headers, footers, and framed objects in page layout view. This is useful for recognizing various text areas when viewing or editing complex layouts.

Picture Placeholders   Select this option to display rectangles in place of graphics to speed up scrolling through a document. Graphics still print correctly with this option selected.

Field Codes   You can have Word display field codes instead of field results. For instance, with this option selected, Word displays a DATE field as {DATE}. With this option cleared, Word displays the date itself, such as 10/25/91.

Line Breaks And Fonts As Printed   Select this option to display line breaks and fonts the way they will appear when printed. If you choose a font or size not available on the selected printer, Word displays the closest one available.

Nonprinting Characters

Select which nonprinting characters will be visible on the screen.

Tabs   Select this to display tab characters (→).

Spaces   Select this to display space marks (··).

Paragraph Marks   Select this to display paragraph marks (¶), end-of-cell characters (⌧), and newline breaks (SHIFT+ENTER) (↵).

Optional Hyphens   Select this to display optional hyphens (¬)—those you have added by pressing CTRL+HYPHEN and those added by Word when you use the Hyphenate command. Selecting this option also displays non-breaking hyphens you have added using CTRL+SHIFT+HYPHEN; they appear as a longer line (—).

Hidden Text   Select this option if you want hidden text displayed. Hidden text is indicated on the screen by a dotted underline. Displaying hidden text affects line wrapping and page breaks in normal and page layout view, but not in print preview or when printing. Selecting this option determines only whether or not hidden text is displayed. To print hidden text, you must select the Hidden Text option in the Print category of the Options dialog box.

All   Select this option if you want to display all nonprinting characters.

Full Screen (No Menus)

When you select the Full Screen (No Menus) check box, Word hides all screen elements, including menus, the Toolbar, ribbon, ruler, scroll bars, title bar, style area, and status bar. Press ESC to restore all hidden elements to the Word screen.

General

Select the General category to set defaults regarding typing and editing.

Settings

Background Repagination   If you select this option, Word automatically repaginates documents when the program is idle; that is, when you are not typing or editing. Selecting Background Repagination may slow some operations. If this happens, clear this option and use the Repaginate Now command on the Tools menu when you want to repaginate your document.

Typing Replaces Selection   Select this option if you want Word to replace selected text with the new text you type.

Drag-And-Drop Text Editing   When this option is selected, you can use the mouse to drag a selection—text or a graphic—to a new location in the document. Clear this option if you don't want the mouse to function in that manner.

Confirm File Conversions   Select this option if you want to confirm which converter Word uses when you are converting a file to Word. If you leave this option cleared, Word uses what is most likely the appropriate converter without getting your confirmation.

Use The INS Key For Paste   Select this option if you want to use the INS key as the shortcut key for the Paste command.

Overtype Mode   Select this option if you want Word to replace existing text as you type. You can also switch between normal and overtype mode by pressing the INS key (if the Use The INS Key For Paste option is not selected). When overtype mode is on, "OVR" appears in the status bar at the bottom of the screen.

WordPerfect Help   Select this option if you want to access commands with the keys used in WordPerfect and learn how to perform the same operations in Word.

WordPerfect Document Navigation Keys   Select this option if you want to move around your document with the keys used in WordPerfect.

Measurement Units

Select the unit of measure you want to be used on the ruler, in dialog boxes, and for measurements such as margins and tab settings. You can choose inches, centimeters, points, or picas. The ruler and measurements displayed in text boxes change to reflect the unit you choose. Note, however, that spacing measurements, such as superscript and subscript, expand and condense, and line spacing, continue to use points, even if you change the default measurement.

Print

Select the Print category to specify printing defaults. The printing options you select remain in effect for all documents until you change them. These options also appear when you choose the Options button in the Print dialog box.

Printing Options

Use these options to control how Word prints documents.

Draft Output   With this option selected, Word prints documents without formatting. Character formatting is printed as underlining and graphics are printed as empty box frames. This option gives you the fastest printing, to review the text of a document without formatting.

Reverse Print Order   Select this option to have documents printed from the end to the beginning. This option is useful for printers that stack the printed pages face up.

Update Fields   Selecting this option directs Word to update all fields in the document before printing.

Include With Document

Select options to have additional information and elements, such as summary information or hidden text, printed with documents.

Summary Info   You can have Word print the information you provided about the document in the Summary Info dialog box, such as the document title, subject, author, and keywords. The summary information is printed on a separate page.

Field Codes   With this option selected, Word prints field codes instead of field results. For example, Word displays a DATE field as {DATE}. With this option cleared, Word displays the date itself; for example, 9/5/91.

Annotations   Select this option to have Word print annotations on separate pages at the end of a document. When you select this option, Hidden Text is automatically selected because the annotations are formatted as hidden text.

Hidden Text   Select this option to print any text that has the hidden text format, even if hidden text is not displayed in the document.

Envelope Options

Printer's Envelope Feeder Has Been Installed   Select this option if you have attached an envelope feeder to the printer and want Word to use it.

Options For Current Document Only

Widow/Orphan Control   Selecting this option prevents a widow (the last line of a paragraph) from being printed by itself at the top of a page or an orphan (the first line of a paragraph) from being printed by itself at the bottom of a page.

Save

Select the Save category to set the default options that Word uses when saving.

Save Options

For more information about backup copies and fast saves, see Chapter 2, "Opening, Saving, and Deleting Documents."

Always Create Backup Copy Select this option to have Word automatically create a backup copy whenever you save a document. Word saves backup copies under the current filename with a .BAK filename extension. Each time you save, Word updates the backup copy with the latest changes. Selecting Always Create Backup Copy does not allow fast saves. You can also change this option whenever you save a document by choosing Save As from the File menu.

Allow Fast Saves Select this option to save documents more quickly than usual. Fast saves attach the changes you make to the end of a document file, rather than updating the entire file as in a normal save. However, with this option selected, your documents grow in size and consume more memory, so Word occasionally performs a normal save to consolidate accumulated changes. If the Always Create Backup Copy option is selected, Word will not perform fast saves.

Prompt for Summary Info If you select this option, Word automatically displays the Summary Info dialog box when you save a new document. In the Summary Info dialog box, you can enter information such as title, subject, author, keywords, and comments. If you clear this option, you can choose Summary Info from the File menu when you want to enter this information.

Automatic Save Every __ Minutes Select this option to have Word save your document at regular intervals. Type or select a time interval in minutes.

Spelling

For more information about using dictionaries with the Spelling command, see Chapter 14, "Proofing a Document."

Select the Spelling category to specify the dictionaries and general rules Word uses when you choose the Spelling command from the Tools menu. This category also appears when you choose the Options button after choosing the Spelling command.

Ignore

During a spell check, Word checks every word in your document, including acronyms and words with numbers. To speed up your spell checks, you can have Word ignore certain types of words by selecting options under Ignore.

Words In UPPERCASE Select this option to have Word ignore words typed in all capital letters. This option is handy if you use a lot of acronyms and abbreviations and don't want Word to question these words during a spell check. Word continues to check the spelling of words that are capitalized by applying the All Caps or Small Caps character format.

Words With Numbers Select this option to have Word ignore any combination of characters containing a number, such as 20mg or 408tx1. Even if this option is not selected, Word ignores combinations of numbers and letters that contain only one letter, such as 3a or 640k.

Custom Dictionaries

Select the custom dictionaries you want Word to use during spell checks. You create custom dictionaries for words in your documents that are not in a main dictionary, such as specialized terms, acronyms and abbreviations, and names of clients and business associates. When you add these words to a custom dictionary and select that dictionary for a spell check, Word doesn't question the words.

Word displays all available custom dictionaries (*.DIC files) located in the Word directory, the current directory, and the spelling path in the WIN.INI file. You can select up to four custom dictionaries at a time.

Add   Use the Add button to create new custom dictionaries or add existing ones to the list of available dictionaries.

Always Suggest

Select this option if you want Word to automatically display suggested spellings every time it encounters an unknown word during a spell check. If you clear this option, you can still choose the Suggest button in the Spelling dialog box to display a list of suggestions for a particular word.

Grammar

For more information about using the Grammar command, see Chapter 14, "Proofing a Document."

Select the Grammar category to specify the rules Word applies when you choose the Grammar command from the Tools menu. This category also appears when you choose the Options button during a grammar check.

Use Grammar And Style Rules

You can select one of three predefined rule groups for Word to use during grammar checks.

Strictly (All Rules)   Select this option if you want Word to apply all available rules during the grammar check.

For Business Writing   Select this option to clear some of the style rules if you want more flexibility in your writing style.

For Casual Writing   Select this option if you want to clear a few additional categories.

Customize Settings

Choose this button if you want to modify the default settings in any of the three grammar checking levels. Word displays a separate dialog box, where you can specify which style and grammar rules are applied during a grammar check. You can also control how Word checks for split infinitives, consecutive nouns, and consecutive prepositional phrases. For specific information about customizing these grammar settings, see Chapter 14, "Proofing a Document."

Show Readability Statistics After Proofing

If you select this option, Word displays a box after a grammar check that provides statistical counts of the words, characters, paragraphs, and sentences in the active document. Word also calculates several readability indexes that help you evaluate how easily your writing can be understood by the average adult reader.

User Info

Select the User Info category to enter information about yourself.

Name

Type the name you want Word to use in the Author text box of the Summary Info dialog box. The default name is the one typed during Word installation.

Initials

Type the initials you want Word to display when an annotation mark is added.

Mailing Address

Type your address, which can automatically be added as the return address when printing envelopes.

Toolbar

Select the Toolbar category to customize the Toolbar so it contains buttons for the commands or macros you use most often. Changes to the Toolbar are stored in the active template, which is identified at the top of the dialog box. If you want to store changes to the Toolbar in a different template, choose Template from the File menu and then select the template you want to modify. For more information, see Chapter 38, "Customizing Menus, the Keyboard, and the Toolbar."

Tool To Change

Select the button you want to modify. If you want to add a new button, select the option [space] where you want the new button to appear.

Show

Commands   Select this option to add or delete Word commands on the Toolbar. The Commands/Macros box displays the commands available in Word

Macros   Select this option to add or delete your own macros on the Toolbar. The Commands/Macros box displays the available macros.

Commands/Macros

The contents of this list box change according to what you select under Show: Commands or Macros. Select the command or macro that you want to add to the Toolbar. If you want to delete a button from the Toolbar, select the first item, [space]. This allows you to replace a selected button with a blank space.

Button

Select the button you want to add to the Toolbar, after selecting the command or macro you want associated with it.

Description

Displays a description of the selected command or macro.

Reset Tool

Choose Reset Tool to restore an individual button to the default assignment originally shipped with Word.

Reset All

Choose this button to restore the original Toolbar shipped with Word.

Context

Global   Select this option if you want the change to the Toolbar to be available to all documents, including those based on the template attached to your document.

Template   Select this option if you want the change to the Toolbar to be available only to documents based on the attached template. This option is unavailable if the template attached to your document is NORMAL.DOT.

Menus

Select the Menus category to add or remove Word commands and macros on menus. Changes you make to the menus are stored in the active template, which is identified at the top of the dialog box. If you want to store changes to the menus in a different template, first choose Template from the File menu and then select the template you want to modify. For information about how to customize menus, see Chapter 38, "Customizing Menus, the Keyboard, and the Toolbar."

Menu

Select the menu you want to change.

Menu Text

When you select a command or macro in the Commands/Macros box or in the list below the Menu Text box, that item is inserted into the Menu Text box. You can then add or remove the item on a selected menu. You can also rename the command or macro or change the access key. To change the access key for the menu item, type an ampersand (&) before the letter of the key you want to use.

Show

Commands   Select this option to add or remove Word commands on menus.

Macros   Select this option to add or remove macros on menus.

Commands/Macros

The contents of this list box change according to which option you select under Show: Commands or Macros. Select the command or macro that you want to add to or remove from a menu.

Description

Displays a description of the selected command or macro.

Add

Choose this button to add the item displayed in the Menu Text box to the selected menu.

Delete

Choose this button to remove the item displayed in the Menu Text box from the selected menu.

Reset All

Choose this button to restore the original menus shipped with Word.

Context

Global   Select this option if you want the change to the menus to be available to all documents, including those based on the template attached to your document.

Template   Select this option if you want the change to the menus to be available only to documents based on the attached template. This option is unavailable if the template attached to your document is NORMAL.DOT.

Keyboard

Select the Keyboard category to customize the keyboard so you can use the shortcut keys you find handiest. Changes you make to the keyboard are stored in the active template, which is identified at the top of the dialog box. If you want to store changes to the keyboard in a different template, choose Template from the File menu and then select the template you want to modify. For information about how to customize the keyboard, see Chapter 38, "Customizing Menus, the Keyboard, and the Toolbar."

Shortcut Key

Select the keys you want to assign to the selected command or macro.

Currently   Shows the name of any command or macro already assigned to the key combination you specify.

Show

Commands   Select this option if you want to assign shortcut keys to Word commands.

Macros   Select this option if you want to assign shortcut keys to macros.

Commands/Macros

The contents of this list box change according to which option you select under Show: Commands or Macros. Select the command or macro to which you want to assign a shortcut key combination.

Current Keys For

Displays the name of the selected command or macro and any keys already assigned.

Add

Choose this button to add the specified keys to the selected command or macro.

Delete

Choose this button to remove the selected keys from the selected command or macro.

Reset All

Choose this button to restore the original shortcut key assignments shipped with Word.

Context

Global   Select this option if you want the change to the key assignments to be available to all documents, including those based on the template attached to your document.

Template   Select this option if you want the change to the key assignments to be available only to documents based on the attached template. This option is unavailable if the template attached to your document is NORMAL.DOT.

WIN.INI

For more information about modifying the WIN.INI file, see Appendix B, "Modifying the WIN.INI File."

Select the WIN.INI category to change startup options for different Word features.

Application

Select the section containing the settings you want to modify.

Startup Options

Select the option you want to modify.

Option

Displays the selected option.

Setting

Edit the setting in this box.

Delete

Choose this button to delete the selected option.

Set

Choose this button to apply the new setting to the selected option.

Chapter 40

Bookmarks and Cross-references

When you insert a bookmark in a Word document, you assign a name to a particular location or selection in the document. The following are some of the things you can do after marking a location with a bookmark:

- Find a marked location quickly using the Go To command on the Edit menu
- Use marked numbers in a calculation and insert the result into your document
- Insert marked text into another document with a link for automatic updating
- Create cross-references within text, page number cross-references, or cross-references to items in automatically numbered lists
- Update linked text automatically

Using Bookmarks

Use bookmarks to mark locations you want to find or easily refer to later. You can insert as many as 450 bookmarks in a single document.

Inserting and Deleting Bookmarks

Inserting a bookmark is like tagging a particular location or selection. A bookmark does not appear on the screen or when you print the document. Instead, Word invisibly marks the location with the name you specify.

To insert a bookmark

1   Position the insertion point where you want to insert a bookmark.

    If you want to mark a location in the document, position the insertion point in that location. If you want to mark a particular amount of text, select the text.

2   From the Insert menu, choose Bookmark (ALT, I, M).

3   In the Bookmark Name box, type a name.

    Bookmark names can be from 1 to 20 characters long, must begin with a letter, and cannot contain spaces—only letters, numbers, and the underscore character (_).

    If you type a bookmark name that is already assigned, the original bookmark is removed, and the current location or selection is marked with this name instead of the location or selection you originally marked.

4   Choose the OK button.

The location or selection is now named, and the name of the bookmark is listed in the Bookmark dialog box.

Important   If you replace all the characters in a block of marked text or delete a marked location, the bookmark no longer exists. If this is not what you intended, choose the Undo command from the Edit menu before taking any other action to restore the marked text or location and its bookmark name.

To delete a bookmark

When you no longer need a location or selection marked, you can delete the bookmark.

1 From the Insert menu, choose Bookmark (ALT, I, M).

2 Type or select the bookmark name you want to delete.

3 Choose the Delete button.

4 Choose the Close button.

Tip   Another way to remove a bookmark from one location is to insert a new bookmark in a different location, giving it the name of the bookmark you want to remove. Word inserts the bookmark in the new location, removing it from the first one.

Working with Marked Locations

Once you have inserted bookmarks, you can use marked locations in a number of ways.

To go to a marked location

1 From the Edit menu, choose Go To (ALT, E, G).

2 In the Go To box, type or select the bookmark name.

3 Choose the OK button.

–Or–

1 Press the Go To key (F5).

2 In the status bar, type the bookmark name.

3 Press ENTER.

Moving Marked Text

If you cut marked text and paste it in a new location, the pasted text is still marked. If you copy marked text and paste it in a new location, the pasted text is marked, but the original text is no longer marked.

If you paste marked text into a different document, the bookmark and bookmark name are also pasted. The bookmark name appears in the Bookmark and Go To dialog boxes when either document is open.

To use marked numbers in a calculation

You can use bookmarks to perform calculations on numbers at different locations in a document.

1 Select a number you want to include in the calculation.

2 Insert a bookmark.

3 Repeat steps 1 and 2 for each number you want to include in the calculation.

4 Position the insertion point where you want the result of the calculation to appear.

5 From the Insert menu, choose Field (ALT, I, D).

6 In the Insert Field Type box, select = Expression, if it's not already selected.

7 In the Field Code box, type an expression using the bookmark names as the values to be calculated.

> For example, if your file contains bookmarks called "income" and "expenses," and you want to calculate net gain and insert the result into your document, type an expression in the Field Code box such as the following:
>
> **= income - expenses**

8 Choose the OK button.

If there is a check mark next to the Field Codes command on the View menu, Word displays field codes. If there is no check mark next to the Field Codes command, Word displays field results instead.

The result of the calculation appears at the location of the field, unless the Field Codes command has been chosen. If you want to look at or modify the expression, position the insertion point immediately in front of the result, and then press the Field Codes key (SHIFT+F9). To see the result again, press the Update Field key (F9).

For more information about fields, see Chapter 41, "Fields," and Chapter 16, "Math Calculations."

To insert marked text into another document

1 In the first document, select the text you want to insert into another document, and then insert a bookmark.

2 In the second document, position the insertion point where you want the marked text to appear.

3 From the Insert menu, choose File (ALT, I, L).

4 In the File Name box, type or select the name of the document that contains the marked text.

5 In the Range box, type the bookmark name.

6   If you want Word to update the inserted text if the text in the first document changes, select the Link To File check box.

7   Choose the OK button.

Word inserts an INCLUDE field whose result is the marked text. If you want to update the field, select it, and then press the Update Field key (F9).

Creating Cross-references

Using bookmarks and fields, you can create three kinds of cross-references. You can create textual cross-references, page number cross-references, or cross-references to an item in an automatically numbered sequence. Then if you later change the marked text, you can have Word update the reference automatically.

To create a cross-reference to text

You can use bookmarks and fields to create a cross-reference to text in another part of the document.

1   Select the text to which you want to refer.

2   Insert a bookmark.

For more information, see "To insert a bookmark," earlier in this chapter.

3   Position the insertion point where you want the reference to appear.

4   From the Insert menu, choose Field (ALT, I, D).

5   Press R to select Reference in the Insert Field Type box.

6   In the Instructions box, select the bookmark name.

7   Choose the Add button.

8   Choose the OK button.

Word inserts a REF field whose result is the text marked with the bookmark. If the marked text changes, you can update the cross-reference by selecting the REF field and then pressing the Update Field key (F9).

To create a page number cross-reference

You can use bookmarks and fields to create a page number cross-reference.

1   Select the text for which you want to create a page number cross-reference.

2   Insert a bookmark.

   For more information, see "To insert a bookmark," earlier in this chapter.

3   Position the insertion point where you want the page number of the referenced text to appear.

4   From the Insert menu, choose Field (ALT, I, D).

5   Press P twice to select Page Ref. in the Insert Field Type box.

6   In the Instructions box, select the bookmark name.

7   Choose the Add button.

8   Choose the OK button.

Word inserts a PAGEREF field whose result is the page number on which the text marked with the bookmark appears. If the location of the marked text changes, you can update the cross-reference by selecting the PAGEREF field and then pressing the Update Field key (F9).

Fields

A field is a set of codes that instruct Word to insert material into a document automatically. The DATE field, for example, inserts the current date, the TIME field, the current time. You can use fields to add text, graphics, page numbers, and other material to your Word document. You can also use fields to automate certain more complex Word functions, such as indexing.

If you've worked with Word, you may have already used fields without knowing it, because many Word commands insert fields. For example, the Page Number command on the Insert menu inserts a PAGE field. Using these commands, you can get much of the benefit of fields without working with them directly.

However, by working with fields directly, you can tailor them to your needs.

The Elements of a Field

The codes used to create a field have three basic parts:

- The *field characters* ({ }) show the beginning and end of a field. They look like braces, but to insert field characters, you use the Insert Field key (CTRL+F9), not the brace keys on the keyboard.

- The *field type* identifies the action you want the field to perform.

- The *instructions* are the details of how you want the action performed. Instructions can contain *switches* that modify the results of the instructions.

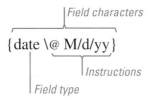

Field Codes and Field Results

Most fields generate field results. The field result is what appears in your document when you print it. The result of the DATE field, for example, is the current date. The result of the PAGE field is the current page number. You can choose to view on-screen either the field's code or its result. You can switch between views using the Field Codes command on the View menu or the Field Codes key (SHIFT+F9). The preceding illustration shows the field code; the result of that field is 12/1/91.

Most often, you'll want to see field results, because they are what appear in your printed document. However, it's useful to see codes if you want to edit a field. For example, you might want to modify the DATE field to produce a date in a different format. To change the date format, you change the format instructions. For example, the modified field {date \@ "MMMM d, yyyy"} produces the current date in the format "December 1, 1991."

Updating Fields

Much of the power of fields lies in the fact that they can be updated. When a field is updated, Word checks to see if the conditions that created the current field result have changed; if they have, Word changes the result accordingly. For example, when the DATE field is updated, Word checks the current date and changes the field result if the date has changed.

Tip   You can find general information on using fields, as well as specific information on field types, in online Help. To gain access to the Help topic quickly, press SHIFT+F1 and then, while the mouse pointer is a question mark, use it to choose Field from the Insert menu. The Help window displays the topic on the Field command.

Common Uses for Fields

For information on specific fields, see the entries on this topic in online Help.

Fields can play a useful part in many tasks. To give you a sense of how to use fields in your work, this section presents an overview of some of their functions.

Time, Date, and Summary Information

Time and date fields insert the time and date in the format you specify. Summary information fields, such as AUTHOR and TITLE, provide a way to insert into your document information from the Summary Info and Document Statistics dialog boxes.

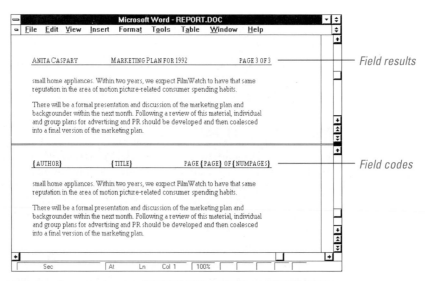

Fields in a document header: AUTHOR, TITLE, PAGE, and NUMPAGES

Numbering

With the automatic numbering fields, you can separately number tables, figures, and lists. You can also have Word automatically number outlines and legal documents.

Cross-references

For information on specific fields, see the entries on this topic in online Help.

Using the REF, PAGEREF, and FTNREF fields, you can create cross-references to text, page numbers, and even footnote numbers. Using the STYLEREF field, you can create dictionary-style headers.

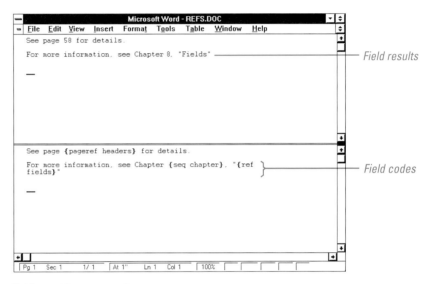

Fields used in a cross-reference

Indexes, Tables of Contents, and Lists

See also Chapter 29, "Indexes and Tables of Contents."

With INDEX and TOC fields, you can compile highly customized indexes and tables of contents, based on entries created with XE (Index Entry) and TC (Table of Contents Entry) fields in your document.

Calculating

For more information, see Chapter 16, "Math Calculations."

Using Expression (=) fields with a Word table, you can set up a simple spreadsheet in your document.

Merge Printing

For information on merge printing, see Part 8, "Merging Documents."

Many fields, such as DATA, NEXT, MERGEFIELD, and MERGEREC, are intended for merge printing.

Linking and Embedding

Using the LINK field, you can establish links to files created in other Windows applications, such as Microsoft Excel. Information inserted from these files can be updated either automatically or when you choose. When you insert into your Word document objects created in other Windows applications, Word inserts an EMBED field. Once having embedded an object, you can easily edit it.

Specialized Uses

Using these fields, you can add some unusual features to your documents.

The FILLIN field   This field provides a useful way to guide someone through filling out a form. The FILLIN field prompts the user to enter information (to "fill in" the blank).

"Button" fields   Word includes two fields that act like buttons: if you double-click them, they produce an action. When you double-click the GOTOBUTTON field, it acts like the Go To command on the Edit menu and positions the insertion point at the location specified in the field. When you double-click the MACROBUTTON field, it runs the macro specified in the field. The macro can be a Word command or a macro.

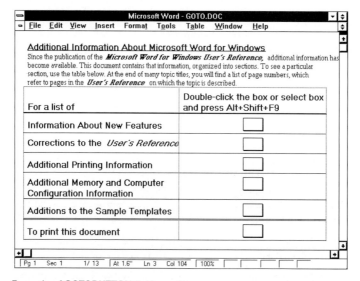

Example of GOTOBUTTON field results

Working with Fields

This section covers inserting, viewing, editing, formatting, and updating fields.

Inserting Fields

The easiest way to insert some fields is indirectly, using a command that inserts them for you. Here is a table listing the Word commands that insert fields and the fields they can insert:

This command	Can insert these fields
Paste (Edit menu)	EMBED
Paste Special (Edit menu)	LINK, EMBED
Header/Footer (View menu)	PAGE, DATE, TIME
Date And Time (Insert menu)	DATE, TIME
Symbol (Insert menu)	SYMBOL
Index Entry (Insert menu)	XE
Index (Insert menu)	INDEX
Table Of Contents (Insert menu)	TOC
File (Insert menu)	INCLUDE
Picture (Insert menu)	IMPORT
Object (Insert menu)	EMBED
Bullets And Numbering (Tools menu)	SYMBOL, AUTONUM, AUTONUMLGL, AUTONUMOUT

Most fields, however, must be inserted directly, using either the Field command on the Insert menu or the Insert Field key (CTRL+F9). The Field dialog box lists all of the available fields, as well as field instructions and switches for some fields. If you know the field name and instructions you want to type, you use the Insert Field key (CTRL+F9) and type the field codes directly into your document.

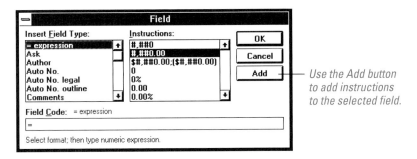

Use the Add button to add instructions to the selected field.

To insert a field from the menu

1 From the Insert menu, choose Field (ALT, I, D).

2 Select a field type.

3 Select instructions, if required, and then choose the Add button.
   –or–
   Type instructions in the Field Code box.

   For information on the instructions used with different fields, see the entries on this topic in online Help.

4 Choose the OK button.

To insert a field without using the menu

1 Press the Insert Field key (CTRL+F9).

2 Type the field type and its instructions.

   For information on the instructions used with different fields, see the entries on this topic in online Help.

3 Press an arrow key to leave the field.

–Or–

▶ Type the contents of the field, select them, and then press the Insert Field key (CTRL+F9).

Note Field instructions must always be separated by a space from the field type—for example:

`{date \@ "M/d/yy"}`

If you type `{date\@ "M/d/yy"}`, the field shows no result instead of the correct result.

To nest a field

You can insert a field within another field—for example, `{set name {fillin "What is your name?"}}`. This is called *nesting*. You can nest fields to as many as 20 levels.

1 Position the insertion point within an existing field, after the field type.

2 Insert the field you want to nest by pressing CTRL+F9 and then typing the field code.

Viewing Field Codes and Field Results

Fields are displayed on screen either as field codes or as results. For example, the DATE field may appear on your screen as {date}—the field code—or as the current date, say 12/1/91—the field result. You can switch the view from field codes to results, and back again, for your entire document or for selected fields.

A few fields have results that are not visible on the screen or in your document. These fields initiate actions that affect the results of other fields. They are the following:

ASK	DATA
NEXT	NEXTIF
SET	SKIPIF
RD (Referenced Document)	TC (TOC Entry)
XE (Index Entry)	

Viewing the "results" of these fields means that the fields are not displayed on your screen.

Sometimes it's useful to view field codes and their results at the same time. You can do this by viewing field codes in one window or pane and their results in another, as shown in the following illustration.

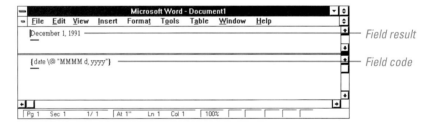

Field result — December 1, 1991

Field code — {date \@ "MMMM d, yyyy"}

To switch between showing field codes and field results for the whole document

Three fields, RD (Referenced Document), TC (TOC Entry), and XE (Index Entry), are automatically formatted as hidden text when you insert them. You can display them only when you display hidden text. The Field Codes command and the Field Codes key (SHIFT+F9) have no effect on them.

For All Fields Except RD, TC, and XE Fields

▶ From the View menu, choose Field Codes (ALT, V, C).

–Or–

▶ In page layout view only, press the Field Codes key (SHIFT+F9).

This displays all fields except those without visible results that are in the document and in the same view.

When the Field Codes command on the View menu has a check mark, all fields show their codes. When it has no check mark, all fields show their results.

For RD, TC, and XE Fields

1 From the Tools menu, choose Options (ALT, O, O).

2 Select the View category.

3 Under Nonprinting Characters, select the Hidden Text check box (ALT+I) to see the field codes.
   –or–
   Clear the Hidden Text check box (ALT+I) to hide the field codes.

Tip   You can also use the Show/Hide ¶ button on the ribbon to show or hide these fields and all other hidden text.

To switch between showing field codes and results for individual fields

1 In normal view, select the field.

2 Press the Field Codes key (SHIFT+F9).

This does not affect RD (Referenced Document) fields, TC (TOC Entry) fields, or XE (Index Entry) fields.

To print field codes

1 From the File menu, choose Print (ALT, F, P).

2 Choose the Options button.

3 Under Include With Document, select the Field Codes check box.

4 Choose the OK button.

Editing a Field

Once you've inserted a field, you can edit it in much the same way you edit regular text. You can edit the field itself—perhaps to change its instructions—or you can edit its result. Suppose, for example, you insert a DATE field in your document. The field code might look like the following:

`{date \@ "MM/DD/YY"}`

Its result looks like this: 12/10/91. In Field Codes view, you can edit the field's instructions. You can change "MM/DD/YY" to "MMMM d, yyyy", for example, and the result looks like this: December 10, 1991.

The main difference in editing a field is that if you select the field characters that surround the field, Word selects the entire field.

Note You cannot overtype a field character, nor can you delete a single field character; field characters must be deleted together. Note also that you cannot add text within a field while you are in overtype mode; you can, however, overtype existing field text.

To edit a field

1 Position the insertion point in the field.

2 If the field is showing its result, press the Field Codes key (SHIFT+F9).

3 Edit the text of the field type or instructions as desired.

4 Press the Update Field key (F9) to test the field codes for the correct result.

To select text within a field

▶ Select text within the field, but do not select either of the field characters.

To delete a field

1   Select the whole field, including the field characters.

2   From the Edit menu, choose Cut (ALT, E, T).
    –or–
    Press DEL.

Formatting a Field

Once you've inserted a field, you may want to format the field's result. Generally, the easiest way is to select the entire field and apply the formatting you want. You can also apply more than one format to the result of a field. For example, you can format the result of a DATE field in this way: December **10**, 1991, making the "10" bold. Usually, if you update this field, the bold formatting would be removed. You can avoid this by adding the * mergeformat switch, which tells the field to use the exact formatting of the previous result when it updates a field. For example:

```
{date \@ "MM/DD/yy" \* mergeformat}
```

Many other switches are provided for formatting fields. For more information, see the entries on this subject in online Help.

To format the result of a field

▶ Select the field and apply the formatting you want.

To format the result of a field with switches

▶ Type the appropriate switches (optional commands) anywhere in the field after the field type.

For information about the unique switches for a field, see that field's entry in online Help.

Updating Fields

Updating a field means asking Word to follow the field instructions and produce a new result or action.

You can update fields directly by pressing the Update Field key (F9), or you can update most fields indirectly through printing, print merge, or pagination. For information on whether a field can be updated indirectly, see the entries for specific fields in online Help. If you want to make sure that all fields are updated when you print, you can select the Update Fields check box in the Print dialog box (File menu).

You can update one field at a time, or select more than one to update all of the fields in the selection.

To update a field

1 Select the field (or its result), or position the insertion point within it.

2 Press the Update Field key (F9).

The Update Field key (F9) does not affect the following fields:

> AUTONUM (automatic arabic number)
>
> AUTONUMLGL (automatic legal number)
>
> AUTONUMOUT (automatic outline number)
>
> EQ (formula)
>
> GOTOBUTTON (jump to destination)
>
> MACROBUTTON (run a macro)
>
> PRINT (send literals to the printer)

To jump to a field

If you want to update fields selectively, you can jump from one field to the next using the Next Field key (F11 or ALT+F1) or the Previous Field key (SHIFT+F11 or ALT+SHIFT+F1).

▶ Press the Next Field key (F11 or ALT+F1).

–Or–

▶ Press the Previous Field key (SHIFT+F11 or ALT+SHIFT+F1).

These keys ignore Index Entry (XE), TOC Entry (TC), and Referenced Document (RD) fields.

Preventing Fields from Being Updated

If you want to prevent a field from being updated—to make the current result permanent—you can either "unlink" the field or "lock" it. When you unlink a field, its result becomes regular text—you can no longer update it. If you lock a field, Word does not update it, but you can still unlock it later if you want to update it then. Locking a field is useful if, for example, you want to protect temporarily the result of a calculation performed by a field.

To unlink a field

1 Select the field.

2 Press the Unlink Field key (CTRL+SHIFT+F9).

To lock or unlock a field

1   Select the field.

2   To lock the field, press the Lock Field key (CTRL+F11 or ALT+CTRL+F1).
    –or–
    To unlock the field, press the Unlock Field key (CTRL+SHIFT+F11 or ALT+CTRL+SHIFT+F1).

Summary of Field Keys

Field key	Action
Insert Field (CTRL+F9)	Inserts the two field characters, { and }, positioning the insertion point between them. If you have a selection in the document when you press the Insert Field key, Word encloses the selection within the field characters.
Update Field (F9)	Follows the field's instructions and produces a new result.
Next Field (F11)	Selects the next field in your document. If you do not have an F11 key, press ALT+F1.
Previous Field (SHIFT+F11)	Selects the previous field in your document. If you do not have an F11 key, press ALT+SHIFT+F1.
Field Codes (SHIFT+F9)	Switches the display of the field between field code and results. This key does not affect Referenced Document (RD) fields, TOC Entry (TC) fields, and Index Entry (XE) fields.
Lock Field (CTRL+F11)	Locks the result of the field so that subsequent update actions do not update the field. This key is useful for keeping a specific result. If you do not have an F11 key, press ALT+CTRL+F1.
Unlock Field (CTRL+SHIFT+F11)	Unlocks a field so that it can be updated. If you do not have an F11 key, press ALT+CTRL+SHIFT+F1.
Unlink Field (CTRL+SHIFT+F9)	Permanently replaces the field code with its last result. The link with the source of the result is broken, and the result becomes document contents— that is, standard text or graphics.
Update Source (CTRL+SHIFT+F7)	Copies changes made in the result of an INCLUDE field to the field's source file; for INCLUDE fields only.
Do Field Click (ALT+SHIFT+F9)	Carries out GOTOBUTTON and MACROBUTTON actions (go to destination or run macro).

Field Code Syntax

A field consists of two or more parts. Every field has field characters and a field type. Fields can also contain additional instructions or switches. In some fields, some parts are required and some are optional.

A field does not have to be on one line only; it can wrap onto more than one line as needed.

For a summary of the requirements and options for each field, see the entries on this topic in online Help.

Field Characters ({ })

Field characters designate the beginning and end of a field. Field characters are a special pair of characters that have the same appearance as braces, but you insert them using the Insert Field key (CTRL+F9). You cannot insert them by typing the brace characters.

When you select one field character, the other is automatically selected with it, as are the contents of the field.

Field Type

The field type identifies the action or result of the field. The first item in a field following the first field character must be one of the following:

- Field type
- Equal sign (=)
- Bookmark name

You can precede a field type, equal sign, or bookmark name with blank space. You can also precede a field type or equal sign (but not a bookmark name) with a backslash (\). Field types must be separated from instructions with a blank space.

All of the field types are listed and summarized in online Help.

Instructions

Instructions are all the parts of a field following the field type. Instructions add information and directions to the field type to tailor the action of the field to your specific needs. Instructions can consist of arguments, bookmarks, expressions, identifiers, text, and switches.

Arguments

Arguments are numbers, text, or graphics that refine the action or result of the field. When an argument contains more than one word, but the separate words make up a single argument, enclose that argument within quotation marks (""). If you want to include quotation marks within an argument, precede each quotation mark with a backslash at the point in the argument where you want the quotation mark to appear. For example:

```
{set motto "to be or \"not\" to be"}
```

The word "not" is in quotation marks.

If you want a backslash included in an argument, double the backslash (\\). If you type a DOS path in a field, you must use double backslashes (\\) between directory names.

Bookmarks

For more information on bookmarks, see Chapter 40, "Bookmarks and Cross-references."

A bookmark is a name you assign to text or a graphic for use as a quick access point within a document. You can refer to a bookmark to provide the results for fields. Some fields use the contents of the bookmark; some use the page number of the bookmark's location; some use the value of the sequence number at the bookmark's location.

Expressions

An expression is a mathematical statement that results in a single number. An expression can contain numbers, bookmarks, and certain numeric or logical operators. For more information, see the entry on this subject in online Help.

Identifiers

Identifiers are labels you assign to parts of a document when you want to distinguish them for purposes of a field action. For example, if you want to number separately a series of tables and a series of charts, you use the SEQ field with one identifier for the tables and another for the charts—for example, {SEQ table} and {SEQ chart}.

Text

Text includes words or graphics you want inserted into a document or displayed on the screen. For example, a field that displays a message when it is time to type some text contains *prompt text*.

Fields may contain text with hidden text character format. If the first field character has the hidden text format, then Word reads the hidden text within the field when it calculates the field's results. If the first field character does not have hidden text character format, then Word ignores hidden text within the field during calculation.

You can use hidden text to insert comments within a field.

Switches

Switches activate specific actions. Generally, switches are options added to fields to modify the result in some way.

Switches always have a backslash (\) as their first character. The second character is usually some mnemonic initial or a pictorial symbol for the name or effect of the switch.

Some switches are followed by arguments that further refine the effect of the switch. Some fields have implied switches with default arguments.

A field can contain as many as 10 field-specific switches and 10 general switches.

Field-Specific Switches

A field-specific switch affects only one field. For example, you might want to modify the DATE field to produce a date in a different format. To change the date format, you change the date-time picture switch.

Switches provide much of the flexibility of fields. The following table shows examples of the different date format switches.

Format	Results
MM/dd/yy	09/01/91
MMM d, yyyy	Sept 1, 1991
MMMM d, yyyy	September 1, 1991
ddd, MMM d, yyyy	Sun, Sept 1, 1991
dddd, MMMM d, yyyy	Sunday, September 1, 1991
d-MMM-yy	1-Sept-91
d MMMM yyyy	1 September 1991

You can even create additional date formats if you want. You change the DATE format using a switch. For information about the switches available for use with this field, see the DATE field entry in online Help.

General Switches

For more information about general switches, see this topic in online Help.

General switches are optional instructions that affect the format of a field's result or lock a field's result. General switches can be used with all field types except the following:

AUTONUM	AUTONUMLGL
AUTONUMOUT	EQ
GOTOBUTTON	IMPORT
MACROBUTTON	RD
TC	XE

The general switches are the following.

Switch	Name	Description
*	Format	Adds formatting such as bold or capitalization to the field's result.
\#	Numeric picture	Formats a numeric result. Specifies separator character, number of decimal places, and so forth.
\@	Date-time picture	Formats a date result as month/day/year, day/month/year, and so forth.
\!	Lock result	Prevents fields that are part of the result of an INCLUDE or REF field from being updated.

Fields Reference

You can find reference information on specific fields and switches in online Help. You can also find information there on general switches. Besides choosing Help Index from the Help menu (ALT, H, I), you can request Help on a field type more directly by pressing F1 from within the Field dialog box, as in the following procedure.

To get Help on a specific field type

1   From the Insert menu, choose Field (ALT, I, D).

2   In the Insert Field Type box, select the field type for which you need Help.

3   Press F1.

Using Macros

A macro is a custom-made command you create to complete your work more quickly and efficiently. A typical macro consists of Word commands and actions that are triggered when you run the macro. Using a macro, you can carry out complicated word-processing tasks with a single command.

Here are some typical uses for macros:

- To select a frequently used option in a dialog box.

  Example: If you often select Draft as an option when printing, you can record that action to create a Print Draft macro.

- To record an often-used sequence of commands and actions.

  Example: If you sometimes transpose letters when you're typing (type "teh" instead of "the"), you can create a macro to fix the transposition for you.

- To modify a Word command.

  Example: If you often change to a certain directory when you save a file, you can record that action to create a macro that changes to the directory automatically.

- To automate a series of tasks.

  Example: If you sometimes have to strip unwanted paragraph marks from a text file, you can automate the process with a macro.

Word comes with a set of macros to help you get started. These macros are useful in themselves and can also be a source of ideas for macros you may want to create.

You can create macros easily using the macro recorder. Just start the recorder, and every key you press is recorded and can be played back as a macro.

For more information, consult the manual *Using WordBasic*. You can order this manual with a coupon included in your Word package.

You can make your macros available globally or store them in individual templates. You can also assign a macro to a menu or give it a key combination.

Word includes a macro editor with special tools for testing macros. Word also includes a separate application, the Dialog Editor, to help create custom dialog boxes.

Word uses a macro language, WordBasic, that is designed to be easy to learn, yet powerful. This chapter includes an overview of the main features of WordBasic to help you get started writing macros. You can also refer to online Help for macros. Within the macro editor, online Help provides context-sensitive Help for individual macro statements and functions.

Creating Macros

You can create a macro by recording a series of actions in Word, writing it from scratch, or recording some parts and writing others. Recording is best for simple macros, while more complex macros typically employ macro instructions that cannot be recorded.

Recording a Macro

The fastest and easiest way to create a macro is to record it. To do so, you start the Word macro recorder by choosing Record Macro from the Tools menu, and then you perform the series of actions that you wish to record as a macro. Word records everything you do until you stop the macro recorder. When you run the macro, it "plays back" what you recorded—but it does it much more quickly.

When the macro recorder is on, you'll notice that you can no longer use the mouse to move the insertion point or select text in your document. That's because the macro recorder cannot record mouse movements in a document window. Otherwise, the only sign that the macro recorder is on is that "REC" appears on the status bar and the Record Macro command on the Tools menu changes to Stop Recorder.

When you choose the Record Macro command to start the macro recorder, the Record Macro dialog box is displayed. Word proposes a name for the macro—such as Macro1, as shown in the following illustration.

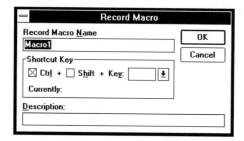

An option in the Template dialog box (File menu) determines if the macro is stored in NORMAL.DOT and available globally or stored in the document template, or whether you are prompted whenever you create a macro to indicate where it should be stored. If the active document is not based on a template, the macro is saved as a global macro, regardless of the setting in the Template dialog box.

The macro is not saved until you save the template in which it is stored, using the Save All command from the File menu or by responding to the message displayed when you quit Word.

To record a macro

1   From the Tools menu, choose Record Macro (ALT, O, R).

2   Under Record Macro Name, type a name for the macro.

 If you prefer to use the name Word proposes, omit this step.

3   If you wish, type in the Description box a description of what the macro does.

 You can type as many as 255 characters.

4   If you wish, you can assign the macro to a key or key combination by selecting the keys you want under Shortcut Keys.

5   Choose the OK button.

6   Working in your main document, perform the actions you want to record.

7   From the Tools menu, choose Stop Recorder (ALT, O, R).

To rename a macro

1   From the Tools menu, choose Macro (ALT, O, M).

2   Select the macro to rename.

3   Choose the Rename button.

4   Type a new name, and then choose the OK button.

5   Choose the Close button.

Writing a Macro

Word provides a macro-editing window for writing and editing macros. The macro-editing window includes a macro-testing bar below the menu, as well as online Help for the macro language. In the macro-editing window, just position the insertion point in a macro statement and then press the Help key (F1) for help on that statement.

For more information about the specifics of writing and testing macros and getting help, see the sections "Editing and Testing Macros," "Using WordBasic Help," and "Using WordBasic," later in this chapter.

To write a macro

1   From the Tools menu, choose Macro (ALT, O, M).

2   In the Macro Name box, type a name for the macro.

 If you want, in the Description box, type a description of what the macro does (maximum 255 characters).

3   Choose the Edit button.

The macro-editing window appears, and you can begin writing the macro.

Running Macros

Word provides four ways to run a macro:

- Choose the Macro command from the Tools menu and select a macro.
- Choose the macro from the menu to which you have assigned it.
- Press the key combination you have assigned to the macro.
- Click the Toolbar button to which you have assigned the macro.

You can use the Macro command on the Tools menu to run any macro. However, if you think you'll use a macro often, it makes sense to put it on a menu or on the Toolbar or assign a key combination to it. That way, you can run the macro directly without having to go through the Macro dialog box.

The Macro command can also be used to "run" commands built into Word. For example, you can use it to run the Open command from the File menu; the effect is the same as choosing Open from the menu. You can see a list of all Word commands if you select the Commands option in the Macro dialog box.

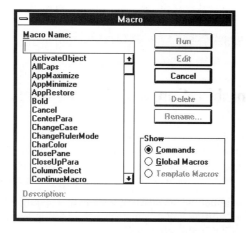

You can always choose a Word command from the Macro dialog box. You might need to do this if you have removed the command from the menu using the Options command on the Tools menu.

To run a macro

1   From the Tools menu, choose Macro (ALT, O, M).

2   Select the macro you want to run, and then choose the Run button.

Shortcuts

You can also press the key combination you assigned to a macro, choose a macro from the menu to which you assigned it, or click a button on the Toolbar to which you have assigned a macro.

Installing the Supplied Macros

For a list of the supplied macros and a description of their functions, see the README.DOC file.

The macros supplied with Word are stored in a file called NEWMACRO.DOC. Before you can run the supplied macros, you must install the macros you intend to use.

To install a supplied macro

1   From the File menu, choose Open (ALT, F, O).

2   If necessary, select the Word program directory, and then select NEWMACRO.DOC in the File Name box.

3   Choose the OK button.

Word runs a macro to install macros you want to use.

Menu, Key Combination, and Toolbar Assignments

Because a macro is meant to help you work quickly and efficiently, running it shouldn't be cumbersome. The best way to make a macro accessible is to assign it to a menu, give it a key combination, or assign it a button on the Toolbar.

To assign a key combination to a macro

1   From the Tools menu, choose Options (ALT, O, O).

2   Under Category, select Keyboard.

3   Under Show, select the Macros option button to display a list of macros.

4   Under Context, select either the Global or Template option button, depending on where the macro is stored. If the template attached to your document is NORMAL.DOT, the Template option is unavailable.

5   In the Macros box, select a macro.

6   Press the key combination you want to assign to the macro, or select the keys you want under Shortcut Key.

7   Choose the Add button, and then choose the Close button.

To assign a macro to a menu

1   From the Tools menu, choose Options (ALT, O, O).

2   Under Category, select Menus.

3   Under Show, select the Macros option button to display a list of macros.

4   Under Context, select either the Global or Template option button, depending on where the macro is stored. If the template attached to your document is NORMAL.DOT, the Template option is unavailable.

5   In the Macros box, select a macro.

6   In the Menu box, select the menu you want to assign the macro to.

    You can change the menu text in the Menu Text box. An ampersand (&) is added to the menu text; the character following the ampersand is the access key. Change the access key by moving the ampersand.

7   Choose the Add button, and then choose the Close button.

When you select the macro from this menu, the first 99 characters of the description are displayed on the status bar.

To assign a macro to a Toolbar button

1   From the Tools menu, choose Options (ALT, O, O).

2   Under Category, select Toolbar.

3   Under Show, select the Macros option button to display a list of macros.

4   Under Context, select either the Global or Template option button, depending on where the macro is stored. If the template attached to your document is NORMAL.DOT, the Template option is unavailable.

5   In the Macros box, select a macro.

6   Under Tool To Change, select the tool you want to change.
    –or–
    In the Macros box, select [Space] to create a new button in one of the empty spaces on the Toolbar.

7   In the Button box, select the button you want to use to represent the macro.

8   Choose the Change button, and then choose the Close button.

Using WordBasic

This section provides an overview of WordBasic. If you've worked with macros or done some programming before, much of the material in this section should be familiar to you. If you haven't had any experience with macros or programming, you may find it helpful to consult a book on basic programming skills or take a class.

When you begin writing macros, you should also refer to online Help, which provides reference information for individual macro statements and functions. A printed version of the macro statements and functions reference is included along with a tutorial for writing advanced macros in the manual *Using WordBasic*. A coupon for this manual is included in your Word package.

A Simple Macro

One way to get started with WordBasic is to look at a simple macro. This one transposes two characters—changing "teh" to "the," for example:

```
Sub MAIN
  CharLeft 1,1
  EditCut
  CharLeft 1
  EditPaste
  CharRight 1
End Sub
```

A macro in Word must begin with `Sub MAIN` and end with `End Sub`. "Sub" stands for "subroutine," which means a subsection of a larger program. Macros are subroutines of Word because they can run only when Word is running. A macro can have its own subroutines, as described in "Subroutines: Tools You Can Reuse," later in this chapter.

Every macro is a series of instructions. Many instructions are directly equivalent to Word commands. `EditCut` and `EditPaste`, for example, are the macro equivalents of the Cut and Paste commands on the Edit menu. Other instructions tell the macro to carry out actions you would do yourself. In the example above, the `CharLeft` and `CharRight` instructions move the insertion point to the left and right. The numbers next to these statements specify how many characters to move the insertion point the left or right. In the instruction `CharLeft 1,1`, the first "1" indicates that the insertion point is to move one character left; the second "1" is a shorthand instruction to select text as well as move the insertion point. Many WordBasic instructions use similar shorthand notations. To learn about them, refer to online Help for WordBasic.

Note WordBasic is not case sensitive; you don't have to type the examples in this chapter with uppercase and lowercase letters exactly as shown. WordBasic recognizes keywords and capitalizes their first letters, leaving everything else as you entered it. The examples in this section are shown as WordBasic formats them.

Statements and Functions

A statement tells the macro to do something. In effect, it's a command; many WordBasic statements are equivalent to Word commands. Each line in the previous example is a statement. Here are two more examples of statements:

```
EditFind .Find = "Yours truly"
Insert "Sincerely yours,"
```

The first statement is equivalent to the Find command on the Edit menu; it tells the macro to search for the phrase "Yours truly." The second statement inserts the phrase "Sincerely yours, " in the active document, just as if someone had typed it.

If a statement is a command, a function is a question. You use functions to find out information that the macro needs. Rather than producing a result in your document like a statement does, a function produces a value that can be used within the macro itself. A function produces, or returns, a value. If a macro needs to know the font size of selected text, you use the FontSize() function. If the text is 12 points, the function returns the number 12. Here are some other function names: ViewOutline(), Selection$(), and StyleName$().

As these examples show, WordBasic functions are identified by their ending parentheses. The first example returns a value that indicates whether or not the document is in outline view. The second returns whatever text is selected in a document. The third example returns the name of the style of the paragraph in which the insertion is located. The $ sign in the last two functions indicates that they return strings of text. The next section describes text strings and numbers in more detail.

Variables and Constants

Variables are placeholders for values that can change while a macro is running. Constants are fixed values and are not changed by the macro or external conditions.

Variables and constants in WordBasic have two forms: numeric and string.

Numeric Variables and Constants

In WordBasic, any variable name that ends with a letter or number is a numeric variable. All numeric variables in WordBasic accept decimal values and are accurate to about 15 decimal places. (They are double-precision, floating-point variables.)

Numeric constants are numbers generally used as part of an expression. Here are some examples of numeric variables and constants:

```
ShortPi = 3.14
Inch = 1
Foot = 12 * Inches
```

In the first example, ShortPi is a numeric variable; 3.14 is a constant. In the second example, Inch is a variable; 1 is a constant. Since variables are equivalent to the values they represent, you can use numeric variables in expressions in the same way you use numbers, as shown in the third example.

String Variables and Constants

Any variable name that ends with $ is a string variableñfor example, Name$. In WordBasic "$" is a "string sign." A string variable can contain any sequence of characters, including letters, numbers, spaces, and punctuation marks. The number of characters is limited to 32,767 or the amount of available memory, whichever is less.

String constants must be surrounded by double quotation marks, for example:

```
Name$ = "Julie Gabor"
Myfont$ = Font$()
```

In the first example, Name$ is the variable; "Julie Gabor" is the constant. In the second example, MyFont$ is the variable; Font$() is a function that returns the name of the font in which the selected text is formatted.

Assigning Values to Variables

You assign a value to a variable with an assignment statement. An assignment statement has three components: the variable to receive the new value, an equal sign (=), and the value itself. The value can be a string, a number, or an expression that produces a string or value. (Expressions are explained later in the chapter.)

These are all valid assignment statements:

```
age = 41
myname$ = "Willie"
result = result3 + leftval + rightval
```

You can use the same variable name on both sides of the equal sign—for example, when you want to change the variable's value:

```
Counter = 6
Counter = Counter + 1
```

The value of Counter in the second line is 7, or the initial value of Counter plus 1.

You cannot assign numeric values to string variables or string values to numeric variables. The following statements are not acceptable; either statement would prevent a macro from running and cause Word to display the message "Type mismatch":

```
Strg$ = 3.14159
```

```
Number= "hi, there"
```

You can use numbers in a string variable, but WordBasic does not interpret them as numeric values. For example, the string "42" simply represents the characters "4" and "2," not their values; if added to a number in a string variable, say "40", the result would not be the sum of the two but rather the string "4240".

Talking with the User

WordBasic includes several ways to communicate with the user. This section explains the Print, Input, MsgBox, MsgBox(), and InputBox$() statements, each of which presents a different way to display a message or to request information.

Print and Input are simple statements you can use to display or prompt for information quickly. MsgBox and InputBox$() offer more control and customization.

You can also create dialog boxes with check boxes, list boxes, and other features. For more information, see "Creating Custom Dialog Boxes," later in this chapter.

Print

The Print statement displays a message in the status bar. For example, Print "Working..." displays the message "Working..." in the status bar at the bottom of the screen.

Because the Print statement doesn't require any response from the user, it can be useful for displaying status messages while a macro is running.

The Print statement can display string or numeric variables or constants, and expressions in any combination. The following are all valid uses of the Print statement:

```
Print Name$
Print Total
Print "Hello"
Print 365.25
Print "Hello", 365.25; Total
```

When you use commas as delimiters to separate multiple items in a Print statement, Word inserts a predefined tab space between the items. When you use semicolons as delimiters, the next item starts immediately after the previous one.

MsgBox and MsgBox( )

The MsgBox statement displays a message in a dialog box that the user must acknowledge before the macro can continue. A MsgBox dialog box can have a title and a symbol to identify the kind of message. For example, the statement:

```
MsgBox "Macro complete", "Sample Macro", 64
```

displays the following message in the dialog box:

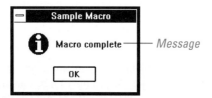

— *Message*

The function MsgBox( ) is just like the MsgBox statement, except that you can use it to give the user a choice or to ask a question. The following statement:

```
a = MsgBox("OK to reformat?", "Two Column Macro", 292)
```

displays the following question:

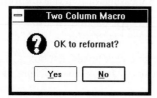

If the user chooses Yes, `MsgBox()` returns one value; if the user chooses No, `MsgBox()` returns a different value. The values are placed in the variable "a." The numeric argument `292` controls which symbol and buttons are displayed and which button is the default. A table of these values, their meanings, and instructions for their use is in online Help for WordBasic. See "Using WordBasic Help," later in this chapter.

Input

The Input statement prompts the user for information in the status bar. For example:

```
Input "What point size for the headline?", Size
```

displays the message "What point size for the headline?" in the status bar.

The user's response is placed in the numeric variable `Size`. `Input` can also prompt for string variables or a combination of string and numeric variables. To prompt for a list of variables, use statements like the following:

```
Input Height, Width
Input UserID$, Password$
```

The user must respond with the appropriate values separated by commas; for example:

```
6,3
KyleM, Qwerty
```

No matter how many variables you use in an `Input` statement, `Input` always attempts to divide the user's response at a comma. If you want to allow responses that contain commas, use a `Line Input` statement. `Line Input` works like `Input`, but with one important difference: you can specify only a single string variable. Here's an example:

```
Line Input Address$
```

If Word encounters a comma in the response, it returns the comma as part of the string. With some imagination and the use of WordBasic string functions, you can use `Line Input` to accept almost any kind of value—numeric or string.

InputBox$( )

Using `InputBox$()`, you prompt the user with a dialog box with a title, a prompt, and a default response. For example, the statement:

```
File$=InputBox$("Name of the file to open?", "Open Macro", "Latest
memo")
```

produces the following dialog box:

The user can replace the default, edit it, or accept it as is. Sometimes when a macro prompts a user for information, the purpose is to confirm something that's true most of the time, but that the user occasionally might want to change. The user's response, or the result of InputBox$( ), is placed in the variable File$.

Expressions

An expression is what most people would call a formula. It can consist of numbers, strings, variables, functions, and operators in any combination that can be evaluated down to a single result. For example, 2+2 is a simple expression that can be evaluated down to the single result 4.

In macros, expressions serve a number of purposes. As in the example above, you can use expressions to perform mathematical calculations. WordBasic supports the standard mathematical operations of addition, subtraction, multiplication, and division, represented by the plus sign (+), minus sign (-), asterisk (*), and forward slash (/), respectively. In addition, WordBasic supports MOD, the remainder operator. MOD performs a special type of division in which the whole-number part of the division result is discarded and the remainder is returned. For example, 7 MOD 3 = 1 (1 is the remainder when you divide 7 by 3).

Expressions can also be used to add strings together.

Operation	Result
"Dear " + "Mr. Jones"	Dear Mr. Jones
"C:\MYFILES\" + Filename$( )	C:\MYFILES\LETTER.DOC

The last example uses the Filename$( ) function to return the name of the active document, which in this example is called LETTER.DOC.

Comparing Values

Some of the most useful macro expressions compare values. Word uses the following relational operators to compare values.

Relational operator	Meaning
=	Equal to
<>	Not equal to
>	Greater than
<	Less than
>=	Greater than or equal to
<=	Less than or equal to

Word evaluates expressions that compare values as either true or false. (These expressions are often referred to as Boolean expressions, after the English mathematician, George Boole.)

Each of the following expressions is either true or false.

Expression	Evaluation
7 = 35	False
7 <> 6	True
7 <= 7	True
"Bob" = "Bob"	True
"Bob" = "bob"	False
"Bob" <> "Jerry"	True

As the examples show, you can compare strings as well as numbers. You can even use an expression such as "Blue" < "Green".

For a list of the ANSI values, see your Windows documentation.

Word evaluates string comparisons character by character until it finds characters that don't match and then compares the ANSI value for each character. In the preceding example, "B" has a smaller value than "G," so the expression is true.

Expressions that are either true or false are useful because they can be used to make decisions. Suppose you want a macro to open a series of documents and perform different actions on different documents. You can include a statement that says, for each document you open, "This document is document A." If the statement is true, the macro can take one action; if it is false, it can take another.

Compound Expressions

You can link two or more expressions together to create a compound expression. The two most commonly used operators to link expressions are And and Or. The And operator requires both expressions to be true in order for the compound expression to be true. The Or operator requires only one of the expressions to be true for the compound expression to be true.

The following compound expressions combine simple expressions by using And or Or.

Expression	Evaluation
10 > 5 And 100 < 200	True
3 < 6 And 7 > 10	False
8 < 7 Or 90 > 80	True
2 < 1 Or 3 > 60	False
"Y" > "N" And "yes" <> "no"	True
"Y" < "N" Or 4 <> 4	False

The Not logical operator evaluates to the opposite of the expression that follows it.

Expression	Evaluation
Not (5 > 10)	True
Not (8 < 7 Or 90 > 80)	False
Not (3 < 6 And 7 > 10)	True
Not (0)	True

The logic of the last example may not be immediately obvious. In WordBasic, false is 0. Therefore, Not (0) means "not (false)," or true. You can use combinations of And, Or, and Not to build complex expressions. There is no practical limit to their complexity—although the more complex the expression, the more difficult it is to read.

When WordBasic evaluates Boolean (true/false) expressions, it proceeds from left to right; all simple expressions are evaluated first, then all compound expressions with And, then all compound expressions with Or. You can use parentheses to control the order of evaluation, as in mathematical expressions.

Arrays of Variables

By assigning a subscript to a variable, you can create an array, which is a table of related variables. You can assign a value to each variable in the array and draw upon these values to perform specific operations. Defining an array can save the time and number of steps it would otherwise take to define each variable separately.

Suppose you want to track the high temperature for each day in January. You could define 31 separately named variables, but it would be more efficient to define a single array, January, with 31 entries. Specific entries are designated by the name of the array followed by their numeric position within the array, enclosed within parentheses. Note that since computers start counting at zero, January(0) is the first entry, January(1) is the second, and January(n) is the last (nth).

In this example, it may be easier to use the array if the first entry—January(0)—is ignored, so that the value of January(1) corresponds to the date January 1, and so forth. You can do this by not assigning a value to the first entry in the array; see "Specifying Array Elements," later in this chapter.

Declaring Arrays

An array of variables must first be "declared" with a Dim (dimension) statement, which establishes the size of the array. You have to include a Dim statement in a macro before you can use the array.

You include in the Dim statement the collective name of the variables and a value that specifies the maximum number of variables that appear in the array. For example, the statement Dim January(31) declares an array of 32 numeric variables named January whose subscripts run from 0 through 31.

Remember that, because the first entry in an array always has the subscript 0, January(31) is actually the thirty-second entry in the array.

Dim can define string variables as well as numeric ones. String-variable array names, like string variables, must end with the $ character; for example:
```
Dim StringVar$(250)
```

You can even use a variable as the value in a Dim statement, leaving it to WordBasic to create an array that is the size needed for a particular task; for example:
```
Dim Month(Days).
```

After declaring the number of variables in an array, you need to assign values to each variable. You can do this with simple assignment statements, with Input statements that request input from the user, or with more complex statements such as the ForNext loop. ForNext loops are explained in "Control Structures," later in this chapter.

Specifying Array Elements

You can instruct WordBasic to use a particular element of an array for a certain operation simply by following the variable name with that elementís subscript or an expression that evaluates to that element's subscript. For example, you can tell WordBasic to use the high temperature value for January 4 by specifying January(4) as the variable.

The following macro fragment prompts the user for a date in January and then prints the high temperature for that day, assuming that all the temperatures have been assigned to the January array:

```
Dim January(28)
January(1) = 34
January(2) = 40
January(3) = 42
[Assignment statements…]
Input "Type the January date for the day's high temperature", Date
Message$ = "The high temperature for January "+ Str$(date) \
+ " was" + Str$(January (date))
MsgBox Message$
```

Note that the first variable assigned a value is January(1) rather than January(0), which is actually the first entry in the array. This is done so that the array variable January(1) matches the date January 1 and the macro is easier to read.

Comments

Comments explain a macro to others and remind you of why you wrote it the way you did. Comments begin with an apostrophe or with the Rem statement:

```
'This is a comment
Rem This is also a comment
Beep    'The Beep statement causes the speaker to beep
```

When WordBasic encounters an apostrophe, it ignores everything between the apostrophe and the end of the line.

Control Structures

Control structures are statements that control the flow of a macro. These control structures enable the macro to take different actions in different situations and to repeat tasks until a condition changes. For example, you can write a macro that asks users whether they want to print an envelope. Depending on the response, the macro either prints an envelope or doesn't print it. Likewise, you can write a macro to repeat the same task in a document until it reaches the end of the document.

ForNext

For *CounterVariable = Start* **To** *End [Increment]*
        Statement(s)
Next *[CounterVariable]*

Word carries out the statements between `For` and `Next` as many times as it takes for the `CounterVariable` to increment from the `Start` value to the `End` value. The `Increment` is the value (usually 1) by which Word increments the counter.

For names the `CounterVariable` and specifies the `Start` and `End` values that constitute the range of the `CounterVariable`. These values can be constants, variables derived before the start of the loop, or expressions from which Word can compute a range of values for the `CounterVariable`.

The `Increment` can be a positive or negative number; positive numbers increase the counter, and negative numbers decrease the counter. If `Increment` is omitted, the default of 1 is used. For example:

```
For Month = 1 To 12
        Print Month
Next Month
```

The following table shows some other valid beginnings of `ForNext` loops and their resulting operations.

Example	Result
`For DayMonth = 1 To 31`	The variable `DayMonth` increments from 1 to 31 in steps of 1.
`For Dozens = 0 To 144 Step 12`	The variable `Dozens` increments from 0 to 144 in steps of 12.
`For CountDown = 10 To 1 Step -1`	The variable `CountDown` decrements from 10 to 1 in steps of -1.
`For Loop = Start To Finish Step Size`	The variable `Loop` increments or decrements from the value of the variable `Start` to the value of the variable `Finish` in steps equal to the variable `Size`.
`For Count = Count To Count + 10`	The initial value of the variable `Count` is increased by 10 in steps of 1.

Note that `Start` and `End` values, as well as the `Increment` value, are checked only once. Changing them once the loop has started does not affect the progress of the loop. The `CounterVariable` itself, however, should not be altered until the loop is completed, or problems such as those produced by the following example can result:

```
For Count = 1 To 10
      Count = 5
Next Count
```

This example creates an endless loop. The value of `Count` never reaches 10 because the statement `Count` = 5 resets the value to 5 each time Word repeats the loop.

The following are not valid `For` statements:

Invalid statement	Invalid because
`For 10 = 1 To 10`	`CounterVariable` needed
`For Count = 300 To 50`	Negative `Step` value needed
`For Count = 1 To 100 Step -1`	Positive `Step` value needed
`For Count = 1000 To 0 Step 5`	Negative `Step` value needed

The `Next` statement can be used with or without the variable name that identifies the loop with which the statement is associated. The `Next` statement always attempts to associate itself with the nearest preceding `For` statement. If you don't specify a `CounterVariable` after `Next`, Word completes the loop without generating an error.

If you do specify a `CounterVariable` after `Next` and the variable does not match the `CounterVariable` of the previous `For` statement, an error is generated. Although it is easier to omit the `CounterVariable`, use of the `CounterVariable` can serve as a good test of your macro's logic. If an error is generated, it may indicate that you omitted a `Next` statement somewhere else in the macro, incorrectly spelled a variable name, or made some other error that would otherwise be difficult to detect. This safeguard is most important in large macros that may have multiple loops and many variables.

Goto

Goto *Label*

In response to this command, Word branches unconditionally to the line in the macro that starts with the label. The syntax for the label is simply

Label: [Statement]

where `Label` is text or a number. Lines beginning with labels cannot be indented with the TAB key, because the label must be the first character in the line.

The following is an example:

```
Goto Bye
   Print "Hello"
Bye:
```

In this case, the statement `Print "Hello"` is not performed. The macro jumps directly from the `Goto Bye` statement to the `Bye` label without carrying out the statement between them.

The label can also occur before the `Goto` statement, as in this example:

```
Bye:
   Print "Hello"
Goto Bye
```

This macro creates another endless loop, because the `Goto Bye` statement always returns to the `Bye:` label. There are situations in which endless loops can be useful, but you usually need to include some sort of option in the macro to enable Word to exit the loop when you want it to. One way of exiting is with an `If` statement, which is discussed next.

If...ElseIf...Else...End If

If *Condition* **Then** *Statement(s)* [**Else** *Statement(s)*]

If *Condition1* **Then**
      Statement(s)
[**ElseIf** *Condition2* **Then**
      Statement(s)]
[**Else**
      Statement(s)]
End If

The `If...Then` control structure carries out an action conditionally or branches actions, depending on its component expressions. The conditions in an `If...ElseIf...Else...End If` block can be any logical expressions that WordBasic can evaluate as true or false. To build conditional expressions, you use the relational operators (=, <>, >, <, >=, and <=) and the logical operators (And, Or, and Not). Each `If...Then` control structure has only one `If Condition Then` statement. Each `If` control structure can have as many `ElseIf Condition Then` statements as needed. WordBasic evaluates the expressions in the order in which they appear and carries out the statements corresponding to the first condition that results in a true (nonzero) value.

If tests for a specified condition. If the condition is true, Word carries out the operations following the `Then` statement. The operations following `Else` are performed if none of the `If` or `ElseIf` conditions evaluate to true.

Here is an example of the If...Then control structure:

```
If Sales > 300 Then Print "Sales were more than 300"
```

and here is an example of the If...ElseIf...Else...End If control structure:

```
If Sales > 300 Then
  Print "Sales were more than 300!"
ElseIf Sales > 280 Then
  Print "Sales were Okay"
Else
  Print "Another year goes by"
End If
```

Select Case

Select Case *Expression*
Case *CaseExpression*
      Statement(s)
[**Case Else**
      Statement(s)]
End Select

This control structure is similar to an If...ElseIf...Else...End If statement in that Word carries out a statement or group of statements based on the result of some expression. However, the result of the Select Case expression is compared with the expressions that follow each repetition of the keyword Case. Each of these expressions may be a single value, a list of values separated by commas, a range of values separated by the keyword To, or a relational expression beginning with the keyword Is, followed by a relational operator (=, <>, <, >, <=, or >=) and an expression.

Word compares the expression with all the values in each case expression until a match is found. If a match is found, Word carries out the statement(s) following that particular case expression. If there is no match and there is a Case Else statement, Word carries out the statement(s) following Case Else. If there is no match and no Case Else statement, Word displays an error message.

Here is an example:

```
Select Case Int(Rnd() * 10) - 5
Case 1,3
  Print "1 or 3"
Case Is > 3
  Print "Greater than 3"
Case -5 To 0
  Print "Between -5 and 0 (inclusive)"
Case Else
  Print "Must be 2"
End Select
```

While...Wend

While *Condition*
   Statement(s)
Wend

The While...Wend loop repeats the statement(s) between While and Wend as long as the condition is true. If the condition is initially false, the loop is never carried out.

A While...Wend loop uses a conditional expression to determine the number of times the statement(s) are carried out. WordBasic evaluates the condition each time the statement(s) are carried out and, as long as the condition is true, continues carrying out the statement(s). When the condition is evaluated as false, WordBasic stops carrying out the statement(s) and exits the loop.

The condition can be any conditional expression. To build conditional expressions, use the relational operators (=, <>, <, >, <=, and >=) and the logical operators (And, Or, and Not). The evaluation results are either -1 for true or 0 for false.

In the following example, WordBasic searches the document for the string "macro" until the function EditFindFound() returns a zero, indicating that the end of the document has been reached. The example illustrates the major distinction between For...Next and While...Wend loops. For...Next loops are most useful when instructions must be repeated a fixed number of times and that number is known or can be calculated in advance. While...Wend loops are most useful when the number of repetitions necessary to satisfy the condition is not known and cannot be calculated in advance. In the example, the document could be of any length and the string "macro" could occur any number of times.

```
Sub MAIN
  Count = 0
  StartOfDocument
  EditFind "macro", .Direction=2
  While EditFindFound()
    Count = Count + 1
    EditFind "macro", .Direction=2
  Wend
  Print "macro was found ";Count; " times"
End Sub
```

Subroutines: Tools You Can Reuse

A subroutine is a group of statements that performs a specific task. Every WordBasic macro is a Word subroutine that must begin with a Sub MAIN statement and end with an End Sub statement. You cannot nest subroutines; that is, you cannot insert one subroutine within another subroutine. The syntax of the Sub and End Sub statements is as follows:

Sub Name *[(ParameterList)]*
   Statement(s)
End Sub

The simplest macro consist of only one subroutine. As macros get more complicated, they are usually broken down into small units and written as separate modules. If you want to perform the same action in different parts of your macro, it makes sense to write the statements that carry out that particular action as a separate subroutine. For example, suppose you want the computer to beep before displaying a message. One way to do this is shown in the following macro:

```
Sub MAIN
  BeepMsg "Are you sure you want to quit?", 0
  BeepMsg "Don't you want to save your work first?", 0
  BeepMsg "This is your last chance. Choose OK to quit.", 65
End Sub
"*** SubRoutine begins here
Sub BeepMsg (msg$, type)
  Beep
  MsgBox msg$, "Microsoft Word", type
End Sub
```

User-Defined Functions

User-defined functions are similar to subroutines in that they are modular units of code that can be called from elsewhere in the macro. They differ from subroutines in that they return a value or string and must be used as part of an expression. You define new functions in a manner similar to subroutines, except that instead of using the Sub keyword, you use the Function keyword. The syntax is as follows:

Function Name *[(ParameterList)]*
> *Statement(s)*
End Function

The ParameterList is a list of the variables, separated by commas, that are being passed as arguments to the function. The statements between Function and End Function are used to produce a value that is returned to the subroutine that called the function. An example follows:

```
Sub MAIN
  Print RndInt(100)
  Print RndInt(200)
End Sub

Function RndInt(n)
  RndInt = Int(Rnd() * n)
End Function
```

The Rnd() function is a built-in WordBasic function that returns a random fractional value between 0 and 1. The user-defined RndInt() function generates a random integer between 0 and a value you specify. The Function RndInt(n) statement tells Word that a new function is being defined and that the function takes a single numeric parameter called "n." The next line indicates that the value of the function is the formula Int(Rnd() * n).

Every user-defined function includes an implied variable with the same name as the function. Assigning a value to that variable defines the value returned from the function. In the preceding example, `Int(Rnd() * n` is assigned to the variable `RndInt`. A function can contain statements above and below the assignment.

The following are also valid ways to call the user-defined `RndInt()` function:

```
NewValue = RndInt(OldValue)
Print RndInt(Number) + 100
If RndInt(50) > 25 Then TailsMsg
```

A user-defined function returns a numeric value unless the function name ends with `$`, in which case the function returns a string.

Using WordBasic Help

The Word Help system includes online reference information for all WordBasic statements and functions. When the macro-editing window is active, you can select any WordBasic function or statement and press F1 for instant Help on it. Each entry in WordBasic Help shows the syntax and other information for the command or function. Some entries include examples that you can paste into the macro-editing window.

To get Help on WordBasic

1   From the Help menu, choose Index (ALT, H, I).

2   Under Reference Information, select WordBasic Programming Language.

3   Select the statement or function for which you want Help.

To get Help on a specific WordBasic statement or function

▶   From within the macro-editing window, select the WordBasic statement or function on which you want Help, and then press F1.

Reference information for the statement or function selected appears in the Help window. If you select more than one statement or function, Help provides information on the first statement or function in the line.

Editing and Testing Macros

It's easiest to edit and test a macro while in the macro-editing window. Using the editing window's macro-testing bar, you can trace a macro as it runs, choose between two different ways to step through it, or display the current values of variables.

The following paragraphs describe the buttons on the macro-testing bar.

Start/Continue   Runs the active macro; changes from Start to Continue when the macro stops—for example, after a step in step mode, or when the macro contains a `Stop` statement.

Step   Runs a single macro instruction and then stops. If the instruction is a subroutine, Word runs each instruction in the subroutine as a single step.

Step SUBs   Runs a single macro instruction and then stops. If the instruction is a subroutine, Word treats the entire subroutine as a single step.

Trace   Trace Runs the active macro, highlighting each instruction as it is carried out.

Vars   Displays the current values of variables in the macro and allows you to modify the contents of a variable. It does not show array variables.

To use the macro-testing bar with the keyboard, press ALT+SHIFT+*underlined letter* in the name of a button. You can also click the buttons with the mouse.

If you discover a syntax error, remember that you can press F1 or choose the Help button in the message box for instant Help on that statement or function.

Finding Where Errors Occur

When the macro-editing window is open and an error occurs in the macro, Word highlights the line in the macro where the error occurred. Usually, you'll find the statement that is the source of the problem on the highlighted line, but sometimes the statements on the highlighted line may have only detected a problem whose actual cause lies elsewhere in the macro.

Checking Variable Contents

It is often useful to inspect the contents of macro variables while the macro is running. There are two ways to do this.

You can insert `Print` statements in the macro that display the values of selected variables in the status bar. In most macros, these statements do not interfere with the operation of the macro; the macro continues to run while you observe its progress.

A second method allows inspection of all the variables in a macro. You insert a `Stop` statement in the macro. The macro stops when it encounters the `Stop` statement and displays a message saying the macro has been interrupted. If you are running the macro with the macro-editing window open, the Vars button is available. Choosing this button opens a dialog box with a list of all the variable names and their values.

If you choose the Set button, you can change the contents of any variable. Making changes can be useful in some kinds of macro testing. When you choose the Close button, you return to the macro editor. You can then choose the Continue button, and the macro continues from the point where it was interrupted.

You can also press ESC to interrupt a running macro so that you can inspect its variable contents, but this method is usually much less precise than using a `Stop` statement.

Using Trace

When you choose the Trace button on the macro-testing bar, Word highlights macro lines in the macro-editing window as they are run. You may experience some difficulty in using this feature—or while using the Start, Step, or Step SUBs functions—because many commands are not available in the macro-editing window.

For example, many formatting commands are unavailable because macros don't have character or paragraph formatting. Other commands are unavailable because they are relevant only to printed documents. As a safety measure, some commands are unavailable to prevent a macro from accidentally modifying itself. If any of these commands is included in your macro and you run the macro while the macro-editing window is active, an error occurs and your macro may display a message telling you the command is unavailable.

To use Trace to follow the operation of a macro that includes unavailable commands, choose the Arrange All command from the Window menu. This splits the screen between the macro-editing window and the document window. Make sure the document window is active, and then choose the Trace button. This time the error will not occur, and you can observe the operation of the macro on the document while tracing its operation in the macro-editing window.

Auto Macros

Word recognizes five macros named AutoExec, AutoClose, AutoNew, AutoOpen, and AutoExit as special macros that run automatically as shown in the following table.

Macro name	When it runs
AutoExec	When you start Word
AutoNew	Each time you create a new document
AutoOpen	Each time you open a document
AutoClose	Each time you close a document
AutoExit	When you quit Word

These "auto" macros can be useful in many ways. One use for AutoNew, for example, would be to automatically present the Save As dialog box for you to name and save the file. Then when you have given the file a name, the macro could insert the file-name in the document header or footer. You could use the AutoExec macro to open automatically the last document used when Word starts.

You can prevent AutoExec from running by typing the / m option when you start Word from the system prompt (for example, **win winword /m**).

You create an auto macro just as you do a regular macro. The only difference is that you must give the macro one of the special auto macro names that Word recognizes.

As with other macros, auto macros can be defined either globally or for a particular template.

Creating Custom Dialog Boxes

You can create custom dialog boxes for Word command macros by using the Dialog Editor, a separate application included with Word. With the Dialog Editor, you can add, arrange, move, or resize items in a dialog box and move or resize the dialog box. You can also group items to show they are related. For example, you can group several option buttons so that only one of the options can be selected at a time. Once you create a group, you can resize and move it as a unit.

You can make your dialog boxes look exactly as you want them to. When you create a dialog box, the Dialog Editor automatically writes a dialog box definition that describes the dialog box and all the items it contains. The definition includes the position of the dialog box, the width and height coordinates of the items contained in the dialog box, and any text labels for those items.

To create and use a custom dialog box, first create the dialog box with the Dialog Editor. Next, copy the dialog box definition to a macro, and then write a macro to use the dialog box.

Creating a New Dialog Box

When you start the Dialog Editor, it automatically creates a blank dialog box. A single custom dialog box can include as many as 32 items and 512 text characters.

For information on a dialog box you are creating with the Dialog Editor, select the dialog box and choose the Info command from the Edit menu. The Info dialog box appears, showing the size and coordinates of the dialog box you are creating. The horizontal position of an item within the dialog box is measured from the left edge of the dialog box to the left edge of the item. The vertical position of an item is measured from the top of the dialog box to the top of the item.

To start the dialog editor

▶ In the Program Manager, double-click the Dialog Editor icon.

– Or –

1 From the Program Manger File menu, choose Run (ALT, F, R).

2 Type **macrode.exe**

3 Choose the OK button.

An empty dialog box is displayed on your screen. You can now add buttons, text boxes, and other items, and you can move them around within the dialog box.

To add an item to a dialog box

All items except group boxes and fixed text have more than one variation. When you choose the item you want from the Item menu, a dialog box appears so you can specify the variation you want.

If you omit either or both of the x and y coordinates for a dialog box or item, Word positions the dialog box or item for you. If you omit either the height or width for a dialog box or item, Word sizes the box or item for you. If you omit just one value, Word automatically adjusts the measurement for that dimension.

▶ From the Item menu, choose the item you want to add.

The item is added to the dialog box and remains selected. You can add a copy of some items by selecting the item and then pressing ENTER or choosing Duplicate from the Edit menu (ALT, D, E).

If you select a group box and press enter, an option button is added to the group box.

Note You can change the default text Word inserts in title bars, text items, option buttons, check boxes, and group boxes. You select the item and then choose Info from the Edit menu (ALT, E, I). In the Text$ box, type the text you want for the item.

To select an item in a dialog box

You must select an item before you can move, resize, or delete it.

▶ Click the item you want to select.

–Or–

▶ Press TAB until the item you want is selected.

To select multiple items in a dialog box

1 Click the first item you want.

2 Hold down SHIFT and click the additional items you want to select.

To delete an item in a dialog box

1 Select the item or items you want to delete.

2 From the Edit menu, choose Clear (ALT, E, E).

You cannot delete a dialog box with the Clear command. If you choose this command when a dialog box is selected, all items in the dialog box are deleted—but not the box itself. A dialog box is selected whenever none of its items are individually selected.

To move an item in a dialog box

You may need to choose Info from the Edit menu and clear the Auto check box for
the x and y coordinates before you can move the dialog box item.

▶ Drag the item to the location you want.

If you hold down SHIFT while you drag an item or its border, you can drag only
vertically or horizontally, depending on which direction you first move the mouse.

Note   You can use the Edit Info dialog box to precisely size and position a dialog box
item. For example, you can align a series of edit boxes by typing the same x coordi-
nate for each of them. Some items have the Auto check box selected for one or more
of the four dimensions and coordinates. You cannot change the width or height of an
item while the Auto check box is selected for that dimension. To change the size of the
item, clear the Auto check box, and then type a new number in the associated box.

To resize an item in a dialog box

You may need to choose Info from the Edit menu and clear the Auto check box for
Height and Width before you can change the size of the dialog box item.

1   Click the item you want to resize.

2   Drag the border of the item until it's the size you want.

To cancel moving or sizing an item

▶ Press ESC before you press ENTER or release the mouse button.

To clear automatic sizing and positioning

Some of the dimensions of dialog box items, such as the height of an OK or Cancel
button, cannot be changed until you clear the Auto check box.

1   Double-click the item.

2   Clear the Auto check box next to the dimension you want to change.

3   Type the size or position you want.

4   Choose the OK button.

Working with a Group of Items

A group is a set of related items placed together in a group box because they share
similar functionality. You can move, resize, or delete an entire group. After you create
a group box, you can add, delete, and move items into and out of the group.

To create a group of items in a dialog box

You create a group box before you create the items you want in it.

1 From the Item menu, choose Group Box (ALT, I, G).

2 Choose the items you want to add.

   You can also add option buttons to a group by selecting the group and pressing ENTER for each option button you want to create. Immediately after creating an option button, type a name for it.

To add an existing item to a group

If you try to drag an existing item into a group box, it does not automatically belong to that group. displayed. Use the following procedure to add the item to the group.

1 Select the item.

2 From the Edit menu, choose Cut (ALT, E, T).

3 Make sure the group box is selected.

4 From the Edit menu, choose Paste (ALT, E, P).

5 Drag the item into the group box, or use the arrow keys to position the item.

6 Press ENTER.

To change a group of items

1 Select the group box.

2 From the Edit menu, choose Select Group (ALT, E, G).

3 Move, resize, or delete the group as you would an individual item.

You can also edit, move, resize, or delete individual items in a group box just as you do items outside of group boxes.

Copying a Dialog Box to a Macro

After you create a dialog box with the Dialog Editor, you copy the resulting dialog box definition to a Word macro so that you can use it box in the macro.

To copy the dialog box definition to a macro

1 From the Edit menu, choose Select Dialog (ALT, E, S).

   With the mouse, you can also click the dialog box border to select the dialog box.

2 From the Edit menu, choose Copy to copy the dialog box to the Clipboard.

3 Switch to Word.

4 Open the macro into which you want to paste the dialog box definition and position the insertion point where you want to insert the definition.

5 From the Edit menu, choose Paste (ALT, E, P).

Note As soon as you copy the dialog box to the Clipboard, any other dialog box already there is deleted. Itís a good idea to paste a dialog box into a macro immediately after copying it to the Clipboard.

Quitting the Dialog Editor

After you copy the dialog box definition to a macro, you can quit the Dialog Editor.

To quit the dialog editor

▶ In the Dialog Editor, choose Exit from the File menu (ALT, F, X).

If you've created a new dialog box or changed an existing one, the Dialog Editor asks if you want to copy your changes to the Clipboard. If you want to use the dialog box in Word and have not already copied it, choose the Yes button. If you choose the No button, any changes made to the dialog box are lost.

Displaying a Dialog Box

To display a dialog box, you need to create a macro that uses the dialog box definition you created. The following example shows a dialog box definition created by the Dialog Editor, followed by two statements required to display the dialog box:

```
Begin Dialog UserDialog 320, 84, "Edit File Macro"
  Text 10, 6,160, 12, "Name of &File To Edit:"
  TextBox 10, 21, 236, 18, .TextBox1
  OKButton 9, 58, 88, 21
  CancelButton 115, 58, 88, 21
End Dialog

Dim TestDialog As UserDialog
Dialog TestDialog
```

The following illustration shows what the dialog box looks like.

For more information on the statements used to create and display a dialog box, see online Help for WordBasic.

Editing an Existing Dialog Box

You can open an existing dialog box in the Dialog Editor to change or delete it.

To delete all contents of a dialog box

▶ From the File menu, choose New (ALT, F, N).

If you've changed the dialog box, the Dialog Editor asks if you want to copy the changes to the Clipboard. To copy the changes, choose the Yes button. To discard your changes, choose the No button.

–Or–

1 From the Edit menu, choose Select Dialog (ALT, E, S).

2 From the Edit menu, choose Cut (ALT, E, T).

A message is displayed asking if you are sure you want to clear the dialog box. Choose the Yes button if you are sure.

After you've cleared the dialog box, an empty dialog box is displayed.

To change an existing dialog box

You can change a custom dialog box that exists in a macro by copying the dialog box definition from the macro to the Clipboard and then pasting it from the Clipboard into the Dialog Editor. You can then edit the dialog box in the Dialog Editor.

1 In your macro, select the the dialog box definition.

The dialog box definition begins with `Begin Dialog UserDialog` and ends with `End Dialog`. Select everything between and including those lines.

2 From the Edit menu, choose Copy (ALT, E, C).

3 Switch to the Dialog Editor.

4 From the Edit menu, choose Paste (ALT, E, P).

5 Add, delete, move, or resize the items you want.

6 From the Edit menu, choose Select Dialog (ALT, E, S).

With the mouse, you can also click the dialog box border to select the dialog box.

7 From the Edit menu, choose Copy to copy the revised dialog box to the Clipboard.

8 Switch to Word.

9 In the macro, select the dialog box definition.

10 From the Edit menu, choose Paste (ALT, E, P).

Setting Up and Using Word on a Network

On a network, many users can share the Word program and documents created in Word. Once Word is set up on the network, the program can be copied onto the hard disks on individual workstations, or it can be run from the network server.

This appendix assumes that you know how to use network software to connect to network drives and how to find files stored on network computers.

Note Every Word user must have a Microsoft Word license. A license is obtained by buying a retail package or a Microsoft License Pack. For more information on network use restrictions, see your Microsoft Word license agreement.

Setting Up Word on a Network

Before you set up Word:

- The network must be operational, and you must have read-write access to the network directory in which you want to install Word. For more information, see your network software documentation.

- You must set up the Windows operating environment version 3.0 or later on the network server and on any workstations that will run the Word program. For information on setting up Windows, see your Windows documentation.

Setting up Word on a network is a two-step process. You first install Word on the network server. Then you set up the workstations, either by installing Word on each workstation's hard disk or by setting up the workstations to run Word from the server.

Note Each workstation should have at least 1 MB of RAM for the basic Word program. To use all features, including the add-on features and grammar checking, 2 MB of RAM is required.

Setting Up Word on a Server

Before setting up Word on your workstation, you should set it up on the network server.

To set up Word on a network server

1   From a workstation, log on to the network and connect to the drive on which you want to install Word.

2   If Windows is not already running, at the DOS prompt, type **win** and press ENTER.
    —or—
    If Windows is running, close any open applications.

3   From the File menu, choose Run (ALT, F, R).

4   Insert the Disk1—Setup disk in drive A.

5   Type **a:\setup** and press ENTER.

6   Type your name and the name of your organization, and then choose the Continue button.

    Each name can be no longer than 50 characters.

7   On the next Setup screen, choose the Continue button to verify the information.
    —or—
    Choose the Change button to return to the previous screen and make changes.

    Setup asks where you want to install Word.

8   Type the path to the directory on the server where the Word program will reside; for example, type **w:\winword**. Then choose the Continue button.

    If there is no directory with that name, Setup asks if you want to create a directory. You can edit the path if you like. Then choose the Yes button.

    If Setup detects a previous version of Word in the directory, it asks if you want to overwrite the program. If you choose to overwrite, Setup installs version 2.0 over the earlier version.

9   Detecting a network drive, Setup provides three installation choices. Choose the Server Installation button.

10 When Setup is complete, choose the OK button to return to Windows.

Although the Word program directory on the server (the directory containing WINWORD.EXE) can be either read-write or read-only, you should make it read-only after installing Word to prevent users from unintentionally overwriting files. For more information, see your operating system documentation.

Using Word with a Novell Network

If you are installing Word on a Novell or NetBIOS-compatible network, you must add the following line to the WIN.INI file on each workstation:

NovellNet=Yes

This entry affects how Word checks for valid directories. Without the entry, Word may not be able to open some files.

In Word, you can make this change by choosing the Options command from the Tool menu and adding the entry to the options in the WIN.INI category. Or edit the WIN.INI file directly, adding the line to the [Microsoft Word 2.0] section. You must save the WIN.INI file in Text Only format. For more information, see Appendix B, "Modifying the WIN.INI File."

Although the Novell network permits directory names with as many as 14 characters, Windows limits directory names to 12 characters. If you are using Word with a Novell network, make sure that your directory names have no more than 12 characters.

Setting Up Word on a Workstation

If you are copying the Word program to a workstation's local hard disk, connect to the drive on the server on which Word is installed. Then install Word as a workstation by following the instructions in *Microsoft Word Getting Started.*

If you plan to run Word from a network server instead of having a copy of the program on the workstation's hard disk, use the following procedure to install Word.

Important   Remember the drive letter you use when you connect to the network and run Setup for the first time from your workstation. Whenever you run Word over the network, you need to connect to the network using the same drive letter.

To install Word on a workstation

1   From the workstation, log on to the network and connect to the drive that contains the Word program directory.

2   If Windows is not already running, at the workstation's DOS prompt, type **win** and press ENTER.
    –or–
    If Windows is running, close any open applications.

3   From the File menu, choose Run (ALT, F, R).

4   Type the complete path to where Word is installed on the network, followed by **setup**

For example, type **w:\winword\setup**

Then press ENTER.

5   Type the name of the person who will use the workstation (a maximum of 50 characters). To correct errors, press the BACKSPACE key. When you finish, choose the Continue button.

This name can be used in Word in return addresses for letters and envelopes and as the author name for documents.

6   On the next Setup screen, choose the Continue button to verify the information.
    –or–
    Choose the Change button to return to the previous screen and make changes.

Setup asks where you want to install Word.

7   Type the path to the user directory on your workstation; for example, type **c:\winword**

Then choose the Continue button.

If there is no directory with that pathname, Setup asks if you want to create a directory. You can edit the path if you like. Then choose the Yes button.

If Setup detects a previous version of Word in the directory, it asks if you want to overwrite the program. If you choose to overwrite, Setup installs version 2.0 over the earlier version.

8   Detecting a network drive, Setup provides three installation choices. Choose the Workstation Installation button.

9   Follow the instructions on the screen. If necessary, you can return to the installation screen (step 7) by choosing Close from the Control menu (ALT+SPACEBAR), or you can exit Setup by pressing F3.

10 Setup asks if you want to update the startup file AUTOEXEC.BAT. Choose the Update button.

If you choose the Do Not Update button, you must update AUTOEXEC.BAT yourself, as explained in Chapter 2, "Setting Up Word," in *Microsoft Word Getting Started*.

The Word program remains on the server; your own copy of the Word settings file, WINWORD.INI, is stored in the directory you specified in step 7. WINWORD.INI contains information that Word needs to run from the network server.

If you have old copies of the add-on features that come with Word, Setup updates them in your WINDOWS\MSAPPS directory. If you don't already have copies of these features on your workstation, these files remain on the network server and are available when you use Word.

11 When Setup is complete, choose the OK button to return to Windows.

Path Settings in WIN.INI

Setup makes changes to the Windows settings file, WIN.INI, which contains information about your Windows applications, including the default locations for Word document files, Word utilities, fonts, and the Word settings file, WINWORD.INI.

You can change any of these paths by editing the WIN.INI file. In Word, you can do this by changing options in the WIN.INI category of the Options dialog box (Tools menu). Or you can edit the file directly, saving it in the Text Only format.

You may want to adjust the following paths, depending on how you want your network to run. The first five settings are always added during installation. You can add the sixth if you don't have it.

Statement	Sets location for	Default location
`programdir=pathname`	WINWORD.EXE	Program directory on server
`INI-path=pathname`	WINWORD.INI	Home directory on workstation (same directory as DOC-path)
`DOC-path=pathname`	User documents	Home directory on workstation (same directory as INI-path)
`DOT-path=pathname`	Template files	DOT-path home directory
`autosave-path=pathname`	Automatically saved files	Directory specified in workstation's TEMP variable
`TOOLS-path=pathname`	Alternate path for tools, converters, filters, autosave files, and user dictionaries	Program directory on server

WIN.INI also contains paths for the proofing tools—including the standard spelling dictionary and the custom dictionary, to which a user can add entries. If you store the standard spelling dictionary in a write-protected directory on the network server, make sure the directory for the custom dictionary is one the user can write to. To see the path for the custom dictionary, display the WIN.INI category in the Options dialog box; then, in the Application box, select MS Proofing Tools.

For more information on Windows settings, see Appendix B, "Modifying the WIN.INI File."

Using Word on a Network

Using Word on a network is essentially the same as using Word from a hard disk on an individual computer. On the network, you can make a document available to other users and allow them to make changes to the file, or you can protect the file from changes. You can use the network server to store and exchange documents between users, and many people can use a printer attached to the network server.

Using Word in a Workgroup

A workgroup is any group of people who work on the same types of documents, belong to the same functional unit within a company, or share documents or information on computers. Word has many features that can increase a workgroup's productivity.

The Find File command on the File menu, using the summary information that a user supplies for a document, can help users locate documents quickly by title, subject, specific text, author, date, and other types of information. For information, see Chapter 26, "Finding and Managing Files."

Annotations, revision marks, and version comparisons can be used to track changes that users make to a shared document. For information, see Chapter 31, "Footnotes, Annotations, and Revision Marks."

Using INCLUDE and RD fields, one person can compile a group of documents that several people create, and can create a table of contents and index for a group of documents. For information on using INCLUDE fields, see Chapter 11, "Setting Up Long Documents." For information on using RD fields, see Chapter 26, "Finding and Managing Files."

By linking a document on a workstation to a shared document on the network, you can automatically update information in the workstation document when it changes in the shared document. You can link Word documents with each other and with documents created in other applications such as Microsoft Excel. For information, see Chapter 36, "Exchanging Information."

You can use password protection to control access to documents containing sensitive information. For information, see Chapter 2, "Opening, Saving, and Deleting Documents."

Starting Word over the Network

Before you can start Word on a workstation, both Windows and Word must be set up on the workstation. If your workstation runs Word from the network server, you must connect to the server before starting Word. Use the following procedure.

To start Word on a network workstation

You must use the same drive letter to connect to the network server and run Word that you used when you set up Word.

1   Using the same drive letter you used when you ran Setup for the first time, connect to the network drive and directory containing the Word program.

2   Start Word in the usual way. For instructions, see *Microsoft Word Getting Started.*

Storing Documents on a Network

You can create documents on your own workstation disks or on the network server. By default, Word saves your documents in your home directory on your workstation's hard disk. You can change this default using the Options command on the Tools menu. The DOC-path option in the WIN.INI category determines where your files are saved by default. For more information, see Appendix B, "Modifying the WIN.INI File."

If you save your documents on the network server, create your own directory to hold them. Do not store work in the directory with the Word program (WINWORD.EXE).

Tip   In Word, you can apply a style quickly by assigning a key combination to the style. This key assignment remains with the document. If you plan to share a document with other users, be careful not to assign key combinations that are already in use by Word. For example, CTRL+I normally applies italic formatting. If you assign CTRL+I to a style, other users may get unexpected results when they press these keys. For a list of key assignments, see the Keyboard category in the Options dialog box (Tools menu).

Sharing Files on a Network

You can protect files that are shared on a network from unintentional changes in several ways. You can assign access permissions at the system or network level. And in Word you can limit users' access and the scope of their write permissions for a document.

System and Network File Protections

At the system level, you can restrict access to a single file or to all files in a directory. For information about how to assign access permissions, see your system
documentation.

To do this	Give this type of access
Prevent changes to all files in a directory	Read-only access for the directory.
Allow users to open a file but not make changes to it under the current filename	Read-only access for the document. This is especially useful for shared documents and dictionaries.
Allow users to open a copy of a document and save changes to it	Read-write permission for the document. The first user to open a document has control of the original until closing it.

Some operating systems and local area networks (LANs) provide additional means of
protecting files. For example, with Novell networks you can set the protection for a
file using the Novell flag command. To find out about additional file protection
features, see your operating system or network documentation.

You can assign system-level read-only or read-write permission for a document in
Windows using the following procedure.

To set the protection for a document

1 In the Program Manager, double-click the File Manager.

2 Select the document you want to make read-only or read-write.

3 From the File menu, choose Change Attributes (ALT, F, G).

4 Select or clear the Read Only check box.

5 Choose the OK button.

Tip   You can also change attributes from the Program Manager by choosing the
Run command from the File menu (ALT, F, R). To make a document read-only,
type **attrib +r** *filename* in the Run dialog box. Type **attrib -r** *filename* to make a
document read-write. You must include the complete path if the file isn't in the current
directory.

Word Document Protections

When a Word user opens a document that has read-write permission, the user can protect the original document from accidental changes by selecting the Read Only check box in the Open dialog box. This does not prevent the user from saving changes under a different document name.

In addition, a document can be *locked* so that it can be opened only by supplying a password or can be annotated but no changes made to the document's text. For information on password protection, see Chapter 2, "Opening, Saving, and Deleting Documents." For information on locking a file while allowing annotations, see Chapter 31, "Footnotes, Annotations, and Revision Marks."

To open a shared document

For information on opening documents, see Chapter 2, "Opening, Saving, and Deleting Documents."

1 Log on to the network computer that contains the document you want to open, and start Word.

2 From the File menu, choose Open (ALT, F, O).

3 In the File Name box, select the file you want to open.

4 If you don't want to make changes to the original shared document, select the Read-Only check box.

5 Choose the OK button.

If you try to open a document that has read-write permission while another user has it open, Word displays a message saying that the document is locked.

6 If you see this message, choose the OK button to open a copy of the document. To make changes to your copy, you must save it under a different name.

While you have a locked document open, the first user who opened the document is able to make changes that won't be reflected in the copy you're using. You can't make changes to the original.

When you open a read-only document, a message tells you that the document is read-only. To save changes to a read-only document, save the document under a different filename.

Note You cannot search for information in a locked file using the Find File command on the File menu . If a locked file is in the search path, Find File displays a message indicating the file cannot be read and was not included in the search.

Printing over a Network

For information on setting up printers, see your Windows documentation. For information on printing with Word, see Chapter 4, "Printing a Document."

The procedures for printing over a network generally are the same as printing procedures for an individual computer. You use the Windows Setup program to set up all printers available to you. Then you use the Print Setup command on the File menu in Word to select a printer for use with Word and to change the settings for the active printer.

If you have installed more than one printer, when you start Word for the first time, make sure you select the printer you will be using for your documents. If you select one printer when you format a document and a different printer when you print the document, some fonts, point sizes, and other character formatting options may not be available when you print.

Note   Your network software may require you to issue a system command to make a network printer available to your computer. For specific procedures for your network, see your network software documentation.

Modifying the WIN.INI File

Windows stores settings and preferences for screen color, mouse double-click speed, default printers, printer ports, font sets, and many other options in the WIN.INI file. The WIN.INI file also contains settings for Windows applications, such as Word. When you start Windows, it reads the WIN.INI file and uses the settings that were in effect at the end of the last Windows session.

If a previous version of Word exists when you set up Word for Windows 2.0, the Word Setup program modifies the WIN.INI file to contain new information and preserves settings that still apply from the earlier version.

There are three ways to modify the WIN.INI file:

For information on the Windows Control Panel, see your Windows documentation.

- Use the Windows Control Panel to adjust settings that apply for all Windows applications—for example, you can customize your desktop, install and configure printers and ports, add and remove fonts, customize the mouse, and set system date and time.

- Use the Word Setup program to install additional text or graphics converters and supplemental applications such as the Equation Editor and Microsoft Draw. When you use Setup to add these items, Setup automatically updates the WIN.INI file.

- In Word, use the WIN.INI category of the Options command on the Tools menu to view and adjust settings that affect Word. For more information about modifying the WIN.INI file, see "Editing the WIN.INI File," later in this appendix.

WIN.INI Options

The WIN.INI file is divided into sections. Each section begins with a title enclosed in brackets. The general Windows settings, for example, are listed in the "[Windows]" section; settings that affect the desktop are listed under "[Desktop]."

Sections that contain options that affect Word are listed in the following table—each section is described in detail later in this appendix.

Section name	Contents
[Microsoft Word 2.0]	Paths for the Word application, proofing tools, and documents.
[MS Graphic Import Filters] [MS Graphic Export Filters]	Paths for the installed graphic filters and filename extensions for each type of graphic filter.
[MS Proofing Tools]	Paths and filenames for custom dictionaries for use with the installed proofing tools.
[MSWord Text Converters]	Paths and filenames for the installed text conversion programs.
[MSWord Editable Sections]	Sections of WIN.INI that appear in the Application list box of the Options dialog box. You can edit these sections when you choose the Options command from the Tools menu and select the WIN.INI category.

[Microsoft Word 2.0]

This section lists the paths and filenames for the Word application files, including proofing tools, and the default directory for Word documents. For each of the proofing tools, the option shows the number for the language and the type of tool. A list of language and tool numbers follows the list of options.

In general, you do not need to edit these options; they are updated by Word or the Setup program. If you lose your WIN.INI file, Word can automatically reinstall the proofing tools.

The options can appear in any order.

Option	Explanation
programdir=*path* Example: programdir=c:\winword	Specifies the directory where Word program files are stored.
DOC-path=*path* Example: DOC-path=c:\winword	Specifies the default directory for documents.
Spelling *language,type=path,path* Example: Spelling 1033,0=c:\winword\spell.dll, c:\winword\sp_am.lex	Specifies the path and filenames for spelling tools.
Hyphenate *language,type=path,path,path* Example: Hyphenate 1033,0=c:\winword\hyph.dll, c:\winword\hy_am.lex, c:\winword\sp_am.lex	Specifies the path and filenames for hyphenation tools.
Thesaurus *language,type=path,path* Example: Thesaurus 1033,0=c:\winword\th_am.dll, c:\winword\th_am.lex	Specifies the path and filenames for the thesaurus tool.
Grammar *language,type=path,path* Example: Grammar 1033,0=c:\winword\grammar.dll, c:\winword\gr_am.lex	Specifies the path and filenames for the grammar tool.
DOC-extension=*filename_extension* Example: DOC-extension=.doc	Specifies the default filename extension for Word documents.
DOT-extension=*filename_extension* Example: DOT-extension=.dot	Specifies the default filename extension for Word templates.
DOT-path=*path* Example: DOT-path=c:\winword	Specifies the directory where document templates are stored.
INI-path=*path* Example: INI-path=c:\winword	Specifies the directory where WINWORD.INI is stored
AUTOSAVE-path=*path* Example: AUTOSAVE-path=c:\winword	Specifies the directory where autosave files are stored.

(continued)

Option	Explanation
TOOLS-path=*path* Example: TOOLS-path=c:\winword	Sets alternative (second and third priority) search paths for proofing tools, converters, graphic filters, autosave files and user dictionaries.
BAK-extension=*filename_extension* Example: BAK-extension=.bak	Specifies the default filename extension for Word backup documents.
DateFormat=*date_template* Example: dateformat=d/m/y	Sets the default date format for the DATE field in Word.
TimeFormat=*time_template* Example: timeformat=hh:mm:ss	Sets the default time format for the TIME field in Word.
BitMapMemory=*n* Example: bitmapmemory=100	Sets the amount of memory reserved for cache memory for bitmaps (in K).
CacheSize=*n* Example: cachesize=200	Sets the amount of memory reserved for cache memory (in K).
DDETIMEOUT=*seconds* Example: ddetimeout=30	Sets the amount of time in seconds Word waits for DDE messages from another application before reporting that the connection can't be made.
NovellNet=yes	Adds this option to use Word on a Novell network.
AskForPrinterPicture=1	Screen picture for color printer. Microsoft Excel uses this for DDE results.
UnderlineMode=1	Enables special code in Word to underline correctly with some printers.
SlowShading=yes	Makes it possible for users to shade graphics by overriding a special drawing function on some Hewlett-Packard printers. Using this option slows printing. If your printer doesn't support the special drawing function, this setting has no effect.
SuppressTopSpacing=yes	Forces the first line at the top of each page to be single-spaced, regardless of the line spacing defined for the current paragraph. This switch is useful if you want to ensure that the top margins of single-spaced and double-spaced pages match precisely.

Language Numbers

The following table lists some commonly used language numbers.

Language	Number
Australian English	3081
British English	2057
Danish	1030
Dutch	1043
French	1036
German	1031
Italian	1040
Norwegian	1044
Portuguese	2070
Spanish	1034
Swedish	1054
U.S. English	1033

Type of Tool

The following table lists standard types of proofing tools.

Tool	Number
Normal	0
Concise	1
Complete	2
Medical	3
Legal	4

[MS Graphic Import Filters] and [MS Graphic Export Filters]

This section lists the directories where the installed graphic filters are stored. The filename extension for each type of graphics file is also listed in this section. When you use Setup to install Word, Setup copies the graphic filters to the directory C:\WINDOWS\MSAPPS\GRPHFLT to make them accessible to Word and other applications.

Graphic filters available with Word include the following.

Graphics file type	Filter filename and extension
Windows Metafile	WMFIMP.FLT,WMF
Computer Graphics Metafile	CGMIMP.FLT,CGM
DrawPerfect	WPGIMP.FLT,WPG
Encapsulated PostScript	EPSIMP.FLT,EPS
Micrografx Designer or Draw	DRWIMP.FLT,DRW
TIFF	TIFFIMP.FLT,TIF
AutoCAD 2-Dimensional	DXFIMP.FLT,DXF
AutoCAD Binary ADI	ADIMPORT.FLT,PLT
PC Paintbrush (PCX)	PCXIMP.FLT,PCX
HP Graphic Language	HPGLIMP.FLT,HGL
Lotus 1-2-3 (PIC)	LOTUSIMP.FLT,PIC

You should use the Setup program to install graphic filters. The entry Setup adds to WIN.INI to install a filter follows the form:

filter_name (.ext)=path,ext

[MS Proofing Tools]

This section lists the paths and filenames of custom user dictionaries. Assuming your program directory is C:\WINWORD, Word adds the following entry to install one custom dictionary during setup:

Custom Dict 1=C:\WINWORD\CUSTOM.DIC

If you create additional custom dictionaries, you can add options to the WIN.INI file using the same form.

[MSWord Text Converters]

This section lists the paths, filenames, and filename extensions of the installed text conversion programs. When you install Word with Setup, Word puts text conversion programs in the Word program directory and adds information about the converters to this section of the WIN.INI file. The list in the [MSWord Text Converters] section of your WIN.INI file depends on which conversions you installed with Setup.

You should use the Word Setup program to install text converters. Installing a text converter just by adding an entry to the WIN.INI file is not recommended; text converters are updated by Word or the Setup program. If you lose your WIN.INI file, Word can automatically reinstall the converters.

Information in the [MSWord Text Converters] section follows this format:

Converter_class_name=application_name, filename, filename_extension

For example, if the Microsoft Word for Windows version 1.x filter is installed in the C:\WINWORD directory, the following option appears in the [MSWord Text Converters] section of the WIN.INI file:

MSWordWin=Word for Windows 1.x,C:\WINWORD\WORDWIN1CNV,DOC

[MSWord Editable Sections]

This section identifies the WIN.INI sections you can edit from within Word. You edit a section in Word by selecting it in the Applications box in the WIN.INI category of the Options dialog box (Tools menu). The following entries are included in Setup.

[Microsoft Word 2.0]	[DCAConv]
[MS Graphic Import Filters]	[TxtLytConv]
[MS Proofing Tools]	[PCWordConv]
[MS Word Text Converters]	[MacWordConv]
[MS Editable Sections]	[PCWorksConv]

You can also add entries to this section. For example, if you add Extensions=yes to the list, you can use the WIN.INI category of the Options dialog box to edit the [Extensions] section of the WIN.INI file.

The specific information you can change in WIN.INI is explained in preceding sections of this appendix. For more information about editing the [DCAConv], [TxtLytConv], [PCWordConv], [MacWordConv], and [PCWorksConv] sections, see "Conversion Options in the WIN.INI File" in the CONVINFO.DOC file located in your Word for Windows program directory.

Search Hierarchy

Word tries to locate the supporting files it needs to complete a command according to the following search order, assuming the Windows directory is C:\WINDOWS.

For this type of file	Word looks in this file/directory
Proofing tools	WIN.INI file TOOLS-PATH Program directory
Text converters	WIN.INI file TOOLS-PATH Program directory C:\WINDOWS\MSAPPS\TEXTCONV
Graphic filters	WIN.INI file C:\WINDOWS\MSAPPS\GRPHFLT TOOLS-PATH Program directory
User dictionaries	WIN.INI file C:\WINDOWS\MSAPPS\PROOF TOOLS-PATH Program directory
Autosave files	AUTOSAVE-PATH TOOLS-PATH Program directory

Editing the WIN.INI File

For more information about using the Options command to customize Word, see Chapter 39, "Setting Preferences."

You can use the Options command on the Tools menu to change the Word settings described in this appendix.

To modify the WIN.INI file

1 From the Tools menu, choose Options (ALT, O, O).

2 Under Category, select WIN.INI.

3 In the Application box, select the section of the WIN.INI file you want to view.

Word displays entries in that section in the Startup Options box.

4 From the list of Startup Options, select individual settings to view or change.

5 To modify a setting, type the new information in the Setting box, and then choose the Set button.
   −or−
   To remove the option from the WIN.INI file, choose the Delete button.

6 Choose the Close button when you've finished.

Operating Limits

Editing documents is easier if you keep within the operating limits recommended for Word. If you exceed the listed limits, Word may display an error message. Some of these limits are determined by the amount of available memory in your computer and whether your computer uses an extended memory manager (EMM). Features with fixed maximums are marked with an asterisk.

Operating parameter	Limit
Number of open windows	9 *
Maximum file size	Available disk space
Number of words in user dictionaries	10,000
Length of bookmark name	20 characters *
Number of bookmarks in a document	450
Length of glossary entry name (including spaces)	31 characters *
Number of glossary entries per document template	150
Number of global glossary entries	150
Length of style name	20 characters *
Number of styles per document or document template	220 *
Number of macros per document template	150
Number of global macros	150
Number of nesting levels in macros	16 *
Number of general switches in a field	10 *
Number of field-specific switches in a field	10 *
Number of nested fields	20 *
Number of fields in a document	2,000
Point size of characters	127
Number of columns in a table	31
Number of newspaper-style columns	100
Number of tabs set in a paragraph	50
Minimum page height	3 inches

Index

A

O

Table **843**